THE
BURDEN OF
RACE

Also by Gilbert Osofsky:

HARLEM: *The Making of a Ghetto*

THE BURDEN
OF RACE

A DOCUMENTARY HISTORY OF

NEGRO-WHITE RELATIONS

IN AMERICA

❁ ❁

Gilbert Osofsky

HARPER & ROW, PUBLISHERS

NEW YORK, EVANSTON, AND LONDON

Grateful acknowledgment is extended to the following for the use of material:

Excerpts from *Dusk of Dawn* by W. E. B. Du Bois, copyright 1940 by Harcourt, Brace & World, Inc.; reprinted with their permission. "A Litany at Atlanta" and "The Riddle of the Sphinx" from *Darkwater: Voices from Within the Veil* by W. E. B. Du Bois, copyright 1920 by Harcourt, Brace & World, Inc.; reprinted by permission of Bernard Jaffe acting for the Du Bois estate. Excerpts from "Postscript" by W. E. B. Du Bois, copyright 1934 by the NAACP; reprinted by permission from the February, 1934, and June, 1934, issues of *The Crisis*. Excerpts from "The Face of the Poor" by Renwick C. Kennedy, copyright 1933 by Christian Century Foundation; reprinted by permission from the June 21, 1933, issue of *The Christian Century*. "Detroit—The Storm Bursts" (editorial), copyright 1943 by Christian Century Foundation; reprinted by permission from the June 30, 1943, issue of *The Christian Century*. "Nonviolence and Racial Justice" by Martin Luther King, Jr., copyright 1957 Christian Century Foundation; reprinted by permission from the February 6, 1957, issue of *The Christian Century*. Excerpts from *Revolt Among the Sharecroppers* by Howard Kester, copyright 1936 by Howard Kester; reprinted by permission of the author. Excerpts from *Message to the Black Man in America* by Elijah Muhammad, copyright 1940 by Elijah Muhammad, reprinted by permission of the author. Two articles by A. Philip Randolph from the March, 1941, and July, 1941, issues of *The Black Worker,* copyright 1941 by the Brotherhood of Sleeping Car Porters, reprinted by permission of the author. Excerpts from *Race and Rumors of Race* by Howard Odum, copyright 1943 by the University of North Carolina Press; reprinted by permission of the publisher. Excerpts from "Jim Crow in the Army" by Lucille B. Milner, reprinted by permission of *The New Republic* copyright 1944, Harrison-Blaine of New Jersey, Inc. Excerpts from *Marching Blacks* by Adam Clayton Powell, Jr., copyright 1945 by Dial Press, Inc., and used by permission of the publisher. Excerpts from *A Rising Wind* by Walter White, copyright 1945 by Walter White; reprinted by permission of Doubleday & Company, Inc. Excerpts from *A Man Called White* by Walter White, copyright 1948 by Walter White; reprinted by permission of The Viking Press, Inc. "The Equalitarian Dogma" by Henry E. Garrett, copyright 1961 by The Mankind Quarterly; reprinted by permission from the 1-4 issue of *The Mankind Quarterly*. Excerpts from *Negro Americans, What Now?* by James Weldon Johnson, copyright 1934 by James Weldon Johnson, copyright 1962 by Grace Nail Johnson; reprinted by permission of The Viking Press, Inc. Excerpts from *Malcolm X Speaks: Selected Speeches and Statements by Malcolm X,* copyright 1965 by Merit Publishers.

FIRST EDITION

LIBRARY OF CONGRESS CATALOG CARD NUMBER: 66-10533

H-R

For

MARCIANKA

Contents

✿

Preface

❁

This is a study of the way Negroes and whites have lived together in America over the last 350 years. It has most often been a sad relationship and sometimes a brutal one. There are relatively few moments of lighthearted relief and joy in this book because these have been rare indeed in our history.

The book is constructed around significant ideas. Each chapter is preceded by an introduction, which presents the themes that are explored in the documents that follow. The introductions to chapters and the statements before each document are heavily interpretive. I have chosen to write the book in this fashion on the premise that these ideas may help place specific documents within the broader framework of America's racial history. I have not intentionally avoided the great documents—the most well-known ones —but whenever I thought a more obscure, though no less representative, illustration might be used I have selected it.

Another point about the structure of this book should be clarified. I have concentrated on Negro-white relations within a national setting, permitting spokesmen from all sections of the country over the centuries to express their views. The book, to choose one example, illustrates racial attitudes in the North when Negroes represented a very small portion of that section's population—in the eighteenth and early nineteenth centuries. Cotton Mather's words of wisdom to the prudent slaveholders of Boston tell us as much about Negro-white relations in America as the mouthings of the most venomous slaver in New Orleans on the eve of the Civil War. And to fathom the meaning of race in our history both must be understood.

It is hazardous to try to find enough pages of the proper words to deal with such a complex subject over many centuries. Some ideas—such as the brilliant and subtle insights of a book like

Lillian Smith's *Killers of the Dream*—are not easily explored in a documentary study. And even if one were blessed with universal vision, there certainly is never enough space to give everyone his day in court. The book is offered, therefore, not as *the* definitive history of Negro-white relations in America, but as my personal and selective vision of some of the most significant ideas that explain America's racial past.

I wish to thank the library staffs at the University of Chicago, the University of Illinois, Chicago Circle, the Manuscript Division of the Library of Congress, the National Archives, the Oral History Research Office at Columbia University, the James Weldon Johnson Collection of Yale University, and Howard University. At a critical stage in the preparation of this book I found the rich source material and the cordial atmosphere of Howard University's Moorland Collection invaluable. Especial thanks are due Mrs. Dorothy B. Porter and her staff. Hugh Van Dusen and Jeannette Hopkins of Harper & Row, and what seemed like an army of anonymous readers, subjected the first draft of the book to searching criticism. In the process, my manuscript, and my learning, were considerably improved. Thanks are also due my colleagues and cronies at the University of Illinois, Chicago, for stealing occasional moments from the time-consuming job of university-building to share their ideas with me. Some of the material in this study is drawn from our valuable Urban Historical Collection. Darrel Simmons made countless trips to the library, Mrs. Joan Trotter did a superb typing job on the first draft of the manuscript, and Mrs. Ethel M. Ellis prepared the index. The University of Illinois Graduate Research Board has again been most generous with financial help. The book is dedicated to my wife, the brains of the outfit.

GILBERT OSOFSKY

University of Illinois, Chicago

THE
BURDEN OF
RACE

CHAPTER I

SLAVERY

World of Sorrow, World of Toil

❁ ❁

To make a contented slave, you must make a thoughtless one. It is necessary to darken his moral and mental vision, and, as far as possible, to annihilate his power of reason. He must be able to detect no inconsistencies in slavery. The man that takes his earnings, must be able to convince him that he has a perfect right to do so. It must not depend upon mere force; the slave must know no Higher Law than his master's will. The whole relationship must not only demonstrate, to his mind, its necessity, but its absolute rightfulness.

FREDERICK DOUGLASS, *My Bondage and My Freedom* (1855)

And there is such a disparity in their Conditions, Colour & Hair, that they can never embody with us, and grow up into orderly Families, to the Peopling of the Land. . . .

SAMUEL SEWALL, *The Selling of Joseph: A Memorial* (1700)

———————

Slavery was a brutal, brutalizing, and alluring institution. Profits from the forced labor of men tempted African chiefs, the great powers of Europe, small traders from Newport, Salem, Charleston, and New York City, the largest commercial companies of the Western world, and Protestants and Roman Catholics, for centuries. Bars of iron, rum, tobacco, crystal beads, spears, tinsel, mirrors, brass pans and cotton cloth were bartered for "likely young boys and girls in good health." Ingenious master

I

builders—Portuguese, Spanish, Dutch, English, French, American—were commissioned to construct vessels which packed together the most people in the least space, to make slaves "lie as close together as it is possible to be crowded," one man wrote in 1705. Blacksmiths of all nations forged padlocks for necks, hands, and legs, chains, shackles, branding irons, and devices to pry open the mouths of Africans who preferred to starve rather than be transported across the Atlantic. A Westminster entrepreneur advertised padlocks "for blacks and dogs." Merchants in eighteenth-century Liverpool adorned their town hall with the bust of a slave, a symbol of the pride they felt in becoming the most prominent slave-trading port in the world. "God be thanked! His name therefore be praised evermore! Amen," a chronicler recorded when Sir John Hawkins returned from England's first successful slave trade venture; "I pity them greatly, but I must be mum/For how could we do without sugar and rum," runs a piece of eighteenth-century doggerel of a West Indian planter—and such words echoed through the Atlantic world from the fifteenth through the nineteenth centuries. (1)*

Centuries of slavery brutalized many slaves as well as their masters. Every aspect of the slave regime attempted to obliterate the slave's being. The simplest and most sacred forms by which humans acquire identity and dignity were denied slaves—the right to a name, knowledge of a birthday, occasional privacy, the ability to maintain the most basic family relationships, protection from physical and sexual savagery, and so on. Frederick Douglass, for example, never knew his father, saw his mother only once before she died, and was never sure of the exact date or even the year of his birth. "By far the largest part of the slaves know as little of their age as horses know of theirs," Douglass wrote, "and it is the wish of most masters . . . to keep their slaves thus ignorant. . . . A want of information concerning my own was a source of unhappiness to me even during my childhood. The white children could tell their ages. I could not tell why I ought to be deprived of the same privilege." Douglass' narrative of his life as a slave, like those of dozens of others, is replete with references to the "dehumanizing," "brutalizing," and "soul-killing" effects of slavery.

Douglass was a man of genius, sensitivity, learning, extraordi-

---

* A theme or a number of themes presented in the introductions to all chapters will be followed by an Arabic numeral. Documents illustrative of such themes will be found under that numeral in each chapter.

nary physical energy, and even he almost succumbed to the system. Shortly before his escape he worked as a field hand under a "nigger breaker"—a specialist in debasing recalcitrant Negroes. "Mr. Covey succeeded in breaking me," Douglass recorded. "I was broken in body, soul and spirit. My natural elasticity was crushed; my intellect languished; the disposition to read departed; the cheerful spark that lingered about my eye died; *the dark night of slavery closed in upon me;* and behold a man transformed into a brute."

That men like Douglass, Henry Bibb, William Wells Brown, Lunsford Lane, and others were able to withstand such pressure and maintain a sense of dignity and self-respect was a measure of their remarkable strength of mind; that others were less able to endure is unquestionable. When J. W. C. Pennington escaped to New York City he wrote that it took him "three years before I had purged my language of slavery's idioms; it was four years before I had thrown off the crouching aspect of slavery. . . ."

An abundance of evidence illustrates the infinite variety of tactics devised by slaves to adjust to their closed world—stealing, truancy, lying, and malingering, for example. That many actually found meaning for their lives in a quasi adoption of their master's values is also true. This is exemplified in the emergence of a slave aristocracy based on skin color and hair texture: "The same little indefinable difference that existed between the social levels of the white folks, existed [among] the colored people," commented Robert Anderson, a Kentucky slave. Slaves sometimes boasted of the value they could bring in the market place, maintained an intense sense of rivalry with each other, occasionally brawled over the relative importance of their masters. "There is much rivalry among the slaves, at times, as to which can do the most work, and masters generally seek to promote such rivalry," Douglass concluded. "To be a SLAVE, was thought to be bad enough; but to be a poor man's slave, was deemed a disgrace, indeed." "It must be confessed," recorded Austin Steward, another slave, "that among the poor, degraded and ignorant slaves there exists a foolish pride, which loves to boast of their master's wealth and influence." (2)

Few Americans in the colonial period bothered to be concerned with slavery and the condition of Negroes. The most audible voices in a placid society were those of Quakers. George Fox, founder of the Society of Friends, and William Edmundson, his much-persecuted disciple, visited Virginia and Rhode

Island in 1671–1672 and counseled religious instruction for slaves. Others followed in their tradition, some demanding absolute emancipation, some amelioration of the slave's status: Germantown Quakers, William Southeby, Ralph Sandiford, John Farmer, Anthony Benezet, the Christ-like John Woolman, to mention a few. Benjamin Lay, the bearded and hunchbacked author of *All Slave-Keepers that Keep the Innocent in Bondage, Apostates* (1737), once stood barefoot before a meetinghouse on a frigid day. When people demonstrated sympathy for his suffering he chastised them for failing to recognize an evil a hundred-fold worse. At another time Lay temporarily kidnaped a slave-holder's child to make him experience the anguish of a slave parent. "Trading in souls would provoke the Vengeance of the Lord," Sandiford wrote in *A Brief Examination of the Practice of the Times* (1729), "and bring the Wrath and Displeasure of God on all those engaged in it."

Yet, for all the anticipated terrors of a righteous deity, Friends represented a minority of the American population, and those who opposed slavery publicly most often criticized slave-holding among other Quakers—they were a minority within a minority. The first hundred years of Quaker antislavery was especially concerned with the evils of the slave trade rather than slavery, and most congregations failed to disown slaveholders prior to the 1760's and 1770's. While some preached the golden rule, others practiced segregation within their own churches; some even carried it to the church pew and the graveyard. Quaker antislavery is clearly important when contrasted with the general colonial disinterest in racial problems; but it hardly reflected a serious national movement toward emancipation or racial reform.

Other Christians sought to ameliorate the lives of slaves by sharing the Gospel with them. Cotton Mather was one, as were preachers of the Society for the Propagation of the Gospel—the most active proselytizing group in the colonies. But the peace and good will offered in this version of Christianity was a slave keeper's piety: "The world is a sorrowful place," slaves were told. "Not one of us ever saw the man yet that had no sorrow, that had no sickness, no hard painful work." Masters were convinced that the words of the Lord, properly interpreted, would help create a more docile and contented slave population. "The deeper the piety of the slave, the more valuable is he in every sense of the word," a South Carolinian argued. "Christianity truly taught and sincerely cherished can not fail to render the slave population more tranquil and happy." Such "Gospel Among the Slaves" served as a crucial bulwark of the slave regime—it never attempted to confront the moral dilemmas inherent in the institution itself. One slave remembered hearing varieties of the same sermon repeated throughout his life. The minister "argued from the Bible," he recalled, "that it was the will of heaven from all eternity we should be slaves. . . ."

Greater secular and religious interest in antislavery was spurred by the Revolutionary War. A heightened faith in the rights of man coincided with a diminution in the economic importance of slavery throughout the North and some sections of the South. Ideology and economic interest fused to touch off the most intense debate over the place of slavery in America that the nation had yet experienced. "At a time when the general rights and liberties of mankind . . . are become so much the subjects of universal consideration," Friend Benezet observed, "can it be an inquiry indifferent to any . . . the treatment of . . . tens of thousands of our fellow men, who . . . are at this very time kept in the most deplorable state of Slavery. . . ."

And Revolutionary rhetoric yielded practical results. Slavery was not permitted in the Northwest Territory, the Constitution allowed the slave trade to be discontinued after twenty years, the Founding Fathers never overtly mentioned the institution in the document (hoping it would die out someday), immediate or gradual emancipation occurred throughout most of the North, and the earliest abolitionist societies were formed in the upper South and North. "Ye ADVOCATES of American Liberty, [rise] up and espouse the cause of Humanity and general Liberty," wrote Benjamin Rush, the distinguished Philadelphian, in 1773.

Despite the temporary emergence of antislavery as a national issue of some importance, few Americans—even supporters of emancipation—envisioned a future nation in which Negroes were granted full rights of citizenship. Rush, it is true, did demand "all the privileges of free-born British subjects" for the prospective freedmen, but Jefferson's views were more representative of the colonial mind. The noted humanitarian supported Negro emancipation in Virginia but coupled it with colonization. Like Samuel Sewall, Jefferson regarded slavery as a malicious institution, but he felt no especial kinship for Negroes. "I advance it . . . as a suspicion only," he wrote, "that the blacks whether originally a distinct race, or made distinct by time and circumstances, are inferior to the whites in the endowments both of body and mind." It was no wonder then that an angry David Walker, in his classic *Appeal to the Colored Citizens of the World* (1829–1830), continually excoriated Jefferson for his racial views and set out to refute them: "Do you know that Mr. Jefferson was one of as great characters as ever lived among the whites?" Walker told other Negroes. "Do you believe that the assertions of such a man, will pass away into oblivion unobserved by . . . the world? If you do you are much mistaken. . . ." The most advanced racial positions of the colonial era, therefore, were themselves often tainted with overtones of racism. (3)

1. THE SLAVE TRADE

A Slave Trader's Description of a Voyage to Africa
Joseph Hawkins*

No one knows how many Africans were transported across the Atlantic in the entire history of the slave trade. Ulrich B. Phillips estimated the number at five million; more recent studies place the figure between fifteen and fifty million; the Muslims usually say one hundred million. It was a nightmare experience that often ended in death. Again, no one will ever know how many slaves died in the process, but the most sophisticated guesses of mortality rates on the Middle Passage alone (the journey from Africa to the West Indies) demonstrate that 13 percent of a typical slave cargo never arrived in the New World. A most unusual and frightening American description of a slaver's voyage is Joseph Hawkins' Voyage to the Coast of Africa. Hawkins not only lost a finger in the fight with his captives (as he describes), but went blind on the return trip to America.

We sailed from Charleston the 1st of Dec. 1793, on board the ship *Charleston,* J. Connelly master, burthen 400 Tons; and after a passage partly boisterous, and frequently becalmed for several days, we made the isles of Delos† on the 17th January 1794.

---

* Joseph Hawkins, *Voyage to the Coast of Africa* (1797). From Elizabeth Donnan, *Documents Illustrative of the History of the Slave Trade to America* (Washington, D.C., 1935), IV, 494–500.
† Hawkins is probably referring to the Isles de Los, off modern Conakry.

These islands are nine in number, and afford harbours and safe anchorage in deep water for ships of any burthen; they are six leagues from the main land of Africa; . . . they are inhabited by French and English factors, who find their account in living on those islands in preference to the main, particularly from the circumstances of accommodation for their ships, which lye here with the greatest safety in all weathers, and that their slaves cannot easily escape. The slaves are in those islands suffered to go at large, without chains, contrary to the customs on the continent. The surface of the islands is barren and rocky, but there is abundance of fine fresh water; and provisions are procured with facility.

From the factors here we learned that the Ebo and Golo Kings had been at war, the latter of whom having been defeated, and a great part of his army had fallen into the hands of the conqueror, they therefore advised us to proceed . . . to the Ebo nation. . . .

On the 6th February we were visited by numbers of the natives, who offered to barter with us fruit and ivory for our hardwares; but finding after we had exchanged a few articles, that they belonged to a nation which had been before represented to us as thinly inhabited, and that we could not accommodate ourselves here as we wished, we made use of them to obtain information concerning the country of the Ebo king. We fortunately found an interpreter acquainted with that country and the trade, him we engaged, and an expedition was immediately determined upon by the captain. . . .

He proposed that I should go and see the prisoners; we accordingly crossed to the southeastern side of the rivulet, where at the lower side of the town, we found them confined in a large area within a thick stockade, on the outside of which was a trench: the inside was divided into parcels, and huts irregularly constructed, and the entrance as well as the whole circuit, was guarded by men with spears.

We commonly find ourselves impressed with emotions of horror or compassion, on entering places where our fellow men are doomed to punishment or thraldom. In the scene before me, the ear was not indeed dinned with the clanking of heavy fetters, but was horrible in its peculiar way. The captives were destitute for the

most part of even their necessary covering, and bound indiscriminately together by the hands and legs, the cords being again
fastened to the ground by stakes; they were loosed a few at a time
once every day, when each was permitted to eat the only meal they
were allowed, consisting of rice and palm oil. Benevolence, however, sometimes broke through the rigours of a savage life, and
occasionally alleviated the sufferings of the weakly, or the
wounded with milk or other necessaries: their condition was on
the whole deplorable.

I had often in the course of the voyage, and of the journey,
rebuked myself for having embarked in the African trade, but
found a consolation in the reflection, that it was not from a malicious
inclination or avaricious disposition, that I had embarked in it, but
from the pressing call of necessity, and at a time when my dissent
could not alter or obstruct the undertaking. On the present occasion, however, I was fully convinced the removal of these poor
wretches even into the slavery of the West-Indies, would be an act
of humanity, rather than one exposed to censure.

We passed through the whole range of the place of confinement,
the old chief pointing out to me those who were the greatest
warriors of the Galla nation. He then intimated to me that I might
chuse such of them as I should think proper and agree on what he
was to receive in return. I agreed to do so, but requested that I
might have an opportunity of conversing with them, and chusing
such as would go with me voluntarily, if any could be found. To
this he readily assented; and for the next week I continued to visit
them daily, and took occasion through my interpreter, to exhibit as
flattering a prospect to their future situation in America, should
they go with me, as I thought was just in itself, and favorable to
their wishes. . . .

Having arranged matters on this subject to my mind, I mentioned to the old king the several articles which I proposed
exchanging with him, and shewing specimens of such few articles
as I had brought, proposed dispatching a person to the ship with a
letter, directing the Captain to send a shallop with goods to the
mouth of the little Congo, and that rafts should be ready with
hands to convey them up the rest of the way. The Galla nation
having suffered so much by their last war, had now become fearful
of molesting or interfering with the Ebo people, a circumstance,

which if we had previously known, would have saved us a long, circuitous and troublesome journey, which might now be performed with ease in one half the time. . . .

On the 3d of April, while I was on an excursion abroad, one of the messengers returned from the ship, and I found him before me at my hut in the evening, with a packet from the Captain, advising me of the goods which he had sent by the shallop, to the mouth of the little Congo, and giving me directions how to proceed.

The information being communicated to the old chief, he informed me he would send a number of experienced old men with me, to chuse such articles as they should approve and after three days, provisions and horses being provided we set out, the company consisting of six of the deputation, with some of their families, a number of persons to carry provisions and goods, and my two wives. We had nearly 100 miles to go, which engaged us six days; riding proved very unpleasant to me, on account of the heat and the want of a saddle. We found the boats as we were directed, and a cargo of brandy, rum, gin, and tobacco, a few coarse guns, some ammunition, swords, knives, spears, and ornament, such as rings of various kinds, for the legs, arms, and fingers, some gilt and plated breast plates for their warriors, tinsel laces, and some glass-ware. An assortment so extensive and rich in their eyes, had never been there before; and bargains were very soon made for goods, in exchange for 100 slaves, being ordered not to bring down more; for the rest I procured ivory and gold, in dust and bars. In these dealings I found my wives of . . . use to me . . . , for they sincerely studied my interest. . . .

The slaves that I had purchased were young men, many of whom being eager to escape from their bondage in Ebo, preferred the evil they "knew not of" to that which they then felt; but the majority were evidently affected with grief at their approaching departure.

Arrangements were made and a sufficient body of the Ebo people undertook to accompany me as a guard to the place of embarkation; provisions were provided for the journey, so that each of the slaves was well fed, and a load of provisions or goods given him to carry. They were tied to poles in rows, four feet apart; a loose wicker bandage round the neck of each, connected him to the pole, and the arms being pinioned by a bandage affixed

behind above the elbows, they had sufficient room to feed, but not
to loose themselves, or commit any violence; and as the guard was
provided with arms, we had nothing to apprehend during the night,
as we divided the Ebo people into parties, one of which slept while
the other watched. . . .

This journey was extremely different in its nature from that in
which I had last passed this way; the giddy pranks of the vain, or
the inebriated Ebo, was woefully contrasted by the sullen melancholy, and deep sighs of the poor Galla prisoners; often did they
look back with eyes flowing with tears, turn sudden round and
gaze, seeming to part with reluctance, even from their former
bondage. It was excessively affecting to me, but I considered that
death might have been their fate otherwise, and I endeavoured to
reconcile them to their condition, by representing flattering accounts of the country to which they were going; that the bonds
they then bore were only to prevent their flight; that they should be
at liberty where they were going, and have plenty to eat, drink, etc.
These assurances occasioned a temporary composure, and we at
length arrived at the place of our embarkation; two boats had been
brought up, as the shallop drew too much water; the slaves were
put on board, and necessarily in irons brought for the purpose.
This measure occasioned one of the most affecting scenes I ever
witnessed: their hopes with my assurances had buoyed them up on
the road; but a change from the cordage to iron fetters, rent their
hopes and hearts together: their wailings were torturing beyond
what words can express: but delay at this crisis would have been
fatal; the boat's crews were acquainted with the duty, and they
were all safely embarked. . . .

We soon lost sight of them in a winding of the river; and
continued going down with the current till night: the slaves seemed
every hour to feel their situation more grievously, and I ordered
them each a dram of liquor which for a while exhilarated their
spirits and quieted their cares. . . . We furnished the slaves with
provisions, but whether through grief or sullenness, very few of
them would partake of any refreshments beside water.

As soon as we had light we unmoored, and before noon we
reached our shallop, extremely fatigued from the heat and close-
ness of the air, the banks of each side as we passed, being over-
grown with wood and thicket, obstructing its free circulation. We

had now another disagreeable piece of duty to execute, *viz.* the removal of the slaves from the small boats into the shallop; they were in want of room, and it was suggested to loose six of them at a time; we accordingly moved to the centre of the river, and being moored by a grappling, began to remove them; they appeared generally more quiet, and willing to act as we directed by the interpreter than usual, and had now all been removed, and placed below, but the last six, whom we suffered to remain on deck; when we had got under weigh, and were passing through a narrow part of the river, two of them found means to jump overboard; a sailor who was in the small boat astern seized one of them by the arms, and the end of a rope being thrown to him, the slave was taken on board, though not without some difficulty. The others who had been at the oars, seeing their fellows, one of them seized, and the other struck on the head with a pole, set up a scream, which was echoed by the rest below; those that were loose made an effort to throw two of the sailors overboard; the rest, except the one in the boat and at the helm, being asleep: the noise had now aroused them, and the scream had impressed them with some degree of terror; they seized on the guns and bayonets that lay ready, and rushed upon the slaves, five of whom from below had got loose, and were endeavouring to set the rest free, while those we had to deal with above, were threatening to sacrifice us to their despair. These transactions were but the events of a moment; I had neither gun nor sword, and to retire in search of either, would have been to give the slaves a decisive superiority; I laid hold of [a] stick, and had raised it to strike one of them who had nearly wrested a gun from one of the sailors, but before I could give the blow, I received a stroke of an oar, which severed my little finger from my hand; I know not how it was that I felt nothing of the severe pain for the moment, a slight twitch on the hand was the only sensation I experienced; the blow was broken that I had intended, but I renewed the effort, and with effect, for I levelled the fellow, and the sailor recovered his gun, whom I could not prevent from running the poor negro through the body; the hatch was open, and he fell among his fellows, who had, crowded, tied, and ironed as they were to assist as far as they were able, by holding our legs, encouraging their companions, and shouting whenever those above did any thing that appeared likely to overcome one or other of us.

We at length overpowered them; one only having escaped and one being killed, the rest were immediately bound in double irons, and took care from thence till our arrival at the ship, not to suffer any of them to take the air without being made fast. Five of the sailors were considerably, but not dangerously hurt, and of the slaves, those who had been riotous above and below, nine were severely wounded.

We reached the ship in five days from our first embarkation, where we were received with much satisfaction; the officers had all provided themselves with three or four wives each, and rebuked me for not bringing mine along, alledging that they would, according to the account given by their messmates, bring a good price when we arrived in America. I was sorry, however, to find that two of our best seamen had expired during my absence, from the excessive fatigue of the ships duty, and the heat of the climate.

While I was away, the Captain had opened a trade in another channel, he had obtained 100 slaves in the place where he lay, beside gold and ivory; and had contracted with some French and English factors . . . for the remainder of his cargo, and for his sea stores. . . .

The whole number of slaves that we had now on board, I found about 500, of whom above 50 were then lying in a dangerous state of illness; it was time for us to depart, being now in the 13th of June, 1795. We accordingly got in our anchors, and procured six of the native boats, with six men in each, to tow us down night and day, when the tide served. . . .

A Slave's Description of the Domestic Slave Trade
William Wells Brown*

Congress outlawed the foreign slave trade in 1807. Although the traffic in men across the Atlantic continued in subterfuge thereafter, the domestic slave trade replaced it in importance in the two generations preceding the Civil War. Slave coffles were marched overland in chains, transported along the coastline in small sloops, or shipped down the Mississippi in steamboats. Slave trading was a

* From *The Narrative of William Wells Brown: A Fugitive Slave* (Boston, 1847), pp. 41–45.

*most profitable business that brought wealth to the Woolfolks of
Virginia and Maryland, to the firms of Franklin & Armfield, Price,
Birch & Co., Overly & Sanders, and thousands of others. Major
trading centers were located in Savannah, St. Louis, the District of
Columbia, Alexandria, Richmond, Charleston, Norfolk and, of
course, New Orleans. Some slaves were raffled off; "fancy girls"
(concubines) went for the highest prices, as did "rattlin' good
breeders" and "prime" field hands. In 1838, the Charleston* Mer-
cury *advertised the sale of a twenty-year-old girl "very prolific in
her generating qualities." This description of the domestic slave
trade was written by William Wells Brown, who was hired-out by
his master to work with a trader.*

On our arrival at St. Louis I went to Dr. Young,* and told him
that I did not wish to live with Mr. Walker any longer. I was heart-
sick at seeing my fellow-creatures bought and sold. But the Dr.
had hired me for the year, and stay I must. Mr. Walker again
commenced purchasing another gang of slaves. He bought a man
of Colonel John O'Fallon, who resided in the suburbs of the city.
This man had a wife and three children. As soon as the purchase
was made, he was put in jail for safe keeping, until we should be
ready to start for New Orleans. His wife visited him while there,
several times, and several times when she went for that purpose
was refused admittance.

In the course of eight or nine weeks Mr. Walker had his cargo
of human flesh made up. There was in this lot a number of old
men and women, some of them with gray locks. We left St. Louis
in the steamboat Carlton, Captain Swan, bound for New Orleans.
On our way down, and before we reached Rodney,† the place
where we made our first stop, I had to prepare the old slaves for
market. I was ordered to have the old men's whiskers shaved off,
and the gray hairs plucked out where they were not too numerous,
in which case we had a preparation of blacking to color it, and with
a blacking brush we would put it on. This was new business to me,
and was performed in a room where the passengers could not see
us. These slaves were also taught how old they were by Mr.
Walker, and after going through the blacking process they looked

* Brown's owner.
† Mississippi.

ten or fifteen years younger; and I am sure that some of those who
purchased slaves of Mr. Walker were dreadfully cheated, especially in the ages of the slaves which they bought.

We landed at Rodney, and the slaves were driven to the pen in
the back part of the village. Several were sold at this place, during
our stay of four or five days, when we proceeded to Natchez.
There we landed at night, and the gang were put in the warehouse
until morning, when they were driven to the pen. As soon as the
slaves are put in these pens, swarms of planters may be seen in and
about them. They knew when Walker was expected, as he always
had the time advertised beforehand when he would be in Rodney,
Natchez, and New Orleans. These were the principal places where
he offered his slaves for sale.

When at Natchez the second time, I saw a slave very cruelly
whipped. He belonged to a Mr. Broadwell, a merchant who kept a
store on the wharf. The slave's name was Lewis. I had known him
several years, as he was formerly from St. Louis. We were
expecting a steamboat down the river, in which we were to take
passage for New Orleans. Mr. Walker sent me to the landing to
watch for the boat, ordering me to inform him on its arrival. While
there I went into the store to see Lewis. I saw a slave in the store,
and asked him where Lewis was. Said he, "They have got Lewis
hanging between the heavens and the earth." I asked him what he
meant by that. He told me to go into the warehouse and see. I
went in, and found Lewis there. He was tied up to a beam, with his
toes just touching the floor. As there was no one in the warehouse
but himself, I inquired the reason of his being in that situation. He
said Mr. Broadwell had sold his wife to a planter six miles from
the city, and that he had been to visit her—that he went in the
night, expecting to return before daylight, and went without his
master's permission. The patrol had taken him up before he
reached his wife. He was put in jail, and his master had to pay for
his catching and keeping, and that was what he was tied up for.

Just as he finished his story, Mr. Broadwell came in, and
inquired what I was doing there. I knew not what to say, and while
I was thinking what reply to make he struck me over the head with
the cowhide, the end of which struck me over my right eye, sinking
deep into the flesh, leaving a scar which I carry to this day. Before
I visited Lewis he had received fifty lashes. Mr. Broadwell gave

him fifty lashes more after I came out, as I was afterwards informed by Lewis himself.

The next day we proceeded to New Orleans, and put the gang in the same negro-pen which we occupied before. In a short time the planters came flocking to the pen to purchase slaves. Before the slaves were exhibited for sale, they were dressed and driven out into the yard. Some were set to dancing, some to jumping, some to singing, and some to playing cards. This was done to make them appear cheerful and happy. My business was to see that they were placed in those situations before the arrival of the purchasers, and I have often set them to dancing when their cheeks were wet with tears. As slaves were in good demand at that time, they were all soon disposed of, and we again set out for St. Louis.

2. THE LAW OF BONDAGE AND ITS PRACTICE

Louisiana's Slave Code*

Slave codes varied from state to state and from generation to generation—yet they always remained essentially the same. They legally transformed people into property. The codification of racial inferiority had begun in the seventeenth century in the North and South. The severity of Virginia's code of 1705—runaway slaves could be dismembered, for example—was paralleled by somewhat milder legislation in New York, Boston, and South Kingstown, Rhode Island. On the eve of the Civil War the proscriptive laws of all Southern states became increasingly malevolent. Historians continue to debate the significance of slave codes; some argue that they were rigidly enforced, others that they were not. It is obvious that all power over a slave's life was placed in the hands of his owner, and very few slaves found legal redress for actions committed against them in violation of the law.

1. The condition of a slave being merely a passive one, his subordination to his master, and to all who represent him, is not susceptible of any modification or restriction, (except in what can

* From the Louisiana code of 1852. *The Consolidation and Revision of the Statutes of the State, 1852* (New Orleans, 1852), pp. 522–557.

incite the said slave to the commission of crimes,) in such a manner that he owes to his master, and to all his family, a respect without bounds, and an absolute obedience; and he is, consequently to execute all the orders he receives from him, his said master, or from them.

2. As the person of a slave belongs to his master, no slave can possess anything in his own right, or dispose in any way of the produce of his industry, without the consent of his master.

3. No slaves shall be parties to a suit in civil matters, either as plaintiffs or defendants, nor be witness in any civil or criminal matters, against any white person: Provided, however, that their masters may act and defend in civil matters, and prosecute in criminal cases, to obtain satisfaction of the outrages and abuses which might have been committed against their slaves.

14. Slaves shall always be reputed and considered real estate, and shall be, as such, subject to be mortgaged, according to the rules prescribed by law; and they shall be seized and sold as real estate.

19. In order to keep slaves in good order and due submission, no person whatever shall allow any slave whose care and conduct are entrusted to him, or her, and residing in New Orleans, to go out of said city; or any slave residing in the country to go out of the plantation to which said slave belongs, or where he is habitually employed, without a permission in the following form, viz:

"The bearer (negro or mulatto) named   has leave to go from   to   for   days," (or hours)   dated the same day of delivery.

Which said permission shall be signed by the owner or other person having charge of the slave, or some other person by his order, or with his consent; and every slave who shall be found beyond the limits of the said city, if said slave habitually works or resides there, or beyond the limits of the plantation to which the said slave belongs, or in which he habitually works, if he resides in the country, without a permission as above mentioned, or without a white person accompanying him, shall receive twenty lashes from the person who will arrest him, and shall be sent back to his master, who shall pay one dollar for his trouble, to whoever shall bring back said slave.

20. Every person is prohibited from permitting in his or her negro quarter, any other assemblies but those of his or her own slaves, under the penalty of paying all the damage which might result to the owner of any strange slave in consequence of such an admittance, and from allowing his or her slaves the liberty to dance during the night.

22. The inhabitants of the State shall be permitted to pursue and search for their runaway slaves in whatsoever place they may be, in such manner and by such white persons residing in the parish, as they may think proper, or may do so themselves if they think fit, even in the fields of other plantations, without being obliged to give notice of the same until after the search be made, except when search is made in the principal dwelling house, and other places under lock and key.

23. No owner of slaves shall hire his slaves to themselves, under the penalty of a fine of five and twenty dollars for every offence.

27. No slave shall be permitted to buy, sell, negotiate, trade or exchange any kind of goods or effects, and no slave shall be permitted to hold any barge, pirogue, or boat, or manage or bring up for his, the said slave's, own use, any horses, mares, or horned cattle, under the penalty of forfeiting the whole; and any person or persons whatsoever shall have authority to seize and carry away from every such slave, such goods, articles, barges, pirogues, boats, horses, mares, and horned cattle, and deliver them to the justice of the peace residing nearest to the place where said seizure shall take place. . . .

29. If any slave shall be found absent from the house or dwelling, or plantation, where he lives, or usually works, without some white person accompanying him, and shall refuse to submit himself to the examination of any freeholder, the said freeholder shall be permitted to seize and correct the said slave as aforesaid;

and if the said slave should resist or attempt to make his escape, the said inhabitant is hereby authorized to make use of arms, but at all events avoiding the killing of said slave; but should the said slave assault and strike the said inhabitant, he is lawfully authorized to kill him.

30. Every slave who shall be found on horseback, shall be liable to be immediately arrested, if he is not the bearer of a permission in writing from his master; and if he has no such permission, the said slave shall receive twenty-five lashes, after which he shall be taken back with the horse to his master, and his said master shall pay twelve cents and a half per mile for the carrying back the said slave.

31. No slave shall, by day or by night carry any visible or hidden arms, not even with a permission for so doing; and in case any person or persons shall find any slave or slaves using or carrying such fire arms, or any offensive weapons of any other kind, contrary to the true meaning of this section, he, she or they, lawfully may seize and carry away such fire arms or other offensive weapons. . . .

34. All persons whatever are prohibited from selling or in any manner whatever giving to any slave any intoxicating liquor, either for cash or in payment of some provisions, without a permission in writing from their master. . . .

40. The patrols ordered by the police juries shall have the right to enter on all plantations to visit the negro huts; and any inhabitant, his overseer or his representative, who shall prevent or forcibly oppose said patrols, when they shall proceed to visit the negro huts, shall, on conviction thereof, be condemned to a fine not exceeding one hundred dollars, nor less than twenty dollars, to be recovered on information before any court of competent jurisdiction, for the use of the parish.

41. The said patrols are hereby authorized to arrest and imprison all persons whom they shall meet committing any disorder or disturbing the public peace, and all vagabonds and suspicious persons; and it shall be the duty of the commander of patrols immediately to inform thereof the neighboring justice of the peace; Provided, that if the individuals arrested are runaway slaves, the

patrols shall have a right to the compensation fixed by law for arresting the same.

56. It shall no longer be lawful to bring into this State any slave entitled to freedom at a future period, or a "statu liber"; and any person who shall bring, or cause to be brought such slave or statu liber, contrary to the true intent and meaning of this section, shall be liable to criminal prosecution, and on conviction shall be punished by a fine not exceeding one thousand dollars, and imprisonment not exceeding six months, or both, at the discretion of the courts, and shall, besides, be compelled to pay the expenses of conveying the said slave back to the place whence he was brought here, or elsewhere out of the State.

106. Any slave who shall wilfully and maliciously strike his or her master or mistress, child or children, or any white overseer appointed by his or her owner to superintend said owner's slaves, so as to cause a contusion or shedding of blood, shall be punished with death.

110. If any slave shall maliciously burn or destroy any stacks of rice, corn, or other grain, or produce, raw or manufactured, of this Territory, or shall set fire to, or willingly or maliciously burn or destroy any building or house, or shall wilfully or maliciously poison, or maliciously administer poison to any free man, woman, child, servant, slave, or shall commit a rape upon the body of any white woman or girl, such slave shall suffer death.

138. Any person or persons who shall emancipate his, her or their slave or slaves, shall enter into bond, with at least one good and sufficient security, in the sum of one thousand dollars for each and every slave intended to be emancipated, conditioned that the slave or slaves emancipated, shall permanently depart from the State within one month from and after the passage of the act of emancipation; and in default of the slave so emancipated refusing or neglecting to depart from the State within the time prescribed by this section, the said bond shall become forfeited, one-half to the person denouncing and the other half to the State, the penalty of

said bond to be recovered by motion before any court of competent jurisdiction. . . .

147. Whosoever shall write, print, publish or distribute any thing having a tendency to produce discontent among the free colored population of the State, or insubordination among the slaves therein, shall, on conviction thereof, before any court of competent jurisdiction, be sentenced to imprisonment at hard labor for life, or suffer death, at the discretion of the court.

149. All persons who shall teach, or permit or cause to be taught, any slave in this State to read or write, shall, on conviction thereof before any court of competent jurisdiction, be imprisoned not less than one month nor more than twelve months.

151. If any person or persons shall harbor or conceal any runaway slave or slaves or fugitives from their masters, knowing that they are such, or shall cut or break any iron chain or collar which any master of slaves should have used in order to prevent the running away or escape of any such slave or slaves, such person or persons so offending shall, on conviction of any such offences, be fined not less than two hundred dollars, nor exceeding one thousand dollars, and suffer imprisonment for a term not exceeding two years nor less than six months, and the offender shall moreover be liable to pay to the master or masters of all slaves, or to his representative, the sum of two dollars for every day that such person or persons shall have concealed the said slave or slaves, and moreover such person or persons shall be responsible in his or their own and proper name for every damage which the said slave or slaves may have committed during the time of his or her concealment at said person's or persons'; and if said person or persons shall not have the means to pay to the master or masters of said slave or slaves the above compensation such person or persons shall, by the judge or justice of the peace, be condemned to an imprisonment which shall not exceed three months, and which shall not be less than fifteen days.

162. No slave shall be admitted as a witness, either in civil or criminal matters, for or against a white person.

The Experience of Slavery

The extent of physical brutality on the plantation is another subject of historical contention. Perhaps the best way to answer the question is to ask another: Have scholars known of a case of a single slave, male or female, who grew to maturity without at least one flogging? There were certainly very few. The whip is the most enduring symbol of the peculiar institution. It was applied for "sauciness," "impudence," tardiness, disobedience of any kind, theft, laziness, independence, and a catalogue of other supposed offenses. "Everybody in the south wants the privilege of whipping somebody else," Douglass recalled. "The whip is all in all." The following documents illustrate the common physical cruelty of the slave regime.

The Subduing of Randall *William Wells Brown**

My master, being a politician, soon found those who were ready to put him into office, for the favors he could render them; and a few years after his arrival in Missouri he was elected to a seat in the legislature. In his absence from home everything was left in charge of Mr. Cook, the overseer, and he soon became more tyrannical and cruel. Among the slaves on the plantation was one by the name of Randall. He was a man about six feet high, and well-proportioned, and known as a man of great strength and power. He was considered the most valuable and able-bodied slave on the plantation; but no matter how good or useful a slave may be, he seldom escapes the lash. But it was not so with Randall. He had been on the plantation since my earliest recollection, and I had never known of his being flogged. No thanks were due to the master or overseer for this. I have often heard him declare that no white man should ever whip him—that he would die first.

Cook, from the time that he came upon the plantation, had frequently declared that he could and would flog any nigger that was put into the field to work under him. My master had repeatedly told him not to attempt to whip Randall, but he was determined to try it. As soon as he was left sole dictator, he

* William Wells Brown, *Narrative*, pp. 16–19.

thought the time had come to put his threats into execution. He soon began to find fault with Randall, and threatened to whip him if he did not do better. One day he gave him a very hard task—more than he could possibly do; and at night, the task not being performed, he told Randall that he should remember him the next morning. On the following morning, after the hands had taken breakfast, Cook called out to Randall, and told him that he intended to whip him, and ordered him to cross his hands and be tied. Randall asked why he wished to whip him. He answered, because he had not finished his task the day before. Randall said that the task was too great, or he should have done it. Cook said it made no difference—he should whip him. Randall stood silent for a moment, and then said, "Mr. Cook, I have always tried to please you since you have been on the plantation, and I find you are determined not to be satisfied with my work, let me do as well as I may. No man has laid hands on me, to whip me, for the last ten years, and I have long since come to the conclusion not to be whipped by any man living." Cook, finding by Randall's determined look and gestures, that he would resist, called three of the hands from their work, and commanded them to seize Randall, and tie him. The hands stood still—they knew Randall—and they also knew him to be a powerful man, and were afraid to grapple with him. As soon as Cook had ordered the men to seize him, Randall turned to them, and said—"Boys, you all know me; you know that I can handle any three of you, and the man that lays hands on me shall die. This white man can't whip me himself, and therefore he has called you to help him." The overseer was unable to prevail upon them to seize and secure Randall, and finally ordered them all to go to their work together.

Nothing was said to Randall by the overseer for more than a week. One morning, however, while the hands were at work in the field, he came into it, accompanied by three friends of his, Thompson, Woodbridge and Jones. They came up to where Randall was at work, and Cook ordered him to leave his work, and go with them to the barn. He refused to go; whereupon he was attacked by the overseer and his companions, when he turned upon them, and laid them, one after another, prostrate on the ground. Woodbridge drew out his pistol, and fired at him, and brought him to the ground by a pistol ball. The others rushed upon him with their clubs, and beat him over the head and face, until they succeeded in tying him. He was then taken to the barn, and tied to a beam. Cook gave him over one hundred lashes with a heavy cowhide, had him washed with salt and water, and left him tied during the day. The next day he was untied, and taken to a blacksmith's shop, and had a ball and chain attached to his leg. He was compelled to labor in the field, and perform the same amount of work that the other hands did. When his master returned home, he was much pleased to find that Randall had been subdued in his absence.

Life on a Plantation *Frederick Douglass**

It is the boast of slaveholders, that their slaves enjoy more of the physical comforts of life than the peasantry of any country in the world. My experience contradicts this. The men and the women slaves on Col. Lloyd's farm, received, as their monthly allowance of food, eight pounds of pickled pork, or their equivalent in fish. The pork was often tainted, and the fish was of the poorest quality—herrings, which would bring very little if offered for sale in any northern market. With their pork or fish, they had one bushel of Indian meal—unbolted—of which quite fifteen percent was fit only to feed pigs. With this, one pint of salt was given; and this was the entire monthly allowance of a full grown slave, working constantly in the open field, from morning until night, every day in the month except Sunday, and living on a fraction more than a quarter of a pound of meat per day, and less than a peck of corn-meal per week. There is no kind of work that a man can do which requires a better supply of food to prevent physical exhaustion, than the field-work of a slave. So much for the slave's allowance of food; now for his raiment. The yearly allowance of clothing for the slaves on this plantation, consisted of two tow-linen shirts—such linen as the coarsest crash towels are made of; one pair of trowsers of the same material, for summer, and a pair of trowsers and a jacket of woolen, most slazily† put together, for winter; one pair of yarn stockings, and one pair of shoes of the

---

* From Frederick Douglass, *My Bondage and My Freedom* (New York, 1855), pp. 100–105.
† Sleazily.

coarsest description. The slave's entire apparel could not have cost more than eight dollars per year. The allowance of food and clothing for the little children, was committed to their mothers, or to the older slave-women having the care of them. Children who were unable to work in the field, had neither shoes, stockings, jackets nor trowsers given them. Their clothing consisted of two coarse tow-linen shirts—already described—per year; and when these failed them, as they often did, they went naked until the next allowance day. Flocks of little children from five to ten years old, might be seen on Col. Lloyd's plantation, as destitute of clothing as any little heathen on the west coast of Africa; and this, not merely during the summer months, but during the frosty weather of March. The little girls were no better off than the boys; all were nearly in a state of nudity.

As to beds to sleep on, they were known to none of the field hands; nothing but a coarse blanket—not so good as those used in the north to cover horses—was given them, and this only to the men and women. The children stuck themselves in holes and corners, about the quarters; often in the corner of the huge chimneys, with their feet in the ashes to keep them warm. The want of beds, however, was not considered a very great privation. Time to sleep was of far greater importance, for, when the day's work is done, most of the slaves have their washing, mending and cooking to do; and, having few or none of the ordinary facilities for doing such things, very many of their sleeping hours are consumed in necessary preparations for the duties of the coming day.

The sleeping apartments—if they may be called such—have little regard to comfort or decency. Old and young, male and female, married and single, drop down upon the common clay floor, each covering up with his or her blanket—the only protection they have from cold or exposure. The night, however, is shortened at both ends. The slaves work often as long as they can see, and are late in cooking and mending for the coming day; and, at the first gray streak of morning, they are summoned to the field by the driver's horn.

More slaves are whipped for oversleeping than for any other fault. Neither age nor sex finds any favor. The overseer stands at the quarter door, armed with stick and cowskin, ready to whip any who may be a few minutes behind time. When the horn is blown, there is a rush for the door, and the hindermost one is sure to get a blow from the overseer. Young mothers who worked in the field, were allowed an hour, about ten o'clock in the morning, to go home to nurse their children. Sometimes they were compelled to take their children with them, and to leave them in the corner of the fences, to prevent loss of time in nursing them. The overseer generally rides about the field on horseback. A cowskin and a hickory stick are his constant companions. The cowskin is a kind of whip seldom seen in the northern states. It is made entirely of untanned, but dried, ox hide, and is about as hard as a piece of well-seasoned live oak. It is made of various sizes, but the usual length is about three feet. The part held in the hand is nearly an inch in thickness; and, from the extreme end of the butt or handle, the cowskin tapers its whole length to a point. This makes it quite elastic and springy. A blow with it, on the hardest back, will gash the flesh, and make the blood start. Cowskins are painted red, blue and green, and are the favorite slave whip. I think this whip worse than the "cat-o'-nine-tails." It condenses the whole strength of the arm to a single point, and comes with a spring that makes the air whistle. It is a terrible instrument, and is so handy, that the overseer can always have it on his person, and ready for use. The temptation to use it is ever strong; and an overseer can, if disposed, always have cause for using it. With him, it is literally a word and a blow, and, in most cases, the blow comes first.

As a general rule, slaves do not come to the quarters for either breakfast or dinner, but take their "ash cake" with them, and eat it in the field. This was so on the home plantation; probably, because the distance from the quarter to the field, was sometimes two, and even three miles.

The dinner of the slaves consisted of a huge piece of ash cake, and a small piece of pork, or two salt herrings. Not having ovens, nor any suitable cooking utensils, the slaves mixed their meal with a little water, to such thickness that a spoon would stand erect in it; and, after the wood had burned away to coals and ashes, they would place the dough between oak leaves and lay it carefully in the ashes, completely covering it; hence, the bread is called ash cake. The surface of this peculiar bread is covered with ashes, to the depth of a sixteenth part of an inch, and the ashes, certainly, do not make it very grateful to the teeth, nor render it very palatable. The bran, or coarse part of the meal, is baked with the fine, and bright scales run through the bread. This bread, with its ashes and bran, would disgust and choke a northern man, but it is quite liked by the slaves. They eat it with avidity, and are more concerned about the quantity than about the quality. They are far too scantily provided for, and are worked too steadily, to be much concerned for the quality of their food. The few minutes allowed them at dinner time, after partaking of their coarse repast, are variously spent. Some lie down on the "turning row," and go to sleep; others draw together, and talk, and others are at work with needle and thread, mending their tattered garments. Sometimes you may hear a wild, hoarse laugh arise from a circle, and often a song. Soon, however, the overseer comes dashing through the field. *"Tumble up! Tumble up,* and to *work, work,"* is the cry; and, now, from twelve o'clock (mid-day) till dark, the human cattle are in motion, wielding their clumsy hoes; hurried on by no hope of reward, no sense of gratitude, no love of children, no prospect of bettering their condition; nothing, save the dread and terror of the slave-driver's lash. So goes one day, and so comes and goes another.

Slave Holidays and Songs *Frederick Douglass* *

Christmas was a time of temporary psychological release for the bondsmen. This annual jubilee, which usually lasted a week, was traditionally a time of abandon, drunkenness, dancing through the night and feasting: "Not to be drunk during the holidays was disgraceful. . . ." Slaves put on their "best attire": women wore some bright ribbons in their hair and perhaps a castaway bonnet or handkerchief; men dressed in their cleanest coats and those with shoes or hats proudly displayed them. It was a time, one slave recalled, to forget our "many sorrows amid the general hilarity. . . ."

Slave songs performed the same function—they helped people endure what Du Bois called the "blight." "Had it not been for my beloved violin, I scarcely can conceive how I could have endured

* From Frederick Douglass, *My Bondage and My Freedom,* pp. 97–100, 251–256.

the long years of bondage," Solomon Northup, a fugitive slave, recorded. "Often, at midnight, when sleep had fled . . . and my soul was disturbed and troubled with the contemplation of my fate, it would sing me a song of peace."

The days between Christmas day and New Year's, are allowed the slaves as holidays. During these days, all regular work was suspended, and there was nothing to do but to keep fires, and look after the stock. This time we regarded as our own, by the grace of our masters, and we, therefore used it, or abused it, as we pleased. Those who had families at a distance, were now expected to visit them, and to spend with them the entire week. The younger slaves, or the unmarried ones, were expected to see to the cattle, and attend to incidental duties at home. The holidays were variously spent. The sober, thinking and industrious ones of our number, would employ themselves in manufacturing corn brooms, mats, horse collars and baskets, and some of these were very well made. Another class spent their time in hunting opossums, coons, rabbits, and other game. But the majority spent the holidays in sports, ball playing, wrestling, boxing, running foot races, dancing, and drinking whisky; and this latter mode of spending the time was generally most agreeable to their masters. A slave who would work during the holidays, was thought, by his master, undeserving of holidays. Such a one had rejected the favor of his master. There was, in this simple act of continued work, an accusation against slaves; and a slave could not help thinking, that if he made three dollars during the holidays, he might make three hundred during the year. Not to be drunk during the holidays, was disgraceful; and he was esteemed a lazy and improvident man, who could not afford to drink whisky during Christmas.

The fiddling, dancing and *"jubilee beating,"* was going on in all directions. This latter performance is strictly southern. It supplies the place of a violin, or of other musical instruments, and is played so easily, that almost every farm has its "Juba" beater. The performer improvises as he beats, and sings his merry songs, so ordering the words as to have them fall pat with the movement of his hands. Among a mass of nonsense and wild frolic, once in a while a sharp hit is given to the meanness of slaveholders. Take the following, for an example:

"We raise de wheat,
　　Dey gib us de corn;
　We bake de bread,
　　Dey gib us de cruss;
　We sif de meal,
　　Dey gib us de huss;
　We peal de meat,
　　Dey gib us de skin,
　And dat's de way
　　Dey takes us in.
　We skim de pot,
　　Dey gib us the liquor,
　And say dat's good enough for nigger.
　　　Walk over! walk over!
　　　Tom butter and de fat;
　　　Poor nigger you can't get over dat;
　　　　　Walk over!"

This is not a bad summary of the palpable injustice and fraud of slavery, giving—as it does—to the lazy and idle, the comforts which God designed should be given solely to the honest laborer. But to the holidays.

Judging from my own observation and experience, I believe these holidays to be among the most effective means, in the hands of slaveholders, of keeping down the spirit of insurrection among the slaves.

To enslave men, successfully and safely, it is necessary to have their minds occupied with thoughts and aspirations short of the liberty of which they are deprived. A certain degree of attainable good must be kept before them. These holidays serve the purpose of keeping the minds of the slaves occupied with prospective pleasure, within the limits of slavery. The young man can go wooing; the married man can visit his wife; the father and mother can see their children; the industrious and money loving can make a few dollars; the great wrestler can win laurels; the young people can meet, and enjoy each other's society; the drunken man can get plenty of whisky; and the religious man can hold prayer meetings, preach, pray and exhort during the holidays. Before the holidays, these are pleasures in prospect; after the holidays, they become pleasures of memory, and they serve to keep out thoughts and wishes of a more dangerous character. Were slaveholders at once to abandon the practice of allowing their slaves these liberties, periodically, and to keep them, the year round, closely confined to the narrow circle of their homes, I doubt not that the south would blaze with insurrections. These holidays are conductors or safety valves to carry off the explosive elements inseparable from the human mind, when reduced to the condition of slavery. But for these, the rigors of bondage would become too severe for endurance, and the slave would be forced up to dangerous desperation. Woe to the slaveholder when he undertakes to hinder or to prevent the operation of these electric conductors. A succession of earthquakes would be less destructive, than the insurrectionary fires which would be sure to burst forth in different parts of the south from such interference.

Thus, the holidays, become part and parcel of the gross fraud, wrongs and inhumanity of slavery. Ostensibly, they are institutions of benevolence, designed to mitigate the rigors of slave life, but, practically, they are a fraud, instituted by human selfishness, the better to secure the ends of injustice and oppression. The slave's happiness is not the end sought, but, rather, the master's safety. It is not from a generous unconcern for the slave's labor that this cessation from labor is allowed, but from a prudent regard to the safety of the slave system. I am strengthened in this opinion, by the fact, that most slaveholders like to have their slaves spend the holidays in such a manner as to be of no real benefit to the slaves. It is plain, that everything like rational enjoyment among the slaves, is frowned upon; and only those wild and low sports, peculiar to semi-civilized people, are encouraged. All the license allowed, appears to have no other object than to disgust the slaves with their temporary freedom, and to make them as glad to return to their work, as they were to leave it. By plunging them into exhausting depths of drunkenness and dissipation, this effect is almost certain to follow. I have known slaveholders resort to cunning tricks, with a view of getting their slaves deplorably drunk. A usual plan is, to make bets on a slave, that he can drink more whisky than any other; and so to induce a rivalry among them, for the mastery in this degradation. The scenes, brought about in this way, were often scandalous and loathsome in the extreme. Whole multitudes might be found stretched out in brutal drunkenness, at once helpless and disgusting. Thus, when the slave asks for a few hours of virtuous freedom, his cunning master takes advantage of his ignorance, and cheers him with a dose of vicious and revolting dissipation, artfully labeled with the name of LIBERTY. We were induced to drink, I among the rest, and when the holidays were over, we all staggered up from our filth and wallowing, took a long breath, and went away to our various fields of work; feeling, upon the whole, rather glad to go from that which our masters artfully deceived us into the belief was freedom, back again to the arms of slavery. . . .

I am the more induced to take this view of the holiday system, adopted by slaveholders, from what I know of their treatment of slaves, in regard to other things. It is the commonest thing for them to try to disgust their slaves with what they do not want them to have, or to enjoy. A slave, for instance, likes molasses; he steals some; to cure him of the taste for it, his master, in many cases, will go away to town, and buy a large quantity of the *poorest* quality, and set it before his slave, and, with whip in hand, compel him to eat it, until the poor fellow is made to sicken at the very thought of molasses. The same course is often adopted to cure slaves of the disagreeable and inconvenient practice of asking for more food, when their allowance has failed them. The same disgusting process works well, too, in other things, but I need not cite them. When a slave is drunk, the slaveholder has no fear that he will plan an insurrection; no fear that he will escape to the north. It is the sober, thinking slave who is dangerous, and needs the vigilance of his master, to keep him a slave.

. . . Slaves are generally expected to sing as well as to work. A silent slave is not liked by masters or overseers. *"Make a noise, make a noise,"* and *"bear a hand,"* are the words usually addressed to the slaves when there is silence amongst them. This may account for the almost constant singing heard in the southern states. There was, generally, more or less singing among the teamsters, as it was one means of letting the overseer know where they were, and that they were moving on with the work. But, on allowance day, those who visited the great house farm were peculiarly excited and noisy. While on their way, they would make the dense old woods, for miles around, reverberate with their wild notes. These were not always merry because they were wild. On the contrary, they were mostly of a plaintive case, and told a tale of grief and sorrow. In the most boisterous outbursts of rapturous sentiment, there was ever a tinge of deep melancholy. I have never heard any songs like those anywhere since I left slavery, except when in Ireland. There I heard the same *wailing notes,* and was much affected by them. It was during the famine of 1845–6. In all the songs of the slaves, there was ever some expression in praise of the great house farm; something which would flatter the pride of the owner, and, possibly, draw a favorable glance from him.

> "I am going away to the great house farm,
>   O yea! O yea! O yea!
> My old master is a good old master,
>   O yea! O yea! O yea!"

This they would sing, with other words of their own improvising —jargon to others, but full of meaning to themselves. I have sometimes thought, that the mere hearing of those songs would do more to impress truly spiritual-minded men and women with the soul-crushing and death-dealing character of slavery, than the reading of whole volumes of its mere physical cruelties. They speak to the heart and to the soul of the thoughtful. I cannot better express my sense of them now, than ten years ago, when, in sketching my life, I thus spoke of this feature of my plantation experience:

"I did not, when a slave, understand the deep meanings of those rude, and apparently incoherent songs. I was myself within the circle, so that I neither saw nor heard as those without might see and hear. They told a tale which was then altogether beyond my feeble comprehension; they were tones, loud, long and deep, breathing the prayer and complaint of souls boiling over with the bitterest anguish. Every tone was a testimony against slavery, and a prayer to God for deliverance from chains. The hearing of those wild notes always depressed my spirits, and filled my heart with ineffable sadness. The mere recurrence, even now, afflicts my spirit, and while I am writing these lines, my tears are falling. To those songs I trace my first glimmering conceptions of the de-humanizing character of slavery. I can never get rid of that conception. Those songs still follow me, to deepen my hatred of slavery, and quicken my sympathies for my brethren in bonds. If any one wishes to be impressed with a sense of the soul-killing power of slavery, let him go to Col. Lloyd's plantation, and, on allowance day, place himself in the deep, pine woods, and there let him, in silence, thoughtfully analyze the sounds that shall pass through the chambers of his soul, and if he is not thus impressed, it will only be because 'there is no flesh in his obdurate heart.' "

The remark is not unfrequently made, that slaves are the most contented and happy laborers in the world. They dance and sing, and make all manner of joyful noises—so they do; but it is a great mistake to suppose them happy because they sing. The songs of the slave represent the sorrows, rather than the joys, of his heart; and he is relieved by them, only as an aching heart is relieved by its tears. Such is the constitution of the human mind, that, when pressed to extremes, it often avails itself of the most opposite methods. . . . The singing of a man cast away on a desolate island, might be as appropriately considered an evidence of his contentment and happiness, as the singing of a slave. Sorrow and desolation have their songs, as well as joy and peace. Slaves sing more to *make* themselves happy, than to express their happiness.

The Quest for Identity *William Wells Brown**

When Muslims today relinquish their "given" names and search for others or replace them with an X, they touch upon one of the most debasing consequences of slavery—the denial of human identity. The right to have or choose one's own name is the right to be; *the power to control a man's name is authority to subjugate the man himself. Most slaves seem to have been given Christian names of a Biblical nature, but some were ridiculed or burlesqued from birth with such labels as Bashful, Virtue, Frolic, Gamesome, Lady, Madame, Duchess, Cowslip, Spring, Summer, Caesar, Pompey, Strumpet, and so on. Nothing better reveals the derisive nature of slavery than the act of naming.*

The quest for identity is clearly evident in the independent experiences of two slaves, William Wells Brown and Frederick Douglass. When each escaped, they permitted those who had befriended them to choose their surnames but insisted on retaining the names by which they had been known all their lives. Douglass,

* William Wells Brown, *Narrative*, pp. 96–104.

for example, acquired his name because Nathan Johnson of New Bedford, Massachusetts, was reading Lady of the Lake *when Douglass knew him. He insisted, however, on being called Frederick: "I gave Mr. Johnson the privilege of choosing me a name, but told him he must not take from me the name of 'Frederick.' I must hold on to that to present a sense of my identity."*

My escape to a land of freedom now appeared certain, and the prospects of the future occupied a great part of my thoughts. What should be my occupation, was a subject of much anxiety to me; and the next thing what should be my name? I have before stated that my old master, Dr. Young, had no children of his own, but had with him a nephew, the son of his brother, Benjamin Young. When this boy was brought to Dr. Young, his name being William, the same as mine, my mother was ordered to change mine to something else. This, at the time, I thought to be one of the most cruel acts that could be committed upon my rights; and I received several very severe whippings for telling people that my name was William, after orders were given to change it. Though young, I was old enough to place a high appreciation upon my name. It was decided, however, to call me "Sandford," and this name I was known by, not only upon my master's plantation, but up to the time that I made my escape. I was sold under the name of Sandford.

But as soon as the subject came to my mind, I resolved on adopting my old name of William, and let Sandford go by the board, for I always hated it. Not because there was anything peculiar in the name; but because it had been forced upon me. It is sometimes common, at the south, for slaves to take the name of their masters. Some have a legitimate right to do so. But I always detested the idea of being called by the name of either of my masters. And as for my father, I would rather have adopted the name of "Friday," and been known as the servant of some Robinson Crusoe, than to have taken his name.* So I was not only hunting for my liberty, but also hunting for a name. . . .

The kind friend that had taken me in was named Wells Brown. He was a devoted friend of the slaves. . . . Before leaving this good Quaker friend, he inquired what my name was besides

* A white man.

William. I told him that I had no other name. "Well," said he, "thee must have another name. Since thee has got out of slavery, thee has become a man, and men always have two names."

I told him that he was the first man to extend the hand of friendship to me, and I would give him the privilege of naming me.

"If I name thee," said he, "I shall call thee Wells Brown, after myself."

"But," said I, "I am not willing to lose my name of William. As it was taken from me once against my will, I am not willing to part with it again upon any terms."

"Then," said he, "I will call thee William Wells Brown."

"So be it," said I; and I have been known by that name ever since I left the house of my first white friend, Wells Brown.

3. ATTITUDES TOWARD SLAVERY IN COLONIAL AMERICA

The Church and Slavery

For three centuries the more liberal forces of American religion worried about the slave's soul. When it had been agreed and codified in the seventeenth century that the Lord permitted Negroes to be both Christians and slaves, ministers in the North and South attempted to convince masters that the Gospel was as essential to their interests as to the slaves'—slaveholders were asked to act as agents of the Divine. Cotton Mather, who founded a school for slaves, told masters in Boston to help convert the "most Bruitish *of Creatures upon Earth." "Will you do nothing to pluck them out of the Jaws of* Satan the Devourer?" *he queried. "Be assured Syrs; Your Servants will be* Better Servants, *for being made* Christian Servants."

The same doctrine was presented in the South. The Reverend Thomas Bacon of the Protestant Episcopal Church in Maryland preached sermons to slaves in the 1740's that were models of others delivered until the Civil War. His works, in fact, were reprinted in the nineteenth century. The Reverend Bacon composed poems on "The Comforts of Religion," "Against Lying," and "The All-Seeing God." Other clergymen, like the author of Sambo and Toney: A Dialogue *(1813), wrote plays—yet the message was always the same. "On Sabbath there was one sermon preached expressly for the colored people," a North Carolina bondsman recorded in the 1840's. "I became quite familiar with the texts. 'Servants be obedient to your masters.' 'Not with eye service as men pleasers.' 'He that knoweth his master's will and doeth it not, shall be beaten with many stripes,' and others of this class. . . . The first commandment impressed upon our minds was to obey our masters, and the second was . . . to do as much work when they or the overseers were not watching us as when they were."*

A Minister's Advice to Boston Slaveholders *Cotton Mather**

. . . Oh! That our Neighbours would consider the incomparable *Benefits* that would follow upon your *Endeavours* to *Christianize* your Negroes, and bring them to a share with your selves in the *Benefits* of the Heavenly *Inheritance*. If your care and cost about the cultivation of your *Negroes,* be laid out upon such a Stony and Barren Soil, that you can see no Fruit of it, yet it is not all thrown away. The blessed God will approve and reward what you have done; Think, *Tho' my* Negroes *will not prove a part of the Israel of God, and will not be gathered unto the Lord, yet my work is with my God, and what I do is glorious in the Eyes of the Lord.* But it is very probable, You may see some good *Success* of your Travail. And *then!* Oh! the *Consolations* that will belong unto you! *Christianity* does Marvellously befriend and enrich and advance Mankind. The greatest *Kindness* that can be done to any Man is to make a *Christian* of him. Your *Negroes* are immediately Raised unto an astonishing Felicity, when you have *Christianized* them. They are become amiable spectacles, & such as the *Angels* of God would gladly repair unto the Windows of Heaven to look upon. Tho' they remain your *Servants,* yet they are become the *Children* of God. Tho' they are to enjoy no *Earthly Goods,* but the small Allowance that your Justice and Bounty shall see proper for them,

---

* From Cotton Mather, *The Negro Christianized: An Essay to Excite and Assist that Good Work, the Instruction of Negro-Servants in Christianity* (Boston, 1706), pp. 18–27.

yet they are become *Heirs* of God, and *joint-Heirs* with the Lord
Jesus Christ. Tho' they are your *Vassals,* and must with a profound subject wait upon you, yet the Angels of God now take them
under their Guardianship, and vouchsafe to tend upon them. Oh!
what have you done for them! Happy *Masters,* who are Instru-
mental to raise their *Servants* thus from the *Dust,* and make them
objects for the *Nobles* of *Heaven* to take Notice of! But it will not
be long before you and they come at length to be together in the
Heavenly City. *Lazarus* there lies down at the same Feast, with his
Master *Abraham.* There was *Joy in Heaven* when your *Servants*
first came to [know] *that the Lord is Gracious:* and it cannot but
be a vast Accession unto your *Joy in Heaven, to meet your Servants* there and hear them forever blessing the gracious God, for
the Day when He first made them your *Servants.* If these *Consolations of God* be *small* unto a Man truly, he has very Bad Symptoms upon him.

    Yea, the pious *Masters,* that have instituted their *Servants* in
Christian Piety, will even in this Life have a sensible Recompense.
The more *Serviceable,* and Obedient and obliging Behaviour their
Servants unto them, will be a sensible & as notable *Recompense.*
Be assured, Syrs; Your *Servants* will be the *Better Servants,* for
being made *Christian Servants.* To *Christianize* them aright, will be
to *fill them with all Goodness. Christianity* is nothing but a very
Mass of Universal *Goodness.* Were your *Servants* well tinged with
the Spirit of *Christianity,* it would render them exceeding *Dutiful*
unto their *Masters,* exceeding *Patient* unto their *Masters,* exceeding faithful in their *Business,* and afraid of speaking or doing any
thing that may justly displease you. It has been observed, that
those *Masters* who have used their *Negroes* with most of *Humanity,* in allowing them all the Comforts of Life, that are necessary
and *Convenient* for them, (Who have remembered, that by the
Law of God, even an *Ass* was to be relieved, When *Sinking under
his Burden,* and an *Ox* might not be *Muzzeled* when *Treading out
the Corn;* and that is a *Just man will regard the Life of his Beast,*
he will much more allow the comforts of life to and not himself
from his own Flesh): have been better *Serv'd,* had more work
done for them, and better done, than those *Inhumane Masters,*
who have used their *Negroes* worse than their *Horses.* And those
Masters doubtless who use their *Negroes* with most of *Christianity,*

and use most pains to inform them in, and conform them to, *Christianity,* will find themselves no losers by it. . . . But many *Masters* whose *Negroes* have greatly vexed them, with miscarriages, may do well to examine, Whether Heaven be not chastising of them, for their failing in their Duty about their *Negroes.* Had they done more, to make their *Negroes* the knowing and willing *Servants* of God, it may be, God would have made their *Negroes* better *Servants* to them. Syrs, you may Read your *Sin* in the *Punishment.*

And now, what *Objection* can any Man Living have, to retund the force of these *Considerations?* Produce *thy cause,* O Impiety, *Bring forth thy strong reasons,* and let all men see what Idle and silly cavils, are thy best *Reasons* against this Work of God.

It has been cavilled, by some, that it is questionable Whether the *Negroes* have *Rational Souls,* or no. But let that *Bruitish* insinuation be never Whispered any more. Certainly, their *Discourse,* will abundantly prove, that they have *Reason. Reason* showes it self in the *Design* which they daily act upon. The vast improvement that *Education* has made upon *some* of them, argues that there is a *Reasonable Soul* in *all* of them. . . . They are *Men,* and not *Beasts* that you have bought, and they must be used accordingly. 'Tis true; They are *Barbarous.* But so were our own *Ancestors.* The *Britons* were in many things as *Barbarous,* but a little before our Saviours Nativity, as the *Negroes* are at this day. . . . Christianity will be the best cure for their Barbarity. Their Complexion sometimes is made an Argument, why nothing should be done for them. A *Gay* sort of argument! As if the great God went by the Complexion of Men, in His Favours to them! As if none but *Whites* might hope to be Favoured and Accepted with God! Whereas it is well known, that the Whites, are the least part of Mankind. The biggest part of Mankind, perhaps, are *Copper-Coloured;* a sort of *Tawnies.* And our English that inhabit some Climates, do seem growing apace to be not much unlike unto them. As if, because a people, from the long force of the African *Sun & Soyl* upon them, (improved perhaps, to further Degrees by maternal imaginations, and other accidents,) are come at length to have the small *Fibres* of their *Veins,* and the Blood in them, a little more interspersed thro their Skin than other People, this must render them less valuable to Heaven than the rest of Mankind?

Away with such Trifles! The God who *looks on the Heart,* is not moved by the colour of the Skin; is not more propitious to one *Colour* than another. Say rather, with the Apostle; . . . *Of a truth I perceive, that God is no respecter of persons; but in every Nation, he that feareth Him and worketh Righteousness, is accepted with Him.* Indeed their *Stupidity* is a *Discouragement.* It may seem, unto as little purpose, to *Teach,* as to *wash an AEthiopian.* But the greater their *Stupidity,* the greater must be our *Application.* If we can't learn them so much as we *Would,* let us learn them as much as we *Can.* A little divine *Light* and *Grace* infused into them, will be of great account. And the more *Difficult* it is, to fetch such *forlorn things* up out of the perdition whereinto they are fallen, the more *Laudable* is the undertaking: There will be the more of a *Triumph,* if we prosper in the undertaking. Let us encourage our selves from that word; *God is able of these Stones, to raise up Children unto Abraham.*

Well, But if the *Negroes* are *Christianized,* they will be *Baptised;* and their *Baptism* will presently entitle them to their Freedom; so our Money is thrown away.

Man, If this were true; that a *Slave* bought with thy *Money,* were by thy means brought unto the *Things that accompany Salvation,* and thou shouldest from this time have no more Service from him, yet thy *Money* were not thrown away. That Mans *Money will perish with him,* who had rather the Souls in his Family should *Perish,* than that he should lose a little *Money.* And suppose it were so, that *Baptism* gave a legal Title to *Freedom.* Is there no guarding against this Inconvenience? You may by sufficient *Indentures,* keep off the things, which you reckon so Inconvenient. But it is all a Mistake. There is no such thing. What *Law* is it, that Sets the *Baptised Slave* at *Liberty?* Not the *Law of Christianity:* that allows of *Slavery;* Only it wonderfully Dulcifies, and Mollifies, and Moderates the Circumstances of it. *Christianity* directs a *Slave,* upon his embracing the *Law of the Redeemer,* to satisfy himself, *That he is the Lords Free-man,* tho' he continues a *Slave.* It supposes, That there are *Bond* as well as *Free,* among those that have been *Renewed in the Knowledge and Image of Jesus Christ.* Will the *Canon-law* do it? No; The *Canons* of Numberless *Councils,* mention, the *Slaves* of *Christians,* without any contradiction. Will the *Civil Law* do it? No: Tell, if you can, any part of *Christendom,* wherein Slaves are not frequently to be met withal. But is not *Freedom* to be claimed for a *Baptised Slave,* by the *English* Constitution? The English *Laws,* about Villeins, or, Slaves, will not say so; for by those Laws, they may be granted for Life, like a Lease, and passed over with a Mannor, like other Goods or Chattels. And by those Laws, the Lords may seize the Bodies of their Slaves even while a Writt . . . is depending. These English Laws were made when the Lords & the Slaves, were both of them Christians; and they stand still unrepealed. If there are not now such Slaves in England as formerly, it is from the Lords, more than from the Laws. The Baptised then are not thereby entitled unto their Liberties.

. . . The way is now cleared, for the work that is proposed: that excellent *WORK, THE INSTRUCTION OF THE NE-GROES IN THE CHRISTIAN RELIGION.*

Sermon to Maryland Slave Congregation *Thomas Bacon**

Having thus shewn you the chief duties you owe to your great master in heaven, I now come to lay before you the duties you owe to your *masters* and *mistresses* here upon earth.

And for this, you have one general rule that you ought always to carry in your minds;—and that is,—*to do all service for them, as if you did it for GOD himself.* —Poor creatures! you little consider, when you are idle and neglectful of your master's business,—when you *steal* and *waste,* and *hurt* any of their substance,—when you are *saucy* and *impudent,*—when you are telling them *lies,* and deceiving them,—or when you prove *stubborn* or *sullen,* and will not do the work you are set about without stripes and vexation;—you do not consider, I say, that what faults you are guilty of towards your masters and mistresses are faults done against GOD himself, who hath set your masters and mistresses over you, in his own stead, and expects that you will do for them, just as you would do for him. —And pray, do not think that I want to deceive you, when I tell you, that your *masters* and *mistresses* are GOD's *overseers,*—and that if you are faulty towards them, GOD himself will punish you severely for it in the next world, unless you repent

* From Thomas Bacon, *Sermons Addressed to Masters and Servants and Published in the Year 1743.* . . . (Winchester, Va., 1813?), pp. 104–111.

of it, and strive to make amends, by your *faithfulness* and *diligence,* for the time to come;—for GOD himself hath declared the same. And you have at the same time this comfort, that if any of your *owners* should prove *wicked overseers,* and use you, who are his under servants here, as they ought not to do;—though you must submit to it, and can have no remedy in this world, yet, when GOD calls you and them together face to face before him in the next world, and examines into these matters, he will do you strict justice, and punish those that have been bad stewards and overseers over you with the greater severity, as they had more of this world entrusted to their care:—and that whatever you have suffered *unjustly* here, GOD will make you amends for it in heaven. I will now read over to you the rules which GOD hath given you, in his own words, that you may see what I say is truth. "Servants, be obedient to them that are your masters according to the flesh, with fear and trembling, in singleness of your heart, as unto Christ:—Not with eye-service, as men-pleasers, but as the servant of Christ, doing the will of GOD from the heart. With good will doing service, as to the LORD and not to men. —Knowing, that whatsoever good thing any man doeth, the same shall he receive of the Lord, whether he be bond or free. —And ye masters, do the same things unto them, forbearing (or moderating) threatening; knowing that your master also is in heaven; neither is there respect of persons with him."

Now, from this great general rule, namely, that you are to *do all service for your masters and mistresses, as if you did it for GOD himself,* there arise several other rules of duty towards your *masters* and *mistresses,* which I shall endeavour to lay in order before you.

1. And in the first place, *you are to be obedient and subject to your masters in all things.* For the rules which GOD hath left us in the scriptures are these—"Servants, obey in all things your masters according to the flesh, not with eye-service as men-pleasers, but in singleness of heart, fearing GOD:—And whatsoever ye do, do it heartily, as to the Lord, and not unto men; knowing, that of the Lord ye shall receive the reward of the inheritance for ye serve the Lord Christ. —But he that doeth wrong shall receive for the wrong he hath done; and there is no respect of persons. — Servants, be subject to your masters, with all fear, not only to the good and gentle, but also to the froward."—And Christian ministers

are commanded to *exhort servants to be obedient unto their own masters, and to please them well in all things, not answering again,* or murmuring, or gainsaying. —You see how strictly GOD requires this of you, that whatever your *masters* and *mistresses* order you to do, you must set about it immediately, and faithfully perform it, without any disputing or grumbling,—and take care to please them well in all things. —And, for your encouragement, he tells you, that he will reward you for it in heaven, because, while you are honestly and faithfully doing your master's business here, you are serving your Lord and master in heaven. You see also, that you are not to take any exceptions to the behaviour of your masters and mistresses, and that you are to be subject and obedient, not only to such as are *good,* and *gentle,* and *mild,* towards you, but also to such as may be *froward, peevish,* and *hard.* —For you are not at liberty to chuse your own masters, but into whatever hands GOD hath been pleased to put you, you must do your duty, and GOD will reward you for it. And if they neglect to do theirs, GOD will punish them for it:—For there is no respect of persons with him. There is only *one case,* in which you may refuse obedience to your owners,—and that is, if they should command you to do any *sinful* thing. —As *Joseph* would not hearken to his mistress, when she tempted him to sin with her. —So that if any master could be so wicked as to command you to *steal,* to *murder,* to *set a neighbour's house on fire,* to *do harm to any bodys goods, or cattle,* or to get *drunk,* or to *curse and swear,* or to *work on sundays,* (unless it should be in a case of great necessity)—or to do any thing that GOD hath forbidden, there it is your duty to refuse them;—because GOD is your *head master,* and you must not do a thing which you know is contrary to his will. —But in every thing else, you must obey your owners; and GOD requires it of you.

2. You are *not* to be *eye-servants.* —Now *eye-servants* are such as will *work hard,* and seem mighty diligent, while they think that any body is taking notice of them, but when their masters and mistresses backs are turned, they are idle, and neglect their business.

—I am afraid that there are a great many such *eye servants* among you,—and that you do not consider how great a sin it is to be so, and how severely GOD will punish you for it. —You may easily deceive your owners, and make them have an opinion of you that you do not deserve, and get the praise of men by it. But remember, that you cannot deceive Almighty GOD, who sees your wickedness and deceit, and will punish you accordingly. For the rule is, that you must *obey your masters in all things,* & do the work they set you about *with fear and trembling, in singleness of heart, as unto Christ, not with eye-service, as men pleasers, but as the servants of Christ, doing the will of God from the heart: With good will doing service, as to the Lord, and not as to men.* —If then, you would but think, and say within yourselves,—"My master hath set me about this work, and his back is turned, so that I may loiter and idle if I please, for he does not see me. —But there is my *great master* in heaven, whose overseer my other master is—and his eyes are always upon me, and taking notice of me, and I cannot get any where out of his sight, nor be idle without his knowing it, and what will become of me if I lose his good will, and make him angry with me." —If, I say, you would once get the way of thinking and saying thus, upon all occasions, you then would do what GOD commands you, and serve your masters with singleness of heart,—that is, with honesty and sincerity; you would do the work you are set about *with fear and trembling,* not for fear of your masters and mistresses upon earth (for you may easily cheat them, and make them believe you are doing their business when you do not)—but with *fear and trembling,* lest GOD, your heavenly master, whom you cannot deceive, should call you to account, and punish you in the next world, for your *deceitfulness,* and *eye-service* in this.

3. You are to be *faithful and honest to your masters and mistresses—not purloining* (or wasting their goods or substance) *but shewing all good fidelity in all things.*

If you were to *rob* or *steal* from others, you know that it would be a very bad thing and how severely the law would punish you for it. —But if your master is robbed of what belongs to him by your wastefulness or negligence, do not you think that it is wicked? —For pray what is the difference to me, when my substance is gone, whether a thief took it away from me, or whether I am robbed of it by my servants negligence? —The loss is the same, and they will have it to answer for. —How then can many of you be so careless about your master's business? —How can you be so unfaithful and wicked, as to see their substance perish and be lost, when a little of your timely care would prevent the loss? —Is not this a very common case among you? —And do not most masters complain, with great justice, that unless they happen to see into every thing themselves, their servants will take no care? —Nay, even when they are told of it, and ordered to do it, they will still neglect, and let the goods perish? —Do not your masters, under GOD, provide for you? —And how shall they be able to do this, to *feed* and to *clothe* you, unless you take honest care of every thing that belongs to them? —Remember that GOD requires this of you, and if you are not afraid of suffering for it here, you cannot escape the vengeance of Almighty GOD, who will judge between you and your masters, and make you pay severely in *the next world* for all the injustice you do them here. —And tho' you could manage so cunningly as to escape the eyes and hands of man, yet think what a dreadful thing it is to fall *into the hands of the living GOD, who is able to cast both soul and body into hell.*

4. You are to *serve your masters with cheerfulness, reverence, and humility.* —You are to do your masters service *with good will,* doing it as *the will of GOD, from the heart,* without any sauciness or answering again. —How many of you do things quite otherwise, and, instead of going about your work with a *good* will and a good heart, *dispute,* and *grumble;* give saucy answers, and behave in a surly manner? —There is something so becoming and engaging in a modest, chearful, good-natured behaviour, that a little work done in that manner, seems better done, and gives far more satisfaction, than a great deal more that must be done with fretting, vexation, and the lash always held over you. It also gains the good will and love of those you belong to, and makes your own life pass with more ease and pleasure. —Besides, you are to consider, that this *grumbling* and *ill will* does not affect your *masters* and *mistresses* only:—They have ways and means in their hands of forcing you to do your work, whether you are willing or not. — But your *murmuring* and *grumbling* is against GOD, who hath placed you in that service, who will punish you severely in the next world for despising his commands.

Thus I have endeavoured to shew you, why you ought to serve GOD, and what duty in particular you owe to him:—I have also shewn you, that while you are serving your masters and mistresses, or doing any thing that GOD hath commanded, you are at the same time *serving* him; and have endeavoured to shew you what duty or service you owe to your owners, in obedience to GOD, and that in so plain a manner, as I hope the greatest part of you did well understand. —The other parts of your duty and the rewards which GOD hath promised to you (if you will honestly set about doing it) I shall endeavour to lay before you at our next meeting here for that purpose. —In the mean time, consider well what hath been said. —Think upon it, and talk about it one with another, and strive to fix it on your memories. —And may GOD of his infinite mercy grant, that it may sink deep into your hearts, and, taking root there, may bring forth in you the fruit of good living, to the honour and praise of his holy name, the spreading abroad of his gospel, and the eternal salvation of your precious souls, through our Lord and Saviour JESUS CHRIST, to whom, with the father, and the holy spirit, be all honor and glory, world without end. — *Amen.*

Race and Natural Rights

Anthony Benezet and John Woolman were abolitionist movements unto themselves. They were undoubtedly the most outspoken American opponents of slavery in the eighteenth century. Both had international reputations for their piety, corresponded throughout the Atlantic world in the interests of Negro emancipation, and devoted their lives to teaching, writing, and preaching against the slave trade and slavery. Benezet's essay "Observations on Slavery" is offered as an illustration of the way Revolutionary rhetoric was used as a weapon of antislavery—he quotes from the Declaration of Independence. The racial views of the author of the Declaration follow that.

A Quaker's Observations on Slavery *Anthony Benezet**

The Slavery which now so largely subsists in the American Colonies, is another mighty evil, which proceeds from the same corrupt root as War; for, however, it may be granted that some, otherwise,

* From Anthony Benezet, "Observations on Slavery" in *Serious Considerations on Several Important Subjects. . . .* (Philadelphia, 1778), pp. 27–40.

well disposed people in different places, particularly in these
provinces, at first fell into the practice of buying and keeping
Slaves, thro' inadvertency, or by the example of others; yet in the
generality it sprang from an unwarrantable desire of gain, a lust
for amassing wealth, and in the pride of their heart, holding an
uncontrollable power over their fellow-men. The observation
which the Apostle makes on War, may well be applied to those
who compelled their fellow-men to become their slaves, *they
lusted,* for wealth and power *and desired to have, that they might
consume it upon their lusts.*

It is a very afflictive consideration, that notwithstanding the
rights and liberties of mankind have been so much the object of
publick notice, yet the same corrupt principles still maintain their
power in the minds of most Slave Holders. Indeed nothing can
more clearly and positively militate against the slavery of the
Negroes, than the several declarations lately published, with so
great an appearance of solemnity, thro' all the colonies, viz. "We
hold these truths to be self evident, that all men are created equal,
that they are endowed by their creator with certain unalienable
rights; that among these are life, liberty, and the pursuit of
happiness." And "That all men are by nature equally free and
independent, and have certain inherent rights, of which when they
enter into a state of society they cannot by any compact, deprive
or divert their property, namely the enjoyment of life and liberty,
with the means of acquiring and possessing property, and pursuing
and obtaining happiness and safety." That after these, and other
declarations of the same kind, have been so publickly made to the
world, Slavery should continue in its full force in the Colonies
. . . is a great aggravation of that guilt which has so long lain
upon America; and which together with the blood of the Native
Indians, so daringly spilt, is likely to be one of the principal causes
of those heavy judgments, which are now so sensibly displayed
over the Colonies. Perhaps nothing will so sensibly teach us to feel
for the affliction of the oppressed Africans, as that ourselves
partake of the same cup of distress, we have so long been instru-
mental in causing them to drink. If we look back to early times,
and bring to our remembrance what we have heard from our
fathers, relating to the first introduction of Negroes amongst us, we
shall have reason to conclude, that there were but few of those

concerned in those purchases, who were not in some measure acquainted with the dreadful calamities introduced in Guinea, in order to procure Slaves for the American Market. They had doubtless heard something of these accounts; they saw their afflicted fellow-men, after being by the ravages of war deprived of all property, and cruelly rent from every tender connection in their native land, brought to America, and there sold like beasts for burden or slaughter; yet we have too much reason to conclude that but little sympathy was extended to them, few, very few, even amongst professors, endeavoured, on their behalf, *"To seek judgment, to relieve the oppressed; to plead for the fatherless, and to judge for the widow; few mourned with those that mourned"*; people saw their affliction and heared the doleful story of their particular cases with little or no fellow feeling, indifferency prevailed; there was too much of a joining in spirit with those who *"had slain with the sword, and had carried into captivity,"* arising from a secret satisfaction, at the prospect of having an opportunity, thro' the Slaves labour, of encreasing their substance, and amassing much wealth, in the acquirement and possession of which, a proper regard not being had, *"to the will of the Lord that reigneth,"* there has been sent *a curse* upon what they esteemed *a blessing;* their riches have proved as wings to raise their children above truth and real happiness: The offspring of many of these are still living in idleness and pride; whilst others are rioting in dissipation and luxury. If the good and just father of mankind is now arisen to plead the cause of the oppressed Africans, and to bring the matter home to ourselves; who can say, what doest thou. Will not the Americans, amongst whom the establishment of religious as well as civil liberty is the present and great object of consideration and debate, be a witness against themselves, so long as they continue to keep their Fellow-Inhabitants in such grievous circumstances, whereby they are not only deprived of their liberty, but of all property and indeed of every right whatsoever?

Here it may not be necessary to repeat what has been so fully declared in several modern publications, of the inconsistence of slavery with every right of mankind, with every feeling of humanity, and every precept of Christianity; nor to point out its inconsistency with the welfare, peace and prosperity of every country, in proportion as it prevails; what grievous sufferings it brings on the poor Negroes; but more especially what a train of fatal vices it produces in their lordly oppressors and their unhappy offspring.

. . . May I speak plainly to you? I must. Love constrains me: Love to you, as well, as those you are concerned with. Is there a God? You know there is. Is he a just God? Then there must be a state of retribution: A state wherein the just God will reward every man according to his work. Then what reward will he render to you. O think betimes! before you drop in eternity: Think how, "He shall have judgment without mercy, that shewed no mercy." Are you a man? Then you should have a human heart. But have you indeed? What is your heart made of? Is there no such principle as compassion there? Do you never feel another's pain? Have you no sympathy? No sense of human woe? No pity for the miserable? When you saw the flowing eyes, the heaving breast, or the bleeding sides and tortured limbs of your fellow-creatures: Was you a stone or a brute? Did you look upon them with the eyes of a tiger? When you squeezed the agonizing creatures down in the ship, or when you threw their poor mangled remains into the sea, had you no relenting? Did not one tear drop from your eye, one sigh escape from your breast? Do you feel no relenting now? If you do not, you must go on, till the measure of your iniquities is full. Then will the great God deal with you, as you have dealt with them, and require all their blood at your hands. And at that day it shall be more tolerable for Sodom and Gomorrah than for you: But if your heart does relent; though in a small degree, know it is a call from the God of love. And to-day, if you hear his voice, harden not your heart—To-day resolve, God being your helper to escape for your life—Regard not money: All that a man hath will he give for his life. Whatever you lose, lose not your Soul; nothing can countervail that loss. Immediately quit the horrid trade: At all events be an honest man.

This equally concerns every merchant who is engaged in the Slave-trade. It is you that induce the African villain to fell his countrymen; and in order thereto, to steal, rob, murder men, women and children without number: By enabling the English villain to pay him for so doing; whom you over pay for his execrable labour. It is your money, that is the spring of all, that impowers him to go on, so that whatever he or the African does in this matter, is all your act and deed. And is your conscience quite reconciled to this? Does it never reproach you at all? Has gold entirely blinded your eyes and stupified your heart? Can you see, can you feel no harm therein? Is it doing as you would be done to? Make the case your own. "Master! (said a Slave at Liverpool to the merchant that owned him) what if some of my countrymen were to come here, and take away my mistress, and master Tommy and master Billy, and carry them into our country and make them slaves, how would you like it?" His answer was worthy of a man: "I will never buy a slave more while I live." O let this resolution be yours! Have no more any part in this detestable business. Instantly leave it to those unfeeling wretches, "Who laugh at humanity and compassion."

And this equally concerns every Person who has an estate in our American plantations: Yea all Slave-holders of whatever rank and degree; seeing menbuyers are exactly on a level with menstealers. Indeed you say, "I pay honestly for my goods; and I am not concerned to know how they are come by." Nay, but you are: You are deeply concerned, to know that they are not stolen: Otherwise you are partaker with a thief, and are not a jot honester than him. But you know they are not honestly come by: You know they are procured by means nothing near so innocent as picking of pockets, house breaking, or robbery upon the highway. You know they are procured by a deliberate series of more complicated villainy, (of fraud, robbery and murder,) than was ever practised either by Mahometans or Pagans; in particular by murders of all kinds; by the blood of the innocent poured upon the ground like water. Now it is your money that pays the merchant, and thro' him the captain and African butchers. You therefore are guilty: Yea, principally guilty, of all these frauds, robberies, and murders. You are the spring that puts all the rest in motion; they would not stir a step without you. —Therefore the blood of all these wretches, who die before their time, whether in their country or else where, lies upon your head. The blood of thy brother, (for whether thou wilt believe it or no, such he is in the sight of him that made him) crieth against thee from the earth, from the ship and from the waters. O! what ever it cost, put a stop to its cry, before it be too late. Instantly, at any price, were it the half of thy goods, deliver thyself from blood guiltiness! Thy hands, thy bed, thy furniture, thy house, thy land, are at present stained with blood. Surely it is enough; accumulate no more guilt: Spill no more the blood of the innocent! Do not hire another to shed blood! Do not pay him for doing it! Whether thou art a christian or no, shew thy self a man; be not more savage than a lion or a bear.

Perhaps thou wilt say, "I do not buy any negroes: I only use those left me by my father." But is it enough to satisfy your own conscience! Had your father, have you, has any man living, a right to use another as a slave? It cannot be, even setting revelation aside. It cannot be, that either war, or contract, can give any man, such a property in another as he has in his sheep and oxen: Much less is it possible, that any child of man, should ever be born a slave. Liberty is the right of every human creature, as soon as he breathes the vital air. And no human law can deprive him of that right, which he derives from the law of nature. If therefore you have any regard to justice, (to say nothing of mercy, nor of the revealed law of God,) render unto all their due. Give liberty to whom liberty is due, that is to every child of man, to every partaker of human nature. Let none serve you but by his own act and deed, by his own voluntary choice. Away with ships, chains and all compulsion. Be gentle towards all men. And see that you invariably do unto every one, as you would he should do unto you.

Racial Views of a Founding Father Thomas Jefferson*

[I proposed] to emancipate all slaves born after passing the act. The bill reported by the revisors does not itself contain this proposition; but an amendment containing it was prepared, to be offered to the legislature whenever the bill should be taken up, and further directing, that they should continue with their parents to a certain age, then be brought up at the public expence, to tillage, arts or sciences, according to their geniuses, till the females should be 18, and the males 21 years of age, when they should be colonized to such place as the circumstances of the time should render most proper, sending them out with arms, implements of household and of the handicraft arts, seeds, pairs of the useful domestic animals, &c. to declare them a free and independent

* From Thomas Jefferson, *Notes on the State of Virginia.* . . . (Baltimore, 1800), pp. 141–147.

people, and extend to them our alliance and protection, till they have acquired strength; and to send vessels at the same time to other parts of the world for an equal number of white inhabitants; to induce whom to migrate hither, proper encouragements were to be proposed. It will probably be asked, Why not retain and incorporate the blacks into the state, and thus save the expense of supplying by importation of white settlers, the vacancies they will leave? Deep rooted prejudices entertained by the whites; ten thousand recollections, by the blacks, of the injuries they have sustained; new provocations; the real distinctions which nature has made; and many other circumstances, will divide us into parties, and produce convulsions, which will probably never end but in the extermination of the one or the other race. To these objections, which are political, may be added others, which are physical and moral. The first difference which strikes us is that of colour. Whether the black of the negro resides in the reticular membrane between the skin and the scarf-skin,* or in the scarf-skin itself; whether it proceeds from the colour of the blood, the colour of the bile, or from that of some other secretion, the difference is fixed in nature, and is as real as if its seat and cause were better known to us. And is this difference of no importance? Is it not the foundation of a greater or less share of beauty in the two races? Are not the fine mixtures of red and white, the expressions of every passion by greater or less suffusions of colour in the one preferable to that eternal monotony, which reigns in the countenances, that immoveable veil of black which covers all the emotions of the other race? Add to these, flowing hair, a more elegant symmetry of form, their own judgment in favour of the whites, declared by their preference of them, as uniformly as is the preference of the Oranootan† for the black women over those of his own species. The circumstance of superior beauty, is thought worthy attention in the propagation of our horses, dogs, and other domestic animals; why not in that of man? Besides those of colour, figure, and hair, there are other physical distinctions proving a difference of race. They have less hair on the face and body. They secrete less by the kidnies, and more by the glands of the skin, which gives them a very strong and disagreeable odour. This greater degree of

---

* Outer layer of the skin; epidermis.
† Orangutan.

transpiration renders them more tolerant of heat, and less so of cold than the whites. Perhaps too a difference of structure in the pulmonary apparatus . . . may have disabled them from extricating, in the act of inspiration, so much of that fluid from the outer air, or obliged them in expiration, to part with more of it. They seem to require less sleep. A black after hard labour through the day, will be induced by the slightest amusements to sit up till midnight, or later though knowing he must be out with the first dawn of the morning. They are at least as brave, and more adventuresome. But this may perhaps proceed from a want of forethought, which prevents their seeing a danger till it be present. When present, they do not go through it with more coolness or steadiness than the whites. They are more ardent after their female: but love seems with them to be more an eager desire, than a tender delicate mixture of sentiment and sensation. Their griefs are transient. Those numberless afflictions, which render it doubtful whether heaven has given life to us in mercy or in wrath, are less felt, and sooner forgotten with them. In general, their existence appears to participate more of sensation than reflection. To this must be ascribed their disposition to sleep when abstracted from their diversions, and unemployed in labour. An animal whose body is at rest, and who does not reflect, must be disposed to sleep of course. Comparing them by their faculties of memory, reason, and imagination, it appears to me that in memory they are equal to the whites; in reason much inferior, as I think one could scarcely be found capable of tracing and comprehending the investigations of Euclid; and that in imagination they are dull, tasteless, and anomalous. It would be unfair to follow them to Africa for this investigation. We will consider them here, on the same stage with the whites, and where the facts are not apocryphal on which a judgment is to be formed It will be right to make great allowances for the difference of condition, of education, of conversation, of the sphere in which they move. Many millions of them have been brought to, and born in America. Most of them indeed have been confined to tillage, to their own homes, and their own society: yet many have been so situated, that they might have availed themselves of the conversation of their masters; many have been brought up to the handicraft arts, and from that circumstance have always been associated with the whites. Some have been

liberally educated, and all have lived in countries where the arts
and sciences are cultivated to a considerable degree, and have had
before their eyes samples of the best works from abroad. The
Indians, with no advantages of this kind, will often carve figures on
their pipes not destitute of design and merit. They will crayon out
an animal, a plant, or a country, so as to prove the existence of a
germ in their minds which only wants cultivation. They astonish
you with strokes of the most sublime oratory; such as prove their
reason and sentiment strong, their imagination glowing and elevated. But never yet could I find that a black had uttered a thought
above the level of plain narration; never see even an elementary
trait of painting or sculpture. In music they are more generally
gifted than the whites with accurate ears for tune and time, and
they have been found capable of imagining a small catch. Whether
they will be equal to the composition of a more extensive run of
melody, or of complicated harmony, is yet to be proved. Misery is
often the parent of the most effecting touches in poetry. Among the
blacks is misery enough, God knows, but no poetry. Love is the
peculiar oestrum of the poet. Their love is ardent, but it kindles the
senses only, not the imagination. Religion indeed has produced a
Phyllis Whately;* but it could not produce a poet. The composi-
tions published under her name are below the dignity of criticism.
The heroes of the Dunciad are to her as Hercules to the author of
that poem. Ignatius Sancho† has approached nearer to merit in
composition; yet his letters do more honour to the heart than the
head. They breathe the purest effusions of friendship and general
philanthropy, and show how great a degree of the latter may be
compounded with strong religious zeal. He is often happy in the
turn of his compliments, and his style is easy and familiar, except
when he affects a Shandean fabrication of words. But his imagination is wild and extravagant, escapes incessantly from every restraint of reason and taste, and in the course of its vagaries, leaves
a tract of thought as incoherent and eccentric, as is the course of a
meteor through the sky. His subjects should often have led him to

---

* Phillis Wheatley (*ca.* 1753–1784), slave-poet of Boston.
† Ignatius Sancho (1729–1780) was a Negro writer who lived in England,
admired Laurence Sterne, corresponded with him and "penned epistles in
Sterne's manner." The allusion to "Shandean fabrication" refers to Sancho's
imitation of the style of *Tristam Shandy*.

a process of sober reasoning: yet we find him always substituting sentiment for demonstration. Upon the whole, though we admit him to the first place among those of his own colour who have presented themselves to the public judgment, yet when we compare him with the writers of the race among whom he lived and particularly with the epistolary class, in which he has taken his own stand, we are compelled to enroll him at the bottom of the column. This criticism supposes the letters published under his name to be genuine, and to have received amendment from no other hand; points which would not be of easy investigation.

The improvement of the blacks in body and mind, in the first instance of their mixture with the whites, has been observed by every one, and proves that their inferiority is not the effect merely of their condition of life. We know that among the Romans, about the Augustan age especially, the condition of their slaves was much more deplorable than that of the blacks on the continent of America. The two sexes were confined in separate apartments, because to raise a child cost the master more than to buy one. Cato, for a very restricted indulgence to his slaves in this particular, took from them a certain price. But in this country the slaves multiply as fast as the free inhabitants. Their situation and manners placed the commerce between the two sexes almost without restraint. —The same Cato, on a principle of oeconomy, always sold his sick and superannuated slaves. He gives it as a standing precept to a master visiting his farm, to sell his old oxen, old waggons, old tools, old and diseased servants, and every thing else become useless. . . . The American slaves cannot enumerate this among the injuries and insults they receive. It was the common practice to expose in the Island of AEsculapius, in the Tyber, diseased slaves, whose cure was like to become tedious. The emperor Claudius, by an edict, gave freedom to such of them as should recover, and first declared that if any person chose to kill rather than expose them, it should be deemed homicide. The exposing them is a crime of which no instance has existed with us; and were it to be followed by death, it would be punished capitally. We are told of a certain Vedius Pollio, who, in the presence of Augustus, would have given a slave as food to his fish, for having broken a glass. With the Romans, the regular method of taking the evidence of their slaves was under torture. Here it has been thought better never to resort to their evidence. When a master was murdered, all his slaves, in the same house, or within hearing, were condemned to death. Here punishment falls on the guilty only, and as precise proof is required against him as against a freeman. Yet notwithstanding these and other discouraging circumstances among the Romans, their slaves were often their rarest artists. They excelled too in science, insomuch as to be usually employed as tutors to their master's children. Epictetus, Terence, and Phaedrus, were slaves. But they were of the race of whites. It is not their condition then, but nature, which has produced the distinction. —Whether further observation will or will not verify the conjecture, that nature has been less bountiful to them in the endowments of the head, I believe that in those of the heart she will be found to have done them justice. That disposition to theft with which they have been branded, must be ascribed to their situation, and not to any depravity of the moral sense. The man, in whose favour no laws of property exist, probably feels himself less bound to respect those made in favour of others. When arguing for ourselves, we lay it down as a fundamental, that laws, to be just, must give a reciprocation of right: that, without this, they are mere arbitrary rules of conduct, founded in force and not in conscience: and it is a problem which I give to the master to solve, whether the religious precepts against the violation of property were not framed for him as well as his slave? And whether the slave may not as justifiably take a little from one, who has taken all from him, as he may slay one who would slay him; That a change in the relations in which a man is placed should change his ideas of moral right and wrong, is neither new, nor peculiar to the colour of the blacks. Homer tells us it was so 2600 years ago.

> Jove fix'd it certain, that whatever day
> Makes man a slave takes half his worth away.

But the slaves of which Homer speaks were whites. Notwithstanding these considerations which must weaken their respect for the laws of property, we find among them numerous instances of the most rigid integrity, and as many as among their better instructed masters, of benevolence, gratitude, and unshaken fidelity.—The opinion, that they are inferior in the faculties of reason and imagination, must be hazarded with great diffidence. To justify a general conclusion, requires many observations, even where the subject may be submitted to the anatomical knife, to optical glasses, to analysis by fire, or by solvents. How much more then where it is a faculty, not a substance, we are examining; where it eludes the research of all the senses; where the conditions of its existence are various and variously combined; where the effects of those which are present or absent bid defiance to calculation; let me add too, as a circumstance of great tenderness, where our conclusion would degrade a whole race of men from the rank in the scale of beings which their Creator perhaps may have given them. To our reproach it must be said, that though for a century and a half we have had under our eyes the races of black and of red men, they have never yet been viewed by us as subjects of natural history. I advance it therefore as a suspicion only, that the blacks whether originally a distinct race, or made distinct by time and circumstances, are inferior to the whites in the endowments both of body and mind. It is not against experience to suppose, that different species of the same genus or varieties of the same species, may possess different qualifications. Will not a lover of natural history then, one who views the gradations in all the races of animals with the eye of philosophy, excuse an effort to keep those in the department of man as distinct as nature has formed them? This unfortunate difference of colour, and perhaps of faculty, is a powerful obstacle to the emancipation of these people. Many of their advocates while they wish to vindicate the liberty of human nature are anxious also to preserve its dignity and beauty. Some of these, embarrassed by the question "What further is to be done with them?" join themselves in opposition with those who are actuated by sordid avarice only. Among the Romans emancipation required but one effort. The slave when made free, might mix with, without staining the blood of his master. But with us a second is necessary unknown to history. When freed, he is to be removed beyond the reach of mixture.

CHAPTER II

PARIAHS

Free Negroes

❀ ❀

A free negro! Why, the very term seems an absurdity.

George Fitzhugh, *"What Shall Be Done with the Free Negroes?"* appended to Sociology for the South, or The Failure of Free Society (*Richmond, Va., 1854*)

It is difficult to distinguish between Northern and Southern race prejudice in the pre–Civil War era. Free Negroes were treated as inferior beings throughout the North and South, doomed as readily to subordinate positions by the mores, laws, and institutions of Connecticut as by those of Mississippi and Georgia. Perhaps an expert mathematician might devise an adequate geometry to measure degrees of prejudice and conclude Negroes were three-quarters free in Massachusetts, one-half free in New York and Ohio, one-quarter free in Illinois, Kentucky, and Oregon. It would necessitate an ingenious scale indeed, as the overwhelming truth was that "free Negroes" were "free" nowhere in the United States. And what function could a calculus of unfreedom have to a society which claimed that the very entity to be divided was indivisible? An all-pervasive and intense race prejudice existed throughout the nation. "In a word," the British traveler William Chambers concluded in 1853, non-slave Negroes, North and South, were "treated from first to last as *Pariahs. . . .*" (1)

Racism tainted every aspect of Negro life and dogged Negroes to the grave in the form of segregated burial grounds. Discrimination was the rule, not the exception, in schools, workshops, churches, homes, polling booths, and courts of law. Only four states permitted Negroes the right to vote on an equal basis with whites prior to the Civil War. "Nigger pews," separate sections of churches specifically assigned to Negroes, characterized many Northern religious institutions. The laws of all the Southern states and five Northern ones—Iowa, California, Ohio, Indiana, and Illinois—denied Negroes the right to testify against whites. Negro migration was restricted in the North by legislative action or constitutional provision in the states of Illinois, Michigan, Iowa, Ohio, Oregon, and Indiana; and in the South by laws which demanded forced emigration of all manumitted slaves. Negroes lucky enough to receive a rudimentary education usually attended segregated and second-rate schools. In 1836, Lydia Maria Child summed up the situation concisely. "It has been shown," she concluded, "that no other people on earth indulge so strong a prejudice with regard to color as we do." The effects of American racism on free Negroes is evident in the description of Philadelphia slums (2) and the shouts of anguish of the Reverend Hosea Easton and Frederick Douglass. (3)

"What shall be done with the free Negroes?" was the rhetorical question Southern philosopher George Fitzhugh posed himself. He replied, in all seriousness, that they should re-enslave themselves. Freedom was a condition utterly detrimental to the welfare of Negroes, Fitzhugh believed—a state antithetical to their beings: "How cruel and unwise . . . not to extend the *blessings of slavery* to the free negroes," he wrote. The founders of the American Colonization Society asked the same question, and concluded there was no hope for racial harmony or advancement in America: "The black man's case is well nigh *hopeless* [in] this country." Colonizationists advocated a return to Africa. Unfortunately for these points of view, neither solution seemed especially palatable to Negroes. (4)

Yet American society was unable to offer any better answers to Fitzhugh's query. Advocates of the simplest and yet most complex answer—full equality—represented an infinitesimal portion of the general population. Justice Taney's position, in the Dred Scott decision, found ample evidence in the history of colonial and Revolutionary America and in the laws of all the states to warrant the conclusion that free Negroes had never been treated as American citizens anywhere in the nation and, therefore, he denied them any right to citizenship. (5) The decision simply formalized and clarified a fact of American life. On the eve of the Civil War just under a half-million free Negroes found themselves in this anomalous position— strangers in the land of their birth.

1. PREJUDICE AND EXCLUSION

An Englishman's Description of America's "Monomania":
Color Consciousness in America William Chambers*

William Chambers, prolific writer, publisher of inexpensive jour-nals and popular books for Great Britain's working classes, toured America in 1853. His journal, Things as They Are in America, *from which the following excerpt is taken, described what he called America's "monomania"—its color consciousness. He later expanded this idea into a book,* American Slavery and Colour *(London and Edinburgh, 1857). Chambers' thesis, that no geo-graphic boundary separated North and South in its image of the Negro, was popular with Southerners and subsequently reprinted in* De Bow's Review, *the leading Southern journal of the pre-Civil War period.*

It is difficult to understand what is the genuine public feeling on this entangled question; for with all the demonstrations in favour of freedom in the north, there does not appear in that quarter to be any practical relaxation of the usages which condemn persons of African descent to an inferior social status. There seems, in short, to be a fixed notion throughout the whole of the states, whether slave or free, that the coloured is by nature a subordinate race; and that, in no circumstances, can it be considered equal to the white. Apart from commercial views, this opinion lies at the root of American slavery; and the question would need to be argued less on political and philanthropic than on physiological grounds. Previ-ous to my departure from Richmond, in Virginia, I had an accidental conversation with a gentleman, a resident in that city, on the subject of slavery. This person gave it as his sincere opinion, founded on close observation, and a number of physio-logical facts, that negroes were an inferior species or variety of

* From William Chambers, *Things as They Are in America* (London and Edinburgh, 1854).

human beings, destined, or at least eminently suited, to be servants to the white and more noble race; that, considering their faculties, they were happier in a state of slavery than in freedom, or when left to their own expedients for subsistence; and that their sale and transfer was, from these premises, legitimate and proper. Such opinions are, perhaps, extreme; but, on the whole, I believe they pretty fairly represent the views of the south on the subject of slavery, which is considered to be not merely a conventional, but an absolutely natural institution, sanctioned by the precept and example of ministers of the Gospel, and derived from the most remote usages of antiquity.

It may have been merely a coincidence, but it is remarkable, that all with whom I conversed in the States on the distinctions of race, tended to the opinion, that the negro was in many respects an inferior being, and his existence in America an anomaly. The want of mental energy and forethought, the love of finery and of trifling amusements, distaste of persevering industry and bodily labour, as well as overpowering animal propensities, were urged as general characteristics of the coloured population; and it was alleged, that when consigned to their own resources, they do not successfully compete with the white Anglo-Americans, or with the immigrant Irish; the fact being added, that in slavery they increase at the same ratio as the whites, while in freedom, and affected with the vices of society, the ratio of increase falls short by one-third. Much of this was new to me; and I was not a little surprised to find, when speaking a kind word for at least a very unfortunate, if not brilliant race, that the people of the northern states, though repudiating slavery, did not think more favourably of the negro character than those further south. Throughout Massachusetts, and other New England States, likewise in the states of New York, Pennsylvania, &c., there is a rigorous separation of the white and black races. In every city, there are white and black schools, and white and black churches. No dark-skinned child is suffered to attend a school for white children. In Boston, celebrated for its piety and philanthropy, all the coloured children [are required] to go to one school, however inconveniently situated it may be for some of them. This school was instituted in 1812, and the following is the existing ordinance respecting it:—"The coloured population in the city not being sufficiently numerous to require more than one school, it has been thought proper to provide in this the means of instruction in all the branches of learning, which are taught in the several schools for white children."* In New York, there are nine public schools exclusively for coloured children, besides a coloured orphan asylum. In the city of Providence, Rhode Island, it is ordained that "there shall be three public schools maintained exclusively for the instruction of coloured children, the grades thereof to be determined from time to time by the school committee." In Philadelphia, there is a similar organisation of district schools for coloured children.

As an explanation of these distinctions, I was informed that white would not sit beside coloured children; and further, that coloured children, after a certain age, did not correspondingly advance in learning—their intellect being apparently incapable of being cultured beyond a particular point. From whatever cause, it was clear that a reluctance to associate with persons of negro descent was universally inculcated in infancy, and strengthened with age. The result is a singular social phenomenon. We see, in effect, two nations—one white and another black—growing up together within the same political circle, but never mingling on a principle of equality.

The people of England, who see a negro only as a wandering curiosity, are not at all aware of the repugnance generally entertained towards persons of colour in the United States: it appeared to me to amount to an absolute monomania. As for an alliance with one of the race, no matter how faint the shade of colour, it would inevitably lead to a loss of caste, as fatal to social position and family ties as any that occurs in the Brahminical system. Lately, a remarkable illustration of this occurred at New Orleans. It was a law case, involving the question of purity of blood. The plaintiff, George Pandelly, a gentleman in a respectable station, sued Victor Wiltz for slander. Wiltz had said that Pandelly had a taint of negro blood; inasmuch as one of his ancestresses was a mulatto of "African combination." In describing the case to the court, the counsel for the plaintiff was so overcome by the enormity of the offence, that he shed tears! He produced several aged witnesses to prove that the ancestress, mentioned by Wiltz as a mulatto, was the great-great-grandmother of the plaintiff, and

* Boston, in 1855, became the first major city to integrate its schools.

was not a mulatto of negro origin, but a woman who had derived her colour from Indian blood! Satisfied with the evidence on this important point, the jury found a verdict for the plaintiff, but no damages; which was considered satisfactory—the sole object of Mr. Pandelly having been to establish the purity of his descent.

All the efforts, in my opinion, which may be made with a view to influencing the south in favour of emancipation, are valueless so long as there exists a determined resolution throughout northern society to consider the coloured race, in all its varieties of shade, as beneath the dignity of human nature, and in no respect worthy to be associated with, countenanced, honoured, or so much as spoken to on terms of equality. Excluded, by such inflexible and carefully nourished prejudices, from entertaining the slightest prospect of ever rising beyond the humblest position; condemned to infamy from birth; not tolerated in the railway-cars which are devoted to the use of the whites; turned away from any of the ordinary hotels, no matter what be their character, means, or style of dress; in a word, treated from first to last as *Pariahs*—how can we expect that objects of so much contumely are to improve in their faculties or feelings, or to possess, in any degree, the virtue of self-respect? The wonder, indeed, is, that they conduct themselves so well as they do, or that they assume anything like the dress or manners of civilised persons.

2. URBAN POVERTY

*A Description of Philadelphia's Slums Society of Friends**

Some free Negroes achieved modest success within the racial restrictions of American culture. Many free Negro artisans and farmers acquired economic independence in the South, especially in the Border States. The free Negro middle class in the North was a seedbed for the abolitionist movement as well as for the National Negro Convention movement, which met sporadically after 1830. The careers of such eminent leaders as James Forten, the Reverend Richard Allen, Charlotte L. Forten, David M. Ruggles, Henry Highland Garnet, Robert Purvis, Charles Lenox Remond, and a

* From Society of Friends, *A Statistical Inquiry into the Condition of the People of Colour, of the City and Districts of Philadelphia* (Philadelphia, 1849), pp. 36–41.

*host of others illustrated that free Negroes of ability could assume
positions of leadership and responsibility.*

*The majority of the free Negro population, however, then as
later, lived in poverty. An inordinate number worked in menial
and service occupations, and these positions were continually
threatened by the masses of immigrants who settled America's
cities throughout the nineteenth century. Documents of the 1820's
to 1860's regularly allude to the declining economic position of
free Negroes. Competition for even the most grueling jobs was
often intense and bred an antagonism between recent immigrants
and Negroes which became a constant theme of America's racial
history. The following description of lower-class Negro slums in
Philadelphia, written by a group of Quakers, clearly depicts a
condition of life which they, and we, find "the power of language"
inadequate to convey.*

The vicinity of the place we sought, was pointed out by a large
number of coloured people congregated on the neighbouring pave-
ments. We first inspected the rooms, yards and cellars of the four
or five houses next above Baker Street on Seventh. The cellars
were wretchedly dark, damp, and dirty, and were generally rented
for 12½ cents per night. These were occupied by one or more
families at the present time; but in the winter season, when the
frost drives those who in summer sleep abroad in fields, in board
yards, in sheds, to seek more effectual shelter, they often contain
from twelve to twenty lodgers per night. Commencing at the back
of each house are small wooden buildings roughly put together,
about six feet square, without windows or fire places, a hole about
a foot square being left in the front along side of the door, to let in
fresh air and light, and to let out foul air and smoke. These
desolate pens, the roofs of which are generally leaky, and their
floors so low, that more or less water comes in on them from the
yard in rainy weather, would not give comfortable winter accommodation to a cow. Although as dismal as dirt, damp, and
insufficient ventilation can make them, they are nearly all inhabited. In one of the first we entered, we found the dead body of
a large negro man, who had died suddenly there. This pen was
about eight feet deep by six wide. There was no bedding in it; but a
box or two around the sides furnished places where two coloured

persons, one said to be the wife of the deceased, were lying, either drunk or fast asleep. The body of the dead man was on the wet floor, beneath an old torn coverlet. The death had taken place some hours before; the coroner had been sent for, but had not yet arrived. A few feet south, in one of the pens attached to the adjoining house, two days before, a coloured female had been found dead. The hole from which she was taken, appeared smaller than its neighbours generally, and had not as yet obtained another tenant.

"Let me introduce you to our Astor House," said our guide, turning into an alley between two of the buildings on Baker street. We followed through a dirty passage, so narrow, a stout man would have found it tight work to have threaded it. Looking before us, the yard seemed unusually dark. This we found was occasioned by a long range of two story pens, with a projecting boarded walk above the lower tier, for the inhabitants of the second story to get to the doors of their apartments. This covered nearly all the narrow yard, and served to exclude light from the dwellings below. We looked in every one of these dismal abodes of human wretchedness. Here were dark, damp holes, six feet square, without a bed in any of them, and generally without furniture, occupied by one or two families: apartments where privacy of any kind was unknown—where comfort never appeared. We endeavoured with the aid of as much light as at mid-day could find access through the open door, to see into the dark corners of these contracted abodes; and as we became impressed with their utter desolateness, the absence of bedding, and of ought to rest on but a bit of old matting on a wet floor, we felt sick and oppressed. Disagreeable odours of many kinds were ever arising; and with no ventilation but the open door, and the foot square hole in the front of the pen, we could scarcely think it possible that life could be supported, when winter compelled them to have fire in charcoal furnaces. With sad feelings we went from door to door, speaking to all, inquiring the number of their inmates, the rent they paid, and generally the business they followed to obtain a living. To this last question the usual answer was, "ragging and boning."* Some of these six by six holes, had six, and even eight persons in them, but more generally two to four. In one or two instances a single man

* Secondhand clothing and junk dealers.

rented one for himself. The last of the lower story of the "Astor" was occupied by a black man, his black wife, and an Irish woman. The white woman was half standing, half leaning against some sort of a box, the blacks were reclining upon the piece of old matting, perhaps four feet wide, which by night furnished the only bed of the three. Passing to the end of the row, we ventured up steps much broken, and very unsafe, to the second story platform, and visited each apartment there. It is not in the power of language to convey an adequate impression of the scene on this property. The filth, the odours, the bodily discomfort, the moral degradation everywhere apparent. Descending with difficulty, we proceeded to examine the cellars and rooms in a building still further back, having the same owner. The same want of accommodations were observed, few, if any there having a trace of bedding. For the pens, 10 cents a night were paid generally, 8 cents for the rest. The miserable apartments in the houses brought about the same prices. Some rooms, however, rented as high as one dollar per week. In the damp double row of the "Astor building," we found, although occupied by apparently young married people, there was no child. Neither were there children to be found, except as a very rare instance, in any of the pens we examined on other property around. Struck with the fact, we concluded, that an infant if born in them, could scarcely survive there many weeks. In those families occupying apartments in buildings, which might by courtesy be called houses, though all in these parts were miserably destitute of comforts, there were a few children. They were not however, either in number or appearance, to be compared with those healthy, happy beings, who swarm around the coloured man's home in country places.

Now for the statistics of this "Astor House," and its appurtenances. The double row of pens cost perhaps $100 to erect; and if they contain twenty apartments renting for 8 and 10 cents per night, they produce an income of $600 per year. When the owner of this property was asked a few years back to sell it, that a House of Industry might be erected there, he declined; but in conversation with the individual who asked to purchase it, he stated that it had cost him $1300. A physician who is frequently called to attend patients in the place, being curious to know what yearly rent the owner was receiving, undertook with another white man to visit the apartments, and inquire the amount paid by the dwellers in each. The aggregate amounted to $1600.

We inquired the daily earnings of those we visited, and the amount they had to pay for a glass of whiskey. Some earned 50, some 75 cents per day; but we have reason to believe that many do not realize on an average more than a few cents over the daily rent. Whiskey, apple or rye, as bests suits the taste of the drinker, is furnished at one cent per glass.

The wretchedness of the condition of these people, is greatly aggravated by the entire want of all legal restrictions upon the cupidity of the landlord. The victims of the typhus fever of 1847, were the inhabitants of rooms and buildings many of which were unfit for the residence of human beings, and most of which were in crowded and filthy courts and alleys; over which no public care is commonly extended. The law protects the poor tenant, from the exactions of the landlord, by placing a certain description of his personal effects out of the power of the constable. Why should it not with equal justice and for greater public ends, the preservation of the health and morals of that portion of the community, interfere to say what amount of ventilation and room, of personal accommodation, and the means of warmth and cleanliness, shall be guaranteed to the humblest individual; and suitably to punish the attempt to crowd human beings, into abodes not fit for domestic animals, and where vice and pestilence are sure to be engendered?

3. EARLY-NINETEENTH-CENTURY AMERICAN RACISM

It would be difficult to find a more sensitive description and analysis of early-nineteenth-century American racism than Hosea Easton's A Treatise on the Intellectual Character, and Civil and Political Condition of the Colored People of the United States; and the Prejudice Exercised Towards Them—*a book that deserves to be known as a classic in the literature of American race relations. At a meeting of the Massachusetts Anti-Slavery Society in 1837 the Reverend Mr. Easton of Hartford, Connecticut, asked that abolitionists speak out against the many forms of racial prejudice that pervaded American culture. "The spirit of slavery will survive,*

*in the form of prejudice, after the system is overturned," he pre-
dicted. "Our warfare ought not to be against slavery alone, but
against the spirit which makes color a mark of degradation."
Frederick Douglass' letter to William Lloyd Garrison—which
follows the selection from Easton—emphasizes similar themes. It
was written on a trip to Ireland and published in the* Liberator,
January 30, 1845.

A Northern Negro Minister on Race Hate *Hosea Easton**

Legal codes, however oppressive, have never as yet been able to
crush the aspiring principles of human nature. The real monster,
slavery, cannot long exist, where it is sustained by legal codes only;
it is forced to stand off, and is capable of imposing its shadow
only, in comparison to what it is capable of doing by collateral aid.
When public sentiment, therefore, has become so morally, civilly,
and politically corrupted by the principles of slavery, as to be
determined in crushing the objects of its malignity, it is under the
necessity of calling prejudice to its aid, as an auxiliary to its
adopted formal code of wickedness, clothed like a semi-devil, with
all the innate principles of the old dragon himself. This auxiliary,
is all powerfully capable of accommodating itself to local circumstances and conditions, and appearing with all the nature of the old
beast, slavery; it is always ready to destroy every aspiration to
civil, political and moral elevation, which arises in the breast of the
oppressed. There is no pretext too absurd, by which to justify the
expenditures of its soul-and-body-destroying energies. The complexion, features, pedigree, customs, and even the attributes and
purposes of God, are made available to its justification.

By this monster, the withering influence of slavery is directed to
the very vitals of the colored people—withering every incentive to
improvement—rendering passive all the faculties of the intellect—
subjecting the soul to a morbid state of insensibility—destroying
the body—making one universal wreck of the best work of nature's God.

Such is its effect at the south, and scarcely less destructive at the

* From Hosea Easton, *A Treatise on the Intellectual Character, and
Civil and Political Condition of the Colored People of the United States;
and the Prejudice Exercised Towards Them* (Boston, 1837).

north. The only difference is this: at the north, there is not so formal a code of laws by which to direct the energies of prejudice as at the south; still the doctrine of *expediency* full well makes up the deficiency of cruel laws, giving prejudice as full toleration to exercise itself, and in lavishing out its withering influence, as law at the south.

It is a remarkable fact that the moment the colored people show signs of life—any indication of being possessed with redeeming principles, that moment an unrelenting hatred arises in the mind which is inhabited by that foul fiend, prejudice; and the possessor of it will never be satisfied, until those indications are destroyed; space, time, nor circumstance, is no barrier to its exercise. Transplant the object of its malignity to Africa, or Canada, or elsewhere, and its poison is immediately transferred from local into national policy, and will exert all possible means it possesses, to accomplish its fell design. It always aims its deadly fangs at the noble and active principles of the immortal mind, which alone enables man to stand forth pre-eminent in all the works of God.

Let the oppressed assume the character of capable men in business, either mercantile, mechanical, or agricultural,—let them assume the right of exercising themselves in the use of the common privileges of the country—let them claim the right of enjoying liberty, in the general acceptation of the term—let them exercise the right of speech and of thought—let them presume to enjoy the privileges of the sanctuary and the Bible—let their souls be filled with glory and of God, and wish to bow the knee at the sacred altar, and commemorate the dying love of Christ the Lord—let them seek a decent burial for their departed friend in the church yard—and they are immediately made to feel that they are as a carcass destined to be preyed upon by the eagles of persecution. Thus they are followed from life's dawn to death's-doom.

I have no language wherewith to give slavery, and its auxiliaries, an adequate description, as an efficient cause of the miseries it is capable of producing. It seems to possess a kind of omnipresence. It follows its victims in every avenue of life.

The principle assumes still another feature equally destructive. It makes the colored people subserve almost every foul purpose imaginable. Negro or nigger, is an opprobrious term, employed to impose contempt upon them as an inferior race, and also to express their deformity of person. Nigger lips, nigger shins, and nigger heels, are phrases universally common among the juvenile class of society, and full well understood by them; they are early learned to think of these expressions, as they are intended to apply to colored people, and as being expressive or descriptive of the odious qualities of their mind and body. These impressions received by the young, grow with their growth, and strengthen with their strength. The term in itself, would be perfectly harmless, were it used only to distinguish one class of society from another; but it is not used with that intent; the practical definition is quite different in England to what it is here, for here, it flows from the fountain of purpose to injure. It is this baneful seed which is sown in the tender soil of youthful minds, and there cultivated by the hand of a corrupt immoral policy.

The universality of this kind of education is well known to the observing. Children in infancy receive oral instruction from the nurse. The first lessons given are, Johnny, Billy, Mary, Sally, (or whatever the name may be,) go to sleep, if you don't the old *nigger* will carry you off; don't you cry—Hark; the old *nigger's* coming—how ugly you are, you are worse than a little *nigger*. This is a specimen of the first lessons given.

The second is generally given in the domestic circle; in some families it is almost the only method of correcting their children. To inspire their half grown misses and masters to improvement, they are told that if they do this or that, or if they do thus and so, they will be poor or ignorant as a *nigger;* or that they will be black as a *nigger;* or have no more credit than a *nigger;* that they will have hair, lips, feet, or something of the kind, like a *nigger*. If doubt is entertained by any, as to the truth of what I write, let them travel twenty miles in any direction in this country, especially in the free States, and his own sense of hearing will convince him of its reality.

See nigger's thick lips—see his flat nose—nigger eye shine—that slick looking nigger—nigger, where you get so much coat?—that's a nigger priest—are sounds emanating from little urchins of Christian villagers, which continually infest the feelings of colored travellers, like the pestiferous breath of young devils; and full grown persons, and sometimes professors of religion, are not unfrequently heard to join in the concert.

A third mode of this kind of instruction is not altogether oral. Higher classes are frequently instructed in school rooms by referring them to the nigger-seat, and are sometimes threatened with being made to sit with the niggers, if they do not behave.

The same or similar use is made of nigger pews or seats in meeting-houses. Professing Christians, where these seats exist, make them a test by which to ascertain the amount of their humility. This I infer from their own language; for, say they, of the colored people, if we are only humble enough, we should be willing to sit any where to hear the word. If our hearts were right we should not care where we sit—I had as lief sit there (meaning the nigger pew,) as any where in the world. This, I admit, is all very good, but comes with rather bad grace. But, as I above observed, this kind of education is not altogether oral. Cuts and placards descriptive of the negroe's deformity, are every where displayed to the observation of the young, with corresponding broken lingo, the very character of which is marked with design.

Many of the popular book stores, in commercial towns and cities, have their show-windows lined with them. The bar-rooms of the most popular public houses in the country, sometimes have their ceiling literally covered with them. This display of American civility is under the daily observation of every class of society, even in New England. But this kind of education is not only systematized, but legalized. At the south, public newspapers are teeming through the country, bearing negro cuts, with remarks corresponding to the object for which they are inserted.

But this system is not carried on without deep design. It has hitherto been a settled opinion of philosophers that a black man could endure the heat better than a white man. Traders in human flesh have even taken the advantage of that opinion, by urging it as a plea of justification of their obtaining Africans, as laborers in warm climates; hence, we may naturally expect, that in a slave country like this, it would be a universally admitted axiom; and the more readily admitted, as it is easily construed into a plea to justify their wicked purposes. If the black can endure the heat, and the white cannot, say they, it must be that God made him on purpose for that; hence, it is no harm for us to act in accordance with the purposes of God, and make him work. These are the simple inferences drawn from the philosophical premises. . . .

What could accord better with the objects of this nation in reference to blacks, than to teach their little ones that a negro is part monkey?

The effect of this instruction is most disastrous upon the mind of the community; having been instructed from youth to look upon a black man in no other light than a slave, and having associated with that idea the low calling of a slave, they cannot look upon him in any other light. If he should chance to be found in any other sphere of action than that of a slave, he magnifies to a monster of wonderful dimensions, so large that they cannot be made to believe that he is a man and a brother. Neither can they be made to believe it would be safe to admit him into stages, steamboat cabins, and tavern dining-rooms; and not even into meeting-houses, unless he have a place prepared on purpose. Mechanical shops, stores, and school rooms, are all too small for his entrance as a man; if he be a slave, his corporeality becomes so diminished as to admit him into ladies' parlors, and into small private carriages, and elsewhere, without being disgustful on account of his deformity, or without producing any other discomfiture. Thus prejudice seems to possess a magical power, by which it makes a being appear most odious one moment, and the next, beautiful—at one moment too large to be on board a steam-boat, the next, so small as to be convenient almost any where.

Mind acts on matter. Contemplate the numerous free people of color under the despotic reign of prejudice—contemplate a young man in the ardor of youth, blessed with a mind as prolific as the air, aspiring to eminence and worth—contemplate his first early hopes blasted by the frost of prejudice—witness the ardor of youth inspiring him to a second and third trial, and as often repelled by this monster foe—hear him appealing to the laws of the land of his birth for protection—the haughty executives of the law spurning him from the halls of justice. He betakes to the temple of God— the last alternative around which his fading, dying hopes are hovering—but here, also, he receives a death thrust, and that by the hand of the priest of the altar of God. Yes—hear ye priests of the altar—it is the death thrust of slavery carried to the hearts of its victims by you. Yes—let it be known to the world, that the colored people who have been stolen, and have lost all allegiance to Africa, are sold in the shambles, and scouted from every privilege that makes life desirable. Under these discouragements they betake themselves to those who are called to preach good tidings to the meek, to bind up the broken-hearted, to proclaim liberty to the captives, and the opening of the prison doors to them that are bound, and they are set at nought by them also. The effect of these discouragements are every where manifest among the colored people.

Slavery, in the form and character of prejudice, is as fatal, yea, more fatal than the pestilence. It possesses imperial dominion over its votaries and victims. It demands and receives homage from priests and people. It drinks up the spirit of the church, and gathers blackness, and darkness, and death, around her brow. Its poison chills the life blood of her heart. Its gigantic tread on the Sabbath day, pollutes the altars of the sanctuary of the Most High. It withholds the word of life from thousands of perishing immortals, and shuts the gate of heaven alike upon those whose hearts it possesses, and those marked out for its victims. It opens wide the way to hell; and as though possessed with more than magic power, coerces its millions down to the pit of woe in defiance of the benevolence of a God, and the dying groans of a Saviour. O Prejudice, thou art slavery in disguise! and couldst thou ascend to heaven, thy pestiferous breath would darken and poison that now healthful and happy clime; and thou wouldst make its inhabitants feel the pains of the lowest hell. If there are degrees of intensity to the misery of the damned, that being must feel it in eternity, in whose heart prejudice reigned in this world. O Prejudice, I cannot let thee pass without telling thee and thy possessors, that thou art a compound of all evil—of all the corrupt passions of the heart. Yea, thou art a participant in all the purposes of the wicked one—thou art the very essence of hell.

"We Don't Allow Niggers in Here" Frederick Douglass*

In the Southern part of the United States, I was a slave, thought of and spoken of as property. In the language of the LAW, *"held, taken, reputed and adjudged to be a chattel in the hands of my*

* From Carter G. Woodson, ed., *The Mind of the Negro as Reflected in Letters Written during the Crisis, 1800–1860* (Washington, D.C., 1926), pp. 392–394.

owners and possessors, and their executors, administrators, and assigns, to all intents, constructions, and purposes whatsoever." In the Northern States, a fugitive slave, liable to be hunted at any moment like a felon, and to be hurled into the terrible jaws of slavery—doomed by an inveterate prejudice against color to insult and outrage on every hand . . . denied the privileges and courtesies common to others in the use of the most humble means of conveyance—shut out from the cabins on steamboats—refused admission to respectable hotels—caricatured, scorned, scoffed, mocked and maltreated with impunity by any one, (no matter how black his heart,) so he has a white skin. But now behold the change! Eleven days and a half gone, and I have crossed three thousand miles of the perilous deep. Instead of a democratic government, I am under a monarchical government. Instead of the bright blue sky of America, I am covered with the soft grey fog of the Emerald Isle. I breathe, and lo! the chattel becomes a man. I gaze around in vain for one who will question my equal humanity, claim me as his slave, or offer me an insult. I employ a cab—I am seated beside white people—I reach the hotel—I enter the same door—I am shown into the same parlor—I dine at the same table—and no one is offended. No delicate nose grows deformed in my presence. I find no difficulty here in obtaining admission into any place of worship, instruction or amusement, on equal terms with people as white as any I ever saw in the United States. I meet nothing to remind me of my complexion. I find myself regarded and treated at every turn with the kindness and deference paid to white people. When I go to church, I am met by no upturned nose and scornful lip to tell me, *"We don't allow niggers in here"!*

I remember, about two years ago, there was in Boston, near the southwest corner of Boston Common, a menagerie. I had long desired to see such a collection as I understood were being exhibited there. Never having had an opportunity while a slave, I resolved to seize this, my first, since my escape. I went, and as I approached the entrance to gain admission, I was met and told by the door-keeper, in a harsh and contemptuous tone, *"We don't allow niggers in here."* I also remember attending a revival meeting in the Rev. Henry Jackson's meeting-house, at New-Bedford, and going up the broad aisle to find a seat. I was met by a good deacon, who told me, in a pious tone, *"We don't allow niggers in here"!* Soon after my arrival in New-Bedford from the South, I had a strong desire to attend the Lyceum, but was told, *"They don't allow niggers in here"!* While passing from New York to Boston on the steamer Massachusetts, on the night of 9th Dec. 1843, when chilled almost through with the cold, I went into the cabin to get a little warm. I was soon touched upon the shoulder, and told, *"We don't allow niggers in here"!* On arriving in Boston from an anti-slavery tour, hungry and tired, I went into an eating-house near my friend Mr. Campbell's, to get some refreshments. I was met by a lad in a white apron, *"We don't allow niggers in here"!* A week or two before leaving the United States, I had a meeting appointed at Weymouth, the home of that glorious band of true abolitionists, the Weston family,* and others. On attempting to take a seat in the Omnibus to that place, I was told by the driver, (and I never shall forget his fiendish hate,) *"I don't allow niggers in here"!* Thank heaven for the respite I now enjoy! I had been in Dublin but a few days, when a gentleman of great respectability kindly offered to conduct me through all the public buildings of that beautiful city; and a little afterwards, I found myself dining with the Lord Mayor of Dublin. What a pity there was not some American democratic Christian at the door of his splendid mansion, to bark out at my approach, *"They don't allow niggers in here!"* The truth is, the people here know nothing of the republican negro hate prevalent in our glorious land. They measure and esteem men according to their moral and intellectual worth, and not according to the color of their skin. Whatever may be said of the aristocracies here, there is none based on the color of a man's skin. This species of aristocracy belongs pre-eminently to "the land of the free, and the home of the brave." I have never found it abroad, in any but Americans. It sticks to them wherever they go. They find it almost as hard to get rid of it as to get rid of their skins.

The second day after my arrival at Liverpool . . . I went to

* Maria Weston Chapman and her husband, Henry Grafton Chapman, were dedicated Garrisonians. Mrs. Chapman, a firebrand of an abolitionist, was most active in the Boston Female Anti-Slavery Society and the author of a number of antislavery works. Her sisters, Anne Warren Weston and Caroline Weston, were also Garrisonians.

Eaton Hall, the residence of the Marquis of Westminster, one of the most splendid buildings in England. On approaching the door, I found several of our American passengers, who came out with us in the Cambria, waiting at the door for admission, as but one party was allowed in the house at a time. We all had to wait till the company within came out. And of all the faces, expressive of chagrin, those of the Americans were pre-eminent. They looked as sour as vinegar, and bitter as gall, when they found I was to be admitted on equal terms with themselves. When the door was opened, I walked in, on an equal footing with my white fellow-citizens, and from all I could see, I had as much attention paid me by the servants that showed us through the house, as any with a paler skin. As I walked through the building, the statuary did not fall down, the pictures did not leap from their places, the doors did not refuse to open, and the servants did not say, *"We don't allow niggers in here"!*

4. NEGRO RESISTANCE TO EXPATRIATION

The Colonization Movement:
*Letters to William Lloyd Garrison from Free Negroes**

The American Colonization Society, founded in 1817, claimed that expatriation was the only viable solution to America's racial dilemma, and established a colony for American Negroes at Liberia in 1821. All would benefit, they rationalized: white America, American Negroes, and Africans who would learn the Gospel from Negro immigrants. "I know this scheme is from God," a founder of the Colonization Society believed. Free Negroes, many of whose forefathers had come to America before those of colonizationists, called the scheme a racial ploy and denounced it bitterly. Although some fifteen thousand free Negroes did return to Africa, including America's first Negro college graduate, John B. Russwurm, the American Colonization Society was a failure. "The . . . indisposition of the free people of colour to emigrate," colonizationists learned, "constituted one of the . . . most prominent objections to our plan." The following de-

* From Woodson, *The Mind of the Negro*, pp. 224–227.

nunciations of the back-to-Africa movement, written to William Lloyd Garrison in 1831, represent the majority opinion of free Negroes on the subject.

How long, oh! ye boasters of freedom, will ye endeavor to persuade us, your derided, degraded fellow countrymen, to the belief that our interest and happiness are prized in high estimation among you? Be it known, that we are not all such misguided, deluded mortals as to be duped by your plans; that we will not suffer ourselves to become so infatuated as to "hurl reason from her throne," and succumb to your glittering, showy, *dissimulating* path to eminence. We spurn with contempt your unrighteous schemes, and point the finger of derision at your fruitless attempts. You have commenced them in a day, when liberty, justice and equality are claimed by almost all, as Nature's rights; for behold! a beam of science, lucid as the sun, has divinely fallen upon the lightless intellects of a portion of that ignoble part of your fellow creatures, who have been so long the victims of your fell injustice and inhumanity. Would to God that conscience might subdue your malignant prejudices. Tell us not that our condition can never be bettered in the land of our birth: you know it not. Make but the attempt in consecrating a portion of your time, talents and money upon us here, and you would soon find the cause of Afric's injured race vindicated by her descendants; and the day which now dawns would be speedily ushered into blazing light, declaring in its effulgence the joyful sound of Liberty—Justice—Equality to all mankind.

To the Editor of the Liberator.

Sir—I have read the several numbers of your excellent paper with much pleasure, and cannot refrain from tendering my sincere thanks to you for the active part that you have taken in behalf of myself and colored brethren of this country.

That we are not treated as freemen, in any part of the United States, is certain. This usage, I should say, is in direct opposition to the [Declaration of Independence]; which positively declares, that all men are born equal, and endowed with certain inalienable rights—among which are life, liberty, and the pursuit of happiness.

I would ask some of our pretended white friends, and the members of the American Colonization Society, why they are so interested in our behalf as to want us to go to Africa? They tell us that it is our home; that they desire to make a people of us, which we can never be here; that they want Africa civilized; and that we are the very persons to do it, as it is almost impossible for any white person to exist there. I deny it. Will some of those guardian angels of the people of color tell me how it is that we, who were born in the same city or state with themselves, can live any longer in Africa than they? I consider it the most absurd assertion that any man of common sense could make, unless it is supposed, as some have already said, that we are void of understanding. If we had been born on that continent, the transportation would be another matter; but as the fact is the reverse, we consider the United States our home, and not Africa as they wish to make us believe;—and if we do emigrate, it will be to a place of our own choice.

I would also mention to the supporters of the Colonization Society, that if they would spend half the time and money that they do, in educating the colored population and giving them lands to cultivate here, and secure to them all the rights and immunities of freemen, instead of sending them to Africa, it would be found, in a short time, that they made as good citizens as the whites. Their traducers would hear of fewer murders, highway robberies, forgeries, &c. &c. being committed, than they do at present among some of the white inhabitants of this country.

If a man of color has children, it is almost impossible for him to get a trade for them, as the journeymen and apprentices generally refuse to work with them, even if the master is willing, which is seldom the case. Even among laborers, there is a distinction. During the late snow storm, thousands of persons were employed in cleaning the gutters, leveling the drifts, &c. Among the whole number, there was not a man of color to be seen, when hundreds of them were going about the streets with shovels in their hands, looking for work and finding none. I mention this fact merely to show what a great distinction exists, more or less, between the whites and blacks, in all classes—and as much among aliens who have been in this country three or four months, or perhaps a year, as any class of persons that I can mention.

5. JUDICIAL EXCLUSION

The Question of Negro Citizenship:
Dred Scott vs Sandford Justice Taney*

One may question the justice and morality of the majority opinion of the Supreme Court in the Dred Scott case, made public in March, 1857, but not the evidence marshaled by Chief Justice Roger B. Taney. Taney demonstrated, with only slight exaggeration, that Negroes had traditionally been excluded from full and equal participation in American life and institutions in all sections of the country. The selections from his opinion offered here are presented not only because Dred Scott vs. Sandford *was a seminal constitutional decision, but because Taney used accurate evidence from Northern and Southern states to demonstrate his thesis.*

The question is simply this: Can a negro, whose ancestors were imported into this country, and sold as slaves, become a member of the political community formed and brought into existence by the Constitution of the United States, and as such become entitled to all the rights, and privileges, and immunities, guaranteed by that instrument to the citizen? One of which rights is the privilege of suing in a court of the United States in the cases specified in the Constitution.

It will be observed, that the plea applies to that class of persons only whose ancestors were negroes of the African race, and imported into this country, and sold and held as slaves. The only matter in issue before the court, therefore, is, whether the descendants of such slaves, when they shall be emancipated, or who are born of parents who had become free before their birth, are citizens of a State, in the sense in which the word citizen is used in the Constitution of the United States.

We proceed to examine the case as presented by the pleadings.

The words "people of the United States" and "citizens" are synonymous terms. . . . They both describe the political body who, according to our republican institutions, form the sovereignty, and who hold the power and conduct the Government

* *Dred Scott vs. Sandford,* 19 Howard 393 (1857).

through their representatives. They are what we familiarly call the "sovereign people," and every citizen is one of this people, and a constituent member of this sovereignty. The question before us is, whether the class of persons described in the plea in abatement compose a portion of this people, and are constituent members of this sovereignty? We think they are not, and that they are not included, and were not intended to be included, under the word "citizens" in the Constitution, and can therefore claim none of the rights and privileges which that instrument provides for and secures to citizens of the United States. On the contrary, they were at that time considered as a subordinate and inferior class of beings, who had been subjugated by the dominant race, and, whether emancipated or not, yet remained subject to their authority, and had no rights or privileges but such as those who held the power and the Government might choose to grant them.

In the opinion of the court, the legislation and histories of the times, and the language used in the Declaration of Independence, show, that neither the class of persons who had been imported as slaves, nor their descendants, whether they had become free or not, were then acknowledged as a part of the people, nor intended to be included in the general words used in that memorable instrument.

It is difficult at this day to realize the state of public opinion in relation to that unfortunate race, which prevailed in the civilized and enlightened portions of the world at the time of the Declaration of Independence, and when the Constitution of the United States was framed and adopted. But the public history of every European nation displays it in a manner too plain to be mistaken.

They had for more than a century before been regarded as beings of an inferior order, and altogether unfit to associate with the white race, either in social or political relations; and so far inferior, that they had no rights which the white man was bound to respect; and that the negro might justly and lawfully be reduced to slavery for his benefit. He was bought and sold, and treated as an ordinary article of merchandise and traffic, whenever a profit could be made by it. This opinion was at that time fixed and universal in the civilized portion of the white race. It was regarded as an axiom in morals as well as in politics, which no one thought of disputing, or supposed to be open to dispute; and men in every grade and position in society daily and habitually acted upon it in their private pursuits, as well as in matters of public concern, without doubting for a moment the correctness of this opinion.

And in no nation was this opinion more firmly fixed or more uniformly acted upon than by the English Government and English people. They not only seized them on the coast of Africa, and sold them or held them in slavery for their own use; but they took them as ordinary articles of merchandise to every country where they could make a profit on them, and were far more extensively engaged in this commerce than any other nation in the world.

The opinion thus entertained and acted upon in England was naturally impressed upon the colonies they founded on this side of the Atlantic. And, accordingly, a negro of the African race was regarded by them as an article of property, and held, and bought and sold as such, in every one of the thirteen colonies which united in the Declaration of Independence, and afterwards formed the Constitution of the United States. The slaves were more or less numerous in the different colonies, as slave labor was found more or less profitable. But no one seems to have doubted the correctness of the prevailing opinion of the time.

The legislation of the different colonies furnishes positive and indisputable proof of this fact.

It would be tedious, in this opinion, to enumerate the various laws they passed upon this subject. It will be sufficient, as a sample of the legislation which then generally prevailed throughout the British colonies, to give the laws of two of them; one being still a large slaveholding State, and the other the first State in which slavery ceased to exist.

The province of Maryland, in 1717, . . . passed a law declaring "that if any free negro or mulatto intermarry with any white woman, or if any white man shall intermarry with any negro or mulatto woman, such negro or mulatto shall become a slave during life, excepting mulattoes born of white women, who, for such intermarriage, shall only become servants for seven years, to be disposed of as the justices of the county court, where such marriage so happens, shall think fit; to be applied by them towards the support of a public school within the said country. And any white man or white woman who shall intermarry as aforesaid, with any negro or mulatto, such white man or white woman shall become servants during the term of seven years, and shall be disposed of by the justices as aforesaid, and be applied to the uses aforesaid."

The other colonial law to which we refer was passed by Massachusetts in 1705. . . . It is entitled "An act for the better preventing of a spurious and mixed issue," &c.; and it provides, that "if any negro or mulatto shall presume to smite or strike any person of the English or other Christian nation, such negro or mulatto shall be severely whipped, at the discretion of the justices before whom the offender shall be convicted."

And "that none of her Majesty's English or Scottish subjects, nor of any other Christian nation, within this province, shall contract matrimony with any negro or mulatto; nor shall any person, duly authorized to solemnize marriage, presume to join any such in marriage, on pain of forfeiting the sum of fifty pounds; one moiety thereof to her Majesty, for and towards the support of the Government within this province, and the other moiety to him or them that shall inform and sue for the same, in any of her Majesty's courts of record within the province, by bill, plaint, or information."

We give both of these laws in the words used by the respective legislative bodies, because the language in which they are framed, as well as the provisions contained in them, show, too plainly to be misunderstood, the degraded condition of this unhappy race. They were still in force when the Revolution began, and are a faithful index to the state of feeling towards the class of persons of whom they speak, and of the position they occupied throughout the thirteen colonies, in the eyes and thoughts of the men who framed the Declaration of Independence and established the State Constitutions and Governments. They show that a perpetual and impassable barrier was intended to be erected between the white race and the one which they had reduced to slavery, and governed as subjects with absolute and despotic power, and which they then looked upon as so far below them in the scale of created beings, that intermarriages between white persons and negroes or mulattoes were regarded as unnatural and immoral, and punished as crimes, not only in the parties, but in the person who joined them in marriage. And no distinction in this respect was made between the free negro or mulatto and the slave, but this stigma, of the deepest degradation, was fixed upon the whole race.

This state of public opinion had undergone no change when the Constitution was adopted, as is equally evident from its provisions and language.

It is very true, that in that portion of the Union where the labor of the negro race was found to be unsuited to the climate and unprofitable to the master, but few slaves were held at the time of the Declaration of Independence; and when the Constitution was adopted, it had entirely worn out in one of them, and measures had been taken for its gradual abolition in several others. But this change had not been produced by any change of opinion in relation to this race; but because it was discovered, from experience, that slave labor was unsuited to the climate and productions of these States: for some of the States, where it had ceased or nearly ceased to exist, were actively engaged in the slave trade, procuring cargoes on the coast of Africa, and transporting them for sale to those parts of the Union where their labor was found to be profitable, and suited to the climate and productions. And this traffic was openly carried on, and fortunes accumulated by it, without reproach from the people of the States where they resided. And it can hardly be supposed that, in the States where it was then countenanced in its worst form—that is, in the seizure and transportation—the people could have regarded those who were emancipated as entitled to equal rights with themselves.

We need not refer, on this point, particularly to the laws of the present slaveholding States. Their statute books are full of provisions in relation to this class, in the same spirit with the Maryland law which we have before quoted. They have continued to treat them as an inferior class, and to subject them to strict police regulations, drawing a broad line of distinction between the citizen and the slave races. . . .

And if we turn to the legislation of the States where slavery had worn out, or measures taken for its speedy abolition, we shall find the same opinions and principles equally fixed and equally acted upon.

Thus, Massachusetts, in 1786, passed a law similar to the colonial one of which we have spoken. The law of 1786, like the law of 1705, forbids the marriage of any white person with any negro, Indian, or mulatto, and inflicts a penalty of fifty pounds upon any one who shall join them in marriage; and declares all such marriages absolutely null and void, and degrades thus the unhappy issue of the marriage by fixing upon it the stain of bastardy. And this mark of degradation was renewed, and again impressed upon the race, in the careful and deliberate preparation of their revised code published in 1836. This code forbids any person from joining in marriage any white person with any Indian, negro, or mulatto, and subjects the party who shall offend in this respect, to imprisonment, not exceeding six months, in the common jail, or to hard labor, and to a fine of not less than fifty nor more than two hundred dollars; and, like the law of 1786, it declares the marriage to be absolutely null and void. It will be seen that the punishment is increased by the code upon the person who shall marry them, by adding imprisonment to a pecuniary penalty.*

So, too, in Connecticut. We refer more particularly to the legislation of this State, because it was not only among the first to put an end to slavery within its own territory, but was the first to fix a mark of reprobation upon the African slave trade. The law last mentioned was passed in October, 1788, about nine months after the State had ratified and adopted the present Constitution of the United States; and by that law it prohibited its own citizens, under severe penalties, from engaging in the trade, and declared all policies of insurance on the vessel or cargo made in the State to be null and void. But, up to the time of the adoption of the Constitution, there is nothing in the legislation of the State indicating any change of opinion as to the relative rights and position of the white and black races in this country, or indicating that it meant to place the latter, when free, upon a level with its citizens. And certainly nothing which would have led the slaveholding States to suppose, that Connecticut designed to claim for them, under the new Constitution, the equal rights and privileges and rank of citizens in every other State.

The first step taken by Connecticut upon this subject was as early as 1774, when it passed an act forbidding the further

---

* In 1843 Massachusetts rescinded this law under pressure from the Garrisonians.

importation of slaves into the State. But the Section containing the prohibition is introduced by the following preamble:

"And whereas the increase of slaves in this State is injurious to the poor, and inconvenient."

This recital would appear to have been carefully introduced, in order to prevent any misunderstanding of the motive which induced the Legislature to pass the law, and places it distinctly upon the interest and convenience of the white population—excluding the inference that it might have been intended in any degree for the benefit of the other.

And in the act of 1784, by which the issue of slaves, born after the time therein mentioned, were to be free at a certain age, the section is again introduced by a preamble assigning a similar motive for the act. It is in these words:

"Whereas sound policy requires that the abolition of slavery should be effected as soon as may be consistent with the rights of individuals, and the public safety and welfare"—showing that the right of property in the master was to be protected, and that the measure was one of policy, and to prevent the injury and inconvenience, to the whites, of a slave population in the State.

And still further pursuing its legislation, we find that in the same statute passed in 1774, which prohibited the further importation of slaves into the State, there is also a provision by which any negro, Indian, or mulatto servant, who was found wandering out of the town or place to which he belonged, without a written pass such as is therein described, was made liable to be seized by any one, and taken before the next authority to be examined and delivered up to his master—who was required to pay the charge which had accrued thereby. And a subsequent section of the same law provides, that if any free negro shall travel without such pass, and shall be stopped, seized, or taken up, he shall pay all charges arising thereby. And this law was in full operation when the Constitution of the United States was adopted, and was not repealed till 1797. So that up to that time free negroes and mulattoes were associated with servants and slaves in the police regulations established by the laws of the state.

And again, in 1833, Connecticut passed another law, which made it penal to set up or establish any school in that State for the instruction of persons of the African race not inhabitants of the State, or to instruct or teach in any such school or institution, or board or harbor for that purpose, any such person, without the previous consent in writing of the civil authority of the town in which such school or institution might be.

By the laws of New Hampshire, collected and finally passed in 1815, no one was permitted to be enrolled in the militia of the State, but free white citizens; and the same provision is found in a subsequent collection of the laws, made in 1855. Nothing could more strongly mark the entire repudiation of the African race. The alien is excluded, because, being born in a foreign country, he cannot be a member of the community until he is naturalized. But why are the African race, born in the State, not permitted to share in one of the highest duties of the citizen? The answer is obvious; he is not, by the institutions and laws of the State, numbered among its people. He forms no part of the sovereignty of the State, and is not therefore called on to uphold and defend it.

Again, in 1822, Rhode Island, in its revised code, passed a law forbidding persons who were authorized to join persons in marriage, from joining in marriage any white person with any negro, Indian, or mulatto, under penalty of two hundred dollars, and declaring all such marriages absolutely null and void; and the same law was again re-enacted in its revised code of 1844. So that, down to the last-mentioned period, the strongest mark of inferiority and degradation was fastened upon the African race in that State.

The legislation of the States therefore shows, in a manner not to be mistaken, the inferior and subject condition of that race at the time the Constitution was adopted, and long afterwards, throughout the thirteen States by which that instrument was framed; and it is hardly consistent with the respect due to these States, to suppose that they regarded at that time, as fellow-citizens and members of the sovereignty, a class of beings whom they had thus stigmatized; whom, as we are bound, out of respect to the State sovereignties, to assume they had deemed it just and necessary thus to stigmatize, and upon whom they had impressed such deep and enduring marks of inferiority and degradation. . . .

CHAPTER III

CONFLICTING IDEOLOGIES

Abolitionism vs. Proslavery

❋ ❋

We have offended, Oh! my countrymen!
We have offended very grievously,
And been most tyrannous. From east to west/ A groan of accusation pierces Heaven!

LYDIA MARIA CHILD, *An Appeal in Favor of that Class of Americans Called Africans* (New York, 1836)

A knowledge of the great primary truth, that the negro is a slave by nature, and can never be happy, industrious, moral or religious, in any other condition than the one he was intended to fill, is of great importance to the theologian, the statesman, and to all those who are at heart seeking to promote his . . . future welfare.

DR. SAMUEL A. CARTWRIGHT, "Diseases and Peculiarities of the Negro Race," *De Bow's Review*, IV (July, 1851)

───────────

The heated debate over slavery and its place in American life was waged for a generation preceding the Civil War. The number of books, speeches, scientific tracts, essays, sermons, poems, diatribes, songs, lectures, and editorials devoted to the discussion is staggering. Although the literature is voluminous, it is possible to isolate the major themes around which opponents and defenders of the peculiar institution centered their concern. The documents in this chapter have been arranged to create a debate between abolitionists and supporters of slavery.

There were three dominant themes that pervaded the discussion. In order of importance they were: (1) Was slavery a sin in the eyes of God and the Bible?; (2) Was slavery antithetical to the institutions of American democracy and a free society?—the freest of all societies, Jacksonian Democrats maintained; and (3) Were Negroes racially inferior to whites? The following documents have been grouped around these questions. As abolitionists generally took the initiative in raising the issues involved, their positions will be presented first in each section— followed immediately by their opponents' views.

1. SLAVERY AND THE BIBLE

Theodore Dwight Weld was the evangelist of abolition. He and his followers held abolition camp meetings night after night, hour after hour—as long as the spirit moved them—in the tier of states between Massachusetts and Ohio. They preached the gospel of anti-slavery revival-style, and left a trail of converted Northerners in most of the places they visited. Harriet Beecher Stowe was abolition's most famous propagandist. Ten thousand copies of Uncle Tom's Cabin *were sold in its first days off the press in March, 1852; 300,000 during its first year. Adapted as a play, it became one of the most successful American dramas of the nineteenth century. Weld and Stowe had both grown to intellectual maturity in highly religious settings: Weld in New York's early-nineteenth-century center of new awakening, the "Burned-Over District," and later in Cincinnati—Ohio's hub of revivalism and abolition; Stowe, the daughter of the Reverend Lyman Beecher, the sister of a veritable brood of abolitionist clergymen and the wife of a Biblical scholar, came from a family that had preached a vigorous Calvinism to wayward New Englanders, and others, since the seventeenth century. Both considered slavery the worst form of sin in the eyes of God, and argued that nonslaveholding Christians who remained*

*silent on the issue were as guilty as slaveholders themselves:
"Neutrality in such a struggle is the abhorrence of God. . . .
Silence is* CRIME!*" In Weld's* The Bible Against Slavery: An Inquiry into the Patriarchal and Mosaic Systems on the Subject of Human Rights, *he argues that the essential spirit of the Bible opposes slavery. The concluding pages of Stowe's* Uncle Tom's Cabin; or, Life Among the Lowly *warns Christians of the wrath of a righteous and avenging God and clearly presents the dominant theme that united antislavery people of conflicting views.*

Evangelical Abolitionism Theodore Dwight Weld*

The spirit of slavery never seeks refuge in the Bible of its own accord. The horns of the altar are its last resort—seized only in desperation, as it rushes from the terror of the avenger's arm. Like other unclean spirits, it "hateth the light, neither cometh to the light, lest its deeds should be reproved." Goaded to phrenzy in its conflicts with conscience and common sense, denied all quarter, and hunted from every covert, it vaults over the sacred inclosure and courses up and down the Bible, "seeking rest, and finding none." THE LAW OF LOVE, glowing on every page, flashes around it an omnipresent anguish and despair. It shrinks from the hated light, and howls under the consuming touch, as demons quailed before the Son of God, and shrieked, "Torment us not." At last, it slinks away under the types of the Mosaic system, and seeks to burrow out of sight among their shadows. Vain hope! Its asylum is its sepulchre; its city of refuge, the city of destruction. It flies from light into the sun; from heat, into devouring fire; and from the voice of God into the thickest of His thunders.

ENSLAVING MEN IS REDUCING THEM TO ARTICLES OF PROPERTY —making free agents, chattels—converting *persons* into *things*— sinking immortality into *merchandize*. A *slave* is one held in this condition. In law, "he owns nothing, and can acquire nothing." His right to himself is abrogated. If he say *my* hands, *my* body, *my* mind, MY*self,* they are figures of speech. To *use himself* for his

* From Theodore Dwight Weld, *The Bible Against Slavery: An Inquiry into the Patriarchal and Mosaic Systems on the Subject of Human Rights,* 4th ed. (New York, 1838).

own good, is a *crime*. To keep what he earns, is *stealing*. To take his body into his own keeping, is *insurrection*. In a word, the profit of his master is made the END of his being, and he, a *mere means* to that end—a mere means to an end into which his interests do not enter, of which they constitute no portion. MAN, sunk to a *thing!* the intrinsic element, the *principle* of slavery; MEN, bartered, leased, mortgaged, bequeathed, invoiced, shipped in cargoes, stored as goods, taken on executions, and knocked off at a public outcry! Their *rights,* another's conveniences; their interests, wares on sale; their happiness, a household utensil; their personal inalienable ownership, a serviceable article or a plaything, as best suits the humour of the hour; their deathless nature, conscience, social affections, sympathies, hopes—marketable commodities! We repeat it, THE REDUCTION OF PERSONS TO THINGS! Not robbing a man of privileges, but of *himself;* not loading him with burdens, but making him a *beast of burden;* not restraining liberty, but his neighbour of a *cent,* yet commission him to rob his neighbour of *himself?* . . . Slaveholding is the highest possible violation of the eight[h] commandment. To take from a man his earnings, is theft. But to take the *earner,* is a compound, life-long theft—supreme robbery that vaults up the climax at a leap—the dread, terrific, giant robbery, that towers among other robberies a solitary horror. The eight[h] commandment forbids the taking away, and the tenth adds, "Thou shalt not *covet* any thing that is thy neighbor's"; thus guarding every man's right to himself and property, by making not only the actual taking away a sin, but even that state of mind which would *tempt* to it. Who ever made human beings slaves, without *coveting* them? Why take from them their time, labor, liberty, right of self-preservation and improvement, their right to acquire property, to worship according to conscience, to search the Scriptures, to live with their families, and their right to their own bodies, if they do not *desire* them? They COVET them for purposes of gain, convenience, lust of dominion, of sensual gratification, of pride and ostentation. THEY BREAK THE TENTH COMMANDMENT, and pluck down upon their heads the plagues that are written in the book. *Ten* commandments constitute the brief compend of human duty. *Two* of these brand slavery as sin.

An Avenging Lord Harriet Beecher Stowe*

What do you owe to these poor unfortunates, O Christians? Does not every American Christian owe to the African race some effort at reparation for the wrongs that the American nation has brought upon them? Shall the doors of churches and school-houses be shut upon them? Shall States arise and shake them out? Shall the Church of Christ hear in silence the taunt that is thrown at them, and shrink away from the helpless hand that they stretch out; and, by her silence, encourage the cruelty that would chase them from our borders? If it must be so, it will be a mournful spectacle. If it must be so, the country will have reason to tremble, when it remembers that the fate of nations is in the hands of One who is very pitiful, and of tender compassion.

This is an age of the world when nations are trembling and convulsed. A mighty influence is abroad, surging and heaving the world, as with an earthquake. And is America safe? Every nation that carries in its bosom great and unredressed injustice has in it the elements of this last convulsion.

For what is this mighty influence thus rousing in all nations and languages those groanings that cannot be uttered, for man's freedom and equality?

O Church of Christ, read the signs of the times! Is not this power the spirit of HIM whose kingdom is yet to come, and whose will to be done on earth as it is in heaven?

But who may abide the day of his appearing? "For that day shall burn as an oven: and he shall appear as a swift witness against those that oppress the hireling in his wages, the widow and the fatherless, and that *turn aside the stranger in his right: and he shall break in pieces the oppressor.*"

Are not these dread words for a nation bearing in her bosom so mighty an injustice? Christians! Every time that you pray that the kingdom of Christ may come, can you forget that prophecy associates in dread fellowship, the *day of vengeance* with the year of his redeemed?

A day of grace is yet held out to us. Both North and South have

* From Harriet Beecher Stowe, *Uncle Tom's Cabin* (Boston, 1852), pp. 507–516.

been guilty before God; and the *Christian Church* has a heavy account to answer. Not by combining together, to protect injustice and cruelty, and making a common capital of sin, is this Union to be saved,—but by repentance, justice, and mercy; for, not surer is the eternal law by which the mill-stone sinks in the ocean, than that stronger law by which injustice and cruelty shall bring on nations the wrath of Almighty God!

Slavery as a Divine Trust *Rev. B. M. Palmer**

Southerners had Bibles too, and read them to advantage. Some believed the obvious allusions to slavery in the Old Testament guaranteed divine sanction for the institution in all ages. The most common defense portrayed Negroes as the cursed descendants of Ham, destined to be "servants of servants" for all time. More imaginative exegesis came from the pen of Dr. Thornton String-fellow, whose excursions in Hebrew etymology convinced him that Negroes were created separately from whites, that the serpent who deluded Eve in the Garden of Eden was a Negro, that "the ancestors of the negroes now in the United States were the slaves of serpent," and literally and metaphorically, that black people were destined to eat dust "all the days of thy life." The following sermon, delivered at the First Presbyterian Church of New Orleans shortly after Lincoln's election in 1860, takes the higher ground. It insists that God entrusted the care of "the black race" to Southern slaveholders. This "providential duty," the Reverend Dr. B. M. Palmer wrote, was in the higher interest of Negroes themselves and Southern culture generally, and should be fulfilled without fear of consequence.

In determining our duty in this emergency, it is necessary that we should first ascertain the nature of the trust providentially committed to us. A nation often has a character as well-defined and intense as that of the individual. This depends, of course, upon a variety of causes, operating through a long period of time. It is due largely to the original traits which distinguish the stock from which it springs, and to the providential training which has formed its

* From the Reverend B. M. Palmer, "Slavery A Divine Trust: Duty of the South to Preserve and Perpetuate It," in *Fast Day Sermons: The Pulpit on the State of the Country* (New York, 1861).

education. But however derived, this individuality of character alone makes any people truly historic, competent to work out its specific mission, and to become a factor in the world's progress. The particular trust assigned to such a people becomes the pledge of Divine protection, and their fidelity to it determines the fate by which it is finally overtaken. What that trust is must be ascertained from the necessities of their position, the institutions which are the out-growth of their principles, and the conflicts through which they preserve their identity and independence. If, then, the South is such a people, what, at this juncture, is their providential trust? I answer, that it is *to conserve and to perpetuate the institution of slavery as now existing.*

For us, as now situated, the duty is plain of conserving and transmitting the system of slavery, with the freest scope for its natural development and extension. Let us, my brethren, look our duty in the face. With this institution assigned to our keeping, what reply shall we make to those who say that its days are numbered? My own conviction is, that we should at once lift ourselves, intelligently, to the highest moral ground, and proclaim to all the world that we hold this trust from God, and in its occupancy we are prepared to stand or fall as God may appoint. If the critical moment has arrived at which the great issue is joined, let us say that, in the sight of all perils, we will stand by our trust: and God be with the right!

The argument which enforces the solemnity of this providential trust is simple and condensed. It is bound upon us, then, by the *principle of self-preservation,* that "first law" which is continually asserting its supremacy over others. Need I pause to show how this system of servitude underlies and supports our material interest? That our wealth consists in our lands, and in the serfs who till them? That from the nature of our products they can only be cultivated by labor which must be controlled in order to be certain? That any other than a tropical race must faint and wither beneath a tropical sun? Need I pause to show how this system is interwoven with our entire social fabric? That these slaves form parts of our households, even as our children; and that, too, through a relationship recognized and sanctioned in the scriptures of God even as the other? Must I pause to show how it has fashioned our modes of life, and determined all our habits of thought and feeling, and moulded the very type of our civilization? How, then, can the hand of violence be laid upon it without involving our existence? The so-called free States of this country are working out the social problem under conditions peculiar to themselves. These conditions are sufficiently hard, and their success is too uncertain, to excite in us the least jealousy of their lot. With a teeming population, which the soil cannot support—with their wealth depending upon arts, created by artificial wants—with an eternal friction between the grades of their society—with their labor and their capital grinding against each other like the upper and nether millstones—with labor cheapened and displaced by new mechanical inventions, bursting more asunder the bonds of brotherhood; amid these intricate perils we have ever given them our sympathy and our prayers, and have never sought to weaken the foundations of their social order. God grant them complete success in the solution of all their perplexities! We, too, have our responsibilities and our trials; but they are all bound up in this one institution, which has been the object of such unrighteous assault through five and twenty years. If we are true to ourselves, we shall, at this critical juncture, stand by it, and work out our destiny.

This duty is bound upon us again *as the constituted guardians of the slaves themselves.* Our lot is not more implicated in theirs, than is their lot in ours; in our mutual relations we survive or perish together. The worst foes of the black race are those who have intermeddled on their behalf. We know better than others that every attribute of their character fits them for dependence and servitude. By nature, the most affectionate and loyal of all races beneath the sun, they are also the most helpless; and no calamity can befall them greater than the loss of that protection they enjoy under this patriarchal system. Indeed, the experiment has been grandly tried of precipitating them upon freedom, which they know not how to enjoy; and the dismal results are before us, in statistics that astonish the world. With the fairest portions of the earth in their possession, and with the advantage of a long discipline as cultivators of the soil, their constitutional indolence has converted the most beautiful islands of the sea into a howling waste. It is not too much to say, that if the South should, at this moment, surrender every slave, the wisdom of the entire world, united in solemn council, could not solve the question of their disposal. Their transportation to Africa, even if it were feasible, would be but the most refined cruelty; they must perish with starvation before they could have time to relapse into their primitive barbarism. Their residence here, in the presence of the vigorous Saxon race, would be but the signal for their rapid extermination before they had time to waste away through listlessness, filth and vice. Freedom would be their doom; and equally from both they call upon us, their providential guardians, to be protected. I know this argument will be scoffed abroad as the hypocritical cover thrown over our own cupidity and selfishness; but every Southern master knows its truth and feels its power. My servant, whether born in my house or bought with my money, stands to me in the relation of a child. Though providentially owing me service, which, providentially, I am bound to exact, he is, nevertheless, my brother and my friend; and I am to him a guardian and a father. He leans upon me for protection, for counsel, and for blessing; and so long as the relation continues, no power, but the power of almighty God, shall come between him and me. Were there no argument but this, it binds upon us the providential duty of preserving the relation that we may save him from a doom worse than death.

2. SLAVERY AND DEMOCRACY

A Pro-Slavery Constitution William Lloyd Garrison*

The abolitionist Theodore Parker imagined a conversation between a reincarnated Socrates and Brother Jonathan, the early nineteenth-century folk-symbol of America. "Is not this a land of freedom?" Socrates inquires. "The only free country in the world," Jonathan replies. "Three million slaves in the only free country in the world! I begin to understand a little," Socrates replies cynically.

This was another central issue in the pre-Civil War confrontation of ideologies. How could America profess to be an open society, a nation destined to carry the message of freedom to the world, when it permitted slavery, the essence of anti-democracy, to

* From "The United States Constitution," in *Selections from the Writings and Speeches of William Lloyd Garrison* (Boston, 1852), pp. 307–315.

*exist? Even the Constitution, as William Lloyd Garrison points out
in the following essay, compromised on this most crucial of
questions. No professedly free society could live honorably with
slavery or the Constitution which helped guarantee it. Garrison
said: "what the Constitution may become a century hence, we
know not; we speak of it as it is, and repudiate it as it is." On
Independence Day, 1854, he publicly burned the Constitution at
an abolitionist meeting to symbolize his opposition to "compromises with tyranny" and "covenants with death."*

Away with all verbal casuistry, all legal quibbling, the idle parade
of Lord Mansfield's decision in the case of Somerset, the useless
appeals to Blackstone's Commentaries, and the like, to prove that
the United States Constitution is an Anti-Slavery instrument! It is
worse than labor lost, and, as a false issue, cannot advance, but
must rather retard, the Anti-Slavery movement. Let there be no
dodging, no shuffling, no evasion. Let us confess the sin of our
fathers, and our own sin as a people, in conspiring for the degradation and enslavement of the colored race among us. Let us be
honest with the facts of history, and acknowledge the compromises
that were made to secure the adoption of the Constitution, and the
consequent establishment of the Union. Let us, who profess to
abhor slavery, and who claim to be freemen indeed, dissolve the
bands that connect us with the Slave Power, religiously and politically; not doubting that a faithful adherence to principle will be the
wisest policy, the highest expediency, for ourselves and our posterity, for the miserable victims of Southern oppression, and for
the cause of liberty throughout the world.

We charge upon the present national compact, that it was
formed at the expense of human liberty, by a profligate surrender
of principle, and to this hour is cemented with human blood.

We charge upon the American Constitution, that it contains
provisions, and enjoins duties, which make it unlawful for freemen
to take the oath of allegiance to it, because they are expressly
designed to favor a slaveholding oligarchy, and, consequently, to
make one portion of the people a prey to another.

It was pleaded at the time of its adoption, it is pleaded now,
that, without such a compromise, there could have been no union;
that, without union, the colonies would have become an easy prey

to the mother country; and, hence, that it was an act of necessity, deplorable indeed when viewed alone, but absolutely indispensable to the safety of the republic.

To this we reply: The plea is as profligate as the act was tyrannical. It is the . . . doctrine, that the end sanctifies the means. It is a confession of sin, but the denial of any guilt in its perpetration. This plea is sufficiently broad to cover all the oppression and villainy that the sun has witnessed in his circuit, since God said, "Let there be light." It assumes that to be practicable which is impossible, namely, that there can be freedom with slavery, union with injustice, and safety with bloodguiltiness. A union of virtue with pollution is the triumph of licentiousness. A partnership between right and wrong is wholly wrong. A compromise of the principles of justice is the deification of crime.

Better that the American Union had never been formed, than that it should have been obtained at such a frightful cost! If they were guilty who fashioned it, but who could not foresee all its frightful consequences, how much more guilty are they, who, in full view of all that has resulted from it, clamor for its perpetuity! If it was sinful at the commencement to adopt it, on the ground of escaping a greater evil, is it not equally sinful to swear to support it for the same reason, or until, in process of time, it be purged from its corruption?

It is absurd, it is false, it is an insult to the common sense of mankind, to pretend that the Constitution was intended to embrace the entire population of the country under its sheltering wings; or that the parties to it were actuated by a sense of justice and the spirit of impartial liberty; or that it needs no alteration, but only a new interpretation, to make it harmonize with the object aimed at by its adoption. As truly might it be argued, that because it is asserted in the Declaration of Independence, that all men are created equal, and endowed with an inalienable right to liberty, therefore none of its signers were slaveholders, and since its adoption slavery has been banished from the American soil! The truth is, our fathers were intent on securing liberty to themselves, without being very scrupulous as to the means they used to accomplish their purpose. They were not actuated by the spirit of universal philanthropy; and though in words they recognized occasionally the brotherhood of the human race, in practice they continually denied it. They did not blush to enslave a portion of their fellow-men, and to buy and sell them as cattle in the market, while they were fighting against the oppression of the mother country, and boasting of their regard for the rights of man. Why, then, concede to them virtues which they did not possess? Why cling to the falsehood, that they were no respecters of persons in the formation of the government?

Three millions of the American people are crushed under the American Union! They are held as slaves, trafficked as merchandise, registered as goods and chattels! The government gives them no protection—the government is their enemy, the government keeps them in chains! Where they lie bleeding, we are prostrate by their side—in their sorrows and sufferings we participate—their stripes are inflicted on our bodies, their shackles are fastened on our limbs, their cause is ours! The Union which grinds them to the dust rests upon us, and with them we will struggle to overthrow it! The Constitution which subjects them to hopeless bondage is one that we cannot swear to support. Our motto is, "No UNION WITH SLAVEHOLDERS," either religious or political. They are the fiercest enemies of mankind, and the bitterest foes of God! We separate from them, not in anger, not in malice, not for a selfish purpose, not to do them an injury, not to cease warning, exhorting, reproving them for their crimes, not to leave the perishing bondman to his fate—O no! But to clear our skirts of innocent blood—to give the oppressor no countenance—and to hasten the downfall of slavery in America, and throughout the world!

The Conservative Reaction *George Fitzhugh**

George Fitzhugh, the most able and learned advocate of Negro slavery, was essentially a critic of democracy, an opponent of the major progressive tenets of thought in Jacksonian America, a philosopher of reaction. All advanced societies are founded on exploitation, "slavery" in essence if not in name, he claimed. "Fanatics," "schemers," as he and others popularly called Northern reformers, attempted to deny this truth. "Liberty and equality are new things

* From George Fitzhugh, *Sociology for the South, or The Failure of Free Society* (Richmond, Va., 1854).

*under the sun," Fitzhugh wrote. "In France and in our own North-
ern states the experiment has already failed." The burden of Fitzhugh's position is that it is utopian to strive to institute free society
anywhere. Recognizing this, and also that Negroes are "human
beings who have all the physical powers of men, with the wants
only of brutes," slavery is seen as their most beneficial condition.
Northern slaves, wage earners, were worse off than Southern, he
said. To prove that "free society is a failure and its philosophy
false," Fitzhugh wrote one of the most interesting books of the ante-
bellum period,* Sociology for the South, or The Failure of Free
Society.

Free society has continued long enough to justify the attempt to
generalize its phenomena, and calculate its moral and intellectual
influences. It is obvious that, in whatever is purely utilitarian and
material, it incites invention and stimulates industry. Benjamin
Franklin, as a man and a philosopher, is the best exponent of the
working of the system. His sentiments and his philosophy are low,
selfish, atheistic and material. They tend directly to make man a
mere "featherless biped," well-fed, well-clothed and comfortable,
but regardless of his soul as "the beasts that perish."

Since the Reformation the world has as regularly been retro-
grading in whatever belongs to the departments of genius, taste
and art, as it has been progressing in physical science and its
application to mechanical construction. Mediaeval Italy rivalled if
it did not surpass ancient Rome, in poetry, in sculpture, in painting, and many of the fine arts. Gothic architecture reared its
monuments of skill and genius throughout Europe, till the 15th
century; but Gothic architecture died with the Reformation. The
age of Elizabeth was the Augustan age of England. The men who
lived then acquired their sentiments in a world not yet deadened
and vulgarized by puritanical cant and levelling demagoguism.
Since then men have arisen who have been the fashion and the go
for a season, but none have appeared whose names will descend to
posterity. Liberty and equality made slower advances in France.
The age of Louis XIV was the culminating point of French genius
and art. It then shed but a flickering and lurid light. Frenchmen are
servile copyists of Roman art, and Rome had no art of her own.
She borrowed from Greece; distorted and deteriorated what she

borrowed; and France imitates and falls below Roman distortions. The genius of Spain disappeared with Cervantes; and now the world seems to regard nothing as desirable except what will make money and what costs money. There is not a poet, an orator, a sculptor, or painter in the world. The tedious elaboration necessary to all the productions of high art would be ridiculed in this money-making, utilitarian, charlatan age. Nothing now but what is gaudy and costly excites admiration. The public taste is debased.

But far the worst feature of modern civilization, which is the civilization of free society, remains to be exposed. Whilst labor-saving processes have probably lessened by one half, in the last century, the amount of work needed for comfortable support, the free laborer is compelled by capital and competition to work more than he ever did before, and is less comfortable. The organization of society cheats him of his earnings, and those earnings go to swell the vulgar pomp and pageantry of the ignorant millionaires, who are the only great of the present day. These reflections might seem, at first view, to have little connexion with negro slavery; but it is well for us of the South not to be deceived by the tinsel glare and glitter of free society, and to employ ourselves in doing our duty at home, and studying the past, rather than in insidious rivalry of the expensive pleasures and pursuits of men whose sentiments and whose aims are low, sensual and grovelling.

Human progress, consisting in moral and intellectual improvement, and there being no agreed and conventional standard weights or measures of moral and intellectual qualities and quantities, the question of progress can never be accurately decided. We maintain that man has not improved, because in all save the mechanic arts he reverts to the distant past for models to imitate, and he never imitates what he can excel.

We need never have white slaves in the South, because we have black ones. Our citizens, like those of Rome and Athens, are a privileged class. We should train and educate them to deserve the privileges and to perform the duties which society confers on them. Instead, by a low demagoguism depressing their self-respect by discourses on the equality of man, we had better excite their pride by reminding them that they do not fulfil the menial offices which white men do in other countries. Society does not feel the burden of providing for the few helpless paupers in the South. And we should recollect that here we have but half the people to educate, for half are negroes; whilst at the North they profess to educate all. It is in our power to spike this last gun of the abolitionists. We should educate all the poor. The abolitionists say that it is one of the necessary consequences of slavery that the poor are neglected. It was not so in Athens, and in Rome, and should not be so in the South. If we had less trade with and less dependence on the North, all our poor might be profitably and honorably employed in trades, professions and manufactures. Then we should have a rich and denser population. Yet we but marshal her in the way that she was going. The South is already aware of the necessity of a new policy, and has begun to act on it. Every day more and more is done for education, the mechanic arts, manufactures and internal improvements. We will soon be independent of the North.

We deem this peculiar question of negro slavery of very little importance. The issue is made throughout the world on the general subject of slavery in the abstract. The argument has commenced. One set of ideas will govern and control after awhile the civilized world. Slavery will every where be abolished, or every where be re-instituted. We think the opponents of practical, existing slavery, are estopped by their own admission; nay, that unconsciously, as socialists, they are the defenders and propagandists of slavery, and have furnished the only sound arguments on which its defence and justification can be rested. We have introduced the subject of negro slavery to afford us a better opportunity to disclaim the purpose of reducing the white man any where to the condition of negro slaves here. It would be very unwise and unscientific to govern white men as you would negroes. Every shade and variety of slavery has existed in the world. In some cases there has been much of legal regulation, much restraint of the master's authority; in others, none at all. The character of slavery necessary to protect the whites in Europe should be much milder than negro slavery, for slavery is only needed to protect the white man, whilst it is more necessary for the government of the negro even than for his protection. But even negro slavery should not be outlawed. We might and should have laws in Virginia, as in Louisiana, to make the master subject to presentment by the grand jury and to punishment, for any inhuman or improper treatment or neglect of his slave.

We abhor the doctrine of the "Types of Mankind";* first, because it is at war with scripture, which teaches us that the whole human race is descended from a common parentage; and, secondly, because it encourages and incites brutal masters to treat negroes, not as weak, ignorant and dependent brethren, but as wicked beasts, without the pale of humanity. The Southerner is the negro's friend, his only friend. Let no intermeddling abolitionist, no refined philosophy, dissolve this friendship.

3. ENVIRONMENTALISTS AND RACISTS

An Abolitionist on the Equality of Mankind Theodore Tilton†

Theodore Tilton's The Negro: A Speech at Cooper Institute, New York, May 12, 1863 *ranks with Lydia Maria Child's* An Appeal in Favor of that Class of Americans Called Africans *(New York, 1836), Martin R. Delany's* The Condition, Elevation and Destiny of the Colored People of the United States *(Philadelphia, 1852), and William Wells Brown's* The Black Man: His Antecedents, His Genius, and His Achievements *(New York, 1863) for its vindication of racial equality. If the slave was morally or intellectually backward, Tilton said, as had Child and Brown and Delany, it was the product of his environment, not his genes. This editor of the antislavery Congregationalist journal* The Independent *advocated complete Negro equality and assimilation into American life. When the "brutalization of immortal souls" ended, he predicted, the Negro would emerge a productive and competent citizen. Tilton's wittiness, evident here, made him a popular lecturer on the lyceum circuit.*

MY FRIENDS: I bring to you the Negro! Not the slave—not the contraband—not the freedman—but the negro? You and I will never meet slavery in the future as we have met it in the past. The times have changed. Like St. Margaret in Raphael's picture, our

---

* A book by Josiah C. Nott and George R. Gliddon criticizing the Biblical account of creation and arguing that Negroes are a separate species of man.

† From Theodore Tilton, *The Negro: A Speech at Cooper Institute,* New York, May 12, 1863 (New York, 1863)

feet are now upon the Great Dragon, and the palm-branch of victory is in our hands. . . . As *The Journal of Commerce* says, "The opposition is no longer to the Slave: it is to the Negro." That is, there is a sworn enmity to the black man whether in his chains or out—whether under the yoke or free. Men dislike the color of his skin—so they lift their hands to smite his cheek. Our plea, therefore, is no longer for the Slave. That argument has passed. It passed on the First of January.* The needful plea now is for the Negro. . . .

Who, then, is the Negro? What is his rank among mankind? Send men to search for the negro, and where will they look? Under other men's feet—for they keep him to trample on! Lift him up and ask who is he? and what is the answer? An inferior man—a sunken humanity—a half-gifted child of God. A white man, looking down upon a negro, straightens himself an inch higher into a fool's pride!

But settle as you will who are *above* the negro, I will tell you who are *below* him. The Esquimaux are below him. The Pacific Islanders are below him. The South American tribes poleward from the La Plata are below him. The ground castes of India are below him. . . . The natives of Van Dieman's Land are below him. Is the negro's skull thick? The Van Dieman's Lander breaks fire-wood over *his!* He could be his own schoolmaster! (Laughter.) I can count you twenty races of men—and as many editors of newspapers—who rank below the negro (laughter).

Do you call the negro race inferior? No man can yet pronounce that judgment safely. How will you compare races, to give each its due rank? There is but one just way. You must compare them in their fulfilments, not in their beginnings—in their flower, not in their bud. How will you estimate the rank of the Roman people? By its beginnings? By its decline? By neither. You rank it at the height of its civilization—when it attained to jurisprudence, to statesmanship, to eloquence, to the beautiful arts. Otherwise you rank it unjustly. The Germans, to-day, give philosophy to Europe—but you can count the years backward when the Germans, now philosophers, were barbarians. Who could say, eight or nine centuries ago, what was to be the intellectual rank of the French

* Emancipation Day, January 1, 1863.

nation? So no man can now predict the destiny of the negro race. That race is yet so undeveloped—that destiny is yet so unfulfilled—that no man can say, and no wise man pretends to say, what the negro race shall finally become.

Inferior? What is human inferiority? Will you look at a child in his cradle and say, that is an inferior man? No. You wait for his growth—you will not judge him till his manhood. Will you look upon a race yet in its ungrowth and say, that is an inferior humanity? No. The time has not yet come to judge that infant child; the time has not yet come to judge this infant race. As in the nursery song, so these stormy times are yet only rocking its cradle in the tree-tops. It may be that negroes—on their original continent—in the long future—growing strong as other nations grow weak—holding the soil in one hand and the sea in the other—may yet stand the dominant, superior race of the world. I do not say this will so be—but I say no man can prove that this will *not* so be. You may read . . . the whole library of Ethnology—and in the confusion of knowledge one thing is plain—and that is, science has not yet proved that the negro race is not to be a high-cultured, regnant race—masters of their own continent, and perhaps dictators to the world. Who knows but each continent may, in turn, become chief of the whole five in power and civilization? Asia once outranked Europe, but Europe now outranks Asia. North America, once a wilderness, now nearly equals Europe. Who knows but Africa may yet overtop them all? For, as the least shall be greatest in the Kingdom of Heaven, it may be also that the least shall be greatest among the kingdoms of the earth (applause).

But whatever is to be the destiny of the negro race in Africa, every man sees that the future is not to find a negro race in America—I mean a strictly negro race, of unmingled blood. We have no isolated race here. . . . The American people are all peoples—a nation of many nations. The four quarters of the earth send us their sons and daughters. As all tongues enter into the English tongue, so all nations enter into the English-speaking race on this continent.

Three stupendous processes of intermingling are going forward in this country. First, we are absorbing the Irish race. Second, we are absorbing the German race. Third, are we absorbing the Negro race? No, just the opposite. Look at the facts. It is not black blood that pours itself into white veins. It is white blood that pours itself into black veins. It is not, therefore, a philosophical statement to say . . . that the negro race is being absorbed by the white. On the contrary, the negro race is receiving and absorbing part of the white. A large fraction of the white race of the South is melting away into the black. I am not stating any theory on the subject—I am stating only the fact. And this is the plain fact, which no man can gainsay.

Now what is it that I ask for the negro? I ask nothing more than for the white man—nothing less. I ask nothing more than for myself—nothing less. First of all, I ask that he shall not be held as a slave. Break the yokes; burst the chains; open the prison-doors; let the oppressed go free! (Applause.) I ask, then, that after he is free, he shall not be oppressed by those cruel laws which degrade him to a secondary slavery in the free States. I ask that in the State of New York he shall go to the ballot-box, subject to the same restrictions as white men, and subject to no other (applause). On the day when the people of this State gave, with their right hand, 100,000 majority for Abraham Lincoln, they gave, with their left, 100,000 majority against negro suffrage.* Now we must help the negro up from under the weight of that injustice (applause). I ask, also, that he shall take his seat in the jury-box, to perform a part in those honorable services from which no white man escapes. . . . I ask, also, that the negro shall be eligible to every political office to which white men are eligible. . . . But, remember, I do not ask simply that *competent* black men shall hold office. I ask that *incompetent* black men shall hold office—for only so will they be on a level with the whites (laughter).

We speak of social equality and inequality—of high and low—of rich and poor—of white and black. If you had walked down Broadway at six o'clock this evening—stemming that stream of humanity that pours hitherward after the mill-wheels of the day's work are stopped—you would have seen the merchant, the scholar, the lawyer—you would have seen the mechanic, the beggar, the outcast—all grades of men. You would have rendered them varying respect according to their varying grade. But how soon shall all these distinctions fade away, and all men stand equal

* A $250 freehold remained a requirement for Negro voting in New York State until after the Civil War.

before the bar of Him who is no respecter of persons? If, then, these distinctions avail so little there, why should they avail so much here? My thought wanders out to that great multitude of God's lowly children who are soon to be lifted to a higher estate on earth—that great race who, for 240 years, have been slaves on the same soil where we are free—whose bondage is thrice older than the Republic—whose fathers, for eight generations, have worn the chain, and borne the burden, and gone down with sorrow into merciful graves! What a record will be revealed against this guilty nation in that day when the books shall be opened, and the graves shall burst, and God shall avenge his own elect! I dare not think of it! Veil the picture! It is too awful for human sight! Look, rather, toward the far South, to the living children of these eight generations of the dead—children more blessed than their fathers, having now a hope in this world! Behold them emerging out of the valley of the shadow of death into the light and liberty of the sons of God! My countrymen, give them a greeting of good cheer! Throw words of Christian welcome like roses under their feet, to make fragrant the pathway of their coming! For they come guided of Him whose reward is with Him—who has said, "Inasmuch as ye do it unto the least of these, my little ones, ye do it unto me" (applause).

A Scientific Proof of the Biological Inferiority of the Negro
J. H. Van Evrie*

Dr. J. H. Van Evrie's Negroes and Negro Slavery: The First, An Inferior Race—The Latter, Its Normal Condition *represents the Southern pseudoscientific school of writers who attempted to prove the Negro biologically inferior to the Caucasian and incapable of major advancement. "Where we once apologized and extenuated," the editor of* De Bow's Review *proudly acknowledged, "we now boldly defend." Van Evrie, like his contemporaries, Josiah C. Nott, Thornton Stringfellow, and Samuel A. Cartwright, insisted that slavery was the natural and beneficent state of an innately savage people: "It has elevated him from the depths of barbarism and brutalism to a degree of civilization and usefulness, and*

* From Dr. J. H. Van Evrie, *Negroes and Negro Slavery: The First, an Inferior Race—The Latter, Its Normal Condition* (Baltimore, 1853).

happiness, which he never would have reached through any other instrumentality."

The hypocritical and false issue presented to the credulous friends of liberty every where [is] . . . that the Negro is a BLACK WHITE MAN, or that two widely separated, unmistakenly marked, and perpetually different things are the SAME THING!! This single fallacy, which is in reality an absurdity, as well as a lie, once exploded, and the mighty edifice which fraud and imposture, and popular credulity, have united to magnify into such fearful proportions, instantly collapses and disappears forever. The Negro once comprehended, as he is, as God has made him, as he must perpetually remain, and instantly, "philanthropy," "humanity," that which men have worshipped as a divinity, becomes . . . a hideous monstrosity.

Fortunately for the cause of truth and real "humanity," this question is resolvable into *fact* and wholly unlike the "divinity" of kings, or "infallibility" of priests, or other lying *abstractions,* which could only be exploded by appeals to reason, the absolute falsity and utter absurdity of the single race dogma is demonstrable to the senses.

The human creation like the animal creation, like all the families or forms of being, is composed of a certain number of races, all generally resembling each other, yet each specifically different from all others.

This simple, though mighty truth, hitherto obscured by ignorance and covered by a monstrous falsehood, underlies all our sectional troubles and needs only to be recognized by our people to end them forever.

The Negro is a man, but an inferior *species* of man, who could no more originate from the same parentage with us than could the owl from the eagle, or the shad from the salmon, or the cat from the tiger, and can no more be *forced* by human power, to manifest the qualities or fulfil the duties imposed by the Almighty on the Caucasian man than can either of these forms of life be forced to manifest qualities other than those eternally impressed upon them by the hand of God.

The Caucasian brain measures 92 cubic inches—with the cerebrum, the centre of the intellectual functions, relatively predominating over the cerebellum, the centre of the animal instincts; thus, it is capable of indefinite progression, and transmits the knowledge or experience acquired by one generation to subsequent genera-tions—the record of which is history.

The Negro brain measures from 65 to 75 cubic inches—with the cerebellum, the centre of the animal instincts relatively pre-dominating over the cerebrum, the centre of the intellectual powers; thus, its acquisition of knowledge is limited to a single generation, and incapable of transmitting this to subsequent ones, *it can have no history.* A single glance at eternal and immutable *facts,* which perpetually separate these forms of human existence will be sufficient to cover the whole ground—thus, could the deluded people who propose to improve on the works of the Creator, and *elevate* the Negro to the standard of the white, actually perform an act of omnipotence, and, add 20 or 30 percent to the totality of the Negro brain, they would still be at as great a distance as ever from their final object, while the relations of the anterior and posterior portions of the brain remained as at present.

And were they capable of performing a second act of creative power, to diminish the posterior portion, and add to the anterior portion of the Negro brain, to make it in form, as well as size, correspond to that of the Caucasian man, they would even then, after all this effort, and all this display of omnipotent force, come back again to the starting point, for such a brain could no more be born of a negress, than an elephant pass the eye of a needle. Historical fact is in perfect accordance with these physiological facts; thus, while there are portions, nationalities or branches of the Caucasian race that have relapsed, become effete, decayed, lost—the *race* has steadily progressed, and from the banks of the Nile, to those of the Mississippi, civilization, progress, intellectual development, the *specific* characteristics of the Caucasian have alone changed locations. The Negro on the contrary is at this moment just where the race was three thousand years ago, when sculptured on Egyptian monuments. Portions of it in contact with the superior race have been temporarily advanced; but invariably, without exception, they have returned to the African standard as soon as this contact has ceased, or as soon as the results of amalgamation between them have disappeared.

The Abyssinians originally pure Caucasian, the Lybians, the Numidians of Roman history, and Ethiopians, the two latter, and doubtless the Lybians also of mixed Caucasian blood are often confounded with the Negro or the typical woolly haired, and thus it has been claimed that the latter were capable of progress; but it is a historical truth beyond contradiction or doubt even that the typical African, *the race now in our midst,* has never of its own volition passed beyond the hunter condition, that condition which it now occupies in Africa, when isolated from all other races.

The Creator has beneficently and wisely permitted amalgamation to a certain extent between the extremes of "humanity," the Caucasian and Negro—otherwise there would be slavery, oppression, brutality, death, but this is limited within fixed boundaries; thus, the Mulatto or Hybrid of the fourth generation, is as sterile as the mule or most *animal* hybrids are in the first generation.

These two races thus widely diverging, one the most superior and the other the most inferior of all the human races, exist at the South in juxtaposition. What does fact, reason, common sense, the evident design of the Almighty as written upon the structure of each indicate as their true social relations?

Why manifestly those *peculiar* institutions which actually do exist. The superior and predominating race adopt for themselves a system of Democracy—that is those that are equal by nature are declared equal by the law—those organized alike and endowed alike, and thus, evidently designed by the Creator for like purposes, for the exercise of the same rights and performance of the same duties, are protected in these rights and compelled to perform these duties. For the inferior race inferiorly organized and inferiorly endowed, as incapable of fulfilling the purposes assigned to the superior organization by the Almighty Creator of all as it is to change the color of its skin a *peculiar* system adapted to its *specific* nature, and which provides for that eternal subordination to the Caucasian man, fixed from the beginning, is not merely a necessity of human existence but an imperative *duty* devolving on the superior race.

This system, these *peculiar* institutions, ignorance, popular credulity and the followers of European opinion confound with Roman and other systems of *slavery,* to which it has just as complete a resemblance as black has to white; but this term unfortunately

fixed upon it, has deceived millions of men—thus we see multitudes among ourselves impotently as blindly butting their brains
against a present, normal, vital, organization of Southern society
with the confident belief that they are battling with monstrosities
dead and buried centuries ago! To be sure it does not necessarily
follow because the white is superior and the Negro inferior, that
therefore the present relations of the races or the social system of
the South is exactly right or in precise conformity to the wants or
the natural rights of both; but it is a *fact,* that this condition
assures to the Negro a greater amount of happiness than any other
ever known; therefore for precisely the reasons that New York
claims her institutions to be founded in truth, may Mississippi do
the same; and if the "greatest good to the greatest number" proves
that "equality" is a natural relation where white men exist only, a
similar result wherever whites and Negroes exist together, equally
proves that the relation of master and "slave" is a fundamental law
of human existence.

The Negroes at the South are even acknowledged by the dupes
of delusion to be in a good material condition, which in truth is
acknowledging every thing, for it is true in all cases with whites as
well as blacks that those in the best physical condition are also in
the best moral condition.

Material and moral well being is an inseparable unity, that
cannot be divided or isolated any more than can mind and body,
or life and organized matter; therefore the Negro in Mississippi
who has plenty to eat, who is not over-worked, who rapidly mul-
tiplies, is also from the necessity of things in the best moral condition possible for *him.*

Those writers among us who sometimes undertake to defend
Southern institutions by comparing the condition of the Negro with
the condition of the British laborer, and who think they have made
out their case when they shew it to be no *worse* than the latter,
thus make a vital mistake. The fact is no comparison is allowable
or possible. The Negro is governed by those *naturally* superior,
and is in the *best* condition of any portion or branch of his race;
while the British laborer, governed by those *naturally* his equals,
and even sometimes his inferiors, is in the *worst* condition of any
portion or branch of *his* race. The first is secure in all the rights
that nature gives him; the latter is *practically* denied all or nearly

all of his;—the first is protected and provided for by those the Creator has designed should govern him; the latter is kept in ignorance, brutalized, over-worked and plundered by those it is designed should only *govern themselves;—one is a normal condition, the other an infamous usurpation.*

The notion that so-called slavery is an "evil" is equally a fallacy as that which supposes it a wrong. It arises to a great extent from confounding two very different things—the presence of a Negro population with the *peculiar* institutions necessary for its governance; thus, while it might be desirable in certain localities to get rid of the former, to destroy the latter would be as absurd and indeed as *wrong* as it would be to tear all boys of a certain age from their parents and guardians and to turn them loose upon the world.

Instead of an "evil" in any sense whatever it is an unmixed good to the Negro, to the master, to the North, to civilization, to the world; it is "the best relation between capital and labor ever known," the "corner stone of our Republican edifice," and the presence of the inferior race on this continent, the most fortunate conjuncture that has ever happened in human affairs.

The American School of Ethnology *Samuel George Morton**

Van Evrie was a Southerner and a popular writer. Such views as he expressed, however, had wider currency in the pre-Darwinian scientific world outside the South. Some of the most distinguished scientists of the pre–Civil War era questioned the essentially equalitarian image of man that pervaded eighteenth-century thought. Some were eventually considered heretics for challenging the Biblical interpretation of the creation of man. Samuel George Morton, Louis Agassiz, and E. George Squier, among others, found evidence in assorted crania, Indian burial mounds, and Egyptian tombs to conclude that there were inherent and unchangeable physical, moral, and intellectual differences among the races of men. The dean of this influential American school of ethnology was the Philadelphia physician and anthropologist, Samuel George Morton. Morton's writings had none of the emo-

* From Samuel George Morton, *Brief Remarks on the Diversities of the Human Species.* . . . (Philadelphia, 1842), pp. 5–11.

*tionalism of Van Evrie's or Nott's—he always considered himself
a detached and objective man of science. Nonetheless, his conclusion that Negroes represented the lowest order of man differed
little from the position of his Southern counterparts. The following
paper was read at the Pennsylvania Medical College in Philadelphia on November 1, 1842.*

Ours is essentially a science of facts. In Anatomy little should be
taken for granted that cannot be made manifest to observation;
while, in Physiology, we are not called upon to believe any thing
that does not follow as an obvious and reasonable result of
demonstrable facts. Like the Geographer who goes forth to study
the seas, the rivers and the mountains of the earth, so do we search
into the varied and multiform tissues of the human body,—so
wisely constructed, so harmoniously blended, and so mutely eloquent of the hand that made them.

My province is to teach the structure and functions of the
human body; that inimitable contrivance which we are assured, on
the strongest testimony, was created in the image of its Maker. To
comprehend disease we must first become familiar with that fabric
which is subject to its influences; we must study man in all the
phases of his development, from childhood to senility; and we
must acquaint ourselves with those varied circumstances of climate
and locality which act on the springs of life, and modify their
numberless functions.

Man, regarded in his general character, is the same in every
zone; he possesses the same general conformation, and notwithstanding some striking diversities of organization, the whole human family is to be regarded as a single species. Yet, notwithstanding this approximation of mankind in essential and specific characteristics, I firmly believe that they were originally, or, in other
words, before their dispersion into different latitudes, endowed
with those varied traits of mind and body which alone could adapt
them to their various allotments on the face of the earth. The more
I have reflected on these diversities, the more I am confirmed in
the conclusion, that they have not resulted from physical causes
acting on constitutions originally the same, but that, on the contrary, there has been a primeval difference among men; not an
accidental occurrence, but a part of that all-pervading design

which has adapted man, in common with animals and plants, to those diverse conditions which form a necessary part of the economy of creation. Some intelligent minds, influenced more, perhaps, by feeling than by reflection, are unwilling to admit these differences among the several races of men; regarding them as incompatible with the equal wisdom and justice of Providence. Yet, on the other hand, it requires but little observation to convince oneself that these very differences form a universal, and no doubt essential feature in the social organization of our species. In the same family, for example, some individuals are precocious of intelligence from infancy itself, while others are imbecile from their very birth. In the one the mind develops itself in defiance of every obstacle; while in the other, care and culture are unavailing, and the intellect, if it deserves that name, remains in hopeless torpor till the end of life. How numberless are the gradations between these two extremes! Nor are these diversities confined to the physical and intellectual man; they are also conspicuous in his moral character, and pervade, in fact, every attribute of his existence. What is undeniable on the small scale, is not less true of the great; and although we may not perceive the fitness of things, this is no proof of the absence of wisdom in their adaptation.

The inspired historian has depicted the moral and physical beauty of our first parents in the gardens of Paradise, among the vallies of Mesopotamia. But temptation and sorrow soon blighted this primeval happiness; the earth became filled with iniquity, and, by a universal calamity, the race of man, excepting a single family, was swept from the face of creation. Is it to be supposed that this family, which had been preserved from the common fate of humanity by a series of divine interpositions, would be sent forth on the wide world to struggle with the vicissitudes of *chance?* Is it not more probable that the same Infinite power that conducted them unharmed through the Deluge itself, would adapt them, before their dispersion, to those varied physical circumstances with which they were henceforward to contend? The strongest moral contrasts are coeval with the descent of mankind from the ark;* and we may reasonably infer that equally strong physical diversities were then established, constituting what are called in modern language, the *Races of Men*. Now, as these views form a legitimate

* See Genesis, chap. ix., 25, 26, 27, and chap. lxix., 1 to 27.

and philosophical department of Physiological inquiry, let us pause and devote a few moments to their consideration.

In the first place, then, we may remark, that if the black complexion was the mere consequence of the action of the sun's rays in a hot climate, the Indians of our own continent, who inhabit the torrid zone, ought to be as dark-skinned as the inter-tropical Africans; which is very far from being the fact, for these American tribes are no darker than others who live on the shores of the Rio de la Plata, in the cold region of Patagonia. Again, if climate caused the peculiar texture of the hair in the African, a similar temperature in the same latitudes of America, ought to produce an analogous result in at least some portion of the indigenous population; but the hair of the Indian, in all his localities, is long and lank, like that of the Mongolian: nor, on the other hand, does there appear to be the smallest tendency in any American climate to change the hair of the Negro; for we have the experience of three centuries in the West India Islands, in disproof of any such mutation.

If the African derives his complexion from the causes to which we have adverted, how does it happen that he becomes no fairer in a colder climate? Real Negroes constitute the indigenous population of Van Diemen's Land, which is nearly as cold as Ireland; and yet these very people are among the most strongly marked tribes of the African race. In many islands of the Indian Archipelago, the Nigritos, a race of Negroes of small stature, inhabit the hill-country, and the Malays the low-lands nearer the coast; and yet the Malay, under these circumstances, does not approximate to the Negro in any one of his physical characteristics.

So also the Dutch inhabitants of the Cape of Good Hope, who have lived for three centuries among the Hottentots, have preserved their natural traits unaltered; and this remark is also true of the Arabs who have lived during many generations among the Negroes in the heart of Africa, yet have lost none of the distinctive features of their race. Analogous examples might be multiplied to a great extent; but these may suffice the purpose of present illustration.

That climate has a certain and obvious effect on the human body, I most certainly admit; and, taking the skin for an illustration, we all know the effect of the sun's rays in producing a darker complexion, as seen in our own latitudes, and which is more strikingly manifest in those Caucasian or white nations who inhabit inter-tropical regions. They become of a dark brown complexion, not unfrequently as sable as mulattoes; but the children of such parents, if protected from the sun's rays, preserve the complexion which is characteristic of their progenitors, as in the instance of the Arabs to whom I have already adverted. But, with regard to the permanence of those organic characters which mark the different races of men, a conclusive source of evidence has within a few years been disclosed to us in the monuments of Egypt. These venerable and truly wonderful remains of human ingenuity, embrace numberless legends, of which the knowledge of hieroglyphic literature has established not only the meaning, but the dates themselves; and by their evidence we discover the interesting fact, that the several races of men were as perfectly distinct in Egypt upwards of three thousand five hundred years ago as they are now. The white man and the Negro are there depicted, side by side, with the same physical characteristics which are now familiar to our daily observation. This vast period of thirty-five centuries, has made no appreciable change in either; and as less than seven hundred years could have intervened between the positive existence of these distinctions and the epoch of the Deluge according to the Hebrew chronology, we come to the unavoidable conclusion, as already stated, that these diversities of organization were coeval with the dispersion of our species. Let me repeat, therefore, my admonition, that we may not hastily attribute to mere chance those singular phenomena which bear the impress of obvious and original design.

The negro presents us, moreover, with a remarkable example of the adaptation of constitution to climate. Thus, there are vast tracts on both the eastern and western coasts of inter-tropical Africa, in which the European constitution at once becomes the victim of enervating and destroying fevers; and although it may, for a time, resist the fatal effect of these subtle influences, it sooner or later becomes a prey to them. No precautions can prevent them; and no manner of life accustoms an exotic constitution to contend with its unseen but indomitable enemy. In these very climates, in the midst of these lethal exhalations, in this foul and poisoned atmosphere, the negro reaches the acme of his physical nature, and scorns those precautionary restraints which are necessary to the European.

This remark applies to the negro not only in his native African regions, to which we presume his constitution is essentially assimilated, but also in exotic climates; for I believe the fact has been satisfactorily proved, that he is much less subject than the white man to the yellow fever of our own country, and also to those destroying epidemics which infest the rice plantations and other marshy districts of the southern states.

. . . Do not these and similar facts point to an original adaptation of the physical man to the local position he was ordained to inhabit? I apprehend that without such adaptation, the patriarchal germs of our species would have been utterly destroyed in the effort to contend with those pestilential influences which appear to be inherent to certain localities on the surface of our earth.

I have chiefly adverted to the negro in the preceding remarks, because his physical characteristics contrast more strongly with our own than those of the people of the other races; yet the same remarks are, on the general principle, applicable to any of the permanent varieties of mankind, as a moment's reflection will prove.

CHAPTER IV

THE UNFULFILLED

REVOLUTION

❁ ❁

I do not think the work is finished, so long as the word "white"
is allowed to play any part in legislation. . . .

CHARLES SUMNER, 1870

The social revolution that accompanied the Civil War was
unfulfilled because it was unanticipated. Full equality for Negroes, as C. Vann Woodward has shown, was not a commitment
of the Northern war effort. The abolition of slavery and the
subsequent enfranchisement of the Negro through the Fourteenth and Fifteenth Amendments were byproducts of situations
which only peripherally reflected the moral issue of equal justice
for black people: the former came as a necessary war measure;
the latter, as a Northern response to an adamant and recalcitrant South, and a political act to bolster the Republican party.
Abolition of slavery, and especially Negro suffrage, met considerable opposition in the North. Frederick Douglass and other
antislavery leaders recognized that these changes would come *in*
spite of a hesitant public opinion. As Douglass put it, "When
Seward said the status of no man in the country would be
changed by the war, the negro did not believe him."

As the major political parties began to splinter in the early
1850's, the Republican party was able to mobilize mass support
as a result of its opposition to slavery expansion, not to slavery
itself. The distinction is crucial, as Republicans incessantly

reminded their opponents. Slavery was considered an evil to
whites, a system which degraded and humiliated the white
working classes unable to compete with it. It is a striking fact of
the 1850's that the more popular Republican quasi-abolitionism
became, the more intense was national antipathy toward Negroes and abolitionists. The decade immediately preceding the
Civil War was a most trying period for advocates of Negro
freedom and equality. "The 'negro question,' as I understand
it," an Ohio Republican asserted, "is a *white man's question,*
the question of the right of free white laborers to the soil of the
territories. It is not to be crushed or retarded by shouting
'Sambo' at us. We have no Sambo in our platform. . . . We
object to Sambo. We don't want him about."* Similar attitudes
are evident in the positions of David Wilmot and Abraham
Lincoln. When emancipation came, Lincoln publicly emphasized that freedom for slaves was used as a weapon of war.
(1)

   This is the background against which to evaluate the mael-
strom that followed the Civil War. The dominant political party,
confused in its racial goals, faced the most perplexing social
problem in all American history. Questions of Negro civil rights
became deeply enmeshed in sectional and presidential politics.
Abolitionists continually prodded Northern sensitivity by claiming that the North had won the war but was losing the peace.
After much debate, a minimal program of Negro citizenship was
embodied in the Reconstruction amendments to the Constitution, the bevy of laws subsequently passed to enforce them, and
the emasculated Civil Rights Act of 1875. Fulfillment of this
program depended on a persistently enlightened and interested
public opinion, and on Northern military force. By the 1870's
the country recoiled from the seemingly endless concern with
postwar issues and permitted the constitutional provisions to
become largely dead letters. Southern resistance had proven a
successful barrier to racial reform. As Edward A. Pollard
contended in 1868, the "Lost Cause" was "Regained." (2)

   A concomitant tragedy of the era was the failure of even the
most advanced social reformers to recognize clearly the debili-
tating and dehumanizing effects on slaves of some two and a
half centuries of bondage. Wendell Phillips, Frederick Douglass,

* Quoted in James M. McPherson, *The Struggle for Equality: Abolitionists and the Negro in Civil War and Reconstruction* (Princeton, N.J., 1964),
p. 24.

Stephen S. Foster and practically all other radical abolitionists considered their work completed in 1870 when the Fifteenth Amendment was passed, and permitted the American Anti-Slavery Society to disband. Charles Sumner, with little support from others in the 1870's, continued the struggle for Negro equality. A laissez-faire society was firmly convinced that emancipation and the suffrage alone contained semimagical qualities which would imbue the slaves with ambition and permit them "to rise." "Slavery has left them in a most deplorable condition," a New Englander wrote, "but liberty *can* and must restore them." It is a vacuous freedom that exists without an economic base and we have since come to realize that the middle-class ethic of social progress, embodied in such temporary programs as those of the Freedmen's Bureau, was hardly an adequate social philosophy for a propertyless people denied human aspirations by a system which "classed the black man and the ox together." (3)

1. REPUBLICANISM AND THE NEGRO

*No Slavery, No Negroes David Wilmot***

The Republican party was a congeries of conflicting groups—Democrats, Whigs, Free Soilers, immigrants, nativists—united in part in their opposition to the expansion of slavery into the Territories of the United States. The career of David Wilmot, a founder of the party, first Republican gubernatorial candidate in Pennsylvania and Republican senator from the state during the Civil War, mirrors the forces that called Republicanism into existence. A Jacksonian by conviction, Wilmot followed Van Buren into the Free Soil party and then became a Republican. In the following address to Congress, delivered at the time of debate over the Wilmot Proviso, he presents the underlying motivation for his opposition to slavery expansion. George Fitzhugh believed that his speech demonstrated that "the Wilmot Proviso [was] directed against the negro race—not against slavery." The substance of the Proviso, forbidding slavery in the Territories, was enacted into law in 1862.

* From *Congressional Globe*, 29th Cong., 2nd sess. (1847), XVI, 353–355; and *ibid.*, 30th Cong., 1st sess. (1848), XVII, 1076–1080.

What . . . do we ask? Sir, we ask the neutrality of this Government on this question of slavery. I have stood up at home . . . and fought, time and again, against the abolitionists of the North. I have denounced them publicly, upon all occasions, when it was proper to do so. I have met them in their own meetings, and assailed them. And, sir, the efforts that may be made, here or elsewhere, to give an abolition complexion to this movement, cannot . . . have the least effect. And efforts made to give me the character of an abolitionist, will fall harmless when they reach my constituency. They know me upon this question distinctly. I stand by every compromise of the Constitution. I adhere to its letter and its spirit. And I would never invade one single right of the South. So far from it am I, that I stand ready, at all times and upon all occasions, as do nearly the entire North, to sustain the institutions of the South as they exist, with our money and with our blood, when that day comes, as many—many southern men—fear it may come. When that day comes, sir, the North stands with them. We go for every compromise of the Constitution.

But, sir, this is another question—entirely another question. We ask that this Government preserve the integrity of free territory against the aggressions of slavery—against its wrongful usurpations.

My colleague[s] tell me, however, Wait till the people meet together to form their own Constitution, and let them then decide whether they will have slavery in that Territory or not. Sir, I am willing it should be so. All I ask is—and my amendment goes no further—(for we can legislate over this Territory only as long as it is a Territory)—that slavery shall be prevented from entering there, and getting a foothold before that time. When we surrender it up, and States are formed within it and admitted, they come into the Union with all the attributes of sovereign States, and have the right to act for themselves upon this question, as upon all others. I suppose that Pennsylvania could establish slavery to-day, if she chose; and so could Ohio, in spite of the ordinance of 1787. But all we demand is, that while this is a Territory, and while it is under the control of the Government of the United States, that this Government should religiously preserve its character. Free it is now; and free, with God's help, it shall remain. It shall not be fettered; it shall not be trampled upon: it is ours by destiny; and we will keep it, and keep it free. When territory presents itself for annexation with slavery already established, I stand ready to take it, if national considerations require it, as they did in the case of Texas. I will not change its institutions, then. I make no war upon the South. I have no squeamish sensitiveness on the subject of slavery—no morbid sympathy for the slave. But I stand for the integrity of the territory. It shall remain free, so far as my voice and vote can aid in the preservation of its free character.

And that is what we ask. And yet the majority of this House, the majority of the Republicans of the North, are called upon to yield—what? To make concession of things that ought to be conceded? No. They are called upon to yield up rights clearly their own. Where is the northern gentleman prepared to do it? I will go for concession, for compromise; but to compromise on this question is to compromise the right, and establish the wrong. It is to carry slavery where it does not now exist; to violate the integrity of this territory. If you refuse to make it slave territory, is that an invasion of the rights of the South? While I have, as I before remarked, no squeamish sensitiveness on the subject—none whatever—I am nevertheless one of those who believe that the future destiny and glory of this Republic depend in a great measure upon letting the institution remain within its present limits.

But, upon this point, one other thought. The North has ever been ready to yield when the cry of disunion came from the South. And, by-the-by, when southern gentlemen sit down and revise their estimates of the value of this Union, _ have no fears of dissolution from that quarter. Not that I doubt the bravery of the South. I know they dare do all brave men dare do in vindication of their rights. But they will not, when the North is right, when they stand on the broad, firm ground of justice and right, dissolve the Union for such a cause. I would be afraid to invade their rights; I would expect, from their known character, from their chivalry, and from the position they have heretofore taken upon the question of State-rights, a manful resistance. I would be afraid that trouble would grow out of such a controversy. I say, I would be afraid to invade their rights. This we are not disposed to do. But I am not afraid to do right; I am not afraid to insist upon this position, that territo y now free shall remain free while under the control of this Gov-ernment.

Sir, my reasons for moving in this matter have been in part given. Because I saw the policy of the Administration—every man with his eyes open sees it, and must see it. There is no concealment. Territory we will have, and money we ask of you to buy it with. I am ready, I am anxious to give this money. I will vote for it. But I seek in the act which gives this money, that the territory shall be preserved from the aggressions of slavery; that the territory, so far as the act of this Government can do it, shall be sealed up for freedom. This is what I seek.

But, sir, in reference to slavery, while, as I said before, I have no morbid sympathies on this subject, I do believe it is a great political and a great social evil. I believe it is the most difficult problem which we will have to work out in our free Government here. Why, if you go back to the days of the Revolution, or rather after the establishment of peace and of our independence, you find there were six slave States and seven free States; the slave States containing an area of some fifty thousand square miles more than the free States, and with about equal population. This is shown by the census of 1790. Now, in 1840, these seven free States have double the population of these six slave States. How, and why is it? Why, in the Revolution, Massachusetts furnished more men for . . . carrying on the war than the entire slave States. How happened this? Not from want of patriotism on the part of the South—for they were foremost in that glorious struggle—but from the want of ability, growing out of this question of slavery. Where the men who labor in the field are slaves, you cannot place arms in their hands; and it is the laboring man, the man who toils in the field, who constitutes and will constitute the strength and defence of his country on the field of battle. That is the reason. Why, if this war continue, Pennsylvania, I believe, will send more men into the field than the entire six original slave States. Not that Pennsylvania feels any more interest in the vindication of the honor and the glory of the country than they do; but because she has the men to do it, and, owing to the peculiar institution of the South, they have them not: their laborers cannot take arms. Why is it that Virginia, the "mother of States"—that State which has ever been foremost, since the adoption of the Constitution, in the vindication of the rights of the States and the liberties of the people—why is it that the sun of the glorious "Old Dominion" is not still in the ascendant? She used to be first: before New York, before Pennsylvania; and now she is outstripped by some States that have grown up within the memory and lives of the present generation. How is it? Why, owing to this institution. This is the whole secret. I believe it. Contrast again Ohio with Kentucky. Why is it that the one has left the other in the race of prosperity and growth in greatness? It is owning entirely to this institution in the one, and not in the other. There is always a lack of energy, a want of enterprise in slave labor, which are found in free labor. Why, I verily believe that the poor man of the North, who goes into the woods to hew himself out a home, does more work than three slaves, while he consumes less. Nothing is neglected by him; his eye catches everything that requires attention. It is their enterprise, their diligence, their economy, that builds up new empires in the West, while the South has been falling back. Why, sir, contrast Michigan and Arkansas. In twenty years, Michigan has assumed a high position among the States of this Union. She has all the elements of a great State; cities, flourishing towns, and highly cultivated fields; with a population that outnumbers three or four times that of Arkansas. And yet Arkansas has even a better soil, even superior natural advantages. What is the cause of this disparity? It is owning to this institution in Arkansas, and the absence of it in Michigan.

Now, as a friend of the Union, and in no spirit of hostility to the South, but as a friend of the American Union, I offered this proposition. . . . To insist upon your own, is to infringe upon no man's rights. To demand that slavery shall not invade the field that of right belongs to free labor, is not to make war upon the South, or the institutions of the South.

Slaves are like any other stock, of which merchandise is made. Widen the market for their sale, and you stimulate the production. Increase their value, and you prolong the years of their bondage. The extension of slavery and the increase of slaves are identical and inseparable—one and the same thing. It is the influence and effect of this policy upon white labor of which I especially complain. It gives up to the cupidity of the slaveholder, and to the unproductive tillage of his human cattle, that which of right belongs to free labor, and which is necessary for the support and happiness of our own race and people. It brings dishonor and degradation upon the poor white man, who is brought in close contact with the servile labor of the black. It mars his manhood. It destroys his self-respect and dignity of character. He feels a sense of humiliation when he looks up to the vast distance between himself and the lordly planter, in the shadow of whose aristocratic possessions he lives an inferior, if not a dependent. He lives in the midst of a social system, made up of lords and vassals; and if he cannot rise to the condition of the former, he must sink to a level with the latter.

Lincoln and the Free Negroes *Abraham Lincoln**

Abraham Lincoln, as politician, made conflicting statements about Negroes at different times in his career. Racists can and have culled his writings in an attempt to gather him into their fold; Negroes have searched the same tomes and collected contradictory data in a desire to emphasize Lincoln's abolitionist tendencies. Neither is right, or perhaps both are half right.

Lincoln, on racial matters, is most accurately categorized as a middle-of-the-road Republican. His views fell somewhere between the overt racism of the majority of the party, typified by David Wilmot, and the minority antislavery views of men like Charles Sumner. Lincoln always believed slavery an immoral institution, but was perplexed about the role of Negroes in American society and seriously doubted they might be assimilated as readily as "Hans, Baptiste and Patrick." "If all earthly power were given me," he once said, "I should not know what to do as to the existing institution. My first impulse would be to free all the slaves and send them to Liberia—to their own native land. But a moment's reflection would convince me that, whatever of high hope (as I think there is) there may be in this, in the long run its sudden execution is impossible." Perhaps the fairest estimate of Lincoln's position was the one made by Frederick Douglass some ten years after the martyr's assassination: "President Lincoln was a white man, and shared the prejudices common to his countrymen towards the colored race. Looking back to his times and to the condition of his country, we are compelled to admit that this un-

---

* From a paraphrase of Lincoln's address to a group of free Negroes: "Address on Colonization to a Deputation of Negroes," August 14, 1862, in Roy P. Basler, ed., *The Collected Works of Abraham Lincoln* (New Brunswick, N.J., 1953), V, 370–375.

*friendly feeling on his part may be safely set down as one element
of his wonderful success in organizing the loyal American people
for the tremendous conflict before them. . . . Viewed from the
genuine abolition ground, Mr. Lincoln seemed tardy, cold, dull,
and indifferent; but measuring him by the sentiment of his country,
a sentiment he was bound as a statesman to consult, he was swift,
zealous, radical, and determined. . . . In his heart of hearts he
loathed and hated slavery."*

Throughout the Civil War Lincoln toyed with the idea of
compensated emancipation for slaveholders and Negro colonization—and incorporated both ideas into the law that emancipated
slaves in the District of Columbia in April, 1862. He mentions
these schemes regularly in his annual messages to Congress and
was finally granted $600,000 to experiment with Negro coloniza-
tion. The Chiriqui Project, mentioned in the following document,
and the subsequent tragic settlement, in 1863–1864, of American
Negroes on Cow Island, off Haiti, were both failures.

This afternoon the President of the United States gave audience to
a Committee of colored men at the White House. They were introduced by the Rev. J. Mitchell, Commissioner of Emigration.* E.
M. Thomas,† the Chairman, remarked that they were there by
invitation to hear what the Executive had to say to them. Having
all been seated, the President, after a few preliminary observations,
informed them that a sum of money had been appropriated by
Congress, and placed at his disposition for the purpose of aiding
the colonization in some country of the people, or a portion of
them, of African descent, thereby making it his duty, as it had for
a long time been his inclination, to favor that cause; and why, he
asked, should the people of your race be colonized, and where?
Why should they leave this country? This is, perhaps, the first
question for proper consideration. You and we are different races.
We have between us a broader difference than exists between
almost any other two races. Whether it is right or wrong I need not

* The Reverend James Mitchell, of Indiana, worked on colonization programs in the Interior Department and had long been associated with the
colonization movement in his home state.

† Edward M. Thomas, a free Negro of the District of Columbia, was
president of the Anglo-African Institute for the Encouragement of Industry
and Art.

discuss, but this physical difference is a great disadvantage to us both, as I think your race suffer very greatly, many of them by living among us, while ours suffer from your presence. In a word we suffer on each side. If this is admitted, it affords a reason at least why we should be separated. You here are freemen I suppose.

A Voice: Yes, sir.

The President—Perhaps you have long been free, or all your lives. Your race are suffering, in my judgment, the greatest wrong inflicted on any people. But even when you cease to be slaves, you are yet far removed from being placed on an equality with the white race. You are cut off from many of the advantages which the other race enjoy. The aspiration of men is to enjoy equality with the best when free, but on this broad continent, not a single man of your race is made the equal of a single man of ours. Go where you are treated the best, and the ban is still upon you.

I do not propose to discuss this, but to present it as a fact with which we have to deal. I cannot alter it if I would. It is a fact, about which we all think and feel alike, I and you. We look to our condition, owing to the existence of the two races on this continent. I need not recount to you the effects upon white men, growing out of the institution of Slavery. I believe in its general evil effects on the white race. See our present condition—the country engaged in war!—our white men cutting one another's throats, none knowing how far it will extend; and then consider what we know to be the truth. But for your race among us there could not be war, although many men engaged on either side do not care for you one way or the other. Nevertheless, I repeat, without the institution of Slavery and the colored race as a basis, the war could not have an existence.

It is better for us both, therefore, to be separated. I know that there are free men among you, who even if they could better their condition are not as much inclined to go out of the country as those who being slaves could obtain their freedom on this condition. I suppose one of the principal difficulties in the way of colonization is that the free colored man cannot see that his comfort would be advanced by it. You may believe you can live in Washington or elsewhere in the United States the remainder of your life [as easily], perhaps more so than you can in any foreign country, and hence you may come to the conclusion that you have nothing to do with the idea of going to a foreign country. This is (I speak in no unkind sense) an extremely selfish view of the case.

But you ought to do something to help those who are not so fortunate as yourselves. There is an unwillingness on the part of our people, harsh as it may be, for you free colored people to remain with us. Now, if you could give a start to white people, you would open a wide door for many to be made free. If we deal with those who are not free at the beginning, and whose intellects are clouded by Slavery, we have very poor materials to start with. If intelligent colored men, such as are before me, would move in this matter, much might be accomplished. It is exceedingly important that we have men at the beginning capable of thinking as white men, and not those who have been systematically oppressed.

There is much to encourage you. For the sake of your race you should sacrifice something of your present comfort for the purpose of being as grand in that respect as the white people. It is a cheering thought throughout life that something can be done to ameliorate the condition of those who have been subject to the hard usage of the world. It is difficult to make a man miserable while he feels he is worthy of himself, and claims kindred to the great God who made him. In the American Revolutionary war sacrifices were made by men engaged in it; but they were cheered by the future. Gen. Washington himself endured greater physical hardships than if he had remained a British subject. Yet he was a happy man, because he was engaged in benefiting his race—something for the children of his neighbors, having none of his own.

The colony of Liberia has been in existence a long time. In a certain sense it is a success. The old President of Liberia . . . has just been with me—the first time I ever saw him. He says they have within the bounds of that colony between 300,000 and 400,000 people, or more than in some of our old States, such as Rhode Island or Delaware, or in some of our newer States, and less than in some of our larger ones. They are not all American colonists, or their descendants. Something less than 12,000 have been sent thither from this country. Many of the original settlers have died, yet, like people elsewhere, their offspring outnumber those deceased.

The question is if the colored people are persuaded to go anywhere, why not there? One reason for an unwillingness to do so is that some of you would rather remain within reach of the country of your nativity. I do not know how much attachment you may have toward our race. It does not strike me that you have the greatest reason to love them. But still you are attached to them at all events.

The place I am thinking about having for a colony is in Central America. It is nearer to us than Liberia—not much more than one-fourth as far as Liberia, and within seven days' run by steamers. Unlike Liberia it is on a great line of travel—it is a highway. The country is a very excellent one for any people, and with great natural resources and advantages, and especially because of the similarity of climate with your native land—thus being suited to your physical condition.

The particular place I have in view is to be a great highway from the Atlantic or Caribbean Sea to the Pacific Ocean, and this particular place has all the advantages for a colony. On both sides there are harbors among the finest in the world. Again, there is evidence of very rich coal mines. A certain amount of coal is valuable in any country, and there may be more than enough for the wants of the country. Why I attach so much importance to coal is, it will afford an opportunity to the inhabitants for immediate employment till they get ready to settle permanently in their homes.

If you take colonists where there is no good landing, there is a bad show; and so where there is nothing to cultivate, and of which to make a farm. But if something is started so that you can get your daily bread as soon as you reach there, it is a great advantage. Coal land is the best thing I know of with which to commence an enterprise.

To return, you have been talked to upon this subject, and told that a speculation is intended by gentlemen, who have an interest in the country, including the coal mines. We have been mistaken all our lives if we do not know whites as well as blacks look to their self-interest. Unless among those deficient of intellect everybody you trade with makes something. You meet with these things here as elsewhere.

If such persons have what will be an advantage to them, the question is whether it cannot be made of advantage to you. You are intelligent, and know that success does not as much depend on external help as on self-reliance. Much, therefore, depends upon yourselves. As to the coal mines, I think I see the means available for your self-reliance.

I shall, if I get a sufficient number of you engaged, have provisions made that you shall not be wronged. If you will engage in the enterprise I will spend some of the money intrusted to me. I am not sure you will succeed. The Government may lose the money, but we cannot succeed unless we try; but we think, with care, we can succeed.

The political affairs in Central America are not in quite as satisfactory condition as I wish. There are contending factions in that quarter; but it is true all the factions are agreed alike on the subject of colonization, and want it, and are more generous than we are here. To your colored race they have no objection. Besides, I would endeavor to have you made equals, and have the best assurance that you should be the equals of the best.

The practical thing I want to ascertain is whether I can get a number of able-bodied men, with their wives and children, who are willing to go, when I present evidence of encouragement and protection. Could I get a hundred tolerably intelligent men, with their wives and children, to "cut their own fodder," so to speak? Can I have fifty? If I could find twenty-five able-bodied men, with a mixture of women and children, good things in the family relation, I think I could make a successful commencement.

I want you to let me know whether this can be done or not. This is the practical part of my wish to see you. These are subjects of very great importance, worthy of a month's study [instead] of a speech delivered in an hour. I ask you then to consider seriously not pertaining to yourselves merely, nor for your race, and ours, for the present time, but as one of the things, if successfully managed, for the good of mankind—not confined to the present generation, but as

> "From age to age descends the lay,
>   To millions yet to be,
>   Till far its echoes roll away,
>   Into eternity."

The Chairman of the delegation briefly replied that "they would hold a consultation and in a short time give an answer." The President said: "Take your full time—no hurry at all."

The delegation then withdrew.

The Emancipation Proclamation *Abraham Lincoln**

Forced by the exigencies of war and the threat of foreign interven-
tion to reconsider the Republican party's attitude toward the
sanctity of slavery in the Southern states, Lincoln sketched the first
draft of the Emancipation Proclamation on July 22, 1862, and
issued the Preliminary Emancipation Proclamation on September
22, 1862, after the Battle of Antietam. The President continued to
hold out the lure of compensated emancipation for rebel states that
returned to the Union and adopted voluntary programs of gradual
abolition prior to January 1, 1863. When the Proclamation was
issued, loyal slave states and the counties or parishes already in
Union hands were exempted from its provisions.

By the President of the United States of America:
A Proclamation.

Whereas, on the twentysecond day of September, in the year of
our Lord one thousand eight hundred and sixty two, a proclamation was issued by the President of the United States, containing,
among other things, the following, towit:

"That on the first day of January, in the year of our Lord one
thousand eight hundred and sixty-three, all persons held as slaves
within any State or designated part of a State, the people whereof
shall then be in rebellion against the United States, shall be then,
thenceforward, and forever free; and the Executive Government of
the United States, including the military and naval authority
thereof, will recognize and maintain the freedom of such persons,
and will do no act or acts to repress such persons, or any of them,
in any efforts they may make for their actual freedom.

"That the Executive will, on the first day of January aforesaid,
by proclamation, designate the States and parts of States, if any, in
which the people thereof, respectively, shall then be in rebellion
against the United States; and the fact that any State, or the people
thereof, shall on that day be, in good faith, represented in the
Congress of the United States by members chosen thereto at
elections wherein a majority of the qualified voters of such State

* "Emancipation Proclamation," January 1, 1863, in Basler, *Lincoln,* VI,
28–31.

shall have participated, shall, in the absence of strong countervailing testimony, be deemed conclusive evidence that such State, and the people thereof, are not then in rebellion against the United States."

Now, therefore I, Abraham Lincoln, President of the United States, by virtue of the power in me vested as Commander-in-Chief, of the Army and Navy of the United States in time of actual armed rebellion against authority and government of the United States, and as a fit and necessary war measure for suppressing said rebellion, do, on this first day of January, in the year of our Lord one thousand eight hundred and sixty three, and in accordance with my purpose so to do publicly proclaimed for the full period of one hundred days, from the day first above mentioned, order and designate as the States and parts of States wherein the people thereof respectively, are this day in rebellion against the United States, the following, towit:

Arkansas, Texas, Louisiana, (except the Parishes of St. Bernard, Plaquemines, Jefferson, St. Johns, St. Charles, St. James[,] Ascension, Assumption, Terrebonne, Lafourche, St. Mary, St. Martin, and Orleans, including the City of New-Orleans) Mississippi, Alabama, Florida, Georgia, South-Carolina, North-Carolina, and Virginia, (except the fortyeight counties designated as West Virginia, and also the counties of Berkley, Accomac, Northampton, Elizabeth-City, York, Princess Ann, and Norfolk, including the cities of Norfolk & Portsmouth[)]; and which excepted parts are, for the present, left precisely as if this proclamation were not issued.

And by virtue of the power, and for the purpose aforesaid, I do order and declare that all persons held as slaves within said designated States, and parts of States, are, and henceforward shall be free; and that the Executive government of the United States, including the military and naval authorities thereof, will recognize and maintain the freedom of said persons.

And I hereby enjoin upon the people so declared to be free to abstain from all violence, unless in necessary self-defence; and I recommend to them that, in all cases when allowed, they labor faithfully for reasonable wages.

And I further declare and make known, that such persons of suitable condition, will be received into the armed service of the

United States to garrison forts, positions, stations, and other places, and to man vessels of all sorts in said service.

And upon this act, sincerely believed to be an act of justice, warranted by the Constitution, upon military necessity, I invoke the considerate judgment of mankind, and the gracious favor of Almighty God.

2. RECONSTRUCTION

The Black Code of St. Landry's Parish*

Amid the complex and confusing issues of Reconstruction, one point is clear: the white South refused to accept any changes in its racial views. Slavery was dead, but most Southerners still had "a settled belief in the negro's inferiority" and sought through law, violence and intimidation to continue the system of white supremacy. Southern Black Codes were passed at every level of government— from the smallest rural parish and municipality to the Statehouse. These laws proscribed the lives of freedmen and forced them to accept the position of a permanently degraded caste. Although Southern truculence in the face of military defeat helped shock the North into passing the Reconstruction amendments and laws, the spirit of Southern defiance was ultimately successful. The Black Code of St. Landry's Parish, Louisiana, including its provisions for summary punishment, is typical of laws passed throughout the South.

Whereas it was formerly made the duty of the police jury to make suitable regulations for the police of slaves within the limits of the parish; and whereas slaves have become emancipated by the action of the ruling powers; and whereas it is necessary for public order, as well as for the comfort and correct deportment of said freedmen, that suitable regulations should be established for their government in their changed condition, the following ordinances are adopted, with the approval of the United States military authorities commanding in said parish, viz:

* From 39th Cong., 1st sess., *Senate Executive Document No. 2* (1865), pp. 93–94.

SECTION 1. *Be it ordained by the police jury of the parish of St. Landry,* That no negro shall be allowed to pass within the limits of said parish without a special permit in writing from his employer. Whoever shall violate this provision shall pay a fine of two dollars and fifty cents, or in default thereof shall be forced to work four days on the public road, or suffer corporeal punishment as provided hereinafter.

SECTION 2. *Be it further ordained,* That every negro who shall be found absent from the residence of his employer after 10 o'clock at night, without a written permit from his employer, shall pay a fine of five dollars, or in default thereof, shall be compelled to work five days on the public road, or suffer corporeal punishment as hereinafter provided.

SECTION 3. *Be it further ordained,* That no negro shall be permitted to rent or keep a house within said parish. Any negro violating this provision shall be immediately ejected and compelled to find an employer; and any person who shall rent, or give the use of any house to any negro, in violation of this section, shall pay a fine of five dollars for each offence.

SECTION 4. *Be it further ordained,* That every negro is required to be in the regular service of some white person, or former owner, who shall be held responsible for the conduct of said negro. But said employer or former owner may permit said negro to hire his own time by special permission in writing, which permission shall not extend over seven days at any one time. Any negro violating the provisions of this section shall be fined five dollars for each offence, or in default of the payment thereof shall be forced to work five days on the public road, or suffer corporeal punishment as hereinafter provided.

SECTION 5. *Be it further ordained,* That no public meetings or congregations of negroes shall be allowed within said parish after sunset; but such public meetings and congregations may be held between the hours of sunrise and sunset, by the special permission in writing of the captain of patrol, within whose beat such meetings shall take place. This prohibition, however, is not intended to prevent negroes from attending the usual church services, conducted by white ministers and priests. Every negro violating the provisions of this section shall pay a fine of five dollars, or in default thereof shall be compelled to work five days on the public road, or suffer corporeal punishment as hereinafter provided.

SECTION 6. *Be it further ordained,* That no negro shall be permitted to preach, exhort, or otherwise declaim to congregations of colored people, without a special permission in writing from the president of the police jury. Any negro violating the provisions of this section shall pay a fine of ten dollars, or in default thereof shall be forced to work ten days on the public road, or suffer corporeal punishment as hereinafter provided.

SECTION 7. *Be it further ordained,* That no negro who is not in the military service shall be allowed to carry fire-arms, or any kind of weapons, within the parish, without the special written permission of his employers, approved and indorsed by the nearest or most convenient chief of patrol. Any one violating the provisions of this section shall forfeit his weapons and pay a fine of five dollars, or in default of the payment of said fine, shall be forced to work five days on the public road, or suffer corporeal punishment as hereinafter provided.

SECTION 8. *Be it further ordained,* That no negro shall sell, barter, or exchange any articles of merchandise or traffic within said parish without the special written permission of his employer, specifying the articles of sale, barter or traffic. Any one thus offending shall pay a fine of one dollar for each offence, and suffer the forfeiture of said articles, or in default of the payment of said fine shall work one day on the public road, or suffer corporeal punishment as hereinafter provided.

SECTION 9. *Be it further ordained,* That any negro found drunk within the said parish shall pay a fine of five dollars, or in default thereof shall work five days on the public road, or suffer corporeal punishment as hereinafter provided.

SECTION 10. *Be it further ordained,* That all the foregoing provisions shall apply to negroes of both sexes.

SECTION 11. *Be it further ordained,* That it shall be the duty of every citizen to act as a police officer for the detection of offences and the apprehension of offenders, who shall be immediately handed over to the proper captain or chief of patrol.

SECTION 12. *Be it further ordained,* That the aforesaid penalties shall be summarily enforced, and that it shall be the duty of the captains and chiefs of patrol to see that the aforesaid ordinances are promptly executed.

SECTION 13. *Be it further ordained,* That all sums collected from the aforesaid fines shall be immediately handed over to the parish treasurer.

SECTION 14. *Be it further ordained,* That the corporeal punishment provided for in the foregoing sections shall consist in confining the body of the offender within a barrel placed over his or her shoulders, in the manner practiced in the army, such confinement not to continue longer than twelve hours, and for such time within the aforesaid limit as shall be fixed by the captain or chief of patrol who inflicts the penalty.

SECTION 15. *Be it further ordained,* That these ordinances shall not interfere with any municipal or military regulations inconsistent with them within the limits of said parish.

SECTION 16. *Be it further ordained,* That these ordinances shall take effect five days after their publication in the Opelousas Courier.

A Visit from the Ku Klux Klan*

When ordinances were ineffective, vigilante tactics were used. Members of the Klan patrolled the South and enforced the social code of white supremacy—and they continued to do so after Congress passed the Ku Klux Klan Act in April, 1871. The following testimony is an infinitesimal portion of the closely printed thirteen volumes of hearings on "The Ku-Klux Conspiracy."

* From Joint Committee to Inquire into the Condition of Affairs in the Late Insurrectionary States, *The Ku-Klux Conspiracy* (Washington, D.C., 1872), XI, 482–483.

Question. Where do you live?

Answer. I live in Macon.

Question. How long have you lived here?

Answer. I came here about the last of April.

Question. Where did you come from?

Answer. I came from Winston County.

Question. What occasioned your coming here?

Answer. I got run by the Ku-Klux.

Question. Give the particulars to the committee.

Answer. Give the particulars?

Question. Tell how it occurred; give a statement of the circumstances.

Answer. Well, I don't know anything that I had said or done that injured any one, further than being a radical in that part of the land, and as for interrupting any one, I didn't, for I had plenty of my own of anything I wanted myself. I had done bought my land and paid for it, and I had a great deal of hogs; I had eighteen head of hogs to kill this fall. I had twelve head of sheep, and one good milk-cow, and a yearling, and the cow had a right young calf again, and I had my mule and my filly, and all of it was paid for but my mule, and I had my brother hired to pay for him. The mule cost me $65, and I had him hired out to pay for him. It was like I was getting the mule from you, and you wanting a hand to work the value of the mule out in work.

Question. Did any of the Ku-Klux come to your house?

Answer. They did.

Question. In the night-time?

Answer. They came about a half hour or more before day, as nigh as I can recollect by my brains, being frightened at their coming up in this kind of way. They were shooting and going on at me through the house, and when they busted the door open, coming in shooting. I was frightened, and I can only tell you as nigh as my recollection will afford at this time that it was about a half hour to day.

Question. What did they do to you?

Answer. None of the shot hit me, but they aimed to hit me; but I had one door just like that at the side of the house and the other at this side, and there was the chimney, and there was my bed in that corner opposite, and they came to the door first, [illustrating,] and hollered "Hallo"; bum, bum, bum, on the lock. I jumped up and said, "Hallo." Then one at the door said, "Raise a light in there." "What for; who is you?" I said. He says, "Raise a light in there, God damn you; I'll come in there and smoke my pipe in your ear." He said that just so. I said, "Is that you, uncle Davy?" Says he, "No, God damn you, it isn't uncle Dave; open this door." Says I, "I am not going to open my door to turn nobody on me that won't tell me who they are before I do it. Who are you?" He says, "God damn you, we didn't come to tell you who we are." I was peeping through the little crack in the door. I had bored a gimlet-hole about as big as that pen to put a string through, and had a latch inside so that when I had been off at work anywhere, and happened to come home at night, I could open the door without my wife having to get up, and she would put the string through the door and I would pull, and that was the way I would get in.

Question. That was the hole you looked through?

Answer. Yes, sir.

Question. What did you see?

Answer. I saw men out there standing with horns and faces on all of them, and they all had great, long, white cow-tails way down the breast. I said it was a cow-tail; it was hair, and it was right white. They told me they rode from Shiloh in two hours, and came to kill me. They shot right smart in that house before they got in, but how many times I don't know, they shot so fast outside; but when they come in, they didn't have but three loads to shoot. I know by the way they tangled about in the house they would have put it in me if they had had it. They only shot three times in the house. The men behind me had busted in through the door; both doors were busted open. By the time the fellows at the back door got in the door, these fellows at the front door busted in, and they all met in the middle of the floor, and I didn't have a thing to fight with, only a little piece of ax-handle; and when I started from the first door to the second, pieces of the door flew and met me. I jumped for a piece of ax-handle and fought them squandering about, and they were knocking about me with guns, and firing balls that cut several holes in my head. The notches is in my head now. I dashed about among them, but they knocked me down several times. Every time I would get up, they would knock me down again. I saw they were going to kill me, and I turned in and laid there after they knocked me down so many times. The last time they knocked me down I laid there a good while before I moved, and when I had strength I jumped to split through a man's legs that was standing over me, and, as I jumped, they struck at me jumping between his legs, and they struck him and, he hollered, "Don't hit me, God damn you," but they done knocked him down then, but they hadn't knocked him so he couldn't talk. I jumped through and got past him. They didn't hit him a fair lick, because he was going toward them, and it struck past his head on his shoulder. If it had struck his head, it would have busted it open. I didn't catch that lick. I got up then; they had shot out the loads. I grabbed my ax-handle, and commenced fighting, and then they just took and cut me with knives. They surrounded me in the floor and tore my shirt off. They got me out on the floor; some had me by the legs and some by the arms and the neck and anywhere, just like dogs string out a coon, and they took me out to the big road before my gate and whipped me until I couldn't move or holler or do nothing, but just lay there like a log, and every lick they hit me I grunted just like a mule when he is stalled fast and whipped; that was all. They left me there for dead, and what it was done for was because I was a radical, and I didn't deny my profession anywhere and I never will. I never will vote that conservative ticket if I die.

Question. Did they tell you they whipped you because you were a radical?

Answer. They told me, "God damn you, when you meet a white man in the road lift your hat; I'll learn you, God damn you, that you are a nigger, and not to be going about like you thought yourself a white man; you calls yourself like a white man, God damn you."

A Report on Reconstruction *Carl Schurz*[*]

From July to September, 1865, Carl Schurz traveled through the South as an emissary of President Johnson. His report on Southern

[*] *Report of Carl Schurz on the States of South Carolina, Georgia, Alabama, Mississippi, and Louisiana,* 39th Cong., 1st sess., *Senate Executive Document No. 2* (1865), pp. 16–20.

conditions and attitudes is one of the most enlightening documents of the post–Civil War era. Schurz was impressed with two major factors. "Confusion," he wrote, pervaded the atmosphere of every state he visited: "All elements of society being afloat, the difficulties were immense." Secondly, he concluded that the majority of whites in the South were unwilling to accept Negroes in any other status than as slaves: "The whites esteem the blacks their property by natural right, and, however much they may admit that the relations of masters and slaves have been destroyed . . . they still have an ingrained feeling that the blacks at large belong to the whites. . . ." President Johnson was so dissatisfied with Schurz's report and his suggestion that Negroes be enfranchised that he refused to have it published until Congress demanded it. It is offered here as an analysis and summary of Southern racial views in the Reconstruction period.

That the result of the free labor experiment made under circumstances so extremely unfavorable should at once be a perfect success, no reasonable person would expect. Nevertheless, a large majority of the southern men with whom I came into contact announced their opinions with so positive an assurance as to produce the impression that their minds were fully made up. In at least nineteen cases of twenty the reply I received to my inquiry about their views on the new system was uniformly this: "You cannot make the negro work without physical compulsion." I heard this hundreds of times, heard it wherever I went, heard it in nearly the same words from so many different persons, that at last I came to the conclusion that this is the prevailing sentiment among the southern people. There are exceptions to this rule, but, as far as my information extends, far from enough to affect the rule.

Unfortunately the disorders necessarily growing out of the transition state continually furnished food for argument. I found but few people who were willing to make due allowance for the adverse influence of exceptional circumstances. By a large majority of those I came in contact with, and they mostly belonged to the more intelligent class, every irregularity that occurred was directly charged against the system of free labor. If negroes walked away from the plantations, it was conclusive proof of the incorrigible instability of the negro, and the impracticability of free negro labor. If some individual negroes violated the terms of their contract, it proved unanswerably that no negro had, or ever would have, a just conception of the binding force of a contract, and that this system of free negro labor was bound to be a failure. If some negroes shirked, or did not perform their task with sufficient alacrity, it was produced as irrefutable evidence to show that physical compulsion was actually indispensable to make the negro work. If negroes, idlers or refugees crawling about the towns, applied to the authorities for subsistence, it was quoted as incontestably establishing the point that the negro was too improvident to take care of himself, and must necessarily be consigned to the care of a master. I heard a Georgia planter argue most seriously that one of his negroes had shown himself certainly unfit for freedom because he impudently refused to submit to a whipping. I frequently went into an argument with those putting forth such general assertions, quoting instances in which negro laborers were working faithfully, and to the entire satisfaction of their employers, as the employers themselves had informed me. In a majority of cases the reply was that we northern people did not understand the negro, but that they (the southerners) did; that as to the particular instances I quoted I was probably mistaken; that I had not closely investigated the cases, or had been deceived by my informants; that they *knew* the negro would not work without compulsion, and that nobody could make them believe he would. Arguments like these naturally finished such discussions. It frequently struck me that persons who conversed about every other subject calmly and sensibly would lose their temper as soon as the negro question was touched.

A belief, conviction, or prejudice, or whatever you may call it, so widely spread and apparently so deeply rooted as this, that the negro will not work without physical compulsion, is certainly calculated to have a very serious influence upon the conduct of the people entertaining it. It naturally produced a desire to preserve slavery in its original form as much and as long as possible—and you may, perhaps, remember the admission made by one of the provisional governors, over two months after the close of the war, that the people of his State still indulged in a lingering hope slavery might yet be preserved—or to introduce into the new system that element of physical compulsion which would make the negro work. Efforts were, indeed, made to hold the negro in his old state of subjection, especially in such localities where our military forces had not yet penetrated, or where the country was not garrisoned in detail. Here and there planters succeeded for a limited period to keep their former slaves in ignorance, or at least doubt, about their new rights; but the main agency employed for that purpose was force and intimidation. In many instances negroes who walked away from the plantations, or were found upon the roads, were shot or otherwise severely punished, which was calculated to produce the impression among those remaining with their masters that an attempt to escape from slavery would result in certain destruction. A large proportion of the many acts of violence committed is undoubtedly attributable to this motive. The documents attached to this report abound in testimony to this effect. For the sake of illustration I will give some instances:

Brigadier General Fessenden reported to Major General Gillmore from Winnsboro', South Carolina, July 19, as follows: "The spirit of the people, especially in those districts not subject to the salutary influence of General Sherman's army, is that of concealed and, in some instances, of open hostility, though there are some who strive with honorable good faith to promote a thorough reconciliation between the government and their people. A spirit of bitterness and persecution manifests itself towards the negroes. They are shot and abused outside the immediate protection of our forces *by men who announce their determination to take the law into their own hands, in defiance of our authority.* To protect the negro and punish these still rebellious individuals it will be necessary to have this country pretty thickly settled with soldiers." I received similar verbal reports from other parts of South Carolina. To show the hopes still indulged in by some, I may mention that one of the sub-district commanders, as he himself informed me, knew planters within the limits of his command who had made contracts with their former slaves *avowedly* for the object of keeping them together on their plantations, so that they might have them near at hand, and thus more easily reduce them to their former condition, when, after the restoration of the civil power, the "unconstitutional emancipation proclamation" would be set aside.

Cases in which negroes were kept on the plantations, either by

ruse or violence, were frequent enough in South Carolina and
Georgia to call forth from General Saxton a circular threatening
planters who persisted in this practice with loss of their property,
and from Major General Steedman, commander of the department
of Georgia, an order bearing upon the same subject. At Atlanta,
Georgia, I had an opportunity to examine some cases of the nature
above described myself. While I was there, 9th and 10th of
August, several negroes came into town with bullet and buckshot
wounds in their bodies. From their statements, which, however,
were only corroborating information previously received, it appeared that the reckless and restless characters of that region had
combined to keep the negroes where they belonged. Several freedmen were shot in the attempt to escape, others succeeded in
eluding the vigilance of their persecutors; large numbers, terrified
by what they saw and heard, quietly remained under the restraint
imposed upon them, waiting for better opportunities. The commander of the sub-district and post informed me that bands of
guerillas were prowling about within a few miles of the city,
making it dangerous for soldiers and freedmen to show themselves
outside of the immediate reach of the garrison, and that but a few
days previous to my arrival a small squad of men he had sent out
to serve an order upon a planter, concerning the treatment of
freedmen, had been driven back by an armed band of over twenty
men, headed by an individual in the uniform of a rebel officer.

As our troops in Georgia were at that time mostly concentrated
at a number of central points, and not scattered over the State in
small detachments, but little information was obtained of what was
going on in the interior of the country. A similar system was
followed in Alabama, but enough has become known to indicate
the condition of things in localities not immediately under the eye
of the military. In that State the efforts made to hold the negro in a
state of subjection appear to have been of a particularly atrocious
nature. Rumors to that effect which reached me at Montgomery
induced me to make inquiries at the post hospital. The records of
that institution showed a number of rather startling cases which
had occurred immediately after the close of the war, and some of a
more recent date; all of which proved that negroes leaving the
plantations, and found on the roads, were exposed to the savagest

treatment. An extract from the records of the hospital . . . also a statement signed by the provost marshal at Selma, Alabama . . . says: "There have come to my notice officially twelve cases, in which I am morally certain the trials have not been had yet, that negroes were killed by whites. In a majority of cases the provocation consisted in the negroes' trying to come to town or to return to the plantation after having been sent away. The cases above enumerated, I am convinced, are but a small part of those that have actually been perpetrated." In a report to General Swayne, assistant commissioner of the Freedmen's Bureau, in Alabama, communicated to me by the general, Captain Poillon, agent of the bureau at Mobile, says of the condition of things in the southwestern part of the State, July 29: "There are regular patrols posted on the rivers, who board some of the boats; after the boats leave they hang, shoot, or drown the victims they may find on them, and all those found on the roads or coming down the rivers are almost invariably murdered. . . . The bewildered and terrified freedmen know not what to do—to leave is death; to remain is to suffer the increased burden imposed upon them by the cruel taskmaster, whose only interest is their labor, wrung from them by every device an inhuman ingenuity can devise; hence the lash and murder is resorted to to intimidate those whom fear of an awful death alone cause to remain, while patrols, negro dogs and spies, disguised as Yankees, keep constant guard over these unfortunate people." In a letter addressed to myself, September 9, Captain Poillon says: "Organized patrols, with negro hounds, keep guard over the thoroughfares; bands of lawless robbers traverse the country, and the unfortunate who attempts to escape, or he who returns for his wife or child, is waylaid or pursued with hounds, and shot or hung."

In Mississippi I received information of a similar character. Lieutenant Colonel P. J. Yorke, post commander at port Gibson, Mississippi, reported to General Davidson, on August 26, that a "county patrol" had been organized by citizens of his sub-district, which, for reasons given, he had been obliged to disband; one of these reasons was, in his own language, that: "The company was formed out of what they called picked men, *i.e.,* those only who had been actually engaged in the war, and were known as strong disunionists. The negroes in the sections of country these men controlled were kept in the most abject slavery. . . . As late as September 29, Captain J. H. Weber, agent of the Freedmen's Bureau, reported to Colonel Thomas, assistant commissioner of the bureau, in the State of Mississippi, as follows: "In many cases negroes who left their homes during the war, and have been within our military lines, and having provided homes here for their families, going back to get their wives and children, have been driven off, and told that they could not have them. In several cases guards have been sent to aid people in getting their families; in many others it has been impracticable, as the distance was too great. In portions of the northern part of this district the colored people are kept in slavery still. The white people tell them that they were free during the war, but the war is now over, and they must go to work again as before. The reports from sub-commissioners nearest that locality show that the blacks are in a much worse state than ever before, the able-bodied being kept at work under the lash, and the young and infirm driven off to care for themselves. As to protecion from the civil authorities, there is no such thing outside of this city."

The conviction, however, that slavery in the old form cannot be maintained has forced itself upon the minds of many of those who ardently desired it preservation. But while the necessity of a new system was recognized as far as the right of property in the individual negro is concerned, many attempts were made to introduce into that new system the element of physical compulsion, which, as above stated, is so generally considered indispensable. This was done by simply adhering, as to the treatment of the laborers, as much as possible to the traditions of the old system, even where the relations between employers and laborers had been fixed by contract. The practice of corporal punishment was still continued to a great extent, although, perhaps, not in so regular a manner as it was practiced in times gone by. The habit is so inveterate with a great many persons as to render, on the least provocation, the impulse to whip a negro almost irresistible. It will continue to be so until the southern people will have learned, so as never to forget it, that a black man has rights which a white man is bound to respect.

3. NORTHERN ATTITUDES TOWARD
THE FREEDMEN

The Search for a Solution

Southern views on the future condition of the freedmen were clear; the attitudes of Northerners were amorphous. Republican politicians throughout the North shied away from the issue of Negro suffrage in the first major state elections after the Civil War. The electorates of Connecticut, Wisconsin, and Minnesota rejected constitutional amendments proposing Negro enfranchisement in the elections of 1865. Confronted with Northern racism, abolitionists strenuously campaigned for equal voting rights and were eventually successful. The most progressive social reformers firmly believed the vote would prove a crucial wedge to Negro social and economic advancement in American culture.

And yet many feared "doing too much" for the former slaves. Their arguments flowed from two premises. One was an almost religious faith in the ideology of self-help. "Let all the natural laws of labor, wages, competition . . . come into play," a Northern educator among the freedmen at Port Royal wrote, "and the sooner will habits of responsibility, industry, self-dependence and manliness be developed." To expropriate land and give it to ex-slaves, he argued, "would be most unwise *and* injurious*. . . ." Although some abolitionists advocated land distribution, the idea was never seriously considered. In addition, abolitionists were apprehensive that a program of temporary paternalism might actually become a subterfuge for continuing slavery in reality, if not in name, as it had proven in the West Indies, 1834–1838.*

From the vantage point of the twentieth century it may safely be said that few, if any, Americans of the mid-nineteenth century clearly envisioned the depth of human blight produced by the slave system. Freedom alone was a deficient social policy for the slaves. By way of defense, however, it is also clear that the type of full equality for Negroes suggested by abolitionists as a basis for free economic competition never came into being. The demand that "the freedman should be treated at once as any other free man" *was not implemented. Faith in the salutary consequences of Negro competition in the open market was never tested fairly.*

The following two documents illustrate these generalizations. The first, a program of racial reform in the South prepared by three abolitionists, Robert Dale Owen, James McKaye, and Samuel Gridley Howe, was presented to the War Department in 1863; the second, a speech of Frederick Douglass to the Massachusetts Anti-Slavery Society, was delivered shortly before the end of the Civil War.

A Program for Racial Reform *Robert Dale Owen, James McKaye, and Samuel Gridley Howe**

Let us beware the temptation to treat the colored people with less than even justice, because they have been, and still are, lowly and feeble. Let us bear in mind that, with governments as with individuals, the crucial test of civilization and sense of justice is their treatment of the weak and the dependent.

God is offering to us an opportunity of atoning, in some measure, to the African for our former complicity in his wrongs. For our own sakes, as well as for his, let it not be lost. As we would that He should be to us and to our children, so let us be to those whose dearest interests are, by His providence, committed for the time to our charge.

As regards the question, What amount of aid and interference is necessary or desirable to enable the freedmen to tide over the stormy transition from slavery to freedom? we have chiefly to say that there is as much danger in doing too much as in doing too little. The risk is serious that, under the guise of guardianship, slavery, in a modified form, may be practically restored. Those who have ceased, only perforce, to be slave-holders, will be sure to unite their efforts to effect just such a purpose. It should be the earnest object of all friends of liberty to anticipate and prevent it. Benevolence itself, misdirected, may play into the hands of freedom's enemies, and those whose earnest endeavor is the good of

* From American Freedman's Inquiry Commission, *Final Report;* in *War of the Rebellion,* ser. 3, Vol. IV, pp. 380–382.

the freedman may, unconsciously, contribute to his virtual re-enslavement.

The refugees from slavery, when they first cross our lines, need temporary aid, but not more than indigent Southern whites fleeing from secessionism, both being sufferers from the disturbance of labor and the destruction of its products incident to war. The families of colored men, hired as military laborers or enlisted as soldiers, need protection and assistance, but not more than the families of white men similarly situated. Forcibly deprived of education in a state of slavery, the freedmen have a claim upon us to lend a helping hand until they can organize schools for their children. But they will soon take the labor and expense out of our hands, for these people pay no charge more willingly than that which assures them that their children shall reap those advantages of instruction which were denied to themselves.

For a time we need a freedman's bureau, but not because these people are negroes, only because they are men who have been, for generations, despoiled of their rights. The Commission has heretofore . . . recommended the establishment of such a bureau. . . .

Extensive experience in the West Indies has proved that emancipation, when it takes place, should be unconditional and absolute.* The experiment of a few years' apprenticeship, plausible in theory, proved, in practice, a failure so injurious in its effects that the provincial legislatures, though they had been opposed to the abolition of slavery, voted, after trial, for the abolition of apprenticeship.

The freedman should be treated at once as any other free man. He should be subjected to no compulsory contracts as to labor. There should not be, directly or indirectly, any statutory rates of wages. There should be no interference between the hirers and the hired. Nor should any regulations be imposed in regard to the local movements of these people, except such regulations, incident to

* This is a restatement of the thesis of a classic and commonly overlooked antislavery tract, James A. Thome and Joseph H. Kimball, *Emancipation in the West Indies: A Six Months' Tour in Antigua, Barbadoes, and Jamaica in the Year 1837* (New York, 1838). Thome and Kimball made a comparative study of emancipation on three West Indian islands and concluded that it had been most successful on Antigua, where it was immediate and unconditional, and where former slaves were given full constitutional guarantees.

war, relative to vagrancy or otherwise, as apply equally to whites. The natural laws of supply and demand should be left to regulate rates of compensation and places of residence.

But when freedmen shall have voluntarily entered into any agreement to work, they may at first usefully be aided in reducing that agreement to writing, and, for a time, we may properly see to it that such freedmen do not suffer from ill-treatment or failure of contract on the part of their employers, and that they themselves perform their duty in the premises.

It is of vital importance that the leasing and supervision of abandoned real estate in insurrectionary districts should be intrusted to the same persons who have in charge the interests of the freedmen who are likely to cultivate the lands in question. Between two sets of agents, one having in charge the lands, and another the interests of the freedmen, jarrings and conflicts of authority would be sure to ensue.

The Commission is confirmed in the opinion that all aid given to these people should be regarded as a temporary necessity; that all supervision over them should be provisional only, and advisory in its character. The sooner they shall stand alone and make their own unaided way, the better both for our race and for theirs.

The essential is that we secure to them the means of making their own way; that we give them, to use the familiar phrase, "a fair chance." If, like whites, they are to be self-supporting, then, like whites, they ought to have those rights, civil and political, without which they are but laboring as a man labors with hands bound.

There will for some time to come be a tendency on the part of many among those who have heretofore held them in bondage still to treat them in an unjust and tyrannical manner. The effectual remedy for this is, not special laws or a special organization for the protection of colored people, but the safeguard of general laws, applicable to all, against fraud and oppression.

The sum of our recommendations is this: Offer the freedmen temporary aid and counsel until they become a little accustomed to their new sphere of life; secure to them, by law, their just rights of person and property; relieve them, by a fair and equal administration of justice, from the depressing influence of disgraceful prejudice; above all, guard them against the virtual restoration of slavery in any form, under any pretext, and then let them take care of themselves. If we do this, the future of the African race in this country will be conducive to its prosperity and associated with its well-being. There will be nothing connected with it to excite regret or inspire apprehension.

The Power of the Franchise *Frederick Douglass* *

I have had but one idea for the last three years, to present to the American people, and the phraseology in which I clothe it is the old abolition phraseology. I am for the "immediate, unconditional, and universal" enfranchisement of the black man, in every State in the Union. (Loud applause.) Without this, his liberty is a mockery; without this, you might as well almost retain the old name of slavery for his condition; for, in fact, if he is not the slave of the individual master, he is the slave of society, and holds his liberty as a privilege, not as a right. He is at the mercy of the mob, and has no means of protecting himself.

It may be objected, however, that this pressing of the negro's right to suffrage is premature. Let us have slavery abolished, it may be said, let us have labor organized, and then, in the natural course of events, the right of suffrage will be extended to the negro. I do not agree with this. The constitution of the human mind is such, that if it once disregards the conviction forced upon it by a revelation of truth, it requires the exercise of a higher power to produce the same conviction afterwards. The American people are now in tears. The Shenandoah has run blood—the best blood of the North. All around Richmond, the blood of New England and of the North has been shed—of your sons, your brothers and your fathers. We all feel, in the existence of this Rebellion, that judgments terrible, wide-spread, far-reaching, overwhelming, are abroad in the land; and we feel, in view of these judgments, just now, a disposition to learn righteousness. This is the hour. Our streets are in mourning, tears are falling at every fireside, and under the chastisement of this Rebellion we have almost come up to the point of conceding this great, this all-important right of suffrage. I fear that if we fail to do it now, if abolitionists fail to

* From Frederick Douglass, "What the Black Man Wants," in *The Equality of All Men Before the Law* (Boston, 1865), pp. 36–39.

press it now, we may not see, for centuries to come, the same disposition that exists at this moment. (Applause.) Hence, I say, now is the time to press this right.

It may be asked, "Why do you want it? Some men have got along very well without it. Women have not this right." Shall we justify one wrong by another? That is a sufficient answer. Shall we at this moment justify the deprivation of the negro of the right to vote, because some one else is deprived of that privilege? I hold that women, as well as men, have the right to vote (applause), and my heart and my voice go with the movement to extend suffrage to woman; but that question rests upon another basis than that on which our right rests. We may be asked, I say, why we want it. I will tell you why we want it. We want it because it is our *right,* first of all. (Applause.) No class of men can, without insulting their own nature, be content with any deprivation of their rights. We want it, again, as a means for educating our race. Men are so constituted that they derive their conviction of their own possibilities largely from the estimate formed of them by others. If nothing is expected of a people, that people will find it difficult to contradict that expectation. By depriving us of suffrage, you affirm our incapacity to form an intelligent judgment respecting public men and public measures; you declare before the world that we are unfit to exercise the elective franchise, and by this means lead us to undervalue ourselves, to put a low estimate upon ourselves, and to feel that we have no possibilities like other men. Again, I want the elective franchise, for one, as a colored man, because ours is a peculiar government, based upon a peculiar idea, and that idea is universal suffrage. If I were in a monarchical government, or an autocratic or aristocratic government, where the few bore rule and the many were subject, there would be no special stigma resting upon me, because I did not exercise the elective franchise. It would do me no great violence. Mingling with the mass, I should partake of the strength of the mass; I should be supported by the mass, and I should have the same incentives to endeavor with the mass of my fellow-men; it would be no particular burden, no particular deprivation; but here, where universal suffrage is the rule, where that is the fundamental idea of the Government, to rule us out is to make us an exception, to brand us with the stigma of inferiority, and to invite to our heads the missiles of those about us; therefore, I want the franchise for the black man.

There are, however, other reasons, not derived from any consideration merely of our rights, but arising out of the condition of the South, and of the country . . . considerations which must arrest the attention of statesmen. I believe that when the tall heads of this Rebellion shall have been swept down, as they will be swept down, when the Davises and Toombses, and Stephenses, and others who are leading in this Rebellion shall have been blotted out, there will be this rank undergrowth of treason . . . growing up there, and interfering with, and thwarting the quiet operation of the Federal Government in those States. You will see those traitors handing down, from sire to son, the same malignant spirit which they have manifested, and which they are now exhibiting, with malicious hearts, broad blades, and bloody hands in the field, against our sons and brothers. That spirit will still remain; and whoever sees the Federal Government extended over those Southern States will see that Government in a strange land, and not only in a strange land, but in an enemy's land. A post-master of the United States in the South will find himself surrounded by a hostile spirit; a collector in a Southern port will find himself surrounded by a hostile spirit; a United States marshall or United States judge will be surrounded there by a hostile element. That enmity will not die out in a year, will not die out in an age. They will endeavor to circumvent, they will endeavor to destroy, the peaceful operation of this Government. Now, where will you find the strength to counterbalance this spirit, if you do not find it in the negroes of the South? They are your friends, and have always been your friends. They were your friends even when the Government did not regard them as such. They comprehended the genius of this war before you did. It is a significant fact, it is a marvellous fact, it seems almost to imply a direct interposition of Providence, that this war, which began in the interest of slavery on both sides, bids fair to end in the interest of liberty on both sides. (Applause.) It was begun, I say, in the interest of slavery on both sides. The South was fighting to take slavery out of the Union, and the North fighting to keep it in the Union; the South fighting to get it beyond the limits of the United-States Constitution, and the North fighting

to retain it within those limits; the South fighting for new guarantees, and the North fighting for the old guarantees;—both despising the negro, both insulting the negro. Yet, the negro, apparently
endowed with wisdom from on high, saw more clearly the end
from the beginning than we did. When Seward said the status of no
man in the country would be changed by the war, the negro did not
believe him. (Applause.) When our generals sent their underlings
in shoulder-straps to hunt the flying negro back from our lines
into the jaws of slavery, from which he had escaped, the negroes
thought that a mistake had been made, and that the intentions of
the Government had not been rightly understood by our officers in
shoulder-straps, and they continued to come into our lines, thread-
ing their way through bogs and fens, over briers and thorns,
fording streams, swimming rivers, bringing us tidings as to the safe
path to march, and pointing out the dangers that threatened us.
They are our only friends in the South, and we should be true to
them in this their trial hour, and see to it that they have the
elective franchise.

I know that we are inferior to you in some things—virtually
inferior. We walk about among you like dwarfs among giants. Our
heads are scarcely seen above the great sea of humanity. The
Germans are superior to us; the Irish are superior to us; the
Yankees are superior to us (laughter); they can do what we
cannot, that is, what we have not hitherto been allowed to do. But
while I make this admission, I utterly deny that we are originally,
or naturally, or practically, or in any way, or in any important
sense, inferior to anybody on this globe. (Loud applause.) This
charge of inferiority is an old dodge. It has been made available
for oppression on many occasions. It is only about six centuries
since the blue-eyed and fair-haired Anglo-Saxons were considered
inferior by the haughty Normans, who once trampled upon them. If
you read the history of the Norman Conquest, you will find that
this proud Anglo-Saxon was once looked upon as of coarser clay
than his Norman master, and might be found in the highways and
byways of old England laboring with a brass collar on his neck,
and the name of his master marked upon it. *You* were down then!
(Laughter and applause.) You are up now. I am glad you are up,
and I want you to be glad to help us up also. (Applause.)

I hold that the American people are bound, not only in self-defence, to extend this right to the freedmen of the South, but they are bound by their love of country, and by all their regard for the future safety of those Southern States, to do this—to do it as a measure essential to the preservation of peace there. But I will not dwell upon this. I put it to the American sense of honor. The honor of a nation is an important thing. It is said in the Scriptures, "What doth it profit a man if he gain the whole world, and lose his own soul?" It may be said, also, What doth it profit a nation if it gain the whole world, but lose its honor? I hold that the American government has taken upon itself a solemn obligation of honor, to see that this war—let it be long or let it be short, let it cost much or let it cost little—that this war shall not cease until every freedman at the South has the right to vote. (Applause.) It has bound itself to it. What have you asked the black men of the South, the black men of the whole country, to do? Why, you have asked them to incur the deadly enmity of their masters, in order to befriend you and to befriend this Government. You have asked us to call down, not only upon ourselves, but upon our children's children, the deadly hate of the entire Southern people. You have called upon us to turn our backs upon our masters, to abandon their cause and espouse yours; to turn against the South and in favor of the North; to shoot down the Confederacy and uphold the flag—the American flag. You have called upon us to expose ourselves to all the subtle machinations of their malignity for all time. And now, what do you propose to do when you come to make peace? To reward your enemies, and trample in the dust your friends? Do you intend to sacrifice the very men who have come to the rescue of your banner in the South, and incurred the lasting displeasure of their masters thereby? Do you intend to sacrifice them and reward your enemies? Do you mean to give your enemies the right to vote, and take it away from your friends? Is that wise policy? Is that honorable? Could American honor withstand such a blow? I do not believe you will do it. I think you will see to it that we have the right to vote. There is something too mean in looking upon the negro, when you are in trouble, as a citizen, and when you are free from trouble, as an alien. When this nation was in trouble, in its early struggles, it looked upon the negro as a citizen. In 1776 he was a citizen. . . . In 1812 Gen. Jackson addressed us as citizens—"fellow-citizens." He wanted us to fight.

We were citizens then! And now, when you come to frame a con-
scription bill, the negro is a citizen again. He has been a citizen just
three times in the history of this government, and it has always
been in time of trouble. In time of trouble we are citizens. Shall we
be citizens in war, and aliens in peace? Would that be just?

I ask my friends who are apologizing for not insisting upon this
right, where can the black man look, in this country, for the
assertion of this right, if he may not look to the Massachusetts
Anti-Slavery Society? Where under the whole heavens can he look
for sympathy, in asserting this right, if he may not look to this
platform? Have you lifted us up to a certain height to see that we
are men, and then are any disposed to leave us there, without
seeing that we are put in possession of all our rights? We look
naturally to this platform for the assertion of all our rights, and for
this one especially. I understand the anti-slavery societies of this
country to be based on two principles,—first, the freedom of the
blacks of this country; and, second, the elevation of them. Let me
not be misunderstood here. I am not asking for sympathy at the
hands of abolitionists, sympathy at the hands of any. I think the
American people are disposed often to be generous rather than
just. I look over this country at the present time, and I see Educational Societies, Sanitary Commissions, Freedmen's Associations,
and the like,—all very good: but in regard to the colored people
there is always more that is benevolent, I perceive, than just,
manifested towards us. What I ask for the negro is not benevolence, not pity, not sympathy, but simply *justice*. (Applause.) The
American people have always been anxious to know what they
shall do with us. Gen. Banks was distressed with solicitude as to
what he should do with the negro.* Everybody has asked the
question, and they learned to ask it early of the abolitionists,
"What shall we do with the negro?" I have had but one answer
from the beginning. Do nothing with us! Your doing with us has
already played the mischief with us. Do nothing with us! If the
apples will not remain on the tree of their own strength, if they are
worm-eaten at the core, if they are early ripe and disposed to fall,
let them fall! I am not for tying or fastening them on the tree in
any way, except by nature's plan, and if they will not stay there, let

* General Nathaniel P. Banks outraged most abolitionists by instituting a
modified form of the apprenticeship system in Louisiana.

them fall. And if the negro cannot stand on his own legs, let him fall also. All I ask is, give him a chance to stand on his own legs! Let him alone! If you see him on his way to school, let him alone,—don't disturb him! If you see him going to the dinner-table at a hotel, let him go! If you see him going to the ballot-box, let him alone,—don't disturb him! (Applause.) If you see him going into a work-shop, just let him alone,—your interference is doing him a positive injury. Gen. Banks's "preparation" is of a piece with this attempt to prop up the negro. Let him fall if he cannot stand alone! If the negro cannot live by the line of eternal justice . . . the fault will not be yours, it will be his who made the negro, and established that line for his government. (Applause.) Let him live or die by that. If you will only untie his hands, and give him a chance, I think he will live. He will work as readily for himself as the white man. A great many delusions have been swept away by this war. One was, that the negro would not work; he has proved his ability to work. Another was, that the negro would not fight; that he possessed only the most sheepish attributes of humanity; was a perfect lamb, or an "Uncle Tom"; disposed to take off his coat whenever required, fold his hands, and be whipped by anybody who wanted to whip him. But the war has proved that there is a great deal of human nature in the negro, and that "he will fight . . . when there is a reasonable probability of his whipping anybody." (Laughter and applause.)

Advice to the Freedmen from the Freedmen's Bureau
*Clinton B. Fisk**

The Freedmen's Bureau represented the major national effort to assist the ex-slaves and regulate employer-employee relations in the South. Its program followed closely the suggestions of the American Freedmen's Inquiry Commission. As a temporary agency, its appropriations were renewed year-to-year, and it went out of existence formally in 1872—although its power had declined significantly two years earlier. President Johnson even opposed the efforts of this so-modest-a-body. "A system for the support of indigent persons in the United States," he maintained in

* *Reports of the Assistant Commissioners of the Freedmen's Bureau,*
39th Cong., 1st sess., *Senate Executive Document No. 27* (1866), pp. 4–5.

his 1866 veto, "was never contemplated by the authors of the Constitution. . . ." The following address to the "Freedmen of Kentucky," by Clinton B. Fisk, assistant commissioner of the Bureau for Tennessee and Kentucky and an ardent Methodist, illustrates the middle-class orientation of the organization.

Freedmen of Kentucky:

The Constitution of the United States has been so amended that hereafter no one can be held as a slave anywhere in the country, except in punishment for crime. All the colored people, therefore, in the State of Kentucky, are free, and your friend, the assistant commissioner of the Freedmen's Bureau, desires to address you a few plain words:

1. First of all, you should be grateful to your Heavenly Father, who has broken your bonds and conferred upon you the inestimable boon of freedom.

2. You should recognize your high obligations to the federal government, which, in its mighty struggle with the great rebellion and in its triumph, has been true to the interests of freedom, and has fulfilled its pledges to the oppressed.

3. You should love Kentucky, for it is a noble old State—your native State, your home and the home of your children, and now a free State.

4. I advise you to remain in your old homes, and that you enter into good contracts with your former owners and masters. You have been associated with them for many years; you are bound to the old home by many ties, and most of you I trust will be able to get on as well with your late masters as with any one else. If your former owners will not make good contracts with you—giving you good wages, or a share of the crop—you will have a perfect right to go where you can do better.

5. Let me warn you specially against flocking into the towns and cities. There are too many people in the towns and cities already. Hundreds, unless they speedily remove to the country, will, I fear, fall victims of pestilence. The small-pox is now prevalent, and in a few weeks the cholera may be among us. In the crowded cities you will wear your lives away in a constant struggle to pay high rent for miserable dwellings and scanty allowances of food. Many of your children, I greatly fear, will be found wander-

ing through the streets as vagrants—plunging into the worst of vices, and filling the workhouses and jails. By all means seek healthy homes in the country.

6. Now that you are free and will enjoy the fruits of your own industry, enter upon your new life with a hearty will. You begin it with little besides your hands, but by patient industry and economy you may soon earn and save enough money to purchase a home of your own, and to furnish it with many of the comforts of life.

7. Let each man turn his heart and his thoughts toward providing a good home for his wife and children, and to aid in the care of his aged and dependent parents; carefully guard and keep sacred the marriage relation; be lawfully wedded: "taking up with each other" in an abominable practice, and must perish with the institution which gave it birth.

8. Early attention should be given to the education of your children. Purchase books for them, and employ good teachers. You have numerous friends in the country who will aid you in the establishment of schools. Be resolved that all your children shall be taught reading, writing, and arithmetic.

9. Let the past be forgotten. Treat all men with respect; avoid disputes; demonstrate to Kentucky and to the world, by your faithful observance of the laws, by your sobriety and good morals, and by your thrift, that you are not only qualified for the precious blessing of freedom, but for the high and responsible duties of citizens of the Commonwealth.

10. Until the enactment and enforcement of State laws giving you full protection in person and property, impartial justice will be secured to you by the strong arm of the national government.

A Plea for Equal Rights for All Charles Sumner*

No single national political figure in American history has so fervently advocated "Equal Rights of All"—and he generally capitalized the phrase—as Charles Sumner; and few have seen so much of their work come to fruition. Sumner played a seminal role

* Sumner to John Mercer Langston, April 7, 1872; and Sumner to the final meeting of the American Anti-Slavery Society, April 8, 1870, in *The Works of Charles Sumner* (Boston, 1883), XV, 68–70, and *ibid.*, XIII, 375–376.

*in the desegregation of the Massachusetts schools, abolishing
slavery and Jim Crow transportation facilities in the District of
Columbia, equalizing pay for Negro soldiers, introducing the first
Negro lawyer to practice before the Supreme Court, permitting
Negroes to serve as witnesses in federal courts and as electors
under the District of Columbia charter. He helped shape every
major piece of Reconstruction legislation from the Freedmen's
Bureau Bill to the Civil Rights Act of 1875—passed shortly after
his death. "Be not satisfied with anything less than the Rights of
All," was his advice to Negro leaders. When others lost interest in
the cause of complete Negro equality, Sumner remained adamant
—as evident in the following letter to the National Convention of
Colored People, New Orleans, April 7, 1872, and his suggestion
that the American Anti-Slavery Society continue to work for
freedom after the passage of the Fifteenth Amendment.*

MY DEAR SIR,—In reply to your inquiry, I make haste to say,
that, in my judgment, the Colored Convention should think more
of principles than of men,—except so far as men stand for principles. Above all, let them insist on the rights of their own much-
abused and insulted people.

It is absurd for anybody to say that he "accepts the situation,"
and then deny the equal rights of the colored man. If the "situation" is accepted in good faith, it must be entirely,—including not
merely the abolition of Slavery and the establishment of equal
suffrage, but also all those other rights which are still denied or
abridged. There must be complete equality before the law, so that
in all institutions, agencies, or conveniences, created or regulated
by law, there can be no discrimination on account of color, but a
black man shall be treated as a white man.

In maintaining their rights, it will be proper for the Convention
to invoke the Declaration of Independence, so that its principles
and promises shall become a living reality, never to be questioned
in any way, but recognized always as a guide of conduct and a
governing rule in the interpretation of the National Constitution,
being in the nature of a Bill of Rights preceding the Constitution.

It is not enough to "proclaim liberty throughout all the land
unto all the inhabitants thereof." Equality must be proclaimed
also; and since both are promised by the great Declaration, which

is a national act, and as from their nature they should be uniform throughout the country, both must be placed under the safeguard of national law. There can be but one liberty and one equality, the same in Boston and New Orleans, the same everywhere throughout the country.

The colored people are not ungenerous, and therefore will incline to any measures of good-will and reconciliation; but I trust no excess of benevolence will make them consent to any postponement of those equal rights which are still refused. The disabilities of colored people, loyal and long-suffering, should be removed before the disabilities of former Rebels; or at least the two removals should go hand in hand.

It only remains that I should say, "Stand firm!" The politicians will then know that you are in earnest, and will no longer be trifled with. Victory will follow soon, and the good cause be secure forever.

GENTLEMEN,—You propose to celebrate the triumph of Equal Rights at the ballot-box, and at the same time to abandon that famous shibboleth by which you once rallied the country against Slavery.

It was said of Wolfe, the conqueror at Quebec, that he died in the arms of Victory; and such will be the fortune of your noble Society. "They run!" was the voice that fell on the ears of the expiring General. "Who run?" he exclaimed. "The enemy," was the answer. "Now, God be praised, I shall die in peace," said he, and his battle ended.

The Antislavery Society may now die in peace. Slavery is ended. But I do not doubt that the same courage and fidelity which through long years warred against this prodigious Barbarism will continue determined to the end in protecting and advancing the work begun.

I do not think the work finished, so long as the word "white" is allowed to play any part in legislation,—so long as it constrains the courts in naturalization,—so long as it rules public conveyances, steamboats, and railroads,—so long as it bars the doors of houses bound by law to receive people for food and lodging, or licensed as places of amusement,—so long as it is inscribed on our common schools;—nor do I think the work finished until the power of the Nation is recognized, supreme and beyond question, to fix the definition of a "republican government," and to enforce the same by the perfect maintenance of rights everywhere throughout the land, according to the promises of the Declaration of Independence, without any check or hindrance from the old proslavery pretension of State Rights. It must be understood that every State, while perfectly free in its local administration, is subject to the supremacy of the Nation, whenever it touches the Rights of Man,—so that, according to the ancient words of Demosthenes, the law shall be "a general ordinance, *equal and alike to all.*" Let there be Equality before the Law, and all rights are assured. In this cause count me always as your devoted and grateful fellow-worker.

Letters from Yankee Teachers*

Perhaps the most important source of antislavery thought had been the deep strain of Christian piety and benevolence that was generated by the New Awakening of the 1820's. Those individuals who experienced conversion were admonished to find practical outlets for their zeal. Some discovered in abolitionism the field best suited for their blessed work, others became devoted advocates of other reform movements. After the 1830's, however, the missionary enterprise flagged seriously—to be revived, in part, by the Civil War. It was no longer necessary to go to Africa, India, or Hawaii to locate a choice area of Christian endeavor when such promising territory now lay so close to home.

This was the setting for one of the most important social and racial movements of the Reconstruction period: the creation of schools for the freedmen. In the years immediately following the war, some 10,000 teachers set up makeshift classrooms in barns, churches, tents, old barracks, hotels, and confiscated mansions. Books and other educational materials were sent south in crates and barrels. Northern teachers blended training in reading and writing with lessons in equalitarianism and religious piety. And

* These letters are taken from scattered issues of *The American Freedman,* II (1867), and the *American Missionary,* XIII (1869).

everywhere they went they found the ex-slaves hungry for knowledge. As Harriet Beecher Stowe said, the freedmen "rushed not for the grog-shop but for the schoolroom—they cried for the spelling-book as for bread." Some of the dominant attitudes, problems, and reactions of former slaves and their teachers are revealed in these letters of Yankee educators.

> *Newbern, North Carolina*
> *January 1, 1867*

I must tell you of an evening last week, spent so pleasantly that, simply for the enjoyment, I could wish you to have been present. The occasion was an "Exhibition," solely under the charge of the colored people, the proceeds of which were for lighting their school room with gas. Three years ago these children knew nothing, and now they give us evening entertainments. There was one admirable little actress, a beautiful child, of perhaps six years, who elicited the warmest applause—a highly accomplished officer, sitting near me exclaiming, "It makes me ashamed of my own children!"

We gather together, daily, a motley crowd of humanity, from infancy almost to old age, bringing in, as well, every grade of mental ability, from the small boy, who seems to swallow the alphabet whole, to the poor deformed creature, who cannot remember a letter from one week to another, but who steadfastly perseveres, hoping that she may sometime be able to trace out the Word of God.

Our most faithful and diligent scholars seem, as in all the rest of the world, to be those who are laboring under the greatest difficulties; one of these is "Dumpey," a boy of twelve years, in whom one cannot fail to be interested. He "commenced his education" with us about six weeks ago, and has gone on with wonderful rapidity, until now, he reads intelligently, and is one of the first in arithmetical calculation. He lives with a widowed mother, some distance from the city, and is her only support. He is a grave, serious child, with his weighty responsibility always looking out from his large, cloudy eyes.

Bare footed, bare shouldered, bare headed little things, we find bundled together at the church door these cold winter mornings, but all cheerful, all ready to shiver over their books as soon as the time comes. Nothing seems to diminish their eagerness to learn, in many cases, nothing to *satisfy* it, and a scrap of an old book, or a single leaf, is treasured as sacredly as a miser's gold.

Among our scholars is one class of adults, who are taking two or three months rest from labor, for the purpose of "getting an education." It is really painful to see them toiling so faithfully at their primers, knowing, as we do, that, with all their earnestness, they will never see more than a glimmer of the light that has been shut out from them, and it is a relief to turn from them to the children who stride from alphabet to primer, and from primer to reader, in a wonderfully short time.

Staunton, Virginia
May 1, 1869

Six or eight left school a few days ago because they could not pay their tuition, and although I called and informed them that while I desired them to pay if they could I should not send any away who were actually unable to, they had too much pride to accept my offer and still refused to come until they could pay.

One little boy about eight years old, who had not paid for a month, and who began to think I was going to send him home, after hearing me urge the children to bring their ten cents, came next morning with forty cents, which he handed to me with more pride than a Wall St. broker has with his millions. "Well," said I, "how did you get this money?" "I made it dis mornin' down town holdin horses for ge'm'an." And sure enough I found he had been out on the street ever since sun-rise to watch for jobs, lest he should lose his place in the schoolroom. Indeed the interest manifested on the part of those who still attend school is greater than at any time previous. Neither rain, darkness, or anything else, prevents them from coming, though many are compelled to come late, being hired out to those who care more for their labor than their education.

The old minister who commenced his alphabet last December, is still poring over the Primers, but now begins to read short words quite readily. Last Monday night, when I called to hear him recite, I found him studying with the greatest enthusiasm. "O," said he, "if I could only read a chapter in the Bible, or give out a hymn to be sung, I would give all that I am worth," and that is perhaps $2000, which he has saved since his freedom. The day before he had been out to a neighboring town to preach, and such is his memory of Scripture that several of the white people who were present declared that he must have been able to read; yet his only means of getting information from the Bible as yet is by having his little boy read to him. He declares he will succeed.

Macon, Georgia
April, 1869

I had not come South prepared to see more than a little imperfect scholarship, on the part of the colored people. At least I did not expect to find pupils studying Algebra, Latin and Geometry. But there they were doing it.

I did not look for very excellent map drawing and penmanship, but I saw it there.

It seems to have been the plan and study of our Superintendent to introduce those methods of study and instruction which shall advance the pupils most thoroughly, and yet, most expeditiously, and I think his three years work here since the schools were first established, has been a success. In every room there is the same method, showing an under-current of thought on the part of some grand manager, and all works well.

For instance, map drawing is taught on Guyot's plan. Children are taught to add and multiply by contracted methods and in the primary rooms to read by the Phonetic system of sounds rather than the names of letters. Every means is taken to contract the methods of education into as small a space as possible.

Towards the end of the second term, I had four normal pupils placed under my care for training. I gave up my classes into their hands, and to the best of my ability taught them how to teach. They adapted themselves to the wants of the situation and achieved a success within the next four weeks as marked as could perhaps be attained. One of them then went out from here to teach by himself in the country. Two others were put over two small schools in the same building, and one is still with me, acting as my assistant. She is about seventeen, very black . . . very faithful.

Augusta, Georgia
April 29, 1869

I cannot tell you how glad I was to get back here after my four
month's vacation; not that I was made particularly welcome by the
"Southern chivalry," whose hospitality is so renowned—on the
contrary, the very first time I went out, Miss B——, who had
never before been South, was startled by hearing a lady say, for
our benefit, "Here are those mean Yankee school-ma'ams come
back to cheat the niggers! I can teach niggers to work, but not to
read and spell." (Perhaps she could not.) A few weeks ago Miss
Williams and I were quietly walking along, when a splendid
barouche passed, with four elegantly dressed ladies (?) in it, and a
colored driver. We had scarcely noticed it till one of the four rose
and shook her fist at us, calling out in a tone that made us start,
"See those Yankees! Oh you——————," using words too
profane and vile to write. We took no notice, but trembled to hear
such language from the lips of a female.

Valentine's day many precious missives were put in under our
hall door, illustrated with pen drawings in which we were represented with our "carpet bags" full of gold, and saying: "I cheat
every nigger I can get hold of."

How differently I was welcomed by my dusky friends! One little
fellow on seeing me in the street ran home, crying "Mother, sister,
good news! good news! Miss Emma dun come back!" A woman
whose children attended my school last year, threw up her arms,
saying; "Well, well, well! I'm as proud to see you as if you was my
mother."

A tailor and his wife, who belonged to different masters, were
destitute even of necessary clothing when "freedom cum," as they
express it here. They have since not only taken care of their four
children, sent them to school, etc. but have accumulated enough to
buy two sewing-machines, and to build a nice little house, which is
very neatly furnished.

I cannot forbear telling you how much I enjoy my work. Many
in my school are Christians and although some of them *do* think
"religion ain't got nothing to do with studying and behaving at
school," yet they try to do right. When I arrived at school this
morning some one came to meet me, saying that one of my
scholars had got religion.

Every Friday we have a prayer-meeting after school.

Thursday evenings Miss Merrick has a Bible-class which, I think, will be the means of doing a great deal of good. All who are in the habit of coming are very regular, and seem to enjoy it exceedingly.

One of my most advanced scholars, a boy of fifteen, whose father is a drunkard, said one day, "I never thought studying the Bible could be made so interesting! All the week I look forward with longing for Bible-class night to come. Often I have work to do in the shop, and then I run every step of the way for fear of being late."

Poor boy! I wish he could be taken from here and surrounded by good influences—something could be made of him, for he is very bright. His father allows him to go to school two hours a day, whenever it is convenient for him; the rest of the time he works in his barber shop. Nearly all the boys, and some of the girls in my school support themselves by working out of school hours. My Sunday School is very pleasant. All in my class are very intelligent, and not only able to read, but also to reason for themselves, and their interest is evident from the numerous questions they ask.

Altogether I have never spent a happier two years in my life than the two I spent teaching the Freedmen.

CHAPTER V

AN ERA OF HATE
AND VIOLENCE

❀   ❀

It sometimes seems we are deserted by earth and Heaven.

FREDERICK DOUGLASS, 1895

The late nineteenth and early twentieth centuries were a period
of racial barbarism. In the South, Negroes were practically
disfranchised by a variety of subterfuges which nullified the
protections of the Fourteenth and Fifteenth Amendments. (1)
Segregation in all areas of life was instituted on a massive scale
throughout the South. More Negroes were shot, lynched, and
burned in these years than ever before or since. (3) Negro convicts were "farmed out," as contemporaries termed it, to work
as field hands on plantations, as railroad laborers, or in the
hideous turpentine camps of Georgia and elsewhere. (2) Many
tenant farmers who desired to leave the land were restricted
in movement by law or force in every Southern state and reduced to a condition of practical peonage. The debate over
the place of the Negro in the human community was revived
and helped produce an abundant racial literature strikingly
similar in style and content to the old proslavery argument
of natural Negro inferiority. (4) Redneck leaders arose, like
Hoke Smith, Ben Tillman, and James K. Vardaman, whose
vilifications exploited ever-present racial tensions for the political and economic advantage of their poor white constituency—
and for themselves. The short-lived racial moderation of some

Southern Populists was overwhelmed by this dominant trend. "If the American conscience were only half alive," Frederick Douglass lamented shortly before his death in 1895, "if the American church and clergy were only half Christianized, if American moral sensibility were not hardened by persistent infliction of outrage and crime against colored people, a scream of horror, shame, and indignation would rise to Heaven. . . ."

But it would be a mistake to assume that the racial bitterness of these years was of peculiarly Southern vintage. The United States Supreme Court, for example, supported the ingeniously devised white supremacy laws in case after case. The power of the court was an active force in the movement "to keep the Negro down." (5)

And so was Northern racism. The Civil War had ushered in a short-lived period of relatively decent race relations in the North. Many of the legal impediments to Negro equality that had existed since the colonial period were done away with in the 1870's and 1880's—segregated schools, transportation facilities, and public accommodations. This easing of racial tensions in the North came to an end in the 1890's and early twentieth century as Southern Negroes migrated to Northern cities in greater numbers. There were race riots in New York City in 1900 and in Springfield, Illinois, in 1908—and others throughout the North and West as well as the South. Hostility toward Negroes also took the subtler form of burlesquing their supposedly racial characteristics in thousands of vaudeville shows and songs popular in Northern cities at the turn of the century. (6)

1. DISFRANCHISEMENT OF THE NEGRO

*The Politics of White Supremacy Ben Tillman**

The Negro was the pawn of Southern politics in the 1870's and 1880's. Whatever voting strength the Republican party had in the South depended on Negro ballots. In some states, like Mississippi, unholy alliances were made between white Democratic leaders and Negro Republicans in exchange for patronage appointments. More generally, as in South Carolina—the only state with a Negro

* From *Journal of the Constitutional Convention of the State of South Carolina, 1895* (Columbia, S.C., 1895), pp. 462–464.

legislative majority during Reconstruction—Negroes represented a
powerful Republican force. To eliminate or control the Negro vote
by exploiting the theme of white supremacy became a principal
Southern political tactic of the late nineteenth century. "Pitchfork
Ben" Tillman, the "one-eyed plowboy" of South Carolina's white
Democracy, whose abusive racial and class-conscious epithets
made him an appealing figure to the state's mudsill farmers,
describes how Negro disfranchisement began in the 1870's and
1880's.

Now, I have alluded to the fact of this villainy, anarchy, misrule
and robbery, and I cannot, in any words I possess, paint it. There
is no man on this floor living in the country who dared during that
dark period* to leave his fireside without dread that when he
returned he would find some harm to his family; and he dared not
go forth without being armed, fearful of robbery. The sky was lit
almost every night by the glare of burning dwellings and ginhouses.
Our Courts of Justice were filled with bribe-takers, and the Judges
themselves were not free from bribery. How did it come about,
and who must bear the blame? We are told the negroes didn't do it.
"Oh, we didn't do it," they say. [Addressing the negro delegates.]†
You blindly followed and obeyed the orders of the Freedmen's
Bureau and the Union League and ignored the appeals of your
former masters, who treated you with kindness and furnished you
with your daily bread. I myself can testify that appeal after appeal
was made by me, and by almost every white man in this State, with
the negroes with whom he came in contact on his plantation:
"Stop! come back! help us free ourselves from this burden!" But
every one of you, almost up to 1876, blindly followed wherever
these white thieves ordered. Was it negro government? The
negroes furnished the ballots, and that is what we are dealing with.
The negroes put the little pieces of paper in the box that gave the
commission to these white scoundrels who were their leaders and
the men who debauched them; and this must be our justification,
our vindication and our excuse to the world that we are met in
Convention openly, boldly, without any pretense of secrecy, to
announce that it is our purpose, as far as we may, without coming

* Reconstruction.
† Six Negro Republican delegates were present at the convention.

in conflict with the United States Constitution, to put such safe-guards around this ballot in future, to so restrict the suffrage and circumscribe it, that this infamy can never come about again.

The negroes were the tools of designing white men, I acknowl-edge—participators and willing tools. The poor, ignorant cotton field hand, who never reaped any advantage, nor saw anything except a pistol, blindly followed like sheep wherever their black and white leaders told them to go, voted unanimously every time for the Republican ticket during that dark period, and these results were achieved solely and wholly by reason of the ballot being in the hands of such cattle. Is the danger gone? No. How did we recover our liberty? By fraud and violence. We tried to overcome the thirty thousand majority by honest methods, which was a mathematical impossibility.

How did we bring it about? Every white man sunk his personal feelings and ambitions. The white people of the State, illustrating our glorious motto, "Ready with their lives and fortunes," came together as one. By fraud and violence, if you please, we threw it off. In 1878 we had to resort to more fraud and violence, and so again in 1880. Then the Registration Law and eight-box system was evolved from the superior intelligence of the white man to check and control this surging, muddy stream of ignorance and to tell it to back, and since then we have carried our elections without resort to any illegal methods, simply because the whites were united.* If we were to remain united it would still be desirable that we should guard against the possibility of this flood, which is now dammed up, breaking loose; or, like the viper that is asleep, only to be warmed into life again and sting us whenever some more white rascals, native or foreign, come here and mobilize the ignorant blacks. Therefore, the only thing we can do as patriots and as statesmen is to take from them every ballot that we can under the laws of our national government.

I read a moment ago from the report of the Committee that good government can only rest on intelligence and good morals. I

* The Registration Law of 1882 limited the time when eligible voters could register, increased the discretionary powers of electoral officials, and penalized Negro sharecroppers who migrated from one precinct to another. The eight-box system placed a sign on each ballot box directing the voter to a specific one. White illiterates were helped to find the right box, Negroes were not.

will go further and say that good government and the very life of republics rest on virtue, patriotism and intelligence. The chief amongst the three is intelligence. It has been said, and it must be apparent to any one who thinks, that even if we restrict the suffrage as we propose, that with 40,000 Conservatives and 40,000 Reformers, divided and striving for mastery, and 15,000 illiterate white men disfranchised, that the negroes are still here in sufficient numbers to control us. Are we so besotted, so forgetful and oblivious of the record which I have just read to you? Have our memories grown so callous that we as a white race—kinsmen, brothers, common inheritors of the glorious past and of the freedom transmitted to us by our forefathers—have we got to the point where we cannot unite as brothers, throwing aside the petty bickerings and animosities that have been engendered in the last five years, and, without regard to personal ambition or partisan advantage to anybody, can we not provide so that we will not have to appeal to these people as arbiters of our fate? Can we not rise to the necessities of the occasion and put into this Constitution such an Article in reference to suffrage as will guarantee, as far as the law can guarantee, to future generations that they shall have the blessings of Anglo-Saxon civilization and liberty in this State? How pitiable, how puerile, how ineffably, unutterably contemptible appear the personal ambitions and petty spites of men alongside of this grand and glorious purpose!

Southern Constitutional Conventions

The somewhat haphazard system of restricting the Negro franchise employed in Southern politics in the 1870's and 1880's developed into a fine art in Mississippi in 1890. The "Mississippi Plan" was avidly studied by every other Southern state when it was conspicuously evident, after the defeat of the Lodge Force Bill in 1890, that the federal government would do nothing to guarantee black suffrage. The Mississippi Constitutional Convention of 1890 set itself the task of eliminating the Negro vote without violating the Fourteenth and Fifteenth Amendments. Residence requirements, poll taxes, the "understanding clause"—which called for an accurate reading and understanding "of any section of the Constitution of this State"—and the disfranchisement of certain criminals, served the same purpose without mentioning Negroes specifi-

*cally. Southern states followed Mississippi's pattern—with a few
added nuances—so that the Negro was eliminated as a significant
force in Southern politics by the first decade of the twentieth
century. The following keynote addresses at the constitutional
conventions of Mississippi, Louisiana, and Alabama demonstrate
the motivation which called the sessions into being.*

Mississippi*

Who knows better than the gentlemen before me what is the
occasion and the object of this solemn assembly.

I must in the expression of my thanks for the distinction
bestowed upon me, say that I am deeply sensible of the honor, and
in accepting this elevated position I enter upon the discharge of its
duties with very much diffidence of my qualifications, tempered
however with the assurance I feel that so magnanimous and
distinguished and able a body will make my work less and easier.
It is useless to say now that we have been convened for conference
and conciliation for the promotion of public and not private ends.

Mississippi, our common mother, whom we all love, requires us
to do our duty for the people now living and who are yet to live
within our borders. She requires that. Do not entertain any opinion
but such as seek that end; reject none except upon maturest
consideration, unshackled to the stone floor of fixed opinion,
unchained to the walls of prejudice and passion. She expects that,
with magnanimity for the opinions of each, we will throw all
opinions into the common crucible of thought. She says to us that
our position is so peculiar as to have attracted the curious examination of the outside world. She has assembled us together to look
into that situation calmly and with no other consideration than the
weal of the State.

You are confronted by a colossal fact which cannot be obscured
by the clouds of maudlin sentiment or pseudo philanthropy. That
fact cannot be argued away or speculated upon; it will remain in
spite of all discussion, of all criticism from outside parties, in spite
of all reflection made by ourselves; that fact remains that there
exists here in this State two distinct and opposite types of mankind. We find ourselves together and we must live together and the

* From *Journal of the Proceedings of the Constitutional Convention of
the State of Mississippi, 1890* (Jackson, Miss., 1890), pp. 9–11.

question is how it shall be arranged so that we may live harmoniously.

This unfortunate fact exists and it is a fact that needs no argument of mine that there has not heretofore been in the history of the world, certainly not in the history of Mississippi, anything but heterogeneousness between those races. It is a fact that each race is fond of the other. There is no man who hears me who does not understand that the individuals of the opposite race are his friends in all the various transactions of life. There is no black man or colored man in the State of Mississippi who does not feel that in all the business of life the whites are his friends. That is one statement that is true; how is it then that we cannot have political homogeneity?

How is it then that one finds them massed on one side to the other whenever it comes to any matter of Government policy? It does not arise from any dislike each for the other, nor from lack of confidence each in the other. It arises, gentlemen of this Convention, in that principle of human nature, in that principle which has its root deep in human nature—that when any of the five distinct races encounter each other in the matter of government, that from the instinct implanted in its nature, it desires to be in the ascendency.

This is so true, so general, such a historic fact that it may be said to be a law of God. This shows the difficulty of one of the problems you have to encounter.

This ballot system must be so arranged as to effect one object, permit me to say—for we find the two races now together, the rule of one of which has always meant economic and moral ruin; we find another race whose rule has always meant prosperity and happiness, and prosperity and happiness to all races.

What does the instinct of self-protection require us to do? We have been twenty-five long years endeavoring to have strictly homologous political relations between those races. We have failed.

We must never pass any ordinance, of course, that will work any injustice or oppression, but be full of benefit to all the citizens of this State and those who are to come. The policy must be so just and necessary that ruin shall not result but we shall have prosperity for all if possible.

That is the great problem for which we are called together; that is the great question for you to solve, and the outside world is looking anxiously and our sister States of the South are looking at the solution we arrive at in reference to that question.

Louisiana*

In the first place, my fellow-citizens, we are all aware that this convention has been called by the people of the State of Louisiana principally to deal with one question, and we know that but for the existence of that one question this assemblage would not be sitting here to-day. We know that this convention has been called together by the people of the State to eliminate from the electorate the mass of corrupt and illiterate voters who have during the last quarter of a century degraded our politics. I care nothing for details. The people of this State are not concerned as to details in this matter, but they have expressed themselves upon a principle. With a unanimity unparalleled in the history of American politics, they have intrusted to the Democratic party of this State the solution of the question of the purification of the electorate. They expect that question to be solved, and to be solved quickly. (Applause.) You know, my fellow-delegates, that all over this State the people are listening to the click of the telegraph instrument and waiting for news as to the course which this convention will adopt upon the great question with which the hustings have rung for the past three months. You know that the people of this State will watch your deliberations hour by hour, until they learn, as I believe they will, that you intend to devote yourselves, first, and before all else, to the solution of the suffrage question.

That you will allow naught else to interfere between you and it until you have settled the provisions upon that question which you will insert in the new Constitution which you are to frame for the people of Louisiana. (Applause.)

That question, my fellow-citizens, is one that reaches beyond State lines to-day. I believe that our Northern fellow-citizens begin to feel the race sympathy stilling within their breasts. They know that the question which we are trying to solve here is one which

* From *Official Journal of the Proceedings of the Constitutional Convention of the State of Louisiana, 1898* (New Orleans, 1898), pp. 9–10.

imperils not only the integrity of the future government of the State of Louisiana and those of eight or ten other Southern States, but that we, sitting here as a deliberate assembly, and the assemblies of the other Southern States, are to decide whether the presidential office is to be put up for barter and sale on account of the irresponsible character of the constituency in these Southern States. (Applause.) And of the venality and corruption of the delegations which they send to certain national conventions.

Only a few years back, it might have been considered impolite to say what I am now saying, but there are men standing high to-day in the councils of the nation, who have seen the doors of the White House barred to them by the ignorant and corrupt delegations of Southern negroes, and we know that they cannot but feel a sympathy with us in our aspirations and efforts. (Applause.)

My fellow-delegates, let us not be misunderstood! Let us say to the large class of the people of Louisiana who will be disfranchised under any of the proposed limitations of the suffrage, that what we seek to do is undertaken in a spirit, not of hostility to any particular men or set of men, but in the belief that the State should see to the protection of the weaker classes; should guard them against the machinations of those who would use them only to further their own base ends; should see to it that they be not allowed to harm themselves. We owe it to the ignorant, we owe it to the weak, to protect them just as we would protect a little child and prevent it from injuring itself with sharp-edged tools placed in its hands.

May this hall, where, thirty-two years ago, the negro first entered upon the unequal contest for supremacy, and which has been reddened with his blood, now witness the evolution of our organic law which will establish the relations between the races upon an everlasting foundation of right and justice. (Applause.)

Alabama*

And what is it that we do want to do? Why, it is, within the limits imposed by the Federal Constitution, to establish white supremacy in this State.

This is our problem, and we should be permitted to deal with it,

* From *Journal of the Proceedings of the Constitutional Convention of the State of Alabama, 1901* (Montgomery, 1901), pp. 8–15.

unobstructed by outside influences, with a sense of our responsibilities as citizens, and our duty to posterity.

. . . If we would have white supremacy, we must establish it by law—not by force or fraud. If you teach your boy that it is right to buy a vote, it is an easy step for him to learn to use money to bribe or corrupt officials or trustees of any class. If you teach your boy that it is right to steal votes, it is an easy step for him to believe that it is right to steal whatever he may need or greatly desire. The results of such an influence will enter every branch of society; it will reach your bank cashiers, and affect positions of trust in every department; it will ultimately enter your courts, and affect the administration of justice.

I submit it to the intelligent judgment of this Convention that there is no higher duty resting upon us, as citizens and as delegates, than that which requires us to embody in the fundamental law such provisions as will enable us to protect the sanctity of the ballot in every portion of the State.

The justification for whatever manipulation of the ballot that has occurred in this State has been the menace of negro domination. After the war, by force of Federal bayonets, the negro was placed in control of every branch of our government. Inspired and aided by unscrupulous white men, he wasted money, created debts, increased taxes until it threatened to amount to confiscation of our property. While in power, and within a few years, he increased our State debt from a nominal figure to nearly thirty millions of dollars. The right of revolution is always left to every people. Being prostrated by the effects of the war, and unable to take up arms in their own defense, in some portions of this State, white men, greatly in the minority, it is said, resorted to stratagem—used their great intellect to overcome the greater numbers of their black opponents. If so, such a course might be warranted when considered as the right of revolution, and as an act of necessity for self-preservation. But a people cannot always live in a state of revolution. The time comes when, if they would be a free, happy and contented people they must return to a constitutional form of government, where law and order prevail, and where every citizen stands ready to stake his life and his honor to maintain it.

Upon the threshold of our deliberations, I will not undertake to indicate to you how you should solve this new and difficult question of Constitutional reform. At the outset of this movement, I

venture to suggest that delegates should be cautious in undertaking
to define just what provisions would be or should be embodied in
the Constitution; that the new Constitution, when made and placed
before the people for ratification, would be and ought to be the
result of the united action of the Convention; that if one came here
with his mind made up and his Constitution in his pocket, he
would hardly be in a fit condition to confer with his fellow-
delegates on this important subject. I still hold this view. I fail to
appreciate the idea of those who seem to think it the duty of
delegates to this Convention to write out and publish their views
before the Convention meets. Under this plan, we would be liable
to have as many Constitutions as delegates. What the people want,
in my judgment, is an earnest consideration of and consultation
upon these important questions, so that the finished work will
represent the united wisdom and experience of the Convention.

Mississippi is the pioneer State in this movement. In addition to
the payment of a poll tax, there it is provided that only those can
vote who have been duly registered, and only those can register
who can read, or understand when read to them, any clause in the
Constitution. The decision as to who are sufficiently intelligent to
meet the requirements of the understanding clause is exclusively in
the hands of the registrars.

But to this plan, the objection has been urged with force that it
perpetuates the very form of abuse from which we are seeking to
escape; that elections by managers or registrars is not what we
want. Our aim should be for a correction of all evils which
threaten the purity of the ballot and the morals of the people.

The provision adopted in South Carolina requires the payment
of the poll tax, assessed against him for the previous year, six
months before any election, and that the voter shall be duly
registered. To be qualified for registration up to January 1st, 1898,
voters must have been able to read a clause in the Constitution, or
understand or explain it when read by the registration officer; and
all who register subsequent to that time must be able both to read
and write any section of the Constitution, or else show ownership
of property assessed at three hundred dollars or more, and the
payment of all taxes assessed against him and collectable during
the previous year.

In Louisiana and North Carolina, the methods of relief adopted are substantially the same, and require in addition to the poll tax clause, that the voter shall register in accordance with the provisions of the Constitution, and only those are authorized to register who are able to read and write any section of the Constitution in the English language, with the further proviso that no male person who was, on January 1st, 1867, or at any time prior thereto, entitled to vote under the laws of any State in the United States wherein he then resided, and no lineal descendant of any such person shall be denied the right to register and vote at any election by reason of his failure to possess the educational qualifications prescribed, provided he registers within the time limited by the terms of the Constitution, which in Louisiana is about six months, in North Carolina about eight years.

It is contended in defense of this provision, that while in effect, it will exclude the great mass of ignorant negro voters, it does not, in terms, exclude them, and applies generally to all classes of voters, without reference to their race, color or previous condition of servitude; that all negroes who were voters prior to January, 1867,—of whom it was claimed, there were quite a number— could vote, and the descendants—whether slaves or not—of these free negroes, were entitled to vote, and that these were quite numerous. And, on the other hand, that white people born in other countries—emigrants—who cannot read and write, could not vote, nor could white people who were unable to vote in the State in which they lived prior to 1867, unless they were able to read and write. If it be said that this exception permits many more white people to vote than negroes, the answer was that this would be equally true of any proper qualification which might be proposed. It would be true of an educational qualification, and it would be true of a property qualification, the validity of which has never been questioned.

These provisions are justified in law and in morals, because it is said that the negro is not discriminated against on account of his race, but on account of his intellectual and moral condition. There is a difference it is claimed with great force, between the un-educated white man and the ignorant negro. There is in the white man an inherited capacity for government which is wholly wanting in the negro. Before the art of reading and writing was known, the ancestors of the Anglo-Saxon had established an orderly system of government, the basis, in fact, of the one under which we now live. That the negro, on the other hand, is descended from a race lowest in intelligence and moral perception of all the races of men.

2. THE CONVICT-LEASE SYSTEM

*McDonald's Camp, Mississippi**

The convict-lease system ranks among the more ingenious systems of malicious oppression devised by man. Southern judges were given discretionary power to sentence petty thieves to long terms in the penitentiary. Mississippi's infamous "pig law," for example, subjected thieves to a maximum term of five years in prison for stealing swine or cattle. The state profited from the system by leasing the convicts, the majority of whom were Negro, as laborers. A lucrative commission business developed, similar to that which flourished in the pre–Civil War domestic slave trade, as middlemen sometimes assumed responsibility for large numbers of prisoners and subsequently subleased them. Trafficking in convict labor also became a means of paying political debts. "The negro has a constitutional propensity to steal," a South Carolinian said in justification of the system. "The State should farm out such convicts . . . rather than compel taxpayers to support them in idleness."† That more than twice as many Negro criminals died in Southern prisons as whites is clearly understood after reading the following description of life in a Mississippi convict-lease camp in 1887.

McDonald, sub-contractor, has about 196 convicts in Monroe county, 16 miles from Aberdeen, on Birmingham R.R., at railroad work. The convicts are worked on Sundays.

2. They are whipped cruelly and often for slight offenses. Bullwhips and sole-leather straps attached to wooden handles used.

---

* From "Report of the House Committee to Investigate the State Penitentiary, 1887," in *Journal of the House of Representatives of the State of Mississippi, 1888* (Jackson, 1888), Appendix, 12–14.

† Quoted in George Brown Tindall, *South Carolina Negroes, 1877–1900* (Columbia, S.C., 1952), p. 267.

The whipping is applied to the naked flesh. The marks on the convicts show the punishment inflicted.

3. It is generally believed in the camp that one of [the] guards whipped a convict to death. . . .

4. McDonald, Sr., is the most cruel and brutal man I ever knew. He drinks heavily. Some of his "bosses" are very cruel men, while some are kind. McDonald, Sr., whips the convicts with his own hands, and all the bosses whip. I have seen him whip convicts cruelly several times. On one occasion he ordered a convict to carry a sack of oats to the top tier of a pile of oats. The man was too weak to do it. Indeed a stout man could not have performed this task. McDonald whipped the man with an ox-whip, with the whip part doubled back on the pole. He snatched the whip from a wagon-driver standing near.

5. It is the general practice to *curse* the convicts.

6. The convicts are badly clothed; about two thirds, on an average, are bare-footed, and were so during March while I was at the camp. They were worked then on the railroad construction, in the wet, water, mud and cold. Numbers had sore and swollen feet.

7. McDonald has two "shack" houses about two miles apart for the convicts to live in. The convicts are sometimes in two squads, and divided between these houses, and sometimes all are kept in one house.

These houses are made of upright poles stuck in the ground to make the walls. No windows in them, but there are large gaps between the poles 4 to 6 inches wide, all around the sides, nothing to obstruct the wind and cold; houses covered with pine boards; dirt floor. There are two or three planks, one above the other, on which the men sleep. These houses are cold. There is one stove in each, but this does not begin to warm the house. There are no separate bunks, but these plank platforms, one above the other, are put across the house, and the men lie side by side close together, with no division between them. These houses are about 35 or 40 by 75 feet in size, and in one of them the whole number of convicts are sometimes kept. There is no stockade around these "shacks," but guards are placed around them. The convicts eat and sleep in the shackhouse. When they are not worked on Sunday they are kept in the shackhouse. Each convict has one blanket, and lies on a bare plank for a bed.

The convicts are waked at 4:30 o'clock A.M., get their breakfast immediately (it being already prepared for them by convict cooks) and at once are put to work. They rest 40 minutes for dinner. This includes going and coming for dinner and eating the meal. They are then worked until after sundown, and as long as it is light enough for a guard to see how to shoot. They are worked every day, rain or shine, cold or wet.

9. No hospital at all. The sick are left in the "shacks" with the well—sleep right with them on these planks, and when they die, they die among the living. There are always sick convicts on hand. The diet for the sick is just the same as for the well, prepared the same way. There are no nurses for the sick. The shackhouse is filthy and has a horrible stench all the time. No paint, whitewash, or disinfectants are used. The convicts are dirty—if they ever have a chance to wash or cleanse themselves, I do not know it.

10. All the time I was there (about a month) there was no official inspection of the camp. McDonald employed all the guards, and he and his bosses have absolute control. They work men constantly who are complaining of being sick and who are not able to work, and this is an every-day occurrence.

3. RULE BY VIOLENCE

A Negro Journalist's Description of a Lynching Bee Ida B. Wells

Late-nineteenth-century statistics of lynching are unreliable. The "Miscellaneous Items" sections of contemporary Southern newspapers carry sentences like these: "Four negroes were lynched in Grenada last week; also one at Oxford." Whatever the inadequacies of statistics, however, there is no doubt that the late nineteenth and early twentieth centuries were a heyday of Negro murder.

Contemporaries justified "lynching bees," as they called them, for every violation of the Southern etiquette of racial inferiority. Negroes who were supposedly insolent or "uppity," attempted to vote or campaign for office, used abusive language to white women, murdered white men and so on were subject to Judge Lynch's law. The lynching bee *(the term is significant) became a social institution, a community gathering spontaneously mobilized to expiate a sin; and its perpetrator was considered beyond the pale of normal judicial process. When the accused was hung, castrated, shot, tortured, or burned "in a business-like manner," a neighborhood returned to its normal state assured that true justice had been done. Lynching acted as a community catharsis. The supposed rape of white women by Negro men touched the most sensitive psychological nerve of Southern white society and was popularly considered the most common cause for lynch law.* Very few Negroes charged with killing whites or raping white women ever entered courts of law.*

The Negro journalist Ida B. Wells (later Ida Wells Barnett) led an almost single-handed movement to outlaw the crime in the 1890's. Driven from Memphis for her views in 1892, she settled in Chicago and gathered material on Southern lynching from the press. Her Central Anti-Lynching League distributed literature and won the support of Negro women's groups in the North, but did little to effect change. The following description of a human burning is drawn from her classic, A Red Record: Lynchings in the United States, 1892–1893–1894.†

Never in the history of civilization has any Christian people stooped to such shocking brutality and indescribable barbarism as that which characterized the people of Paris, Texas, and adjacent communities on the 1st of February, 1893. The cause of this awful outbreak of human passion was the murder of a four year old child, daughter of a man named Vance. This man, Vance, had been a police officer in Paris for years, and was known to be a man of bad temper, overbearing manner and given to harshly treating the prisoners under his care. He had arrested Smith and, it is said, cruelly mistreated him. Whether or not the murder of his child was an act of fiendish revenge, it has not been shown, but many persons who know of the incident have suggested that the secret of

---

* Studies of the NAACP and the Commission on Interracial Cooperation in the twentieth century demonstrated that only one-sixth of those lynched since the 1880's were accused of sexual crimes, yet the popular myth endured.

† Chicago, 1895, pp. 25–29.

the attack on the child lay in a desire for revenge against its father.

In the same town there lived a Negro, named Henry Smith, a well known character, a kind of roustabout, who was generally considered a harmless, weak-minded fellow, not capable of doing any important work, but sufficiently able to do chores and odd jobs around the houses of the white people who cared to employ him. A few days before the final tragedy, this man, Smith, was accused of murdering Myrtle Vance. The crime of murder was of itself bad enough, and to prove that against Smith would have been amply sufficient in Texas to have committed him to the gallows, but the finding of the child so exasperated the father and his friends, that they at once shamefully exaggerated the facts and declared that the babe had been ruthlessly assaulted and then killed. The truth was bad enough, but the white people of the community made it a point to exaggerate every detail of the awful affair, and to inflame the public mind so that nothing less than immediate and violent death would satisfy the populace. As a matter of fact, the child was not brutally assaulted as the world has been told in excuse for the awful barbarism of that day. Persons who saw the child after its death, have stated, under the most solemn pledge to truth, that there was no evidence of such an assault as was published at that time, only a slight abrasion and discoloration was noticeable and that mostly about the neck. In spite of this fact, so eminent a man as Bishop Haygood deliberately and, it must also appear, maliciously falsified the fact by stating that the child was torn limb from limb, or to quote his own words, "First outraged with demoniacal cruelty and then taken by her heels and torn asunder in the mad wantonness of gorilla ferocity."*

Nothing is farther from the truth than that statement. It is a cold blooded, deliberate, brutal falsehood which this Christian (?) Bishop uses to bolster up the infamous plea that the people of Paris were driven to insanity by learning that the little child had been viciously assaulted, choked to death, and then torn to pieces by a demon in human form. It was a brutal murder, but no more

* Bishop Atticus Green Haygood of the Methodist Episcopal Church, South, president of Emory College and director of the John F. Slater Fund's educational program for Negroes in the South, wrote on lynching in "The Black Shadow in the South," *The Forum,* XVI (October, 1893), 167–175.

brutal than hundreds of murders which occur in this country, and which have been equalled every year in fiendishness and brutality, and for which the death penalty is prescribed by law and inflicted only after the person has been legally adjudged guilty of the crime. Those who knew Smith, believe that Vance had at some time given him cause to seek revenge and that this fearful crime was the outgrowth of his attempt to avenge himself of some real or fancied wrong. That the murderer was known as an imbecile, had no effect whatever upon the people who thirsted for his blood. They determined to make an example of him and proceeded to carry out their purpose with unspeakably greater ferocity than that which characterized the half crazy object of their revenge.

For a day or so after the child was found in the woods, Smith remained in the vicinity as if nothing had happened, and when finally becoming aware that he was suspected, he made an attempt to escape. He was apprehended, however, not far from the scene of his crime and the news flashed across the country that the white Christian people of Paris, Texas and the communities thereabout had deliberately determined to lay aside all forms of law and inaugurate an entirely new form of punishment for the murder. They absolutely refused to make any inquiry as to the sanity or insanity of their prisoner, but set the day and hour when in the presence of assembled thousands they put their helpless victim to the stake, tortured him, and then burned him to death for the delectation and satisfaction of Christian people.

Lest it might be charged that any description of the deeds of that day are exaggerated, a white man's description which was published in the white journals of this country is used. The *New York Sun* of February 2d, 1893, contains an account, from which we make the following excerpt:

PARIS, Tex., Feb. 1, 1893.—Henry Smith, the negro ravisher of 4-year-old Myrtle Vance, has expiated in part his awful crime by death at the stake. Ever since the perpetration of his awful crime this city and the entire surrounding country has been in a wild frenzy of excitement. When the news came last night that he had been captured at Hope, Ark., that he had been identified by B. B. Sturgeon, James T. Hicks, and many other of the Paris searching party, the city was wild with joy over the apprehension of the brute. Hundreds of people poured into the city from the ad-

joining country and the word passed from lip to lip that the punishment of the fiend should fit the crime—that death by fire was the
penalty Smith should pay for the most atrocious murder and terrible
outrage in Texas history. Curious and sympathizing alike, they
came on train and wagons, on horse, and on foot to see if the frail
mind of a man could think of a way to sufficiently punish the
perpetrator of so terrible a crime. Whisky shops were closed,
unruly mobs were dispersed, schools were dismissed by a proclamation from the mayor, and everything was done in a business-like
manner.

About 2 o'clock Friday a mass meeting was called at the courthouse and captains appointed to search for the child. She was
found mangled beyond recognition, covered with leaves and brush
as above mentioned. As soon as it was learned upon the recovery
of the body that the crime was so atrocious the whole town turned
out in the chase. The railroads put up bulletins offering free
transportation to all who would join in the search. Posses went in
every direction, and not a stone was left unturned. Smith was
tracked to Detroit on foot, where he jumped on a freight train and
left for his old home in Hempstead County, Arkansas. To this
county he was tracked and yesterday captured at Clow, a flag
station on the Arkansas & Louisiana railway about twenty miles
north of Hope. Upon being questioned the fiend denied everything,
but upon being stripped for examination his undergarments were
seen to be spattered with blood and a part of his shirt was torn off.
He was kept under heavy guard at Hope last night, and later on
confessed the crime.

This morning he was brought through Texarkana, where 5,000
people awaited the train. . . . At that place speeches were made
by prominent Paris citizens, who asked that the prisoner be not
molested by Texarkana people, but that the guard be allowed to
deliver him up to the outraged and indignant citizens of Paris.
Along the road the train gathered strength from the various towns,
the people crowded upon the platforms and tops of coaches
anxious to see the lynching and the negro who was soon to be
delivered to an infuriated mob.

Arriving here at 12 o'clock the train was met by a surging mass
of humanity 10,000 strong. The negro was placed upon a carnival
float in mockery of a king upon his throne, and, followed by an

immense crowd, was escorted through the city so that all might see
the most inhuman monster known in current history. The line of
march was up Main street to the square, around the square down
Clarksville street to Church street, thence to the open prairies
about 300 yards from the Texas & Pacific depot. Here Smith was
placed upon a scaffold, six feet square and ten feet high, securely
bound, within the view of all beholders. Here the victim was
tortured for fifty minutes by red-hot iron brands thrust against his
quivering body. Commencing at the feet the brands were placed
against him inch by inch until they were thrust against the face.
Then, being apparently dead, kerosene was poured upon him,
cottonseed hulls placed beneath him and set on fire. In less time
than it takes to relate it, the tortured man was wafted beyond the
grave to another fire, hotter and more terrible than the one just
experienced.

Curiosity seekers have carried away already all that was left of
the memorable event, even to pieces of charcoal. The cause of the
crime was that Henry Vance when a deputy policeman, in the
course of his duty was called to arrest Henry Smith for being
drunk and disorderly. The Negro was unruly, and Vance was
forced to use his club. The Negro swore vengeance, and several
times assaulted Vance. In his greed for revenge, last Thursday, he
grabbed up the little girl and committed the crime. The father is
prostrated with grief and the mother now lies at death's door, but
she has lived to see the slayer of her innocent babe suffer the most
horrible death that could be conceived.

Words to describe the awful torture inflicted upon Smith cannot
be found. The Negro, for a long time after starting on the journey
to Paris, did not realize his plight. At last when he was told that he
must die by slow torture he begged for protection. His agony was
awful. He pleaded and writhed in bodily and mental pain. Scarcely
had the train reached Paris than this torture commenced. His
clothes were torn off piecemeal and scattered in the crowd, people
catching the shreds and putting them away as mementos. The
child's father, her brother, and two uncles then gathered about the
Negro as he lay fastened to the torture platform and thrust hot
irons into his quivering flesh. It was horrible—the man dying by
slow torture in the midst of smoke from his own burning flesh.
Every groan from the fiend, every contortion of his body was

cheered by the thickly packed crowd of 10,000 persons. The mass of beings 600 yards in diameter, the scaffold being the center. After burning the feet and legs, the hot irons—plenty of fresh ones being at hand—were rolled up and down Smith's stomach. back, and arms. Then the eyes were burned out and irons were thrust down his throat.

The men of the Vance family have wreaked vengeance, the crowd piled all kinds of combustible stuff around the scaffold, poured oil on it and set it afire. The Negro rolled and tossed out of the mass, only to be pushed back by the people nearest him. He tossed out again, and was roped and pulled back. Hundreds of people turned away, but the vast crowd still looked calmly on. People were here from every part of this section. They came from Dallas, Fort Worth, Sherman, Denison, Bonham, Texarkana, Fort Smith, Ark., and a party of fifteen came from Hempstead County, Arkansas, where he was captured. Every train that came in was loaded to its utmost capacity, and there were demands at many points for special trains to bring the people here to see the unparalleled punishment for an unparalleled crime. When the news of the burning went over the country like wildfire, at every country town anvils boomed forth the announcement.

4. THE LITERATURE OF NEGRO INFERIORITY

A View of the Negro as a Beast*

Pseudo-Darwinism fused with an intense turn-of-the-century Anglo-Saxon racism to produce a babble of literature aimed at proving the Negro innately inferior to the white man. Education, the majority of white Southerners believed, would only "spoil the nigger." They used this rationalization to deprive Negroes equal access to the admittedly poverty-stricken public school system of the South. "I have seen the circus-horse Champion dance," one Southerner wrote. "He danced most infamously, but without doubt

* From *"The Negro A Beast"* or *"In the Image of God"*: *The Reasoner of the Age, the Revelator of the Century! The Bible As It Is! The Negro and His Relation to the Human Family!* . . . (St. Louis, Mo., 1900), pp. 288–292.

*his education had cost him ten thousand lashes. Negroes some-
times learn to read about as well as Champion danced, for their
organs of speech are as unfitted for reading as the horse's legs for
dancing." The following excerpt, published by the American Book
and Bible House, confronts the theory of evolution, "explodes" it,
and suggests the Negro is an ape, not man. A contemporary called
the book "the most sacrilegious ever issued from the press of the
country. . . ." The Negro was no longer considered a child or a
lower order of man—as proslavery writers maintained—but
simply and clearly a beast. Gory illustrations accompanied the
tome.*

As a matter of fact, the Negro was never a slave. To conceive
the design of enslaving an individual we must presuppose that he is
free; the first act of enslavement is to deprive him of his liberty.
This the Negro never had since the creation of man. The Negro is
an ape; hence, his status in the universe, his relation to Man, like
that of every other animal, was fixed irrevocably by God in the
Creation, and no act upon man's part, whether legislative, executive or judicial, can change it. The will of God upon this important
subject, as expressed in those original statutes given man in the
Creation, "Have dominion over the fish of the sea, and over the
fowl of the air, and over every living thing that moveth upon the
earth," is the supreme law of the universe; and in the eyes of this
great law there is not today, there never was and there never can
be on this earth, such a thing as a free Negro. To illustrate:
Suppose a man commits a felony and is arraigned, convicted and
sentenced to prison for a term of years, but makes his escape, flees
to some foreign country, where he lives out his days without being
apprehended. Did that man in his exile live out his days and die—
a free man? No jurist would so decide. From the hour of his
conviction that man lived and died the property of the state. So it
is in this case; under the law of God the Negro, like every other
animal, is the property of man, without reference to whether he is
ever brought in contact with him or not. The mere fact that man in
his blind, criminal folly, declines to exert that control over the
Negro, in common with the rest of the animals, which God
designed him to have and commanded him to exercise, does not
free the Negro, it can only damn man, for his shameless contempt

for God's plan of creation, and for his wanton violation of Divine law.

Man was created free. His personal liberty was implied in his assignment to dominion over all the earth, and over the animals. Hence, man can never be enslaved; but since you cannot enslave the horse or the dog, how can you enslave the ape? They all belong to "one kind of flesh," and were placed under man's dominion in the Creation. This absurd idea that it is optional with man to enslave, or to emancipate the Negro, is another result of placing man and the ape in the same family.

Had the Negro been imported here as an ape, as God made him, and had we maintained only such relations with him as were legitimate, the combined world would have been powerless to have taken the Negro from the South; God would have stood by the south to defend and maintain the relation of master and servant which he established between man and the Negro in Creation. But instead of this, under the influence of the theory of development, combined to a certain extent with the equally anti-scriptural church theory that the Negro is the son of Ham, he was brought here as a "lower race of man"—the Ham race—whom it was legitimate to enslave as a means of civilizing, educating and Christianizing; as might have been expected, an amalgamation at once began; and soon it transformed every farm, and many a home in the southland into a harem; it debauched the youth and manhood of the land; it sent many a fond, devoted wife and mother broken-hearted to the grave; it corrupted the flesh and defiled the earth, and brought our country under the curse of heaven, until God in His wrath and disgust, decreed the so-called "slavery system," which was conceived in crime, brought forth in iniquity, and was based solely on his violated law, should be blotted from the face of the earth; then "angels wept and devils laughed" at the spectacle presented here by a continent drenched in the blood of its sons, hemispheres in mourning, the civilized world in tears. And just so long as we allow the Negro and his amalgamated progeny imposed upon us as "lower races of men," with whom we may associate on terms of social, political and religious equality, just so long will we labor under the curse of God, just so long will these degraded creatures have more or less political dominion over us, just so long will the youth and manhood of the land be debauched by amalgamation, just so long will the chastity of our wives and the virginity of our daughters be subjected to their brutal assaults.

The emancipation of the Negro in the United States was not the work of an anti-slavery party, nor of a pro-slavery party, nor of a Lincoln, nor of a Davis, nor of a Grant, nor of a Lee, nor of "the boys in blue," nor of the "boys in gray." These, one and all, were mere instruments, wielded by our outraged God, to compel us to recognize and respect His plan of Creation, and to live in obedience to His law. Realizing that even the horrors of a four years' war had failed to dissipate our mad dream of forming man, the ape and their amalgamated progeny into "one universal brotherhood," God determined that our depraved lust for social, political and religious equality with the Negro and the mixed-bloods should be fully satisfied. As a result, these degraded creatures were promptly declared free; were at once clothed with the suffrage and recklessly thrust into the legislative, executive and judicial departments of our national and State governments. In the last thirty years the Whites of the South have spent about one hundred millions of dollars on the public schools for the education of the so-called Negroes—these mixed bloods, to say nothing of the millions of dollars that have been spent on colleges, churches, etc. And what is the result? To-day our wives and our daughters are not safe from their brutal assaults beyond the range of our shot-guns. They degrade our religion, demoralize our politics, debauch our youths, plunder our citizens, murder our officials, rape our women, and conduct themselves generally as the curse they are and will always be so long as they are allowed to defile our land with their presence.

*A White Man's Republic Rev. Thomas Dixon, Jr.**

The most prominent propagandist of racism was the Reverend Thomas Dixon, Jr. A Baptist minister from North Carolina, Dixon came to New York City in 1889 to assume charge of the Twenty-third Street Baptist Church. A prolific novelist, he won greatest acclaim for his first book, The Leopard's Spots *(1902)—which*

* From Thomas Dixon, Jr., "Booker T. Washington and the Negro," *The Saturday Evening Post*, CLXXVIII (August 19, 1905), 1–3.

was part of the trilogy used as a basis for D. W. Griffith's famous silent film, Birth of a Nation. *Dixon was convinced that whites and Negroes could never live in harmony, and that the Negro represented the most serious threat to the fulfillment of American democracy. He joined the revitalized group of racists at the turn of the century who tried to revive the colonization movement.*

If allowed to remain here the Negro race in the United States will number 60,000,000 at the end of this century by their present rate of increase. Think of what this means for a moment and you face the gravest problem which ever puzzled the brain of statesman or philosopher. No such problem ever before confronted the white man in his recorded history. It cannot be whistled down by opportunists, politicians, weak-minded optimists or female men. It must be squarely met and fought to a finish.

Several classes of people at present obstruct any serious consideration of this question—the pot-house politician, the ostrich man, the pooh-pooh man, and the benevolent old maid. The politician is still busy over the black man's vote in doubtful States. The pooh-pooh man needs no definition—he was born a fool. The benevolent old maid contributes every time the hat is passed and is pretty sure to do as much harm as good in the long run to any cause. The ostrich man is the funniest of all this group of obstructionists, for he is a man of brains and capacity.

I have a friend of this kind in New York. He got after me the other day somewhat in this fashion:

"What do you want to keep agitating this infernal question for? There's no danger in it unless you stir it. Let it alone. I grant you that the Negro race is a poor, worthless parasite, whose criminal and animal instincts threaten society. But the Negro is here to stay. We must train him. It is the only thing we can do. So what's the use to waste your breath?"

"'But what about the future when you have educated the Negro?" I asked timidly.

"Let the future take care of itself!" the ostrich man snorted. "We live in the present. What's the use to worry about Hell? If I can scramble through this world successfully I'll take my chances with the Hell problem!"

My friend forgets that this was precisely the line of argument of our fathers over the question of Negro slavery. When the constructive statesmen of Virginia (called pessimists and infidels in their day) foresaw the coming baptism of fire and blood ('61 to '65) over the Negro slave, they attempted to destroy the slave trade and abolish slavery. My friend can find his very words in the answers of their opponents. "Let the future take care of itself! The slaves are here and here to stay. Greater evils await their freedom. We need their labor. Let the question alone. There is no danger in it unless you stir it."

The truth which is gradually forcing itself upon thoughtful students of our national life is that no scheme of education or religion can solve the race problem, and that Mr. Booker T. Washington's plan, however high and noble, can only intensify its difficulties.

This conviction is based on a few big fundamental facts, which no pooh-poohing, ostrich-dodging, weak-minded philanthropy or political rant can obscure.

The first one is that no amount of education of any kind, industrial, classical or religious, can make a Negro a white man or bridge the chasm of the centuries which separate him from the white man in the evolution of human civilization.

Expressed even in the most brutal terms of Anglo-Saxon superiority there is here an irreducible fact. It is possibly true, as the Negro, Professor Kelly Miller, claims, that the Anglo-Saxon is "the most arrogant and rapacious, the most exclusive and intolerant race in history." Even so, what answer can be given to his cold-blooded proposition: "Can you change the color of the Negro's skin, the kink of his hair, the bulge of his lip or the beat of his heart with a spelling-book or a machine?"

Whence this physical difference? Its secret lies in the gulf of thousands of years of inherited progress which separates the child of the Aryan from the child of the African.

Judged by this supreme test, what contribution to human progress have the millions of Africans who inhabit this planet made during the past four thousand years? Absolutely nothing. And yet, Mr. Booker T. Washington in a recent burst of eloquence over his educational work boldly declares:

"The Negro race has developed more rapidly in the thirty years of its freedom than the Latin race has in one thousand years of freedom."

Think for a moment of the pitiful puerility of this statement falling from the lips of the greatest and wisest leader the Negro race has yet produced!

Education is the development of that which *is*. The Negro has held the Continent of Africa since the dawn of history, crunching acres of diamonds beneath his feet. Yet he never picked one up from the dust until a white man showed to him its light. His land swarmed with powerful and docile animals, yet he never built a harness, cart or sled. A hunter by necessity, he never made an ax, spear or arrowhead worth preserving beyond the moment of its use. In a land of stone and timber, he never carved a block, sawed a foot of lumber or built a house save of broken sticks and mud, and for four thousand years he gazed upon the sea yet never dreamed a sail.

Who is the greatest Negro that ever lived according to Mr. Booker T. Washington? Through all his books he speaks this man's name with bated breath and uncovered head—"Frederick Douglass of sainted memory!" And what did Saint Frederick do? Spent a life in bombastic vituperation of the men whose genius created the American Republic, wore himself out finally drawing his salary as a Federal officer-holder, and at last achieved the climax of Negro sainthood by marrying a white woman!

I repeat, education is the development of that which *is*. Behold the man whom the rags of slavery once concealed—nine millions strong! This creature, with a racial record of four thousand years of incapacity, half-child, half-animal, the sport of impulse, whim and conceit, pleased with a rattle, tickled with a straw, a being who, left to his will, roams at night and sleeps in the day, whose native tongue has framed no word of love, whose passions once aroused are as the tiger's—equality is the law of our life!—when he is educated and ceases to fill his useful sphere as servant and peasant, what are you going to do with him?

The second big fact which confronts the thoughtful, patriotic American is that the greatest calamity which could possibly befall this Republic would be the corruption of our national character by the assimilation of the Negro race. I have never seen a white man of any brains who disputes this fact. I have never seen a Negro of any capacity who did not deny it.

One thought I would burn into the soul of every young American (and who thinks of a Negro when he says "American"?)—

this: Our Republic is great not by reason of the amount of dirt we possess, or the size of our census roll, but because of the genius of the race of pioneer white freemen who settled this continent, dared the might of kings, and blazed the way through our wilderness for the trembling feet of liberty.

The trouble with Mr. Booker T. Washington's work is that he is silently preparing us for the future heaven of Amalgamation—*or he is doing something equally dangerous,* namely, he is attempting to build a nation inside a nation of two hostile races. In this event he is storing dynamite beneath the pathway of our children—the end at last can only be in bloodshed.

We have spent about $800,000,000 on Negro education since the War. One-half of this sum would have been sufficient to have made Liberia a rich and powerful Negro state. Liberia is capable of supporting every Negro in America. Why not face this question squarely? We are temporizing and playing with it. All our educational schemes are compromises and temporary makeshifts. Mr. Booker T. Washington's work is one of noble aims. A branch of it should be immediately established in Monrovia, the capital of Liberia. A gift of ten millions would do this, and establish a colony of half a million Negroes within two years. They could lay the foundations of a free black republic which within twenty-five years would solve our race problem on the only rational basis within human power. Colonization is not a failure. It has never been tried.

We owe this to the Negro. At present we are deceiving him and allowing him to deceive himself. He hopes and dreams of amalgamation, forgetting that self-preservation is the first law of Nature. Our present attitude of hypocrisy is inhuman toward a weaker race brought to our shores by the sins of our fathers. We owe him a square deal, and we will never give it to him on this Continent.

5. THE ROLE OF THE SUPREME COURT

From 1876 through 1898 the United States Supreme Court curtailed the human protections of the Fourteenth Amendment while it expanded the amendment's meaning in terms of property. The Court's rulings on the Reconstruction amendments helped sanctify individual acts of racial discrimination, permitted Negro segrega-

tion in public facilities, and allowed Negroes to be disfranchised. *The Court was an active participant in the national movement to deny Negroes full equality. As Justice John Marshall Harlan predicted in his dissenting opinion in* Plessy vs. Ferguson, *"the judgment this day rendered will, in time, prove to be quite as pernicious as the decision made by this tribunal in the* Dred Scott case." *What follows are the majority opinions of the Court in the* Civil Rights Cases *of 1883—declaring the Civil Rights Act of 1875 unconstitutional—and in* Plessy vs. Ferguson *(1896), the well-known Louisiana separate-but-equal controversy.*

Civil Rights Cases*

We must not forget that the province and scope of the Thirteenth and Fourteenth Amendments are different; the former simply abolished slavery: the latter prohibited the States from abridging the privileges or immunities of citizens of the United States; from depriving them of life, liberty, or property without due process of law, and from denying to any the equal protection of the laws. The amendments are different, and the powers of Congress under them are different. What Congress has power to do under one, it may not have power to do under the other. Under the Thirteenth Amendment, it has only to do with slavery and its incidents. Under the Fourteenth Amendment, it has power to counteract and render nugatory all State laws and proceedings which have the effect to abridge any of the privileges or immunities of citizens of the United States, or to deprive them of life, liberty or property without due process of law, or to deny to any of them the equal protection of the laws. Under the Thirteenth Amendment, the legislation, so far as necessary or proper to eradicate all forms and incidents of slavery and involuntary servitude, may be direct and primary, operating upon the acts of individuals, whether sanctioned by State legislation or not; under the Fourteenth . . . it must necessarily be, and can only be, corrective in its character, addressed to counteract and afford relief against State regulations or proceedings.

The only question under the present head, therefore, is, whether the refusal to any persons of the accommodations of an inn, or a

* From 109 U.S. 3 (1883).

public conveyance, or a place of public amusement, by an individual, and without any sanction or support from any State law or regulation, does inflict upon such persons any manner of servitude, or form of slavery, as those terms are understood in this country? Many wrongs may be obnoxious to the prohibitions of the Fourteenth Amendment which are not, in any just sense, incidents or elements of slavery. Such, for example, would be the taking of private property without due process of law; or allowing persons who have committed certain crimes (horse stealing, for example) to be seized and hung by the *posse comitatus* without regular trial; or denying to any person, or class of persons, the right to pursue any peaceful avocations allowed to others. What is called class legislation would belong to this category, and would be obnoxious to the prohibitions of the Fourteenth Amendment, but would not necessarily be so to the Thirteenth, when not involving the idea of any subjection of one man to another. The Thirteenth Amendment has respect, not to distinctions of race, or class, or color, but to slavery. The Fourteenth Amendment extends its protection to races and classes, and prohibits any State legislation which has the effect of denying to any race or class, or to any individual, the equal protection of the laws.

Now, conceding, for the sake of the argument, that the admission to an inn, a public conveyance, or a place of public amusement, on equal terms with all other citizens, is the right of every man and all classes of men, is it any more than one of those rights which the states by the Fourteenth Amendment are forbidden to deny to any person? And is the Constitution violated until the denial of the right has some State sanction or authority? Can the act of a mere individual, the owner of the inn, the public conveyance or place of amusement, refusing the accommodation, be justly regarded as imposing any badge of slavery or servitude upon the applicant, or only as inflicting an ordinary civil injury, properly cognizable by the laws of the State, and presumably subject to redress by those laws until the contrary appears?

After giving to these questions all the consideration which their importance demands, we are forced to the conclusion that such an act of refusal has nothing to do with slavery or involuntary servitude, and that if it is violative of any right of the party, his redress is to be sought under the laws of the State; or if those laws are adverse to his rights and do not protect him, his remedy will be found in the corrective legislation which Congress had adopted, or may adopt, for counteracting the effect of State laws, or State action, prohibited by the Fourteenth Amendment. It would be running the slavery argument into the ground to make it apply to every act of discrimination which a person may see fit to make as to the guests he will entertain, or as to the people he will take into his coach or cab or car, to admit to his concert or theatre, or deal with in other matters of intercourse or business. Innkeepers and public carriers, by the laws of all the States, so far as we are aware, are bound, to the extent of their facilities, to furnish proper accommodation to all unobjectionable persons who in good faith apply for them. If the laws themselves make any unjust discrimination, amenable to the prohibitions of the Fourteenth Amendment, Congress has full power to afford a remedy under that amendment and in accordance with it.

When a man has emerged from slavery, and by the aid of beneficent legislation has shaken off the inseparable concomitants of that state, there must be some stage in the progress of his elevation when he takes the rank of a mere citizen, and ceases to be the special favorite of the laws, and when his rights as a citizen, or a man, are to be protected in the ordinary modes by which other men's rights are protected. There were thousands of free colored people in this country before the abolition of slavery, enjoying all the essential rights of life, liberty and property the same as white citizens; yet no one, at that time, thought that it was any invasion of his personal status as a freeman because he was not admitted to all the privileges enjoyed by white citizens, or because he was subjected to discriminations in the enjoyment of accommodations in inns, public conveyances and places of amusement. Mere discriminations on account of race or color were not regarded as badges of slavery. If, since that time, the enjoyment of equal rights in all these respects has become established by constitutional enactment, it is not by force of the Thirteenth Amendment (which merely abolishes slavery), but by force of the [Fourteenth] and Fifteenth Amendments.

On the whole we are of opinion, that no countenance of authority for the passage of the law in question can be found in either the Thirteenth or Fourteenth Amendment of the Constitution; and no other ground of authority for its passage being suggested, it must necessarily be declared void, at least so far as its operation in the several States is concerned.

*Plessy v. Ferguson**

So far, then, as a conflict with the Fourteenth Amendment is concerned, the case reduces itself to the question whether the statute of Louisiana is a reasonable regulation, and with respect to this there must necessarily be a large discretion on the part of the legislature. In determining the question of reasonableness it is at liberty to act with reference to the established usages, customs and traditions of the people, and with a view to the promotion of their comfort, and the preservation of the public peace and good order. Gauged by this standard, we cannot say that a law which authorizes or even requires the separation of the two races in public conveyances is unreasonable, or more obnoxious to the Fourteenth Amendment than the acts of Congress requiring separate schools for colored children in the District of Columbia, the constitutionality of which does not seem to have been questioned, or the corresponding acts of state legislatures.

We consider the underlying fallacy of the plaintiff's argument to consist in the assumption that the enforced separation of the two races stamps the colored race with a badge of inferiority. If this be so, it is not by reason of anything found in the act, but solely because the colored race chooses to put that construction upon it. The argument necessarily assumes that if, as has been more than once the case, and is not unlikely to be so again, the colored race should become the dominant power in the state legislature, and should enact a law in precisely similar terms, it would thereby relegate the white race to an inferior position. We imagine that the white race, at least, would not acquiesce in this assumption. The argument also assumes that social prejudices may be overcome by legislation, and that equal rights cannot be secured to the negro except by an enforced commingling of the two races. We cannot accept this proposition. If the two races are to meet upon terms of social equality, it must be the result of natural affinities, a mutual appreciation of each other's merits and a voluntary consent of

* From *Plessy vs. Ferguson*, 163 U.S. 537 (1896).

individuals. As was said by the Court of Appeals of New York in *People* v. *Gallagher,* 93 N.Y. 438, 448, "this end can neither be accomplished nor promoted by laws which conflict with the general sentiment of the community upon whom they are designed to operate. When the government, therefore, has secured to each of its citizens equal rights before the law and equal opportunities for improvement and progress, it has accomplished the end for which it was organized and performed all of the functions respecting social advantages with which it is endowed." Legislation is powerless to eradicate racial instincts or to abolish distinctions based upon physical differences, and the attempt to do so can only result in accentuating the difficulties of the present situation. If the civil and political rights of both races be equal one cannot be inferior to the other civilly or politically. If one race be inferior to the other socially, the Constitution of the United States cannot put them upon the same plane.

6. THE NEGRO STEREOTYPE

A Negro Vaudeville Sketch*

In the 1840's Frederick Douglass deplored the willingness of whites to treat Negroes as comic figures, "as buffoons." Popular racial attitudes toward Negroes were embodied in the minstrelsy that entertained American audiences from the Jacksonian period through the twentieth century. Negro vaudeville underwent a revival at the turn of the century, as did the bawdy and farcical "coon songs." The importance of the image of the Negro evident in vaudeville material is that it represented, in exaggerated form, the common stereotype of the Negro held throughout the North in the late nineteenth century. The Gentlemen Coons' Parade is a particularly good illustration of this derisive image.

Sketch for Three Characters and Chorus—Black

(*Copyright 1879, by* CLINTON T. DEWITT.)

(SCENE: *A drill room, or street. A dozen, more or less, gather on the stage, dressed and armed in every imaginable way.*)

* *The Gentlemen Coons' Parade* (New York, 1879).

(*Enter* CAPT. HORACE JOHNSON.)

HORACE: Good ebening, gentlemen. Hab my fuss and second lef-
tenants arrived?

ALL: No, sar.

HORACE: Den I shall be put to de 'scruciating trouble to put dem
under arrest.

(*Enter 1st Lieut.* CHARLES ALONZO.)

CHARLES: Bon sure, Captain. (*Saluting.*)

HORACE: Why are you late, sar?

CHARLES: I just done quit dat whitewashing job.

HORACE: You're 'cused, sar.

(*Enter 2d Lieut.* THADDEUS JAMES.)

THAD: Gentlemen, I have de honor. (*Saluting.*)

HORACE: Late, sar.

THAD: Couldn't help it. Washin' dishes.

HORACE: 'Cused, sar. Call de roll.

THAD: (*Pulls out a big book.*) Jeff. Thomps.

A DARKEY: Here, sar.

THAD: Lem. Goodwin.

A DARKEY: Here, sar.

THAD: Dick Honeygum.

A DARKEY: Here, sar.

THAD: Henry Ward Simmons.

A DARKEY: He's out ob de city, sar. Gone to Elizabeth.

THAD: Samuel J. Cipher.

A DARKEY: Here, sar.

THAD: Rutherford B. Haymaker.

A DARKEY: Here, sar.

THAD: John Jacob White.

A DARKEY: Here, sar.

THAD: Sim Dipsy.

A DARKEY: Here, sar.

THAD: Ezra Somerndike.

A DARKEY: Here, sar.

THAD: Wendel Phillips.

A DARKEY: Here, sar.

THAD: William Gumshoe.

A DARKEY: Here, sar.

THAD: All the rest who are not here will please answer, and tole de reason whyfore. Captain, de company am formed. (*Salutes.*)

HORACE: Men ob de company ob gentlemen, I wish to 'spress my thanks for de manner in which you perform de noble duties ob de soldier.

ALL: Hear! Hear!

HORACE: Please don't interrupt your captain. You all said you was here once before. Dar's no use in disrepeating dat fact. I say, gentlemen, dat I am proud ob your soldierly bearing, and ob de 'nificent way in which you 'pear on grand parade. Your actions is beyond all praise. Dar's only one regiment dat can 'proach you, and dat am de seventh! You am de observed ob all observers when you march. Ladies sigh to see your manly forms. Boquets are shied from de windows ob Sullivan street by dar fair occupants. To day, gentlemen, I want you to excel all de rest, as in de past, likewise. And I would say tenthly, that any man caught drinking spruce beer on de march shall be presented wid a club. Fall in!

(*All take places awkwardly.*)

Shoulder arms!

(*Muskets assume various positions.*)

You Jeff! Take dat musket out of dat coon's eye! Order arms!

(*Muskets fall one after another.*)

A DARKEY: Say, hyer, sar, dat's my foot.

HORACE: Steady there. Carry arms!

(*All hold muskets differently.*)

Right shoulder shift arms.

(*More confusion.*)

Shoulder arms.

A DARKEY: Dat's my head, you awkward nigger, you.

HORACE: Charge bayonets!

(*They advance and drive the Captain, 1st and 2d Lieutenants all over the stage.*)

1ST L.: Halt! say, stop that.

2D L.: Halt! you black scoundrels.

HORACE: You nigs, halt I say. Don't you know dat comes under de head ob insurrection? Sure's you born. Halt.

(*They return to their places.*)

Prepare to load. Load.

(*One after another makes an awkward attempt at loading.*)

Shoulder arms. Make ready. Fire!

(*The hammers come down with a click, the darkies dodge, etc.*)

Fooled you dat time. Dem guns are all plugged up, for our mutual protection!

*(The symphony of song is played, and the drill goes on as before.
The song is then sung by all the coons, and at its end they march
off.)*

Gentlemen Coons' Parade

Words by GEO. THATCHER.   Music by W. S. MULLALY.
Copyright, 1878, by FREDERICK BLUME.
Published by permission of FREDERICK BLUME, owner of copyright.
Tempo di Marcia.

1. There's a band of cullered
    citizens,
    Who are known both far
    and near;
    Their Captain's name is
    Horace
    Johnson Morrison St. Clair;
    Array'd in gorgeous uni-
    form,
    He draws his trusty blade,
    He looks divine, he cuts a
    shine,
    In the gentlemen coons' pa-
    rade.

2. There is Charles Alonzo
    Martineau,
    Who has hair sleek as a
    mouse;
    And Thaddeus James St.
    Albans,
    Waiter from the Sturtevant
    House;
    You scarce would recog-
    nize them,
    Since they've their toilets
    made;
    With lots of cash, they cuts
    a shine,
    In the gentlemen coons' pa-
    rade.

Chorus

Order arms! yah! yah!
Shoulder arms! yah! yah!
Keep your toes turn'd out,
And march, don't be afraid;
Order arms! yah! yah!
Shoulder arms! yah! yah!
You'll find no common second-class nigs
In the gentlemen coons' parade. *(Drill.)*
Order arms! yah! yah!
Shoulder arms! yah! yah!
Keep your toes turn'd out,

And march, don't be afraid;
Order arms! yah! yah!
Shoulder arms! yah! yah!
You'll find no common second-class nigs
In the gentlemen coons' parade,
You'll find no common second-class nigs
In the gentlemen coons' parade,
You'll find no common second-class nigs
In the gentlemen coons' parade,
The gentlemen coons' parade,
The gentlemen coons' parade! ...

A Description of Racial Violence in the North William English Walling*

"Abe Lincoln brought the niggers to Springfield and we will drive them out," shouted the mob of whites that wreaked havoc in the Illinois state capitol in August, 1908. In their frenzy, stores were looted, innocent people shot, homes burned and two aged Negro men—one was eighty-four—mutilated and lynched. The immediate cause of the riot was the transfer of George Richardson, a Negro accused of having raped a white woman, from the Springfield jail to one in Bloomington, Illinois. The woman, Mrs. Hallam, later confessed that Richardson hadn't assaulted her. When the craze ended, however, only one rioter was convicted— and she committed suicide.

William English Walling—journalist, social reformer, socialist, writer—came to Springfield from Chicago to survey the wreckage and was appalled to find no sense of guilt in the town. His famous essay, "The Race War in the North," called for a revival of abolitionist spirit and set in motion the planning which led to the founding of the NAACP in 1909.

"LINCOLN freed you, we'll show you where you belong," was one of the cries with which the Springfield mob set about to drive the negroes from town. The mob was composed of several thousand of Springfield's white citizens, while other thousands, includ-

* "The Race War in the North," *The Independent*, LXV (September 3, 1908), 529–534.

ing many women and children, and even prosperous business men in automobiles, calmly looked on, and the rioters proceeded hour after hour and on two days in succession to make deadly assaults on every negro they could lay their hands on, to sack and plunder their houses and stores, and to burn and murder on favorable occasion.

The American people have been fairly well informed by their newspapers of the action of that mob; they have also been told of certain alleged political and criminal conditions in Springfield and of the two crimes in particular which are offered by the mob itself as sufficient explanation why six thousand peaceful and innocent negroes should be driven by the fear of their lives from a town where some of them have lived honorably for half a hundred years. We have been assured by more cautious and indirect defenders of Springfield's populace that there *was* an exceptionally criminal element among the negroes encouraged by the bosses of both political parties. And now, after a few days of discussion, we are satisfied with these explanations, and demand only the punishment of those who took the most active part in the destruction of life and property. Assuming that there were exceptionally provocative causes for complaint against the negroes, we have closed our eyes to the whole awful and menacing truth—that a large part of the white population of Lincoln's home, supported largely by the farmers and miners of the neighboring towns, have initiated a permanent warfare with the negro race.

We do not need to be informed at great length of the character of this warfare. It is in all respects like that of the South, on which it is modeled. Its significance is threefold. First, that it has occurred in an important and historical Northern town; then, that the negroes, constituting scarcely more than a tenth of the population, in this case could not possibly endanger the "supremacy" of the whites, and, finally, that the public opinion of the North, notwithstanding the fanatical, blind and almost insane hatred of the negro so clearly shown by the mob, is satisfied that there were "mitigating circumstances," not for the mob violence, which, it is agreed, should be punished to the full extent of the law, but for the race hatred, which is really the cause of it all. If these outrages had happened thirty years ago, when the memories of Lincoln, Garrison and Wendell Phillips were still fresh, what would not have happened in the North? Is there any doubt that the whole country would have been aflame, that all flimsy explanations and "mitigating circumstances" would have been thrown aside, and that the people of Springfield would have had to prove to the nation why they proposed to drive the negroes out, to hold a whole race responsible for a handful of criminals, and to force it to an inferior place on the social scale?

For the underlying motive of the mob and of that large portion of Springfield's population that has long said that "something was bound to happen," and now approves of the riot and proposes to complete its purpose by using other means to drive as many as possible of the remaining two-thirds of the negroes out of town, was confessedly to teach the negroes their place and to warn them that too many could not obtain shelter under the favorable traditions of Lincoln's home town. I talked to many of them the day after the massacre and found no difference of opinion on the question. "Why, the niggers came to think they were as good as we are!" was the final justification offered, not once, but a dozen times.

On the morning after the first riot I was in Chicago and took the night train for Springfield, where I have often visited and am almost at home. On arriving in the town I found that the rioting had been continued thruout the night, and was even feared for the coming evening, in spite of the presence of nearly the whole militia of the State. Altho we visited the Mayor, military headquarters, the leading newspaper, and some prominent citizens, my wife and I gave most of our attention to the hospital, the negro quarters and the jail.

We at once discovered, to our amazement, that Springfield had no shame. She stood for the action of the mob. She hoped the rest of the negroes might flee. She threatened that the movement to drive them out would continue. I do not speak of the leading citizens, but of the masses of the people, of workingmen in the shops, the storekeepers in the stores, the drivers, the men on the street, the wounded in the hospitals and even the notorious "Joan of Arc" of the mob, Kate Howard, who had just been released from arrest on $4,000 bail. [She has since committed suicide. —*Editor*.] The *Illinois State Journal* of Springfield exprest the prevailing feeling even on its editorial page:

"While all good citizens deplore the consequences of this out-burst of the mob spirit, many even of these consider the outburst was *inevitable,* at some time, from existing conditions, needing only an overt act, such as that of Thursday night, to bring it from latent existence into active operation. The implication is clear that conditions, not the populace, were to blame and that many good citizens could find no other remedy than that applied by the mob. It was not the fact of the whites' hatred toward the negroes, but of the negroes' own misconduct, general inferiority or unfitness for free institutions that were at fault."

On Sunday, August 16th, the day after the second lynching, a leading white minister recommended the Southern disfranchise-ment scheme as a remedy for *negro* (!) lawlessness, while all four ministers who were quoted in the press proposed swift "justice" for *the negroes,* rather than recommending true Christianity, democ-racy and brotherhood to the whites. Even the Governor's state-ment of the situation, strong as it was on the whole, was tainted in one place with a concession to Springfield opinion. He said that Burton, the first negro lynched, was killed after he had incensed the crowd by firing into it to protect his home from incendiaries. But when Burton's home was attacked there had already been considerable shooting between the blacks and the whites. More-over, according to his daughters, men had entered the house and threatened him with an axe and other weapons, while his firing of buckshot at random into a mob is by no means necessarily a murderous procedure. The Governor made, then, an understate-ment of the character of the mob, suggesting that the negroes had lost their heads and were accepting the mob's challenge to war. It is probable that Burton was defending not his home, but his life.

Either the spirit of the abolitionists, of Lincoln and of Lovejoy must be revived and we must come to treat the negro on a plane of absolute political and social equality, or Vardaman and Tillman will soon have transferred the race war to the North.

Already Vardaman boasts "that such sad experiences as Spring-field is undergoing will doubtless cause the people of the North to look with more toleration upon the methods employed by the Southern people."

The day these methods become general in the North every hope of political democracy will be dead, other weaker races and classes will be persecuted in the North as in the South, public education will undergo an eclipse, and American civilization will await either a rapid degeneration or another profounder and more revolutionary civil war, which shall obliterate not only the remains of slavery but all the other obstacles to a free democratic evolution that have grown up in its wake.

Yet who realizes the seriousness of the situation, and what large and powerful body of citizens is ready to come to their aid?

CHAPTER VI

VOICES OF PROTEST, MODERATION, ACCOMMODATION

❁ ❁

What we need is a revival of the spirit *of democracy, both South and North.*

RAY STANNARD BAKER, 1909

―――――――

The brutality of late-nineteenth-century thought and action mobilized men of conscience to oppose it—Negroes and whites, Northerners and Southerners. *Ad hoc* Negro meetings and conventions were called, similar in style to the Negro conventions of the abolitionist era and those of Reconstruction, to denounce the Supreme Court's decisions. "O for a Supreme Court of the United States which shall be as true to the claims of humanity as the Supreme Court formerly was to the demands of slavery!" Frederick Douglass said after the Civil Rights decision was handed down. Negroes in many Southern cities boycotted segregated streetcars and denounced lynch law. In 1890 the Afro-American League was formed, through the initiative of Negro newspaper editor T. Thomas Fortune, at a national gathering of Negro leaders in Chicago. The League, and its successor, the Afro-American Council, represented the initial stages of mass Negro opposition to burgeoning American racism.

Yet the Council and League were wracked by internal dissension throughout the two short decades of their existence. The major problems revolved around the style, form, and tactics of Negro protest. Booker T. Washington and his supporters who attempted to control the League insisted that Negro demands be couched in the accommodationist tones that had made Washington's message appealing to white philanthropy. The white world "recognized gladly," as W. E. B. Du Bois noted, a modest program of racial advancement modestly proclaimed—and Washington used his enormous energy and ability to exploit this feeling to build a political and economic empire for himself of considerable proportions. For those Negroes unwilling to accept anything less than full racial equality in American society, Washington's tune seemed a threnody. Du Bois, William Monroe Trotter, George Forbes, and others denounced the "Tuskegee Machine." They insisted that Washington's program questioned the essential manhood of Negro America. If Washington's statesmanship was set in the tradition of the shrewdness of ante-bellum slave house-servants, his opponents' methods were rooted in the uncompromising demands for racial justice typical of Negro abolitionist leaders. Washington was the latter-day embodiment of the crafty folk hero "John"—the trusted Negro slave who generally manipulated and outwitted "Old Massa"; his critics were the ideological descendants of Frederick Douglass. (I)

An all-Negro movement of moral protest, no matter how heroic or aggressive, could make little headway in an America where money and power were overwhelmingly the possessions of white men. Race progress at the turn of the century necessarily demanded interracial involvement and commitment. The white world had to recognize that the position of Negroes called into question the very meaning of American democracy. To permit the degradation of any citizen, to silently allow constitutional provisions to atrophy for any group, to have a double standard of freedom, was to concede the failure of the democratic system. The heightened spirit of social justice that pervaded the Progressive Era focused national attention on racial inequities. A significant minority of socially conscious white reformers, motivated by a broad concern with America's destiny, joined forces with militant Negroes to insist on Negro equality. The creation of the NAACP was the culmination of their efforts. The confluence of interest in social democracy with civil rights was clearly evident in the writings of Ray Stannard Baker. " 'To science there is no poison; to botany no weed; to chemistry no dirt,' " he quoted Emerson as saying. "To this we may add: 'To democracy, no negro.' " (2)

If white racial liberalism remained a minority movement in the North, it had even less stature in the South. When the Southern clergyman and child labor reformer, Edgar Gardner Murphy, convened what was to be a seminal conference on race relations at Montgomery, Alabama, in 1900, it served as a platform for airing the dominant themes of Southern racism. In unending tautophony speakers arose at the misnamed Southern Society for the Promotion of the Study of Race Conditions and Problems to proclaim the Negro biologically, politically, morally, economically, and socially inferior to the white man. The tone of the conference was set by the keynote address of Hilary A. Herbert, former Confederate colonel, congressman from Alabama, and prominent Montgomery lawyer. "The Negro is not the equal of the white man," Herbert concluded. "Science and history alike proclaim this truth." Others predicted race extinction: "In my opinion," a University of Virginia professor augured, "nothing is more certain than that the Negro will go as the Tasmanian and the Carib have gone. . . ." No clearer evidence of the absence of Southern moderation at the turn of the century is needed than the speeches delivered at the Montgomery Conference. In this atmosphere Southerners like Atticus Green Haygood, J. L. M. Curry, Thomas Nelson Page, and Edgar Gardner Murphy—who merely supported a minimal program of public school education for Negroes—were considered radicals.

But Progressivism was a national movement and, as the spirit of social reform intensified in the early twentieth century, it increasingly affected the South. The most advanced racial views were centered in the very small group of Southern social workers and liberal clergymen responsive to the call of the social gospel. The dominant conviction of this group was a faith in the religious sanctity of each human soul; to brutalize a single man, they said, was to brutalize mankind: "The most marked characteristic of the thought of the first decade of this century is a new appreciation of the value and sacredness of the person," W. D. Weatherford noted at the first Southern Sociological Congress in 1912. The annual meetings of the Congress offered other white Southerners the opportunity to speak out on racial affairs, and respect for the holiness of the individual motivated Will Alexander to organize, after World War I, the Commission on Interracial Corporation. The Interracial Commission attempted to promote racial harmony in the South for a quarter century thereafter. (3)

1. SHIFTING MOOD AND TACTICS

Atlanta Exposition Address Booker T. Washington*

Booker T. Washington was the most powerful Negro leader in American history. Under his direction Tuskegee became the Negro's race capital. Everyone who met Washington was impressed with his thoroughness and shrewd ability to analyze individuals. He carefully fostered alliances with some of the wealthiest industrial and financial magnates of the nation and his voluminous correspondence demonstrated that he was keenly aware of the consequences of every action he took, every word and phrase he used in his speeches. As Will Alexander once said, "Booker Washington never overlooked anything."

Washington was a man confronted with an almost impossible ideological riddle. He had to devise a program that assuaged the consciences and mores of Northern and Southern white leadership during a period of violent race hatred and, at the same time, satisfied the demands of the Negro people. These goals were antithetical and he bartered away the Negro's voting and constitutional rights in exchange for economic support from industrial philanthrophy. Washington, curiously, didn't realize he had discovered the solution to the enigma until he experienced the effusive white response to his Atlanta Exposition Address in 1895; and his deferential words yielded cornucopia unimaginable—as Du Bois accurately described it: "Not only did presidents of the United States consult Booker Washington, but governors and congressmen; philanthropists conferred with him, scholars wrote to him. Tuskegee became a vast information bureau and center of advice. It was not merely passive in these matters but . . . suave and far-

* "Atlanta Exposition Address," in Booker T. Washington, *Up From Slavery: An Autobiography* (New York, 1901), pp. 153–158.

seeing[;] active efforts were made to concentrate influence at Tuskegee. After a time almost no Negro institution could collect funds without the recommendation or acquiescence of Mr. Washington. Few political appointments were made anywhere in the United States without his consent. Even the careers of rising young men were very often determined by his advice and certainly his opposition was fatal."

MR. PRESIDENT AND GENTLEMEN OF THE BOARD OF DIRECTORS
AND CITIZENS.

One-third of the population of the South is of the Negro race. No enterprise seeking the material, civil, or moral welfare of this section can disregard this element of our population and reach the highest success. I but convey to you, Mr. President and Directors, the sentiment of the masses of my race when I say that in no way have the value and manhood of the American Negro been more fittingly and generously recognized than by the managers of this magnificent Exposition at every stage of its progress. It is a recognition that will do more to cement the friendship of the two races than any occurrence since the dawn of our freedom.

Not only this, but the opportunity here afforded will awaken among us a new era of industrial progress. Ignorant and inexperienced, it is not strange that in the first years of our new life we began at the top instead of at the bottom; that a seat in Congress or the state legislature was more sought than real estate or industrial skill; that the political convention of stump speaking had more attractions than starting a dairy farm or truck garden.

A ship lost at sea for many days suddenly sighted a friendly vessel. From the mast of the unfortunate vessel was seen a signal, "Water, water; we die of thirst!" The answer from the friendly vessel at once came back, "Cast down your bucket where you are." A second time the signal, "Water, water; send us water!" ran up from the distressed vessel, and was answered, "Cast down your bucket where you are." And a third and fourth signal for water was answered, "Cast down your bucket where you are." The captain of the distressed vessel, at last heeding the injunction, cast down his bucket, and it came up full of fresh, sparkling water from the mouth of the Amazon River. To those of my race who depend on bettering their condition in a foreign land or who underestimate the importance of cultivating friendly relations with the Southern white man, who is their next-door neighbour, I would say: "Cast down your bucket where you are"—cast it down in making friends in every manly way of the people of all races by whom we are surrounded.

Cast it down in agriculture, mechanics, in commerce, in domestic service, and in the professions. And in this connection it is well to bear in mind that whatever other sins the South may be called to bear, when it comes to business, pure and simple, it is in the South that the Negro is given a man's chance in the commercial world, and in nothing is this Exposition more eloquent than in emphasizing this chance. Our greatest danger is that in the great leap from slavery to freedom we may overlook the fact that the masses of us are to live by the productions of our hands, and fail to keep in mind that we shall prosper in proportion as we learn to dignify and glorify common labour and put brains and skill into the common occupations of life; shall prosper in proportion as we learn to draw the line between the superficial and the substantial, the ornamental gewgaws of life and the useful. No race can prosper till it learns that there is as much dignity in tilling a field as in writing a poem. It is at the bottom of life we must begin, and not at the top. Nor should we permit our grievances to overshadow our opportunities.

To those of the white race who look to the incoming of those of foreign birth and strange tongue and habits for the prosperity of the South, were I permitted I would repeat what I say to my own race, "Cast down your bucket where you are." Cast it down among the eight millions of Negroes whose habits you know, whose fidelity and love you have tested in days when to have proved treacherous meant the ruin of your firesides. Cast down your bucket among these people who have, without strikes and labour wars, tilled your fields, cleared your forests, builded your railroads and cities, and brought forth treasures from the bowels of the earth, and helped make possible this magnificent representation of the progress of the South. Casting down your bucket among my people, helping and encouraging them as you are doing on these grounds, and to education of head, hand, and heart, you will find that they will buy your surplus land, make blossom the waste places in your fields, and run your factories. While doing this, you can be sure in the future, as in the past, that you and your families will be surrounded by the most patient, faithful, law-abiding, and unresentful people that the world has seen. As we have proved our loyalty to you in the past, in nursing your children, watching by the sickbed of your mothers and fathers, and often following them with tear-dimmed eyes to their graves, so in the future, in our humble way, we shall stand by you with a devotion that no foreigner can approach, ready to lay down our lives, if need be, in defence of yours, interlacing our industrial, commercial, civil, and religious life with yours in a way that shall make the interests of both races one. In all things that are purely social we can be as separate as the fingers, yet one as the hand in all things essential to mutual progress.

There is no defence or security for any of us except in the highest intelligence and development of all. If anywhere there are efforts tending to curtail the fullest growth of the Negro, let these efforts be turned into stimulating, encouraging, and making him the most useful and intelligent citizen. Effort or means so invested will pay a thousand per cent interest. These efforts will be twice blessed—"blessing him that gives and him that takes."

There is no escape through law of man or God from the inevitable:—

> The laws of changeless justice bind
> Oppressor with oppressed;
> And close as sin and suffering joined
> We march to fate abreast.

Nearly sixteen millions of hands will aid you in pulling the load upward, or they will pull against you the load downward. We shall constitute one-third and more of the ignorance and crime of the South, or one-third its intelligence and progress; we shall contribute one-third to the business and industrial prosperity of the South, or we shall prove a veritable body of death, stagnating, depressing, retarding every effort to advance the body politic.

Gentlemen of the Exposition, as we present to you our humble effort at an exhibition of our progress, you must not expect overmuch. Starting thirty years ago with ownership here and there in a few quilts and pumpkins and chickens (gathered from miscellane-

ous sources),* remember the path that has led from these to the
inventions and production of agricultural implements, buggies,
steam-engines, newspapers, books, statuary, carving, paintings,
the management of drug-stores and banks, has not been trodden
without contact with thorns and thistles. While we take pride in
what we exhibit as a result of our independent efforts, we do not
for a moment forget that our part in this exhibition would fall far
short of your expectations but for the constant help that has come
to our educational life, not only from the Southern states, but
especially from Northern philanthropists, who have made their
gifts a constant stream of blessing and encouragement.

The wisest among my race understand that the agitation of
questions of social equality is the extremest folly, and that progress
in the enjoyment of all the privileges that will come to us must be
the result of severe and constant struggle rather than of artificial
forcing. No race that has anything to contribute to the markets of
the world is long in any degree ostracized. It is important and right
that all privileges of the law be ours, but it is vastly more important that we be prepared for the exercises of these privileges. The
opportunity to earn a dollar in a factory just now is worth infinitely
more than the opportunity to spend a dollar in an opera-house.

In conclusion, may I repeat that nothing in thirty years has
given us more hope and encouragement, and drawn us so near to
you of the white race, as this opportunity offered by the Exposition; and here bending, as it were, over the altar that represents the
results of the struggles of your race and mine, both starting
practically empty-handed three decades ago. I pledge that in your
effort to work out the great and intricate problem which God has
laid at the doors of the South, you shall have at all times the
patient, sympathetic help of my race; only let this be constantly in
mind, that, while from representations in these buildings of the
product of field, of forest, of mine, of factory, letters, and art,
much good will come, yet far above and beyond material benefits
will be that higher good, that, let us pray God, will come, in a
blotting out of sectional differences and racial animosities and
suspicions, in a determination to administer absolute justice, in a
willing obedience among all classes to the mandates of law. This,

* Note the self-denigration of this statement—an allusion to Negro
thievery.

then, coupled with our material prosperity, will bring into our beloved South a new heaven and a new earth.

W. E. B. Du Bois and the Niagara Movement

"In other periods of intensified prejudice all the Negro's tendency to self-assertion has been called forth; at this period a policy of submission is advocated." So judged W. E. B. Du Bois in his celebrated essay, "Of Mr. Washington and Others."

The personalities of the two Negro leaders were markedly in contrast: Washington the Southern slave, Du Bois the free Northern Negro; Washington the young boy who worked in the mines, cleaned stairs and latrines, slept in the streets to acquire an education, Du Bois the brilliant intellectual, recipient of scholarships, Harvard Ph.D.; Washington the organization man, Du Bois the individualist supreme; Washington the self-effacing spokesman of a humble people, Du Bois the militant advocate of a proud race, a man who lived fourscore years and fifteen and never doubted the self-proclaimed superiority of his own ego; Washington the politician, Du Bois the poet and mystic. It was inevitable that such men, and their racial ideologies, would clash.

The Niagara Movement was the institutional expression of these differences. From 1905 to 1909—when most supporters of Niagara principles moved into the NAACP—Du Bois and other leading Negro intellectuals and professionals conducted a loud and caustic propaganda war against Washington, his power and his principles. As Du Bois put it, "We talked some of the plainest English that has been given voice to by black men in America." Although their practical accomplishments were few, Washington's opponents touched the most crucial issues of American race relations and raised questions which our society is yet attempting to answer. The spirit of the confrontation is evident in the following documents. The "Declaration of Principles" of the Niagara Movement and the resolutions of the 1906 barefooted pilgrimage to John Brown's grave are offered first. Du Bois wrote "A Litany at Atlanta" as his response to a violent four-day race riot in September, 1906. "The Riddle of the Sphinx" ranks with Du Bois's "The Souls of White Folk" as perhaps the clearest expression of his rage against white America.

The Niagara Movement: Declaration of Principles*

The members of the conference, known as the Niagara Movement, assembled in annual meeting at Buffalo, July 11th, 12th, and 13th, 1905,

Progress

congratulate the Negro-Americans on certain undoubted evidences of progress in the last decade, particularly the increase of intelligence, the buying of property, the checking of crime, the uplift in home life, the advance in literature and art, and the demonstration of constructive and executive ability in the conduct of great religious, economic and educational institutions.

Suffrage

At the same time, we believe that this class of American citizens should protest emphatically and continually against the curtailment of their political rights. We believe in manhood suffrage; we believe that no man is so good, intelligent or wealthy as to be entrusted wholly with the welfare of his neighbor.

Civil Liberty

We believe also in protest against the curtailment of our civil rights. All American citizens have the right to equal treatment in places of public entertainment according to their behavior and deserts.

Economic Opportunity

We especially complain against the denial of equal opportunities to us in economic life; in the rural districts of the South this amounts to peonage and virtual slavery; all over the South it tends to crush labor and small business enterprises; and everywhere American prejudice, helped often by iniquitous laws, is making it more difficult for Negro-Americans to earn a decent living.

Common school education should be free to all American children and compulsory. High school training should be adequately provided for all, and college training should be the monopoly of no class

* "Declaration of Principles" of the Niagara Movement, 1905 (Schomburg Collection).

or race in any section of our common country. We believe that, in defense of our own institutions, the United States should aid common school education, particularly in the South, and we especially recommend concerted agitation to this end. We urge an increase in public high school facilities in the South, where the Negro-Americans are almost wholly without such provisions. We favor well-equipped trade and technical schools for the training of artisans, and the need of adequate and liberal endowment for a few institutions of higher education must be patent to sincere well-wishers of the race.

Education

We demand upright judges in courts, juries selected without discrimination on account of color and the same measure of punishment and the same efforts at reformation for black as for white offenders. We need orphanages and farm schools for dependent children, juvenile reformatories for delinquents, and the abolition of the dehumanizing convict-lease system.

Courts

We note with alarm the evident retrogression in this land of sound public opinion on the subject of manhood rights, republican government and human brotherhood, and we pray God that this nation will not degenerate into a mob of boasters and oppressors, but rather will return to the faith of the fathers, that all men were created free and equal, with certain unalienable rights.

Public Opinion

We plead for health—for an opportunity to live in decent houses and localities, for a chance to rear our children in physical and moral cleanliness.

Health

We hold up for public execration the conduct of two opposite classes of men: The practice among employers of importing ignorant Negro-American laborers in emergencies, and then affording them neither protection nor permanent employment; and the practice of labor unions in proscribing and boycotting and oppressing thousands of their fellow-toilers, simply because they are black. These methods have accentuated and will accentuate the

Employers and Labor Unions

war of labor and capital, and they are disgraceful to both sides.

Protest

We refuse to allow the impression to remain that the Negro-American assents to inferiority, is submissive under oppression and apologetic before insults. Through helplessness we may submit, but the voice of protest of ten million Americans must never cease to assail the ears of their fellows, so long as America is unjust.

Color-Line

Any discrimination based simply on race or color is barbarous, we care not how hallowed it be by custom, expediency, or prejudice. Differences made on account of ignorance, immorality, or disease are legitimate methods of fighting evil, and against them we have no word of protest; but discriminations based simply and solely on physical peculiarities, place of birth, color of skin, are relics of that unreasoning human savagery of which the world is and ought to be thoroughly ashamed.

"Jim Crow"
Cars

We protest against the "Jim Crow" car, since its effect is and must be to make us pay first-class fare for third-class accommodations, render us open to insults and discomfort and to crucify wantonly our manhood, womanhood and self-respect.

Soldiers

We regret that this nation has never seen fit adequately to reward the black soldiers who, in its five wars, have defended their country with their blood, and yet have been systematically denied the promotions which their abilities deserve. And we regard as unjust, the exclusion of black boys from the military and navy training schools.

War
Amendments

We urge upon Congress the enactment of appropriate legislation for securing the proper enforcement of those articles of freedom, the thirteenth, fourteenth and fifteenth amendments of the Constitution of the United States.

We repudiate the monstrous doctrine that the oppressor should be the sole authority as to the rights of the oppressed.

The Negro race in America stolen, ravished and

Oppression

degraded, struggling up through difficulties and oppression, needs sympathy and receives criticism; needs help and is given hindrance, needs protection and is given mob-violence, needs justice and is given charity, needs leadership and is given cowardice and apology, needs bread and is given a stone. This nation will never stand justified before God until these things are changed.

The Church

Especially are we surprised and astonished at the recent attitude of the church of Christ—on the increase of a desire to bow to racial prejudice, to narrow the bounds of human brotherhood, and to segregate black men in some outer sanctuary. This is wrong, unchristian and disgraceful to the twentieth century civilization.

Agitation

Of the above grievances we do not hesitate to complain, and to complain loudly and insistently. To ignore, overlook, or apologize for these wrongs is to prove ourselves unworthy of freedom. Persistent manly agitation is the way to liberty, and toward this goal the Niagara Movement has started and asks the co-operation of all men of all races.

Help

At the same time we want to acknowledge with deep thankfulness the help of our fellowmen from the abolitionist down to those who to-day still stand for equal opportunity and who have given and still give of their wealth and of their poverty for our advancement.

Duties

And while we are demanding, and ought to demand, and will continue to demand the rights enumerated above, God forbid that we should ever forget to urge corresponding duties upon our people:

> The duty to vote.
> The duty to respect the rights of others.
> The duty to work.
> The duty to obey the laws.
> The duty to be clean and orderly.
> The duty to send our children to school.

The duty to respect ourselves, even as we respect others.

This statement, complaint and prayer we submit to the American people, and Almighty God.

*"The Land of the Thief—and the Home of the Slave"**

The men of the Niagara Movement, coming from the toil of the year's hard work, and pausing a moment from the earning of their daily bread, turn toward the nation and again ask in the name of ten million the privilege of a hearing. In the past year the work of the Negro hater has flourished in the land. Step by step the defenders of the rights of American citizens have retreated. The work of stealing the black man's ballot has progressed and the fifty and more representatives of stolen votes still sit in the nation's capital. Discrimination in travel and public accommodation has so spread that some of our weaker brethren are actually afraid to thunder against color discrimination as such and are simply whispering for ordinary decencies.

Against this the Niagara Movement eternally protests. We will not be satisfied to take one jot or tittle less than our full manhood rights. We claim for ourselves every single right that belongs to a freeborn American, political, civil, and social; and until we get these rights we will never cease to protest and assail the ears of America. The battle we wage is not for ourselves alone, but for all true Americans. It is a fight for ideals, lest this, our common fatherland, false to its founding, become in truth the land of the Thief and the home of the Slave—a by-word and a hissing among the nations for its sounding pretensions and pitiful accomplishment.

Never before in the modern age has a great and civilized folk threatened to adopt so cowardly a creed in the treatment of its fellow-citizens, born and bred on its soil. Stripped of verbiage and subterfuge and in its naked nastiness, the new American creed says: fear to let black men even try to rise lest they become the equals of the white. And this is the land that professes to follow Jesus Christ. The blasphemy of such a course is only matched by its cowardice.

In detail our demands are clear and unequivocal. First, we

* From W. E. B. Du Bois, *Dusk of Dawn* (New York, 1940), pp. 89–91.

would vote; with the right to vote goes everything: freedom, manhood, the honor of your wives, the chastity of your daughters, the right to work, and the chance to rise, and let no man listen to those who deny this.

We want full manhood suffrage, and we want it now, henceforth and forever.

Second. We want discrimination in public accommodation to cease. Separation in railway and street cars, based simply on race and color, is un-American, undemocratic, and silly. We protest against all such discrimination.

Third. We claim the right of freemen to walk, talk, and be with them that wish to be with us. No man has a right to choose another man's friends, and to attempt to do so is an impudent interference with the most fundamental human privilege.

Fourth. We want the laws enforced against rich as well as poor; against Capitalist as well as Laborer; against white as well as black. We are not more lawless than the white race, we are more often arrested, convicted and mobbed. We want justice even for criminals and outlaws. We want the Constitution of the country enforced. We want Congress to take charge of the Congressional elections. We want the Fourteenth Amendment carried out to the letter and every State disfranchised in Congress which attempts to disfranchise its rightful voters. We want the Fifteenth Amendment enforced and no State allowed to base its franchise simply on color.

The failure of the Republican Party in Congress at the session just closed to redeem its pledge of 1904 with reference to suffrage conditions at the South seems a plain, deliberate, and premeditated breach of promise, and stamps that party as guilty of obtaining votes under false pretense.

Fifth. We want our children educated. The school system in the country districts of the South is a disgrace and in few towns and cities are the Negro schools what they ought to be. We want the national government to step in and wipe out illiteracy in the South. Either the United States will destroy ignorance, or ignorance will destroy the United States.

And when we call for education, we mean real education. We believe in work. We ourselves are workers, but work is not necessarily education. Education is the development of power and ideal. We want our children trained as intelligent human beings should be, and we will fight for all time against any proposal to educate black boys and girls simply as servants and underlings, or simply for the use of other people. They have a right to know, to think, to aspire.

These are some of the chief things which we want. How shall we get them? By voting where we may vote; by persistent, unceasing agitation; by hammering at the truth; by sacrifice and work.

We do not believe in violence, neither in the despised violence of the raid nor the lauded violence of the soldier, nor the barbarous violence of the mob; but we do believe in John Brown, in that incarnate spirit of justice, that hatred of a lie, that willingness to sacrifice money, reputation, and life itself on the altar of right. And here on the scene of John Brown's martyrdom, we reconsecrate ourselves, our honor, our property to the final emancipation of the race which John Brown died to make free."

"A Litany at Atlanta"*

O Silent God, Thou whose voice afar in mist and mystery hath left our ears an-hungered in these fearful days—

Hear us, good Lord!

Listen to us, Thy children: our faces dark with doubt are made a mockery in Thy Sanctuary. With uplifted hands we front Thy Heaven, O God, crying:

We beseech Thee to hear us, good Lord!

We are not better than our fellows, Lord; we are but weak and human men. When our devils do deviltry, curse Thou the doer and the deed,—curse them as we curse them, do to them all and more than ever they have done to innocence and weakness, to womanhood and home.

Have mercy upon us, miserable sinners!

And yet, whose is the deeper guilt? Who made these devils? Who nursed them in crime and fed them on injustice? Who ravished and debauched their mothers and their grandmothers?

* W. E. B. Du Bois, "A Litany at Atlanta," *Darkwater: Voices from Within the Veil* (New York, 1920), p. 25–28.

Who bought and sold their crime and waxed fat and rich on public iniquity?

Thou knowest, good God!

Is this Thy Justice, O Father, that guile be easier than innocence and the innocent be crucified for the guilt of the untouched guilty?

Justice, O Judge of men!

Wherefore do we pray? Is not the God of the Fathers dead? Have not seers seen in Heaven's halls Thine hearsed and lifeless form stark amidst the black and rolling smoke of sin, where all along bow bitter forms of endless dead?

Awake, Thou that sleepest!

Thou art not dead, but flown afar, up hills of endless light, through blazing corridors of suns, where worlds do swing of good and gentle men, of women strong and free—far from the cozenage, black hypocrisy, and chaste prostitution of this shameful speck of dust!

Turn again, O Lord; leave us not to perish in our sin!

From lust of body and lust of blood,—

Great God, deliver us!

From lust of power and lust of gold,—

Great God, deliver us!

From the leagued lying of despot and of brute,—

Great God, deliver us!

A city lay in travail, God our Lord, and from her loins sprang twin Murder and Black Hate. Red was the midnight; clang, crack, and cry of death and fury filled the air and trembled underneath the stars where church spires pointed silently to Thee. And all this was to sate the greed of greedy men who hide behind the veil of vengeance!

Bend us Thine ear, O Lord!

In the pale, still morning we looked upon the deed. We stopped our ears and held our leaping hands, but they—did they not wag

their heads and leer and cry with bloody jaws: *Cease from Crime!*
The word was mockery, for thus they train a hundred crimes while
we do cure one.

Turn again our captivity, O Lord!

Behold this maimed and broken thing, dear God; it was an
humble black man, who toiled and sweat to save a bit from the
pittance paid him. They told him: *Work and Rise!* He worked. Did
this man sin? Nay, but someone told how someone said another
did—one whom he had never seen nor known. Yet for that man's
crime this man lieth maimed and murdered, his wife naked to
shame, his children to poverty and evil.

Hear us, O heavenly Father!

Doth not this justice of hell stink in Thy nostrils, O God? How
long shall the mounting flood of innocent blood roar in Thine ears
and pound in our hearts for vengeance? Pile the pale frenzy of
blood-crazed brutes, who do such deeds, high on Thine Altar,
Jehovah Jireh, and burn it in hell forever and forever!

Forgive us, good Lord; we know not what we say!

Bewildered we are and passion-tossed, mad with the madness of
a mobbed and mocked and murdered people; straining at the
armposts of Thy throne, we raise our shackled hands and charge
Thee, God, by the bones of our stolen fathers, by the tears of our
dead mothers, by the very blood of Thy crucified Christ: What
meaneth this? Tell us the plan; give us the sign!

Keep not Thou silent, O God!

Sit not longer blind, Lord God, deaf to our prayer and dumb to
our dumb suffering. Surely Thou, too, art not white, O Lord, a
pale, bloodless, heartless thing!

Ah! Christ of all the Pities!

Forgive the thought! Forgive these wild, blasphemous words!
Thou art still the God of our black fathers and in Thy Soul's Soul
sit some soft darkenings of the evening, some shadowings of the
velvet night.

But whisper—speak—call, great God, for Thy silence is white
terror to our hearts! The way, O God, show us the way and point
us the path!

Whither? North is greed and South is blood; within, the coward, and without, the liar. Whither? To death?

Amen! Welcome, dark sleep!

Whither? To life? But not this life, dear God, not this. Let the cup pass from us, tempt us not beyond our strength, for there is that clamoring and clawing within, to whose voice we would not listen, yet shudder lest we must,—and it is red. Ah! God! It is a red and awful shape.

Selah!

In yonder East trembles a star.

Vengeance is Mine; I will repay, saith the Lord!

Thy Will, O Lord, be done!

Kyrie Eleison!

Lord, we have done these pleading, wavering words.

We beseech Thee to hear us, good Lord!

We bow our heads and hearken soft to the sobbing of women and little children.

We beseech Thee to hear us, good Lord!

Our voices sink in silence and in night.

Hear us, good Lord!

In night, O God of a godless land!

Amen!

In silence, O Silent God.

Selah!

"The Riddle of the Sphinx"*

Dark daughter of the lotus leaves that watch the Southern Sea!
Wan spirit of a prisoned soul a-panting to be free!
  The muttered music of thy streams, the whisper of the deep,
  Have kissed each other in God's name and kissed a world to
    sleep.

* W. E. B. Du Bois, "The Riddle of the Sphinx," *Darkwater: Voices from Within the Veil* (New York, 1920), pp. 53–55.

The will of the world is a whistling wind, sweeping a cloud-swept
    sky,
And not from the East and not from the West knelled that soul-
    waking cry,
    But out of the South,—the sad, black South—it screamed from
      the top of the sky,
      Crying: "Awake, O ancient race!" Wailing, "O woman, arise!"
And crying and sighing and crying again as a voice in the midnight
    cries,—
But the burden of white men bore her back and the white world
    stifled her sighs.

The white world's vermin and filth:
              All the dirt of London,
              All the scum of New York;
              Valiant spoilers of women
              And conquerors of unarmed men;
              Shameless breeders of bastards,
              Drunk with the greed of gold,
              Baiting their blood-stained hooks
              With cant for the souls of the simple;
              Bearing the white man's burden
              Of liquor and lust and lies!

Unthankful we wince in the East,
Unthankful we wail from the westward,
Unthankfully thankful, we curse,
In the unworn wastes of the wild:
              I hate them, Oh!
              I hate them well,
              I hate them, Christ!
              As I hate hell!
              If I were God,
              I'd sound their knell
              This day!
Who raised the fools to their glory,
But black men of Egypt and Ind,
Ethiopia's sons of the evening,
Indians and yellow Chinese,

Arabian children of morning,
And mongrels of Rome and Greece?

                    Ah, well!
And they that raised the boasters
Shall drag them down again,—
Down with the theft of their thieving
And murder and mocking of men;
Down with their barter of women
And laying and lying of creeds;
Down with their cheating of childhood
And drunken orgies of war,—

                    down

                              down

                                        deep down,
Till the devil's strength be shorn,
Till some dim, darker David, a-hoeing of his corn,
And married maiden, mother of God,
Bid the black Christ be born!
Then shall our burden be manhood,
Be it yellow or black or white;
And poverty and justice and sorrow,
The humble and simple and strong
Shall sing with the sons of morning
And daughters of even-song:
   Black mother of the iron hills that ward the blazing sea,
Wild spirit of a storm-swept soul, a struggling to be free,
Where 'neath the bloody finger-marks thy riven bosom quakes,
Thicken the thunders of God's Voice and lo! a world awakes!

Black Nationalism *Bishop Henry M. Turner**

*If the intensity of Negro outrage were measured in decibels and
virulence, none would equal the declamations of Georgia's Henry
M. Turner of the African Methodist Episcopal Church. His language had the tone of a latter-day Garrisonian attack on the Constitution. Bishop Turner had served as Negro chaplain with the
Union army and was subsequently active in Reconstruction poli-*

* Bishop Henry M. Turner, *The Black Man's Doom: The Two Barbarous
and Cruel Decisions of the United States Supreme Court. . . .* (Philadelphia, 1896).

tics in Georgia. From the expulsion of Negro members in the Georgia legislature in 1868 to the eve of World War I he denounced the American flag, American Christianity, the Republican party, and the Supreme Court. Like other black nationalists, Turner believed emigration was one viable solution to the racial dilemma. As Garvey was willing to negotiate with the K.K.K., Turner was able to deal with Ben Tillman. White men were white men North or South, he believed, and this Negro vice-president of the American Colonization Society found it difficult to envision racial peace or advancement in America. An example of his resentment is his rankling attack on the Supreme Court's decisions of 1883 and 1896.

The Brutal Decision of the United States Supreme Court—The most Infamous Piece of Judicial Jugglery known since time began —A Decision Unknown in Hell Itself—The Barbarous Ages Revived and Surpassed—Black Nurses and Dogs can Ride in First-class Cars, but Colored Gentlemen and Ladies Ruled Out by a Banditti of Tyrants—Fool Judges Distort and Debauch the United States Constitution to further Degrade the Race that has been Loyal to the Nation in every Struggle for its Existence—Judge Taney's Decision is but a Bagatelle compared to this latter-day Fulmination—Justice Harlan the only Righteous Judge in the Corrupt Conclave—An Angel among Demons—Let us Teach our Children to Revere his Name and Keep it in Everlasting Remembrance.

Why Publish This Decision

The reason I have gone to the United States Supreme Court library at Washington, D.C., and procured a true and correct copy of the revolting decision, which declared the Civil Rights Bill unconstitutional, and entails upon the colored people of the United States every species of indignities known to proscription, persecution and even death itself, and will culminate in their leaving the United States or occupying the status of *free* slaves, until extermination follows, is because the great mass of our people in this country, including black and white, appear to be so profoundly ignorant of the cruel, disgraceful and inhuman condition of things affecting the colored race, and sustaining the brutal laws, which are degrading and goring their very lives out; I have met hundreds of persons, who, in their stupid ignorance, have attempted to justify the action of the Supreme Court in fettering the arms of justice and disgracing the nation by transforming it into a savage country. The world has never witnessed such barbarous laws entailed upon a free people as have grown out of the decision of the United States Supreme Court, issued October 15, 1883. For that decision alone authorized and now sustains all the unjust discriminations, proscriptions and robberies perpetrated by public carriers upon millions of the nation's most loyal defenders. It fathers all the *"Jim-Crow cars"* into which colored people are huddled and compelled to pay as much as the whites, who are given the finest accommodations. It has made the ballot of the black man a parody, his citizenship a nullity and his freedom a burlesque. It has engendered the bitterest feeling between the whites and blacks, and resulted in the deaths of thousands, who would have been living and enjoying life to-day. And as long as the accompanying decision remains the verdict of the nation, it can never be accepted as a civil, much less a Christian country.

The colored man or woman who can find contentment, menaced and shackled by such flagrant and stalking injustice as the Supreme Court has inflicted upon them, must be devoid of all manliness and those self-protecting instincts that prompt even animals to fight or run. If the negro, as a race, intends to remain in this country, and does not combine, organize and put forth endeavors for a better condition of things here or leave it and search for a land more congenial, he is evidently of the lowest type of human existence, and slavery would be a more befitting sphere for the exercise of his dwarfed and servile powers than freedom. When colored people were forced into "Jim-Crow cars" and deprived of any right, which the whites enjoyed in the days of slavery, they were charged half fare. Now they have to pay for first-class fare, and in thousands of instances are compelled to accept half accommodations; but it is needless to enter into further detail, for the same principle or unprinciple runs throughout the entire series.

Therefore, I have compiled and published these documents*
upon the same for the information of my race everywhere, and

---

* Turner printed the majority opinions of the Court in the Civil Rights Cases and *Plessy vs. Ferguson.*

their friends, that they may see their odious and direful surroundings, and ask themselves whether they can submit to them or not.

A Reply to Thomas Dixon *Kelly Miller**

Kelly Miller's reply to Thomas Dixon, "As to the Leopard's Spots," was written in response to Dixon's essay in the Saturday Evening Post. *Dean Miller, as he was generally known, was a professor of mathematics and dean at Howard University for almost half a century and a prolific writer and lecturer. As Carter G. Woodson said at the time of Miller's death in 1939, "On every important public question concerning the Negro he delivered a lecture or wrote a pamphlet." Miller's racial views fell somewhere between those of Washington and Du Bois. He probably came closest to typifying the majority opinion of Negro intellectuals in the following article, one of his most impassioned statements.*

Dear Sir: I am writing you this letter to express the attitude and feeling of ten million of your fellow-citizens toward the evil propagandism of race animosity to which you have lent your great literary powers. Through the widespread influence of your writings you have become the chief priest of those who worship at the shrine of race hatred and wrath. This one spirit runs through all your books and published utterances, like the recurrent theme of an opera. As the general trend of your doctrine is clearly epitomized and put forth in your contribution to the *Saturday Evening Post* of August 19, I beg to consider chiefly the issues therein raised. You are a white man born in the midst of the Civil War; I am a Negro born during the same stirring epoch. You were born with a silver spoon in your mouth; I was born with an iron hoe in my hand. Your race has afflicted accumulated injury and wrong upon mine; mine has borne yours only service and good will. You express your views with the most scathing frankness; I am sure you will welcome an equally candid expression from me.

In your article in the *Post* you make several references to me and to other colored men with entire personal courtesy. So far as I

* "As to the Leopard's Spots," in *The Everlasting Stain* (Washington, D.C., 1924), pp. 28–41.

know you have never varied from this rule in your personal dealings with members of my race. You are merciless, however, in excoriating the race as a whole, thus keenly wounding the sensibilities of every individual of that blood. I assure you that this courtesy of personal treatment will be reciprocated in this letter, however sharply I may be compelled to take issue with the views you set forth and to deplore your attitude. I shall endeavor to indulge in no bitter word against your race or against the South, whose exponent and special pleader you assume to be.

I fear that you have mistaken personal manners, the inevitable varnish of any gentleman of your antecedents and rearing, for friendship to a race which you hold in despite. You tell us that you are kind and considerate to your personal servants. It is somewhat strange that you should deem such assurance necessary, any more than it is necessary for you to assure us that you are kind to your horse or your dog and fond of them. But when you write yourself down as "one of their best friends," you need not be surprised if we retort the refrain of the ritual, "From all such proffers of friendship, good Lord deliver us." An astronomer once tried to convince a layman, unlearned in astronomical lore, that the North Star was bigger than the moon. The unsophisticated reply was, "It might be so, but it has a mighty poor way of showing it." The reconciliation of your apparently violent attitude with your profession of friendship is, I confess, too subtle a process for the African intellect.

Your fundamental thesis is that "no amount of education of any kind, industrious, classical or religious, can make a Negro a white man or bridge the chasm of the centuries which separates him from the white man in the evolution of human history." This doctrine is as old as human oppression. Calhoun made it the archstone in the defense of Negro slavery—and lost.

This is but a recrudescence of the doctrine which was exploited and exploded during the anti-slavery struggle. Do you recall the school of pro-slavery scientists who demonstrated beyond doubt that the Negro's skull was too thick to comprehend the substance of Aryan knowledge? Have you not read in the now discredited scientific books of that period with what triumphant acclaim it was shown that the shape and size of the Negro's skull, facial angle, and cephalic configuration rendered him forever impervious to the white man's civilization? But all enlightened minds are now as ashamed of that doctrine as they are of the one-time dogma that the Negro had no soul. We become aware of mind through its manifestations. Within forty years of only partial opportunity, while playing, as it were, in the back yard of civilization, the American Negro has cut down his illiteracy by over fifty per cent; has produced a professional class, some fifty thousand strong, including ministers, teachers, doctors, editors, authors, architects, engineers, and is found in all higher lines of listed pursuits in which white men are engaged; some three thousand Negroes have taken collegiate degrees, over three hundred being from the best institutions in the North and West established for the most favored white youth; there is scarcely a first-class institution in America, excepting some three or four in the South, that is without colored students, who pursue their studies generally with success, and sometimes with distinction; Negro inventors have taken out four hundred patents as a contribution to the mechanical genius of America; there are scores of Negroes who, for conceded ability and achievements, take respectable rank in the company of distinguished Americans.

The inherent, essential and unchangeable inferiority of the Negro to the white man lies at the basis of your social philosophy. You disdain to examine the validity of your fondly cherished hope. You follow closely in the wake of Tom Watson, in the June number of his homonymous magazine.* You both hurl your thesis of innate racial inferiority at the head of Booker T. Washington. You use the same illustrations, the same arguments, and you set them forth in the same order of recital, and for the most part in identical language. This seems to be an instance of great minds, or at least of minds of the same grade, running in the same channel.

These are your words: "What contribution to human progress have the millions of Africans, who inhabit this planet, made during the past four thousand years? Absolutely nothing." These are the words of Thomas Watson spoken some two months previous: "What does civilization owe to the Negro race? Nothing! Nothing!!

---

* Tom *Watson's Jeffersonian Magazine* specialized in anti-Catholicism and racism in the early twentieth century, although Watson's class consciousness had earlier led him to support unity among the black and white agrarian masses.

Nothing!!!" You answer the query with the most emphatic negative noun and the strongest qualifying adjective in the language. Mr. Watson, of a more ecstatic temperament, replies with the same noun and six exclamation points. One rarely meets, outside of yellow journalism, with such lavishness of language wasted upon a hoary dogma. A discredited doctrine that has been bandied about the world from the time of Canaan to Calhoun, is revamped and set forth with as much ardor and fervency of feeling as if revealed for the first time and proclaimed for the enlightenment of a waiting world.

There is no hard and fast line dividing the two races on the scale of capacity. There is the widest possible range of variation within the limits of each. A philosopher and a fool may not only be members of the same race but of the same family. No scheme of classification is possible which will include all white men and shut out all Negroes. According to any test of excellence that your and Mr. Watson's ingenuity can devise, some Negroes will be superior to most white men; no stretch of ingenuity or strain of conscience has yet devised a plan of franchise which includes all of the members of one race and excludes all those of the other.

Our own country has not escaped the odium of intellectual inferiority. The generation has scarcely passed away in whose ears used to ring the standing sneer, "Who reads an American book?" It was in the day of Thomas Jefferson that a learned European declared: "America has not produced one good poet, one able mathematician, one man of genius in a single art or science." In response to this charge Jefferson enters an eloquent special plea. He says: "When we shall have existed as a people as long as the Greeks did before they produced a Homer, the Romans, a Virgil, the French, a Racine, the English, a Shakespeare and Milton, should this reproach be still true, we will inquire from what un- friendly cause it has proceeded." How analogous to this is the reproach which you and Mr. Watson, treading the track of Thomas Nelson Page, and those of his school of thought, now hurl against the Negro race? The response of Jefferson defending the American colonies from the reproach of innate inferiority will apply with augmented emphasis to ward off similar charges against the despised and rejected Negro. A learned authority tells us:

"Hardly two centuries have passed since Russia was covered with a horde of barbarians among whom it would have been as difficult to find any example of intellectual cultivation and refinement as at this day to find the same phenomenon at Timbuctoo or among the Negroes of Georgia or Alabama." It is well for the good fame of the Russian people that *Tom Watson's Magazine* did not exist in those days.

According to a study of the distribution of ability in the United States, a study made by Hon. Henry Cabot Lodge, the little State of Massachusetts has produced more men of distinction and achievement than all the South combined. "In architecture, agriculture, manufacture, finance, legislation, sculpture, religion, organization, painting, music, literature, science, the wedding of the fine arts of religion," the South is relatively backward as compared with other sections of the country.

It would evidently be unfair to conclude that the white race in Georgia is inherently inferior to the people of New England because it has failed to produce names of like renown. The difference in wealth, culture and bracing tone of environments are quite sufficient to account for the difference in results. I think that you and Mr. Watson will be generous enough to concede to the Negro the benefit of the same argument which the defenders of the South resort to in justification of its own relative backwardness. The Negro has never, during the whole course of history, been surrounded by those influences which tend to strengthen and develop the mind. To expect the Negroes of Georgia to produce a great general like Napoleon when they are not even allowed to carry arms, or to deride them for not producing scholars like those of the Renaissance when a few years ago they were forbidden the use of letters, verges closely upon the outer rim of absurdity. Do you look for great Negro statesmen in States where black men are not allowed to vote? . . . Above all, for Southern white men to berate the Negro for failing to gain the highest rounds of distinction reaches the climax of cruel inconsistency. One is reminded of the barbarous Teutons in "Titus Andronicus," who, after cutting out the tongue and hacking off the hands of the lovely Lavinia, ghoulishly chided her for not calling for sweet water with which to wash her delicate hands.

2. INTERRACIAL INVOLVEMENT

A Dissenting Voice: Justice Harlan

"The arbitrary separation of citizens, on the basis of race . . . is a badge of servitude wholly inconsistent with the civil freedom and equality before the law established by the Constitution." So ruled a former Kentucky slaveholder, John Marshall Harlan, two generations before Brown v. Board of Education. *Justice Harlan, "the great dissenter," believed the spirit of the Constitution was "color blind." His quasi-religious view of the document as a guarantor of legal freedom for all men made him the lone dissenter in the historic Civil Rights cases,* Plessy v. Ferguson *and the Berea College decision (1908) accepting racial separation in Kentucky's schools. In thirty-three years on the Supreme Court, Harlan was proudest of his civil rights decisions.*

*Civil Rights Cases**

The opinion in these cases proceeds, it seems to me, upon grounds entirely too narrow and artificial. I cannot resist the conclusion that the substance and spirit of the recent amendments of the Constitution have been sacrificed by a subtle and ingenious verbal criticism. "It is not the words of the law but the internal sense of it that makes the law: the letter of the law is the body; the sense and reason of the law is the soul." Constitutional provisions, adopted in the interest of liberty, and for the purpose of securing, through national legislation, if need be, rights inhering in a state of freedom, and belonging to American citizenship, have been so construed as to defeat the ends the people desired to accomplish, which they attempted to accomplish, and which they supposed they had accomplished by changes in their fundamental law. By this I do not mean that the determination of these cases should have been materially controlled by considerations of mere expedi-

* From 109 U.S. 3 (1883).

ency or policy. I mean only, in this form, to express an earnest conviction that the court has departed from the familiar rule requiring, in the interpretation of constitutional provisions, that full effect be given to the intent with which they were adopted.

The purpose of the first section of the act of Congress of March 1, 1875, was to prevent *race* discrimination in respect of the accommodations and facilities of inns, public conveyances, and places of public amusement. It does not assume to define the general conditions and limitations under which inns, public conveyances, and places of public amusement may be conducted, but only declares that such conditions and limitations, whatever they may be, shall not be applied so as to work a discrimination solely because of race, color, or previous condition of servitude. The second section provides a penalty against any one denying, or aiding or inciting the denial, to any citizen, of that equality of right given by the first section, except for reasons by law applicable to citizens of every race or color and regardless of any previous condition of servitude.

There seems to be no substantial difference between my brethren and myself as to the purpose of Congress; for, they say that the essence of the law is, not to declare broadly that all persons shall be entitled to the full and equal enjoyment of the accommodations, advantages, facilities, and privileges of inns, public conveyances, and theatres; but that such enjoyment shall not be subject to conditions applicable only to citizens of a particular race or color, or who had been in a previous condition of servitude. The effect of the statute, the court says, is, that colored citizens, whether formerly slaves or not, and citizens of other races, shall have the same accommodations and privileges in all inns, public conveyances, and places of amusement as are enjoyed by white persons; and *vice versa.*

The court adjuges, I think erroneously, that Congress is without power, under either the Thirteenth or Fourteenth Amendment, to establish such regulations, and that the first and second sections of the statute are, in all their parts, unconstitutional and void.

My brethren say, that when a man has emerged from slavery, and by the aid of beneficent legislation has shaken off the inseparable concomitants of that state, there must be some stage in the progress of his elevation when he takes the rank of a mere citizen, and ceases to be the special favorite of the laws, and when his rights as a citizen, or a man, are to be protected in the ordinary modes by which other men's rights are protected. It is, I submit, scarcely just to say that the colored race has been the special favorite of the laws. The statute of 1875, now adjudged to be unconstitutional, is for the benefit of citizens of every race and color. What the nation, through Congress, has sought to accomplish in reference to that race, is—what had already been done in every State of the Union for the white race—to secure and protect rights belonging to them as freemen and citizens; nothing more. It was not deemed enough "to help the feeble up, but to support him after." The one underlying purpose of congressional legislation has been to enable the black race to take the rank of mere citizens. The difficulty has been to compel a recognition of the legal right of the black race to take the rank of citizens, and to secure the enjoyment of privileges belonging, under the law, to them as a component part of the people for whose welfare and happiness government is ordained. At every step, in this direction, the nation has been confronted with class tyranny. . . . To-day, it is the colored race which is denied, by corporations and individuals wielding public authority, rights fundamental in their freedom and citizenship. At some future time, it may be that some other race will fall under the ban of race discrimination. If the constitutional amendments be enforced, according to the intent with which, as I conceive, they were adopted, there cannot be, in this republic, any class of human beings in practical subjection to another class, with power in the latter to dole out to the former just such privileges as they may choose to grant. The supreme law of the land has decreed that no authority shall be exercised in this country upon the basis of discrimination, in respect of civil rights, against freemen and citizens because of their race, color, or previous condition of servitude. To that decree—for the due enforcement of which, by appropriate legislation, Congress has been invested with express power—every one must bow, whatever may have been, or whatever now are, his individual views as to the wisdom or policy, either of the recent changes in the fundamental law, or of the legislation which has been enacted to give them effect.

*Plessy v. Ferguson**

By the Louisiana statute, the validity of which is here involved, all
railway companies (other than street railroad companies) carrying
passengers in that State are required to have separate but equal
accommodations for white and colored persons, "by providing two
or more passenger coaches for each passenger train, *or* by dividing
the passenger coaches by a *partition* so as to secure separate
accommodations." Under this statute, no colored person is permitted to occupy a seat in a coach assigned to white persons; nor
any white person, to occupy a seat in a coach assigned to colored
persons. The managers of the railroad are not allowed to exercise
any discretion in the premises, but are required to assign each
passenger to some coach or compartment set apart for the exclusive use of his race. If a passenger insists upon going into a coach
or compartment not set apart for persons of his race, he is subject
to be fined, or to be imprisoned in the parish jail. Penalties are
prescribed for the refusal or neglect of the officers, directors,
conductors and employes of railroad companies to comply with
the provisions of the act.

Only "nurses attending children of the other race" are excepted
from the operation of the statute. No exception is made of colored
attendants travelling with adults. A white man is not permitted to
have his colored servant with him in the same coach, even if his
condition of health requires the constant, personal assistance of
such servant. If a colored maid insists upon riding in the same
coach with a white woman whom she has been employed to serve,
and who may need her personal attention while travelling, she is
subject to be fined or imprisoned for such an exhibition of zeal in
the discharge of duty.

It was said in argument that the statute of Louisiana does not
discriminate against either race, but prescribes a rule applicable
alike to white and colored citizens. But this argument does not
meet the difficulty. Every one knows that the statute in question
had its origin in the purpose, not so much to exclude white persons
from railroad cars occupied by blacks, as to exclude colored

* From *Plessy v. Ferguson,* 163 U.S. 537 (1896).

people from coaches occupied by or assigned to white persons. Railroad corporations of Louisiana did not make discrimination among whites in the matter of accommodation for travellers. The thing to accomplish was, under the guise of giving equal accommodation for whites and blacks, to compel the latter to keep to themselves while travelling in railroad passenger coaches. No one would be so wanting in candor as to assert the contrary. The fundamental objection, therefore, to the statute is that it interferes with the personal freedom of citizens. "Personal liberty," it has been well said, "consists in the power of locomotion, of changing situation, or removing one's person to whatsoever places one's own inclination may direct, without imprisonment or restraint, unless by due course of law." If a white man and a black man choose to occupy the same public conveyance on a public highway, it is their right to do so, and no government, proceeding alone on grounds of race, can prevent it without infringing the personal liberty of each.

It is one thing for railroad carriers to furnish, or to be required by law to furnish, equal accommodations for all whom they are under a legal duty to carry. It is quite another thing for government to forbid citizens of the white and black races from travelling in the same public conveyance, and to punish officers of railroad companies for permitting persons of the two races to occupy the same passenger coach. If a State can prescribe, as a rule of civil conduct, that whites and blacks shall not travel as passengers in the same railroad coach, why may it not so regulate the use of the streets of its cities and towns as to compel white citizens to keep on one side of a street and black citizens to keep on the other? Why may it not, upon like grounds, punish whites and blacks who ride together in street cars or in open vehicles on a public road or street? Why may it not require sheriffs to assign whites to one side of a court-room and blacks to the other? And why may it not also prohibit the commingling of the two races in the galleries of legislative halls or in public assemblages convened for the consideration of the political questions of the day? Further, if this statute of Louisiana is consistent with the personal liberty of citizens, why may not the State require the separation in railroad coaches of native and naturalized citizens of the United States, or of Protestants and Roman Catholics?

The white race deems itself to be the dominant race in this country. And so it is, in prestige, in achievements, in education, in wealth and in power. So, I doubt not, it will continue to be for all time, if it remains true to its great heritage and holds fast to the principles of constitutional liberty. But in view of the Constitution, in the eye of the law, there is in this country no superior, dominant, ruling class of citizens. There is no caste here. Our Constitution is color-blind, and neither knows nor tolerates classes among citizens. In respect of civil rights, all citizens are equal before the law. The humblest is the peer of the most powerful. The law regards man as man, and takes no account of his surroundings or of his color when his civil rights as guaranteed by the supreme law of the land are involved. It is, therefore, to be regretted that this high tribunal, the final expositor of the fundamental law of the land, has reached the conclusion that it is competent for a State to regulate the enjoyment by citizens of their civil rights solely upon the basis of race.

In my opinion, the judgment this day rendered will, in time, prove to be quite as pernicious as the decision made by this tribunal in the *Dred Scott case.*

The arbitrary separation of citizens, on the basis of race, while they are on a public highway, is a badge of servitude wholly inconsistent with the civil freedom and the equality before the law established by the Constitution. It cannot be justified upon any legal grounds.

Progressivisim and the Negro *Ray Stannard Baker*[*]

An increasing concern with the meaning and future of democracy in a pluralistic society dominated Progressive thought. One by-product of this rejuvenated national interest was a re-examination of the position of the Negro in American culture. Of the considerable library of essays and books on race relations produced in the first two decades of the twentieth century, none is more representative of white liberalism than the works of Ray Stannard Baker. Baker's Following the Color Line *(1908) was a thoughtful and reasonable tome, a book that struggled to be fair to the North and*

[*] Ray Stannard Baker, "The Negro in a Democracy," *The Independent,* LXVII (September 2, 1909), 584–588.

South. Its major conclusions were that racism was a national not a sectional phenomenon, and that the "spirit of democracy" demanded a struggle with "the ocean of antagonism between the white and Negro races in this country. . . ." The Progressive journalist's message is succinctly given in his article "The Negro in a Democracy."

The South does not now believe and never has believed in a democracy which applies to every man regardless of race, religion or condition. But neither does the North. Undoubtedly the North possesses more of the democratic spirit than the South; and yet, studying the growth of negro communities in Northern cities, I am convinced that if we had anything like the proportion of negroes that the South struggles with, we should also find ourselves developing a spirit not unlike that of the South. Lynchings, mob-law, discrimination, prejudice, are not unknown today in the North. I found discrimination and separation growing even in Boston, and I could not find that mob-law in Springfield, Ohio, was any less ferocious than in Huntsville, Alabama. The same spirit which drives the man with the colored face out of certain counties in Indiana is found burning negro colleges in Texas.

We of the North do not, most of us, believe in any real sense in a democracy which includes black men as well as white men.

If there were enough colored voters in New York to carry the city, or even to exercise a balance of power, and they all voted one ticket as they do in the South, disfranchisement would immediately become an important issue. As it is, we are contented to disfranchise most of our negro voters at every election by bribery. Let us be willing to face the truth, and not cast stones at our Southern neighbors. The plain fact is, most of us in the North do not believe in any real democracy as between white and colored men. Nor do we believe in it among our own white people, for we are divided into warring classes and societies. Nor does the negro on his part believe in it, for no line among white people is more strictly drawn than the line, in some localities, between the mulatto and his black brother. I have known negroes as intolerably aristocratic in their prejudices as any white men I have had the pleasure of meeting.

The point I am making here is that the *spirit* of democracy, which, after all, is the only thing that really counts, is not exhausted with exercise anywhere in this land. We have made a little relative progress toward democracy; we have exprest its shining ideal in some of our institutions, but for the most part the human heart of us is wofully aristocratic, ungenerous, prejudiced, and it expresses its haughtiness not only in the South, where the negro suffers most, but in the North, where we employ swarms of underpaid women and children, and build selfish palaces out of the labor of wretched foreigners. We have no stones to cast at the South. This is our problem, too. I have heard much talk against the passage of the disfranchisement and "Jim Crow" laws, in the South, but I cannot consider them without feeling that whatever else they may express, they also constitute a genuine protest against the lie of the law. The Supreme Court decision in the Berea College case has been attacked in some quarters, but does it not represent the real view of the mass of American citizens? In Chicago, in St. Paul, in Boston, white parents do not often want their children to sit in schools where many negroes attend. This is the plain truth.

But a tremendous endowment of power follows any effort t arrive at the real truth of things. Thus the discussion in the Sou regarding the limitation of democracy on the statute books as opened the question as to where, having begun to limit, the line shall henceforth be drawn. If you study the political campaigns in the South, if you read the proceedings of the recent legislatures of Southern States, you will discover that, however blindly, the discussions have turned upon these questions:

How many colored men can be cut off from participation in the political rights of the democracy? How many seats at the rear of the car shall the negroes occupy? At what door shall the negro enter the railroad station? Shall negroes be confined in the same prisons with white men, or take the oath with their hands on the same Bible, or be buried in the same cemeteries? How many parts of white blood shall admit a negro to real participation in the democracy? What occupation must negroes pursue in the democracy? Some would compel them all to be servants, others would admit them as small businessmen but not as professional men, others still would let them practise medicine *if* they practise only among their own people.

All these discussions may seem amusingly trivial to the outsider who cannot understand that they are, after all, profoundly and fundamentally educative.

Think what a tremendous experimental laboratory in applied democracy is this South of ours! A whole people trying to draw an elusive line between some men who belong and some who do not! In each legislature, in each campaign, the line wavers, is broken down at some point, is newly drawn. Some awful event like the Atlanta riot comes along and the best white men and the best negroes, who have never come together or known one another, are irresistibly forced into common effort. A white man says: "I did not know there were any such intelligent negroes in the country." Another asks: "After all, are we not brothers?"

Or some man arises—a liberator, like Booker T. Washington—who will not be classified, who breaks thru many lines. "What shall be done with such a man?" these campaigners and legislators ask themselves. "He serves the South. He is useful to all of us. How can we legislate such a man out of the democracy? But can we let him in and keep out the dark-skinned man who follows close behind?"

So these Southern men are concerning themselves with real questions; they are being driven onward by the tremendous logic of events. They will see sooner, perhaps, than we see the utter absurdity and impossibility of limiting a democracy. It must either be democracy or else a caste system or graded aristocracy, which, if it is forced, will petrify our civilization as it has petrified that of India. Once an attempt is made to draw lines and it is discovered that the whole attention of the people is centered, as it is today in the South, on drawing and redrawing the lines—to let a few more in or to keep a few more out. So we shall discover in time and by painful experience that if the negro does not fit into our present sort of democracy, it is not the negro who is wrong, but the democracy. The final test of any democracy is its humblest citizen.

Science has taught us that every atom is necessary to every other atom in the universe. It is also teaching us that every human being is necessary to every other human being; that there can be no real democracy which leaves any one out. Emerson says . . . "To science there is no poison; to botany no weed; to chemistry no dirt." To this we may add: "To democracy, no negro."

The spirit of true democracy is faint in this country; and it is not surprising that the United States Supreme Court should express what the people feel. What we need is a revival of the spirit of democracy, both South and North. How can this be attained? Again only by old-fashioned remedies: I mean by education and the passionate preaching of the religion of service.

Hearing these commonplace things suggested, some of us grow weary; the way seems so long and so hard. What we really need is new fervor in our work along these lines. It is not enough to believe; there must burn behind that belief the true fire of faith. If I have any message to deliver today it lies in the reinforcement of our conviction that these old remedies are the true remedies.

What we need today is not less democracy, but more democracy. We need the constant re-assertion of the validity of the highest ideals of democracy: the sort of democracy which leaves no man out. That must be our religion from now on.

A Description of the Beginning of the NAACP
Mary White Ovington*

A number of white racial liberals active in founding the NAACP were descendants of abolitionists. Mary White Ovington, the New York City social worker and journalist, for example, came from a Massachusetts family committed to Garrisonian abolition. The tales and folklore of antislavery were her childhood fare. These old-line Yankee reformers combined with socially conscious urban Progressives, leaders of New Immigrant groups like Henry Moskowitz, and Negroes, to form the NAACP in 1909, the centennial year of Lincoln's birth. Miss Ovington describes the events which led to the founding of the NAACP in How the National Association for the Advancement of Colored People Began, *which includes Oswald Garrison Villard's "Call" to the convention which founded the organization.*

The National Association for the Advancement of Colored People is five years old—old enough, it is believed, to have a history; and I, who am perhaps its first member, have been chosen as the person to recite it.

* From *How the National Association for the Advancement of Colored People Began* (New York, 1914).

In the summer of 1908, the country was shocked by the account of the race riots at Springfield, Illinois. Here, in the home of Abraham Lincoln, a mob containing many of the town's "best citizens," raged for two days, killed and wounded scores of Negroes, and drove thousands from the city. Articles on the subject appeared in newspapers and magazines. Among them was one in the *Independent* of September 3d, by William English Walling, entitled "Race War in the North." After describing the atrocities committed against the colored people, Mr. Walling declared:

"Either the spirit of the abolitionists, of Lincoln and of Lovejoy must be revived and we must come to treat the Negro on a plane of absolute political and social equality, or Vardaman and Tillman will soon have transferred the race war to the North." And he ended with these words, "Yet who realizes the seriousness of the situation, and what large and powerful body of citizens is ready to come to their aid?"

It so happened that one of Mr. Walling's readers accepted his question and answered it. For four years I had been studying the status of the Negro in New York. I had investigated his housing conditions, his health, his opportunities for work. I had spent many months in the South, and at the time of Mr. Walling's article, I was living in a New York Negro tenement on a Negro street. And my investigations and my surroundings led me to believe with the writer of the article that "the spirit of the abolitionists must be revived."

So I wrote to Mr. Walling, and after some time, for he was in the West, we met in New York in the first week of the year 1909. With us was Dr. Henry Moskowitz, now prominent in the administration of John Purroy Mitchell, Mayor of New York.* It was then that the National Association for the Advancement of Colored People was born.

It was born in a little room of a New York apartment. It is to be regretted that there are no minutes of the first meeting, for they would make interesting if unparliamentary reading. Mr. Walling had spent some years in Russia where his wife, working in the cause of the revolutionists, had suffered imprisonment; and he ex-

---

* Moskowitz later became a member of the ethnic coterie that supported the political ambitions of Al Smith.

pressed his belief that the Negro was treated with greater inhumanity in the United States than the Jew was treated in Russia.
As Mr. Walling is a Southerner we listened with conviction. I knew
something of the Negro's difficulty in securing decent employment
in the North and of the insolent treatment awarded him at Northern hotels and restaurants, and I voiced my protest. Dr. Moskowitz, with his broad knowledge of conditions among New York's
helpless immigrants, aided us in properly interpreting our facts.
And so we talked and talked, voicing our indignation.

Of course, we wanted to do something at once that should move
the country. It was January. Why not choose Lincoln's birthday,
February 12, to open our campaign? We decided, therefore, that a
wise, immediate action would be the issuing on Lincoln's birthday
of a call for national conference on the Negro question. At this
conference we might discover the beginnings, at least, of that
"large and powerful body of citizens" of which Mr. Walling had
written.

And so the meeting adjourned. Something definite was determined upon, and our next step was to call others into our councils.
We at once turned to Mr. Oswald Garrison Villard, president of
the N.Y. Evening Post Company. He received our suggestions with
enthusiasm, and aided us in securing the co-operation of able and
representative men and women. It was he who drafted the Lincoln's birthday call and helped to give it wide publicity. I give the
Call in its entirety . . . since it expresses, I think, better than
anything else we have published, the spirit of those who are active
in the Association's cause.

"The celebration of the Centennial of the birth of Abraham
Lincoln, widespread and grateful as it may be, will fail to justify
itself if it takes no note of and makes no recognition of the colored
men and women for whom the great Emancipator labored to
assure freedom. Besides a day of rejoicing, Lincoln's birthday in
1909 should be one of taking stock of the nation's progress since
1865.

"How far has it lived up to the obligations imposed upon it by
the Emancipation Proclamation? How far has it gone in assuring
to each and every citizen, irrespective of color, the equality of
opportunity and equality before the law, which underlie our American institutions and are guaranteed by the Constitution?

"If Mr. Lincoln could revisit this country in the flesh, he would be disheartened and discouraged. He would learn that on January 1, 1909, Georgia had rounded out a new confederacy by disfranchising the Negro, after the manner of all the other Southern States. He would learn that the Supreme Court of the United States, supposedly a bulwark of American liberties, had refused every opportunity to pass squarely upon this disfranchisement of millions, by laws avowedly discriminatory and openly enforced in such manner that the white men may vote and black men be without a vote in their government; he would discover, therefore, that taxation without representation is the lot of millions of wealth-producing American citizens, in whose hands rests the economic progress and welfare of an entire section of the country.

"He would learn that the Supreme Court, according to the official statement of one of its own judges in the Berea College case, has laid down the principle that if an individual State chooses, it may 'make it a crime for white and colored persons to frequent the same market place at the same time, or appear in an assemblage of citizens convened to consider questions of a public or political nature in which all citizens, without regard to race, are equally interested.'

"In many states Lincoln would find justice enforced, if at all, by judges elected by one element in a community to pass upon the liberties and lives of another. He would see the black men and women, for whose freedom a hundred thousand of soldiers gave their lives, set apart in trains, in which they pay first-class fares for third-class service, and segregated in railway stations and in places of entertainment; he would observe that State after State declines to do its elementary duty in preparing the Negro through education for the best exercise of citizenship.

"Added to this, the spread of lawless attacks upon the Negro, North, South, and West—even in the Springfield made famous by Lincoln—often accompanied by revolting brutalities, sparing neither sex nor age nor youth, could but shock the author of the sentiment that 'government of the people, by the people, for the people; shall not perish from the earth.'

"Silence under these conditions means tacit approval. The indifference of the North is already responsible for more than one assault upon democracy, and every such attack reacts as unfavorably upon whites as upon blacks. Discrimination once permitted cannot be bridled; recent history in the South shows that in forging chains for the Negroes the White voters are forging chains for themselves. 'A house divided against itself cannot stand'; this government cannot exist half-slave and half-free any better to-day than it could in 1861.

"Hence we call upon all the believers in democracy to join in a national conference for the discussion of present evils, the voicing of protests, and the renewal of the struggle for civil and political liberty."

It was thus decided that we should hold a conference, and the next two months were busily spent arranging for it. . . . It was agreed that the conference should be by invitation only, with the one open meeting at Cooper Union. Over a thousand people were invited, the Charity Organization Hall was secured, and, on the evening of May 30th, the conference opened with an informal reception at the Henry Street Settlement, given by Miss Lillian D. Wald, one of the Association's first and oldest friends. The next morning our deliberations began.

We have had five conferences since 1909, but I doubt whether any have been so full of a questioning surprise, mounting swiftly to enthusiasm, on the part of the white people in attendance. These men and women, engaged in religious, social and educational work, for the first time met the Negro who demands, not a pittance, but his full rights in the commonwealth. They received a stimulating shock and one which they enjoyed. They did not want to leave the meetings. We conferred all the time, formally and informally, and the Association gained in those days many of the earnest and uncompromising men and women who have since worked unfalteringly in its cause. Mr. William Hayes Ward, senior editor of the *Independent,* opened the conference, and Mr. Charles Edward Russell, always the friend of those who struggle for opportunity, presided at the stormy session at the close.

Out of this conference we formed a committee of forty and secured the services of Miss Frances Blascoer,* as secretary. We were greatly hampered by lack of funds. Important national work would present itself which we were unable to handle. But our

---

* Miss Blascoer was a social worker and author of *Colored School Children in New York* (New York, 1915).

secretary was an excellent organizer, and at the end of a year we had held four mass meetings, had distributed thousands of pamphlets, and numbered our membership in the hundreds. In May, 1910, we held our second conference in New York, and again our meetings were attended by earnest, interested people. It was then that we organized a permanent body to be known as the National Association for the Advancement of Colored People.

The securing of a sufficient financial support to warrant our calling Dr. Du Bois from Atlanta University into an executive office in the Association was the most important work of the second conference.

When Dr. Du Bois came to us we were brought closely in touch with an organization of colored people, formed in 1905 at Niagara and known as the Niagara Movement. This organization had held important conferences at Niagara, Harpers Ferry, and Boston, and had attempted a work of legal redress along very much the lines upon which the National Association for the Advancement of Colored People was working.

The Niagara Movement, hampered as it was by lack of funds and by a membership confined to one race only, continued to push slowly on, but when the larger possibilities of this new Association were clear, the members of the Niagara Movement were advised to join, as the platforms were practically identical. Many of the most prominent members of the Niagara Movement thus brought their energy and ability into the service of the Association, and eight are now serving on its Board of Directors.

Our history, after 1910, may be read in our annual reports, and in the numbers of THE CRISIS. We opened two offices in the *Evening Post* building. With Dr. Du Bois came Mr. Frank M. Turner, a Wilberforce graduate, who has shown great efficiency in handling our books. In November of 1910 appeared the first number of THE CRISIS, with Dr. Du Bois as editor, and Mary Dunlop MacLean, whose death has been the greatest loss the Association has known, as managing editor. Our propaganda work was put on a national footing, our legal work was well under way, and we were in truth, a National Association, pledged to a nation-wide work for justice to the Negro race.

I remember the afternoon that THE CRISIS received its name. We were sitting around the conventional table that seems a necessary adjunct to every Board, and were having an informal talk regarding the new magazine. We touched the subject of poetry.

"There is a poem of Lowell's," I said, "that means more to me to-day than any other poem in the world—'The Present Crisis.'"

Mr. Walling looked up. "The Crisis," he said. "There is the name for your magazine, THE CRISIS."

And if we had a creed to which our members, black and white, our branches North and South and East and West, our college societies, our children's circles, should all subscribe, it should be the lines of Lowell's noble verse, lines that are as true to-day as when they were written seventy years ago:

"Once to every man and nation comes the moment to decide,
In the strife of Truth with Falsehood for the good or evil side;
Some Great cause, God's new Messiah, offering each the bloom or
    blight,
Parts the goats upon the left hand, and the sheep upon the right,
And the choice goes by forever 'twixt that darkness and that light.

"Then to side with Truth is noble when we share her wretched
    crust,
Ere her cause bring fame and profit, and 'tis prosperous to be
    just;
Then it is the brave man chooses, while the coward stands aside,
Doubting in his abject spirit, till his Lord is crucified,
And the multitude make virtue of the faith they had denied."

3. EARLY ORGANIZATIONS IN
THE SOUTH

*Southern Society for the Promotion of the
Study of Race Conditions**

*Edgar Gardner Murphy had high expectations for the Southern
Society for the Promotion of the Study of Race Conditions and*

* From the Southern Society for the Promotion of the Study of Race Conditions and Problems in the South, *The Race Problems of the South: Report of the Proceedings of the First Annual Conference* (Montgomery, Ala., 1900), pp. 10–12.

Problems. Southern white men, he hoped, would find "real solutions to our race problem"; membership would be open to citizens "of every creed and political party"; meetings were to be held annually; the organization would become self-supporting and permanent. The "Official Statement" convening the Montgomery Conference emphasized this optimism; the results dampened and stifled it. The Southern Society was born and died at its initial meeting.

At a recent meeting of a committee of twenty-five, selected from the representative men of Montgomery, it was resolved to inaugurate in May next a series of annual meetings in this city for discussion, in the interest of both elements of our population, of various phases of our race problems in the South.

A SOUTHERN INSTITUTION

We feel that much of true progress in connection with our racial difficulties has been embarrassed by the fact that the leadership of Southern opinion has been too largely attempted merely from the North. The solution of our problems in the South must come from the Southern people themselves. We are persuaded that the people of the South are best fitted by knowledge and experience to deal with these difficulties intelligently and helpfully. Suggestions from the North, offered with the best motives, have frequently been based upon inadequate acquaintance with our conditions.

A COMPREHENSIVE PROGRAM

We wish to create a perfectly free arena for the expression of every serious phase of Southern opinion. We shall not expect the speakers in this conference to agree, for we are not agreed ourselves, on the various questions to be presented. We believe, however, in discussion. Through the conflict of opinions, and the courteous expression of honest differences, we believe that we shall advance the education of the public mind North and South. If most of the debates revolve about the Negro, it is not because we are solely bent upon his especial welfare. Our interest is primarily enlisted for the people of the South as a whole. We are concerned in the broadest sense for the prosperity and happiness of our Southern country. We shall not forget the neglected elements of our white population. In our general situation, however, the Negro is an important factor, industrially as well as in other ways, and we feel that the difficulties of the situation cannot be dissipated by a policy of silence. We hope, therefore, to secure frank and thorough discussion of such questions as these:

I. THE FRANCHISE. Should the Franchise be limited by law? If so, how? If limitation is desirable, should such limitation be based on educational or on property qualifications, or on both?

2. THE NEGRO IN RELATION TO EDUCATION. Should the education of the Negro be wholly or chiefly industrial? What is the relation of the Negro who has had industrial training to the untrained white laborer of the South? What is the extent of the need for the industrial training of the white population? What are the advantages and disadvantages to the South of the Negro as a laborer?

3. THE NEGRO IN RELATION TO RELIGION. Should we advise the raising of the standard of ordination for the Negro clergy? How much is expended by the white race in behalf of religious work among the Negroes? How much of money for religious purposes is administered by Negro leaders? How much is administered by white leaders? What religious work is showing the truest results—that under the auspices of white agencies, or that administered under the auspices of Negroes? How can we increase and better the religious guidance of the Negro? What is the religious condition of the Negro to-day compared with that of ante-bellum days? What are the most hopeful lines of progress for the future?

4. THE NEGRO IN RELATION TO THE SOCIAL ORDER. Is the Negro to remain as a permanent element in Southern life? Is there antipathy to the Negro in the South? If so, is it industrial or racial, or both? Is race antipathy a curse, or a blessing to both races? How far has the agitation of the question of "social equality" increased difficulties, and resulted to the disadvantage of both races? Is the crime of rape increasing or decreasing in the South? Is lynching an effective remedy? If not, why not? Are there adequate legal penalties for the offences often punished by lynching? How can the legal provisions for the punishment of crimes against

women be improved? What is the effect of lynching, as a remedy, on the public mind—of the whites?—of the blacks? Has the increased severity of mob penalties tended to the greater security of the home?

A REPRESENTATIVE ARENA

As the Committee have explained, they are themselves divided as to the answers which should be given to many of these questions. They would also welcome expressions from men who honestly think that nothing can be done through discussion to aid in the solution of our racial difficulties. The questions, moreover, are entirely suggestive, as merely indicating the general lines which the discussion may be expected to take. As we have declared, our sole purpose is to represent and to serve the South. We expect to find Southern speakers who may ably and fully and fairly give due representation to all sides of the great questions which are demanding solution at our hands. In order to give general distinction to the gathering, a few speakers representative of the broader and more sympathetic phases of Northern thought, will be asked to be present as our guests. By giving a just opportunity to the opposing advocates in each debate, we shall hope to aid in the establishment of the truth and in the education of public opinion. The South has nothing to lose and everything to gain from a fearless, scholarly, and patriotic discussion of her own problems by her own sons.

Southern Sociological Congress *W. D. Weatherford**

A glimmer of hope for racial progress in the South was sparked at the May, 1912, meeting of the Southern Sociological Congress in Nashville. Attended predominantly by social workers and liberal Protestant ministers, the Congress tried to breathe social and economic meaning into the hazy concept of a "New South." Lectures were delivered on the evils of child labor, the intensified problems of health in urban areas, and the desperate need for expanded public school facilities. One of the modest successes of

* From James E. McCulloch, ed., *The Human Way: Addresses on Race Problems at the Southern Sociological Congress, Atlanta* (Washington, D.C., 1918), pp. 8–18.

social welfare Progressivism in the South was the movement to end the convict-lease system. By the twenties many Southern states had abolished the horror—although life on the chain gang was no joy afterward.

Among white advocates of a racial New South in the twentieth century, few have spoken more clearly and forcefully than W. D. Weatherford. Weatherford has been an oracle of what was once called "Christian sociology." His Negro Life in the South *(1910) was an unusual book for its time. It has been used as a primer on race relations in some Southern colleges. Motivated by a Christian conscience, and influenced by the social gospel, Weatherford helped direct the activities of the YMCA throughout the South, was a "professor of applied anthropology," and was president of the YMCA Graduate School in Nashville from 1919 to 1936. Subsequently he headed Fisk University's Department of Religion and Humanities. Weatherford was a missionary to his own people and played a leading role in the University Commission on Race Questions, established at Nashville, and dedicated to improving race relations through scientific analysis, annual interracial conferences, and distribution of relevant publications. He participated in the founding of the Commission on Interracial Cooperation at Atlanta after World War I and continues his efforts today by working with the people of Appalachia. The following speech was presented at the second annual meeting of the Southern Sociological Congress.*

I wish to make clear in the very beginning that the same type of agency which can improve the conditions for the white people can also improve the conditions of life for the negro. Humanity is humanity whether the color be black or white, and I know no fiat of God that makes white any more valuable as a color or any easier to deal with than black. Every social agency which is working for the uplift of the white race should also be working for the uplift of the colored race, unless there is a special branch of that organization working for the negroes. Let us take for granted in this paper that we believe the negro needs help in practically every way that the white man needs help.

First, we would mention the Church as the greatest of all social and welfare agencies. We do not now speak of the Church as a dispenser of charity or the builder of orphanages and asylums. We speak of the Church as a social agent in a much truer and deeper sense than any of these. The great social mission of the Church is the bringing in of a new appreciation of the sacredness and value of the individual man. This means brotherhood. It means equal safety of life. It means an equal chance to make a living and build a life. Now the equal opportunity can only come when every man is recognized as a real man, as a person. The Church, and the Church alone, can bring about any such estimate of humanity. No amount of legislation can ever make us value the individual; it can only prevent or deter us from harming that individual. Law can never change our essential attitude toward humanity. To this problem the Church holds the key. Its message of the Fatherhood of God and the brotherhood of man puts new meaning into every life and guarantees a new safety and security.

Now it is high time that the white Churches were awaking to the responsibility of extending this sense of sacredness to all men; to the ignorant as well as to the learned, to the wicked as well as to the righteous, to the black as well as to the white.

In a paper last year before this Congress, I called attention to the fact that this very attitude of man to man is the Gibraltar on which the Southern Church and State may wreck themselves. I wish to repeat here that we can not hope to have any real respect for law, we can not build up any civilized community so long as personality is not held sacred. So long as we grind up our children in the mill, so long as we stifle our poor ones in the damp cellars and cheap tenement houses, so long as we allow negroes to be lynched—just so long will we fail to have any genuine appreciation of the sacredness and value of the person. We can not despise some persons and value others, for personality is personality, whether it is poor or rich, whether black or white; and we despise any portion of humanity at the risk of losing our sense of the sacredness of all men, and hence breaking down our laws, destroying our civilization, giving the lie to our Christian ethics, and damning our own souls.

I want to maintain here and now that every minister of the gospel, every Secretary of the Young Men's Christian Association or of the Young Women's Christian Association, every teacher in our schools, every social worker in the South has a sacred and solemn obligation to instill into the hearts of all those whom they lead this principle of the value and sacredness of the person. We need more sermons preached on this theme. We need more addresses in our Associations, we need more emphasis on this in our schools. If we can not win the day here, we are hopelessly lost. And we are not now winning the day. We are not growing as we should in our appreciation of the sacredness of human personality. The horrible lynchings that have been taking place in the South during the last few months are enough to make our blood run cold with despair. More of us must speak out on this topic. It is not opposition to lynching we are talking about—we must all oppose that, God knows—but we must go deeper than that. We must cure the horrible cancer that eats at the heart of our civilization, this horrible lack of appreciation for the sacredness of the individual person. This is our malady, and so long as we do nothing to cure it we may expect it to flower forth in bloody lynchings, in underfed women, in starved and neglected children, and in a criminal system which is more cruel than raw barbarism.

We need a new crusade of a "Peter the Hermit," not to rescue an empty tomb from the hands of an infidel power, but a crusade to wrench the helpless and the belated from the hands of a maddened mob which puts money above man, which puts prejudice above persons, which puts license instead of law, which uses immoral mobs to uphold morality, which despises and degrades all personality in a so-called attempt to vindicate the wrong of a single person. If the churches, the schools, and the associations would throw themselves into this great crusade, we should have a new appreciation of the Godhood in man and hence less of injustice, inequality, and crime. I should like to see this Congress send out a call for such a crusade as this, which would set a thousand pulpits ringing with a new message of humanity, and would give new meaning to the teaching in ten thousand schoolrooms, because God and humanity had found a defending voice.

The second social agency which must be used for the uplift of the negro is the school. We do not always think of the Church and the school as social and welfare agencies, but they are the strong twin brothers, without which all other agencies would be absolutely helpless. The school touches more classes of people, more members of each class, and each member for a longer time, and at a most favorable period, than does any other social agency. It takes the children of the rich and of the poor alike, the cultured and the uncultured, the moral and the morally deficient, and deals with them together in such a fashion as to give a unique opportunity to really serve. Our task, therefore, is to socialize the school, to so fill it with the message of social uplift that it will minister to the whole life of the community in which it exists.

One can think of no greater and more far-reaching influence than that of a socialized school—a school into which the conception of the value of humanity has found its way; a school where the course of study fits its pupils to take their place in the life of the community; a school where health and housing, morals and manners, efficiency and service are given full presentation. The negro school must be made an effective agent for uplifting the race. We must set forth some standards for it, we must have some convictions about it, we must write some policies for it, and we must put our shoulders to the wheel and swear by all that is holy that these things shall come to pass.

In conclusion, I would like to say one more thing. The South is a solid South in more than a political sense. We are a solid South in a social sense. I mean whatever affects the social welfare of one man affects the social welfare of every other man in the section. We are bound together by the fact of proximity, we are bound together by economic relations, we are bound together by the traditions of the past, we are bound together by all the forces of present life which demand the guarding of our health, our ideals, and our civilization. We are not eight million negroes and twenty million whites; we are twenty-nine million human beings, and whatever affects one of our company must of necessity affect all the other 28,999,999. The sin of the immoral will destroy the safety of the moral, the disease of the weakest will destroy the health of the strongest, the prejudice of the most ignorant will warp the judgment of the most learned, the lawlessness of the most criminal will blacken the fair name and drag into criminal action the law-abiding instincts of the highest citizens. We must stand or fall together. Thank God, this is true! This insures that the learned shall not despise the ignorant, that the physically sound shall not despise the physically weak, the rich man can not scorn the poverty-stricken, the righteous can not become self-righteous in their contempt for the morally weak. Every welfare movement for whites must become a welfare movement for negroes as well. This interest in the whole will keep us from dying with the dry-rot of complacency. God has put upon the religious, educational, and social workers of both races of the South a tremendous load of responsibility; but by His help we will carry it like men, and be all the stronger because of our manly exertion.

Commission on Interracial Cooperation *Will W. Alexander**

Weatherford's respect for the "sacredness of the individual person" was shared by Will W. Alexander, founder and director of the Commission on Interracial Cooperation and a Methodist minister. The Commission was formed at Atlanta in the tense racial atmosphere that followed World War I when, as Alexander said, "everybody knew there was trouble in the air." This agency was the key voice of Southern racial moderation until World War II. Prominent Negroes like R. R. Moton, John Hope, and Bishop Robert Elijah Jones cooperated with white Southern educators, clergymen, and social workers in attempts to prevent lynchings and outlaw peonage, provide better community services for Negroes, and generally improve race relations in the South. It was the first significant time that an interracial group in the South operated in this manner. One of the most sustained drives of the Interracial Commission was its campaign against lynching. Will Alexander describes the way some Southern church women organized to prevent the crime.

I put one of these women on my staff and set her to work.† This is what she did: One, undertook to increase the contact between the organized white women of the South and these organized Negro women who appeared on the board. The YWCA was one of the organizations that was represented. She began, in the states, to get groups of white women of the same type together with groups of colored women, and get them to sit down and talk about what went on in their states. Then she began to get all kinds of white

* "The Reminiscences of Will W. Alexander" (Oral History Research Office, Columbia University, 1952), pp. 239–243.

† In response to the request of some organized Southern women's groups, Alexander permitted Negro and white women to work with the Commission.

women's organizations to invite Negro women of that type to come in and tell their story. . . . Most of these women's organizations had some sort of study groups, so she began to try to create a literature. The church outfits had one book that the women studied each year during a two or three month period. She soon got a book produced on this question, to be used by the women of the churches as their annual study book. The women's organizations had little magazines, newspapers or periodicals through which they got things for their programs and their organizations. She began to see that the proper informative material got into those papers.

Then I brought onto the staff a younger woman who was a college graduate—the wife of an army doctor. Her husband had been with [Walter] Reed in the yellow fever training in Cuba. He had died. This woman had been a very intelligent woman who had been in politics in Texas—had been a delegate to the national Democratic convention—and she knew a good deal about women's organizations and had been an ardent suffragette. She had fought the battles of women for voting, and she'd had a lot of experience. Her name was Mrs. Jesse Daniel Ames.* I finally brought Mrs. Ames in to organize a special section of these women. I think she finally named that the Association of Southern Women for the Prevention of Lynching. She started out to find out what these women could do about lynching. The first thing that these white women had written . . . was that they renounced and denounced in the name of all the decent white women in the South the habit of saying that lynching was for the protection of white women. They said that they needed no such protection and would make war on that sort of thing until it didn't any longer exist. Those resolutions began to appear in women's organizations all over the country.

Then they began to see what they could actually do about it. They had common sense. It became very apparent that you could make more headway in preventing lynchings than you could in punishing lynchers. The strategy was to keep the lynchings from happening. So they set up a lot of schools on what women could do about lynching, and they got thousands of women all across the South alerted to watch for the lynchings. They got intensely interested in it. They had some sort of a pledge that they got these

* Mrs. Ames was also an advocate of Negro suffrage.

women to sign saying that they would do everything humanly possible to watch the situation, and if there were a lynching they would go out, themselves, and try to stop it. They had a card file of several thousand women spread all over the South who had taken the pledge.

Then they hit on the wonderful idea of getting these women to take a similar pledge to the chief of police, sheriff, and important officers in their county and get them to sign it, that they as public officials would commit themselves to these women to do everything they could, and would call these women to help, and so on. When the church women of each county came and said, "We want you to sign a pledge that you'll stop lynching," naturally the sheriff said yes. Not only that, but these women learned to watch the papers and they also had ways of getting word, and when an incident happened that might result in a lynching, those women got hold of the sheriff, and a great many of them went out themselves.

We had one little woman down in Mississippi that was a cousin of half the sheriffs in south Mississippi. She was a very strong-willed person. She was the wife of a jeweler in McComb, Mississippi. She took four or five counties which were in the lynching area, and if she heard there was anything going on in any county in the surrounding area, she'd get in her car and go out there, day and night, and just follow through.

I remember one Christmas there was a threatened lynching in Georgia. They were chasing a colored man with hounds down in some small settlement. It had all the earmarks of a lynching. One of the things I always did when those things happened was to get in touch with the governor's office as soon as I could. It was Christmas, and nobody was in the governor's office. I couldn't find anybody when I phoned down. Finally I called Mrs. Ames and I said, "Have you got in your card file in the office any names from this county?"

She said, "I don't know, but I'll go down there and see." On Christmas morning she went to the office early, found the names of women in that county—fifteen or twenty of them—and on Christmas day called those people on the phone long distance. Those women left their Christmas dinners and got out there and followed that mob that was chasing this Negro. They spent the day keeping them in hand.

CHAPTER VII

THE GHETTO

❀ ❀

Many students of the race problem in America have looked to urbanization and northern migration as one possible solution. But in deserting the country for the city, the Negro appears to have merely jumped from the frying pan into the fire.

JAMES H. HUBERT, New York Urban League, 1933

One of the most important racial changes of the twentieth century has been the urbanization of an essentially rural Negro population. Large-scale Negro migration to urban centers began in the late nineteenth century, continues today, and may be anticipated for at least another generation. A people more than three-quarters rural at the turn of the century has become a population three-quarters urban. Many migrants hoped they were "bound for the Promised Land," but too often the land turned out to be a place of tainted promise.

Although considerable numbers of Negroes settled in Northern cities after the 1890's, the crucial years of Negro urbanization occurred between the Great Migration and the Great Depression. The colored population of most Northern cities increased phenomenally in little more than a decade as the First World War and the immigration laws of the twenties constricted the nation's labor supply. To understand modern racial problems in the city one must return to these years to view the social dislocations in the Negro community and the tensions among whites and Negroes created by the rapid population movements. Experiences similar to those described in this chapter have been relived during each subsequent period of Negro migration.

Everywhere the migrants went in the twenties their story was the same: high rents, overcrowded apartments, low wages, poor health, inadequate schools, infant mortality, working mothers. People nurtured in rural poverty and superstition fell easy prey to the varieties of conjure men and religious charlatans whose magic herbs and roots or blessed incantations offered easy remedies at modest prices for life's most complex problems. What has since been called the "social pathology of the ghetto" was clearly evident in the twenties. (1)

Into these communities came Marcus Garvey, an obscure and rotund Negro educator from Jamaica—a most unlikely messiah. He spoke of the failure of traditional Negro leadership, pilloried the integrationist ideology of the NAACP, boasted of the glories of black men in history and the great work that was yet to be done. Most white people laughed at him, called him a comic, a buffoon. His harshest critics were the Negro leaders (Garvey always called them "mis-leaders") he attacked. To them he was a "charlatan," a "thief," a "racist," a "lunatic," a "jackass," a "traitor," a "madman." An NAACP official delivered a public lecture on "The Madness of Marcus Garvey" that illustrates the intensity of this contemporary hostility. Garvey, said Dr. Robert W. Bagnall, was a "Jamaican Negro of unmixed stock, squat, stocky, fat and sleek, with protruding jaws, and heavy jowls, small bright pig-like eyes and rather bulldog-like face. Boastful, egotistical, tyrannical, intolerant, cunning, shifty, smooth and suave, avaricious; . . . gifted at self-advertisement, without shame in self-laudation, . . . without regard for veracity, a lover of pomp and tawdry, finery and garish display."

To accept the judgments of such contemporaries is to blind oneself to Garvey's meaning in the racial history of our country. Garvey was neither a charlatan nor a racist. Beneath the bombast, magniloquent titles, and showy uniforms was a simple message of race pride and love; the glorification of blackness in a society which despised it. Garvey was an evangelist of race pride whose meetings had the tone of great religious revivals, whose followers believed him to be sanctified, whose speeches were full of mystical Christian and African symbolism: "The man had the magic in him by which the Negro masses were bewitched," poet Claude McKay wrote. At a time of great social disruption and racial alienation Garvey offered American Negroes temporary psychological escape from what many believed to be a hopelessly racist nation. No Negro leader in American history has been able to mobilize the Negro masses into a movement anywhere near the size of the Garvey crusade.* At a time when the NAACP annual budget amounted to some $50,000 to $60,000, Garvey was able to raise more than $1,000,000 *within* the Negro community itself. As Gunnar Myrdal wrote, his success "tells of a dissatisfaction so deep that it mounts to hopelessness of ever gaining a full life in America." (2)

The movement for racial separation within the Negro community coincided with an intensification of race hatred among many whites. Nineteen hundred nineteen was a hellish year of Negro-white warfare; especially, but not only, in the Northern industrial cities that were centers of job competition. W. E. B. Du Bois described the atmosphere in his autobiography, *Dusk of Dawn:* "The facts concerning the year 1919 are almost unbelievable as one looks back on them today. During that year seventy-seven Negroes were lynched, of whom one was a woman and eleven were soldiers; of these, fourteen were publicly burned, eleven of them being burned alive. That year there were race riots large and small in twenty-six American cities including thirty-eight killed in a Chicago riot in August; from twenty-five to fifty killed in Phillips County, Arkansas; and six killed in Washington. For a day, the city of Washington in July 1919, was actually in the hands of a black mob fighting the aggression of the whites with hand grenades."

The twenties also witnessed race warfare over questions of Negro housing—the most prominent case, the Sweet trial, involved a Negro dentist and his family in Detroit who shot into a crowd of hostile whites threatening their home. Racially restrictive housing covenants became the typical device used by white realtors and property owners to restrict expansion of the black ghettos. "Neighborhood Improvement Associations" flourished. When they didn't seem to work, as in Chicago, houses were bombed. From 1917 to 1921 Chicago had an average of one racially motivated bombing every twenty days. It was no wonder then that the revived Klan boasted of its expansion into the North and West. (3, 4)

There seemed to be at least one hopeful sign for broader interracial understanding amid the difficulties of the twenties.

* Estimates of Garvey's strength usually range between 100,000 and the lower millions. The most meaningful statement of the size of his following was made by Garvey himself: "No one will ever know accurately the membership of the UNIA, because every second Negro you meet if not an actual member is one in spirit."

Negro writers, musicians, actors, and artists were encouraged by a growing interest in their work among white intellectuals. Rebelling against the strictures and materialism of their world, white aesthetes considered the ghetto a place of artistic and moral freedom. A "vogue in things Negro" was established among these literati which lasted until the Great Depression. Negro intellectuals like Alain Locke and James Weldon Johnson expected that this enhanced interest in the "New Negro" would serve as a bridge to Negro assimilation into American culture. As the 1930's proved, they were mistaken. (5)

1. CONDITIONS IN THE GHETTO

The Negro Urban Press

Among the important by-products of Negro migration was the reinvigoration and expansion of the Negro urban press. Mass circulation journals appealed to working-class audiences through the usual lurid tales and yet, at the same time, the Negro press acted as a force for race solidarity and justice. No better example of this tabloid-reformist mixture can be found than Robert S. Abbott's Chicago Defender. *The* Defender *was the most widely circulated Negro newspaper at the time of the First World War. Its editorial pages emphasized a single major theme: "Good-bye, Dixie Land, Good-bye"; the* Defender *encouraged Southern Negroes to come north. Thousands of readers sent letters to Abbott asking about the possibilities of employment in Chicago and elsewhere, and describing conditions in the South. What follows are two representative* Defender *editorials in 1917 and 1918, and a few letters by migrants.*

Chicago Defender Editorials*

To die from the bite of frost is far more glorious than at the hands of a mob. I beg you, my brother, to leave the benighted land. You are a free man. Show the world that you will not let false leaders lead you. Your neck has been in the yoke. Will you continue to keep it there because some "white folks' nigger" wants you to?

* The first editorial is from the *Defender* of 1917 and is taken from Emmett J. Scott's *Negro Migration During the War* (New York, 1920), p. 31; the second, called "Migration and Its Effects," appeared in the Chicago *Defender*, April 20, 1918.

Leave for all quarters of the globe. Get out of the South. Your being there in the numbers in which you are gives the southern politician too strong a hold on your progress. . . . So much has been said through the white papers in the South about the members of the race freezing to death in the North. They freeze to death down South when they don't take care of themselves. There is no reason for any human being staying in the Southland on this bugaboo handed out by the white press.

If you can freeze to death in the North and be free, why freeze to death in the South and be a slave, where your mother, sister and daughter are raped and burned at the stake; where your father, brother and sons are treated with contempt and hung to a pole, riddled with bullets at the least mention that he does not like the way he is treated. Come North then, all you folks, both good and bad. If you don't behave yourselves up here, the jails will certainly make you wish you had. For the hard-working man there is plenty of work—if you really want it. The *Defender* says come.

Various estimates have been made of the number of people who have left the South from other parts of the country in the past eighteen months, the figures ranging from 500,000 to 2,000,000.* Whatever the number, it was great enough to upset the labor field in this country and establish us as permanent factors in the economic world. Naturally, we say supply and demand regulate everything, and in a great measure, it is true, the war came and left a great gap in the industries of the North, East and West. When shops, mills and factories close for want of labor, the pocketbooks of the owners suffer, and when a man's pocketbook is touched everything else is forgotten in the mad rush to replenish it.

With foreign immigration cut off and no prospect of being able to draw on foreign countries for labor for some years to come, the captains of industry LOWERED THEIR GLASSES, AND INSTEAD OF LOOKING OVER OUR HEADS, AS THEY HAVE BEEN DOING FOR YEARS, GAZED DIRECTLY AT US AND, CATCHING OUR EYE, BECKONED TO US TO COME TO THEM, SHOWING A PICTURE THE WHILE THAT LURED US ON. THOUSANDS LEFT THEIR SUNNY SOUTHERN HOMES

---

* These numbers reflected a tendency in the popular mind to exaggerate the impact and the novelty of the Great Migration. Negro migration from the South to the North for the entire decade 1910–1920 amounted to 330,000 people.

with bitter-sweet, mostly the bitter, memories. Anxiety was felt on all sides. The employers of the rest of the country were experimenting with what the South has pronounced a failure. They were experimenting, not because they wished to prove the South in error, but because it was either the black workmen or no workmen at all, and between the two evils they wisely chose to have workmen.

The black workmen left the South with trembling and fear. They were going—they didn't know where—among strange people, with strange customs. The people who claimed to know best how to treat them painted frightful pictures of what would befall the [migrants] if they left the land of cotton and sugar cane. But they left in droves, are still leaving, and only a few have returned. The effect has been to paralyze the industries of the South, while the other sections of the country have prospered.

There is no denying the fact that prejudice is rife everywhere; but we, like other animate persons and things, follow the line of least resistance. What has been established for several hundred years cannot be broken down in a day. There is a long fight ahead of us—a fight with brains, not brawn. Our entrance into the economic world sounds the death knell of discrimination and oppression. We must hold fast every inch we have gained, remembering always the many are judged by the few in our case. There is such a thing as STAYING IN ONE PLACE TOO LONG, and while the rolling stone never gathers any moss, when it stops rolling, IT IS MORE POLISHED THAN WHEN IT BEGAN. The scattering of the South's shaded population all over the country is a real blessing. Every day fresh evidence of this fact is apparent. THE WHITE MAN SEEKS THE FARTHEST CORNERS OF THE GLOBE IF HE THINKS HE CAN BETTER HIMSELF. WHY SHOULD WE NOT DO LIKEWISE?

*Letters of Negro Migrants**

MIAMI, FLA., May 4, 1917.

Dear Sir: Some time ago down this side it was a rumour about the great work going on in the north. But at the present time every thing is quite there, people saying that all we have been hearing was false until I caught hold of the Chicago Defender I see where

* From the *Journal of Negro History,* IV (July, 1919), 296–297; and IV (October, 1919), 417–440.

its more positions are still open. Now I am very anxious to get up there. I follows up cooking. I also was a stevedor. I used to have from 150 to 200 men under my charge. They thought I was capable in doing the work and at the meantime I am willing to do anything. I have a wife and she is a very good cook. She has lots of references from the north and south. Now dear sir if you can send me a ticket so I can come up there and after I get straightened out I will send for my wife. You will oblige me by doing so at as early date as possible.

I am now looking for a location and am a man hunting work and there is so many has left the South for the north and Seemes as they are all gone to one place now please send the names of some firms that wants labor i am a Man who Beleave in right and Beleave in work and has worked all of my days and mean to work till i die and Never been No kind of trouble and never has to be made work.

Now i will Cloes, hoping to here from you Soon Yours Very Truly,

NEW ORLEANS, LA., 4/24/17

Dear Sirs: Being desirous of leaving the South for the beterment of my condition generaly and seeking a Home Somewhere in Ill' Chicago or some other prosperious Town I am at sea about the best place to locate having a family dependent on me for support. I am informed by the Chicago Defender a very valuable paper which has for its purpose the Uplifting of my race, and of which I am a constant reader and real lover, that you were in position to show some light to one in my condition.

Seeking a Northern Home. If this is true Kindly inform me by next mail the next best thing to do Being a poor man with a family to care for, I am not coming to live on flowry Beds of ease for I am a man who works and wish to make the best I can out of life   I do not wish to come there hoodwinked not knowing where to go or what to do so I Solicite your help in this matter and thanking you in advance for what advice you may be pleased to Give I am yours for success.

P.S. I am presently imployed in the ICRR.* Mail Department at Union Station this city.

* Illinois Central Railroad.

LUTCHER, LA., May 13, 1917.

Dear Sir: I have been reading the Chicago defender and seeing so many advertisements about the work in the north I thought to write you concerning my condition. I am working hard in the south and can hardly earn a living. I have a wife and one child and can hardly feed them. I thought to write and ask you for some information concerning how to get a pass for myself and family. I don't want to leave my family behind as I cant hardly make a living for them right here with them and I know they would fare hard if I would leave them. If there are any agents in the south there havent been any of them to Lutcher if they would come here they would get at least fifty men. Please sir let me hear from you as quick as possible. Now this is all. Please dont publish my letter, I was out in town today talking to some of the men and they say if they could get passes that 30 or 40 of them would come. But they havent got the money and they dont know how to come. But they are good strong and able working men. If you will instruct me I will instruct the other men how to come as they all want to work. Please dont publish this because we have to whisper this around among our selves because the white folks are angry now because the negroes are going north.

NEW ORLEANS, LA., June 10, 1917.

Kind Sir: I read and hear daly of the great chance that a colored parson has in Chicago of making a living with all the priveleg that the whites have and it mak me the most ankious to want to go where I may be able to make a liveing for my self. When you read this you will think it bery strange that being only my self to support that it is so hard, but it is so. everything is gone up but the poor colerd peple wages. I have made sevle afford to leave and come to Chicago where I hear that times is good for us but owing to femail wekness has made it a perfect failure. I am a widow for 9 years. I have very pore learning altho it would not make much diffrent if I would be throughly edacated for I could not get any better work to do, such as house work, washing and ironing and all such work that are injering to a woman with femail wekness and they pay so little for so hard work that it is just enough to pay room rent and a little some thing to eat. I have found a very good remady that I really feeling to belive would cure me if I only could make enough money to keep up my madison and I dont think that I will ever be able to do that down hear for the time is getting worse evry day. I am going to ask if you peple hear could aid me in geting over her in Chicago and seeking out a position of some kind. I can also do plain sewing. Please good peple dont refuse to help me out in my trouble for I am in gret need of help God will bless you. I am going to do my very best after I get over here if God spair me to get work I will pay the expance back. Do try to do the best you can for me, with many thanks for so doing I will remain as ever.

Yours truly.

GRANVILLE, MISS., May 16, 1917.

Dear Sir: This letter is a letter of information of which you will find stamp envelop for reply. I want to come north some time soon but I do not want to leve here looking for a job wher I would be in dorse all winter. Now the work I am doing here is running a gauge edger in a saw mill. I know all about the grading of lumber. I have abeen working in lumber about 25 or 27 years My wedges here is $3.00 a day 11 hours a day. I want to come north where I can educate my 3 little children also my wife. Now if you cannot fit me up at what I am doing down here I can learn anything any one els can. also there is a great deal of good women cooks here would leave any time all they want is to know where to go and some way to go. please write me at once just how I can get my people where they can get something for their work. there are women here cookeing for $1.50 and $2.00 a week. I would like to live in Chicago or Ohio or Philadelphia. Tell Mr Abbott that our pepel are tole that they can not get anything to do up there and they are being snatched off the trains here in Greenville and a rested but in spite of all this, they are leaving every day and every night 100 or more is expecting to leave this week. Let me here from you at once.

MACON, GA., April 1, 1917.

Dear Sir: I am writing you for information I want to come north east but I have not sufficient funds and I am writing you to see if there is any way that you can help me by giving me the names of some of the firms that will send me a transportation as we are down here where we have to be shot down here like rabbits for every little orfence as I seen an orcurince hapen down here this after noon when three depties from the shrief office an one Negro spotter come out and found some of our raice mens in a crap game and it makes me want to leave the south worse than I ever did when such things hapen right at my door. hopeing to have a reply soon and will in close a stamp from the same.

TROY, ALA., Oct. 17, 1916.

Dear Sir: I am enclosing a clipping of a lynching again which speaks for itself. I do wish there could be sufficient presure brought about to have federal investigation of such work. I wrote you a few days ago if you could furnish me with the addresses of some firms or co-opporations that needed common labor. So many of our people here are almost starving. The government is feeding quite a number here would go any where to better their conditions. If you can do any thing for us write me as early as possible.

BHAM, ALA., May 13, 1917.

Sir: the edeater of the paper i am in the darkness of the south and i am trying my best to get out do you no where about i can get a job in new york. i wood be so glad if cood get a good job hear in this beautifull city o please help me to get out of this low down county i am counted no more thin a dog help me please help me o how glad i wood be if some company wood send me a ticket to come and work for them no joking i mean business i work if i can get a good job.

Report of Hoover's Committee on Negro Housing*

The first major federal investigation of Negro housing was made in the Hoover Administration. The Committee on Negro Housing of the President's Conference on Home Building and Home Owner-ship found conditions "desperate" throughout the country. Most of the pioneering suggestions for urban rehabilitation and renewal recommended by the Committee in 1931 were ignored. That

* From the President's Conference on Home Building and Home Owner-ship, *Negro Housing* (Washington, D.C., 1931), pp. 122–130.

tenement life was as hopeless in Albany, New York, as in Kansas City, Missouri, is attested by these excerpts from housing surveys in various cities.

ALBANY, NEW YORK

With the exception of a relatively small number of homes built by Negro owners for their own use, not one new structure has been made available for the Negro tenant since 1900. A large portion of the houses occupied by Negroes are very old brick buildings and their death, barring accidental destruction, is so lingering and drawn out over so many years of decline and decay that they are undesirable from external appearances alone. In some cases essential repairs were made and the life of the building prolonged, while in other cases no repairs have been made and the buildings remain occupied. The houses do not represent what the city approves according to its Building Ordinance, but it does represent what Albany tolerates and offers to the increasing Negro population group. The Negro population is widely scattered in Albany, being distributed throughout 17 of the 19 wards of the city.

In general there is a low standard of housing for the Negro population in Albany. The scanty equipment and poor repair of the average Negro dwelling make the rent paid comparatively high.

CHICAGO, ILLINOIS

A selection was made of 274 Negro families living in all sections of Chicago. . . .

For the most part the physical surroundings of the Negro family, as indicated by these family histories, are poor. . . .

On the South Side, where most of the Negro population lives, the low quality of housing is widespread, although there are some houses of a better grade which are greatly in demand.

The ordinary conveniences, considered necessities by the average white citizen, are often lacking. Bathrooms are often missing. Gas lighting is common, and electric lighting is a rarity. Heating is commonly done by wood or coal stoves, and furnaces are rather exceptional; when furnaces are present, they are sometimes out of commission. . . .

An almost complete cessation in the building of dwellings in Chicago extended over the greater part of the period when Negro migration was heaviest. As the most recent comers into the tenement districts of the city, Negroes and Mexicans have found shelter in the most used, most outworn and derelict housing which the city keeps. The old tenement districts have long been experiencing a steady encroachment by industry and commerce. In whole or in part as residence sections they are destined for extinction. Already deterioration is general in them, both in their houses and in their neighborhood conditions. It is unlikely that anything will be done to make these districts more fit for dwelling places. Although in many cases it seems hardly conceivable, it nevertheless is probable that further decline and deterioration are all that can be predicted with certainty for much of the renting property in them. . . .

About 8 per cent of the 770 buildings in which the families included in this study dwelt occupied the rear of the lots and had another building in front of them. Almost six out of every ten buildings (59 per cent) had not more than two floors. Fifty-six per cent had only one or two dwellings in them. Fully half were of frame construction though within the fire limits. These are characteristics of older buildings rather than of recent construction in the thickly populated sections of a large city. As a city grows, the one-family frame houses give way to larger multi-family buildings of brick. Land values increase and the ideal of having a city of one-family homes fades into impracticability. . . .

COLUMBUS, OHIO

It is well known that unsatisfactory housing conditions are associated with poverty, both as a cause and as an effect. The very poor man, especially if he has lived only under rural conditions, does not know how to care for modern equipment when he secures a good house. He justifies the landlord's claim that poor people have poor ways. On the other hand, the lack of sanitary facilities is a real reason for dirt and disorder. The housewife who must carry all water from a distant well or hydrant cannot be held entirely to blame if the house is not immaculate. Under such conditions good habits of housekeeping are likely to suffer degeneration.

Negro migrants are poor. Their poverty and the barriers of race restrict them severely in their selection of a home. To this home they bring their country habits, thus helping to keep housing standards low; especially is this true in a district like Champion Avenue, where many of the lots are almost entirely taken up with cheap structures built primarily to produce income from rentals. . . .

Two types of dwellings prevail in this district. There is the old, solidly built house which was originally built for the use of its owner. Some of these houses have been remodeled and modernized by their present owners; others have been divided into tenements; still others remain unchanged—substantial, but not modern. There is also the type of dwelling which had been built more recently and less substantially, not to house its owner, but rather to supply him with an income from rents. Dwellings of this type are usually built at the least possible cost and with the fewest possible conveniences. Costs of repair on such houses would be heavy if repairs were made, but it is seldom found necessary to keep such houses in repair in order to rent them. Several cases can be pointed out in which the landlord has built two four-family flats on one lot with a sixty-foot frontage on the street. One flat is built close to the sidewalk and facing the street, and the other is built on the rear of the lot, facing the alley. The prevailing size of these flats is four rooms. Practically all of them are rental properties, as is shown by the fact that of the 84 households living in four-room apartments, only three were reported as living in their own homes.

These built-up alleys are often dignified by the term "court." A row of sheds built between the two flats, over the sewer-main, contains the fuel supply and the toilets. The latter are generally of the long-hopper type, with a funnel tile connected directly with the sewer-main, but with no flush arrangement to clear the funnel, which in many cases becomes clogged, especially in freezing weather or when used as a garbage receiver. When this happens, such a "toilet" becomes in fact a poor kind of vault privy, in violation of the real intent of the public health laws.

DETROIT, MICHIGAN

Housing is one of the most serious problems of the Negro in Detroit. For some years the fluctuating shortage in the number of houses for the population in general has had its greatest effect upon the Negro group. . . .

This St. Antoine district (which holds the largest Negro population) may be termed a deteriorating area from the standpoint of family housing. Bordering on the main commercial center of the city, it is no longer a favorable location for residential purposes, as factories, garages and other commercial establishments have been built. The paving is not generally of the best and traffic is heavy. Land values are high since the area is chiefly used for manufacturing or commercial purposes. A preponderance of the houses are old frame dwellings, and as the landlords are interested in them only as a temporary source of income until the property can be sold for other than residential purposes, sanitary conditions are often far from the best. In some blocks the houses are so dilapidated that expenditure on the part of the owner to make them suitable for living purposes would be useless. However, since houses still remain and Negro tenants can be obtained for them at any reasonable rent, most of them are still occupied.

The fact that the whites in Detroit feel that the presence of a Negro in a neighborhood depreciates property values is one of the most important factors in "the race problem."

ELIZABETH, NEW JERSEY

In Elizabeth, as in many other northern cities, there are no new houses built for occupancy by Negro tenants. Today a number of the houses occupied by Negroes, particularly in Elizabethport, are unfit for human habitation. The life of such houses is so long and their death, barring accidental destruction, is so lingering and drawn out over so many years of decline and decay that they are undesirable on external appearances alone. In some cases essential repairs have been made, and the buildings have remained occupied. Such conditions do not represent what the City of Elizabeth approves as satisfactory according to its ordinances, but they do represent what Elizabeth tolerates and offers to the ever-increasing Negro population.

KANSAS CITY, MISSOURI

. . . Few cities in the United States have better housing for the middle classes and for a large part of the working class; yet, in spite of these hopeful conditions, Kansas City has a housing problem of sufficient gravity to call for a vigorous movement to eradicate the evils which now exist. The housing problem as related to the Negro is an especially serious one, since only limited districts are available to him for residence purposes; and, as the population increases, these districts must either be enlarged or become overcrowded. The latter course has usually prevailed, and as a result the conditions have been gradually growing worse. . . .

Toilet accommodations are also totally inadequate. The present requirements of the sanitary ordinances of the city provide that not less than one water-closet or privy shall be furnished for every twenty persons, while the new building code provides that there must be one of these for every fifteen persons. Little effort has been made to enforce these provisions, especially in the old buildings where the mass of the Negroes are living. . . .

Only a small percentage of the houses in the congested Negro districts are provided with baths, either tub or shower, though the nature of the daily work done by both the Negro men and the Negro women makes it absolutely necessary for them to keep clean, if they are to retain their health and self-respect; yet the houses in which they are forced to live are not provided with the means. In an investigation made by the Board of Public Welfare near Garrison Square only two bathtubs were found in 827 Negro houses. However, the conditions are not so bad in the other sections of the city. Since baths are not provided by the Negro in his house, there remains no place in the entire city, save the free baths in the Allen Chapel African Methodist Church and a few Negro barber shops, where the Negro can secure a bath.

A Survey of the Effects of Urbanization James H. Hubert*

The demoralization bred in the ghetto affected every aspect of community life. The Negro slums of the twenties were noted for their high crime rates, poor health, juvenile delinquency, and others forms of urban disorder. Social workers made an intensive effort to alleviate the chaos of the ghetto, but were far from successful in doing so. James H. Hubert, executive secretary of the

* "Urbanization and the Negro," *Proceedings of the National Conference of Social Work, 1933* (Chicago, 1933), pp. 420–425.

New York Urban League, presented the following survey of racial problems in the city to the 1933 National Conference of Social Work.

Urbanization on a large scale is comparatively new among Negroes. Up to 1900, 77 per cent of Negroes were rural dwellers. Since 1910, they have been making up for lost time. . . . In spite of the fact that many of the forces pulling the Negroes to cities during the last two decades have diminished in intensity, the drift has continued. Attempts to arouse interest in the "back-to-the-farm movement" have generally fallen on deaf ears. The story is told of a labor agent from the South who went to Chicago some years ago to recruit workers in lumber mills. He was asked, "Mister, where did you say them logs is?" When told "Mississippi," his reply was, "If you'll bring them up here we'll saw them for you." The Negro in the North was predominantly urban before the opening of the present century. In 1920 he was 70 per cent urban in sharp contrast to native whites, who were only 38.6 per cent.

The movement was primarily to the four centers—New York, Chicago, Philadelphia, and Detroit. . . . Whatever influence Horace Greeley may have exerted on the Negro question before and during the Civil War, his advice to young men to go west has apparently not been taken seriously by the Negro of the present generation. For in 1930 there were only 130,000 Negroes in the entire western area. In about fifteen years Detroit's Negro population jumped from 6,000 to over 100,000. New York City rose from 150,000 in 1920 to 327,000 in 1930—an increase of 115 per cent against a 20 per cent increase for its white population.

What has been the effect of this new, unassimilated group on the community life? Everywhere this concentration of Negroes in segregated colonies has been followed by an aggravation of social problems.

According to the White House Conference on Child Health, tuberculosis among Negro children under five years of age is double that of white children; for those between the ages of five and nine, it is four times as great; and from ten to nineteen years of age, it is five times that of whites.

In Chicago, Negro girls and young women have constituted

nearly one-third of females confined in the jails. The Department of Correction of New York reported for 1930 that of 59,000 males arraigned in the four courts, 16,391, or about 28 per cent, were Negroes—five times as great as the population should warrant. One would think that Negroes are especially fond of going to jail. According to studies made by the National Urban League, unemployment runs all the way from four to six times that of the city as a whole. In juvenile delinquency, crime, disease, and the other ills that so vitally affect family life, the story is generally the same. Harlem is referred to in a report of the New York Vice Committee as a place where whites go on a moral vacation.

The causes are not far to seek. A study of 4,000 Negro families of Harlem in 1920 revealed that one-half the income of the heads of these families ($102 per month average) was expended for rent. To supplement this income, over 80 per cent of mothers worked away from home; 65 per cent resorted to taking in of lodgers.

Restriction to definite areas and denial of opportunities to work at the more remunerative jobs were the main contributing factors. A study just completed by the New York Building Congress divides Manhattan into four rental zones. Although the majority of the Negro population falls within the lowest-income group, 75 per cent of them live in the fifty- to one-hundred-dollar-per-month rental zone—the third highest rental section for the city.

Negroes . . . have usually taken over declining areas, houses abandoned as undesirable in the general forward movement of whites to other sections and supply tenants for houses that would otherwise remain unoccupied. Strange as it may seem, these newcomers have been compelled to pay from 10 to 40 per cent more for these houses than was paid by white tenants who preceded them. In Chicago, Negro tenants paid from $8.00 to $20.00 for the same room for which white tenants formerly paid $4.00 to $5.00. In New York, Negroes were found paying, in some instances, $110.00 per month for the same apartments for which whites had previously paid $55.00. Similar conditions were found in Philadelphia and Buffalo. . . .

The mobility of the urbanized Negro within the city is also greater than that of whites. It is estimated that the average Negro tenant in New York moves once every fifteen months, while the average white family moves only once in five years.

A study of census tracts by the President's Research Commission on recent social trends shows a pronounced tendency for immigrants to abandon their colonies and disperse among the general populaton. Negro colonies, on the contrary, show a different history. Instead of scattering, they tend to become more compact and racially more homogeneous.

Many students of the race problem in America have looked to urbanization and northern migration as one possible solution. But in deserting the country for the city, the Negro appears to have merely jumped from the frying pan into the fire. . . . Urbanization has accentuated the growing conviction that, regardless of efforts, the Negro finds it increasingly difficult to "make it on the level"; that he cannot beat the color line; that the barrier of race has condemned him to the lower level of life.

The Influence of Quackery Samuel M. Auerbach*

The history of the peasantry of all nations abounds in tales of superstition, quackery, magic. Slave narratives allude to local wise men, "conjurers," whose roots, powders, and spells were supposed to guarantee protection from wicked masters or act as love charms. "Just Returned from the South," where they apparently rejuvenated their divining powers, is a line used by Negro quacks today—their advertisements appear regularly in the Negro press. Quackery has played a continually harmful role in Negro urban life throughout the twentieth century. The American Social Hygiene Association studied the influence of quackery on Negroes in the twenties, and this is the report of its findings.

That enemy to true healing—the charlatan—is as old as time, and the fight against him is equally ancient. Jeremiah exhorted Israel "hearken not to the sorcerer"; in the Middle Ages, impostors were persecuted because their art seemed to partake of the supernatural; later on in an excess of zeal witches were burned. Today, less revengeful, but still aware of the danger, we make laws to protect the scientist and to suppress the charlatan.

In spite of the age-long combat he remains a factor to be

* Samuel M. Auerbach, "Quackery," *Opportunity*, VII (December, 1929), 373–375.

reckoned with in present-day medicine, and no field of medical practice is so often invaded by the impostor as that of the venereal diseases.

A nation-wide investigation of medical "quackery" in connection with syphilis and gonorrhea conducted by the American Social Hygiene Association has revealed the fact that the more ignorant Negroes are among the numerous victims of these practices. Many experienced public health workers consider the Negro's high morbidity and mortality rate to be due in part to his susceptibility to quack practices. He is not only the victim of the white quacks and charlatans, but he is exploited frequently by members of his own race. The ignorant Negro is easily influenced by the quack and charlatans through the traveling Indian medicine faker, the local wise woman and fortune teller, signs in drug store windows, circulars, posters, and advertisements in a considerable number of national and local Negro newspapers which have a wide circulation.

Many so-called Indian remedy companies, which are reputed to have hundreds of agents canvassing for victims for their cure-all, issue literature listing remedies for all possible or impossible pathological conditions. Local "wise women," "Hoodoo Doctors," witches and fortune tellers, "evil-eye" specialists and others sell charms which frequently have a strong appeal to the superstitious and ignorant.

During a six months' period over 150 "quacks" and charlatans, located in 20 states and 2 foreign countries, and advertising in various publications were investigated. Special investigations were made of advertisements appearing in Negro newspapers and certain types of periodicals for young men.

The advertisers may be roughly divided into the following groups:

1. "Specialists for men" who are licensed physicians and reach their clients through advertisements in newspapers, through pamphlets distributed on street corners or through museums for men, the latter being feeders for a medical office located above the museum.

2. "Hoodoo doctors," "witchcraft professors," "evil-eye specialists," "herbalists" and hypnotists who treat in person or through the mails.

3. So-called "medical institutes" or "clinics" which are run by laymen for diagnosis and treatment of venereal diseases, and "sexual rejuvenation" or to sell "cures" or treatment by mail. The "herbalists" also come under this grouping.

4. "Remedy companies" operated by individuals or companies which do not diagnose or treat, but sell and send remedies, instruments or apparatus through the mail for the guaranteed "cure" of diseases described by their correspondents.

5. Medical offices and "institutes" owned by laymen employing unscrupulous licensed medical practitioners, who lend their names to comply with the law, but where the "free advice" and "treatments" are not given by them.

The methods most frequently employed by quacks to secure patients are advertisements, correspondence and personal appeal. In the case of correspondence which frequently is national in scope the patient answers an advertisement. In reply a letter, circular, or perhaps a catalog, is sent to him with a request for money and an impressive but guarded statement is made and absolute assurance of complete recovery is given if the patient will take the treatment suggested and make the necessary payments. Frequently the "remedy" is sent C.O.D. Quite often the disease is not called by name and usually syphilis is called a "blood disease."

It is essential also to understand that there are large numbers of quacks and charlatans who conduct their business in an elaborate way. They spend thousands of dollars a year for newspaper advertising and for the maintenance of offices and museums. The offices are usually equipped with electric and other appliances which are calculated to lead the gullible victims to believe that it is possible to perform miracles. Many take it for granted that a charm worn around one's neck, or the spraying of a powder in the air, or treatment from an electric machine, is a much easier and quicker road to health than a treatment which requires intravenous and other medications over a long period of time. These people adopting the simpler easier means, think they will become cured, when as a matter of fact, the conditions become chronic if not already so, and they become a danger, not only to themselves, but to the community in which they live.

The following are the texts of typical advertisements copied from certain Negro newspapers and periodicals:

"I Can Cure You TRY ME! Call or write Dr. XX. With his soul power and with the aid of Herb Medicines, heals and banishes diseases given up by doctors as incurable, as if by magic brings success to those who are down and out."

"BLOOD DISEASES—NO MATTER HOW BAD AND OLD THE CASE OR WHAT'S THE CAUSE send for FREE booklet about Dr. X's Treatment successfully used over 25 years in the most severe and chronic cases. Write now."

"See or write to Dr. X for Questionnaire. You can roughly examine yourself and take home treatments for chronic complaints by mail C. O. D. *** Specific for syphilis, blood, aching bones, lost vitality, etc."

"PROF. XXX. Noted Oriental healer and spiritual psychic. Private and confidential readings. Will advise you on all matters and guarantee you results."

"BLOOD AND SKIN PURIFIER. Recommended to be the best Tonic on the Market for Blood and Skin Diseases. GOOD FOR—Pimples, Pustels; Tetter and Salt Rheumatism, Blotches, Boils, Sores, Ringworms, SYPHILITIC AFFECTIONS, Ulcerousness, Rheumatism and all Blood and Skin Disorders. Why not take several bottles and get relieved of those dreadful diseases? Price $1.00 per bottle; 75 cents per package. Manufactured and Guaranteed by ***."

"TOO WEAK TO MARRY? Order XX French Pep. Restores vitality, pep, and youthful energy. Corrects exhaustion ***."

"Are you in hard luck? Are you discouraged? Are you unhappy? Are you disappointed in Business, Health and Love Affairs? Try Dr. . . . .'s Incense and Holy Oil. A secret from the Orient 1000 years a mystery. Each package contains your Horoscope—Lucky Day and Lucky Numbers Sure Winners. No Matter What Your Problem may be, No Matter How Dark the World May Seem There is a Bright Day Ahead for You. Thousands made Happy Daily."

A few cases cited here illustrate the type of fraud uncovered by the investigation:

1. A man in an eastern city conducts a "private clinic." He advertises in newspapers from coast to coast, requesting that those suffering from venereal and other sex diseases write to him for

information enclosing 25 cents in stamps. He especially urges those intending to get married to apply to him for advice. He diagnosed a case through the mail as "chronic gonorrhea," stating that the "microscopic urinalysis and a smear" confirmed this. The sample sent him contained only a spot of the white of an egg and a bottle with a little pure water colored with tobacco juice. He offered to cure the disease in two weeks for $200.

2. An advertiser in a middle western newspaper offers to cure both chronic and acute diseases, especially "diseases that have been given up as incurable by other specialists." He claims to restore hearing to the deaf, sight to the blind, and to perform miracles. He also treats "diseases of men and women." Investigation showed that this man was not a licensed practitioner, and that in addition to his medical office he runs a diploma mill for magnetic healers, hypnotists, etc. This "specialist" offered to treat and cure a case of syphilis through the mail for $120 payable in advance.

3. Another advertiser in various publications states that he has "a powerful constructive, vim, vigor, vitality—nerve body building remedy," and is an expert on "diseases of both sexes." With each remedy he offers as an inducement a free reading of the patient's future. The amount asked for, to cure a venereal disease was "$25 and up."

4. Two "professors" advertise in newspapers from coast to coast. A conservative estimate of the amount of money paid by each of them for advertising is $3,000 a month. Each claims to be the "world's greatest witchcraft and evil-eye specialist" endowed with supernatural powers, and offers among other things to give "victory in everything, including diseases, evil-eye, sorcery, witchcraft spells, enemies, lost love. . . ." The preliminary investigation showed that one layman operated both these enterprises. A letter was written to each of these "professors." One of them replied, "I can liberate you surely from the disease with the utmost of secrecy for $60"; the second "professor" offered a cure for $55 but wanted additional information as to the kind of disease.

5. From a middle western state comes the advertisement of a former "victim of syphilis, cancer and tuberculosis" given up as incurable by famous medical specialists who discovered a preparation with which he cured himself of these three diseases. He offers

his discovery to suffering humanity for $38.00 a gallon of remedy
—one month's treatment—to be forwarded on receipt of the
money. No C.O.D. orders accepted.

6. From the Pacific Coast comes an advertisement of a certain
person claiming supernatural power. Inquiry as to whether the
advertiser could cure a disease "gotten from a woman" brought a
reply that this disease could be cured by correspondence for $25.

Many Chinese herb specialists on the Pacific Coast advertise
that they cure all chronic diseases given up by other doctors. These
are "herbalists" and none of them are licensed physicians. A
Negro (who uses the title "Doctor" without authority), diagnosed
as primary syphilis a case which had been described so as to
preclude an honest opinion that it would be syphilis. He stated that
his medicine, at a price of from $2.95 to $8.95 per dose, would
cure the disease.

From another city comes an advertisement from a man, who
claims to be able to cure all diseases because he was "born on
Good Friday, under the sign of the Seven Stars, with my mouth
full of teeth, and haven't ever seen my father." A letter was written
to him in which he was asked whether he could cure a venereal
disease, and if so, how long it would take and how much it would
cost. No mention was made of the kind of disease nor was he given
any symptoms. The following reply was received. The spelling is
reproduced exactly as in the letter:

Dear Sir:
  i Exknowledge your letter of the 10th please be advise to the said
case witch you have it is a matter of bad blood and the spylner cord
of your back now i want to say to you, that Sygyraer trouble is a bad
thing now you did not explain to me like it is your back are giveing
you trouble and you have a pain that are following you in your Chest
and you are suffering with acking joints at time. now if you will send
me the some of $10.00 i will stard your case and you need other work
did to so if you wish to send me the money and wish to enroll your
name under my administrations. for your help and advises i am in my
office awaiting a reply from you.
  i remain your helping friend.
                              very truly
                              Signature
                              ExKnowledgethrilltoo

In addition to the charlatans who advertise nationally through the mail, there are many pseudo specialists who advertise in local newspapers. Some of them conduct offices which are run by laymen who employ registered physicians to lend their names. They specialize in noisy electrical apparatus and offer to perform the impossible. Some of these medical offices have so-called "museums for men" where admission is free. The experience of an investigator who visited one of these museums is interesting:

I visited the free museum for men only of Dr. X., an advertising specialist. It consists of various specimen show cases, exhibiting charts and wax models of the human body, especially diseased sex organs. One of the employees asked, "Is there anything I can do for you?" I replied that I knew of nothing. He said, "You don't look well. Don't be bashful. Don't be ashamed. Tell me all about yourself." I asked him what he meant. He replied, "Don't you know what I mean? It's very dangerous for a man of your age. You look as if you had gonorrhea. My advice is to go up and see the doctor at once. It won't cost you anything." When I wanted to know how he could tell that I was infected with gonorrhea and whether he was a doctor, he replied, "I have been here long enough to know. I can tell you are sick by looking at you."

Many young men who contract venereal diseases or believe themselves suffering from such diseases apply to the corner drugstore for relief. Druggists in certain localities sometimes examine the patient and "counter-prescribe" something to "cure" the disease. . . .

What is the solution to the problem? What can be done to protect the public against "quackery"? To meet this situation it is necessary that there should be a more vigorous application of the Federal and State laws; namely: those dealing with the use of the mails for fraudulent medical practices; the false branding of drugs; medical licensure and practice; and the control of advertisements of drugs for the treatment of syphilis and gonorrhea. The application of the Government and State machinery is often hindered by lack of sufficient personnel and funds.

An active interest on the part of medical societies and social agencies would be an important contribution to the repressions of quack medical practice. Since cases dealing with quackery can be acted upon most easily if evidence is presented to the responsible officials, complaints might be presented by such groups as timidity, ignorance, or lack of interest on the part of the victim frequently prevents any action being taken.

The refusal of questionable advertisements by all newspapers, including Negro newspapers, would contribute towards protection of the health and welfare of the Negro race. If they would go a step further and give publicity to the methods of quacks and charlatans, the situation would be greatly helped.

Education is one of the most strategic methods of combating quackery. Negro ministers, physicians, editors, educators, and social workers can cooperate in the solution of this difficult problem by advising and guiding those with whom they work. In New York City the Negro physicians through their various organizations have taken a step in the right direction. They are filing complaints against quacks with the Health authorities and are attempting to educate the people with reference to this important problem.

The Storefront Church *Ira De Augustine Reid**

All migrant people attempt to ease their way into a new culture by retaining as much of the substance and spirit of their former institutions and lives as possible. This was evident most clearly among Negro migrants in the proliferation of storefront churches that emerged in all the black ghettos. A walk through Harlem or Chicago's South Side today will attest to the fascination that a fervent, soul shaking, fundamentalist religious service holds for recent Negro settlers in the city. The type of religious institutions that Ira De Augustine Reid describes in the twenties are still active today.

Incredible as it may seem there are within the radius of one hundred and fifty blocks of that section of Harlem occupied by the colored population more than one hundred and forty churches. At the time of the count there were exactly that number. Since then more have been instituted or have moved into the district. These churches have an estimated membership of more than forty thousand.

* Ira De A. Reid, "Let Us Prey!" *Opportunity*, IV (September, 1926), 274–278.

In this large collection of religious institutions one may find the church respected and the church reviled, the church militant and the church penitent, the church "modern" and the church "fundamental," the church esoteric and the church exoteric. One may also find a diversified assortment of denominations—Baptist, Methodist, Presbyterian as well as Moravian, Lutheran, Apostolic and African Orthodox. And here is the mother church of the African Methodist Episcopal Zion Church, and the National Headquarters of the Eureka Oasis Discipleship.

There is no doubt that there are churches in each denomination rendering valuable service to the community. . . . However, these churches have an arduous task. Not only are they called upon to minister to the social and religious needs of their people, but they must also keep established a defense mechanism to offset the subtle encroachments of a large number of smaller institutions called churches, whose leaders have advertently or inadvertently revised the well known entreaty to prayer. For them it reads "Let us prey."

Only fifty-four of these churches are housed in regular church edifices, or residences that have been converted to a peculiar style of church architecture. The churches remaining are in the class known as house churches. They are to be found occupying the first floor of a private dwelling, a site formerly used for business purposes, or the back room of a flat. In fact they are anywhere and everywhere. Yet one cannot register a wholesale criticism against a church because it is located in a house, for there are many larger churches whose general conduct is less moral. It is likewise true that many of the larger churches have had their beginning in houses. Nor can one evade the fact that in this same group there is found a large number of so-called churches that do little or no good and much harm in the community.

Ministers of the leading churches in this section have been opposed to this spurious growth of so-called Christian churches for some time, and have violently condemned the esoteric cults that have arisen. The latter are in most cases conducted by exploiters and charlatans. But they are dynamically opposed to the activities of the "one-man" church. The pastor of one of the largest churches said in a sermon a few weeks ago: "No we haven't too many churches in Harlem. We do have too many house churches.

Somebody wants to be a leader, deacon or preacher and if the large church doesn't give it to him he will establish a little church of his own where he can be seen. Selfishness is really the cause of so many of these house churches." Thus speaks one. And many others have been more violent. Yet these churches have increased.

The churches that spasmodically arise from nowhere and in many cases disappear in much the same fashion are a general nuisance. Neither their appearance nor their character warrants the respect of the community. Their ministers are familiarly called "jack-legs," while their poorly written sign-boards advertising the name of the pastor with his title and degrees, and incidentally the name of the church and the order of service have become the butt of many jokes. Look at one. This holy tabernacle of God is in the very heart of Harlem. One thinks of all save church as he sees a dilapidated frame structure panting beneath the crush of two brick buildings that have been erected on either side of it. There is a yard. A hungry cat slinks through the gate. She reposes on an old push cart in the yard. One sees a rusty milk can, a cot, and several well-aged pieces of wood scattered promiscuously in front of the entrance. An old stone walk leads to the door. It is well worn and cracked. The crevices have been worn to the level of the walk. The steps have been patched so often that little of the original framework seems to remain. The house is paintless except in isolated spots. A dry-rotted trellis hangs dejectedly down the side. In the basement a carpenter plies his trade awaiting the coming of such persons as will follow his teachings blatantly expressed on the shingle which reads:

We Believe That All Manner of Disease Can
Be Cured

by the power of GOD divine. Healing is always
needed; no matter what your ailment may be
it can always be cured. This place is open day
and night for the healing of the sick and prayer.

Jesus is the Doctor
Services on Sunday

In this group of churches there were fifty meeting in places that had outlived their usefulness as homes or places of business. These places rarely if ever seat fifty persons at the utmost, and are poorly lighted and ventilated. They are chiefly immediate neighborhood affairs, support depending upon the activity of the pastor in securing members from the surrounding apartments and tenements. It is because of this fact that the turnover among these churches is very high. They are forced to follow their members, secure new ones, or go out of business. Six weeks after the preliminary list of the churches was made seven of the churches previously listed could not be found.

The wrath of the public when it is active is centered upon the ministers of these churches rather than at the churches themselves. It is the feeling that they are the ones responsible for such a condition. But they must live and despite what may be said against them it is true that in them you find one group that is doing the thing it wants to do. There is no doubt that the assertion made by a minister that selfishness was the underlying motive of many of the organizations is true. One is reminded of the incident relating to the young swain who had come to the church meeting to show good reason why he should be ordained as a Christian minister. He stated that he had a dream. In this dream a still small voice told him to "G. P. C." and when he heard it he knew that he was instructed to "Go preach Christ." After further questioning by the council the chairman told him that he had misinterpreted his dream, for it certainly meant "Go plant corn."

A Southern minister had lost his charges because all of the members had moved North. For five years he had travelled from Georgia to Cincinnati to Chicago to Detroit, thence to New York, where he would assemble his old members for Sunday services. He would exhort and extort in each place. Recently his New York followers became weary of contributing to his wanderlust and suggested that he establish himself here and organize a church. He did not think it wise to do this because his many members in other cities would be neglected. As a result the members failed to transport him South again. Then was he willing to accept their suggestion. It was too late. At present he represents himself as a "pastor at large." He is the supply minister for many of the smaller churches in the city. He boasts that he is a pioneer and has never pastored the church that another has held. He is going to establish the ideal church in Harlem, and has his plans well laid.

Meanwhile others of the ministers are merrily engaged in deploring the vices of sinners and Christians and forewarning them of the wrath that is to come, only to find themselves apprehended on the morrow for the alleged violation of civil and criminal codes. Some of them have found temporary resting places in the unclerical confines of the police station.

All these things do not loom as large upon the horizon of church problems as does the rapid growth of the church esoteric in Harlem. Within the last six years there has been a tidal wave of these groups, many of them sincere in their beliefs but hampered and degraded by a large number of exploiters and charlatans. There are they who dabble in spiritualism, exhibiting their many charms and wares in the form of Grand Imperial incense, prayer incense, aluminum trumpets, luminous bands and other accessories. Among the exploiters in this group one is wont to find as many men as women engaged as pastors, directors and leaders.

It is astounding to note the growth and variety of these movements. Here one finds "The Commandment Keepers, Holy Church of the Living God, The Pillar and the Ground of the Truth," "The Temple of the Gospel of the Kingdom," "The Metaphysical Church of the Divine Investigation," "Prophet Bess," "Mt. Zion Pentecostal Church," "St. Matthew's Church of the Divine Silence and Truth," "Tabernacle of the Congregation of the Disciples of the Kingdom," "Congregation of Beth B'Nai Abraham," "Holy Temple of God in Christ," "The Church of the Temple of Love," and many others—all practicing various doctrines and creeds provocative of no good save the financial returns obtained by the leader.

A visit to the average fake spiritualist meeting proves to be of an innocent if not stupid nature. There are possibly ten or twelve believers present when the service begins. Terrible discords and hymns that were deserving of a better fate were sung. Then the plate was passed and the leader or the assistant passed the plate, appealing for funds to pay the rent already past due. Then the messages started.

This medium, who chanced to be an immense fat man, used none of the regular tricks of the trade. He relied upon the stupidity of the audience and his own. After a few convulsive shivers he started to get messages. Standing in front of each person in turn, and holding some article belonging to him, he proceeded to bring him the good word from those who had passed beyond. Half of the time the messages were wrong, most of the time they were so general they could be applied to any one, and the rest of the time they were so jumbled nobody could understand them. The whole thing was a farce yet one old man sat in the meeting, paid the medium his two dollars—that he evidently needed very badly for himself—and listened with tears in his eyes to the message from a dead relative. The medium failed to mention just which relative it was.

This medium belonged to the "piker" class. There are some who charge larger fees and work with all the paraphernalia of the profession. They get their messages in the dark and have various ways of speaking through collapsible trumpets, and tapping those who are to receive the messages. They prey upon people whose better judgment has been deadened by worry or sorrow, and reap an immense profit. Most of the people thus engaged are in the business for easy personal gain, and are out and out frauds, although there are some sincere mediums and some sincere spiritualists.

This prostitution does not stop here. There have infested Harlem, groups that to all appearances have "acquired" the distinguishing features of the Jews and have called themselves Black Jews. They claim to have come from Damascus, Palestine, and various parts of the Orient. Their activities range from a grocery store to a conservatory of music.

Recently the head of one of these cults has been sent to the Federal Penitentiary for the violation of the Mann Act. This group conducted a "baby farm" in Abescon, N.J. Here was said to be the home of the many children of the "Messiah" (who was their leader). They were borne by such "virgins" as had been elected by him to give themselves to the propagation of the cause. Here are Elder Lazarus, Elder Kauffman, Rosenthal, Goldberg, and many other interesting characters. Under their leadership the Temple of the Gospel of the Kingdom continues.

Then there are other cults that function in their own peculiar fashion. A former minister of the Methodist church, who resigned in 1913, conducts a clannish thing called a Discipleship. There are associated and initiated members. When this minister became the founder and head of the sect he assumed the title of Bishop and the degree of D.D.T.

In this group when one has earned the title of Disciple there is erected in his or her home an altar. The Disciple is now qualified to minister to the physical and spiritual wants of those who are willing to believe. Their services are conducted under such high-sounding phrases as "The Sanctiloquent Equity Exposition," "Inquisition and Information Service," "Practical Biblical Deliberation," and "Ethical Development Classes."

The whole group is characterized by the machinations of impostors who do their work in great style. Bishops without a diocese, those who heal with divine inspiration, praying circles that charge for their services, American Negroes turned Jews "over night," theological seminaries conducted in the rear of "railroad" apartments, Black Rev. Wm. Sundays, Ph.D., who have escaped the wrath of many communities, new denominations built upon the fundamental doctrine of race—all these and even more contribute to the prostitution of the church. And there seems to be no end to their growth. Already have five new institutions been opened for business. One thinks of the much advertised cinema production "Hell Bent For Heaven."

It is unfortunate that the efforts of sincere and well-established churches in Harlem, both small and large, have to be hampered by the manipulations of these groups—both orthodox and pagan—of the outer fringe. While the one steadily prods at social problems with instruments both spiritual and physical, and methods religious and humanitarian, the others are saying "Let us prey." And they do.

2. MARCUS GARVEY'S UNIVERSAL NEGRO IMPROVEMENT ASSOCIATION

"An Appeal to the Conscience of the Black Race" Marcus Garvey*

Marcus Garvey had great respect for Booker T. Washington. Reading Washington's autobiography Up From Slavery *shaped the*

---

* From Amy Jacques-Garvey, *Philosophy and Opinions of Marcus Garvey, or Africa for the Africans* (New York, 1925), II, 22–26.

course of his life and Garvey originally came to America to see Washington—he hoped to establish a Tuskegee-like institution in Jamaica. The two men shared many ideological precepts. Of these the most important was their faith in racial separation and self-help. The businesses Garvey founded were supposed to prove to the world that Negroes could run successful economic enterprises; and only black men were permitted to buy stock in these companies. Unfortunately for this ideal Garvey had an abundance of charisma but a total lack of entrepreneurial common sense. "An Appeal to the Conscience of the Black Race to See Itself"— including its bitter words for Garvey's Negro opponents—is representative of his broader racial philosophy.

It is said to be a hard and difficult task to organize and keep together large numbers of the Negro race for the common good. Many have tried to congregate us, but have failed, the reason being that our characteristics are such as to keep us more apart than together.

The evil of internal division is wrecking our existence as a people, and if we do not seriously and quickly move in the direction of a readjustment it simply means that our doom becomes imminently conclusive.

For years the Universal Negro Improvement Association has been working for the unification of our race, not on domestic-national lines only, but universally. The success which we have met in the course of our effort is rather encouraging, considering the time consumed and the environment surrounding the object of our concern.

It seems that the whole world of sentiment is against the Negro, and the difficulty of our generation is to extricate ourselves from the prejudice that hides itself beneath, as well as above, the action of an international environment.

Prejudice is conditional on many reasons, and it is apparent that the Negro supplies, consciously or unconsciously, all the reasons by which the world seems to ignore and avoid him. No one cares for a leper, for lepers are infectious persons, and all are afraid of the disease, so, because the Negro keeps himself poor, helpless and undemonstrative, it is natural also that no one wants to be of him or with him.

PROGRESS AND HUMANITY

Progress is the attraction that moves humanity, and to whatever people or race this "modern virtue" attaches itself, there will you find the splendor of pride and self-esteem that never fail to win the respect and admiration of all.

It is the progress of the Anglo-Saxons that singles them out for the respect of all the world. When their race had no progress or achievement to its credit, then, like all other inferior peoples, they paid the price in slavery, bondage, as well as through prejudice. We cannot forget the time when even the ancient Briton was regarded as being too dull to make a good Roman slave, yet today the influence of that race rules the world.

It is the industrial and commercial progress of America that causes Europe and the rest of the world to think appreciatively of the Anglo-American race. It is not because one hundred and ten million people live in the United States that the world is attracted to the republic with so much reverence and respect—a reverence and respect not shown to India with its three hundred millions, or to China with its four hundred millions. Progress of and among any people will advance them in the respect and appreciation of the rest of their fellows. It is such a progress that the Negro must attach to himself if he is to rise above the prejudice of the world.

The reliance of our race upon the progress and achievements of others for a consideration in sympathy, justice and rights is like a dependence upon a broken stick, resting upon which will eventually consign you to the ground.

SELF-RELIANCE AND RESPECT

The Universal Negro Improvement Association teaches our race self-help and self-reliance, not only in one essential, but in all those things that contribute to human happiness and well-being. The disposition of the many to depend upon the other races for a kindly and sympathetic consideration of their needs, without making the effort to do for themselves, has been the race's standing disgrace by which we have been judged and through which we have created the strongest prejudice against ourselves.

There is no force like success, and that is why the individual makes all efforts to surround himself throughout life with the evidence of it. As of the individual, so should it be of the race and nation. The glittering success of Rockefeller makes him a power in the American nation; the success of Henry Ford suggests him as an object of universal respect, but no one knows and cares about the bum or hobo who is Rockefeller's or Ford's neighbor. So, also, is the world attracted by the glittering success of races and nations, and pays absolutely no attention to the bum or hobo race that lingers by the wayside.

The Negro must be up and doing if he will break down the prejudice of the rest of the world. Prayer alone is not going to improve our condition, nor the policy of watchful waiting. We must strike out for ourselves in the course of material achievement, and by our own effort and energy present to the world those forces by which the progress of man is judged.

A NATION AND COUNTRY

The Negro needs a nation and a country of his own, where he can best show evidence of his own ability in the art of human progress. Scattered as an unmixed and unrecognized part of alien nations and civilizations is but to demonstrate his imbecility, and point him out as an unworthy derelict, fit neither for the society of Greek, Jew nor Gentile.

It is unfortunate that we should so drift apart, as a race, as not to see that we are but perpetuating our own sorrow and disgrace in failing to appreciate the first great requisite of all peoples—organization.

Organization is a great power in directing the affairs of a race or nation toward a given goal. To properly develop the desires that are uppermost, we must first concentrate through some system or method, and there is none better than organization. Hence, the Universal Negro Improvement Association appeals to each and every Negro to throw in his lot with those of us who, through organization, are working for the universal emancipation of our race and the redemption of our common country, Africa.

No Negro, let him be American, European, West Indian or African, shall be truly respected until the race as a whole has emancipated itself, through self-achievement and progress, from universal prejudice. The Negro will have to build his own government, industry, art, science, literature and culture, before the world will stop to consider him. Until then, we are but wards of a superior race and civilization, and the outcasts of a standard social system.

The race needs workers at this time, not plagiarists, copyists and mere imitators; but men and women who are able to create, to originate and improve, and thus make an independent racial contribution to the world and civilization.

Monkey Apings of "Leaders"

The unfortunate thing about us is that we take the monkey apings of our "so-called leading men" for progress. There is no progress in aping white people and telling us that they represent the best in the race, for in that respect any dressed monkey would represent the best of its species, irrespective of the creative matter of the monkey instinct: The best in a race is not reflected through or by the action of its apes, but by its ability to create of and by itself. It is such a creation that the Universal Negro Improvement Association seeks.

Let us not try to be the best or worst of others, but let us make the effort to be the best of ourselves. Our own racial critics criticise us as dreamers and "fanatics," and call us "benighted" and "ignorant," because they lack racial backbone. They are unable to see themselves creators of their own needs. The slave instinct has not yet departed from them. They still believe that they can only live or exist through the good graces of their "masters." The good slaves have not yet thrown off their shackles; thus, to them, the Universal Negro Improvement Asociation is an "impossibility."

It is the slave spirit of dependence that causes our "so-called leading men" (apes) to seek the shelter, leadership, protection and patronage of the "master" in their organization and so-called advancement work. It is the spirit of feeling secured as good servants of the master, rather than as independents, why our modern Uncle Toms take pride in laboring under alien leadership and becoming surprised at the audacity of the Universal Negro

Improvement Association in proclaiming for racial liberty and independence.

But the world of white and other men, deep down in their hearts, have much more respect for those of us who work for our racial salvation under the banner of the Universal Negro Improvement Association, than they could ever have in all eternity for a group of helpless apes and beggars who make a monopoly of undermining their own race and belittling themselves in the eyes of self-respecting people, by being "good boys" rather than able men.

Surely there can be no good will between apes, seasoned beggars and independent minded Negroes who will at least make an effort to do for themselves. Surely, the "dependents" and "wards" (and may I not say racial imbeciles?) will rave against and plan the destruction of movements like the Universal Negro Improvement Association that expose them to the liberal white minds of the world as not being representative of the best in the Negro, but, to the contrary, the worst. The best of a race does not live on the patronage and philanthropy of others, but makes an effort to do for itself. The best of the great white race doesn't fawn before and beg black, brown or yellow men; they go out, create for self and thus demonstrate the fitness of the race to survive; and so the white race of America and the world will be informed that the best in the Negro race is not the class of beggars who send out to other races piteous appeals annually for donations to maintain their coterie, but the groups within us that are honestly striving to do for themselves with the voluntary help and appreciation of that class of other races that is reasonable, just and liberal enough to give to each and every one a fair chance in the promotion of those ideals that tend to greater human progress and human love.

The work of the Universal Negro Improvement Association is clear and clean-cut. It is that of inspiring an unfortunate race with pride in self and with the determination of going ahead in the creation of those ideals that will lift them to the unprejudiced company of races and nations. There is no desire for hate or malice, but every wish to see all mankind linked into a common fraternity of progress and achievement that will wipe away the odor of prejudice, and elevate the human race to the height of real godly love and satisfaction.

"Declaration of Rights of the Negro Peoples of the World"
Marcus Garvey*

*The usual standards by which one evaluates the success or failure
of a social movement cannot readily be applied to the Garvey
movement. Garvey, as mystic and dreamer, hoped to unite all
black people of the world in what he called spiritual harmony. He
conceived himself the oracle of an abused people who would speak
out against every form of racial injustice in every country in the
world. His mission, as he said, was to "arouse the sleeping
consciousness of Negroes everywhere . . . and appeal to the
spirit of racial pride and love." No earthly being could have
accomplished all the things Garvey set out to do. An example of
the breadth of his demands is the following "Declaration of Rights
of the Negro Peoples of the World."*

Drafted and adopted at Convention held in New York, 1920, over
which Marcus Garvey presided as Chairman, and at which he was
elected provisional President of Africa.

(PREAMBLE)

"Be it Resolved, That the Negro people of the world, through their
chosen representatives in convention assembled in Liberty Hall, in
the City of New York and United States of America, from August
1 to August 31, in the year of our Lord, one thousand nine
hundred and twenty, protest against the wrongs and injustices they
are suffering at the hands of their white brethren, and state what
they deem their fair and just rights, as well as the treatment they
propose to demand of all men in the future."

We complain:

I. "That nowhere in the world, with few exceptions, are black
men accorded equal treatment with white men, although in the
same situation and circumstances, but, on the contrary, are discriminated against and denied the common rights due to human
beings for no other reason than their race and color."

* In Amy Jacques-Garvey, *Philosophy and Opinions of Marcus Garvey,
or Africa for the Africans* (New York, 1925), II, 135–142.

"We are not willingly accepted as guests in the public hotels and inns of the world for no other reason than our race and color."

II. "In certain parts of the United States of America our race is denied the right of public trial accorded to other races when accused of crime, but are lynched and burned by mobs, and such brutal and inhuman treatment is even practised upon our women."

III. "That European nations have parcelled out among ·them and taken possession of nearly all of the continent of Africa, and the natives are compelled to surrender their lands to aliens and are treated in most instances like slaves."

IV. "In the southern portion of the United States of America, although citizens under the Federal Constitution, and in some states almost equal to the whites in population and are qualified land owners and taxpayers, we are, nevertheless, denied all voice in the making and administration of the laws and are taxed without representation by the state governments, and at the same time compelled to do military service in defense of the country."

V. "On the public conveyances and common carriers in the Southern portion of the United States we are jim-crowed and compelled to accept separate and inferior accommodations and made to pay the same fare charged for first-class accommodations, and our families are often humiliated and insulted by drunken white men who habitually pass through the jim-crow cars going to the smoking car."

VI. "The physicians of our race are denied the right to attend their patients while in the public hospitals of the cities and states where they reside in certain parts of the United States."

"Our children are forced to attend inferior separate schools for shorter terms than white children, and the public school funds are unequally divided between the white and colored schools."

VII. "We are discriminated against and denied an equal chance to earn wages for the support of our families, and in many instances are refused admission into labor unions, and nearly everywhere are paid smaller wages than white men."

VIII. "In Civil Service and departmental offices we are everywhere discriminated against and made to feel that to be a black man in Europe, America and the West Indies is equivalent to being an outcast and a leper among the races of men; no matter what the character and attainments of the black man may be."

IX. "In the British and other West Indian Islands and colonies, Negroes are secretly and cunningly discriminated against, and denied those fuller rights of governments to which white citizens are appointed, nominated and elected."

X. "That our people in those parts are forced to work for lower wages than the average standard of white men and are kept in conditions repugnant to good civilized tastes and customs."

XI. "That the many acts of injustices against members of our race before the courts of law in the respective islands and colonies are of such nature as to create disgust and disrespect for the white man's sense of justice."

XII. "Against all such inhuman, unchristian and uncivilized treatment we here and now emphatically protest, and invoke the condemnation of all mankind."

"In order to encourage our race all over the world and to stimulate it to a higher and grander destiny, we demand and insist on the following Declaration of Rights:

1. "Be it known to all men that whereas, all men are created equal and entitled to the rights of life, liberty and the pursuit of happiness, and because of this we, the duly elected representatives of the Negro peoples of the world, invoking the aid of the just and Almighty God do declare all men women and children of our blood throughout the world free citizens, and do claim them as free citizens of Africa, the Motherland of all Negroes."

2. "That we believe in the supreme authority of our race in all things racial; that all things are created and given to man as a common possession; that there should be an equitable distribution and apportionment of all such things, and in consideration of the fact that as a race we are now deprived of those things that are morally and legally ours, we believe it right that all such things should be acquired and held by whatsoever means possible.

3. "That we believe the Negro, like any other race, should be governed by the ethics of civilization, and, therefore, should not be deprived of any of those rights or privileges common to other human beings."

4. "We declare that Negroes, wheresoever they form a community among themselves, should be given the right to elect their

own representatives to represent them in legislatures, courts of law, or such institutions as may exercise control over that particular community."

5. "We assert that the Negro is entitled to even-handed justice before all courts of law and equity in whatever country he may be found, and when this is denied him on account of his race or color such denial is an insult to the race as a whole and should be resented by the entire body of Negroes."

6. "We declare it unfair and prejudicial to the rights of Negroes in communities where they exist in considerable numbers to be tried by a judge and jury composed entirely of an alien race, but in all such cases members of our race are entitled to representation on the jury."

7. "We believe that any law or practice that tends to deprive any African of his land or the privileges of free citizenship within his country is unjust and immoral, and no native should respect any such law or practice."

8. "We declare taxation without representation unjust and tyrannous, and there should be no obligation on the part of the Negro to obey the levy of a tax by any law-making body from which he is excluded and denied representation on account of his race and color."

9. "We believe that any law especially directed against the Negro to his detriment and singling him out because of his race or color is unfair and immoral, and should not be respected."

10. "We believe all men entitled to common human respect, and that our race should in no way tolerate any insults that may be interpreted to mean disrespect to our color."

11. "We deprecate the use of the term 'nigger' as applied to Negroes, and demand that the word 'Negro' be written with a capital 'N.' "

12. "We believe that the Negro should adopt every means to protect himself against barbarous practices inflicted upon him because of color."

13. "We believe in the freedom of Africa for the Negro people of the world, and by the principle of Europe for the Europeans and Asia for the Asiatics; we also demand Africa for the Africans at home and abroad."

14. "We believe in the inherent right of the Negro to possess

himself of Africa, and that his possession of same shall not be regarded as an infringement on any claim or purchase made by any race or nation."

15. "We strongly condemn the cupidity of those nations of the world who, by open aggression or secret schemes, have seized the territories and inexhaustible natural wealth of Africa, and we place on record our most solemn determination to reclaim the treasures and possession of the vast continent of our forefathers."

16. "We believe all men should live in peace one with the other, but when races and nations provoke the ire of other races and nations by attempting to infringe upon their rights, war becomes inevitable, and the attempt in any way to free one's self or protect one's rights or heritage becomes justifiable."

17. "Whereas, the lynching, by burning, hanging or any other means, of human beings is a barbarous practice, and a shame and disgrace to civilization, we therefore declare any country guilty of such atrocities outside the pale of civilization."

18. "We protest against the atrocious crime of whipping, flogging and overworking of the native tribes of Africa and Negroes everywhere. These are methods that should be abolished, and all means should be taken to prevent a continuance of such brutal practices."

19. "We protest against the atrocious practice of shaving the heads of Africans, especially of African women or individuals of Negro blood, when placed in prison as a punishment for crime by an alien race."

20. "We protest against segregated districts, separate public conveyances, industrial discrimination, lynchings and limitations of political privileges of any Negro citizen in any part of the world on account of race, color or creed, and will exert our full influence and power against all such."

21. "We protest against any punishment inflicted upon a Negro with severity, as against lighter punishment inflicted upon another of an alien race for like offense, as an act of prejudice and in-justice, and should be resented by the entire race."

22. "We protest against the system of education in any country where Negroes are denied the same privileges and advantages as other races."

23. "We declare it inhuman and unfair to boycott Negroes from industries and labor in any part of the world."

24. "We believe in the doctrine of the freedom of the press, and we therefore emphatically protest against the suppression of Negro newspapers and periodicals in various parts of the world, and call upon Negroes everywhere to employ all available means to prevent such suppression."

25. "We further demand free speech universally for all men."

26. "We hereby protest against the publication of scandalous and inflammatory articles by an alien press tending to create racial strife and the exhibition of picture films showing the Negro as a cannibal."

27. "We believe in the self-determination of all peoples."

28. "We declare for the freedom of religious worship."

29. "With the help of Almighty God, we declare ourselves the sworn protectors of the honor and virtue of our women and children, and pledge our lives for their protection and defense everywhere, and under all circumstances from wrongs and outrages."

30. "We demand the right of unlimited and unprejudiced education for ourselves and our posterity forever."

31. "We declare that the teaching in any school by alien teachers to our boys and girls, that the alien race is superior to the Negro race, is an insult to the Negro people of the world."

32. "Where Negroes form a part of the citizenry of any country, and pass the civil service examination of such country, we declare them entitled to the same consideration as other citizens as to appointments in such civil service."

33. "We vigorously protest against the increasingly unfair and unjust treatment accorded Negro travelers on land and sea by the agents and employees of railroad and steamship companies and insist that for equal fare we receive equal privileges with travelers of other races."

34. "We declare it unjust for any country, State or nation to enact laws tending to hinder and obstruct the free immigration of Negroes on account of their race and color."

35. "That the right of the Negro to travel unmolested throughout the world be not abridged by any person or persons, and all

Negroes are called upon to give aid to a fellow Negro when thus molested."

36. "We declare that all Negroes are entitled to the same right to travel over the world as other men."

37. "We hereby demand that the governments of the world recognize our leader and his representatives chosen by the race to look after the welfare of our people under such governments."

38. "We demand complete control of our social institutions without interference by any alien race or races."

39. "That the colors, Red, Black and Green, be the colors of the Negro race."

40. "Resolved, That the anthem 'Ethiopia, Thou Land of Our Fathers,' etc., shall be the anthem of the Negro race."

THE UNIVERSAL ETHIOPIAN ANTHEM

(Poem by Burrell and Ford.)

I

Ethiopia, thou land of our fathers,
Thou land where the gods loved to be,
As storm cloud at night suddenly gathers
Our armies come rushing to thee.
We must in the fight be victorious
When swords are thrust outward to gleam;
For us will the vict'ry be glorious
When led by the red, black and green.

Chorus

Advance, advance to victory,
Let Africa be free;
Advance to meet the foe
With the might
Of the red, the black and the green.

II

Ethiopia, the tyrant's falling,
Who smote thee upon thy knees,
And thy children are lustily calling
From over the distant seas.
Jehovah, the Great One has heard us,
Has noted our sighs and our tears,

With His spirit of Love he has stirred us
To be One through the coming years.
CHORUS—Advance, advance, etc.

III

O Jehovah, thou God of the ages
Grant unto our sons that lead
The wisdom Thou gave to Thy sages
When Israel was sore in need.
Thy voice thro' the dim past has spoken,
Ethiopia shall stretch forth her hand,
By Thee shall all fetters be broken,
And Heav'n bless our dear fatherland.
CHORUS—Advance, advance, etc.

41. "We believe that any limited liberty which deprives one of the complete rights and prerogatives of full citizenship is but a modified form of slavery."

42. "We declare it an injustice to our people and a serious impediment to the health of the race to deny to competent licensed Negro physicians the right to practise in the public hospitals of the communities in which they reside, for no other reason than their race and color."

43. "We call upon the various governments of the world to accept and acknowledge Negro representatives who shall be sent to the said government to represent the general welfare of the Negro peoples of the world."

44. "We deplore and protest against the practice of confining juvenile prisoners in prisons with adults, and we recommend that such youthful prisoners be taught gainful trades under humane supervision."

45. "Be it further resolved, that we as a race of people declare the League of Nations null and void as far as the Negro is concerned, in that it seeks to deprive Negroes of their liberty."

46. "We demand of all men to do unto us as we would do unto them, in the name of justice; and we cheerfully accord to all men all the rights we claim herein for ourselves."

47. "We declare that no Negro shall engage himself in battle for an alien race without first obtaining the consent of the leader of the Negro people of the world, except in a matter of national self-defense."

48. "We protest against the practice of drafting Negroes and sending them to war with alien forces without proper training, and demand in all cases that Negro soldiers be given the same training as the aliens."

49. "We demand that instructions given Negro children in schools include the subject of 'Negro History,' to their benefit."

50. "We demand a free and unfettered commercial intercourse with all the Negro people of the world."

51. "We declare for the absolute freedom of the seas for all peoples."

52. "We demand that our duly accredited representatives be given proper recognition in all leagues, conferences, conventions or courts of international arbitration wherever human rights are discussed."

53. "We proclaim the 31st day of August of each year to be an international holiday to be observed by all Negroes."

54. "We want all men to know we shall maintain and contend for the freedom and equality of every man, woman and child of our race, with our lives, our fortunes and our sacred honor."

These rights we believe to be justly ours and proper for the protection of the Negro race at large, and because of this belief we, on behalf of the four hundred million Negroes of the world, do pledge herein the sacred blood of the race in defense and we hereby subscribe our names as a guarantee of the truthfulness and faithfulness hereof in the presence of Almighty God, on the 13th day of August, in the year of our Lord one thousand nine hundred and twenty.

3. RACIAL CONFLICT

Description of a Race Riot in Chicago*

James Weldon Johnson called the summer of 1919 the "Red Summer"—red with the blood of those killed or injured in racial clashes. The hope that a broader acceptance of democracy would emerge from America's participation in World War I was stifled.

* *The Negro in Chicago: A Study of Race Relations and a Race Riot* (Chicago, 1922), pp. 1–4, prepared under the direction of the Chicago Commission on Race Relations.

In the South there was a revival of the Klan and an increase in lynching; in the North, a multiplication of savage racial warfare.

Chicago's race riot was the worst of the year—it ranks with the East St. Louis horror of 1917 and the Watts debacle of 1965 as one of the bloodiest racial confrontations in American history.

Thirty-eight persons killed, 537 injured, and about 1,000 rendered homeless and destitute was the casualty list of the race riot which broke out in Chicago on July 27, 1919, and swept uncontrolled through parts of the city for four days. By August 2 it had yielded to the forces of law and order, and on August 8 the state militia withdrew.

A clash between whites and Negroes on the shore of Lake Michigan at Twenty-ninth Street, which involved much stone-throwing and resulted in the drowning of a Negro boy, was the beginning of the riot. A policeman's refusal to arrest a white man accused by Negroes of stoning the Negro boy was an important factor in starting mob action. Within two hours the riot was in full sway, had scored its second fatality, and was spreading throughout the south and southwest parts of the city. Before the end came it reached out to a section of the West Side and even invaded the "Loop," the heart of Chicago's downtown business district. Of the thirty-eight killed, fifteen were whites and twenty-three Negroes; of 537 injured, 178 were whites, 342 were Negroes, and the race of seventeen was not recorded.

In contrast with many other outbreaks of violence over racial friction the Chicago riot was not preceded by excitement over reports of attacks on women or of any other crimes alleged to have been committed by Negroes. It is interesting to note that not one of the thirty-eight deaths was of a woman or girl, and that only ten of the 537 persons injured were women or girls. In further contrast with other outbreaks of racial violence, the Chicago riot was marked by no hangings or burnings.

The rioting was characterized by much activity on the part of gangs of hoodlums, and the clashes developed from sudden and spontaneous assaults into organized raids against life and property.

In handling the emergency and restoring order, the police were effectively reinforced by the state militia. Help was also rendered by deputy sheriffs, and by ex-soldiers who volunteered.

In nine of the thirty-eight cases of death, indictments for murder were voted by the grand jury, and in the ensuing trials there were four convictions. In fifteen other cases the coroner's jury recommended that unknown members of mobs be apprehended, but none of these was ever found.

The Commission's inquiry concerning the facts of the riot included a critical analysis of the 5,584 pages of the testimony taken by the coroner's jury; a study of the records of the office of the state's attorney; studies of the records of the Police Department, hospitals, and other institutions with reference to injuries, and of the records of the Fire Department with reference to incendiary fires; and interviews with many public officials and citizens having special knowledge of various phases of the riot. Much information was also gained by the Commission in a series of four conferences to which it invited the foreman of the riot grand jury, the chief and other commanding officers of the Police Department, the state's attorney and some of his assistants, and officers in command of the state militia during the riot.

BACKGROUND OF THE RIOT

The Chicago riot was not the only serious outbreak of interracial violence in the year following the war. The same summer witnessed the riot in Washington, about a week earlier; the riot in Omaha, about a month later; and then the week of armed conflict in a rural district of Arkansas due to exploitation of Negro cotton producers.

Nor was the Chicago riot the first violent manifestation of race antagonism in Illinois. In 1908 Springfield had been the scene of an outbreak that brought shame to the community which boasted of having been Lincoln's home. In 1917 East St. Louis was torn by a bitter and destructive riot which raged for nearly a week, and was the subject of a Congressional investigation that disclosed appalling underlying conditions.

Chicago was one of the northern cities most largely affected by the migration of Negroes from the South during the war. The Negro population increased from 44,103 in 1910 to 109,594 in 1920, an increase of 148 percent. Most of this increase came in the years 1916–19. It was principally caused by the widening of

industrial opportunities due to the entrance of northern workers
into the army and to the demand for war workers at much higher
wages than Negroes had been able to earn in the South. An added
factor was the feeling, which spread like a contagion through the
South, that the great opportunity had come to escape from what
they felt to be a land of discrimination and subserviency to places
where they could expect fair treatment and equal rights. Chicago
became to the southern Negro the "top of the world."

It is necessary to point out . . . that friction in industry was
less than might have been expected. There had been a few strikes
which had given the Negro the name of "strike breaker." But the
demand for labor was such that there were plenty of jobs to absorb
all the white and Negro workers available. This condition continued even after the end of the war and demobilization.

In housing, however, there was a different story. Practically no
new building had been done in the city during the war, and it was a
physical impossibility for a doubled Negro population to live in the
space occupied in 1915. Negroes spread out of what had been
known as the "Black Belt" into neighborhoods near-by which had
been exclusively white. This movement . . . developed friction,
so much so that in the "invaded" neighborhoods bombs were
thrown at the houses of Negroes who had moved in, and of real
estate men, white and Negro, who sold or rented property to the
newcomers. From July 1, 1917, to July 27, 1919, the day the riot
began, twenty-four such bombs had been thrown. The police had
been entirely unsuccessful in finding those guilty, and were accused
of making little effort to do so.

A third phase of the situation was the increased political
strength gained by Mayor Thompson's faction in the Republican
party. Negro politicians affiliated with this faction had been able to
sway to its support a large proportion of the voters in the ward
most largely inhabited by Negroes. Negro aldermen elected from
this ward were prominent in the activities of this faction. The part
played by the Negro vote in the hard-fought partisan struggle is
indicated by the fact that in the Republican primary election on
February 25, 1919, Mayor Thompson received in this ward 12,-
143 votes, while his two opponents, Olson and Merriam, received
only 1,492 and 319 respectively. Mayor Thompson was re-elected
on April 1, 1919, by a plurality of 21,622 in a total vote in the

city of 698,920; his vote in this ward was 15,569, to his nearest
opponent's 3,323, and was therefore large enough to control the
election. The bitterness of this factional struggle aroused resentment against the race that had so conspicuously allied itself with
the Thompson side.

As part of the background of the Chicago riot, the activities of
gangs of hoodlums should be cited. There had been friction for
years, especially along the western boundary of the area in which
the Negroes mainly live, and attacks upon Negroes by gangs of
young toughs had been particularly frequent in the spring just
preceding the riot. They reached a climax on the night of June 21,
1919, five weeks before the riot, when two Negroes were murdered. Each was alone at the time and was the victim of un-
provoked and particularly brutal attack. Molestation of Negroes
by hoodlums had been prevalent in the vicinity of parks and
playgrounds and at bathing-beaches.

On two occasions shortly before the riot the forewarnings of
serious racial trouble had been so pronounced that the chief of
police sent several hundred extra policemen into the territory
where trouble seemed imminent. But serious violence did not
break out until Sunday afternoon, July 27, when the clash on the
lake shore at Twenty-ninth Street resulted in the drowning of a
Negro boy.

Events followed so fast in the train of the drowning that this
tragedy may be considered as marking the beginning of the riot.

It was four o'clock Sunday afternoon, July 27, when Eugene
Williams, seventeen-year-old Negro boy, was swimming offshore at
the foot of Twenty-ninth Street. This beach was not one of those
publicly maintained and supervised for bathing, but it was much
used. Although it flanks an area thickly inhabited by Negroes, it
was used by both races, access being had by crossing the railway
tracks which skirt the lake shore. The part near Twenty-seventh
Street had by tacit understanding come to be considered as reserved for Negroes, while the whites used the part near Twenty-
ninth Street. Walking is not easy along the shore, and each race
had kept pretty much to its own part, observing, moreover, an
imaginary boundary extending into the water.

Williams, who had entered the water at the part used by
Negroes, swam and drifted south into the part used by the whites.
Immediately before his appearance there, white men, women, and

children had been bathing in the vicinity and were on the beach in considerable numbers. Four Negroes walked through the group and into the water. White men summarily ordered them off. The Negroes left, and the white people resumed their sport. But it was not long before the Negroes were back, coming from the north with others of their race. Then began a series of attacks and retreats, counterattacks, and stone-throwing. Women and children who could not escape hid behind debris and rocks. The stone-throwing continued, first one side gaining the advantage, then the other.

Williams, who had remained in the water during the fracas, found a railroad tie and clung to it, stones meanwhile frequently striking the water near him. A white boy of about the same age swam toward him. As the white boy neared, Williams let go of the tie, took a few strokes, and went down. The coroner's jury rendered a verdict that he had drowned because fear of stone-throwing kept him from shore. His body showed no stone bruises, but rumor had it that he had actually been hit by one of the stones and drowned as a result.

On shore guilt was immediately placed upon a certain white man by several Negro witnesses who demanded that he be arrested by a white policeman who was on the spot. No arrest was made.

The tragedy was sensed by the battling crowd and, awed by it, they gathered on the beach. For an hour both whites and Negroes dived for the boy without results. Awe gave way to excited whispers. "They" said he was stoned to death. The report circulated through the crowd that the police officer had refused to arrest the murderer. The Negroes in the crowd began to mass dangerously. At this crucial point the accused policeman arrested a Negro on a white man's complaint. Negroes mobbed the white officer, and the riot was under way.

Restrictive Housing Covenants*

Although in 1917 the Supreme Court outlawed municipal zoning codes which restricted residential areas by race, it was not until 1948 that the court held private racially restrictive contracts unenforceable through judicial action. Given the pressure of Negro

* From the Chicago Commission on Race Relations, *The Negro in Chicago: A Study of Race Relations and a Race Riot* (Chicago, 1922), pp. 121–122.

urban population growth, and the sanction of American institutions and mores, realtors and property owners organized white neighborhoods to protect themselves from Negro settlement through race covenants. "The use of these agreements as a restriction upon Negro housing opportunities is a dominant characteristic of the decade between 1920 and 1930," a study of such codes concluded.* Three of every four convenants in force in St. Louis after World War II, and three of every five in Chicago, were initiated in the twenties. The tone of the racial confrontation in housing is evident in the following excerpts from the Hyde Park (Chicago) Property Owners' Journal of 1919 and 1920, and in the letters of the Near North Side (Chicago) Property Owners' Association to a prospective member in 1936.

To damage a man's property and destroy its value is to rob him. The person who commits that act is a robber. Every owner has the right to defend his property to the utmost of his ability with every means at his disposal.

Any property owner who sells property anywhere in our district to undesirables is an enemy to the white owner and should be discovered and punished.

Protect your property!

Property conservatively valued at $50,000,000 owned by some 10,000 individuals is menaced by a possible Negro invasion of Hyde Park. The thing is simply impossible and must not occur.

* * * * * *

As stated before, every colored man who moves into Hyde Park knows that he is damaging his white neighbors' property. Therefore, he is making war on the white man. Consequently, he is not entitled to any consideration and forfeits his right to be employed by the white man. If employers should adopt a rule of refusing to employ Negroes who persist in residing in Hyde Park to the damage of the white man's property, it would soon show good results.

The Negro is using the Constitution and its legal rights to abuse the moral rights of the white.

* Herman H. Long and Charles S. Johnson, *People vs. Property: Race Restrictive Covenants in Housing* (Nashville, 1947), pp. 13–14.

* * * * * *

There is nothing in the make-up of a Negro, physically or mentally, which should induce anyone to welcome him as a neighbor. The best of them are insanitary, insurance companies class them as poor risks, ruin alone follows in their path. They are as proud as peacocks, but have nothing of the peacock's beauty. Certain classes of the Negroes, such as the Pullman porters, political heelers and hairdressers, are clamoring for equality. They are not content with remaining with the creditable members of their race, they seem to want to mingle with the whites. Their inordinate vanity, their desire to shine as social lights caused them to stray out of their paths and lose themselves. We who would direct them back where they belong, towards their people, are censured and called "unjust." Far more unjust are their actions to the members of their race who have no desire to interfere with the homes of the white citizens of this district. The great majority of the Negroes are not stirred by any false ambition that results only in discord. Wherever friction arises between the races, the suffering is usually endured by the innocent. If these misleaders are sincere in their protestations of injustice, if they are not hypocritical in their pretence of solving the race question, let them move. Their actions savour of spite against the whites, whose good will can never be attained by such tactics. The place for a Negro aristocrat is in a Negro neighborhood.

* * * * * *

People who sell their property to Negroes and take first and second mortgages and promises to pay monthly sums do not know what risks they are taking in trying to collect the money. Mrs. Nora Foster of 4207 Prairie sold her house to some niggers and when she went to collect she was assaulted and thrown down a flight of stairs. This is not a case of saying it served her right because more than seven of her neighbors sold before Mrs. Foster did, but it does serve as a splendid example of the fact that niggers are undesirable neighbors and entirely irresponsible and vicious.

The Negroes' innate desire to "flash," to live in the present, not reckoning the future, their inordinate love for display has resulted in their being misled. . . . In their loud mouthing about equality with the whites they have wormed their course into white neighborhoods, where they are not wanted and where they have not the means to support property.

Keep the Negro in his place, amongst his people and he is healthy and loyal. Remove him, or allow his newly discovered importance to remove him from his proper environment and the Negro becomes a nuisance. He develops into an overbearing, inflated, irascible individual, overburdening his brain to such an extent about social equality, that he becomes dangerous to all with whom he comes in contact, he constitutes a nuisance, of which the neighorhood is anxious to rid itself.

* * * * * * *

February 18, 1936*

Dear Sir:

We are sending you herewith some information concerning the work planned to prevent colored occupancy in the Near North Side area south of Chicago Avenue through the use of a property owners' agreement. Under the terms of this agreement all property owners in the area agree not to sell or rent their premises to negroes for a period of approximately twenty-one years.

A number of the property owners have indicated their willingness to subscribe $100.00 each toward the expense of this work and we are wondering if we can look forward to a contribution on behalf of the property at 630–40 N. Dearborn Street. All subscriptions will be made payable to the Treasurer of this Association (anonymously if desired) subject to the following conditions:

1. All moneys collected to be expended in restricting the area bounded roughly as follows: Chicago Avenue to the Chicago River, Wells St. to Michigan Ave.

2. All work to be done and funds expended under the direction of a special committee. . . .

Field work in this area is now going forward. During the past year our Association has been restricting the area north of Chicago Avenue and the enclosed copy of letter of January 5, last, sets forth in detail the streets completed and the amount of work done

* Copy in Chicago Historical Society.

in that district. May we look forward to a favorable response in the near future?

Yours very truly,

NEAR NORTH SIDE PROPERTY OWNERS ASSN.

[January 5, 1936]

As one of the supporters of this Association I am sure you will be interested in the following report of progress made by us in restricting the Near North Side area. The restriction work has been proceeding for a little over a year. In that time we have completed the following streets:

Wells Street, Chicago Avenue to North Avenue
La Salle Street, Chicago Avenue to North Avenue
Clark Street, Chicago Avenue to North Avenue
Sedgwick Street, Division Street to North Avenue
Orleans Street, Schiller Street to North Avenue
North Park Avenue, Schiller Street to North Avenue
Wieland Street, Schiller Street to North Avenue
Division Street, La Salle Street to Sedgwick Street
Beethoven Place, Wells Street to Sedgwick Street
Goethe Street, Wells Street to Sedgwick Street
Sigel Street, Wells Street to Sedgwick Street
Schiller Street, Wells Street to Sedgwick Street

The restriction agreements covering the above streets are now on record in the County Recorder's office with considerably over 90% of the total frontage joining in the restriction.

East of Clark Street work is proceeding steadily and we have taken a great deal of frontage on such streets as Dearborn, State, Wabash, Rush, Astor and intervening cross streets.

To date, all expense of the work has been borne from contributions made by interested property owners such as yourself. Great economy has been used to the end that our limited funds produced the greatest possible results. I believe you will agree with me that the results obtained thus far are most gratifying indeed. May I say that the support and cooperation which you have given is very greatly appreciated.

4. THE REVIVAL OF THE KU KLUX KLAN

*A Proposal from the KKK William Joseph Simmons**

On a cold Thanksgiving night in 1915 some fifteen white men visited Stone Mountain outside Atlanta to awake the Invisible Empire "from its slumber of half a century." The K.K.K. was born again, a reflection of the intensified racism, anti-Catholicism, and anti-Semitism that pervaded the war and postwar years. Klan strength was evident in the North and South, and its founder, William Joseph Simmons, continually reminded the public of the national importance of the Klan's program. "We are the best friends the Negro has, here or anywhere," Simmons wrote in The Klan Unmasked. *He proposed to treat American Negroes as children.*

Grover Cleveland once declared that one American problem for which he saw no solution whatever was the problem of the Negro. If we were in "The land of the beginning again, that country of our dreams, we should, of course, not bring the Negro to our shores. It is easy to idealize our American ancestors, but no doubt they made enough errors in their time. Their most gigantic blunder, one to make Providence himself almost despair of humanity, was the Afro-American slave trade. Man's inhumanity to man brings at last the greatest of all sorrows upon him who works the inhumanity."

The first emotion that thought of the great problem of the Negro must awaken in the hearts of all Americans is humility. Before Almighty God we must resolve in this matter to do justice, and more than justice. Here more than any other place, we must be moved by Christlike kindness and love. The bane of us Americans, in all periods of our history, has been carelessness. We have a tendency to let things drift from bad to worse. Such has been particularly the case with reference to our attitude toward the Negro. It is high time that we applied to our public thinking some

* From William Joseph Simmons, *The Klan Unmasked* (Atlanta, 1923), pp. 147–157.

of that sounder knowledge of society and social laws which recent years have given to us.

Why should the simple truth give offense to anybody? The Negro in Africa is a childish barbarian. Left to himself, he has never at any time or place evolved even the beginning of a civilization. Do what we may in the way of an education, the mind of the pure Negro, compared to the white, on the average does not get beyond the age of twelve years. To ignore this fact is to get into error from the start. Continue to ignore this fact, especially in the execution of larger national policies, and we shall invite, as we have done in the past, trouble that is deep and dangerous. Two facts should be remembered if we would make real progress in this discussion. The first is that only those who live among the Negro and so learn to know him at first hand can really understand his manifold traits. To sit down five hundred miles from the nearest considerable Negro population and write books about the Negro is not likely to help much.

The second fact to be kept constantly in mind relates to our population of mixed blood. Every distinguished leader of the Negro race in the United States has been part white. In fact, a majority of the more distinguished have contained only a small infusion of Negro blood. It is the presence of this Mulatto element which clothes the whole problem in porcupine quills. It is this portion of our colored population which is restless and often unhappy to the point of bitterness because of our present policy with reference to the Negro. If there were no mixed population to consider our problem would not be nearly so difficult.

I have always felt that superficial minds have a peculiar tendency to lay hold of the Negro problem. For instance, witness the illogical claims of some of those who think they are the special friends of the Negro and who continually emphasize the necessity for an enlarged sphere for Negro opportunity. On the one hand they boast of the very great progress the Negro has made during his half century of freedom. On one page they will emphasize Negro accomplishment. More than half of our adult Negro population, for instance, can read and write. Tens of thousands of Negro families own their own farms or city homes. An even greater number of Negroes are attending high schools and colleges. Then, on the very next page, the same author will take pains to show that the Negro is most foully treated. He is kept in ignorance and poverty. The wicked white population which surrounds him denies him every advantage and means of progress. Of course both of these tales can not be true at the same time.

Those of us who grew up among the Negroes and have lived with them on terms of mutual kindness and of helpfulness all our lives are inclined to the conclusion that it is easy to exaggerate the progress of the Negro. The record of what we people of the South have done and have tried to do for the Negro during these fifty years is an open book to all the world. It need not be described or analyzed here. Our task has not been easy. In general, I think we have tried to do it in a way to win both the approval of our own conscience and the commendation of our fellow citizens of other sections of the country. Yet we have acted not only according to our means, but also according to our knowledge of what could be accomplished. In so far as we have failed we simply ask that our fellow citizens of the North and West make special effort to understand the true cause of our failure.

This brings us to the main issue of this discussion. The Negro problem is not peculiar to the South. The Negro problem is the burden of the nation as a whole. . . . In maintaining that the Negro is a ward of the nation I wish to place emphasis upon WARD. The Negro's presence among us requires an ever greater interest and care on our part. It is high time that the people of the South made a wider appeal to their fellow citizens of the North and West. A stupendous moral responsibility is involved in the presence of these ten millions of black people. Not only the past, but the future, too, is looking down upon us. All Americans may well realize that in this, as in so many other matters, we are being weighed in the balance as a nation. As a people we are fortunate in being quick to let bygones be bygones. We of the South know that if other sections come to understand us and our peculiar problem better, not only we, but they also, will be the ultimate gainers. The sooner the nation unites in looking upon our ten millions of colored folk as ten millions of children for whose protection and care we are morally responsible, the sooner we shall all be placed upon solid ground.

The maxims of our democracy are not for universal application. Some Europeans are a hundred years, others five hundred years, behind us in the process of democratic evolution. We may guess, but we can not know, how long they will be in catching up. How far behind them the Negro may be in these things I leave for the anthropologists to determine or surmise. But what we of the South assuredly know, because of our experience, is just this—to treat the Negro as the political equal of the white is to do grave injustice not only to the white, but to the Negro as well. We can not justly enforce the laws among children that we make for adults. To enforce the white man's law, in all cases, upon the Negro is an injustice so great that the effort often causes sorrow to every normal mind among us. Cared for and protected as a child, the Negro's better qualities are developed and made evident by his works. But when he is burdened by moral and legal responsibilities which neither his mind nor his character is prepared to bear, in the vast majority of cases he breaks and falls under the load.

5. THE NEGRO ARTIST AND HIS RECEPTION

James Weldon Johnson and Alain Locke were two of the most gifted Negro intellectuals in our history. In the twenties, both believed they saw a New Negro artist class emerging in the cities of America and anticipated a broader acceptance of Negroes by white society as a result of it. In the minds of Locke and Johnson, assimilation was like a bank account. Negroes would acquire credit by contributing their creative gifts to the nation. When a sufficient capital had accumulated, they believed, white Americans would deem Negroes worthy of full citizenship. Although social scientists demonstrated a serious interest in Negro culture in the twenties, the concern of the majority of white literati was superficial and faddish.

The Negro as a Creator   *James Weldon Johnson**

We are still on the job of getting over into the American consciousness the idea that in our cultural world the Negro is a creator as well as a creature—that he is a giver as well as a receiver—that

---

* From a letter, March 6, 1927, to his close friend Carl Van Vechten, from the James Weldon Johnson Collection, Yale University.

he has aesthetic values as well as values physical, economic and otherwise. This is a vitally important job—perhaps the most important connected with the race question and prejudice. In recent years great advance has been made on it. You have done brave service . . . and the greatest of Negro artists—Hayes, Robeson. But as I look back I believe I can claim to be a pioneer in this particular field. I have just been glancing through the Autobiography*—on pages 84–85 I mention the 4 folk art creations of the Negro—and among them I place the cake walk (the fore-runner of all these modern dances). I can see now that it took both courage and foresight to declare the cake walk to be a form of art, when the Autobiography was written. . . . I started doing for ragtime and the Negro dances what you have more recently done almost singlehanded for the Blues—to prove that they were art creations and not expressions and that their creators were . . . *artists*. And I am coming to believe that nothing can go farther to destroying race prejudice than the recognition of the Negro as a creator and a contributor to American civilization.

The Negro's Contribution *Alain Locke†*

Only in the last decade has there been any considerable recognition of the Negro as a contributor to American life, and the impression is still general that his career as a contributor has hardly more than commenced.

The reason his influence has not been apparent is that until recently Negro contributions have been silent and anonymous—they have been folk-gifts—and although they may on that account have been all the more effective, the race has proportionately lost the credit for them. Later we shall try to list them. But the present point is that the chief expectation for a significant role on the part of the present-generation Negro in American life depends not upon mere dreams but upon actual past performance. Indeed, the one great ground of hope for future influence and constructiveness rests upon the rather startling extent to which the Negro has already contributed to American life.

* James Weldon Johnson, *The Autobiography of An Ex-Coloured Man* (Boston, 1912).

† From Alain Locke, "Negro Contributions to America," *The World Tomorrow*, XII (June, 1929), 255–257.

And if the Negro could be as originally creative and influential as he has been under unfavorable cultural conditions, under more favorable ones he should be many-fold more.

From the usual angles of assessment, the American Negro is a passive recipient and humble beneficiary. The political and economic institutions of America are not of his making, and the formal culture and tradition of the land are his by adoption only. In relation to these, he is a minority group in the second generation stage of assimilation, still below average in the mastery of some phases of American institutional life, especially the economic and industrial. But it should be realized that the Negro's debt to America is not peculiar in kind nor extremely different in degree. It is his longer period of dependence as a slave and his handicap of economic power that are mainly responsible for the conviction of many persons that the Negro is entirely a passive receiver. The reactionary mind capitalizes this condition, assumes him to be a permanent dependent, and for that reason thinks of him in the column of the nation's liabilities rather than its assets. Many of the Negro's best practical friends and benefactors share this view, and the major premise of most missionary efforts in his behalf has been an assumption of his dependence upon a civilization in which he is merely a consumer. Philanthropy's charitable minor premise "even so, it is our duty to share with him"—only compounds this grave misunderstanding. What the present generation is beginning to protest and to revise is the major premise itself. It can indeed be shown to be contrary to fact.

To avoid any possibility of sentimental distortion, however, let us be realists and not presume that the gifts we shall mention were conscious, deliberate, or wholly original. The Negro's contributions have been made as reactions to white civilization, its elements have been the basis of these reactions and its attitudes often the stimulus thereto. Christianity, the plantation, freedom, democracy, justice were all imposed ideas, ideals, and social facts. But to each of these the Negro has given a peculiar and definite contribution from a double point of view: first, as a passive presence influencing the institutional development of each of these basic social ideas; in the second place, actually making, in many instances, a constructive contribution to these same ideas. All of them are characteristically different because of the presence of the

Negro in American life, and all of them have been enriched by his peculiar impress.

To realize this fully, one must notice the Negro's fundamental reaction to American life. Though a virtue of necessity on the part of a people introduced into a civilization by the hard way of slavery, it is a virtue nevertheless of great positive effect. The Negro has consistently from the beginning accepted almost without reservation the values and institutions of American life. Negative merit though it is, feeble as it seems to be, alien attitudes retained by the Negro could have introduced factors of non-conformity into the very heart of American civilization which would have prevented on the one hand, his rapid cultural assimilation, and, on the other, would have put the basic values of American life on the defensive. Even a dependent class has great negative power in this direction, and had his reaction been different, the Negro might presumably have exercised such power. America has gained profoundly then, from the Negro's humble assent to the fundamental values of her civilization. His domestication—for he was taken into the very heart of the American family under the plantation regime—would otherwise have been impossible or dangerous. This is a gift which will only be appreciated in time when it is realized that the whole trend of Negro life in America has been determined by this attitude of willing and loyal conformity.

Conformity to the material side of American life was perhaps necessary; but that of the Negro mind to the spiritual side of our civilization proves my first contention. The first constructive reaction of the Negro was to Christianity. From it the Negro gained a spiritual compensation of inestimable practical value, but to it he gave his own unique spiritual gifts—one emotional, and the other artistic. The latter is well-known and highly prized; but the spirituals, although the most original and universally effective expressions of elemental Christian faith and feeling, are merely the artistic by-products of an emotional interpretation of Christianity that in time may be regarded as a greater gift. At present the vogue of appreciation for them is artistic—they have been lauded as "America's most notable folk music." Later it will be seen that, as an interpretation of Christianity in direct feeling and elemental mood, they are profound. A reaction to religion of similar character, but on a plane above that of the peasant mind, would be a major contribution and influence. There is still in this group tradition and heritage the latent possibilities of a spiritual dynamic of great force. It is to this that our present generation thinkers refer when they claim that the Negro's group experience in America has given him a special discipline and spiritual heritage which may eventually make him the protagonist in our culture of the more spiritual and mystical values of life.

For the time being, this heritage has only made the Negro slightly more of an artist than his fellow white American. No better catalogue of his contribution on this plane can be made than James Weldon Johnson's now famous list of four art gifts—the Uncle Remus body of folk-lore, the spirituals, and the basic idioms of American popular music and dance to the extent that these are distinctively different from the borrowed forms of the ancestral European cultures. The irony of the situation is that in folk-lore, folk-song, folk-dance, and popular music the things recognized as characteristically and uniquely American are products of the despised slave minority. Nor is this confined to the products of the old slave regime. In the two latter cases it is the constant creativeness and influence of the present-day Negro with an increasing extension of this artistic activity from the level of instinctive folk-art to that of formal art. The trained Negro musician, the literary Negro poet, the legitimate Negro actor, and the skilled Negro artist are becoming more and more figures in the foreground of American culture. This revival of artistic creativeness after a fallow period in the transition from slavery to freedom is the well known "Negro Renaissance." Apart from its being an important aspect of minority self-expression, it is a movement that has already made substantial contributions of general artistic significance and value. It begins to appear that the Negro as artist will disproportionately influence American culture in the present and future as in the past.

This artistic sway of the Negro race has been most obvious in music. Few people recognize its potentialities in other artistic fields. No special innate artistic endowments have to be assumed for this. What accounts for it in the past and promises great momentum to it in the future is the simple fact of the intensification of the emotional side of life by persecution and suffering, and the concentration of the group life-force at a point and in channels where the practical disabilities of social and economic handicaps are relatively powerless and inoperative. This is the Negro's compensation for his hard lot and generation-long sacrifice.

It is fair to list potential contributions if they inhere logically in the present race situation. Much of common consequence to America is clearly involved in the attitude of the rest of the nation toward this peculiarly situated minority group. The conditions of the Negro are so unique in some respects that they must be the pivot of a general adjustment of American society in given directions. The Negro's position in America makes him the acid test both of practical democracy and of the practical application of Christianity to the social order. Negro leaders are never tired of pointing out that the failure of the Negro in America will mean the failure of democracy and Christianity. Although at present such a view suggests very painfully the problems and discrepancies of contemporary American institutions, in the long term view these very situations are challenging opportunities involving the practical working-out of the basic ideals of our common civilization. It would be playing a decidedly important national role merely to be the passive means or rough material for the solution of such problems. But Negro progress is in a very vital way a substantial contribution in these directions.

It is obvious, in spite of the great necessity for practical and economic contributions in the future on the part of the Negro, that the main line of Negro development must necessarily be artistic, cultural, moral, and spiritual. Because of the complementary character of such contributions in contrast with the predominantly practical, economic, and scientific trend of the nation, the part which the Negro will play is all the more desirable and promising. Although he must qualify in all branches of American life and activity, the Negro can be of more general good in supplementing Nordic civilization than through merely competitively imitating or extending it along lines in which it is at present successful and preeminent. Indeed, as what seems to be the special race genius matures and gains momentum, it becomes increasingly apparent that the Negro's unique experience and heredity combined may have fitted him for a special creative role in American life as an artist class, as a social re-agent, and as a spiritual leaven.

*Images of the Negro Renaissance George Chester Morse**

The Ladies Missionary Society of a local church, becoming tired of the usual program, thought they would introduce novelty by having a young colored girl speak for them. She spoke perfect English, discussed Negro poetry intelligently and her physical attractiveness was coupled with a serene poise which some of her audience envied. When she had finished speaking, the applause she received was that of an astonished audience. It seemed so unusual to this audience of white Americans to hear a Negro speak without dialect, and without manifesting certain characteristics which they term Negroid.

It seems strange in this Twentieth Century, at a time when we boast of enlightenment and sophistication, that business men's wives should be amazed that a person of color should be intelligent and quite as human as they. It reminds one of the time when Paul Laurence Dunbar, another member of this misunderstood race, was discovered to be a poet and consequently exhibited around the country as a Negro poet, . . . a rare bird. That the Negro is regarded not as a human being amenable to the same influences as his white brother, but as a concept, can be easily accepted if one . . . studies the colored minority of these United States of America. My mother is a laundress who is sometimes asked questions by her employers; they seem to think they will find something bizarre in her life. In asking about me, they stared at her when she told them that I wanted to be a journalist after finishing school. This itself was bold effrontery on my part; I, whose forefathers have done the chores for their white folks, seemed bold indeed to desire to use my brains instead of my muscles. And my mother fears that her employers might discover that we dwell in a well-furnished apartment with books and other features of the average middle-class American home. Such discovery might mean instant dismissal from their employ for daring to live contrary to this concept, different from the fictitious Negro.

They are legion who believe that if a native band from the

* From George Chester Morse, "The Fictitious Negro," *Outlook and Independent*, CLII (August, 1929), 648–649, 678–679.

jungles of Africa should parade the streets beating their tom-toms,
all the black inhabitants of our cities would . . . dance to its
rhythm by virtue of inheritance alone. And though young Negro
poets suffer the pathetic fallacy of yearning for palm trees and
jungle-nights in their outburst of sentiment, this is but a fad that
appeals to a definite sentiment because of frustration here in
America. . . .

Now that we have received a deluge of books dealing with
Negro life *ad nauseam,* let us consider what all these volumes
. . . reveal to us. Without doubt, the placement of the Negro in
particular roles as either comedian, imbecile, or creature of superstition is quite entertaining. This entertainment value decides the
success or failure of many who endeavor to write about Negro life.
Since publishers are chiefly business men, one should not expect
them to accept manuscripts that lack these essential entertaining
features. They know they can sell only the concept.

Let a writer treat of Negro characters who seem to be foreign to
this concept . . . and we find the Negro less interesting. . . .

The credulity of the masses is still exploited by Octavus Roy
Cohen in his *Saturday Evening Post* stories, known for overdone
humor. There are Negro comedians and imbeciles, but they don't
constitute the Negro race as Mr. Cohen would have us believe.
And when the directors at Hollywood prepare for a photoplay with
a ghost plot, the casting director must telephone for one or two
Negroes to be used to register fear for our benefit. Even the much
improved movie has not forsaken all of the stereotypes.

. . . Some critics are prone to interpret Negro life as a particular racial propensity instead of interpreting it in the light of
sociology and psychology. Few are the reviews that do not contain
the words, primitive and exotic. These critics often mistake moral
laxity among Negroes as a racial trait, as though it is a tendency
that has its roots in the jungles of Africa. But in doing so, they
display ignorance of tribal morality. . . . One wonders if tribal
morality is less degrading than the morality of Western civilization.
There are jungles in America called Black Belts where Negroes are
forced to contend with economic and social disadvantages that
encourage animalism.

At present, one of the outstanding successes, not from a standpoint of merit but from a standpoint of longevity . . . is a play

entitled *Harlem,* which without the rent party* scene would have little box-office attraction. To this play the hordes come to feast upon one exotic scene of Negro life, youth in primitive abandon, seeking recreation and diversion dancing in a stuffy Harlem flat.

The rent party is just a social by-product of an economic system. Though reviewers would have us believe that the rent party is a recreation which has its roots in the jungle, . . . rent parties are due to economic difficulties. When Mrs. Johnson and Mr. Brown have to pay seventy-five or eighty dollars for rooms that are worth not half that much in other localities, they must meet this exorbitant rental by some method. Since their wages fall to the minimum scale, some ingenious person originated the rent party as a method of meeting this high cost of living in their proverbial Mecca.

How soon this common theme shall reach the nauseating state is not easy to foretell. We have had this deluge of books, we're entertained and probably are better acquainted with the fictitious Negro. But the Negro remains misunderstood. White Americans still show signs of amazement when Negroes prove themselves worthy members of *homo sapiens* in respect to achievement and culture.

---

* Tickets of admission sold to those who came to the party helped raise money to pay the rent.

CHAPTER VIII

THE ROOSEVELT ERA

A Time of Trial, A Time of Hope

❀ ❀

We live in a year of unparalleled disaster, and . . . the plight of the great masses of the colored people is little less than desperate.
OSWALD GARRISON VILLARD, 1934

During the Roosevelt era . . . Negro Americans made more progress toward their goal of full citizenship than under any other administration.
The Crisis, 1945

The Great Depression and World War II were years of trial in the racial history of America—but they were always mixed with leaven of hope. No single inclusive theme can easily explain the era of the Roosevelt presidency. It was a time when Southern senators repeatedly filibustered the NAACP's anti-lynching and anti–poll-tax legislation to death; when Senator Bilbo hoped to revive the movement to colonize Negroes in Africa; when New Deal agencies accepted racial differentials in NRA codes. But the thirties and early forties also saw the rise, for the first time, of large-scale interracial industrial unionism; the emergence of mass Negro militancy that led to the March on Washington

Movement; picketing, rent strikes, and economic boycotts throughout Northern ghettos; the formation of the Southern Tenant Farmers' Union—a union of white and black Southern sharecroppers welded together by economic desperation.

The most obvious tragedy of the era could be read in the faces of the poor. Traditionally Negroes shared least in American abundance and suffered most in hard times. A federal government survey in 1934 disclosed the shocking facts that more than half the Negro families in Northern and Border cities, and more than a third in Southern cities, were on relief rolls. The corresponding national figures for whites were 10 to 13 percent. In May, 1934, Negro families represented 70 to 80 percent of the households receiving public aid in Washington, D.C., Norfolk, Virginia, and Charlotte, North Carolina. In towns that had been dominated by a single industry which went bankrupt, such as mining communities in southern Illinois and West Virginia, people were found starving to death. The same was true in areas of the South that witnessed the collapse of cotton tenancy. "The economic structure of the Negro race is in an alarming state of threatened disintegration," wrote Forrester B. Washington, head of Atlanta University's School of Social Work. (1)

And how to find a way out? Traditional answers were inadequate. The Urban League's familiar emphasis on the need for increased economic opportunity and education for Negroes was overwhelmed by the absence of work and the magnitude of social dislocation. Lester Granger of the Urban League broke tradition by advocating the formation of Workers' Councils— unions of the black employed and unemployed—but the movement failed. The NAACP pressed unsuccessfully for federal anti-lynching legislation and, more rewardingly, for desegregated institutions of higher learning and equal pay for Negro public school teachers in the South. When Negro economist Abram Harris suggested that the Association subordinate its essentially legal approach to a program of greater involvement with the black masses, his proposal was discussed at length and finally rejected. In despair over the relative inadequacy of NAACP tactics in a time of great crisis, W. E. B. Du Bois resigned from the organization and published a brutal attack on its program: "Today this organization . . . finds itself in a time of crisis and change, without a program," Du Bois wrote, "without effective organization, without executive officers who have the ability or disposition to guide the NAACP in the right direction." Du Bois shocked his colleagues by advocating the establishment of all-Negro economic cooperatives; "organized and deliberate self-segregation," he termed it. The goal of achieving an integrated society was not only hopeless for the present, Du Bois reasoned, but it it also dissipated energy that might be effectively used in building a black state. "Not since Reconstruction days," an Urban League official wrote in 1934, "has there been such an utter bankruptcy of effective leadership among Negroes as exists today." (2)

This judgment must be accepted with caution. It is true that limited budgets and perhaps limited imaginations prevented some organizations from adding flexibility to their customary programs of racial reform. As long as the need for dynamic leadership existed, however, this only left a power vacuum which was filled by new forces—the CIO, the Communist party, and the March on Washington Movement, for example. The competition for leadership of the Negro masses, and the variety of programs it evoked—even conflicting ones—often expanded the meaning of interracial justice in America. The Communists established the interracial Sharecroppers Union in Tallapoosa County, Alabama; doggedly punished what they called "white chauvinism" in their own ranks; worked for interracial unions throughout the country; and helped organize tenants and the unemployed in black ghettos. The CIO broke with labor's traditional racism and openly courted Negro support. By the early forties some half million black workers were organized. A. Philip Randolph's threat to march 10,000 to 100,000 Negroes to Washington led President Roosevelt to establish the FEPC. These were considerable achievements. Rather than argue that there was a "bankruptcy of effective leadership among Negroes" in the thirties and early forties, it would be more accurate to say there was a greater diffusion of effective leadership among Negroes then. (3)

And, although the story is again complex, Negroes made solid advances under the Roosevelt Administrations. Hesitant to alienate powerful white Southern committee chairmen, F.D.R. rarely made public statements on civil rights; and when he did his language was compromising. The strictures that applied to the President, however, didn't effect his wife. Eleanor Roosevelt, as private citizen, won great acclaim for her views in the Negro community. No public figure of the New Deal era spoke more often and more clearly on the demands of racial justice in a democratic society than she did. At the Second National Conference on the Problems of the Negro and Negro Youth (1939), for example, she publicly supported anti-lynching legislation, the coverage of domestic workers by Social Security, equal treatment for Negroes in all the armed services, and the right of minority groups to criticize the government openly in times of crisis. For most Negroes she became "the First Lady indeed!"

Many decisions involving racial questions in the Roosevelt years were left to the prerogatives of state administrators or agency directors. Such decentralization of power sometimes led to the discrimination evident in the Civilian Conservation Corps and the implementation of the National Industrial Recovery and Federal Emergency Relief Acts. It also, however, placed significant power in the hands of individuals who desired fair treatment of Negroes: Aubrey Williams, Harold Ickes, Clark Foreman, Will W. Alexander, Hallie Flanagan. Negroes became an essential part of the Democratic political coalition in the thirties and were rewarded with appointments to federal administrative positions of consequence. Mary McLeod Bethune, Robert C. Weaver, Eugene Kinckle Jones, Alfred E. Smith, Henry Hunt, Robert L. Vann, Forrester B. Washington, and others constituted what the Negro press like to call the "Black Cabinet." The Federal Theater Project brought imaginative classic and contemporary drama and dance to the ghettos, and the Federal Writers Project produced interesting studies in Negro history and sociology. When Du Bois studied the record of the Roosevelt era he concluded that Negroes made greater progress under FDR than in any administration since Lincoln's; and the Negro masses usually expressed the same point of view in the polling booths. (4)

The coming of World War II, however, had a halting effect on much of the racial progress made under F.D.R. Most programs of domestic reform within the national government were subordinated to the demands of the international crisis. Segregation and discrimination in all branches of the military, for example, had been institutionalized—with some exceptions —since the Revolutionary War. When World War II began Negroes were excluded from the air corps and marines, and permitted to serve in the navy only in menial capacities. Although there was some modification of racism in the services during World War II, especially in the closing months of battle, most of the changes were token reforms. "The policy of the War Department is not to intermingle colored and white enlisted personnel in the same regimental organization," a 1940 communiqué stated. "It is the opinion of the . . . Department that no experiments should be tried with the organizational setup of these units at this critical time." Throughout the war there were Jim Crow blood banks, air raid shelters, recreational facilities, and officers' clubs. Perhaps the most flagrant iniquity occurred on a troop train passing through Texas when Negro soldiers had to eat in the Jim Crow section as German prisoners of war dined with the whites. As the historian Rayford W. Logan said in 1944, race relations were "more strained [then] than they have been in years."*

Nor were conditions more promising on the home front. The war created economic opportunities for Negroes and whites and stimulated the migration of a new wave of Southerners—Negro and white—to urban-industrial centers in the North and West. White Southerners and working-class immigrants often objected to and feared increased Negro economic competition. These racial tensions led to serious riots in Los Angeles, New York City, and Detroit in 1943, and minor conflicts throughout the nation. The entire Philadelphia transit system came to a halt in August, 1944, as whites protested the upgrading of Negro workers to motormen. The U.S. Army had to assume control of the system before order was established three weeks later. Those who anticipated the emergence of a racially liberal democracy as a consequence of the war with Hitler saw their expectations dissipate. "Thinking people had hoped that the war on fascism and nazism was sufficiently educational to foreclose the bigotry, intolerance and persecution of minority groups," a *Crisis* editorial stated. "The war has not achieved that." (5)

1. THE NEGRO POOR

A West Virginia Mining Community†

Poverty knew no section, no occupation, no age. The Negro middle class as well as the lower class was decimated by the Great

* Rayford W. Logan, ed., *What the Negro Wants* (Chapel Hill, N.C., 1944), p. vii.
† From FERA, "Confidential Research Bulletin," July 19, 1934 (National Archives).

*Depression. Competition for even the most menial po   de-
stroyed the concept of "Negro jobs"—employment s҆   ꭆding
or repulsive that many whites refused to do it. H   ꭆas as
prevalent among Negro sharecroppers in Alabama ҆   among
those who queued up at bread lines in Detroit. T҆   ꭆl face of
Negro poverty is presented in the following docꭆ   ꭆhe first, a
description of an abandoned West Virginia n   ꭆpulation, is
from a confidential report of the Federal F   y Relief Administration. The report was marked "C   ꭆl—Not to be
Shown to* Anyone!" *Its contents explain w҆*

July 19, 1934

Subject: FIFTEEN WAGE EARNERS,   ҆OM ARE DYING OF
SILICOSIS, PROVIDE SUSTENANC. ꭆOR ENTIRE COMMU-
NITY OF 91 PERSONS AT VANETTA, WEST VA.

Source: REPORT OF LEON BROWER, STATISTICIAN FOR WEST
VIRGINIA E. R. A.

In the early months of 1930 large numbers of able-bodied Negroes
were brought to Vanetta, West Virginia, an abandoned coal
mining settlement which was prosperous as late as 1925, to engage
in the drilling of a three-mile tunnel required by an electric power
development. The mountain to be pierced was found to consist of
pure silicate. In spite of the warnings of the West Virginia
Department of Mines the contractors took no precautions against
the consequences to the workers of breathing the dust, which
causes silicosis, a disease which destroys lung tissues and ultimately causes suffocation. As early as the fall of 1930 thousands
of workers died, allegedly of pneumonia, but exact figures are not
available as many of the sick were allowed to wander away. The
labor turnover on the job was estimated at more than 300 percent.

On the completion of the project in September 1932 Vanetta
reverted to the status of an abandoned village. In 1934 there were
91 persons in residence, occupying 41 tumble-down hovels, 14
children, 44 adult females, and 43 adult males. Of the latter all but
ten have silicosis. Support for the community comes from the
earnings of 15 of the males, 14 of whom suffer from silicosis.
Thirteen are engaged on a road construction project 18 miles away
and are forced to walk to and from work, leaving them but 5 hours
a day for labor. Moreover many, because of their illness, must lay

off work every other day and are frequently too weak to lift a sledge hammer.

Quoting Mr. Brower:

"Coupled with all these hardships is starvation. Relief has always been spasmodic and irregular, and more irregular than is warranted. Every family related the lack of food, and for days at a time during the last winter, they had nothing to eat. One white person living in Vanetta kept many from starving. Many of the negroes went to Gauley and begged for food and work. Several white people in Gauley contributed regularly to the support of some families. Clothing was always inadequate and there were numerous cases of slightly frozen limbs; also several families were evicted during winter, and nearly every family was served with eviction notices.

"Upon coming to the community, the people were accustomed to three meals a day. During the last two winters, if they had one meal a day, they considered themselves fortunate. The food consisted of white and red beans, corn bread, and syrup. Occasionally they had some sowbelly "white meat"—that is the cheap white pork. No variety existed even for the sick or the children. Milk has been unheard of for at least two years.

"Several men, gathered in a group, related how at first the older folks would economize on food so that the children could have more. And then the men would cut their allowance to practically nothing so that the women could eat.

"Direct relief was seldom given. Many families received commodities, but very irregularly. Just three men were given C.W.A. work and these three worked a few weeks only.

"The Relief Office is fourteen miles from the community. These people would get up at four o'clock and trudge through the heavy snow to the office inadequately clothed and hungry. Too often they found that the relief agency was in no position to give assistance."

The author makes the following recommendations concerning rehabilitation of these destitute Negroes:

"Since these persons are not normally unemployed employables,* they will not remain under the F.E.R.A. But for the time being the position of the W. V. R. A. in dealing with all the persons having silicosis should be as follows:

---

* One of the standard relief categories.

"I. To discourage any person from work if the medical problem indicates the necessity.

"2. To provide for all in need by Direct Relief. The relief should be adequate despite the protests of the white people.

"3. To improve the housing and sanitation programs immediately. A public health nurse should spend a considerable amount of time in Vanetta.

"If these people desire to return home, they should be assisted, probably by the Transient Bureau. Since these men have a short period to live, as much security as possible should be provided for them. A trained qualified worker should be in this community to assist in the transportation, and to arrange inter-community contact.

"At any rate, it is inadvisable socially, to keep a community of dying persons intact. Every means should be exerted to move these families, so that they may be in communities where they will be accepted, and where the wives and children will find adjustment easier."

Negro Sharecroppers *Renwick C. Kennedy**

The Negro community at Gee's Bend, Alabama, had remained largely intact since the end of the Civil War. Traditions of plantation ownership and Negro subordination reminiscent of the antebellum era continued relatively unchanged into the twentieth century. The Depression, however, led to mass evictions of sharecroppers and tenant farmers. The situation described by the Reverend Renwick C. Kennedy, a Presbyterian minister from Camden, Alabama, became so desperate that the federal government eventually interceded and helped establish an all-Negro cooperative community there.

"Cap'n, you want to buy a dozen eggs for ten cents?"

He was a Negro of forty-five or fifty. In the Alabama country where he and I live there are 20,000 Negroes and 5,000 whites. It is a daily matter to buy and sell and barter with Negroes at one's

* From Renwick C. Kennedy, "The Face of the Poor," *Christian Century*, L (June 21, 1933), 811–812.

door. Even in prosperous times the Negroes bring their eggs and chickens and peanuts and vegetables to white men's back doors. Their stories are so pathetic this year and their calls so frequent that one buys more than one needs and spends more than one is able.

There was nothing unusual about the man's visit with his dozen eggs, but there was something about him that compelled attention. Six feet in height, slightly stout, light brown in color, a small mustache upon his lip, intelligent eyes, and facial features less heavy than in most local Negroes, he was a fine specimen of brown America, but a familiar type. Clad in blue overalls and jacket, khaki shirt, battered shoes, ragged army leggins, and a worn cap, he still was typical unless he escaped the average by being a little less dirty and a little less ragged than most Negroes this winter.

But you knew that this man had a story to tell. You read instinctively the misery, the despair, the desperation of his spirit.

"Well, I don't know. I bought two dozen eggs yesterday. Take them uptown. The stores will buy them."

"Yassuh, Cap'n, the stores'll take 'em. But they takes 'em in trade an' I wants a dime to pay my ferry cross the river, a nickel each way. He won't let me cross on credit an' I got to have a dime to git home. He won't take nuthin' at that ferry but money."

"Let me see the eggs." He shifted a heavy double sack from his shoulders to the ground and at the same time handed me a small lard tin. There were a dozen fresh eggs in it, packed in lint cotton. I took the eggs in the house and brought him his bucket and a dime.

"Where do you live?" I asked.

"Over in Gee's Bend."

"Oh yes, that's where they closed out so many folks last fall. Did they get you?"

"Cap'n, they're gittin' me now. Takin' everything I got."

"Good Lord! Old man Welch still at it, is he? I thought he got through with that dirty work."

"Naw-suh, he ain't through. Hit were lak this. They's 8,000 acres in that Jones place over there an' sixty colored fam'lies on hit. They broke up all but three fam'lies last fall, taken everything they had, corn, cotton, 'taters, cows, hogs, mules, plows, everything. They even gathered up old sweeps an' hoes. Course they may of left them a little dab of corn but not more'n a few bushels.

But me an' two other mens what had farmed in a bigger way than
the rest an' what didn't owe any big amount, ol' man Welch tol' us
us could keep our mules an' cows an' plows an' four barrels of
corn. But he done changed. He sho' God done changed. They
come an' got my cows an' mules an' plows yestiddy."

"He told you you could keep the cows and mules and plows,
and now he has come back and taken them?"

"Yassuh. He sho' done it. White folks, I'm tellin' you, the
Lawd's goin' to even this thing up some day. They's people starvin'
in Gee's Bend right now."

"Well, what are you going to do?"

"Lawd God, Cap'n, I don't know. If it was just me and my wife
we could make out someway, but I got eight head of chillen. If a
little two year ol' chillen cries for sumpin' to eat, she don't know
no better. They's people over yonder in the Bend ain't got nuthin'
for they chillen or theyselves either."

"How much did you owe Mr. Welch?"

"Cap'n, Mr. Welch says to me last spring, you bring me eleven
bales of cotton this fall an' you'll pay out all you owe me. I brung
him eleven bales an' 118 pound of lint besides an', bless God, he
done broke me up anyway. He been advancin' me for ten years,
an' he's made money outen hit. In 1927 I paid him ten hundred
and fifty dollars. He ain't got no right to be closin' me out. But
what kin a pore nigger do when white mens come aroun' in wagons
an' totin' guns to clean him up?"

"Who's going to advance you folks in the Bend this year?"

"Cap'n, I don't know. Here hit's the middle of March an' time
to begin a crop, but us don't know nuthin' about what us goin' to
do. Mr. Welch done broke us up an' say he ain't going' to do no
more advancin', an' us ain't got nobody to help us this year.
Whitefolks say they can't do no advancin' with cotton so low.
Somebody got to run us or us can't farm. They ain't no hosses, no
mules, no plows, no seed, no nuthin' on all that Jones place. They
done took my two mules. They warn't no 'count, old an' crippled,
but I made eleven bales of cotton with 'em last year. Now they's
gone an' I ain't got nuthin' to plow."

"How about Mr. Jones? Has he said anything about running the
place himself?"

"Naw-suh. He say he ain't got no money. He say he would do
hit if he could but he can't buy mules an' plows for sixty fam'lies,

an' advance to 'em too. I hear 'em say Mr. Jones ain't paid taxes for last year yet. But us been payin' him his rent."

"It looks bad. Have you tried the Red Cross for help?"

"Yassuh. I been two times but they ain't give me nuthin'. You see, I ain't been closed out all the time lak them other people. Them as has been closed out all winter has been gittin' a little flour an' lard from the Red Cross. They ain't been gittin' enough but they been gittin' sumpthin', enough to keep 'em from starvin' to death. Then Mr. Wilson what owns a place back of the Bend in the hills has been helpin' a little. He been lettin' the men work one day a week cleanin' up his land an' givin' 'em a peck of meal an' three pound of meat. But, Lawd God, what good do a peck of meal an' three pound of meat do when you got eight head of chillen? Hit don't go nowhere."

"I don't know, of course, but I believe somebody is going to run that Jones place. That land is too good to lie out."

"Cap'n, they ain't no better land on the Alabamy river. Just give me some mules an' a plow an' a little backin' an' I'll make any man ten bales of cotton disregardin' the weather. If us has a good year I'll make him fifteen bales. If somebody'll back me up, I'd feel lak I could just fly. I'd work harder'n I ever worked befo', an' I always been a steady worker. All them folks over there feels the same way. Us ain't askin' nobody to give us nuthin'. Us just askin' for a chancet to farm. But us can't farm without mules an' plows an' a little bread an' meat."

"What you got at home to eat now?"

"Cap'n, I'll tell you the God's truth, I got a side of meat left from a hog I killed, an' a few chickens in the yard, an' a little dust o' meal, an' that's all."

"Don't you need those eggs you sold me?"

"Yassuh, us sho' needs 'em. But I got to pay my ferry cross the river. I ain't got no money."

"What do you have in that sack?"

"Corn. Hit's the last bushel of them four barrels they left me."

"Are you going to sell it?"

"Naw-suh. Takin' hit to the mill to git me some meal."

"You carried a bushel of corn on your shoulder? How far is it?"

"Hit's seven mile from here to where I live."

"Goin home tonight?"

"Yassuh."

"Got to walk?"

"Onless I picks up a ride on a wagon."

"What are you going to do when you eat up that bushel?"

"God knows, whitefolks."

2. FINDING A WAY OUT

Black Unity and W. E. B. Du Bois

W. E. B. Du Bois came to the NAACP shortly after its founding and made Crisis *a highly successful organ of his personal views as well as those of the Association. Occasionally the two conflicted but matters were ironed out privately. A major break, however, came in 1934 when Du Bois resigned from the Association, relinquished the editorship of* The Crisis, *and publicly dissected the Association's often inconsistent position on the role of segregated institutions in American society. Du Bois wanted more of them, not less, and devised a program of Negro economic and psychological independence that can only be understood after a careful analysis of the major themes of Du Bois's philosophy since the late nineteenth century. His Negro cooperative commonwealth reflected Du Bois's socialism, his pride in the accomplishments of all-Negro institutions, his anticipation of the eventual collapse of capitalism throughout the world. The new racial loyalty and solidarity, he said, would dramatize the Negro's faith in himself, and even recall kinship traditions of African tribal groups. It was a magnificent-sounding scheme, a leap into racial utopia, but few outside Du Bois himself understood the intricate logic of his call for black unity. He never quite knew why others misunderstood him and refused to follow his program.*

The NAACP and Segregation W. E. B. DuBois*

There is a good deal of misapprehension as to the historic attitude of the National Association for the Advancement of Colored

* From W. E. B. Du Bois, *The Crisis,* XLI (February, 1934), 52–53.

People and race segregation. As a matter of fact, the Association, while it has from time to time discussed the larger aspects of this matter, has taken no general stand and adopted no general philosophy. Of course its action, and often very effective action, has been in specific cases of segregation where the call for a definite stand was clear and decided. For instance, in the preliminary National Negro Convention which met in New York May 31st and June 1st, 1909, segregation was only mentioned in a protest against Jim-Crow car laws and that because of an amendment by William M. Trotter. In the First Annual Report, January 1, 1911, the Association evolved a statement of its purpose, which said that "it seeks to uplift the colored men and women of this country by securing to them the full enjoyment of their rights as citizens, justice in all courts, and equality of opportunity everywhere." Later, this general statement was epitomized in the well-known declaration: "It conceives its mission to be the completion of the work which the great Emancipator began. It proposes to make a group of ten million Americans free from the lingering shackles of past slavery, physically free from peonage, mentally free from ignorance, politically free from disfranchisement, and socially free from insult." This phrase which I first wrote myself for the Annual Report of 1915 still expresses pregnantly the object of the N.A.A.C.P. and it has my own entire adherence.

It will be noted, however, that here again segregation comes in only by implication. Specifically, it was first spoken of in the Second Report of the Association, January 1, 1912, when the attempt to destroy the property of Negroes in Kansas City because they had moved into a white section was taken up. This began our fight on a specific phase of segregation, namely, the attempt to establish a Negro ghetto by force of law. This phase of segregation we fought vigorously for years and often achieved notable victories in the highest courts of the land.

But it will be noted here that the N.A.A.C.P. expressed no opinion as to whether it might not be a feasible and advisable thing for colored people to establish their own residential sections, or their own towns; and certainly there was nothing expressed or implied that Negroes should not organize for promoting their own interests in industry, literature or art. Manifestly, here was opportunity for considerable difference of opinion, but the matter never was thoroughly threshed out.

The Association moved on to other matters of color discrimination: the "Full Crew" bills which led to dismissal of so many Negro railway employees;* the "Jim-Crow" car laws on railway trains and street cars; the segregation in government departments. In all these matters, the stand of the Association was clear and unequivocal: it held that it was a gross injustice to make special rules which discriminated against the color of employees or patrons.

In the Sixth Annual Report issued in March, 1916, the seven lines of endeavor of the Association included change of unfair laws, better administration of present laws, justice in the courts, stoppage of public slander, the investigation of facts, the encouragement of distinguished work by Negroes, and organizations.

Very soon, however, there came up a more complex question and that was the matter of Negro schools. The Association had avoided from the beginning any thoroughgoing pronouncement on this matter. In the resolutions of 1909, the conference asked: "Equal educational opportunities for all and in all the states, and that public school expenditure be the same for the Negro and white child." This of course did not touch the real problem of separate schools. Very soon, however, definite problems were presented to the Association: the exclusion of colored girls from the Oberlin dormitories in 1919; the discrimination in the School of Education at the University of Pennsylvania; and the Cincinnati fight against establishing a separate school for colored children, brought the matter squarely to the front. Later, further cases came: the Brooklyn Girls' High School, the matter of a colored High School in Indianapolis, and the celebrated Gary case.†

Gradually, in these cases the attitude of the Association crystallized. It declared that further extension of segregated schools for particular races and especially for Negroes was unwise and dangerous, and the Association undertook in all possible cases to oppose such further segregation. It did not, however, for a moment feel called upon to attack the separate schools where most colored

* After World War I.
† Gary, Indiana, established separate high schools for Negroes.

children are educated throughout the United States and it refrained from this not because it approved of separate schools, but because it was faced by a fact and not a theory. It saw no sense in tilting against windmills.

The case at Cheyney was a variation; here was an old and separate private school which became in effect though not in law a separate public normal school; and in the city of Philadelphia a partial system of elementary Negro schools was developed with no definite action on the part of the N.A.A.C.P.

It will be seen that in all these cases the Association was attacking specific instances and not attempting to lay down any general rule as to how far the advancement of the colored race in the United States was going to involve separate racial action and segregated organization of Negroes for certain ends.

To be sure, the overwhelming and underlying thought of the N.A.A.C.P. has always been that any discrimination based simply on race is fundamentally wrong, and that consequently purely racial organizations must have strong justification to be admissable. On the other hand, they faced certain unfortunate but undeniable facts. For instance, War came. The Negro was being drafted. No Negro officers were being commissioned. The N.A.A.C.P. asked for the admission of Negroes to the officers' schools. This was denied. There was only one further thing to do and that was to ask for a school for Negro officers. There arose a bitter protest among many Negroes against this movement. Nevertheless, the argument for it was absolutely unanswerable, and Joel E. Spingarn, Chairman of the Board, supported by the students of Howard University, launched a movement which resulted in the commissioning of seven hundred Negro officers in the A.E.F. In all the British Dominions, with their hundreds of millions of colored folk, there was not a single officer of known Negro blood. The American Negro scored a tremendous triumph against the Color Line by their admitted and open policy of segregation. This did not mean that Mr. Spingarn or any of the members of the N.A.A.C.P. thought it right that there should be a separate Negro camp, but they thought a separate Negro camp and Negro officers was infinitely better than no camp and no Negro officers and that was the only practical choice that lay before them.

Similarly, in the question of the Negro vote, the N.A.A.C.P.

began in 1920 an attempt to organize the Negro vote and cast it in opposition to open enemies of the Negro race who were running for office. This was without doubt a species of segregation. It was appealing to voters on the grounds of race, and it brought for that reason considerable opposition. Nevertheless, it could be defended on the ground that the election of enemies of the Negro race was not only a blow to that race but to the white race and to all civilization. And while our attitude, even in the Parker case,* has been criticized, it has on the whole found abundant justification.

The final problem in segregation presented to us was that of the Harlem Hospital. Here was a hospital in the center of a great Negro population which for years did not have and would not admit a single Negro physician to its staff. Finally, by agitation and by political power, Negroes obtained representation on the staff in considerable numbers and membership on the Board of Control. It was a great triumph. But it was accompanied by reaction on the part of whites and some Negroes who had opposed this movement, and an attempt to change the status of the hospital so that it would become a segregated Negro hospital, and so that presumably the other hospitals of the city would continue to exclude Negroes from their staffs. With this arose a movement to establish Negro hospitals throughout the United States.

Here was an exceedingly difficult problem. On the one hand, there is no doubt of the need of the Negro population for wider and better hospitalization; and of the demand on the part of Negro physicians for opportunities of hospital practice. This was illustrated by the celebrated Tuskegee hospital where nearly all the Negro veterans are segregated but where an efficient Negro staff has been installed. Perhaps nothing illustrates better than this the contradiction and paradox of the problem of race segregation in the United States, and the problem which the N.A.A.C.P. faced and still faces.

The N.A.A.C.P. opposed the initial establishment of the hospital at Tuskegee although it is doubtful if it would have opposed such a hospital in the North. On the other hand, once established,

---

* The NAACP and the AF of L successfully opposed the appointment of John J. Parker to the Supreme Court in 1930. Parker, in 1920, had praised the exclusion of Negroes from Southern politics.

we fought to defend the Tuskegee hospital and give it widest opportunity.

In other words, the N.A.A.C.P. has never officially opposed separate Negro organizations—such as churches, schools and business and cultural organizations. It has never denied the recurrent necessity of united separate action on the part of Negroes for self-defense and self-development; but it has insistently and continually pointed out that such action is in any case a necessary evil involving often a recognition from within of the very color line which we are fighting without. That race pride and race loyalty, Negro ideals and Negro unity, have a place and function today, the N.A.A.C.P. never has denied and never can deny.

But all this simply touches the whole question of racial organization and initiative. No matter what we may wish or say, the vast majority of the Negroes in the United States are born in colored homes, educated in separate colored schools, attend separate colored churches, marry colored mates, and find their amusement in colored Y.M.C.A.'s and Y.W.C.A.'s. Even in their economic life, they are gradually being forced out of the place in industry which they occupied in the white world and are being compelled to seek their living among themselves. Here is segregation with a vengeance, and its problems must be met and its course guided. It would be idiotic simply to sit on the side lines and yell: "No segregation" in an increasingly segregated world.

On the other hand, the danger of easily and eagerly yielding to suggested racial segregation without reason or pressure stares us ever in the face. We segregate ourselves. We herd together. We do things such as this clipping from the *Atlanta Constitution* indicates:

A lecture on the raising of Lazarus from the dead will be delivered at the city auditorium on Friday night. The Big Bethel choir will sing and the Graham Jackson band will give additional music. Space has been set aside for white people.

The "Jim Crow" galleries of Southern moving picture houses are filled with some of the best Negro citizens. Separate schools and other institutions have been asked by Negroes in the north when the whites had made no real demand.

Such are the flat and undeniable facts. What are we going to do about them? We can neither yell them down nor make them disappear by resolutions. We must think and act. It is this problem which THE CRISIS desires to discuss during the present year in all its phases and with ample and fair representation to all shades of opinion.

The Need for Racial Pride W. E. B. Du Bois*

Many persons have interpreted my reassertion of our current attitude toward segregation as a counsel of despair. We can't win, therefore, give up and accept the inevitable. Never, and nonsense. Our business in this world is to fight and fight again, and never to yield. But after all, one must fight with his brains, if he has any. He gathers strength to fight. He gathers knowledge, and he raises children who are proud to fight and who know what they are fighting about. And above all, they learn that what they are fighting for is the opportunity and the chance to know and associate with black folk. They are not fighting to escape themselves. They are fighting to say to the world: the opportunity of knowing Negroes is worth so much to us and is so appreciated, that we want you to know them too.

Negroes are not extraordinary human beings. They are just like other human beings, with all their foibles and ignorance and mistakes. But they are human beings, and human nature is always worth knowing, and withal, splendid in its manifestations. Therefore, we are fighting to keep open the avenues of human contact; but in the meantime, we are taking every advantage of what opportunities of contact are already open to us, and among those opportunities which are open, and which are splendid and inspiring, is the opportunity of Negroes to work together in the twentieth century for the uplift and development of the Negro race. It is no counsel of despair to emphasize and hail the opportunity for such work.

The assumptions of the anti-segregation campaign have been all wrong. This is not our fault, but it is our misfortune. When I went to Atlanta University to teach in 1897, and to study the Negro problem, I said, confidently, that the basic problem is our racial ignorance and lack of culture. That once Negroes know civiliza-

* The Crisis, XLI (June, 1934), p. 182.

tion, and whites know Negroes, then the problem is solved. This proposition is still true, but the solution is much further away than my youth dreamed. Negroes are still ignorant, but the disconcerting thing is that white people on the whole are just as much opposed to Negroes of education and culture, as to any other kind, and perhaps more so. Not all whites, to be sure, but the overwhelming majority.

Our main method, then, falls flat. We stop training ability. We lose our manners. We swallow our pride, and beg for things. We agitate and get angry. And with all that, we face the blank fact: Negroes are not wanted; neither as scholars nor as business men; neither as clerks nor as artisans; neither as artists nor as writers. What can we do about it? We cannot use force. We cannot enforce law, even if we get it on the statute books. So long as overwhelming public opinion sanctions and justifies and defends color segregation, we are helpless, and without remedy. We are segregated. We are cast back upon ourselves, to an Island Within; "To your tents, Oh Israel!"

Surely then, in this period of frustration and disappointment, we must turn from negation to affirmation, from the ever-lasting "No" to the ever-lasting "Yes." Instead of sitting, sapped of all initiative and independence; instead of drowning our originality in imitation of mediocre white folks; instead of being afraid of ourselves and cultivating the art of skulking to escape the Color Line; we have got to renounce a program that always involves humiliating self-stultifying scrambling to crawl somewhere where we are not wanted; where we crouch panting like a whipped dog. We have got to stop this and learn that on such a program they cannot build manhood. No, by God, stand erect in a mud-puddle and tell the white world to go to hell, rather than lick boots in a parlor.

Affirm, as you have a right to affirm, that the Negro race is one of the great human races, inferior to none in its accomplishment and in its ability. Different, it is true, and for most of the difference, let us reverently thank God. And this race, with its vantage grounds in modern days, can go forward of its own will, of its own power, and its own initiative. It is led by twelve million American Negroes of average modern intelligence; three or four million educated African Negroes are their full equals, and several million Negroes in the West Indies and South America. This body of at least twenty-five million modern men are not called upon to commit suicide because somebody doesn't like their complexion or their hair. It is their opportunity and their day to stand up and make themselves heard and felt in the modern world.

Indeed, there is nothing else we can do. If you have passed your resolution, "No segregation, Never and Nowhere," what are you going to do about it? Let me tell you what you are going to do. You are going back to continue to make your living in a Jim-Crow school; you are going to dwell in a segregated section of the city; you are going to pastor a Jim-Crow Church; you are going to occupy political office because of Jim-Crow political organizations that stand back of you and force you into office. All these things and a thousand others you are going to do because you have got to.

If you are going to do this, why not say so? What are you afraid of? Do you believe in the Negro race or do you not? If you do not, naturally, you are justified in keeping still. But if you do believe in the extraordinary accomplishment of the Negro church and the Negro college, the Negro school and the Negro newspaper, then say so and say so plainly, not only for the sake of those who have given their lives to make these things worthwhile, but for those young people whom you are teaching, by that negative attitude, that there is nothing that they can do, nobody that they can emulate, and no field worthwhile working in. Think of what Negro art and literature has yet to accomplish if it can only be free and untrammeled by the necessity of pleasing white folks! Think of the splendid moral appeal that you can make to a million children tomorrow, if once you can get them to see the possibilities of the American Negro today and now, whether he is segregated or not, or in spite of all possible segregation.

A Critique of W. E. B. Du Bois James Weldon Johnson*

Du Bois's attitude on segregation was a blow to his Negro and white admirers. The most prominent Negro leader in America alienated himself from those who most respected him: "Oh, for a leader," the Chicago Defender *pleaded. The public response*

* From James Weldon Johnson, *Negro Americans, What Now?* (New York, 1935), pp. 12–18.

to Du Bois's position was almost uniformly critical. "His latest battle cry is that the Negro must recognize the curse of segregation and build a black economy of his own," a writer in The Nation *said. "With what? Is Wall Street colored? Is finance capital high yaller? Today Du Bois winds up pretty much where Booker T. Washington started. And so the colored people are leaderless."*

The most thorough critique of Du Bois's stand came from the pen of James Weldon Johnson. Johnson was a man of unusual talent. At various times in his too-short life he was an educator, journalist, poet, novelist, song writer, diplomat, NAACP official, professor, and literary critic.

. . . We have reduced choices of a way out to two. There remain, on the one hand, the continuation of our efforts to achieve integration and, on the other hand, an acknowledgment of our isolation and the determination to accept and make the best of it.

Throughout our entire intellectual history there has been a division of opinion as to which of these two divergent courses the race should follow. From early times there have been sincere thinkers among us who were brought to the conclusion that our only salvation lies in the making of the race into a self-contained economic, social, and cultural unit; in a word, in the building of an *imperium in imperio.*

All along, however, majority opinion has held that the only salvation worth achieving lies in the making of the race into a component part of the nation, with all the common rights and privileges, as well as duties, of citizenship. This attitude has been basic in the general policy of the race—so far as it has had a general policy—for generations, the policy of striving zealously to gain full admission to citizenship and guarding jealously each single advance made.

But this question of direction, of goal, is not a settled one. There is in us all a stronger tendency toward isolation than we may be aware of. There come times when the most persistent integrationist becomes an isolationist, when he curses the White world and consigns it to hell. This tendency toward isolation is strong because it springs from a deep-seated, natural desire—a desire for respite from the unremitting, grueling struggle; for a place in which refuge might be taken. We are again and again confronted by this question. It is ever present, though often dormant. Recently it was emphatically brought forward by the utterances of so authoritative a voice as that of Dr. Du Bois.

The question is not one to be lightly brushed aside. Those who stand for making the race into a self-sufficient unit point out that after years of effort we are still Jim-Crowed, discriminated against, segregated, and lynched; that we are still shut out from industry, barred from the main avenues of business, and cut off from free participation in national life. They point out that in some sections of the country we have not even secured equal protection of life and property under the laws. They declare that entrance of the Negro into full citizenship is as distant as it was seventy years ago. And they ask: What is the Negro to do? Give himself over to wishful thinking? Stand shooting at the stars with a popgun? Is it not rather a duty and a necessity for him to face the facts of his condition and environment, to acknowledge them as facts, and to make the best use of them that he can? These are questions which the thinkers of the race should strive to sift clearly.

To this writer it seems that one of the first results of clear thinking is a realization of the truth that the making of the race into a self-sustaining unit, the creating of an *imperium in imperio,* does not offer an easier or more feasible task than does the task of achieving full citizenship. Such an *imperium* would have to rest upon a basis of separate group economic independence, and the trend of all present-day forces is against the building of any foundation of that sort.

After thoughtful consideration, I cannot see the slightest possibility of our being able to duplicate the economic and social machinery of the country. I do not believe that any other special group could do it. The isolationists declare that because of imposed segregation we have, to a large degree, already done it. But the situation they point to is more apparent than real. Our separate schools and some of our other race institutions, many of our race enterprises, the greater part of our employment, and most of our fundamental activities are contingent upon our interrelationship with the country as a whole.

Clear thinking reveals that the outcome of voluntary isolation would be a permanent secondary status, so acknowledged by the race. Such a status would, it is true, solve some phases of the race question. It would smooth away a good part of the friction and bring about a certain protection and security. The status of slavery carried some advantages of that sort. But I do not believe we shall ever be willing to pay such a price for security and peace.

If Negro Americans could do what reasonably appears to be impossible, and as a separate unit achieve self-sufficiency built upon group economic independence, does anyone suppose that that would abolish prejudice against them and allay opposition, or that the struggle to maintain their self-sufficiency would be in any degree less bitter than the present struggle to become an integral part of the nation? Taking into account human nature as it is, would not the achievement be more likely to arouse envy and bring on even more violent hatreds and persecutions?

Certainly, the isolationists are stating a truth when they contend that we should not, ostrich-like, hide our heads in the sand, making believe that prejudice is non-existent; but in so doing they are apostles of the obvious. Calling upon the race to realize that prejudice is an actuality is a needless effort; it is placing emphasis on what has never been questioned. The danger for us does not lie in a possible failure to acknowledge prejudice as a reality, but in acknowledging it too fully. We cannot ignore the fact that we are segregated, no matter how much we might wish to do so; and the smallest amount of common sense forces us to extract as much good from the situation as there is in it. Any degree of sagacity forces us at the same time to use all our powers to abolish imposed segregation; for it is an evil *per se* and the negation of equality either of opportunity or of awards. We should by all means make our schools and institutions as excellent as we can possibly make them—and by that very act we reduce the certainty that they will forever remain schools and institutions "for Negroes only." We should make our business enterprises and other strictly group undertakings as successful as we can possibly make them. We should gather all the strength and experience we can from imposed segregation. But any good we are able to derive from the system we should consider as a means, not an end. The strength and experience we gain from it should be applied to the objective of *entering into,* not *staying out of* the body politic.

Clear thinking shows, too, that, as bad as conditions are, they are not as bad as they are declared to be by discouraged and pessimistic isolationists. To say that in the past two generations or more Negro Americans have not advanced a single step toward a fuller share in the commonwealth becomes in the light of easily ascertainable facts, an absurdity. Only the shortest view of the situation gives color of truth to such a statement; any reasonably long view proves it to be utterly false.

With our choice narrowed down to these two courses, wisdom and far-sightedness and possibility of achievement demand that we follow the line that leads to equal rights for us, based on the common terms and conditions under which they are accorded and guaranteed to the other groups that go into the making up of our national family. It is not necessary for our advancement that such an outcome should suddenly eradicate all prejudices. It would not, of course, have the effect of suddenly doing away with voluntary grouping in religious and secular organizations or of abolishing group enterprises—for example, Negro newspapers. The accordance of full civil and political rights has not in the case of the greater number of groups in the nation had that effect. Nevertheless, it would be an immeasurable step forward, and would place us where we had a fair start with the other American groups. More than that we do not need to ask.

3. THE DIFFUSION OF LEADERSHIP

*Communism and the Negro**

So many shifts occurred in Communist ideology on racial questions that it is easy to denounce the party for having failed to accomplish any of its stated goals, or criticize it for opportunism. It takes no especial insight, for example, to poke fun at the idea of "self-determination in the black belt"—the concept of a black, independent nation in areas of the South with a Negro majority. One might also hold up for display the obsequious call for a truce on demands for racial justice in World War II, or the changing Communist attitude on the role of the Negro middle class in the civil rights movement. This would only prove the obvious: the party's stand on what it called the "Negro question," as on others, was subordinate to its commitment to international Communism.

* "The Communist International Resolution on the Negro Question in U.S.," *The Communist*, IX (January, 1930), 48–55.

When the requirements of world politics demanded it, all had to be prepared for self-sacrifice.

But once this is admitted, it is necessary to recognize that there is more to be said. The party's call for full racial equality and its attempts to devise methods of achieving it were rare in the history of American radicalism. No national organization since the abolitionist era, excepting all-Negro and civil rights groups, had made Negroes the center of such intense concern and activity. Negroes such as James W. Ford and others acquired positions of prominence in party circles. Party workers in the South refused to acquiesce to Southern codes of racial etiquette when they worked with sharecroppers or the unemployed, and many paid the consequences of such heresy. The wide scope of Communist planning on racial matters is evident in the following resolutions of the Communist International.

1. The industrialization of the South, the concentration of a new Negro working class population in the big cities of the East and North and the entrance of the Negroes into the basic industries on a mass scale, create the possibility for the Negro workers, under the leadership of the Communist Party, to assume the hegemony of all Negro liberation movements, and to increase their importance and role in the revolutionary struggle of the American proletariat.

The Negro working class has reached a stage of development which enables it, if properly organized and well led, to fulfill successfully its double historical mission:

(a) To play a considerable role in the class struggle against American imperialism as an important part of the American working class; and

(b) To lead the movement of the oppressed masses of the Negro population.

2. The bulk of the Negro population (86 percent) live in the southern states: of this number 74 per cent live in the rural districts and are dependent almost exclusively upon agriculture for a livelihood. Approximately one-half of these rural dwellers live in the so-called "Black Belt," in which area they constitute more than 50 per cent of the entire population. The great mass of the Negro agrarian population are subject to the most ruthless exploitation and persecution of a semi-slave character. In addition to the

ordinary forms of capitalist exploitation, American imperialism utilized every possible form of slave exploitation (peonage, share-cropping, landlord supervision of crops and marketing, etc.) for the purpose of extracting super-profits. On the basis of these slave remnants, there has grown up a super-structure of social and political inequality that expresses itself in lynching, segregation, Jim Crowism, etc.

NECESSARY CONDITION FOR NATIONAL REVOLUTIONARY MOVEMENT

3. The various forms of oppression of the Negro masses, who are concentrated mainly in the so-called "Black Belt," provide the necessary conditions for a national revolutionary movement among the Negroes. The Negro agricultural laborers and the tenant farmers feel the pressure of white persecution and exploitation. Thus, the agrarian problem lies at the root of the Negro national movement. The great majority of Negroes in the rural districts of the South are not "reserves of capitalist reaction," but potential allies of the revolutionary proletariat. Their objective position facilitates their transformation into a revolutionary force, which, under the leadership of the proletariat, will be able to participate in the joint struggle with all other workers against capitalist exploitation.

4. It is the duty of the Negro workers to organize through the mobilization of the broad masses of the Negro population the struggle of the agricultural laborers and tenant farmers against all forms of semi-feudal oppression. On the other hand, it is the duty of the Communist Party of the U.S.A. to mobilize and rally the broad masses of the white workers for active participation in this struggle. For that reason the Party must consider the beginning of systematic work in the south as one of its main tasks, having regard for the fact that the bringing together of the workers and toiling masses of all nationalities for a joint struggle against the land-owners and the bourgeoisie is one of the most important aims of the Communist International, as laid down in the resolutions on the national and colonial question of the Second and Sixth Congresses of the Comintern.

FOR COMPLETE EMANCIPATION OF OPPRESSED NEGRO RACE

5. To accomplish this task, the Communist Party must come out as the champion of the right of the oppressed Negro race for full emancipation. While continuing and intensifying the struggle under the slogan of full social and political equality for the Negroes, which must remain the central slogan of our Party for work among the masses, the Party must come out openly and unreservedly for the right of Negroes to national self-determination in the southern states, where the Negroes form a majority of the population. The struggle for equal rights and the propaganda for the slogan of self-determination must be linked up with the economic demands of the Negro masses, especially those directed against the slave remnants and all forms of national and racial oppression. Special stress must be laid upon organizing active resistance against lynching, Jim Crowism, segregation and all other forms of oppression of the Negro population.

6. All work among the Negroes, as well as the struggle for the Negro cause among the whites, must be used, based upon the changes which have taken place in the relationship of classes among the Negro population. The existence of a Negro industrial proletariat of almost two million workers makes it imperative that the main emphasis should be placed on these new proletarian forces. The Negro workers must be organized under the leadership of the Communist Party, and thrown into joint struggle together with the white workers. The Party must learn to combine all demands of the Negroes with the economic and political struggle of the workers and the poor farmers.

AMERICAN NEGRO QUESTION PART OF WORLD PROBLEM

7. The Negro question in the United States must be treated in its relation to the Negro questions and struggles in other parts of the world. The Negro race everywhere is an oppressed race. Whether it is a minority (U.S.A., etc.), majority (South Africa) or inhabits a so-called independent state (Liberia, etc.), the Negroes are oppressed by imperialism. Thus, a common tie of interest is

established for the revolutionary struggle of race and national liberation from imperialist domination of the Negroes in various parts of the world. A strong Negro revolutionary movement in the U.S.A. will be able to influence and direct the revolutionary movement in all those parts of the world where the Negroes are oppressed by imperialism.

8. The proletarianization of the Negro masses makes the trade unions the principal form of mass organization. It is the primary task of the Party to play an active part and lead in the work of organizing the Negro workers and agricultural laborers in trade unions. Owing to the refusal of the majority of the white unions in the U.S.A., led by the reactionary leaders, to admit Negroes to membership, steps must be immediately taken to set up special unions for those Negro workers who are not allowed to join the white unions. At the same time, however, the struggles for the inclusion of Negro workers in the existing unions must be intensified and concentrated upon, special attention must be given to those unions in which the statutes and rules set up special limitations against the admission of Negro workers. The primary duty of the Communist Party in this connection is to wage a merciless struggle against the A. F. of L. bureaucracy, which prevents the Negro workers from joining the white workers' unions. The organization of special trade unions for the Negro masses must be carried out as part and parcel of the struggle against the restrictions imposed upon the Negro workers and for their admission to the white workers' unions. The creation of separate Negro unions should in no way weaken the struggle in the old unions for the admission of Negroes on equal terms. Every effort must be made to see that all the new unions organized by the left wing and by the Communist Party should embrace the workers of all nationalities and of all races. The principle of one union for all workers in each industry, white and black, should cease to be a mere slogan of propaganda, and must become a slogan of action.

Party Trade Union Work Among Negroes

9. While organizing the Negroes into unions and conducting an aggressive struggle against the anti-Negro trade union policy of the A. F. of L., the Party must pay more attention than it has hitherto done to the work in the Negro workers' organizations, such as the

Brotherhood of Sleeping Car Porters, Chicago Asphalt Workers Union, and so on. The existence of two million Negro workers and the further industrialization of the Negroes demand a radical change in the work of the Party among the Negroes. The creation of working class organizations and the extension of our influence in the existing working class Negro organizations, are of much greater importance than the work in bourgeois and petty-bourgeois organizations, such as the National Association for the Advancement of Colored People, the Pan-African Congress, etc.

10. The American Negro Labor Congress* continues to exist only nominally. Every effort should be made to strengthen this organization as a medium through which we can extend the work of the Party among the Negro masses and mobilize the Negro workers under our leadership. After careful preparatory work, which must be started at once, another convention of the American Negro Labor Congress should be held. A concrete plan must also be presented to the Congress for an intensified struggle for the economic, social, political and national demands of the Negro masses. The program of the American Negro Labor Congress must deal specially with the agrarian demands of the Negro farmers and tenants in the South.

11. The importance of trade union work imposes special tasks upon the Trade Union Unity League. The T.U.U.L. has completely neglected the work among the Negro workers, notwithstanding the fact that these workers are objectively in a position to play a very great part in carrying through the program of organizing the unorganized. The closest contact must be established between the T.U.U.L. and the Negro masses. The T.U.U.L. must become the champion in the struggle for the rights of the Negroes in the old unions, and in the organizing of new unions for both Negroes and whites, as well as separate Negro unions.

WHITE CHAUVINISM EVIDENCED IN THE AMERICAN PARTY

[12.] The C.E.C.† of the American Communist Party itself stated in its resolution of April 30, 1928, that "the Party as a

* Founded in 1925.
† Central Executive Committee.

whole has not sufficiently realized the significance of work among the Negroes." Such an attitude toward the Party work among the Negroes is, however, not satisfactory. The time is ripe to begin within the Party a courageous campaign of self-criticism concerning the work among the Negroes. Penetrating self-criticism is the necessary preliminary condition for directing the Negro work along new lines.

13. The Party must bear in mind that white chauvinism, which is the expression of the ideological influence of American imperialism among the workers, not only prevails among different strata of the white workers in the U.S.A., but is even reflected in various forms in the Party itself. White chauvinism has manifested itself even in open antagonism of some comrades to the Negro comrades. In some instances where Communists were called upon to champion and to lead in the most vigorous manner the fight against white chauvinism, they instead, yielded to it. In Gary, white members of the Workers Party protested against Negroes eating in the restaurant controlled by the Party. In Detroit, Party members, yielding to pressure, drove out Negro comrades from a social given in aid of the miners' strike.

While the Party has taken certain measures against these manifestations of white chauvinism, nevertheless those manifestations must be regarded as indications of race prejudice even in the ranks of the Party, which must be fought with the utmost energy.

14. An aggressive fight against all forms of white chauvinism must be accompanied by a widespread and thorough educational campaign in the spirit of internationalism within the Party, utilizing for this purpose to the fullest possible extent the Party schools, the Party press and the public platform, to stamp out all forms of antagonism, or even indifference among our white comrades toward the Negro work. This educational work should be conducted simultaneously with a campaign to draw the white workers and the poor farmers into the struggle for the support of the demands of the Negro workers.

TASKS OF PARTY IN RELATION TO NEGRO WORK

15. The Communist Party of the U.S.A., in its treatment of the Negro question must all the time bear in mind this twofold task:

(a) To fight for the full rights of the oppressed Negroes and for their right to self-determination and against all forms of chauvinism, especially among the workers of the oppressing nationality.

(b) The propaganda and the day-to-day practice of international class solidarity must be considered as one of the basic tasks of the American Communist Party. The fight—by propaganda and by deeds—should be directed first and foremost against the chauvinism of the workers of the oppressing nationality as well as against bourgeois segregation tendencies of the oppressed nationality. The propaganda of international class solidarity is the necessary prerequisite for the unity of the working class in the struggle.

"The center of gravity in educating the workers of the oppressing countries in the principles of internationalism must inevitably consist in the propaganda and defense by these workers of the right of segregation by the oppressed countries. We have the right and duty to treat every socialist of an oppressing nation, who does not conduct such propaganda, as an imperialist and as a scoundrel." (Lenin, selected articles on the national question.)

16. The Party must seriously take up the task of training a cadre of Negro comrades as leaders, bring them into the Party schools in the U.S.A. and abroad, and make every effort to draw Negro proletarians into active and leading work in the Party, not confining the activities of the Negro comrades exclusively to the work among Negroes. Simultaneously, white workers must specially be trained for work among the Negroes.

17. Efforts must be made to transform the "Negro Champion"* into a weekly mass organ of the Negro proletariat and tenant farmers. Every encouragement and inducement must be given to the Negro comrades to utilize the Party press generally.

Negro Work Part of General Work of Party

18. The Party must link up the struggle on behalf of the Negroes with the general campaigns of the Party. The Negro problem must be part and parcel of all and every campaign conducted by the Party. In the election campaigns, trade union

* Communist newspaper founded in the twenties.

work, the campaigns for the organization of the unorganized, anti-imperialist work, labor party campaign, International Labor Defense, etc., the Central Executive Committee must work out plans designed to draw the Negroes into active participation in all these campaigns, and at the same time to bring the white workers into the struggle on behalf of the Negroes' demands. It must be borne in mind that the Negro masses will not be won for the revolutionary struggles until such time as the most conscious section of the white workers show, by action, that they are fighting with the Negroes against all racial discrimination and persecution. Every member of the Party must bear in mind that "the age-long oppression of the colonial and weak nationalities by the imperialist powers, has given rise to a feeling of bitterness among the masses of the enslaved countries as well as a feeling of distrust toward the oppressing nations in general and toward the proletariat of those nations." (See resolution on Colonial and National Question of Second Congress.)

19. The Negro women in industry and on the farms constitute a powerful potential force in the struggle for Negro emancipation. By reason of being unorganized to an even greater extent than male Negro workers, they are the most exploited section. The A.F. of L. bureaucracy naturally exercises toward them a double hostility, by reason of both their color and sex. It therefore becomes an important task of the Party to bring the Negro women into the economic and political struggle.

20. Only by an active and strenuous fight on the part of the white workers against all forms of oppression directed against the Negroes, will the Party be able to draw into its ranks the most active and conscious Negro workers—men and women—and to increase its influence in those intermediary organizations which are necessary for the mobilization of the Negro masses in the struggle against segregation, lynching, Jim Crowism, etc.

21. In the present struggle in the mining industry, the Negro workers participate actively and in large numbers. The leading role the Party played in this struggle has helped greatly to increase its prestige. Nevertheless, the special efforts being made by the Party in the work among the Negro strikers cannot be considered as adequate. The Party did not send enough Negro organizers into the

coal fields, and it did not sufficiently attempt, in the first stages of the fight, to develop the most able Negro strikers and to place them in leading positions. The Party must be especially criticized for its failure to put Negro workers on the Presidium of the Pittsburgh Miners' Conference,* doing so only after such representation was demanded by the Negroes themselves.

22. In the work among the Negroes, special attention should be paid to the role played by the churches and preachers who are acting on behalf of American imperialism. The Party must conduct a continuous and carefully worked out campaign among the Negro masses, sharpened primarily against the preachers and the churchmen, who are the agents of the oppressors of the Negro race.

PARTY WORK AMONG NEGRO PROLETARIAT AND PEASANTRY

23. The Party must apply united front tactics for specific demands to the existing Negro petty bourgeois organizations. The purpose of these united front tactics should be the mobilizing of the Negro masses under the leadership of the Party, and to expose the treacherous petty bourgeois leadership of those organizations.

24. The Negro Miners Relief Committee and the Harlem Tenants League are examples of joint organizations of action which may serve as a means of drawing the Negro masses into struggle. In every case the utmost effort must be made to combine the struggle of the Negro workers with the struggle of the white workers, and to draw the white workers' organizations into such joint campaigns.

25. In order to reach the bulk of the Negro masses, special attention should be paid to the work among the Negroes in the South. For that purpose, the Party should establish a district organization in the most suitable locality in the South.† Whilst continuing trade union work among the Negro workers and the agricultural laborers, special organizations of tenant farmers must be set up. Special efforts must also be made to secure the support

* A T.U.U.L. affiliate.
† Birmingham became the center of party activity in the South.

of the share croppers in the creation of such organizations. The Party must undertake the task of working out a definite program of immediate demands, directed against all slave remnants, which will serve as the rallying slogans for the formation of such peasant organizations.

Henceforth the Communist Party must consider the struggle on behalf of the Negro masses, the task of organizing the Negro workers and peasants and the drawing of these oppressed masses into the proletarian revolutionary struggle, as one of its major tasks, remembering, in the words of the Second Congress resolution, that "the victory over capitalism cannot be fully achieved and carried to its ultimate goal unless the proletariat and the toiling masses of all nations of the world rally of their own accord in a concordant and close union."

The Scottsboro Case Stephen R. Roddy*

Next to the trials of Sacco and Vanzetti and perhaps the Rosenbergs, the Scottsboro case was the most prominent international cause célèbre in American history. The Scottsboro boys—many of whom became men in the twenty years the case dragged its way through courts, parole boards, and negotiating tables—were accused of having raped two white women dressed as tramps on a freight train near Scottsboro, Alabama, in 1931. The Communist legal bureau, the International Labor Defense, immediately came to the aid of the Negro youngsters and party machinery transformed the many trials into a showcase of American racism throughout the world. A march on Washington was held, delegations came to the White House, Scottsboro mothers (real and bogus) spoke in Latvia, Germany, England, and France. The following unique report of the atmosphere at the first trial of the Scottsboro defendants is by Stephen R. Roddy. Roddy, a Southern white man, was hired by the Negro Interdenominational Minister's Alliance of Chattanooga, Tennessee, as soon as the boys were arrested. He attended the trial as an observer and later entered the case as an NAACP lawyer.

* From the NAACP manuscripts, Manuscript Division, Library of Congress.

April 11, 1931

To the Friends and Relatives of the Nine Negro Boys, Charged with Rape, in Jackson County, Alabama.

In compliance with my promise to submit a written report to you upon the proceedings in this matter, I herewith submit the following brief summary of the cases from the beginning to end, as I recall them, tried in Scottsboro, Ala.

The defendants were charged with rape of two white girls on the 25th day of March, in Jackson County, Ala. The rape was supposedly committed on a southbound freight train between Stevenson and Paint Rock, Ala. The nine defendants were taken from the train on its arrival at Paint Rock, by a Deputy Sheriff and several others who were especially deputized for that purpose, and taken to Gadsden, Ala. and confined in the County Jail there. The Grand Jury of Jackson County was called especially for the purpose of considering this case and indictments were returned in all nine cases on the 30th day of March. On that day the defendants were brought by a company of State militia to Scottsboro and arraigned and their cases set for trial for the 6th day of April. On the day of their arraignment, I was in Court and the Judge appointed all members of the Scottsboro Bar, except officials, to represent the defendants. Excuses were presented to the Court by several members of the Bar as to why they could not assist the defendants. I stated to the Court that I had not been employed to represent the defendants in the trial of the cases and requested that his appointment of the local members of the Bar stand as I was not at all sure that I would be, or would accept such employment, if offered. On that statement the Court agreed to appoint Mr. Milo Moody, upon his statement [that] it was satisfactory with him to be an assistant to the defense, if the Court so desired. Immediately after the defendants were taken back by the National Guard to Gadsden, and in Company with Mr. Moody who had been appointed as above stated. I returned to Chattanooga. Mr. Moody and I, as you recall, met some of you that night and agreed to appear and defend these boys on April 6th. On April 6th, Mr. Moody and I filed motions for a change of venue, which motions alleged that the feeling against the defendants was so intense in Jackson County, and many other reasons, that the defendants could not receive a fair trial. The motions were promptly overruled. Also, I had previously asked the Court not to set the trials on April 6th, but to allow a week or two longer for the preparation by the defense, but this request was, of course, overruled.

Juries were then drawn and exceptions to the methods were entered by defense attorneys. The State demanded a severance and proceeded to bring Charlie Weems and Clarence Norris to trial. In this case the jury was out for about two hours and then returned a verdict which carried the death penalty. Haywood Patterson was next brought to trial with the same result. The State then placed on trial Andy Wright, Olin Montgomery, Willie Roberson, Ozie Powell, and Eugene Williams. This case went to the jury about four o'clock on Wednesday afternoon and about ten o'clock Thursday morning it reported a verdict carrying the death penalty. In the case of Roy Wright, aged 14, the solicitor made a proposition that he plead guilty and take a life sentence. Defense counsel suggested that he be placed on trial with the understanding that the State not ask for a sentence that carried the death penalty. This was agreed and the solicitor, in compliance with the agreement, announced to the Court and the jury the State did not ask for a sentence greater than life imprisonment. However, the jury was out all night and late the next day a mis-trial was entered. Upon the poll of the jury, it was shown seven stood for the death penalty and five for life sentence. It might be explained the reason for not accepting the State's proposition the defendant plead guilty and take a life sentence, the defendant would have been deprived of his right of appeal. Under the agreement that he go to trial with the understanding that he not be given more than a life sentence, he reserved his right of appeal. It may be that it will be necessary to try him again, but there is no need to entertain fear that he will be electrocuted.

Regarding the evidence, it was about the same in all the cases. The two girls alleged to have been raped, Victoria Price and Ruby Bates, were the principal witnesses for the State. There were many contradictory statements made by them, particularly in the testimony of Victoria Price. She seemed ready and willing to swear anything to the detriment of the defendants. She was the only witness who identified any of the defendants. Ruby Bates admitted she could not identify the defendants. Both girls stated there were seven white boys and seventeen or eighteen negroes on the train and a fight was started between the whites and blacks with the result that all but two of the white boys were thrown from the train. Each girl testified she was raped by six different negroes; that all of the negroes except two were armed with open knives and the other two with pistols. Two men who reside near Stevenson, Ala., testified for the State, that they saw a fight going on as the train passed, but could not say whether the men were white or black but there were anywhere from seventeen or eighteen to perhaps twenty-five or thirty men on the train engaged in the fight. The arresting officers testified for the State to the effect that they arrested nine negroes, all that could be found on the train when it arrived at Paint Rock. They of course could not identify these negroes as the ones who had committed the rape, except by what the girls told them, which was incompetent. There were two Doctors placed on the witness stand who testified they examined and treated the girls within a short time after their arrival at Paint Rock and found them in good condition both mentally and physically. They did state that on one of the girls they found two small bruises about the size of a dime and a few minor scratches and bruises on their arms just above the wrists; that both girls showed evidence of intercourse but were not lacerated or bruised about the sexual organs; that Ruby Bates was slightly inflamed but Victoria Price appeared normal. That spermatozoa was taken from the vagina of the girls. All nine of the defendants testified and told a positive story as to their positions on the train and stoutly denied that they had any part in the rape and only participated in the fight to the extent that some two or three of the defendants went to the car where the fight was in progress to be of assistance if needed. Two of them further stated they helped to pull two of the white boys from between the cars and thereby saved their lives. The white boys were present at the trial but were not used by the State. On cross examination the negroes stuck to their original stories in every detail and did not accuse each other as stated in an Associated Press dispatch. The whole insistence of the negroes was that the ones who might have had anything to do with the white girls made their escape from the train immediately afterwards and that they did not leave because they had done nothing and did not anticipate the accusation by the white girls; that they had the same opportunity to leave the train as the other negroes.

Regarding the general conditions surrounding the trial of these cases, thousands of people were in Scottsboro during the first day of the trial. Machine guns were placed around the Court House yard and militia men were everywhere in evidence. Spectators who entered the Court room were searched at the door. Everything was orderly until the Clerk of the Court read the verdict of the jury in the first two cases. Instantly, a wild and thunderous roar went up from the audience and was heard by those in the Court House yard where thousands took up the demonstration and carried it on for fifteen or twenty minutes. Within ten minutes after the announcement of the verdict, a brass band made its appearance on the street and entertained the crowd until after dark. The next day the crowd was not nearly so large, however, unusual interest was kept up until after the last defendant was tried, the verdict announced, and the prisoners taken from Scottsboro.

Every exception possible was made by defense counsel to evidence and procedure deemed improper. Motions were promptly made for new trials on many grounds, particularly that of the demonstration by the assembled crowd. Notices of appeals have been made in all cases. In other words everything has been done to get the cases properly before the higher courts and maintain all rights of the defendants. Looking at the cases as tried without prejudice it seems that the cases of the State are very weak and verdicts rendered on the unsupported evidence of Victoria Price, whose word is absolutely unreliable, as will appear in the transcript of the record.

It is my opinion that the Supreme Court or the prison board of Alabama will be very reluctant to permit the death penalty to be imposed upon these defendants after reading the record and deliberating calmly and soberly upon it. To impose such a penalty would amount to wholesale slaughter, the like of which has never been known in this country. I have much confidence that it may be avoided if the defendants and their attorneys are properly supported by you people.

I wish to say that I cannot approve of any organization sending telegrams to the Trial Judge or any of the Judges of the Supreme Court or the Governor, at this time. If they care to be represented, I would suggest that they communicate with Mr. Moody or myself as we will be glad to have them act with us and associate [with] any lawyer they may select.

The C.I.O. and the National Negro Congress *Philip Murray**

Perhaps the most significant break in the color line in the thirties and forties came through the initiative of the CIO. The racial hostility evident in most AF of L unions since the 1890's had often transformed Negro workers into weapons of capital—they were frequently brought in as strikebreakers in times of crisis. Industrial unionism needed Negro allies to survive, and awareness of this economic reality forced such unions as the National Maritime Union, the United Packing House Workers, and the United Automobile Workers to court Negro support. As Joseph Curran, NMU president, wrote in 1939: "Trade Union history has proved that racial, color and religious discrimination has always been an obstacle in the path of unity, dividing workers into small groups which are vulnerable to all types of employer attacks."† The Steel Workers Organizing Committee (SWOC) was a cutting edge of interracial as well as industrial unionism. In 1937 Philip Murray, SWOC chairman, came before the National Negro Congress—a federation of many Negro organizations at that time—and pleaded for Negro support of the new unions. The National Negro Congress played a prominent role in the steel drive and in other CIO strikes and organizing campaigns. Murray's speech follows.

Since the founders of the Committee for Industrial Organization met in Atlantic City two years ago to form that Committee, they set out to organize the great mass production industries of this nation upon the firm belief that each international and each national union should admit to membership upon a basis of absolute

* From Second National Negro Congress, *Official Proceedings, 1937* (Washington, D.C., 1937).

† *Equality for All: The Stand of the NMU on Discrimination* (New York, 1948), p. 3.

equality every man and woman eligible to membership, regardless of race, creed, political or religious belief.

Eight international unions, in November, 1935, founded the Committee for Industrial Organization—having a total membership of one million. Now our membership is four million constituting 32 internationals. We have reduced hours of labor, increased wages for the wage earners who are members of the Committee for Industrial Organization by a sum of money approximating one billion dollars. We admit into our international and national unions colored workers upon the same basis of economic equality as white workers. All members of our several unions enjoy the same economic provisions as the others. That is one of the reasons why the CIO is extremely popular with the workers of this nation. This is true because it is the kind of union that the wage earners want.

Let us analyze in a few situations just what this great organization has done to help the poor. Some eighteen months ago, I was assigned by the CIO to assume the chairmanship of the Steel Workers Organizing Committee. For a period of approximately fifty years, the steel industry has been completely non-union. The steel industry represents the greatest and most powerful combination of wealth in American industry—five billion dollars. That five billion dollars has been utilized with all of its influence—to prevent steel workers from getting membership in independent labor unions; to prevent the enactment of social legislation of all kinds and descriptions, not only in our state legislatures, but in the seat of our federal government as well; to corrupt our courts and to corrupt men holding important public office; to depress wages and worsen the condition of employment of steel workers, not only in the steel industry, because the repercussions of what this powerful combination was doing in steel was felt in every industry, small and large, and in every enterprise where people were working. And this is the steel industry with its power, lust and greed.

Eighteen months ago, when we set out to organize the steel workers, there was nothing. Let us look at the picture today. A crusade on the part of the CIO and the Steel Workers Organizing Committee has resulted in the following: We have organized 1052 lodges in the United States and Canada. We have a signed membership of 532,000. We have 785 independent grievance committees which are peacefully adjusting all grievances affecting the men in those plants. We have reduced hours of labor from 48 to 40. We have improved conditions of labor. Last, but not least, our Research Bureau has found, resulting from our efforts, that the wages of the steel workers have increased by a sum of $236,000,-000 annually.

Surely, trade unions along industrial lines or any other lines if they fulfill their mission in life, have but one service to render—a better distribution of the world's goods, a greater opportunity to improve your status economically, socially and politically. Unions without this purpose are useless. But a union such as the Steel Workers Organizing Committee rendering such a service has made friends in the steel industry and among the workers of the nation generally.

Let us visualize another union in the CIO—the United Automobile Workers of America. For fifty years the AFL tried to organize steel and couldn't succeed. And when they did set up unions in steel, what did they do? They barred colored workers from their unions and they still exercise the same form of discrimination. Recently they decided, and I speak now of the AFL, to amend their organizing policy in craft unions so that colored workers may be brought into what is known as Class B membership—the other people can be Class A, thereby separating them and establishing unjust wage differentials for colored wage earners.

To return to the auto workers. I met with the United Auto Workers at their national office in Detroit where the President told me that they had 23,000 members. I asked him how long the AFL had been trying to organize. He told me they started to organize in 1933 when the National Recovery Act came about and Section 7A gave the workers the right to organize. They established a few federal labor unions here and then left. The workers regretted the unwillingness of the AFL to take advantage of its opportunities during the NRA to organize this industry. So when the CIO was formed, they immediately affiliated with this Committee for the protection and for the assistance which the CIO promptly gave them.

There is only one large automobile manufacturer in this country who has not executed a written agreement with the union—Henry

Ford. But the officers and members of the union will convince Mr. Ford of the need of establishing a different kind of relationship than he has now.*

Another situation—you have in Philadelphia the International Brotherhood of Electrical Workers, a powerful craft organization that undoubtedly has rendered some service to the labor movement. But never in its history has it attempted to organize the electrical manufacturing industry. Nothing was done to organize the large plants of Westinghouse, General Electric, etc., but this small group of men in Philadelphia working in Philco Radio just a year ago determined to affiliate to the CIO and set out on their own union to organize the electrical industry, and the President of the Electrical Union reported to the CIO conference this week that they now have 135,000 members dues paying with contracts for closed shops.

Who ever heard of the AFL attempting to organize the rubber industry? Never, except in Akron where a few men established a federal labor union and divided that union into six separate crafts. That small union, 2,800 in number, rebelled against the autocratic leadership of the A. F. of L.

I could follow industry after industry. There is a striking example in New York. The great transport system in the city of New York operating for years—no organization. Finally just about eighteen months ago a few men formed a small local union. They went to Mr. Green of the A. F. of L. and asked for an industrial charter to organize all the workers on that system. Mr. Green replied that they couldn't do it, and that the only basis on which those workers could be organized is on a basis of eighteen craft unions. Mr. Quill, President of the Transport Workers Union replied that they couldn't be organized that way. These men were, after this, determined to ask the CIO for a charter. That was only six months ago. Now this company is completely organized.

I could continue down the list, giving you the history of the international and national unions that have been formed by the CIO in the past eighteen months. Behind it all lies your opportunity. I speak now particularly with reference to the Negro workers. It is the only labor organization in this country that affords the

---

* The National Negro Congress cooperated with Walter P. Reuther and the UAW in their fight with Ford.

Negro worker the gain that we are entitled to in this life. I might say to you that since we have started this campaign, we have had small conventions of Negro workers and the representatives of Negro organizations in almost every large city throughout the country. Your distinguished chairman, Mr. Randolph, has participated in these conferences and attended the last conference with your Secretary, Mr. John P. Davis, held in Pittsburgh.

But what has happened in the past eighteen months? We have organized the steel towns. I have often maintained that no nation can be politically free unless it is economically free. The Steel Workers Organizing Committee and the CIO gave to the steel workers of all the steel communities throughout the state their economic freedom, and when the people of those towns realized and appreciated the fact that economic freedom had come, they then set in motion an organism, the mechanism, the instrument that might make possible their political freedom. In recent primaries in the State of Pennsylvania in every steel town or almost every steel town the lodges of steel workers that had been set up nominated their own candidates—nominated them in the primaries and have taken from the steel corporations the political control which they formerly held over the people residing in the towns. Thus, the CIO has given every wage earner also the right to exercise his franchise without danger of interference.

Now I have attempted to describe to you the nature of the work now being done by the CIO. We have come to regard this institution as the most powerful labor movement in America. We regard its leaders as the type of leadership that the wage earners want, its policies as the policies which workers also want. We contend that our efforts have had their effect in great non-union industries and enterprises, that many men and women who were not and are not affiliated with unions have enjoyed some of the benefits given to members of the CIO. And I am going to ask your Congress, representing the great Negro population of the United States to take action in the labor division of the Congress; to return to your homes and communities and render every assistance you can to this crusade.

There is no other labor organization in this country that affords the Negro worker the same opportunity as do the great international and national unions affiliated with the CIO. I can conceive your situation—90 to 95% of our entire colored population poor. Thousands of them are undernourished and underprivileged. They have the same ideals and aspirations and the same hopes beating within their breasts that beat within the breast of a white man. Their wives and children have the same feelings and emotions and they are entitled by all the laws of nature itself to the same opportunity in the game of life as any white man.

We tell you your economic and political salvation lies in assisting the CIO in the course of its activities. I speak to you today as an officer of the CIO without prejudices, without passions. I do have a deep-rooted feeling that you can do much in your communities and towns and in your organizations, societies, churches—in all your activities—to assist the CIO in the furtherance of its campaign to help you.

So, my friends, I am happy to have had this opportunity of being with you this afternoon. I want to encourage you. I want you to believe that the CIO is ready to lend every effort to help you in your efforts. And I beseech your support and the support of your officers (many of whom I know personally and whom I have collaborated with in the development of institutions such as you are interested in) in this great undertaking which the CIO has now begun.

The Southern Tenant Farmers' Union *Howard Kester**

An English traveler, Naomi Mitchison, who visited Arkansas in the early 1930's, was shocked at the conditions of life of white and Negro sharecroppers. "They are dressed in rags, they have barely enough food to keep them alive," she wrote. "Their children get no education; they are a prey to diseases which the scientific resources of modern civilization could easily eliminate." These were the economic and social realities which brought into existence the most successful interracial organization of Southern farmers since the Populist era—the Southern Tenant Farmers' Union. Headed by Socialists Harry L. Mitchell and Henry Clay East, the STFU, at the height of its power, had some thirty-one thousand members in Arkansas, Tennessee, Mississippi, Texas, Oklahoma, Missouri,

* Howard Kester, *Revolt Among the Sharecroppers* (New York, 1936), pp. 55-71.

and North Carolina. It followed Mitchell's admonition to "raise plenty of hell" and had some success in adapting trade union tactics to the cotton fields. The STFU was a working-class crusade; its meetings were held in a revival atmosphere which mixed "We Shall Not Be Moved" with the Lord's Prayer. Harsh repression, murder, a disastrous alliance with the CIO's United Cannery Workers Union, and the end of the Depression finally destroyed the STFU—although it continued in name after this time. Howard Kester, a white Southerner, a Methodist minister, a member of the Socialist party's executive council and Mitchell's assistant, describes how the STFU was organized. Kester, a forgotten figure of the civil rights movement and a man of great courage, devoted his life to the cause of interracial justice.

Just south of the little town of Tyronza, in Poinsett County, Arkansas, the Southern Tenant Farmers' Union had its beginning. In the early part of July, 1934, twenty-seven white and black men, clad in overalls, gathered in a rickety and dingy little schoolhouse called Sunnyside. The schoolhouse was old and it had witnessed many strange sights but none so strange as the one being enacted between its four leaning walls that hot summer night. Dimly lighted kerosene lamps cast strange shadows upon the faces of the men as they talked. On rough-hewn benches sat white and colored men discussing their common problems in a spirit of mutual regard and understanding.

Little time was lost in agreeing that they should form some sort of union for their mutual protection. Their main problem was to secure for themselves and their fellow-sharecroppers their share of the benefits granted under the AAA contracts. The contracts entered into between the landlords and the Secretary of Agriculture gave the tenant farmer very little and the sharecropper next to nothing but something, and they considered it worth struggling for anyway. Wholesale violations of the contracts by the planters were occurring daily. Tenants were not getting their "parity payments"; they were being made to sign papers making the landlords trustees of the bale tags; landlords were turning to day labor at starvation wages; the AAA was making things worse. They knew they could not get anything trying to dicker with the landlord individually: he would just "kick them off the place." Most of them had never been in a union and they scarcely knew how to go about organizing one. Anyway, they had to have one and they were sure that they could find someone who would know how and who would help them.

The meeting had not been in progress long when the inevitable question, which always rises when Negro and white men come together to consider joint action, arose. "Are we going to have two unions," someone asked, "one for the whites and one for the colored?" It had been many a day since the ancient walls of the schoolhouse had heard such silence. The men had thought about this before they came together, but now they had to face it and it was not an easy question to answer. A lot depended on their answer, certainly the future of their organization and maybe the future of a whole people. It was time for deep silence and exhaustive thinking. Finally the men began to speak. One man believed that since the churches divided the races that maybe the union should do likewise. He wasn't sure though, for he had noticed that the churches hadn't done very much to help the sharecroppers and that some of the church members were the cause of their suffering. Another observed that it would be dangerous for the white and colored people to mix together in their union and he was sure that the planters wouldn't stand for it. An old man with cotton-white hair overhanging an ebony face rose to his feet. He had been in unions before, he said. In his seventy years of struggle the Negro had built many unions only to have them broken up by the planters and the law. He had been a member of a black man's union at Elaine, Arkansas. He had seen the union with its membership wiped out in the bloody Elaine Massacre of 1919. "We colored people can't organize without you," he said, "and you white folks can't organize without us." Continuing he said, "Aren't we all brothers and ain't God the Father of us all? We live under the same sun, eat the same food, wear the same kind of clothing, work on the same land, raise the same crop for the same landlord who oppresses and cheats us both. For a long time now the white folks and the colored folks have been fighting each other and both of us has been getting whipped all the time. We don't have nothing against one another but we got plenty against the landlord. The same chain that holds my people holds your people too. If we're chained together on the outside we ought to stay chained together in the union. It won't do no good for us to divide because there's where the trouble has been all the time. The landlord is always betwixt us, beatin' us and starvin' us and makin' us fight each other. There ain't but one way for us to get him where he can't help himself and that's for us to get together and stay together." The old man sat down. The men decided that the union would welcome Negro and white sharecroppers, tenant farmers and day laborers alike into its fold.

When this question had been cared for the men turned toward the formation of their new organization. A white sharecropper of great ability, Alvin Nunally, was elected chairman. A Negro minister, C. H. Smith, was chosen vice-chairman. An Englishman with a ready hand for keeping minutes and writing letters was chosen secretary. A holiness preacher was elected chaplain. Some of the men had belonged to lodges and they wanted to introduce all of the secret rigamarole of the fraternal societies into the union. Some of them had formerly ridden with the Ku Klux Klan and they thought it would be a good idea for the union to operate in secret and for the sharecroppers to ride the roads at night punishing dishonest landlords and oppressive managers and riding bosses. One of the men had formerly been a member of the Farmers' Educational and Co-operative Union and advanced the idea that it would be best to have the union made a legal organization and for it to operate in the open. The men agreed that this was the best policy and they turned their minds toward getting it accomplished.

They did not know exactly how to go about having the union made legal. They could not expect any aid from any of the planter-retained lawyers and they did not have any money for fees anyway. Someone suggested that H. L. Mitchell and Clay East might help them. Mitchell was the proprietor of a small dry-cleaning establishment in Tyronza and, next door to him, Clay East ran a filling station. The two men were known throughout the countryside as "square-shooters" who always gave the underdog the benefit of the doubt, and who were, to the amusement of most people, always discussing strange ideas about labor, politics, economics and most everything else. Mitchell had once been a share-cropper himself and all of his people were farmers. He knew something about almost everything. He was known generally as a Socialist but to the landlords and planters as a "Red." Some months before Mitchell had brought Norman Thomas down to

Tyronza to speak to an overflow audience at the schoolhouse. After Thomas had visited some of the plantations, had talked with the sharecroppers in the fields and at their homes, he told the audience gathered in the schoolhouse what he had seen. The planters were there *en masse* and so were the sharecroppers. The planters writhed in their seats and the mouths of the sharecroppers stood agape as Thomas denounced the system of semi-slavery under which they all lived. The planters did not forget Mitchell for this nor did the sharecroppers.

A committee from the sharecroppers called on Mitchell and East. The two men told them that while they did not know much about running a union they would be glad to help all they could. Mitchell subsequently became the secretary of the union and East its president. Mitchell wrote letters to people all over the country asking for help and advice. J. R. Butler, an ex-school teacher, sawmill hand, hill farmer, or as he prefers to be known, "just an Arkansas Hill Billy," came down to write the first constitution and to help spread the organization among the cottonfield workers. Ward H. Rodgers, a young Methodist minister with an eye to social justice, who had been preaching in the Ozark Mountains, decided to come down and preach to the sharecroppers and planters. He gave up his churches and soon became Mitchell's right-hand man.

Each night would witness Mitchell's and East's battered old automobiles loaded down with sharecroppers going to some outlying church or schoolhouse to organize a local. Enthusiasm among the sharecroppers ran high and they talked "union" with the abandon of a backwoods' revivalist. New locals sprang up everywhere the organizers went. The people were hungry for the "New Gospel of Unionism."

When the union was first formed the idea of organizing sharecroppers rather amused the planters. They generally poked fun at the boys who were scouring over the country in all kinds of weather organizing new locals. One man was heard to say, "Oh, well, let them try to organize the sharecroppers; they won't succeed for the sharecroppers are too lazy and shiftless to ever amount to anything worth-while." But as the union continued to grow and the planters saw the Negro and white people getting together they were not quite so amused as formerly. When a carload of white and colored sharecroppers would start off together to a union meeting someone would say, "The Socialists and the Republicans (meaning the Negroes) have joined hands." It had been rumored that Mitchell and East had "political ambitions," and that they were going to run for office in the forthcoming elections. The politicians and planters could not quite understand though why men who had "political ambitions" would bother with Negroes who had been disenfranchised and could not vote, and poor white sharecroppers who had not been disenfranchised but were too poor to pay the poll tax. Gradually the planters got the right idea. These men were not even mildly interested in the kind of politics for which Joe Robinson and Hattie Caraway had made Arkansas famous; they were interested in organizing the sharecroppers to abolish the planters' organized system of semi-slavery.

On July 26, 1934, the organization was incorporated under the laws of the state of Arkansas as the Southern Tenant Farmers' Union. The papers were taken out in White County and a certificate of incorporation received. The movement rapidly became a sort of sharecroppers' crusade and every day new applications for membership in the Union were received. Men came from all over the countryside asking for organizers' papers. The union was definitely on the move.

When the first sharecroppers came together at the little schoolhouse in the early part of July, they had talked about the dangers involved in Negro and white sharecroppers organizing together. They knew trouble was coming sooner or later and they rather expected it sooner than later. Trouble was an old word with them. That was about all that they had ever known. It followed them as doggedly as their own shadow. Whatever trouble the planters might bring down upon their heads could not add much to what they had known all their lives. Trouble was as common as the air they breathed.

Scarcely a month had passed after that memorable meeting at Sunnyside when the first dark shadows of the black terror which was to later sweep over all northeastern Arkansas entered their lives. The union was holding a meeting in a Negro church near Tyronza. The chairman was explaining to the crowded audience the purpose of the union when into the church strode a plantation owner, H. F. Loan. Mr. Loan, from past experience, evidently expected to see a general exodus of the sharecroppers as he and his four riding bosses, with the inevitable guns swinging from their belts, came into the meeting. No one made a move to leave. Instead, someone asked him and his escort to have seats. The chairman continued with the meeting, explaining that the union was legal, that it operated in the open and that all they wanted was their rights which had been guaranteed to them by the Constitution of the United States and more lately by Section 7A of the Cotton Contracts.* The time came for the local to be organized and Mr. Loan and his men were told that their presence was no longer desired or acceptable. Mr. Loan flushed all the way down to his boots, for he had never had anything like this happen to him before. Sharecroppers were ordering him out of *their* meeting. What insolence! However, Mr. Loan was placed at a disadvantage. There were hundreds of sharecroppers on the inside and outside of the building. They were enthusiastic too; even Mr. Loan could see that. He decided to leave peaceably. Before going he *demanded* a copy of the constitution of the union. He was quietly told that he could have one for five cents, the cost of printing.

It came through the grapevine telegraph that before dawn Mr. Loan was on his way to the state capitol at Little Rock to try to get the state officials to revoke the charter of the union. It was reported that he offered a thousand dollars to anyone who would outlaw the union.

From Poinsett County the union gradually spread to adjoining counties where the organizers met with stiff resistance on the part of the planters and officials of the law.

True to its name, Mississippi County had been one of the most difficult counties to penetrate and organize. Here they are at least consistent, in that the planters and "the law" have never allowed a prominent outside speaker for the union to address a public gathering. No section of Arkansas is more slave-ridden or barren of anything that remotely resembles what we ordinarily think of as being culture than Mississippi County. For this reason, if for no other, the sharecroppers of Mississippi County were among the first to ask for a local of the union. Four men went to Birdsong, seat of a church, a few stores and a couple of dwellings. The

---

* This section provided for direct rental and parity payments to tenants and sharecroppers.

meeting had scarcely gotten under way when a mob of planters and deputy sheriffs led by a riding boss invaded the meeting. The organizers were bustled out of the church into their automobiles and told to "git and don't never come back here for we ain't goin' to have our niggers spoiled by no damn union." The men were escorted to the county line which is a regular part of the reception given union organizers.

Preacher Rodgers "thumbed his way" over the state spreading the gospel of social justice for the oppressed sharecroppers. Rodgers and another preacher, C. H. Smith, went to Crittenden County to organize a large local. They succeeded in holding the meeting without any trouble, but two days later Smith was caught while riding with a land salesman and dragged from the car by a group of riding bosses and deputies. He was taken to the woods and beaten and finally thrown in jail. The union officials were in a jam.

Preacher Smith was to be tried in three days. They had no one to defend him and they had no money with which to pay an attorney's fee. It meant that Preacher Smith would be sent to the county farm for six months or a year and that the work of the union would be slowed down among the sharecroppers. They racked their brains. Someone told them about a lawyer in Memphis who had a good record for justice toward the working-man. They went to see several lawyers in Memphis. One of them told Mitchell that he had lost his courage fighting in the Argonne Forest and he did not think he could recapture it in Crittenden County, Arkansas. Finally someone suggested that C. T. Carpenter, a Marked Tree attorney, who was known far and wide for his fair-mindedness, courage and ability, might help them. Carpenter, they remembered, had a distinguished record before the higher courts of the state; he had long ago defended some strikers at the Singer Sewing Machine plant at Truman; and some twenty years ago he had fought a peonage case and at the point of a gun the plantation owner had driven him off his place. Mr. Carpenter agreed to take the case and he would not charge any fee.

When the union attorney went to Marion where Smith was lodged in jail, he was accompanied by forty or fifty sharecroppers. They flocked up the courthouse steps and into the corridors of the building. They were not noisy or sullen but they had a business look in their eyes. When "the law" saw the union attorney and this demonstration of comradeship by the sharecroppers they released Preacher Smith without a trial. Preacher Smith had been freed but the beating the riding bosses and deputies gave him injured him for life.

The effect of Preacher Smith's release from jail was electric. The union had won a victory. It could get its organizers out of jail. The officers of the union scheduled a big rally at Sunnyside Church. The sharecroppers declared a holiday, left their farm work and gathered from miles around to hear the speaking and see Preacher Smith. The church was packed and the yards jammed with men, women and children. Preacher Smith was there to tell his story. In his simple way the old man said that "the union" was his "cross" and that he was "glad to bear it for the union. For," said he, "the union is the only thing that will help my people—and all of you people, whether white or black, are my people." Vows of vengeance were made when the old man bared his broken and swollen body to the throng gathered at Sunnyside.

Although the union had won a victory it was increasingly clear to the sharecroppers that the opposition of the planters had hardly begun. The word was passed among the planters that the union was to be stopped. It did not matter particularly how it was done. Churches, where the union had been meeting, were padlocked, windows boarded over and floors removed, and schoolhouses were packed with hay. Tenants who were active in the union were given eviction notices long before the usual moving time, which is about January 1st. Others were sent threatening letters and told not to attend any more union meetings. Still others were unceremoniously driven from the plantations, flogged and beaten. Through the grapevine telegraph came the disturbing information that the planters were buying machine guns. The sharecroppers knew when and how the machine guns were to be used. At this open threat of violence the sharecroppers decided to prepare themselves for a general massacre.

They took down their old shotguns from their resting places, oiled and cleaned them. When they went to the hardware and general merchant-stores to buy cartridges, they were told by the managers that they had been ordered not to sell any tenants or sharecroppers firearms or ammunition. The order had come down from the planters. It was, nevertheless, a common sight during the latter part of the summer of 1934 to see a sharecropper walking along a dusty plantation road or a national thoroughfare with a shotgun slung in a businesslike fashion under his arm. Behind him, following closely, would be his wife and all their children. When the sharecroppers arrived at the meeting place, their guns were safely stacked in a nearby corner of the building in ready access should the alarm be given that the planters were attacking. . . . Thus it was that the sharecroppers sprang to the defense of the *one thing* which offered them hope and freedom and thus it was that the union survived the first onslaught of the enraged plantation aristocracy. Had they not responded as they did, it is altogether likely that the union would have been completely crushed during those first few summer months.

The union officials were aware of the grave dangers which those shotguns represented. They knew and *felt,* perhaps better than anyone else in the world, the terrific consequences of one slight error on the part of a sharecropper. A planter could commit all the crimes in the calendar and more besides, and it would not matter. He represented culture, society, money, "the law," power. He was power. His will ruled the lives of millions of helpless human beings who for seventy years had begged for mercy from him. Now they were no longer begging for mercy. They were standing on their legs demanding justice. The union officials knew the feelings that had been pent-up inside of these men; men whose lives had been shattered, who had almost abandoned hope but who were coming back—coming back like an Arkansas tornado, full of fury. It would not take much to set off a spark that would shake the whole cotton country and drench a land in red blood. The planters, they all knew, were itching for a chance to wade into the union membership and wipe it out as they had done time and again to other unions. Give the planters a pretext and they would holler that the "supremacy of white civilization is challenged: down with the niggers." A race war would be on its way. Probably the presence of white men in nearly all Negro locals saved the Southern Tenant Farmers' Union from a bath of blood. . . . And there were women and children in nearly all the meetings. Even a riding boss hesitates to murder women and children—even if they are sharecroppers.

In order to remove every provocation the union officials asked the men to leave their guns behind. They decided to hold their meetings in the open fields under a bright southern sky. Here they were reasonably sure the planters would not attack them openly. At every meeting the officials stressed the utter necessity of proceeding legally, peaceably and democratically. The sharecroppers, almost to a man, abided by the requests of the organizers and officials.

Hundreds of sharecroppers, their wives and children came to the open meetings. Here under the open sky they heard union organizers explain the union and its aims. When such a meeting was held the planters, riding bosses, deputies, sheriff and others would gather on the fringe of the crowd. During the meeting they would amuse themselves by shooting over the heads of the crowd in an effort to intimidate the speaker and frighten his listeners. At intervals a heavy gun would roar and steel would split the air over the speaker's head. If a tree was nearby the bullets would whistle through its leaves and bits of twigs, bark and leaves would shower the crowd. When the performance had been completed a raucous laugh would emerge from "the southern gentlemen of the best families" who had gathered to terrorize the sharecroppers.

In following a strategy of non-violent resistance the union by no means accepted defeat. The officials immediately took the offensive but in a legal and democratic manner. Their first manœuver was to go into the courts on behalf of twenty-seven men who had been evicted from the five thousand acre Fairview Plantation owned by Hiram Norcross, a former Kansas City lawyer. Section 7 of the Cotton Contracts, which has already been referred to, was the basis for the suit. Mr. C. T. Carpenter was employed by the union to represent the men in the test case. At the first hearing before the Chancery Court the judge decided against the union. The case was appealed to the Supreme Court of Arkansas where the decision also went against the union.

While the sharecroppers lost in the courts, the attempt of the union to secure their rights created in the minds of the sharecroppers a wholesome attitude toward it. It was struggling and fighting for their rights. It made them feel warm and friendly toward each other and furnished them something through which they could express their collective wills.

Winter was coming. They had passed through the first few months of their struggle without any serious mishaps. The air was thick with flying steel and they saw the signs of the gathering storm. The planters had been unsuccessful in their effort to have the charter of the union revoked at Little Rock. Evictions, intimidation, beatings had not stopped the union's steady advance. The planters were to make one last effort to have the organization declared illegal through the courts.

Four union organizers, two white and two colored men, were working together in Cross County. One night they were holding a meeting in a Negro church near Parkin, seat of several recent murders of sharecroppers by plantation owners and managers, when the high sheriff of the county, accompanied by a large band of deputies, riding bosses and planters broke up the meeting and arrested the four organizers. The men were roughly handled and the union chaplain, A. B. Brookins, well past seventy, was brutally kicked in the face and stomach. Brookings, severely injured, was refused medical attention until the next day when the sheriff brought a doctor to see him. Before the union attorney, Mr. Carpenter, could reach the men, they were tried and sentenced. Bail was set at $500 when the case was appealed. The men had been arrested on the order of the prosecuting attorney, James Robertson, who claimed that planters ordered him to have the arrests made. The charges lodged against the men were two-fold: "receiving money under false pretense and disturbing labor." The union had no money with which to make bond for its men. Finally organizations in the East came to the rescue and bond was made. After remaining in jail for forty days the men were released.

The theory upon which the men had been arrested was that the union was an illegal organization; that it had never been issued a charter by the state and that therefore the organizers were receiving money under false pretenses. It was a well known fact that the union had been duly chartered under the laws of the state in White County. No one denies that the organizers were disturbing labor: it was their business to "disturb labor." It will be remembered by some, but the Rev. Mr. Sage of Marked Tree will have to get down his New Testament to read it, that it was said of Jesus that "He stirreth up the people."

The union organizers knew that this effort at strangulation

would be the last straw. People were being evicted for union membership, their meetings were being broken up, the workers were being starved and terrorized and the government contracts violated in every detail by the planters. It was time to lay their grievances before Washington. Full of hope and faith five men were sent to Washington. Pennies were scraped together at every union meeting to send the Sharecroppers' Ambassadors to Washington. Outside of a promise made by AAA officials that a thorough and honest investigation of their grievances would be made the trip was uneventful. The high spot, or perhaps it would be truer to say the "tight-spot" of the trip to Washington occurred on their return journey. On a pitch black night the men lost their way in the Virginia hinterland. Setting out a-foot to discover their whereabouts they finally stumbled upon what they thought was a CCC camp. How they got inside the high wire walls they do not remember. They do remember seeing a window dimly lighted by a kerosene lamp. Up they went to the building and knocked at a door and entered a long room filled with cots upon which shapeless objects lay piled. They saw an old man huddled beside a stove in which the fire had long since spent itself. "We're lost," explained Mitchell. "Is this a CCC camp?" The old man did not reply but looked down at his feet. Tightly locked about his ankles were huge chains welded into a nearby post. The old man slowly raised his head and quietly said, "No, son, this is a convict camp." The boys did not stop to ask the old man how to get out of the prison camp. Over a high wire fence they scrambled to land full upon a blackberry thicket below. Scared and scratched they returned to their automobile and waited patiently for dawn.

When the delegation returned from Washington, the sharecroppers throughout northeastern Arkansas were all ears. What had the boys done? Whom did they see? What was President Roosevelt going to do? Was Secretary Wallace as bad as they thought he was? A thousand questions poured in upon the Ambassadors of the Sharecroppers. There was but one thing to do and that was to call a big public mass meeting where all of the delegates could report what they had found out at Washington and the sharecroppers could ask their unending questions. Word was passed around that on the 15th of January the Washington delegation would be heard on the public platform at Marked Tree.

While the delegation was away in Washington, the planters had kept things lively back in Arkansas. Evictions were increasing; the highways were strewn with ejected families; members were being threatened and whipped; false arrests were occurring almost daily; relief was falling off and people were starving and going half-naked. The hardest part of the winter was not over and madness stalked the land.

When Preacher Rodgers gave up his two little churches at Pumpkin Center in the Ozarks and came down to help in the sharecroppers' crusade for freedom and justice, he failed to bring any of his church members' money with him. He arrived on the scene broke and he remained that way thereafter. When he first came, he lived with Secretary Mitchell in Tyronza but the planters and some of the ladies of the Missionary Society in the local Methodist Church started a boycott against Mitchell and gradually succeeded in cutting his economic roots from under him. With Mitchell's business gone, it became necessary for Preacher Rodgers to find a job. He applied to the Workers' Education Bureau in Washington for a job. His application was accepted there and later honored in Little Rock. He got a job teaching in the FERA schools. It was his duty to teach illiterates how to read and write and to also attempt to give his pupils some idea of what was going on in the sovereign states of the union. His classes consisted of white and colored citizens. Evidently Rodgers was a good teacher or his pupils unusually apt, or it was just the ante-bellum attitude of the slave-owning aristocracy reasserting itself, for shortly after he began instructing the Negro sharecroppers how to read and write and *figure* the planters ordered an investigation. Led by Mr. Lynch, Superintendent of the Schools of Tyronza District, a committee of planters called while Rodgers was holding one of his classes. They found the material which the Washington office had recommended for its teachers and some material which had been handed him by the State Director in Little Rock. The planters had never seen any of the pamphlets before and while it was all as harmless as the usual Sunday morning sermon, Rodgers was henceforth condemned as a "Red" trying to overthrow the government. Teaching illiterate sharecroppers how to read and write and figure would probably destroy the kind of government to which Arkansas is accustomed. The following day Teacher

Rodgers decided to call on Principal Lynch. They had a long conversation. Finally Principal Lynch informed Teacher Rodgers that if he did not leave town at once that a "committee of planters will see that you do." Rodgers remonstrated that this was a Ku Klux method. Smilingly Principal Lynch replied that it was.

The day following was the time for the Washington delegation to report. Before the sun had scarcely driven the morning clouds from its path, sharecroppers from all over northeastern Arkansas were on the roads leading to Marked Tree. They walked, rode mules, wagons, broken-down automobiles, anything to get to Marked Tree. Whole families joined the trek. It was to be a big day. *It was their day*. The men whom they had sent to Washington with their hard-earned pennies were going to talk to them. Men whom they all knew and trusted, men of their own kind, who had suffered as they had suffered, had been to Washington and were going to tell them what they had seen and heard. They had sent them; sharecroppers had sent Ambassadors to Washington to see the high and mighty. They came by the scores and by the hundreds crowding the little town that squatted in the middle of a cotton patch. They spilled over the railroad tracks, parked themselves on roofs of houses, perched themselves in trees, on the tops of trucks, box cars and wagons. A bright January sun spiced with a merry westerly wind added zest to the occasion.

The speakers were a little late arriving. The crowd wanted the speaking to commence: most of them had come a long way to hear what the men had to say—ten, fifteen and twenty miles—and they had to be home by dark. It was a long way, especially if you had to "foot it." Preacher Rodgers was going to preside at the union mass meeting. As the crowd grew restless waiting for the speakers to arrive, Chairman Rodgers decided to talk a little himself. The main body of what he had to say concerned the terrible condition facing the needy and the unemployed in Poinsett County. Relief was utterly inadequate, he said. People were starving to death. He knew. He had been in their homes; had eaten at their humble tables; had slept on their corn-shuck mattresses; had seen their hunger-ridden, starved, emaciated bodies; had heard their heart-rending and agonized cries for food and clothes and work; had felt their intolerable burden weighing down on his own head and heart. His sensitive nature made him intensely aware of the plight in which the sharecropper found himself. He suffered as they did but in a different way. He merged his intellect and emotion into the sharecropper's cause. He heard their cries, saw their anguish and spoke their mind. Preacher Rodger's voice boomed in the winter air like an angry surf at high tide. The sharecroppers crept closer and put their ears to the wind. There was a relief agency at Harrisburg, Preacher Rodgers roared, but a poor sharecropper could not get enough food there to keep the house cat alive, much less a family. When they went there, they were treated like lepers, as if they were not citizens and had no right to government relief. It was *their* money the Federal Government was spending for relief. Hadn't they made it and hadn't the planters robbed them of their wages? Hadn't they made Cotton King and clothed the world's nakedness? Now when they were cold and hungry and their children were slowly dying from starvation they went to the relief station and were treated like animals, and told to "come back next week" or "you got your order last month." Preacher Rodgers said what they needed in Poinsett County was a good hunger march to demand adequate relief. Preacher Rodgers denounced the lawless acts committed against the members of the union and the attempts of the planters to destroy the sharecroppers' only hope of salvation. The Southern Tenant Farmers' Union was a legal organization, he said, chartered under the laws of the State of Arkansas; they worked in the open and only asked for justice. They hadn't committed any crimes, hadn't committed a single unlawful act yet their members had been driven from the plantations and their things dumped on the highway; their organizers had been beaten and whipped, illegally arrested and thrown into jail. The planters and some respectable citizens had threatened to lynch some of the organizers including himself. "Well," Preacher Rodgers said, "that is a game two can play. If necessary I could lead the sharecroppers to lynch every planter in Poinsett County, but I have no intention of doing so." An unutterable quality of stillness fell over the great throng. Men caught their breath and women clutched their breasts and children. The awful silence lasted only a moment and then the air was rent with the voices of thousands of sharecroppers yelling their heads off for Preacher Rodgers. The men threw their hats into the air and their arms around one another. For the first time in many a day they had heard a man say exactly what they had all wanted to say and could not. Like lightning out of the blue sky, a voice had spoken their innermost convictions and thoughts.

Rodgers was not speaking before that great multitude of the disinherited that January afternoon: it was the tens of thousands of disinherited, oppressed but nevertheless defiant sharecroppers who after seventy years of tyranny, terror and suffering were hurling their deepest feelings at the world which had oppressed them—and their voice was that of a young Methodist Preacher.

After the applause subsided and the men had recovered their worn hats, Chairman Rodgers introduced the first speaker. The first speaker for the Washington delegation was the Rev. Mr. E. B. McKinney, pillar of granite in a weary land. Chairman Rodgers as always becomes a true Southern gentleman and Christian introduced the speaker, whose brown face gave assurance to the great throng as "Mr. McKinney." On the outskirts of the crowd where the prosecuting attorney, Fred Stafford, the high sheriff of the county and all the "Better Americans" were assembled, a murmur stirred the already stiffening breeze, "He called that nigger mister."

Preacher Rodgers walked to the edge of the platform. As he jumped down the deputy prosecuting attorney, Fred Stafford, formerly of Detroit and a native of Canada, placed him under arrest. He was charged with "anarchy," "attempting to overthrow and usurp the Government of Arkansas," and "blasphemy." . . .

After a lengthy interrogation by the deputy prosecuting attorney, Preacher Rodgers was placed in jail. Shortly after he had been lodged in the small brick structure which serves as the jailhouse, sharecroppers gathered about it by the hundreds. Some wanted to tear down the structure "brick by brick and get Rodgers out." Preacher Rodgers assured his would-be-deliverers that he was much safer in jail than on the outside where he would be a ready victim for mob action by the aroused town farmers. With indignation and resentment burning in their breasts the sharecroppers followed his advice and slowly departed for their homes.

The events of the day had forecast the impending storm which was to break with unprecedented fury over the Arkansas delta country. The sharecroppers had come to Marked Tree in a holiday spirit but they were returning to their cabins sullen and rebellious. One of their best friends had been illegally arrested and thrown into jail. *He had violated no laws, made no criminal remarks; he had, moreover, only said in public what the planters and their representatives frequently did under cover of darkness.* They well understood why Preacher Rodgers had been jailed; it was because he had dared rebuke the powers that be, had condemned their system of tyranny and oppression and had defended the rights of the sharecroppers to life, liberty and the pursuit of happiness. To the plantation interests these things constituted treason, anarchy, blasphemy and sacrilege. Preacher Rodgers had merely turned the tables. Those who had been dealt insults and misery had at last begun to talk about using the same time-honored methods which the planters had used to oppress and enslave them.

It was plainly evident to the hundreds of sharecroppers who gathered in Marked Tree and witnessed the day's proceedings that the planters would tolerate no one who opposed their system. For years the plantation aristocracy had said that sharecroppers were "lazy and shiftless" and that "anything is good enough for them." They were looked upon as so much trash to be trampled underfoot or ruthlessly swept off of the plantations into the highways and swamps at the will of their masters. They were not supposed to have any rights, privileges or feelings. When a friend of the dis-inherited spoke his mind about conditions and used his constitutional right of freedom of speech he was jailed.

The struggle between the sharecroppers and the planters assumed the proportions of a gigantic conflict which swept everything else aside. To the sharecroppers their struggle was a holy crusade for freedom and justice. The planters looked upon the rising of the sharecroppers as the most serious threat on the horizon to their predatory system. They looked upon the Southern Tenant Farmers' Union with loathing and fear because it threatened their very existence. To crush completely this thing which had given the sharecroppers a new estimate of life and power became the consuming passion of those who lived on the backs of the share-croppers. The struggle forced men to take sides. Few men tried to conceal their real feelings. Some were forced to do so in order to maintain their precarious economic position as merchants, traders, etc. Those who had decided opinions were outspoken in their denunciation of the opposing forces. The battle of words was at times as violent as the overt acts of the defenders of the system.

The Greater New York Coördinating Committee
Adam Clayton Powell, Jr.*

*Militancy spread to the Northern ghettos. Tactics of protest com-
mon to the labor movement and the Communist party—picket
lines, boycotts, mass marches, and varieties of direct action techniques—helped win Negroes a fairer share of economic opportunities within and outside the ghetto. Among the more militant and
successful of these urban protest movements was the Greater New
York Coordinating Committee, which operated out of Harlem.
Adam Clayton Powell, Jr., one of its organizers, describes the
Committee's work.*

From the time the Greater New York Coördinating Committee
held its first meeting at my office until the present—the Abyssinian
Baptist Church has been the great foundation upon which many
people's movements were built. Office space has always been
afforded free. Money was ready to underwrite expenses. Eleven
thousand people were available to start things moving. The Coördinating Committee was shunned in the beginning by quite a few
of the so-called big Negroes. One great intellectual giant, however,
stood by my side. Our co-chairman was the Reverend Dr. William
Lloyd Imes, minister of St. James, the nation's largest Negro
Presbyterian church, President of the Alumni Association of
Union Theological Seminary, and now President of Knoxville
College in Tennessee. . . .

Arnold Johnson, a black Cuban, was the secretary of the Coördinating Committee. A suave, handsome young radical who
dressed with impeccable taste. A ladies' man on the surface, at
heart he was a killer set against everything and everyone that was
wrong.

The treasurer, Mrs. Genevieve Chinn, light-skinned West
Virginia socialite, was the wife of one of Harlem's outstanding
professional men. A handsome young woman who presided over
her Whitestone Landing mansion with all the dignity of a person to

* From Adam Clayton Powell, Jr., *Marching Blacks: An Interpretive
History of the Rise of the Black Common Man* (New York, 1945), pp.
95–103.

the manner born. In her heart she was a passionate fighter for the uplifting of the masses.

We were a strange group in those early days. There was James W. Ford, perennial Vice Presidential candidate of the Communist Party fighting side by side with Captain A. L. King, head of the remnant of the Garvey movement. There was Arthur Reid, self-styled and crowned black Nationalist, and Ira Kemp, his partner, working together with Harrison Jackson, able chairman of the legal division and Mrs. Elizabeth Ross Haynes, intellectual middle-roader, the wife of Dr. George E. Haynes.

Most of this strange group used to meet once a week in a Greenwich Village apartment of a Wall Street broker. We called ourselves ante-bellum Negroes, meaning by that not the ante-bellum of before Civil War I but before Civil War II. We dreamed different dreams, but all had one objective—full emancipation of black folk. The Communists dreamed of the day when blacks and whites would unite and through revolt upset the present government and establish a workers' state. (This was before the Party changed its line.)* Captain King and Dr. Lionel Francis dreamed of the day when Negroes would build up their own economy, black capitalism would flourish, ships would be purchased and back to Africa, the mother land, they would sail. Dr. Imes, Arnold Johnson, Mrs. Chinn and I dreamed of the day when Negroes would walk the streets of America with dignity and equality, work at the same jobs with everyone else, and there would be no Jim Crow. All agreed that none of this could come to pass until the black man had economic security.

We set out to blitzkrieg 125th Street. We made it a disgrace for any Negro to cross a picket line. Our picketing was so effective that we could march in front of a corner drug store, such as Liggetts, whose usual traffic was two hundred an hour, and soon clear the store so that only six people would enter of an entire Saturday. We picked the largest five and ten cents stores and picketed them simultaneously. Black phalanxes marched in front with signs crying—"Don't buy where you can't work." Terror struck the exploiters. On one day we picketed ten stores successfully. Flanking us was the militant nationalistic radical Harlem Labor Union. The Street, as 125th is called, was in a turmoil. We

* During World War II.

didn't look like a group of Negroes that could be split; nor did we seem to be the kind whose indignation would pass away over night. The exploiters began to bargain. Some attempted to buy us out, but Uncle Tom was dead. . . .

The Coördinating Committee could pack the largest hall in Harlem in forty-eight hours with 7,000 people and leave 3,000 outside. It was honest because it was poor. The most we ever had in the treasury at one time was $300 for a single week. We never conducted a real membership campaign. We always acted on the assumption that all Harlem belonged. As victories came the band-wagon crowd began to jump on. Cautious but well meaning folks had waited to see how we would make out. They joined and we welcomed them. The committee grew until it represented the mass power of 207 Harlem organizations. . . . One Hundred and Twenty-fifth Street was wide open now, merchants were appealing for so many workers that the Harlem YMCA, the Urban League and the African Patriotic League set up classes training men and women as sales clerks. It was time for the Coördinating Committee to move on. . . .

At this time Governor Herbert Lehman's Committee on the Condition of the Colored Urban Population made its first report to the Legislature of New York. Separate hearings had been held at the local court on Washington Heights. Executive after executive of the big utility companies used every form of subterfuge to wriggle out of the fact that they did not employ Negroes. While the Governor's Committee was reporting, the Coördinating Committee moved. We bombarded the Consolidated Edison Company through its Executive Vice-President, Colonel Stillwell; consulted with the New York Telephone Company; began to work on the beverage industry, including Hoffman's and Canada Dry; went after the bread companies for salesmen, and picketed Liggetts and other drug stores that would not employ Negro pharmacists. We were ready!

The toughest nuts to crack have been the utility companies. Consolidated Edison was not so difficult for it always employed Negroes in various capacities, but the telephone company was fundamentally dishonest. The Vice-President of that company, though he has constantly denied it, told a group of us that he would not employ Negroes and was not particular about the employment of Jews or Catholics. Later on when we held a conference with Stanley Isaacs, then Borough President of Manhattan, acting as mediator, the Vice-President carted in with him a Jewish member of the staff who was probably their lone exhibit A in the field of interracial relationships. Edison finally employed Negroes in white-collar jobs, and the New York Telephone Company took on some Negroes in other than unskilled capacities. Both types of employment were merely tokens. In their great postwar employment drive, Negroes are going to aim at the telephone companies first, not only in New York but throughout the nation.

Beverage industries hired salesmen in such numbers that some of the best wage-earners in town formed the Cork and Bottle Club, composed of representatives of companies doing business in Harlem. When we began the campaign against the drug stores there were scores of Negro pharmacists in New York who were unemployed or working at other occupations. When we finished the job there was not one.

How was all this done? *Through the power of non-violent direct social action.* No blows, no violence, but the steady unrelenting pressure of an increasing horde of people who knew they were right. More and more whites began to join our picket lines. Not only Communists but church members and members of social action groups. . . .

In 1939 Grover Whalen propagandized the world for the New York World's Fair Corporation with the slogan, "Building the World of Tomorrow." The kind of world the Fair Corporation wanted would help bring about World War II. It was a world in which there would be no Negroes. It was early decided not to employ Negroes except in the most menial and unskilled positions. For the first time we moved our Harlem picket line downtown. We struck 34th Street like a blitzkrieg. Not only was there picketing all day, but each Thursday a death watch marched through the night. It was here that the intellectuals, mulattoes and the few remaining upper-class Negroes began to coöperate. Chorus girls coming from Ethel Waters' latest show would hit the Thursday night picket line at midnight. General Sessions' Judge Myles Paige would walk with them. The new Negro sure was something! When we finished the picket campaign scores of Negroes were employed in jobs other than as porters and maids. . . .

Other colored organizations were combined in a unified program which formed the Harlem Chapter for 1940.

In that same year, the New York Telephone Company hired its first Negro. And in 1941 came the crowning victories for the marching hosts of tan Manhattan. Operating on the streets of New York was the Omnibus Corporation. This company, which included nearly all of the North-South bus lines, did not employ any Negroes except for a handful of cleaners in the garages. Its jobs were monopolized by the Irish. On March 10, five hours after the Transport Workers Union concluded its 12-day-old strike, we struck. We had supported the white men in their union strike. We now carried signs at the crossroads of Harlem "WE STAYED OFF THESE BUSES FOR 12 DAYS THAT WHITE MEN MIGHT HAVE A DECENT STANDARD OF LIVING—STAY OFF THEM NOW FOR BLACK MEN." The Harlem Labor Union started the ball rolling. Our committee got together with them and we formed the United Bus Committee with representatives from the National Negro Congress. There were only seventy of us in the beginning. The company officials refused to see us. . . . Finally we had thousands on the streets every day picketing. We laid plans to move our campaign to 42nd Street and the downtown stops. The company sent for us. . . . A tri-party agreement was signed between John D. Ritchie representing the bus company, Michael Quill, representing the Transport Workers Union and I, representing the consumers. The agreement provided that Negroes should be integrated into every phase of the company. They are employed as bus drivers and high-grade mechanics. There has been absolutely no racial trouble between the Irish and the Negroes. They work together as one. The new white man and the new Negro were ready to coöperate. Letters that came from the riding public indicated that the efficiency of the Negro driver was just as good as that of the white. Their courtesy in some cases was considered even better.

The dynamic irresistible force of the new Negro and the new white man began to blast to hell the immovable object of American prejudice. . . . Marching blacks had arrived. They had arrived without striking a blow. They had marched with only picket signs in their hands. They told the Consolidated Edison to give in or a lightless Tuesday would be declared weekly. They told the New York Telephone Company to hire Negroes or 310,000 Harlemites would call for the operator's voice on the dial rather than use the robot mechanism. They coöperated with organized labor in the bus strike and won. . . .

The March on Washington Movement

The March on Washington Movement was the most effective mass Negro protest movement of the Roosevelt era; its founder, A. Philip Randolph, a militant civil rights organization unto himself. Randolph was motivated to threaten the march after a year of national conferences, administrative memoranda, and letters to government contractors had failed to win Negroes a fair share of new jobs in war industry. In the spring of 1941, for example, the president of North American Aviation Company said that "regardless of their training as aircraft workers, we will not employ Negroes in the North American plant. It is against company policy."* Randolph believed that F.D.R. would intercede only if Negroes forced him to and, despite efforts to halt the March, he was prepared to carry it through until the President issued an executive order creating the Committee on Fair Employment Practices. The March on Washington Movement, an all-Negro organization, continued to use its nonviolent direct action methods through the early forties. Randolph considered it "the first demonstration on a national scale of the faith of the Negro people in themselves, in their own capacity to win their rights against opposition." Some hailed F.D.R.'s executive order as a second Emancipation Proclamation, although the FEPC had a tortured history, little power, and was strangled to death financially by Southern congressmen in 1946.

"Let the Negro Masses Speak!" A. Philip Randolph†

Negroes have a stake in National Defense. It is a big stake. It is a vital and important stake.

* Quoted in Louis Ruchames, *Race, Jobs, and Politics: The Story of FEPC* (New York, 1953), p. 12.
† From *The Black Worker*, March, 1941.

But are we getting our stake?

No. Nobody cares anything about us. We are being pushed around.

The stake involves jobs. It involves equal employment opportunities. It involves equal opportunity for integration in the armed forces of the nation.

And what do we get?

Polite promises; sometimes, insults.

How can this stake be protected?

Our answer is:

Let the Negro masses speak!

Yes, thirteen or fifteen million Negroes have a stake of far-reaching economic consequences in the Government's expenditure of twenty, or more, billions for National Defense.

Negroes have a stake in the vast, nation-wide, Government program of vocational training of workers to perform skilled work on contracts to produce munitions and build all types of ships for war.

How can Negroes win their right to equal opportunities to share in this plan of training and retraining for technical services?

Our answer is:

Let the Negro masses speak!

Negroes must not fail to grasp and understand the fact that National Defense is not an ordinary, passing event. They must realize that this world-war crisis is not a temporary, simple, occasional incident.

This world-war crisis and America's scheme of National Defense are destined profoundly to affect the whole economy of our country. Sharp and permanent rearrangements and readjustments in the entire industrial and work setups of business, industry and labor are in the process of development.

If the Negro is shut out of these extensive and intensive changes in industry, labor and business, the race will be set back over fifty years.

Indeed, it is seriously doubtful that if the Negro waits until these economic, trade union and business transformations and innovations, now under way, under the sanction and guidance of the Government, are crystallized and set he may never retrieve lost ground or salvage rights sacrificed.

How can the Negro halt this crystallization of economic and political injustice?

Our answer is:

Let the Negro masses speak!

When they speak, they will speak with the tongues of angels. When they thunder their resentment and revolt against the blighting bottlenecks of race prejudice and hatreds, *their voice will be the Voice of God.*

How shall they speak?

Let us not be beaten, bewildered and bitter. Away with cynicism and defeatism.

Let the Negro masses speak with ten thousand Negroes strong, marching down Pennsylvania Avenue in the Capital of the Nation, singing "John Brown's Body Lies a 'Mouldering in the Grave' " and "Before I'll Be a Slave, I'll Be Buried in My Grave and Go Home to My Father and Be Saved."

In serried ranks, let the Negro masses, as workers, doctors, preachers, lawyers, businessmen, nurses, teachers, women and children, march forward with heads erect, holding banners aloft, inscribed with slogans, preaching the gospel of justice, freedom and democracy, declaring their decisive demands for jobs in National Defense, equal employment and vocational training opportunities, together with equal privileges for integration in all departments of the armed forces.

Let us tear the mask of hypocrisy from America's Democracy!

An able exposé of discrimination against Negroes on National Defense jobs was made by Walter White, Secretary of the National Association for the Advancement of Colored People in the *Saturday Evening Post,* of recent date, and now Negroes must mobilize their might to stop it.

Negroes cannot stop discrimination in National Defense with conferences of leaders and the intelligentsia alone. While conferences have merit, they won't get desired results by themselves.

During the First World War, immigration from Europe was cut off and labor was at a premium. Hundreds of thousands of Negroes were brought up from the South to labor in the factories, mines and mills. They were needed badly. Jobs were seeking them.

Today, it is different. During this World War, there are millions of workers in America unemployed. White workers are in sharp competition now with Negro workers for jobs. Instead of jobs seeking workers, workers are seeking jobs.

Therefore, whatever Negroes get in jobs and vocational training opportunities, they must fight for. Nothing will be given them.

Hence, let the Negro masses speak!

Let the Negro masses march!

Let the Negro masses fight!

When women marched in demonstration in England and America, they won the ballot.

When the American Legions marched on Washington, they secured the bonus.

Let no black man be afraid! We are simply fighting for our constitutional rights as American citizens.

We are not saboteurs.

We are no Quislings.

We hold no allegiance to an alien state. This is our own, our native land. Let us fight to make it truly free, democratic and just.

We are not Trojan Horses.

We are not Fifth Columnists.

We are not traitors.

We are Americans.

We are patriots.

We are fighting for the right to work!

We are fighting for the right to live!

We believe in National Unity.

We believe in National Defense.

We will fight for Uncle Sam!

We are opposed to totalitarian tyranny, Fascist, Nazi and Communist.

We will fight for democracy!

Yes, we will fight!

Indeed, we would rather die on our feet fighting for Negroes' rights than to live on our knees as half-men; as semi-citizens, begging for a pittance.

Therefore, let the Negro masses speak!

Let the Negro masses march!

On to Washington, ten thousand black Americans!

Let them swarm from every hamlet, village and town; from the highways and byways, out of the churches, lodges, homes, schools, mills, mines, factories and fields. Let them come in automobiles, buses, trains, trucks and on feet. Let them come though the winds blow and the rains beat against them, when the date is set.

We call not upon our white friends to march with us. There are some things Negroes must do alone. This is our fight and we must see it through.

If it costs money to finance a march on Washington, let Negroes pay for it. If any sacrifices are to be made for Negro rights in National Defense, let Negroes make them.

If Negroes fail this chance for work, for freedom and training, it may never come again.

Let the Negro masses speak!

Only the masses possess power. Only the voice of the masses will be heard and heeded—Negro America has never yet spoken as a mass, an organized mass.

Top powers of industry, organized white labor and government, have not yet felt the pressure of the Negro masses. They have seen Negro leaders, leaders who are intelligent and well-meaning, pleading for Negro rights.

They have never seen the Negro masses in action.

Thus, let the Negro masses speak!

The Call to the March on Washington *A. Philip Randolph*

JULY 1, 1941

We call upon you to fight for jobs in National Defense.

We call upon you to struggle for the integration of Negroes in the armed forces, such as the Air Corps, Navy, Army and Marine Corps of the Nation.

We call upon you to demonstrate for the abolition of Jim-Crowism in all Government departments and defense employment.

This is an hour of crisis. It is a crisis of democracy. It is a crisis of minority groups. It is a crisis of Negro Americans.

What is this crisis?

To American Negroes, it is the denial of jobs in Government defense projects. It is racial discrimination in Government depart-

* From *The Black Worker,* July, 1941.

ments. It is widespread Jim-Crowism in the armed forces of the Nation.

While billions of the taxpayers' money are being spent for war weapons, Negro workers are being turned away from the gates of factories, mines and mills—being flatly told, "NOTHING DOING." Some employers refuse to give Negroes jobs when they are without "union cards," and some unions refuse Negro workers union cards when they are "without jobs."

What shall we do?

What a dilemma!

What a runaround!

What a disgrace!

What a blow below the belt!

'Though dark, doubtful and discouraging, all is not lost, all is not hopeless. 'Though battered and bruised, we are not beaten, broken or bewildered.

Verily, the Negroes' deepest disappointments and direst defeats, their tragic trials and outrageous oppressions in these dreadful days of destruction and disaster to democracy and freedom, and the rights of minority peoples, and the dignity and independence of the human spirit, is the Negroes' greatest opportunity to rise to the highest heights of struggle for freedom and justice in Government, in industry, in labor unions, education, social service, religion and culture.

With faith and confidence of the Negro people in their own power for self-liberation, Negroes can break down the barriers of discrimination against employment in National Defense. Negroes can kill the deadly serpent of race hatred in the Army, Navy, Air and Marine Corps, and smash through and blast the Government, business and labor-union red tape to win the right to equal opportunity in vocational training and re-training in defense employment.

Most important and vital to all, Negroes, by the mobilization and coordination of their mass power, can cause PRESIDENT ROOSEVELT TO ISSUE AN EXECUTIVE ORDER ABOLISHING DISCRIMINATIONS IN ALL GOVERNMENT DEPARTMENTS, ARMY, NAVY, AIR CORPS AND NATIONAL DEFENSE JOBS.

Of course, the task is not easy. In very truth, it is big, tremendous and difficult.

It will cost money.

It will require sacrifice.

It will tax the Negroes' courage, determination and will to struggle. But we can, must and will triumph.

The Negroes' stake in national defense is big. It consists of jobs, thousands of jobs. It may represent millions, yes, hundreds of millions of dollars in wages. It consists of new industrial opportunities and hope. This is worth fighting for.

But to win our stakes, it will require an "all-out," bold and total effort and demonstration of colossal proportions.

Negroes can build a mammoth machine of mass action with a terrific and tremendous driving and striking power that can shatter and crush the evil fortress of race prejudice and hate, if they will only resolve to do so and never stop, until victory comes.

Dear fellow Negro Americans, be not dismayed in these terrible times. You possess power, great power. Our problem is to harness and hitch it up for action on the broadest, daring and most gigantic scale.

In this period of power politics, nothing counts but pressure, more pressure, and still more pressure, through the tactic and strategy of broad, organized, aggressive mass action behind the vital and important issues of the Negro. To this end, we propose that ten thousand Negroes MARCH ON WASHINGTON FOR JOBS IN NATIONAL DEFENSE AND EQUAL INTEGRATION IN THE FIGHTING FORCES OF THE UNITED STATES.

An "all-out" thundering march on Washington, ending in a monster and huge demonstration at Lincoln's Monument will shake up white America.

It will shake up official Washington.

It will give encouragement to our white friends to fight all the harder by our side, with us, for our righteous cause.

It will gain respect for the Negro people.

It will create a new sense of self-respect among Negroes.

But what of national unity?

We believe in national unity which recognizes equal opportunity of black and white citizens to jobs in national defense and the armed forces, and in all other institutions and endeavors in America. We condemn all dictatorships, Fascist, Nazi and Communist. We are loyal, patriotic Americans, all.

But, if American democracy will not defend its defenders; if

American democracy will not protect its protectors; if American democracy will not give jobs to its toilers because of race or color; if American democracy will not insure equality of opportunity, freedom and justice to its citizens, black and white, it is a hollow mockery and belies the principles for which it is supposed to stand.

To the hard, difficult and trying problem of securing equal participation in national defense, we summon all Negro Americans to march on Washington. We summon Negro Americans to form committees in various cities to recruit and register marchers and raise funds through the sale of buttons and other legitimate means for the expenses of marchers to Washington by buses, train, private automobiles, trucks, and on foot.

We summon Negro Americans to stage marches on their City Halls and Councils in their respective cities and urge them to memorialize the President to issue an executive order to abolish discrimination in the Government and national defense.

However, we sternly counsel against violence and ill-considered and intemperate action and the abuse of power. Mass power, like physical power, when misdirected is more harmful than helpful.

We summon you to mass action that is orderly and lawful, but aggressive and militant, for justice, equality and freedom.

Crispus Attucks marched and died as a martyr for American independence. Nat Turner, Denmark Vesey, Gabriel Prosser, Harriet Tubman and Frederick Douglass fought, bled and died for the emancipation of Negro slaves and the preservation of American democracy.

Abraham Lincoln, in times of the grave emergency of the Civil War, issued the Proclamation of Emancipation for the freedom of Negro slaves and the preservation of American democracy.

Today, we call upon President Roosevelt, a great humanitarian and idealist, to follow in the footsteps of his noble and illustrious predecessor and take the second decisive step in this world and national emergency and free American Negro citizens of the stigma, humiliation and insult of discrimination and Jim-Crowism in Government departments and national defense.

The Federal Government cannot with clear conscience call upon private industry and labor unions to abolish discrimination based upon race and color as long as it practices discrimination itself against Negro Americans.

Executive Order 8802 *Franklin D. Roosevelt**

REAFFIRMING POLICY OF FULL PARTICIPATION IN THE DEFENSE
  PROGRAM BY ALL PERSONS, REGARDLESS OF RACE, CREED,
  COLOR, OR NATIONAL ORIGIN, AND DIRECTING CERTAIN ACTION
  IN FURTHERANCE OF SAID POLICY

WHEREAS it is the policy of the United States to encourage full
participation in the national defense program by all citizens of the
United States, regardless of race, creed, color, or national origin,
in the firm belief that the democratic way of life within the Nation
can be defended successfully only with the help and support of all
groups within its borders; and

WHEREAS there is evidence that available and needed workers
have been barred from employment in industries engaged in defense production solely because of considerations of race, creed,
color, or national origin, to the detriment of workers' morale and
of national unity:

NOW, THEREFORE, by virtue of the authority vested in me by the
Constitution and the statutes, and as a prerequisite to the successful conduct of our national defense production effort, I do hereby
reaffirm the policy of the United States that there shall be no
discrimination in the employment of workers in defense industries
or government because of race, creed, color, or national origin,
and I do hereby declare that it is the duty of employers and of
labor organizations, in furtherance of said policy and of this order,
to provide for the full and equitable participation of all workers in
defense industries, without discrimination because of race, creed,
color, or national origin;

And it is hereby ordered as follows:

1. All departments and agencies of the Government of the
United States concerned with vocational and training programs for
defense production shall take special measures appropriate to
assure that such programs are administered without discrimination
because of race, creed, color, or national origin;

2. All contracting agencies of the Government of the United
States shall include in all defense contracts hereafter negotiated by
them a provision obligating the contractor not to discriminate

* From the *Federal Register*, VI (July 27, 1941).

against any worker because of race, creed, color, or national origin;

3. There is established in the Office of Production Management a Committee on Fair Employment Practice, which shall consist of a chairman and four other members* to be appointed by the President. The Chairman and members of the Committee shall serve as such without compensation but shall be entitled to actual and necessary transportation, subsistence and other expenses incidental to performance of their duties. The Committee shall receive and investigate complaints of discrimination in violation of the provisions of this order and shall take appropriate steps to redress grievances which it finds to be valid. The Committee shall also recommend to the several departments and agencies of the Government of the United States and to the President all measures which may be deemed by it necessary or proper to effectuate the provisions of this order.

FRANKLIN D. ROOSEVELT

THE WHITE HOUSE,
June 25, 1941.

4. F.D.R. AND CIVIL RIGHTS

Anti-Roosevelt Propaganda

Most Presidents are subjected to verbal abuse but few experienced the volume of epithets hurled at F.D.R. and his wife. One leaflet distributed during a strike of Philadelphia transit workers in 1944 included the following supposed message of "Franklin to Eleanor": "You kiss the niggers and I'll kiss the Jews, And we'll stay in the White House as long as we choose." The most inventive tales reflected white Southern hostility for Eleanor Roosevelt. An entire mythology was created in the early years of World War II that blamed all the South's racial tensions on Mrs. Roosevelt. "Eleanor Clubs," rumors maintained, had scattered throughout the South and Negro domestic workers flocked to them. Their purpose?—the preaching of racial equality. The distinguished sociologist Howard W. Odum collected accounts of these imaginary Eleanor Clubs in

* The Committee was increased in size to six members on July 18, 1941.

1942–1943 and published them under the title "The Romance of the Eleanor Clubs" in Race and Rumors of Race: Challenge to American Crisis.*

Perhaps the most remarkable of all the rumors were those relating to the Eleanor Clubs and to the activities and attitude of the First Lady of the Land. These rumors abounded in all their richness and variety wherever southerners abode. Not only in the South but in New York, in Los Angeles, in Chicago, vivacious southerners told the stories as they were told to them. The Eleanor Clubs struck deep at the heart of the South's whole domestic home economy. Basic causes were found in the opportunity for Negro women to work at higher wages, their organization into clubs and branches of organized labor, and the subsequent folk psychology of the South. That the Eleanor Club rumor seemed to reflect the "weakest" and most unfair perhaps of all the folkways of "servants," makes it all the more important as a chronicle of the era. The fact that the folkways of survival here were so strong as to lead the South to forget its manners was again evidence of crisis.

The slogan of the Eleanor Clubs was nearly always a variation of "A white woman in every kitchen by 1943." There were many variations of the same theme, and samplings were offered in abundance because of the richness of their details. Thus, from Mississippi it was reported that an Eleanor Club was found by the sheriff. "My cousin told me that the sheriff went down there and told those 'niggers' that they'd better get back to work, or else." In Georgia, they had heard a special version of the Eleanor Clubs as the "Royal House of Eleanor."

From Georgia it was reported that when an army camp was started "in my town and cooks were asked to cook for the soldiers, receiving as much as $15.00 a week, many housewives decided that this was a project of the Eleanor Clubs to get Negroes out of domestic service, and to give them higher pay." "Here was the way it was: 'Why, all the Negroes are getting so "uppity" they won't do a thing. I hear the cooks have organized Eleanor Clubs and their motto is: A white woman in every kitchen by Christmas.' " This was from North Carolina, where it was also heard that "all the

* Chapel Hill, N.C., 1943, pp. 73–80.

colored maids at a hotel joined Eleanor Clubs and walked out in a body one day because their pay and hours did not suit."

Two major points of emphasis in the Eleanor Club stories were loyalty to the First Lady and her loyalty to the Negroes to the end that they would have better opportunities. Thus, a Negro girl left during the middle of a meal which she was helping to serve because one of the guests had said something she didn't like and "she had been instructed by the Eleanor Club to leave whenever she was insulted." So, too, a very common rumor was that a maid must resign whenever anyone spoke disparagingly of either the First Lady or the President. From Florida came the version that when a Negro applied for a job she first asked if the head of the house liked Eleanor Roosevelt. If not, she replied that she belonged to the Eleanor Club and couldn't work for her.

Another level of the Eleanor Club activities had to do with their influence. One story from North Carolina had it that by the time of the next presidential election the Eleanor Clubs would have enough strength and power to control the election. But always the heart of the situation was in the scarcity of help. Thus, it was said that in a community of two hundred families, who originally had cooks, but two of these families had a cook at that time. "This Eleanor Club is spreading like wildfire all over the South and their motto is 'a white woman in every kitchen,'" And again, "Eleanor Clubs are stirring up troubles that never should have arisen. Clubs are making the Negroes discontented, making them question their status." This was from Georgia, but again the crux of the trouble was reflected in the North Carolina verdict that before the appearance of the Eleanor Club story, back in the early spring, probably in March, 1942, the community buzzed with the story that outside organizers were organizing the colored maids; that they were going to ask for a twelve-dollar-a-week minimum in the wealthier residential section, and eight dollars a week in the middle-class residence area.

Still another type of story reflected the trend toward specialized labor. One woman's maid stopped bringing in any wood for the fire because the other maids in the neighborhood had "jumped on" her and told her that she could not belong to the Eleanor Club and bring in wood. That was not her job, and her employer would have to hire someone else to do the bringing in of the wood or she would have to do it herself. Likewise, the maids refused to wash any windows—that was a man's work—and the maids were to do only the lightest work. Again, a friend reported that "a friend had a maid who had been with them for fifteen years. She joined the Eleanor Club and told her mistress that she would have to leave as she could not work for less than a certain sum, which sum was much more than my friend was paying or could afford to pay."

That was a Florida story, and from Florida came also one telling of a woman who went to the "quarters to see why her maid had not showed up to work. She blew her horn in front of the cottage—no response. She could see there was someone in the place so went to the door. The colored woman was lying down, but said, no, she wasn't sick. When asked why she hadn't come to work, she said, 'because there had been a meeting of the Eleanor Club where they had been told to demand more wages.' The woman told her she would gladly have paid her more if wages had gone up but wanted to know why she hadn't come to tell her. That also had been forbidden. Also, the Club ruler had told them not to answer any more horn calls from a car."

The First Lady was held responsible for these developments and more, although she had appeared in very few towns. Yet a common saying was that in nearly every town in which she had occasion to speak, an Eleanor Club was formed by the Negroes soon thereafter. "They said maids walked out any time of the day with the excuse of going to an Eleanor's meeting."

A variation from South Carolina had it that "a Negro girl came in the front door of a white woman's house. The white woman asked why she came in the front door instead of the back door. The Negro's reply was that she had joined the Eleanor Club and she was supposed to come in the front door instead of the back." In Georgia, it was related that "Eleanor Clubs had drawn up a Black List of white employers and that several Negro servants had stopped working for people on this list. So, also, it was reported that Eleanor Clubs made a practice of investigating their employers and if they found a lack of sympathy for or had a dislike of Mrs. Roosevelt they quit their job and placed the employers' names on a Black List."

A Florida inquiry reported that "since the war started the Negro men had higher incomes and they could afford to have a higher standard of living. Therefore, their wives and children no longer had to cook for the whites. The Negroes had formed unions demanding higher wages and working conditions, so that it was almost impossible to find any help at all. It was thought that the First Lady had a hand in trying to organize the Negroes. It was also rumored in one community that the Eleanor Clubs intended to take an educational grievance to court and that they had money enough to 'fight it out.' It was reported that the money was given to the Eleanor Club by Mrs. Roosevelt who received it from one of her public lectures. They had, it was rumored, more money than one of the larger white high schools had for its entire budget that year."

Sometimes there was more comedy than pathos in the fantastic aspects of the Eleanor Club. A prominent business man who had visited most of the States actually professed to believe there was some relation between the Eleanor Clubs and the zoot-suit young Negroes and their doings.

And in Alabama, they said that "whenever you saw a Negro wearing a wide-brimmed hat with a feather in it, you knew he was wearing the sign of the Eleanor Club." In North Carolina there was a story going around that the number and size of feathers in the new zoot-suit hats being worn by Negroes determined their position in the Eleanor Club. The larger the feather, the greater the number, and the brighter the color were symbols of rating. It was a long way from this to the other Alabama report that the Negroes called Mrs. Roosevelt the "Great White Angel" or the "Great White Mother," and made her sponsor for their Eleanor Clubs.

The intensity of the atmosphere in which the Eleanor Club rumors had grown up was indicated by the response of a very wealthy southerner who said that he would be willing to contribute substantially to a civic fund if it would stop the Roosevelts. His chief complaint was that his large organization could no longer work Negro women on the farm! From Florida came the story that "a gentleman of considerable wealth and position made this remark during a conversation, 'Thanks to Mrs. Roosevelt and the Eleanor Clubs, we're liable to have a race riot here in the South. Mrs. Roosevelt is poking her nose into a situation about which she knows nothing.' " A Louisiana householder reported that her cook at home had been attending meetings of the local Eleanor Club.

"She said they promised the Negro to raise his standards of living as high as that of the whites as soon as the war was over. She spoke of the First Lady as Eleanor this, Eleanor that, and Eleanor the other. There were other rumors to the effect that Negroes in several places had said that they believed after the war there would not only be social equality but that the Negro would be the superior race. They believed that Eleanor Roosevelt would put them on this level."

From the mass of rumors, apparently abundant in all the southern States, it was possible to learn not only the general theme but also the "rules" of the Eleanor Clubs. When it was recalled that the rumor was prevalent in most northern cities, especially in Detroit, it was not surprising that there were variations. Nevertheless, there was generally a common thread running through most of the stories, with the exception of the reference to the zoot suit. "White women were to be in the kitchen by Christmas, 1942, or January, 1943. Negro women were to be out of the kitchen. There must be more pay, more privileges, less hours. There must be no disparaging remarks about either Mrs. Roosevelt or the President. And Negroes must have equal opportunities with whites."

It was clear, of course, that the original Eleanor Clubs were not Eleanor Clubs at all, but new ventures in organization and talk. From these efforts and the accelerated demand for workers and especially Negro women workers, it was an easy step to follow some incidental local club tribute to Mrs. Roosevelt and spread the rumor far and wide. Unfortunately, it was not possible to determine the origin of the clubs with certainty. They appeared inspired by those seeking either to cause trouble or to disparage the President and his wife. The earlier stages did not have the earmarks of the Negro folk story, although many of the later versions were genuine reflections of the folk tale. As a matter of fact, the ideals and aims of the clubs were irreproachable from the folk viewpoint, whether from the vantage point of the Negroes as genuine folk wishes and demands, or for perfect propaganda material, either for the Axis or against the Negro and the First Lady.

A few samplings indicated the range of rules and requirements as rumored. In addition to "Eleanor Clubs," the common designation, they were also called "Daughters of Eleanor," "The Eleanor

Angel Clubs," "The Sisters of Eleanor," "The Royal House of Eleanor."

The clubs were, of course, named after the First Lady of the Land. The early slogan was the previously mentioned "A white woman in every kitchen by Christmas." The club's membership was made up of colored domestic workers. The members agreed not to work for less than a fixed amount a week, varying from rumor to rumor. The members agreed that if they heard any criticism whatsoever of Mrs. Roosevelt or the President they would immediately quit their jobs.

Another summary, featuring Virginia and North Carolina rumors, reported that the members of the Eleanor Clubs refused to work on Sunday. They would not serve extra people without a day's notice. They must be called "Miss" and "Mrs." and not just their first names. Servants must go to work by the front door of their employers' homes. Servants must strike for a dollar or more a day wages. Servants must take a bath in their employer's family bathtub before going home from work.

A South Carolina story reported that in an Army camp in the South a Negro maid was employed by an officer and his wife. "One day the wife entered the dining room and saw three places set at the table. She asked the maid if her husband had called and said he'd bring a friend home for lunch. The maid said, 'no.' The wife then asked what the extra place was for. The maid replied, 'In the Eleanor Club we always sit with the people we work for.' "

A North Carolina version had it that the clubs worked through the church. "When a maid quit work she handed the name of her employer to the church group to which she belonged. The name was read from the pulpit and no person's name which was read could expect to get a maid again. Other than remarks about Mrs. Roosevelt, the maids held grievances for low wages and unfair treatment."

Another summary emphasized the fact that Negro women could work at only one job. "That is, if they were to cook, that was all they were to do. They couldn't help with the house cleaning at all. There must be a butler to put the garbage out and mop the kitchen. A woman could do only one thing, such as wash, scrub, or clean house; the Eleanor Club would not allow her to do general work. The Eleanor Club consisted of Negroes who were going to better themselves and try to be equal to the white race. They believed that the First Lady was their white god and was setting them free. There was coming into existence a 'black list' made up of white employers for whom the Negroes refused to work. It was connected with the Negro women's membership in the Eleanor Clubs and seemed to be gaining ground."

And so the Eleanor Club rumors multiplied. . . .

F.D.R.'s Apologia *Walter White**

Occasional remarks on civil rights may be gleaned from F.D.R.'s speeches. In an address to the Federal Council of Churches of Christ in America (1933), the President denounced lynch law as "collective murder." In a pedestrian talk at the dedication of a new chemistry building at Howard University (1936) he said the federal government knew no "forgotten men and no forgotten races." Roosevelt alluded to the harmful effects of prejudice on Negro youngsters in his keynote address to the Fourth White House Conference on Children in a Democracy (1939). Basically, however, the President remained silent. Walter White, Executive Secretary of the NAACP, offers F.D.R.'s apologia for failing to publicly support a federal anti-lynching bill.

When we renewed and stepped up our fight for the Costigan-Wagner Anti-Lynching Bill,† we found the opposition no less determined, but at the same time we found support for the legislation from some who would have been most unlikely to give support even a few years before. The state legislatures of California, Colorado, Kansas, Minnesota, New Jersey, and Pennsylvania; the state assemblies of Indiana, New York, and Illinois; the Massachusetts state senate, and the city councils of several cities, passed resolutions endorsing the bill. Church, labor, women's, civil rights, fraternal, professional, and other groups, with a total membership of 53,720,593, were lined up in behalf of the legislation. But the archaic Senate rules which permit any senator to

---

* From Walter White, *A Man Called White* (New York, 1948), pp. 167–170.

† This bill, like all those introduced since the end of World War I, was filibustered to death by Southerners with the assistance of Senator William E. Borah.

filibuster by speaking twice on any bill and on each amendment thereto for as long as he wishes again stymied our efforts. We were unable to get the Senate to consider the bill in 1934, despite a favorable report on it by the Senate Judiciary Committee and a tremendous volume of public opinion in its support.

But in 1935 the filibusterers could not prevent its consideration. It was taken up by the Senate on April 16th, and immediately the late Senator "Cotton Ed" Smith of South Carolina launched a venomous attack on the bill and a defense of lynching as necessary "to protect the fair womanhood of the South from beasts." Time and again the bill's opponents attempted to dislodge it from the Senate calendar by motions to adjourn, but we were able to muster votes to defeat the motion each legislative day until May 1st. In the meantime before packed galleries the dismal tragicomedy was played with cynical skill by Southern senators, aided by Senator William E. Borah of Idaho.

It was during this fight that I sought, for a long time unsuccessfully, to obtain an appointment with President Roosevelt to urge him to take a definite stand on the anti-lynching bill. The lean and saturnine Marvin McIntyre,* I learned later, had intercepted my letters and telegrams, showing none of them to the President. When the situation became so critical that the fate of the bill hung in the balance from hour to hour I turned in desperation to Mrs. Roosevelt. I explained the situation over the long-distance telephone and she promptly promised to give the facts I had told her to the President.

The interview thus arranged was a most interesting revelation to me. I had known Mr. Roosevelt as Governor of New York state, but not too well. What I did know of his abilities during that period had caused me to be greatly surprised at the vigor and resourcefulness he had exhibited on becoming President. Since he had entered the White House my contacts with him had been few, but at the conference arranged by his wife on the anti-lynching bill there developed between us a closer relationship, which was destined to last to the day of his death.

The scene of the conference was the south portico of the White House on a warm spring Sunday in 1935. I found Mrs. Sara Delano Roosevelt and the President's wife on the porch, but the

* FDR's secretary.

President had been delayed in returning from a cruise on the Potomac River.

While waiting, Mrs. Eleanor Roosevelt and I discussed some of the arguments being made against the anti-lynching bill. Shortly afterward the President arrived in exuberant good spirits. As was his custom when he wished to avoid discussing a subject, he told many gay and amusing anecdotes to postpone an anticipated ordeal. But finally I was able to bring the conversation to the pending filibuster.

"But Joe Robinson [at the time Senate majority leader] tells me the bill is unconstitutional," the President remarked.

Having heard from Mrs. Roosevelt some of the arguments on this point which had been presented to the President by the bill's opponents, I was ready with the opinions of prominent lawyers who had declared the bill constitutional.

The President then told me of another argument which one of the filibusterers had made and I was able to present facts in refutation. When this had happened three or four times, the President turned sharply and declared, "Somebody's been priming you. Was it my wife?"

I smiled and suggested that we stick to our discussion of the bill.

The President then asked Mrs. Roosevelt if she had coached me, and she too smiled and suggested that the President stick to the subject.

Laughing, the President turned to his mother to say, "Well, at least I know you'll be on my side."

The President's mother shook her head and expressed the opinion that she agreed with Mr. White.

Being a good loser, the President roared with laughter and confessed defeat.

But I gained from the visit only a moral victory, because the President was frankly unwilling to challenge the Southern leadership of his party.

"I did not choose the tools with which I must work," he told me. "Had I been permitted to choose them I would have selected quite different ones. But I've got to get legislation passed by Congress to save America. The Southerners by reason of the seniority rule in Congress are chairmen or occupy strategic places on most of the Senate and House committees. If I come out for the anti-lynching bill now, they will block every bill I ask Congress to pass to keep America from collapsing. I just can't take that risk."

Letters to F.D.R.

One sign of FDR's popularity among Negroes was the volume of mail he received from colored people. No previous Chief Executive seemed as accessible to the Negro working class. FDR and his wife regularly heard from individuals suffering hard times. People whose scrawls often demonstrated that writing was no easy task for them assumed that the President was interested in their troubles and would find some way to help. The letters which follow are typical of this correspondence and come from the WPA Collection at Howard University.

1403 W. 13th Street
Chicago, Illinois
9-14-36

MR. PRES. ROOSEVELT
DEAR SIR:

I am writing you to ask you to ask you can something be done about the eviction of families in this District. People are being sit out in the street, who have large families of small childrens has no place to go and to old people that cant get no job are being evicted and the city relief are not paying any rent and if they do live a rent order the landlords wont except it. I dont know just why they dont except. This is a very bad condition all of which we are asking you to do something to stop this.

We have people that have been in the street, no place to put their things for 10 days. Oh Sir, this is a pitiful condition. Please help us in this condition if you can. I dont know any one to ask but you. We are just trying to live and be loyal Americans hoping to here from you soon in regards to these poor Colored people that are suffering under this condition.

We are on charity and have suffered much because of the change of relief from the state to the city. It was better for the poor when it was in the hands of state.

JAKE HALL
1403 W. 13th Street

4732 Forrestville Avenue
Chicago, Ill.
November 6, 1936

DEAR MADAM:

Will you please be so kind as to do me a more appreciated favor? I am a Negro girl at the age of sixteen and trying to finish high school. I need a coat very badly, and cannot go this winter without a coat, oh I do want to go on to school, for by finishing high school and college I can get some place in the world. I am asking you if you have an old coat that you could give me, I would appreciate it very much. If you dont have a coat handy now, you may send me the money and I will buy the coat. I'll be looking for a return answer as soon as you can spare the time.

SINCERELY,
DOROTHY BUSH.

3608 Green St.
Houston, Texas
Dec. 2, 1936.

DEAR PRESIDENT ROOSEVELT

I know you will be supused to hear from us but we are two little Negro sisters 9 and 7 years old an it is time for Santa Clause to come an our parents are poor and dis able to give us. My Dad doesnt have day work an he is an ex service man will you please tell Santa to come to see us we want even have food.

JOYCE AND VERNA MAE ADAMS.

God Be With You Please Please

Greensboro, Ala.
Sept. 25, 1935.

MR. PRESIDENT:

Dear President all are well and hope when this letter reach you will find you the same. President my little sister and I would like to go to school real bad. Our mother have been dead this year going on 6 years and our father is rupture in his side and cannot do much work and he is not abel to send us to scholl. We have finish out here in the country in the 6th Grade. We would like to finish school. But our father is not abel to send us to town. We haven't any people in town and it is $4 a month for board and we would have to have books, shoes, and clothes and they are high, and the gouverment only alied us 1.50 pound of lint cotton and one acre of cotton and we are not going to make over 100 one Hundre pound of seed cotton by that you know we can not go to school. We are barefeeted and nacked all most. We have some first cousin in Chicago. We would like to go there and go to school with them by are on the relief up there.

Please help us. Our father is getting old and can not work much.

So President if you ever hope any body please sir help us. Any these white people down here can tell you what nice Christian girls we are. We went in the white people church and sang for them. We sweep yards for them and get clothes.

But we can not make enough money at picking cotton for 30¢ a hundred to go to school and cotton is nearly gone. So please help us we would do any thing to go to school to finish. One of us is 15 and the other 16 we miss school a year and a half since mother have ben dead. So we would like to go to school in Chicago where our first cousins they are on the relief and are going to school. So please please sir help poor us. If it is the Lord will he will open your heart towards us two little motherless girls and help us to go to school.

Please write us at onece please help us school in Chicago started Monday.

May God Bless you

Write at once we wnat to here
FROM SISTERS—ISABELL AND MARY LEE EVANS
R. 1, Box 29 Greensboro, Ala.

Nashville, Tenn.
416 11 Ave. N
12, 13, 34

PRESIDENT ROOSEVELT:
DEAR SIR:

I will write a few lines to let you know how I am getting along. I am well at present hope this will find you well at present.

Dera Sir I am askin you for something to eat even some clothes. I went to the Red Cross they tols me they help Ex Service only. The

Community Chest turn me down. The people that need something they the one that don't get anything. I am a hard laborer My wife she makes $2.50 per week. I pay $1.50 per week rent that leaves us just $1.00 to live on. I have not got any work at the time I need clothes. They have stopped me from getting things to eat. Half of the people in this city are hungry. I wish that you could have seen for yourself when you was in Na shville. If you dont think I need anything send the Government men to my house and see for yourself. I want some clothes.

Something to eat I am hungry. Not got changing clothes.

I work for the city 15 years. They taken $3.40 of my money for ten years for charity. Now I need. And I cannot get any at all. Please make some way so I can get Something to eat and wear.

So I will come to a close.
CHARLEY NEAL
Nashville, Tenn.
I am 67 yrs old. But I am hungry.

5. THE WAR YEARS

*Letters from a Segregated Army**

"We are inexpressibly shocked that a President of the United States at a time of national peril should surrender so completely to enemies of Democracy who would destroy national unity by advocating segregation." This is a sentence from a strongly worded telegram sent to F.D.R. by T. Arnold Hill, Walter White, and A. Philip Randolph. The Negro leaders presented a program of their own which aimed at full integration of the armed forces. Although the Commander in Chief arranged some modifications, racism was evident in all branches of the service in World War II. "Just carve on my tombstone," a bitter Negro said, "'Here lies a black man killed fighting a yellow man for the protection of a white man.'" Excerpts in the following essay are from letters of Negro soldiers to the NAACP.

* Lucille B. Milner, "Jim Crow in the Army," *New Republic*, CX (March 13, 1944), 339–342.

"I am a Negro soldier 22 years old. I won't fight or die in vain. If I fight, suffer or die it will be for the freedom of every black . . . man to live equally with other races. . . . If the life of the Negro in the United States is right as it is lived today, then I would rather be dead.

"Any Negro would rather give his life at home fighting for a cause he can understand than against any enemy whose principles are the same as our so-called democracy.

"A new Negro will return from the war—a bitter Negro if he is disappointed again. He will have been taught to kill, to suffer, to die for something he believes in, and he will live by these rules to gain his personal rights."

Statements like these are found over and over in the hundreds of soldiers' letters received by organizations defending the rights of the colored people. It is impossible to read a dozen of these letters picked at random without feeling their tragic significance. The war attitude of the Negro reflects today's dilemma of his race, in an intensified and critical form. The Negro soldier is deeply patriotic, vividly conscious of our aims in this war, eager to get into the fighting areas. That seems an ideal attitude for a soldier to have, but the truth is that the morale of the colored men in our armed forces is far from ideal. For they are not allowed to express their patriotism, their democracy and their militancy freely. They have fought bravely in every war, from the Revolution on, but still they are not treated like Americans.

The sense of being excluded from the mainstream of military service is expressed in their letters in phrases like these: "We really have nothing to soldier for." . . . "It is not like being in a soldier camp. It is more like being in prison." A soldier at an air base wrote: "Segregation in the Army is making enemies of the Negro soldier, demoralizing him. You may wonder why they don't rebel. They do, but individually, and as a result, they are either transferred to Southern parts, placed in the guardhouse or given a dishonorable discharge from the army. . . . We keep constantly in mind that army law is WHITE man's law."

The very set-up in our various services proves that a race that has been three centuries on our soil is still considered Negro, rather than American. The fault is not in our pronouncements but in our practice. The Selective Training and Service Act of 1940 said distinctly that there shall be no discrimination against any person because of race or color.

How is this principle reflected in military practice?

The Navy has refused to commission Negroes in any branch of service—in the Navy proper, the Marine Corps and the Coast Guard.* While it has admitted Negroes to its fighting ranks, Jim Crowism is practised in training and in service.

The Air Corps has discriminated against Negroes in the most complicated and costly way, building a segregated air base for Negroes when there was room in established training centers over the country. The annual output of Negro pilots was 200 when it could easily have been five times that number.

The Army trains and commissions colored and white candidates without discrimination, but Jim Crow rules over every Southern camp.

Colored women are excluded from every auxiliary service but the Wacs,† and here there is segregation.

With the Army calling for thousands of nurses, they have held down the quota of colored nurses to about 200.

Briefly this is the set-up. It reflects no policy on the part of our command, for the simple reason that no policy exists. It reflects merely today's confusion and the inherited tradition of our services from the prewar days. . . . The Negro serviceman feels that the general pattern he must follow is this: to be barred from the sea and the air except on "their" terms; to serve on the land mainly in labor or "service or supply" battalions; to endure Jim Crow in every guise, from subtle slights to brutality and death at the hands of both peace officers and military police; to be kept on American soil and excluded from combat service as long as "they" can contrive retraining, or transfer, or some other run-around; in combat service to be kept if possible behind the lines and always out of the headlines, the newsreels and the glory; to come back as a war casualty and find Jim Crow waiting in most of the hospitals in the South.

The racial attitude of the military is a curious anachronism. Despite the gains made on the civilian front in race relations during the last two decades, actual conditions in our camps, most

---

* Some Negroes were commissioned toward the end of the war.
† Again, some Negroes entered the WAVES before the war was over.

of which are unfortunately in the South, show a reversion to dark
and ignorant prejudice. A corporal writes from the Deep South:
". . . It is no secret that the Negro soldier in the South is as
much persecuted as is his civilian brother; the conditions existing
in this Godforsaken hole which is Camp . . . are intolerable, and
may be considered on a par with the worst conditions throughout
the South since 1865."

Certain inequalities may not seem important until you think
what they mean to the soldiers: post movie theatres and post
exchanges barring Negroes in some camps and segregating them in
others; guest accommodations for whites only in Southern camps;
the fact that in many parts of the South Negro MP's may not carry
arms as the whites do; exclusion from the white USO even when
none exists for the colored men; overwhelming and widespread
troubles about transportation in buses and trains. Candidates for
commissions in a few of the training schools may eat, sleep and
study together without regard to color—but what then? The white
officer is soon sent overseas, the colored officer is apt to be
transferred to another camp for "further training." The practice
seems to be to keep the Negroes, as far as possible, from overseas
duty, to use them at their lowest rather than their highest skills and
to retard promotion.

From a colored officer in the Deep South:

"The only desire the Negro officers could possibly have is to get
completely out of the South. Many of us have never been below
the Mason-Dixon Line, and are now being subjected to chain-gang
practices and disgraceful and embarrassing verbal abuse. . . . No
nursing or recreational facilities have been organized for us. . . .
To go to a nearby city is to invite trouble, not only from civilian
police but more often from the military police, who are upheld in
any discourtesy, breach of discipline, arrogance and bodily assault
they render the Negro officers."

. . . On a crowded troop train going through Texas the colored
soldiers were fed behind a Jim Crow curtain at one end of the
dining car. In the main section, along with the white folks, a group
of German war prisoners dined—and no doubt fed their illusions
of race superiority on that Jim Crow curtain.

The assignment of Negro units in the Army to menial jobs is a
widespread practice. Colored inductees go to camp for military

training and find themselves assigned to service units—cooking, shoveling coal, waiting on the white officers. Entering service, they may find themselves building the Burma Road, or African bases, or encountering winter temperatures of 50 degrees below zero hacking the Alaska Highway or the Canol pipeline out of the Canadian wastes. Meanwhile white units trained at the same time are in the fighting war. . . . "The sight of masses of Negro soldiers constantly blocked off into separate groups and assigned to menial jobs," a white officer writes, "generates in the mind of the average soldier a powerful feeling of superiority and of being 'different.' "

A highly trained Negro technologist . . . was picking up papers around the officers' quarters in a Southern camp. . . . Another inductee, a brilliant bio-chemist, had a fantastic Army career. At the reception center on the Pacific Coast the officers proposed to use his years of medical training to the Army's advantage. He was sent to Camp A for training and assigned to a post in the biological laboratory. Before he could start work he was shipped further east to Camp B, and enrolled for technical training as an armorer. He passed this course with high honors, and was promptly shipped to Camp C—farther west—classed as corporal and assigned to the Army Air Forces. A week later he found himself at Camp D in the Southwest, assigned to labor detail. That meant losing his corporal's stripes gained in another division. He wrote his wife:

"I find that this post is the 'Port of Lost Hope.' . . . Merciful God, I have not been so close to loss of faith as I am at this moment. . . . All this build-up for something to respect, only to be treated like a brainless gorilla fit for nothing more than a post-hole digger and a stringer of wire, a yard bird. . . . I swear if this was Guadalcanal or Australia or North Africa I would expect nothing and would give everything, even my life. . . . It is mockery, let no one tell you differently, this sudden opening up of the so-called exclusive branches of the services to Negroes. We are trained, become skilled—and then the oblivion of common labor."

It is hard to decide which is more cruel—this new pattern of murdering the ambition, the skills, the high potential contributions of the gifted Negro, or the old pattern of physical brutality

which the Negro-baiters and Klan agents use against the colored
man in uniform. Soldiers of both races have been killed in camp
riots which have grown out of unequal conditions and mounting
tensions. But the Negro soldier is much safer in camp than in some
Southern towns or on common carriers. He "finds himself not only
outside the protection of the law but even the object of lawless
aggression by the officers of the law," in the opinion of Judge
William H. Hastie, former Civilian Aide to the Secretary of War,
who felt it necessary to resign his high post in protest against the
Air Corps policy toward Negroes.

For instance, last Memorial Day at Centerville, Mississippi, the
local sheriff intervened in a minor fracas between a white MP and
a Negro soldier whose offense was having lost a sleeve button. The
two were fighting things out, with the other MP's and the Negro's
companions holding back. When the MP began to get the worst of
things, he yelled at the sheriff, "Shoot the nigger." The sheriff fired
point-blank at the Negro's chest, then asked the MP, "Any more
niggers you want killed?"

Another ugly story based on the sworn testimony of eye-
witnesses concerns the murder of a colored private in Hampton,
Arkansas, last spring. He was trying to protect his sister from
assault by a white man who was drunk. A deputy sheriff intervened, and though it was the white man who attacked him, it was
the black man who was shot. The deputy sheriff was never apprehended.

Buses and trains mean even more to the Negro soldier than to
the white in parts of the country where there is no local Negro
population, and he must travel far, or else hope for a visit from his
family, in order to mingle with his own kind. The soldiers' letters
describe endless troubles with buses and trains. Even when they
are being tranferred as troops, they are often refused service in the
railway restaurants and go hungry for twenty-four hours. The wife
and two babies of a Negro chaplain traveled three days to join him
without being able to buy anything but cold milk and sandwiches.
One gentle little Negro woman, whose soldier-husband was refused
coffee at a bus terminal, delivered a sermon to the snappish coun-
tergirl. "Our boys can fight for you," she said. "They are spilling
their blood for you on the battlefield, yet you can't serve them a cup

of coffee." But the management still refused the coffee. "May the Lord forgive them, for they know not what they do," she said in a quiet tone as they turned and left.

From 1770, when the colored boy Crispus Attucks fell in the Boston Massacre, down through the Battle of San Juan Hill and the Meuse-Argonne offensive, the colored Americans have been collecting their traditions of war and their flags and decorations and trophies. As far as we will let them, they are fighting as Americans today, and yet they are fighting with a difference. This, from a soldier's letter, expresses what is in their hearts: "Those of us who are in the armed services are offering our lives and fortunes, not for the America we know today, but for the America we hope will be created after the war."

Detroit's Race Riot*

Negroes had come to Detroit to "work in Mr. Ford's plant" at the time of the First World War. Racial antagonism among working-class and immigrant groups was historically bitter, but even more so in this automobile town which attracted considerable numbers of white Southerners as well as Negroes during the boom years of World War II. Racial clashes over segregated housing and other problems occurred there sporadically from the 1920's on. The worst riot of the war took place in Detroit on June 20, 1943, and is described in this article. Like the misguided analysts of the present who associate Negro discontent with Communism, some contemporaries tried to blame the conflict on Axis propaganda.

Well, it's here. After a night and day of race riots, twenty-eight Detroiters—all but three Negroes—are dead.† More than seven hundred have been injured. Hundreds are in jail. Mobs raging up and down the streets have swept away police, burned houses and automobiles, looted stores, dragged Negroes from streetcars and buses to tear their clothes to bits and beat them into insensibility. For twenty-five blocks along one street in the Negro section not a single window in a dwelling house has been left intact. Now troops, state and federal, have moved in to take over the policing

* "Detroit—The Storm Bursts," *The Christian Century*, LX (June 30, 1943), 759–761.
† The final toll of dead was twenty-five Negroes and nine whites.

of America's fourth city. And President Roosevelt has issued a proclamation calling on the rioters to "disperse and retire peaceably to their respective abodes."

No one can say that Detroit had not been warned. More than a year ago white mob action to prevent colored tenants from moving into the federal Sojourner Truth apartments revealed the racial tension—in that instance largely between Negroes and whites of eastern European extraction. Soon after *Life* magazine roused the country with an article, "Detroit Is Dynamite." Less than three months ago the commanding officer at near-by Selfridge Field shot a Negro soldier who was reporting to him as driver for his car; the officer claimed that he had given orders that no Negro should be assigned to that duty. And less than a month ago . . . twenty thousand workers in the Packard plant struck because three Negroes had been "up-graded"—i.e., promoted—for superior work on the assembly line.

Anyone who has known anything about Detroit has been aware that all the combustibles had been gathered, the fuse laid and the match lit for a gigantic racial explosion. Southern mountaineers, recruited in large numbers to work in the war plants, have brought their sectional feelings with them. European immigrants . . . have seen in the Negroes a threat to their own postwar jobs. And the Negroes, who have responded to the appeals for war labor until they now make up more than a tenth of Detroit's population, have shown a new and disquieting readiness to stand up for their rights. Seeing the danger ahead civic and church circles have responded in familiar ways. There have been some discussions, some resolutions, a few sermons and other admonitions to order. But little of a positive and constructive nature has been attempted. All the while, informed observers have been reporting, old Ku Klux Klan elements have been forming new organizations—most of them led by the old kleagles—pledged to run the Negroes out of the war plants and out of the city.

And no one can say that the nation has not had plenty of warning. City by city, race rioting has been advancing across the country . . . in Mobile, in Beaumont, in Newark, in Philadelphia, in El Paso. And now this throwback to savagery has reached a new height of horror on the blood-drenched streets of Detroit. The *Christian Century* is only one among many voices which have been warning for a long, long time that racial trouble—violent, desperate, deep-seated—threatened the nation. Now it's here.

The worst of it is that this Detroit terror may only mark the beginning of ghastly national tragedy. To be sure, this Detroit outbreak is so terrible that it may produce a salutary revulsion from coast to coast. Some Americans may at last wake up to the way in which such racial outrages play into the hands of Japan's propagandists; they may at last see that for every person of color struck down by a white mob in this country the United States loses the confidence and comradeship of ten thousand Asiatics. Other Americans may awaken to the presence of deep cleavages in the American community; they may at last begin to sense what these must mean to the future of national unity. Still other Americans may see the destruction and anarchy and bloodshed which lie ahead for this land unless the mob is brought under control. Seeing these things, the American people may be shocked into appropriate action.

They may be. But let none be too sanguine. There are elements involved here which will not yield easily to persuasion or policing. For example, white anger must be reckoned with. In many parts of the nation, and particularly in the south, it is clear that a large portion of the white population has been growing more belligerent from week to week, exasperated by what it regards as the assertiveness of colored groups. For some time past this editorial office has been receiving a trickle of letters from frightened ministers in many parts of the south prophesying race riots on a scale hitherto unknown. One of the most disquieting phenomena of the war period is the hatred so commonly expressed for Mrs. Roosevelt all over the south, largely because of her interest in Negro welfare. The southern votes which were cast in the House of Representatives last week to eliminate the appropriation for the domestic activities of the OWI* largely resulted from the anger of Democratic politicians because the OWI had published a booklet relating Negro contributions to the winning of the war.

Nor is this white anger confined to Negroes. A reporter for a Chicago newspaper, investigating the situation in California, wires back from Los Angeles: "Feeling against the Japanese is feverish and high, and a great secret society somewhat reminiscent of the

* Office of War Information.

Ku Klux Klan has been organized to see that no Japanese ever returns to California. 'If he comes,' a member told us, 'he'll not be here twenty-four hours later. No Jap can ever set foot in Los Angeles again, and that includes the nisei.' "

And on the other side there are elements among these racial minorities which also must be taken into account. This is particularly true in the case of the Negroes. There can be no doubt that younger Negroes today feel a racial self-respect which makes them ready to resent any act or word which they construe as containing the slightest racial slight. But with this is coupled a sense of desperation which too often thwarts good judgment. The result may easily be outbursts which better poised Negroes deplore as deeply as do any whites. Yet there seems to be no cessation of incidents diabolically calculated to add to this tension. Such have been, of course, the detention of loyal Japanese-Americans behind barbed wire. And such have been, conspicuously, the various types of run-around which the Negro has received from the navy, the marine corps, the air forces, the army and the FEPC. No one can read the Negro press these days without becoming aware of the rapidity with which this tension is mounting. But how many white Americans bother to read the Negro press?

Under such tension, fed from both sides of the racial lines which stretch back and forth across the country, anything can happen. Unless informed, strong and wise measures are taken immediately to head off further racial outbreaks, even worse riots will occur than have already burst out in Los Angeles and Detroit. But what can be done? The responsibility for action, it seems to us, is fourfold.

First, the government has a responsibility. It can and must make the FEPC work. It must clean up racial discrimination in the army, navy, marines and air force. And it must suppress these new klans which are being organized in areas of tension with the deliberate purpose of fomenting race trouble. If it could suppress the bund as a measure of national security, it can suppress these. Second, leaders of the minority groups have a responsibility. They can counsel patience, forbearance, the dignity which accepts injustice with restraint. They can do something to see that irresponsible or unbalanced zealots are recognized and brought under control before they touch off explosions. Third, responsible citizens of the majority white group have a responsibility. In their civic clubs and in their commercial organizations, they can see that economic opportunities are provided for all citizens of every color and they can demand that local authorities provide minority group members with full protection and their full rights before the law. And the churches have a responsibility. That responsibility involves the instruction and arousing of the national conscience. It is a responsibility which cannot be shifted to other shoulders.

The nation is at war, according to the President, in order to make possible a world in which there shall be, for all people, freedom from fear. Freedom from fear—with mobs sweeping up and down the streets of our cities shouting "Kill the d——n niggers!" "Kill the d——n greasers!" "Kill the d——n Japs!" Freedom from fear! Will not the words stick in our throats . . . ?

CHAPTER IX

THE POSTWAR YEARS

The Spirit Says Do

❀ ❀

We will go to jail, we will walk, we will ride, we will do what the spirit says do until we are free.

MISSISSIPPI FREEDOM DEMOCRATIC PARTY, 1965

When World War II ended, some prophets of disaster envisioned a postwar era of bitter racial hostility similar to the violence of 1919. Evidence of racial tension in the North and South during the war seemed to add weight to these predictions. The same rumors that floated anarchically around in World War I were disinterred and repeated: Negro soldiers had been trained to kill and they would wreak havoc when they returned. "I want you to know I ain't afraid," said a Negro character in a playlet in 1942. "I don't mind fighting. I'll fight Hitler, Mussolini, the Japs all at the same time, but I'm telling you I'll give these crackers down South the same damn medicine." In the minds of some white Southerners the only defense against the anticipated holocaust was to "show the nigger where he stands" as soon as the war was over. One way to do so was to negate whatever modest gains had been made as a result of the war. Eugene Talmadge, John E. Rankin, Theodore G. Bilbo, and others went about this job diligently and choked off federal appropriations for FEPC in 1946. The Committee died and, with it, the hope of a permanent, federal fair employment practices commission.

Other forces, however, operated to mollify a potentially tense situation and transformed the decade that followed the war into one of modest progress instead of retrogression in America's racial history. The most important of these was the ideological and political character of the war itself. World War II was judged by contemporaries not only as a fight with a brutal enemy, but a war against a racist ideology. Democracy had defeated fascism, people believed, freedom vanquished tyranny, brotherhood subdued racism. As Walter White said in the closing days of battle, it wasn't only Hitler that lost, but his "master-race theory" as well. It was a blow against a world system which categorized Jews as sub-human and Negroes as "half-apes."*

And the war reshaped basic tenets of international politics that had endured since the expansion of western Europe in the sixteenth century. The fitful death of Western colonialism was accompanied by the erosion of an essential part of its *raison d'être*. No longer might one justify imperialism by claims to superior civilization, to white supremacy. The emerging nations of Africa and Asia were inhabited by people of color—people who represented a majority of the world's citizens. The expectations of Martin R. Delany had finally come true. Some hundred years earlier Delany, who had a reverence for his African heritage perhaps unequalled by any of his contemporaries, told a convention of free Negroes: "The white races are but one-third of the population of the globe—or one of them to two of us— and it cannot much longer continue that two-thirds will passively submit to the universal domination of the one-third."

The rise of independent nations of nonwhites coincided with America's entry into world politics as an active, proselytizing power. One of the key themes of American foreign policy in the confrontation of ideologies that followed the war was the claim that our side represented the humanistic values of democracy, such concepts as human brotherhood and the unity of mankind. Americans like to believe that people of diverse ethnic backgrounds live here "in peace and harmony and enjoy the benefits of democracy." Racism within the country, therefore, increasingly became a matter of world concern. It challenged one of the

---

* Roy Wilkins, "The Negro Wants Full Equality," in R. W. Logan, ed., *What the Negro Wants* (Chapel Hill, N.C., 1944), p. 113.

key tenets of America's self-image, and hampered our ability to deal with nonwhite nations. Perhaps the first significant effect of this shrinking new world on American race relations was F.D.R.'s Executive Order 8802. The President was concerned that the March on Washington—which was planned at the very time he was bringing the United Nations into existence—would cause the United States "international embarrassment." Since World War II each act of domestic racism has been held up to world view and used as weapon against American foreign policy. This in turn has served as a prod for more forceful executive leadership on questions of racial injustice. Dean Acheson, testifying before the FEPC, pointed to this problem in 1946: ". . . The existence of discrimination against minority groups in this country has an adverse effect upon our relations with other countries," Acheson said. "We are reminded over and over by some foreign newspapers and spokesmen, that our treatment of various minorities leaves much to be desired. . . . Frequently we find it next to impossible to formulate a satisfactory answer to our critics in other countries; the gap getween the things we stand for in principle and the facts of a particular situation may be too wide to bridge." (1)

For American Negroes the emergence of the nonwhite world, especially the nations of Africa, has had added significance. It has created a sense of dignity and respect for an African past that was too often previously considered debased, savage, and unworthy of emulation. It has led to an expanded kinship and pride for people of color throughout the world; an affirmation of Blackness. Horace Cayton put it cogently when he said. "The world is now the scene." To choose another example, the radical contemporary magazine *Liberator* uses the lower-case "n" in referring to Negroes but capitalizes "Black Man" and "Afro-American." The glorification of Blackness was one of the chief sources of Malcolm X's appeal. Lorraine Hansberry described how this change influenced her. During World War II, she said, she began to see herself as a member of a "world majority" rather than an American minority. "As a fairly self-conscious Negro," she told Harold R. Isaacs, "I began to feel this kinship, the feeling from the past summed up in 'aren't we all miserable?' passing to a new and happier feeling: 'Aren't we all moving ahead!' "* (4)

---

* Quoted in Harold R. Isaacs, *The New World of Negro Americans* (New York, 1963), p. 283.

The decade that followed the war also saw the rise of in-creased institutional commitment to the goals of racial justice. President Truman, moved in part by the growth of powerful Negro voting blocs in the Northern cities, spoke more forcefully of civil rights than had F.D.R. The report of the President's Committee on Civil Rights, *To Secure These Rights* (1947), was hailed as a major breakthrough by contemporaries. Walter White called it "the most uncompromising and specific pro-nouncement by a government agency on the explosive issue of racial and religious bigotry." Added to this was the authority of the Supreme Court. In a series of historic decisions the Court attacked white primaries, segregation in interstate transporta-tion, inequality and segregation in institutions of higher learn-ing, followed by the historic decision on segregation in the schools, *Brown* v. *Board of Education,* in 1954. About half the states enacted FEPC laws in these years. None of these activi-ties radically altered the day-to-day relations between the races in America but they did crumble the institutional and legal bulwarks upon which racism had flourished and had been justified for centuries. They were a necessary prelude to the racial revolution which followed. (1)

The School Segregation cases rocked the nation as no other act of the federal government dealing with race since the Emanci-pation Proclamation. There was, however, a glaring disparity be-tween the moral force of the unanimous decision and the methods by which it was to be implemented. The Court left enforcement of its ruling to the torturous process of individual suits for justice in lower federal courts. In essence the Court passed the burden of its decision to NAACP lawyers, Negro parents, and fifty-eight federal district judges. Hope that President Eisenhower would somehow use the prestige of his office and his own personal power to facilitate enforcement of the decision in the South was blunted when the Chief Executive consistently spoke of the inability of stateways to effect folkways. In a variety of different phrases Eisenhower referred to the impossibility of "legislating morality." Hesitant leadership at the national level encouraged the rise of reactionary forces throughout the South.

Although some Border states integrated their schools quickly, the majority of Southern states said "never." Legislatures passed an unending series of laws to circumvent the ruling. The sym-bolic leadership of the resistance movement was assumed, to some people's surprise, by Virginians. The tainted constitutional doctrine of "interposition" was exhumed by Richmond newspaper editor James Jackson Kilpatrick and incorporated into a legislative system by Senator Harry F. Byrd, the principal force behind the "Southern Manifesto" of 1956. In Virginia as in Little Rock some people were willing to destroy the public school system rather than permit schools to operate on an integrated basis. "If Virginia surrenders," Senator Byrd wrote, "if the Virginia line is broken, the rest of the South will go down too."*

A period of massive repression followed. The White Citizens' Councils were founded, the KKK was reactivated, and both attempted to use intimidation and economic reprisals against Negroes who petitioned for integrated schools. When these methods failed, violence was resorted to. Voices of Southern moderation, with a few heroic exceptions, were stifled. Benjamin Muse, of the Southern Regional Council, describes Southern reaction to the decision reminiscent of the constraints of the ante-bellum period. Teachers and clergymen who dissented were fired; library shelves were purged of "questionable" books; controversial public personalities were not permitted to speak; roving preachers of hate, like John Kasper and "Ace" Carter, made a business of stirring up trouble in tense localities; television stations refused to show national programs in which Negroes performed; a new pseudoscientific racism flourished; manuals of instruction for white school children appeared and contained such nuggets of pedagogical wisdom as: "God put the white people off by themselves. He put the yellow, red, and black people by themselves. God wanted the white people to live alone. And He wanted the colored people to live alone. That is why He put them off by themselves. . . . Some people do not think God made men different. But we know God did make men different."† The South's challenge to federal authority represented the most serious questioning of national governmental power since the Civil War. (2)

All these forces in various combinations, steeled Negroes in America to demand, not request, racial justice—and call for it now. The most significant Negro revolution for equality in American history took place in the 1950's and early 1960's. No single strategy of freedom, no one leader or organization dominated the movement. Some, like Martin Luther King, Jr., believed in nonviolence as a philosophic and religious principle.

* Quoted in Benjamin Muse, *Ten Years of Prelude* (New York, 1964), p. 147.
 † Ibid., pp. 160–177.

King and the Southern Christian Leadership Conference spoke of creating a "beloved community" through the power of suffering and love. Others, like the Congress of Racial Equality and the Student Non-Violent Coordinating Committee were able to accept the tactic without its mystique. "Very few of us accept non-violence as a way of life," a SNCC worker in Mississippi said. "We were willing to accept it as long as it was sanity, but it's just not sanity to give your life away." In Monroe, North Carolina, Robert Williams, president of the local NAACP, devised his own strategy by arming his followers and fighting a civil war in miniature.

Paradoxically, the very looseness of the civil rights revolution, even the tensions among competing groups, permitted creative forms of individual protest to arise. The Negro youngsters who began the sit-ins in 1960 had no plan to set off spontaneous protests throughout the South, yet they did. The CORE-sponsored freedom rides of 1961 eventually involved leaders from SNCC, and prodded the NAACP into using techniques of direct action. Bob Moses of SNCC began an almost one-man voter registration project in McComb, Mississippi, in 1961 which became one of the most daring challenges to the whole system of racial inequality in the South, and finally involved the other civil rights groups. If Uncle Tom died during the Montgomery bus boycott his requiem was sung at the SNCC voter-registration project. And if the voices of Negro leadership occasionally sounded cacophonous they still were black voices directing a predominantly Negro freedom movement in America. (3)

The force of Negro protest combined with white Southern recalcitrance and hate to produce the most important legislative victories for racial equality in American history. The communications revolution permitted the entire country to witness the confrontations which became a daily part of American life for a decade—bombed churches, snarling dogs, cattle prods, murders, water hoses, Birmingham, Selma. Many Southern communities grouped reporters and television cameramen with the other "outside agitators" who disturbed their supposed racial harmony, and treated them accordingly. Such brutalism shocked the conscience of the nation and mobilized mass support for the sweeping Civil Rights Act of 1964 and the Voting Rights Act of 1965. There certainly was enough evidence of hesitant federal support—especially in the Deep South—to justify cynicism among civil rights workers. "There is a town in Mississippi called Liberty, there is a Department in Washington called Justice," reads a sign on a SNCC office in Mississippi. Yet, when measured against the myopia of the Eisenhower years the public attitudes of the Kennedy and Johnson Administrations provided a crucial measure of executive leadership on racial matters. They helped transform brutal skirmishes into permanent victories. In the 1960's, for the first significant time since Reconstruction, the question of racial justice became a national, political issue. (4)

In spite of the success of the institutional and legal war on inequality, a number of formidable deterrents to racial freedom remained. The hard-core racist South, schooled by a century of experience, continued to devise ingenious subterfuges to undermine or bypass the requirements of law. The frightful gap between victories in the halls of Congress and day-to-day life in the ghetto led to the despair, which became the violence, of the summers of 1964–1966. Shortly after the passage of the Voting Rights Act of 1965, Watts exploded, to inform those who hadn't realized it that the economic position of the Negro masses actually *retrogressed* during the years of the civil rights revolution. Attempts to resolve problems of housing, employment, and education in the ghetto would demand perceptive, massive, expensive, and long-range effort—the type of program envisioned in A. Philip Randolph's "Freedom Budget"—and a coalition of national conscience and interracial understanding equal to that which had been molded in the early 1960's would be necessary to carry through such meaningful reform. But, as the summer and fall of 1966 demonstrated, lines of communication between the races were hardening, not softening; black nationalism and white racism increased their appeal; the advances of the previous decade were threatened by the possibility of intense racial hostility and economic dislocation in the future. A period of regression and apathy followed the racial changes of Reconstruction; history, some feared, in 1966, could repeat itself. (5)

1. THE FIRST STEPS

A Rising Wind Walter White*

Walter White, the NAACP's volatile executive secretary, toured the European Theater of Operations in the last year of World War II.

* From Walter White, *A Rising Wind* (New York, 1945), pp. 144–155.

He went to investigate rumors of tension between Negro and white troops but, more importantly, came back with a heightened awareness of the international implications of the death of European colonialism. "White nations and peoples had vigorously proclaimed to the world that this war is being fought for freedom," he wrote, "and colored peoples were taking them at face value." The sensitive title of the book he wrote describing his experiences, A Rising Wind, *was adapted from a speech of Eleanor Roosevelt: "a wind is rising throughout the world of free men everywhere. . . ."*

World War II has given to the Negro a sense of kinship with other colored—and also oppressed—peoples of the world. Where he has not thought through or informed himself on the racial angles of colonial policy and master-race theories, he senses that the struggle of the Negro in the United States is part and parcel of the struggle against imperialism and exploitation in India, China, Burma, Africa, the Philippines, Malaya, the West Indies, and South America. The Negro soldier is convinced that as time proceeds that identification of interests will spread even among some brown and yellow peoples who today refuse to see the connection between their exploitation by white nations and discrimination against the Negro in the United States.

The evil effect of misbehavior by a minority and the timorousness of the American Government in meeting such misbehavior will cost America and other white nations dearly so far as colored peoples, constituting two thirds of the earth's population, are concerned. Winston Churchill's recent statement that, as the war nears its end, ideology is being forgotten increasingly means to colored peoples that idealism is being conveniently shelved. Colored peoples, particularly in the Pacific, believed, whether correctly or not, that in its later stages the war was being fought to restore empire to Great Britain, France, Holland, and Portugal. The immediate resumption of control of Hollandia and other sections of Dutch New Guinea by the Dutch, and similar action by the British in Guadalcanal and Tarawa as soon as the Japanese had been driven out, the preparations being made by France to take over again control of Indo-China the minute the Nipponese are ejected, created increasing skepticism of the Allies throughout the Pacific.

Any person of normal intelligence could have foreseen this. With considerable effectiveness, the Japanese by radio and other means have industriously spread in the Pacific stories of lynchings, of segregation and discrimination against the Negro in the American Army, and of race riots in Detroit, Philadelphia, and other American cities. To each of these recitals has been appended the statement that such treatment of a colored minority in the United States is certain to be that given to brown and yellow peoples in the Pacific if the Allies, instead of the Japanese, win the war. No one can accurately estimate at this time the effectiveness of such propaganda. But it is certain that it has had wide circulation and has been believed by many. Particularly damaging has been the circulation of reports of clashes between white and Negro soldiers in the European and other theaters of operation.

Indissolubly tied in with the carrying overseas of prejudice against the Negro is the racial and imperialist question in the Pacific of Great Britain's and our intentions toward India and China. Publication of Ambassador William Phillips' blunt warning to President Roosevelt in May 1944 that India is a problem of the United States as well as of England despite British opposition to American intervention is of the highest significance. It reaffirmed warnings to the Western world by Wendell Willkie, Sumner Welles, Pearl Buck, and Henry Wallace, among others, that grave peril which might bring disaster to the entire world was involved in continued refusal to recognize the just claims for justice and equality by the colored people, particularly in the Orient. These people are not as powerless as some naïve Americans believe them to be. In the first place they have the strength of numbers, unified by resentment against the condescension and exploitation by white nations which Pearl Buck calls "the suppression of human rights to a degree which has not been matched in its ruthlessness outside of fascist-owned Europe," which can and possibly will grow into open revolt. The trend of such awakening and revolution is clearly to be seen in the demand which was made by China at the Dumbarton Oaks Conference of August 1944 that the Allied nations unequivocally declare themselves for complete racial equality. It is to be seen in Ambassador Phillips' warning that though there are four million Indians under arms they are wholly a mercenary army whose allegiance to the Allies will last only as long as they are paid; and in his further revelation that all of these as well as African troops must be used to police other Indians instead of fighting Japan.

Permit me to cite a few solemn warnings of the inevitability of world-wide racial conflict unless the white nations of the earth do an about-face on the issue of race. "Moreover, during the years between 1920 and 1940 a period in the history of the Asiatic and Pacific peoples was in any event drawing to its close," says Sumner Welles, former Undersecretary of State, in his epochal book, *The Time for Decision.*

The startling development of Japan as a world power, and the slower but nevertheless steady emergence of China as a full member of the family of nations, together with the growth of popular institutions among many other peoples of Asia, notably India, all combined to erase very swiftly indeed the fetish of white supremacy cultivated by the big colonial powers during the nineteenth century. The thesis of white supremacy could only exist so long as the white race actually proved to be supreme. The nature of the defeats suffered by the Western nations in 1942 dealt the final blow to any concept of white supremacy which still remained.

While there are British and Dutch colonial administrators who show a "spirit of devotion, of decency and of self-abnegation," Mr. Welles remarks, there also are "yet only too many British representatives in the Far East [who] have demonstrated that type of thinking which is so well exemplified in the words of a high British official in India at the outset of the present century when he expressed a conviction which he asserted 'was shared by every Englishman in India, from the highest to the lowest . . . the conviction in every man that he belongs to a race whom God has destined to govern and subdue.' "

The distinguished former Undersecretary might well have gone on to point out that had not the Russians and Chinese performed miracles of military offense and defense in World War II, or had not the black Governor-General of French Equatorial Africa, Félix Eboué, retained faith in the democratic process when white Frenchmen lost theirs, the so-called Anglo-Saxon nations and peoples would surely have lost this war. And Mr. Welles could have reminded his readers that brown and yellow peoples in Asia and the Pacific and black peoples in Africa and the West Indies and the United States are not ignorant of the truth that the war was won by men and women—white, yellow, black, and brown. Resumption of white arrogance and domination in the face of such facts may be disastrous to the peace of the world.

The distinguished novelist, Pearl Buck, hits hard on the same issue in her *American Unity and Asia* in the chapter ominously captioned, "Tinder for Tomorrow."

The Japanese weapon of racial propaganda in Asia is beginning to show signs of effectiveness [she declares]. This is not because of peculiar skill in the way it is being used, but because it is being presented to persons who have had unfortunate experiences with English and American people. . . . It will be better for us if we acknowledge the danger in this Japanese propaganda. The truth is that the white man in the Far East has too often behaved without wisdom or justice to his fellow man. It is worse than folly—it is dangerous today—not to recognize the truth, for in it lies the tinder for tomorrow. Who of us can doubt it who has seen a white policeman beat a Chinese coolie in Shanghai, a white sailor kick a Japanese in Kobe, an English captain lash out with his whip at an Indian vendor— who of us, having seen such oriental sights or heard the common contemptuous talk of the white man in any colored country, can forget the fearful bitter hatred in the colored face and the blaze in the dark eyes?

Miss Buck tells how such stupid cruelty is put to use by the Japanese among the one billion colored people of the Pacific.

Race prejudice continues unabated among white people today, the Japanese are saying. Tokyo radio programs daily send their broadcasts over Asia in their campaign to drive out the white man. They dwell upon white exploitation of colored troops and cite mistreatment of Filipinos by the American military and similar treatment of Indian troops by the English. . . . "The colored peoples," Japanese propaganda says over and over again in a thousand forms, "have no hope of justice and equality from the white peoples because of their unalterable race prejudice against us." . . . The effect therefore of this Japanese propaganda cannot be lightly dismissed. It lies uneasy in the minds and memories of many at this moment who are loyally allied with Britain and the United States, in the minds and memories of colored peoples of Asia. Yes, and it lies uneasy, too, in the minds and memories of many colored citizens of the United States, who cannot deny the charge and must remain loyal in spite of it. For such minds realize that, though Nazism may give them nothing but death, yet the United States and Britain have given them too little for life in the past and not even promises for the future. Our colored allies proceed to war against the Axis not deceived or in ignorance. They know that it may not be the end of the war for them even when Hitler has gone down and Nazism is crushed and Japan returned to her isles again. The colored peoples know that for them the war for freedom may have to go on against the very white men at whose side they are now fighting.

These are grim words not pleasant to the ears of white America and Britain, who believe that the last shot fired in this war will mean the complete restoration of the way of life which preceded it. But the consequences of denying or ignoring them are solemnly voiced by an Englishman, Harold J. Laski, who bluntly warns that "Englishmen who put imperial power before social justice, Americans who think the color of a man's skin determines his rights— these are only some of the elements in our midst who might easily pervert the great victory into an epoch barren and ugly."

Will the United States after the war perpetuate its racial-discrimination policies and beliefs at home and abroad as it did during the war? Will it continue to follow blindly the dangerous and vicious philosophy voiced in Kipling's poem, *The White Man's Burden,* which Paul Hutchinson characterized in *World Revolution and Religion* as "the most significant cultural expression of the nineteenth century: even more significant than Nietzsche's discovery of the *"Übermensch"*? Will decent and intelligent America continue to permit itself to be led by the nose by demagogues and professional race-hate mongers—to have its thinking and action determined on this global and explosive issue by the lowest common denominator of public opinion?

Or will the United States, having found that prejudice is an expensive luxury, slough off the mistakes of the past and chart a new course both at home and in its relations with the rest of the world? Miss Buck supplies one answer:

This also the Far Eastern Allies are asking. Japan is busily declaring that we cannot. She is declaring in the Philippines, in China, in India, Malaya, and even Russia that there is no basis for hope that colored peoples can expect any justice from the people who rule in the United

States, namely, the white people. For specific proof the Japanese point to our treatment of our own colored people, citizens of generations in the United States. Every lynching, every race riot, gives joy to Japan. The discriminations of the American army and navy and air forces against colored soldiers and sailors, the exclusion of colored labor in our defense industries and trade unions, all our social discriminations, are of the greatest aid today to our enemy in Asia, Japan. "Look at America," Japan is saying to millions of listening ears. "Will white Americans give you equality?"

Who can reply with a clear affirmative? The persistent refusal of Americans to see the connection between the colored American and the colored peoples abroad, the continued, and it seems even willful, ignorance which will not investigate the connection, are agony to those loyal and anxious Americans who know all too well the dangerous possibilities.

Is Japan right in what she says to Asia and the Pacific? And whether right or not, what effect is her propaganda—unhappily based largely on truth—having upon hundreds of millions of people in what were once far places but today are but a few hours away from New York or Washington or San Francisco? Upon people whose good will and faith in our integrity are vital to our own national security?

During the middle stages of the war I made a study of Japanese radio and other propaganda among the people of the Orient and of German propaganda, almost invariably identical in language and content to the Japanese, in Latin America and Africa. Every lynching, every race riot like the one in Detroit in 1943 and the one in Philadelphia in 1944 against employment of qualified Negroes on streetcars, every killing or other mistreatment of a Negro soldier in a Southern training camp or city, every anti-Negro diatribe on the floor of Congress, every refusal to abolish racial segregation in the armed services of the United States was played up over and over again. Significantly enough, there was little embellishment of the details, probably because little was needed. In one form or another this moral was driven home: See what the United States does to its own colored people; this is the way you colored people of the world will be treated if the Allied nations win the war! Be smart and cast your lot with another colored people, the Japanese, who will never mistreat fellow colored people!

What will America's answer be? If already planned race riots and lynchings of returning Negro soldiers "to teach them their place" are consummated, if Negro war workers are first fired, if India remains enslaved, if Eboué's people go back to disease and poverty to provide luxury and ease for Parisian boulevardiers, World War III will be in the making before the last gun is fired in World War II. In *One World,* Wendell Willkie reported that "everywhere I found polite but skeptical people, who met my questions about their problems and difficulties with polite but ironic questions about our own. The maladjustments of races in America came up frequently." Such skepticism is but beginning. The question is posed bluntly: Can the United States, Britain, and other "white" nations any longer afford, in enlightened self-interest, racial superiority?

What to do?

The United States, Great Britain, France, and other Allied nations must choose without delay one of two courses—to revolutionize their racial concepts and practices, to abolish imperialism and grant full equality to all of its people, or else prepare for World War III. Another Versailles Treaty providing for "mandates," "protectorates," and other devices for white domination will make such a war inevitable. One of the chief deterrents will be Russia. Distrustful of Anglo-American control of Europe, many and perhaps all of the Balkan states may through choice or necessity ally themselves with Russia. If Anglo-Saxon practices in China and India are not drastically and immediately revised, it is probable and perhaps certain that the people of India, China, Burma, Malaya, and other parts of the Pacific may also move into the Russian orbit as the lesser of two dangers.

As for the United States, the storm signals are unmistakable. She can choose between a policy of appeasement of bigots—which course she gives every indication now of following—and thus court disaster. Or she can live up to her ideals and thereby both save herself and help to avert an early and more disastrous resumption of war.

A wind *is* rising—a wind of determination by the have-nots of the world to share the benefits of freedom and prosperity which the haves of the earth have tried to keep exclusively for themselves. That wind blows all over the world. Whether that wind develops into a hurricane is a decision which we must make now and in the days when we form the peace.

UNESCO Statement on Race*

As many of the atrocities of World War II were committed in the name of racial superiority the United Nations decided to publicize scientific data on race and create a program of international education based on its findings. "Race hatred and conflict," the UN maintained, "thrive on scientifically false ideas and are nourished by ignorance." UNESCO held its first conference on race in Paris in December, 1949. Anthropologists, psychologists, and sociologists representing Brazil, France, India, Mexico, New Zealand, the United Kingdom, and the United States participated. The statement they prepared in 1950, reproduced below, was the first major pronouncement on the scientific meaning of race issued by the United Nations. Another followed in 1951 and a whole library of pamphlets and books on the meaning of race in the modern world subsequently appeared.

1. Scientists have reached general agreement in recognizing that mankind is one: that all men belong to the same species, *Homo sapiens*. It is further generally agreed among scientists that all men are probably derived from the same common stock; and that such differences as exist between different groups of mankind are due to the operation of evolutionary factors or differentiation such as isolation, the drift and random fixation of the material particles which control heredity (the genes), changes in the structure of these particles, hybridization, and natural selection. In these ways groups have arisen of varying stability and degree of differentiation which have been classified in different ways for different purposes.

2. From the biological standpoint, the species *Homo sapiens* is made up of a number of populations, each one of which differs from the others in the frequency of one or more genes. Such genes, responsible for the hereditary differences between men, are always few when compared to the whole genetic constitution of man and to the vast number of genes common to all human beings regard-

* From UNESCO, *Race and Science* (New York, 1961), pp. 496–501.

less of the population to which they belong. This means that the likenesses among men are far greater than their differences.

3. A race, from the biological standpoint, may therefore be defined as one of the group of populations constituting the species *Homo sapiens*. These populations are capable of interbreeding with one another but, by virtue of the isolating barriers which in the past kept them more or less separated, exhibit certain physical differences as a result of their somewhat different biological histories. These represent variations, as it were, on a common theme.

4. In short, the term "race" designates a group or population characterized by some concentrations, relative as to frequency and distribution, of hereditary particles (genes) or physical characters, which appear, fluctuate, and often disappear in the course of time by reason of geographic and/or cultural isolation. The varying manifestations of these traits in different populations are perceived in different ways by each group. What is perceived is largely preconceived, so that each group arbitrarily tends to misinterpret the variability which occurs as a fundamental difference which separates that group from all others.

5. These are the scientific facts. Unfortunately, however, when most people use the term "race" they do not do so in the sense above defined. To most people, a race is any group of people whom they choose to describe as a race. Thus, many national, religious, geographic, linguistic or cultural groups have, in such loose usage, been called "race," when obviously Americans are not a race, nor are Englishmen, nor Frenchmen, nor any other national group. Catholics, Protestants, Moslems and Jews are not races, nor are groups who speak English or any other language thereby definable as a race; people who live in Iceland or England or India are not races; nor people who are culturally Turkish or Chinese or the like thereby describable as races.

6. National, religious, geographic, linguistic and cultural groups do not necessarily coincide with racial groups; and the cultural traits of such groups have no demonstrated genetic connexion with racial traits. Because serious errors of this kind are habitually committed when the term "race" is used in popular parlance, it would be better when speaking of human races to drop the term "race" altogether and speak of *ethnic groups*.

7. Now what has the scientist to say about the groups of

mankind which may be recognized at the present time? Human races can be and have been differently classified by different anthropologists, but at the present time most anthropologists agree on classifying the greater part of present-day mankind into three major divisions, as follows: the Mongoloid Division, the Negroid Division, the Caucasoid Division. The biological processes which the classifier has here embalmed, as it were, are dynamic, not static. These divisions were not the same in the past as they are at present, and there is every reason to believe that they will change in the future.

8. Many sub-groups or ethnic groups within these divisions have been described. There is no general agreement upon their number, and in any event most ethnic groups have not yet been either studied or described by the physical anthropologists.

9. Whatever classification the anthropologist makes of man, he never includes mental characteristics as part of those classifications. It is now generally recognized that intelligence tests do not in themselves enable us to differentiate safely between what is due to innate capacity and what is the result of environmental influences, training and education. Wherever it has been possible to make allowances for differences in environmental opportunities, the tests have shown essential similarity in mental characters among all human groups. In short, given similar degrees of cultural opportunity to realize their potentialities, the average achievement of the members of each ethnic group is about the same. The scientific investigations of recent years fully support the dictum of Confucius (551–478 B.C.): "Men's natures are alike; it is their habits that carry them far apart."

10. The scientific material available to us at present does not justify the conclusion that inherited genetic differences are a major factor in producing the differences between the cultures and cultural achievements of different peoples or groups. It does indicate, however, that the history of the cultural experience which each group has undergone is the major factor in explaining such differences. The one trait which above all others has been at a premium in the evolution of men's mental characters has been educability, plasticity. This is a trait which all human beings possess. It is indeed, a species character of *Homo sapiens*.

11. So far as temperament is concerned, there is no definite

evidence that there exist inborn differences between human groups. There is evidence that whatever group differences of the kind there might be are greatly over-ridden by the individual differences, and by the differences springing from environmental factors.

12. As for personality and character, these may be considered raceless. In every human group a rich variety of personality and character types will be found, and there is no reason for believing that any human group is richer than any other in these respects.

13. With respect to race-mixture, the evidence points unequivocally to the fact that this has been going on from the earliest times. Indeed, one of the chief processes of race-formation and race-extinction or absorption is by means of hybridization between races or ethnic groups. Furthermore, no convincing evidence has been adduced that race-mixture of itself produces biologically bad effects. Statements that human hybrids frequently show undesirable traits, both physically and mentally, physical disharmonies and mental degeneracies, are not supported by the facts. There is, therefore, no "biological" justification for prohibiting intermarriage between persons of different ethnic groups.

14. The biological fact of race and the myth of "race" should be distinguished. For all practical social purposes "race" is not so much a biological phenomenon as a social myth. The myth "race" has created an enormous amount of human and social damage. In recent years it has taken a heavy toll in human lives and caused untold suffering. It still prevents the normal development of millions of human beings and deprives civilization of the effective co-operation of productive minds. The biological differences between ethnic groups should be disregarded from the standpoint of social acceptance and social action. The unity of mankind from both the biological and social viewpoints is the main thing. To recognize this and to act accordingly is the first requirement of modern man. It is but to recognize what a great biologist wrote in 1875: "As man advances in civilization, and small tribes are united into larger communities, the simplest reason would tell each individual that he ought to extend his social instincts and sympathies to all the members of the same nation, though personally unknown to him. This point being once reached, there is only an artificial barrier to prevent his sympathies extending to the men of all nations and races." These are the words of Charles Darwin in *The Descent of*

Man (2nd ed., 1875, pp. 187–88). And, indeed, the whole of human history shows that a co-operative spirit is not only natural to men, but more deeply rooted than any self-seeking tendencies. If this were not so we should not see the growth of integration and organization of his communities which the centuries and the millennia plainly exhibit.

15. We now have to consider the bearing of these statements on the problem of human equality. It must be asserted with the utmost emphasis that equality as an ethical principle in no way depends upon the assertion that human beings are in fact equal in endowment. Obviously individuals in all ethnic groups vary greatly among themselves in endowment. Nevertheless, the characteristics in which human groups differ from one another are often exaggerated and used as a basis for questioning the validity of equality in the ethical sense. For this purpose we have thought it worth while to set out in a formal manner what is at present scientifically established concerning individual and group differences.

(a) In matters of race, the only characteristics which anthropologists can effectively use as a basis for classifications are physical and physiological.

(b) According to present knowledge there is no proof that the groups of mankind differ in their innate mental characteristics, whether in respect of intelligence or temperament. The scientific evidence indicates that the range of mental capacities in all ethnic groups is much the same.

(c) Historical and sociological studies support the view that genetic differences are not of importance in determining the social and cultural differences between different groups of *Homo sapiens,* and that the social and cultural *changes* in different groups have, in the main, been independent of *changes* in inborn constitution. Vast social changes have occurred which were not in any way connected with changes in racial type.

(d) There is no evidence that race-mixture as such produces bad results from the biological point of view. The social results of race-mixture whether for good or ill are to be traced to social factors.

(e) All normal human beings are capable of learning to share in a common life, to understand the nature of mutual service and reciprocity, and to respect social obligations and contracts. Such biological differences as exist between members of different ethnic groups have no relevance to problems of social and political organization, moral life and communication between human beings.

Lastly, biological studies lend support to the ethic of universal brotherhood; for man is born with drives toward co-operation, and unless these drives are satisfied, men and nations alike fall ill. Man is born a social being who can reach his fullest development only through interaction with his fellows. The denial at any point of this social bond between man and man brings with it disintegration. In this sense, every man is his brother's keeper. For every man is a piece of the continent, a part of the main, because he is involved in mankind.

The original statement was drafted at Unesco House, Paris by the following experts:

> Professor Ernest Beaglehole, New Zealand;
> Professor Juan Comas, Mexico;
> Professor L. A. Costa Pinto, Brazil;
> Professor E. Franklin Frazier, United States of America;
> Professor Morris Ginsberg, United Kingdom;
> Dr. Humayun Kabir, India;
> Professor Claude Levi-Strauss, France;
> Professor M. F. Ashley-Montagu, United States of America
>   (Rapporteur).

The text was revised by Professor Ashley-Montagu, after criticisms submitted by Professors Hadley Cantril, E. G. Conklin, Gunnar Dahlberg, Theodosius Dobzhansky, L. C. Dunn, Donald Hager, Julian S. Huxley, Otto Klineberg, Wilbert Moore, H. J. Muller, Gunnar Myrdal, Joseph Needham, Curt Stern.

President Truman's Committee on Civil Rights*

President Truman's Committee on Civil Rights was appointed by executive order on December 5, 1946. The order itself contained forceful language: "The Constitutional guarantees of individual

* From President's Committee on Civil Rights, *To Secure These Rights* (Washington, D.C., 1947), pp. 151–173.

liberties and of equal protection under the laws clearly place on the Federal Government the duty to act when state and local authorities abridge or fail to protect these Constitutional rights." The strong committee recommendations, which follow, were made the basis of Truman's legislative program in 1948. Although few of the proposals were implemented at that time they did symbolize the increasing national interest in problems of minority rights and race. Some Southerners believed the threat significant enough to bolt the Democratic party in the 1948 elections.

THE COMMITTEE'S RECOMMENDATIONS

I. *To strengthen the machinery for the protection of civil rights, the President's Committee recommends:*

1. The reorganization of the Civil Rights Section* of the Department of Justice to provide for:

The establishment of regional offices;

A substantial increase in its appropriation and staff to enable it to engage in more extensive research and to act more effectively to prevent civil rights violations;

An increase in investigative action in the absence of complaints;

The greater use of civil sanctions;

Its elevation to the status of a full division in the Department of Justice.

The creation of regional offices would enable the Civil Rights Section to provide more complete protection of civil rights in all sections of the country. It would lessen its present complete dependence upon United States Attorneys and local FBI agents for its work in the field. Such regional offices should be established in eight or nine key cities throughout the country, and be staffed with skilled personnel drawn from the local areas. These offices should serve as receiving points for complaints arising in the areas, and as local centers of research, investigation, and preventive action. Close cooperation should be maintained between these offices, local FBI agents, and the United States Attorneys.

* Established in 1939.

The Department of Justice has suggested that heads of these regional offices should have the status of Assistant United States Attorneys, thereby preserving the centralization of federal criminal law enforcement. The President's Committee is fearful that under this plan the goal of effective, courageous, and nonpolitical civil rights protection in the field will not be reached unless satisfactory measures are taken to prevent these assistants from becoming mere political subordinates within the offices of the United States Attorneys.

Additional funds and personnel for research and preventive work would free the Civil Rights Section from its present narrow status as a prosecutive agency. Through the use of properly developed techniques and by the maintenance of continuous checks on racial and other group tensions, much could be done by the Section to reduce the number of lynchings, race riots, election irregularities, and other civil rights violations. Troublesome areas, and the activities of organizations and individuals who foment race tensions could be kept under constant scrutiny.

A larger staff and field-office facilities would also make it possible for the Section to undertake investigations of suspected civil rights violations, without waiting for the receipt of complaints. There are many problems, such as the possible infringement of civil rights resulting from practices used in committing persons to mental institutions, which might be so studied. These investigations in the absence of complaints could also be combined with educational and mediation efforts to check chronic incidents of police brutality or persistent interferences with the right to vote.

The difficulty of winning convictions in many types of criminal civil rights cases is often great. The Committee believes that the Civil Rights Section should be granted increased authority, by Congress if necessary, to make appropriate use of civil sanctions, such as suits for damages or injunctive relief, suits under the Declaratory Judgment Act, and the right of intervention by means of briefs amicus curiae in private litigation where important issues of civil rights law are being determined.

Finally, the Committee urges congressional action raising the Civil Rights Section to full divisional status in the Department of Justice under the supervision of an Assistant Attorney General. We believe this step would give the federal civil rights enforcement program prestige, power, and efficiency that it now lacks. Moreover, acceptance of the above recommendations looking toward increased activity by the Civil Rights Section and the passage by Congress of additional civil rights legislation would give this change added meaning and necessity.

2. The establishment within the FBI of a special unit of investigators trained in civil rights work.

The creation of such a unit of skilled investigators would enable the FBI to render more effective service in the civil rights field than is now possible. At the present time, its investigators are concerned with enforcement of all federal criminal statutes. In some instances, its agents have seemingly lacked the special skills and knowledge necessary to effective handling of civil rights cases, or have not been readily available for work in this area.

These special agents should work in close harmony with the Civil Rights Section and its regional offices.

3. The establishment by the state governments of law enforcement agencies comparable to the federal Civil Rights Section.

There are large areas where, because of constitutional restrictions, the jurisdiction of the federal government as a protector of civil rights is either limited or denied. There are civil rights problems, unique to certain regions and localities, that can best be treated and solved by the individual states. Furthermore, our review of the work of the Civil Rights Section has persuaded us of the cardinal importance of developing specialized units for the enforcement of civil rights laws. We believe that this is true at the state level too. States which have, or will have, civil rights laws of their own, should buttress them with specially designed enforcement units. These would have the further effect of bringing the whole program closer to the people. They would also facilitate systematic local cooperation with the federal Civil Rights Section, and they would be able to act in the areas where it has no authority.

Here and elsewhere the Committee is making recommendations calling for remedial action by the states. The President's Executive Order invited us to consider civil rights problems falling within state as well as federal jurisdiction. We respectfully request the President to call these recommendations to the attention of the states and to invite their favorable consideration.

4. The establishment of a permanent Commission on Civil Rights in the Executive Office of the President, preferably by Act of Congress; and the simultaneous creation of a Joint Standing Committee on Civil Rights in Congress.

In a democratic society, the systematic, critical review of social needs and public policy is a fundamental necessity. This is especially true of a field like civil rights, where the problems are enduring, and range widely. From our own effort, we have learned that a temporary, sporadic approach can never finally solve these problems.

Nowhere in the federal government is there an agency charged with the continuous appraisal of the status of civil rights, and the efficiency of the machinery with which we hope to improve that status. There are huge gaps in the available information about the field. A permanent Commission could perform an invaluable function by collecting data. It could also carry on technical research to improve the fact-gathering methods now in use. Ultimately, this would make possible a periodic audit of the extent to which our civil rights are secure. If it did this and served as a clearing house and focus of coordination for the many private, state, and local agencies working in the civil rights field, it would be invaluable to them and to the federal government.

A permanent Commission on Civil Rights should point all of its work towards regular reports which would include recommendations for action in the ensuing periods. It should lay plans for dealing with broad civil rights problems, such as those arising from the technological displacement and probable migration of southern Negroes to cities throughout the land. It should also investigate and make recommendations with respect to special civil rights problems, such as the status of Indians and their relationship to the federal government.

The Commission should have effective authority to call upon any agency of the executive branch for assistance. Its members should be appointed by the President with the approval of the Senate. They should hold a specified number of regular meetings. A full-time director should be provided with an adequate appropriation and staff.

Congress, too, can be aided in its difficult task of providing the legislative ground work for fuller civil rights. A standing committee, established jointly by the House and the Senate, would provide a central place for the consideration of proposed legislation. It would enable Congress to maintain continuous liaison with the permanent Commission. A group of men in each chamber would be able to give prolonged study to this complex area and would become expert in its legislative needs.

5. The establishment by the states of permanent commissions on civil rights to parallel the work of the federal Commission at the state level.

The states should create permanent civil rights commissions to make continuing studies of prejudice, group tensions, and other local civil rights problems; to publish educational material of a civil rights nature; to evaluate existing legislation; and to recommend new laws. Such commissions, with their fingers on their communities' pulses, would complement at the state level the activities of a permanent federal Commission on Civil Rights.

6. The increased professionalization of state and local police forces.

The Committee believes that there is a great need at the state and local level for the improvement of civil rights protection by more aggressive and efficient enforcement techniques. Police training programs, patterned after the FBI agents' school and the Chicago Park District Program, should be instituted. They should be oriented so as to indoctrinate officers with an awareness of civil rights problems. Proper treatment by the police of those who are arrested and incarcerated in local jails should be stressed. Supplemented by salaries that will attract and hold competent personnel, this sort of training should do much to make police forces genuinely professional.

II. *To strengthen the right to safety and security of the person, the President's Committee recommends:*

1. The enactment by Congress of new legislation to supplement Section 51* of Title 18 of the United States Code which would

---

* Section 51 made it a crime for two or more persons to conspire to "injure, oppress, threaten, or intimidate any citizen in the free exercise of any right or privilege secured him by the Constitution or laws of the United States." Guilty parties were subject to ten years imprisonment and a fine of $5,000.

impose the same liability on one person as is now imposed by that statute on two or more conspirators.

The Committee believes that Section 51 has in the past been a useful law to protect federal rights against encroachment by both private individuals and public officers. It believes the Act has great potential usefulness today. Greater efforts should be made through court tests to extend and make more complete the list of rights safeguarded by this law.

2. The amendment of Section 51 to remove the penalty provision which disqualifies persons convicted under the Act from holding public office.

There is general agreement that this particular penalty creates an unnecessary obstacle to the obtaining of convictions under the Act and that it should be dropped.

3. The amendment of Section 52* to increase the maximum penalties that may be imposed under it from a $1,000 fine and a one-year prison term to a $5,000 fine and a ten-year prison term, thus bringing its penalty provisions into line with those in Section 51.

At the present time the Act's penalties are so light that it is technically a misdemeanor law. In view of the extremely serious offenses that have been and are being successfully prosecuted under Section 52, it seems clear that the penalties should be increased.

4. The enactment by Congress of a new statute, to supplement Section 52, specifically directed against police brutality and related crimes.

This Act should enumerate such rights as the right not to be deprived of property by a public officer except by due process of law; the right to be free from personal injury inflicted by a public officer; the right to engage in a lawful activity without interference by a public officer; and the right to be free from discriminatory law enforcement resulting from either active or passive conduct by a public officer.

This statute would meet in part the handicap in the use of

---

* Section 52 was directed at public officials who used the force of their office to willfully deprive individuals of their constitutional or legal rights.

Section 52 imposed by the Supreme Court in *Screws* v. *United States*. This was the case in which the Court required prosecutors to establish that defendants had willfully deprived victims of a "specific constitutional right." In later prosecutions, the Civil Rights Section has found it very difficult to prove that the accused acted in a "willful" manner. By spelling out some of the federal rights which run against public officers, the supplementary statute would relieve the Civil Rights Section of this extraordinary requirement.

The Committee considered and rejected a proposal to recommend the enactment of a supplementary statute in which an attempt would be made to include a specific enumeration of all federal rights running against public officers. Such an enumeration would inevitably prove incomplete with the passage of time and might prejudice the protection of omitted rights. However, the committee believes that a new statute, such as the one here recommended, enumerating the rights for the protection of which Section 52 is now most commonly employed, is desirable.

5. The enactment by Congress of an antilynching act.

The Committee believes that to be effective such a law must contain four essential elements. First, it should define lynching broadly. Second, the federal offense ought to cover participation of public officers in a lynching, or failure by them to use proper measures to protect a person accused of a crime against mob violence. The failure or refusal of public officers to make proper efforts to arrest members of lynch mobs and to bring them to justice should also be specified as an offense.

Action by private persons taking the law into their own hands to mete out summary punishment and private vengeance upon an accused person; action by either public officers or private persons meting out summary punishment and private vengeance upon a person because of his race, color, creed or religion—these too must be made crimes.

Third, the statute should authorize immediate federal investigation in lynching cases to discover whether a federal offense has been committed. Fourth, adequate and flexible penalties ranging up to a $10,000 fine and a 20-year prison term should be provided.

The constitutionality of some parts of such a statute, particularly those providing for the prosecution of private persons, has been questioned. The Committee believes that there are several constitutional bases upon which such a law might be passed and that these are sufficiently strong to justify prompt action by Congress.

6. The enactment by Congress of a new criminal statute on involuntary servitude, supplementing Sections 443 and 444* of Title 18 of the United States Code.

This statute should make full exercise of congressional power under the Thirteenth Amendment by defining slavery and involuntary servitude broadly. This would provide a basis for federal prosecutions in cases where individuals are deliberately deprived of their freedom by public officers without due process of law or are held in bondage by private persons. Prosecution under existing laws is limited to the narrow, technical offense of peonage or must be based upon the archaic "slave kidnaping" law, Section 443.

7. A review of our wartime evacuation and detention experience looking toward the development of a policy which will prevent the abridgment of civil rights of any person or groups because of race or ancestry.

We believe it is fallacious to assume that there is a correlation between loyalty and race or national origin. The military must be allowed considerable discretionary power to protect national security in time of war. But we believe it is possible to establish safeguards against the evacuation and detention of whole groups because of their descent without endangering national security. The proposed permanent Commission on Civil Rights and the Joint Congressional Committee might well study this problem.

8. Enactment by Congress of legislation establishing a procedure by which claims of evacuees for specific property and business losses resulting from the wartime evacuation can be promptly considered and settled.

* Known as the "Antipeonage Acts," they punished those guilty of holding or returning someone to a condition of peonage with a fine of $5,000 and five years imprisonment.

The government has acknowledged that many Japanese American evacuees suffered considerable losses through its actions and through no fault of their own. We cannot erase all the scars of evacuation; we can reimburse those who present valid claims for material losses.

III. *To strengthen the right to citizenship and its privileges, the President's Committee recommends:*

1. Action by the states or Congress to end poll taxes as a voting prerequisite.

Considerable debate has arisen as to the constitutionality of a federal statute abolishing the poll tax. In four times passing an anti-poll tax bill, the House of Representatives has indicated its view that there is a reasonable chance that it will survive a court attack on constitutional grounds. We are convinced that the elimination of this obstacle to the right of suffrage must not be further delayed. It would be appropriate and encouraging for the remaining poll tax states voluntarily to take this step. Failing such prompt state action, we believe that the nation, either by act of Congress, or by constitutional amendment, should remove this final barrier to universal suffrage.

2. The enactment by Congress of a statute protecting the right of qualified persons to participate in federal primaries and elections against interference by public officers and private persons.

This statute would apply only to federal elections. There is no doubt that such a law can be applied to primaries which are an integral part of the federal electoral process or which affect or determine the result of a federal election. It can also protect participation in federal election campaigns and discussions of matters relating to national political issues. This statute should authorize the Department of Justice to use both civil and criminal sanctions. Civil remedies should be used wherever possible to test the legality of threatened interferences with the suffrage before voting rights have been lost.

3. The enactment by Congress of a statute protecting the right to qualify for, or participate in, federal or state primaries or elections against discriminatory action by state officers based on

race or color, or depending on any other unreasonable classification of persons for voting purposes.

This statute would apply to both federal and state elections, but it would be limited to the protection of the right to vote against discriminatory interferences based on race, color, or other unreasonable classification. Its constitutionality is clearly indicated by the Fourteenth and Fifteenth Amendments. Like the legislation suggested under (2) it should authorize the use of civil and criminal sanctions by the Department of Justice.

4. The enactment by Congress of legislation establishing local self-government for the District of Columbia; and the amendment of the Constitution to extend suffrage in presidential elections, and representation in Congress to District residents.

The American tradition of democracy requires that the District of Columbia be given the same measure of self-government in local affairs that is possessed by other communities throughout the country. The lack of congressional representation and suffrage in local and national elections in the District deprives a substantial number of permanent Washington residents of a voice in public affairs.

5. The granting of suffrage by the States of New Mexico and Arizona to their Indian citizens.

These states have constitutional provisions which have been used to disfranchise Indians. In New Mexico, the constitution should be amended to remove the bar against voting by "Indians not taxed." This may not be necessary in Arizona where the constitution excludes from the ballot "persons under guardianship." Reinterpretation might hold that this clause no longer applies to Indians. If this is not possible, the Arizona constitution should be amended to remove it.

6. The modification of the federal naturalization laws to permit the granting of citizenship without regard to the race, color, or national origin of applicants.

It is inconsistent with our whole tradition to deny on a basis of ancestry the right to become citizens to people who qualify in every other way.

7. The repeal by the states of laws discriminating against aliens who are ineligible for citizenship because of race, color, or national origin.

These laws include the alien land laws and the prohibition against commercial fishing in California. The removal of race as a qualification for naturalization would remove the structure upon which this discriminatory legislation is based. But if federal action on Recommendation 6 is delayed, state action would be eminently desirable.

8. The enactment by Congress of legislation granting citizenship to the people of Guam and American Samoa.

This legislation should also provide these islands with organic acts containing guarantees of civil rights, and transfer them from naval administration to civilian control. Such legislation for Guam and American Samoa has been introduced in the present Congress.

9. The enactment by Congress of legislation, followed by appropriate administrative action, to end immediately all discrimination and segregation based on race, color, creed, or national origin, in the organization and activities of all branches of the Armed Services.

The injustice of calling men to fight for freedom while subjecting them to humiliating discrimination within the fighting forces is at once apparent. Furthermore, by preventing entire groups from making their maximum contribution to the national defense, we weaken our defense to that extent and impose heavier burdens on the remainder of the population.

Legislation and regulations should expressly ban discrimination and segregation in the recruitment, assignment, and training of all personnel in all types of military duty. Mess halls, quarters, recreational facilities and post exchanges should be nonsegregated. Commissions and promotions should be awarded on considerations of merit only. Selection of students for the Military, Naval, and Coast Guard academies and all other service schools should be governed by standards from which considerations of race, color, creed, or national origin are conspicuously absent. The National Guard, reserve units, and any universal military training program should all be administered in accordance with these same standards.

The Committee believes that the recent unification of the armed forces provides a timely opportunity for the revision of present policy and practice. A strong enunciation of future policy should be made condemning discrimination and segregation within the armed services.

10. The enactment by Congress of legislation providing that no member of the armed forces shall be subject to discrimination of any kind by any public authority or place of public accommodation, recreation, transportation, or other service or business.

The government of a nation has an obligation to protect the dignity of the uniform of its armed services. The esteem of the government itself is impaired when affronts to its armed forces are tolerated. The government also has a responsibility for the well-being of those who surrender some of the privileges of citizenship to serve in the defense establishments.

IV. *To strengthen the right to freedom of conscience and expression the President's Committee recommends:*

1. The enactment by Congress and the state legislatures of legislation requiring all groups, which attempt to influence public opinion, to disclose the pertinent facts about themselves through systematic registration procedures.

Such registration should include a statement of the names of officers, sources of financial contributions, disbursements, and the purposes of the organization. There is no question about the power of the states to do this. Congress may use its taxing and postal powers to require such disclosure. The revenue laws should be changed so that tax returns of organizations claiming tax exemption show the suggested information. These returns should then be made available to the public.

The revenue laws ought also to be amended to require the same information from groups and organizations which claim to operate on a non-profit basis but which do not request tax exemption. The Committee also recommends further study by appropriate governmental agencies looking toward the application of the disclosure principle to profit-making organizations which are active in the market place of public opinion.

Congress ought also to amend the postal laws to require those who use the first-class mail for large-scale mailings to file disclosure statements similar to those now made annually by those who use the second-class mail. The same requirement should be adopted for applicants for metered mail permits. Postal regulations ought also to require that no mail be carried by the Post Office which does not bear the name and address of the sender.

2. Action by Congress and the executive branch clarifying the loyalty obligations of federal employees, and establishing standards and procedures by which the civil rights of public workers may be scrupulously maintained.

The Committee recognizes the authority and the duty of the government to dismiss disloyal workers from the government service. At the same time the Committee is equally concerned with the protection of the civil rights of federal workers. We believe that there should be a public enunciation by responsible federal officials of clear, specific standards by which to measure the loyalty of government workers.

It is also important that the procedure by which the loyalty of an accused federal worker is determined be a fair, consistently applied, stated "due process." Specific rules of evidence should be laid down. Each employee should have the right to a bill of particular accusations, representation by counsel at all examinations or hearings, the right to subpoena witnesses and documents, a stenographic report of proceedings, a written decision, and time to prepare a written brief for an appeal. Competent and judicious people should have the responsibility for administering the program.

The Attorney General has stated to the Committee in a letter, "It is my firm purpose, insofar as my office has control over this program, to require substantial observance of the safeguards recommended by the President's Committee."

V. *To strengthen the right to equality of opportunity, the President's Committee recommends:*

1. In general:

The elimination of segregation, based on race, color, creed, or national origin, from American life.

The separate but equal doctrine has failed in three important respects. First, it is inconsistent with the fundamental equalitarianism of the American way of life in that it marks groups with the brand of inferior status. Secondly, where it has been followed, the results have been separate and unequal facilities for minority peoples. Finally, it has kept people apart despite incontrovertible evidence that an environment favorable to civil rights is fostered whenever groups are permitted to live and work together. There is no adequate defense of segregation.

The conditioning by Congress of all federal grants-in-aid and other forms of federal assistance to public or private agencies for any purpose on the absence of discrimination and segregation based on race, color, creed, or national origin.

We believe that federal funds, supplied by taxpayers all over the nation, must not be used to support or perpetuate the pattern of segregation in education, public housing, public health services, or other public services and facilities generally. We recognize that these services are indispensable to individuals in modern society and to further social progress. It would be regrettable if federal aid, conditioned on nonsegregated services, should be rejected by sections most in need of such aid. The Committee believes that a reasonable interval of time may be allowed for adjustment to such a policy. But in the end it believes that segregation is wrong morally and practically and must not receive financial support by the whole people.

A minority of the Committee favors the elimination of segregation as an ultimate goal but opposes the imposition of a federal sanction. It believes that federal aid to the states for education, health, research and other public benefits should be granted provided that the states do not discriminate in the distribution of the funds. It dissents, however, from the majority's recommendation that the abolition of segregation be made a requirement, until the people of the states involved have themselves abolished the provisions in their state constitutions and laws which now require segregation. Some members are against the nonsegregation requirement in educational grants on the ground that it represents federal control over education. They feel, moreover, that the best way ultimately to end segregation is to raise the educational level of the people in the states affected; and to inculcate both the teachings of religion regarding human brotherhood and the ideals of our democracy regarding freedom and equality as a more solid basis for genuine and lasting acceptance by the peoples of the states.

2. For employment:

The enactment of a federal Fair Employment Practice Act prohibiting all forms of discrimination in private employment, based on race, color, creed, or national origin.

A federal Fair Employment Practice Act prohibiting discrimination in private employment should provide both educational machinery and legal sanctions for enforcement purposes. The administration of the act should be placed in the hands of a commission with power to receive complaints, hold hearings, issue cease-and-desist orders and seek court aid in enforcing these orders. The Act should contain definite fines for the violation of its procedural provisions. In order to allow time for voluntary adjustment of employment practices to the new law, and to permit the establishment of effective enforcement machinery, it is recommended that the sanction provisions of the law not become operative until one year after the enactment of the law.

The federal act should apply to labor unions and trade and professional associations, as well as to employers, insofar as the policies and practices of these organizations affect the employment status of workers.

The enactment by the states of similar laws;

A federal fair employment practice statute will not reach activities which do not affect interstate commerce. To make fair employment a uniform national policy, state action will be needed. The successful experiences of some states warrant similar action by all of the others.

The issuance by the President of a mandate against discrimination in government employment and the creation of adequate machinery to enforce this mandate.

The Civil Service Commission and the personnel offices of all federal agencies should establish on-the-job training programs and other necessary machinery to enforce the nondiscrimination policy in government employment. It may well be desirable to establish a government fair employment practice commission, either as a part of the Civil Service Commission, or on an independent basis with authority to implement and enforce the Presidential mandate.

3. For education:

Enactment by the state legislatures of fair educational practice laws for public and private educational institutions, prohibiting discrimination in the admission and treatment of students based on race, color, creed, or national origin.

These laws should be enforced by independent administrative commissions. These commissions should consider complaints and hold hearings to review them. Where they are found to be valid, direct negotiation with the offending institution should be undertaken to secure compliance with the law. Wide publicity for the commission's findings would influence many schools and colleges sensitive to public opinion to abandon discrimination. The final sanction for such a body would be the cease-and-desist order enforceable by court action. The Committee believes that educational institutions supported by churches and definitely identified as denominational should be exempted.

There is a substantial division within the Committee on this recommendation. A majority favors it.

4. For housing:

The enactment by the states of laws outlawing restrictive covenants;

Renewed court attack, with intervention by the Department of Justice, upon restrictive covenants.

The effectiveness of restrictive covenants depends in the last analysis on court orders enforcing the private agreement. The power of the state is thus utilized to bolster discriminatory practices. The committee believes that every effort must be made to prevent this abuse. We would hold this belief under any circumstances; under present conditions, when severe housing shortages are already causing hardship for many people of the country, we are especially emphatic in recommending measures to alleviate the situation.

5. For health services:

The enactment by the states of fair health practice statutes forbidding discrimination and segregation based on race, creed, color, or national origin, in the operation of public or private health facilities.

Fair health practice statutes, following the pattern of fair employment practice laws, seem desirable to the Committee. They should cover such matters as the training of doctors and nurses, the admission of patients to clinics, hospitals and other similar institutions, and the right of doctors and nurses to practice in hospitals. The administration of these statutes should be placed in the hands of commissions, with authority to receive complaints, hold hearings, issue cease-and-desist orders and engage in educational efforts to promote the policy of these laws.

6. For public services:

The enactment by Congress of a law stating that discrimination and segregation, based on race, color, creed, or national origin, in the rendering of all public services by the national government is contrary to public policy;

The enactment by the state of similar laws;

The elimination of discrimination and segregation depends largely on the leadership of the federal and state governments. They can make a great contribution toward accomplishing this end by affirming in law the principle of equality for all, and declaring that public funds, which belong to the whole people, will be used for the benefit of the entire population.

The establishment by act of Congress or executive order of a unit in the federal Bureau of the Budget to review the execution of all government programs, and the expenditures of all government funds, for compliance with the policy of nondiscrimination;

Continual surveillance is necessary to insure the nondiscriminatory execution of federal programs involving use of government funds. The responsibility for this task should be located in the Bureau of the Budget which has the duty of formulating the executive budget and supervising the execution of appropriation acts. The Bureau already checks the various departments and agencies for compliance with announced policy. Administratively, this additional function is consistent with its present duties and commensurate with its present powers.

The enactment by Congress of a law prohibiting discrimination or segregation, based on race, color, creed, or national origin, in interstate transportation and all the facilities thereof, to apply against both public officers and the employees of private transportation companies;

Legislation is needed to implement and supplement the Supreme Court decision in *Morgan* v. *Virginia.** There is evidence that some state officers are continuing to enforce segregation laws against interstate passengers. Moreover, carriers are still free to segregate such passengers on their own initiative since the *Morgan* decision covered only segregation based on law. Congress has complete power under the Constitution to forbid all forms of segregation in interstate commerce. We believe it should make prompt use of it.

The enactment by the states of laws guaranteeing equal access to places of public accommodation, broadly defined, for persons of all races, colors, creeds, and national origins.

Since the Constitution does not guarantee equal access to places of public accommodation, it is left to the states to secure that right. In the 18 states that have already enacted statutes, we hope that enforcement will make practice more compatible with theory. The civil suit for damages and the misdemeanor penalty have proved to be inadequate sanctions to secure the observance of these laws. Additional means, such as the revocation of licenses, and the issuance of cease-and-desist orders by administrative agencies are

---

* Irene Morgan had been convicted in Virginia for failing to move to the rear of a bus. The Supreme Court held "that seating arrangements for the different races in interstate motor travel require a single, uniform rule to promote and protect national travel." The Virginia statute was held invalid and CORE staged its first freedom ride to test the effect of this ruling.

needed to bring about wider compliance. We think that all of the states should enact such legislation, using the broadest possible definition of public accommodation.

7. For the District of Columbia:

The enactment by Congress of legislation to accomplish the following purposes in the District;

Prohibition of discrimination and segregation, based on race, color, creed, or national origin, in all public or publicly-supported hospitals, parks, recreational facilities, housing projects, welfare agencies, penal institutions, and concessions on public property;

The prohibition of segregation in the public school system of the District of Columbia;

The establishment of a fair educational practice program directed against discrimination, based on race, color, creed, or national origin, in the admission of students to private educational institutions;

The establishment of a fair health practice program forbidding discrimination and segregation by public or private agencies, based on race, color, creed, or national origin, with respect to the training of doctors and nurses, the admission of patients to hospitals, clinics, and similar institutions, and the right of doctors and nurses to practice in hospitals;

The outlawing of restrictive covenants;

Guaranteeing equal access to places of public accommodation, broadly defined, to persons of all races, colors, creeds, and national origins.

In accordance with the Committee's division on antidiscrimination laws with respect to private education, the proposal for a District fair education program was not unanimous.

Congress has complete power to enact the legislation necessary for progress toward full freedom and equality in the District of Columbia. The great majority of these measures has been recommended in this report to Congress and to the states to benefit the nation at large. But they have particular meaning and increased urgency with respect to the District. Our nation's capital, the city of Washington, should serve as a symbol of democracy to the entire world.

8. The enactment by Congress of legislation ending the system of segregation in the Panama Canal Zone.

The federal government has complete jurisdiction over the government of the Panama Canal Zone, and therefore should take steps to eliminate the segregation which prevails there.

VI. *To rally the American people to the support of a continuing program to strengthen civil rights, the President's Committee recommends:*

A long term campaign of public education to inform the people of the civil rights to which they are entitled and which they owe to one another.

The most important educational task in this field is to give the public living examples of civil rights in operation. This is the purpose of our recommendations which have gone before. But there still remains the job of driving home to the public the nature of our heritage, the justification of civil rights and the need to end prejudice. This is a task which will require the cooperation of the federal, state, and local governments and of private agencies. We believe that the permanent Commission on Civil Rights should take the leadership in serving as the coordinating body. The activities of the permanent Commission in this field should be expressly authorized by Congress and funds specifically appropriated for them.

Aside from the education of the general public, the government has immediate responsibility for an internal civil rights campaign for its more than two million employees. This might well be an indispensable first step in a large campaign. Moreover, in the armed forces, an opportunity exists to educate men while in service. The armed forces should expand efforts, already under way, to develop genuinely democratic attitudes in officers and enlisted men.

Desegregation of the Armed Forces*

The major recommendation of the President's committee enacted by Truman dealt with segregation in the armed forces, but it took the pressure of Negro protest to force its implementation. "I do not believe," a New Yorker wrote in 1948, "that Negroes will ever again be satisfied with the mere issuance of educational and propaganda material or with the hat-in-hand approach to members of legislative bodies or to the White House itself." A. Philip Randolph proved the point by publicly advising all Negroes to refuse to serve in the military until it was desegregated; he called for civil disobedience. When asked about the possible consequences of such action, Randolph faced the question openly: "I would anticipate Nationwide terrorism against Negroes who refused to participate in the armed forces, but I believe that this is the price we have to pay for democracy," he said. In July, 1948, Truman responded by establishing the President's Committee on Equality of Treatment and Opportunity in the Armed Services; in 1949 the Secretary of Defense supervised the initial program ending military segregation; and the Korean War proved that such an approach was viable. This confrontation of Senator Wayne Morse and Randolph occurred in the Senate, April 12, 1948.

Senator MORSE. Mr. Randolph, I want to question you a bit on your proposal for civil disobedience. Up until now refusal to serve in the military forces of this country in time of national emergency has been limited as far as one's psychological attitudes are concerned, to conscientious objections to war, the participating in war.

It is based upon the legal theory of freedom of religion in this country, that if one's religious scruples are such that in good conscience he cannot bring himself to participate in war, which involves the taking of human life, our Government has protected him in that religious belief, and we have our so-called exemption on the ground of conscientious objection.

Now, this proposal of yours—I am not one to minimize your testimony—your proposal is not based upon conscientious objec-

---

* From 80th Cong., 2nd sess., *Congressional Record* (1948), Part IV, pp. 4312–4318.

tion in the sense that the American law has recognized it to date; am I not right about that?

Mr. RANDOLPH. That is correct.

Senator MORSE. But your proposal, and put me straight on this, your proposal is really based upon conviction that because your Government has not given you certain social, economic, and race protection from discrimination because of race, color, or creed, you feel that even in a time of national emergency, when your Government and the country itself may be at stake, you are justified in saying to any segment of our populace—whether it is the colored group or, as you say in your statement, the white group with like sympathies—that under those circumstances you would be justified then in saying, "Do not shoulder arms in protection of your country in this national emergency"?

Mr. RANDOLPH. That is a correct statement, Mr. Senator.

I may add that it is my deep conviction that in taking such a position we are doing our country a great service. Our country has come out before the world as the moral leader of democracy, and it is preparing its defense forces and aggressive forces upon the theory that it must do this to protect democracy in the world.

Well, now, I consider that if this country does not develop the democratic process at home and make the democratic process work by giving the very people whom they propose to draft in the Army to fight for them democracy, democracy then is not the type of democracy that ought to be fought for, and, as a matter of fact, the policy of segregation in the armed forces and in other avenues of our life is the greatest single propaganda and political weapon in the hands of Russia and international communism today.

Senator MORSE. I understand your position, Mr. Randolph, but for the record I want to direct your attention to certain basic legal principles which I want to say, most kindly, are being overlooked in your position. I want to discuss your position from the standpoint of a couple of hypotheticals and relate them to certain legal principles which I think you ought to give very careful consideration to before you follow the course of action which you have indicated.

Let us assume this hypothetical. A country proceeds to attack the United States or commits acts which make it perfectly clear that our choice is only the choice of war. Would you take the position then that unless our Government granted the demands which are set out in your testimony, or most of the demands set out in your testimony, that you would recommend a course of civil disobedience to our Government?

Mr. RANDOLPH. In answer to that question, the Government now has time to change its policy on segregation and discrimination and if the Government does not change its policy on segregation and discrimination in the interests of the very democracy it is fighting for, I would advocate that Negroes take no part in the Army.

Senator MORSE. My hypothetical assumes that up to the time of the emergency set forth in my hypothetical, our Government does not follow in any degree whatsoever the course of action that you recommend.

Mr. RANDOLPH. Yes.

Senator MORSE. So the facts of the hypothetical then are thrust upon us and I understand your answer to be that under those circumstances even though it was perfectly clear that we would have to fight then to exist as a country, you would still recommend the program of civil disobedience?

Mr. RANDOLPH. Because I would believe that that is in the interest of the soul of our country and I unhesitatingly and very adamantly hold that that is the only way by which we are going to be able to make America wake up and realize that we do not have democracy here as long as one black man is denied all of the rights enjoyed by all the white men in this country.

Senator MORSE. Now, facing realistically that hypothetical situation and the assumption that it has come to pass, do you have any doubt then that this Government as presently constituted under the Constitution that governs us would necessarily follow a legal course of action of applying the legal doctrine of treason to that conduct? Would you question with me that that is the doctrine that undoubtedly will be applied at that time under the circumstances of my hypothetical?

Mr. RANDOLPH. I would anticipate Nationwide terrorism against Negroes who refused to participate in the armed forces, but I believe that that is the price we have to pay for democracy that we want. In other words, if there are sacrifices and sufferings, terrorism, concentration camps, whatever they may be, if that is the only way by which Negroes can get their democratic rights, I unhesitatingly say that we have to face it.

Senator MORSE. But on the basis of the law as it now exists, going back to my premise that you and I know of no legal exemption from participation in military service in the defense of our country other than that of conscientious objection on religious grounds, not on the grounds in which you place your civil disobedience, that then the doctrine of treason would be applied to those people participating in that disobedience?

Mr. RANDOLPH. Exactly. I would be willing to face that doctrine on the theory and on the grounds that we are serving a higher law than the law which applies the act of treason to us when we are attempting to win democracy in this country and to make the soul of America democratic.

I would contend that we are serving a higher law than that law with its legal technicalities, which would include the group which fights for democracy even in the face of a crisis you would portray, I would contend that they are serving a higher law than that law.

Senator MORSE. But you would fully expect that because the law of treason in this country relates to certain specific overt acts on the part of the individual irrespective of what he considers to be his spiritual or moral motivation in justification, that there would not be any other course of action for our Government to follow but indictments for treason?

Mr. RANDOLPH. May I add something there, Mr. Senator?

Senator MORSE. First, do you agree with me that that would be certain to follow?

Mr. RANDOLPH. Let me add here in connection with that that we would participate in no overt acts against our Government, no overt acts of any kind. In other words, ours would be one of nonresistance. Ours would be one of noncooperation; ours would be one of nonparticipation in the military forces of the country.

I want you to know that we would be willing to absorb the violence, to absorb the terrorism, to face the music and to take whatever comes and we, as a matter of fact, consider that we are more loyal to our country than the people who perpetrate segregation and discrimination upon Negroes because of color or race.

I want it thoroughly understood that we would certainly not be guilty of any kind of overt act against the country but we would not participate in any military operation as segregation and Jim Crow slaves in the Army.

Senator MORSE. I think you will agree with me that this is not the time and place for you and me to argue the legal meaning of aiding and abetting the enemy but if you refresh your memory of treason cases, as I have been doing, sitting here this morning, I would only point out to you most kindly that the legal concepts of aiding and abetting are flexible concepts that can be applied to the behavior of individuals which in effect serve the enemy in time of war to the endangerment of the rest of the people of our country.

Furthermore, and I know you are aware of the fact, any such program as you outline would not be a passive program but would be one that would be bound to result in all sorts of overt actions you could not possibly control, but for which you who sponsored it would, as a matter of law, be fixed with the proximate cause of the conduct and, therefore, would be legally responsible for it.

MR. RANDOLPH. I recognize that fact just as for instance a union may call a strike. The union does not promote the violence but the forces that are opposed to the union may create the violence.

Well now, in this instance we are definitely opposed to violence of any kind; we are definitely opposed to any overt acts that would be construed in the form of violence but, nevertheless, we would relentlessly wage a warfare against the Jim Crow armed forces program and against the Negroes and others participating in that program. That is our position.

Now I do not believe the law up to the present time has been faced with such conditions as to enable it to envisage these principles. In other words, American jurisprudence has never been faced with this kind of a condition and consequently its definition of treason could not possibly take in the type and nature of action which we propose in civil disobedience. But however the law may be construed we would be willing to face it on the grounds that our actions would be in obedience and in conformity with the higher law of righteousness than that set forth in the so-called law of treason.

Brown v. Board of Education of Topeka*

"Separate" education had never been financially *"equal."* No single Southern state had ever appropriated as much money for its Negro schools as it had for its white. In *1930,* for example, for every $7.00 spent for a white child in the South, $2.00 was used

* Brown v. Board of Education of Topeka, 347 U.S. 483 (1954).

for Negro youngsters. Since 1938 the Supreme Court handed down a number of decisions that gradually eroded the entire concept that legally separate schools could ever be made fully equal to a non-segregated educational system: Missouri ex rel. *Gaines* v. *Canada (1938), Sweatt* v. *Painter (1950), McLaurin* v. *Oklahoma State Regents (1950). With the handwriting on the wall Southern legislatures began a desperate attempt to equalize Negro school facilities by rapidly increasing expenditures or by providing financial support for the state's Negro students in Northern universities. The Court's finding in the School Segregation cases negated these actions, although some states continued to pour money into all-Negro schools after 1954. "In the field of public education," Chief Justice Warren wrote, "the doctrine of 'separate but equal' has no place. Separate educational facilities are inherently unequal."*

SUPREME COURT OF THE UNITED STATES

NOS. 1, 2, 4 AND 10.—OCTOBER TERM, 1953.

Oliver Brown, et al., Appellants, 1 *v.* Board of Education of Topeka, Shawnee County, Kansas, et al.	On Appeal From the United States District Court for the District of Kansas.
Harry Briggs, Jr., et al., Appellants, 2 *v.* R. W. Elliott, et al.	On Appeal From the United States District Court for the Eastern District of South Carolina.
Dorothy E. Davis, et al., Appellants, 4 *v.* County School Board of Prince Edward County, Virginia, et al.	On Appeal From the United States District Court for the Eastern District of Virginia.
Francis B. Gebhart, et al., Petitioners, 10 *v.* Ethel Louise Belton, et al.	On Writ of Certiorari to the Supreme Court of Delaware.

[May 17, 1954.]

MR. CHIEF JUSTICE WARREN delivered the opinion of the Court. These cases come to us from the States of Kansas, South Carolina, Virginia, and Delaware. They are premised on different facts and different local conditions, but a common legal question justifies their consideration together in this consolidated opinion.[1]

[1] In the Kansas case, *Brown* v. *Board of Education,* the plaintiffs are Negro children of elementary school age residing in Topeka. They brought this action in the United States District Court for the District of Kansas to enjoin enforcement of a Kansas statute which permits, but does not require, cities of more than 15,000 population to maintain separate school facilities for Negro and white students. Kan. Gen. Stat. § 72-1724 (1949). Pursuant to that authority, the Topeka Board of Education elected to establish segregated elementary schools. Other public schools in the community, however, are operated on a nonsegregated basis. The three-judge District Court, convened under 28 U. S. C. §§ 2281 and 2284, found that segregation in public education has a detrimental effect upon Negro children, but denied relief on the ground that the Negro and white schools were substantially equal with respect to buildings, transportation, curricula, and educational qualifications of teachers. 98 F. Supp. 797. The case is here on direct appeal under 28 U. S. C. § 1253.

In the South Carolina case, *Briggs* v. *Elliott,* the plaintiffs are Negro children of both elementary and high school age residing in Clarendon County. They brought this action in the United States District Court for the Eastern District of South Carolina to enjoin enforcement of provisions in the state constitution and statutory code which require the segregation of Negroes and whites in public schools. S. C. Const., Art. XI, § 7; S. C. Code § 5377 (1942). The three-judge District Court, convened under 28 U. S. C. §§ 2281 and 2284, denied the requested relief. The court found that the Negro schools were inferior to the white schools and ordered the defendants to begin immediately to equalize the facilities. But the court sustained the validity of the contested provisions and denied the plaintiffs admission to the white schools during the equalization program. 98 F. Supp. 529. This Court vacated the District Court's judgment and remanded the case for the purpose of obtaining the court's views on a report filed by the defendants concerning the progress made in the equalization program. 342 U. S. 350. On remand, the District Court found that substantial equality had been achieved except for buildings and that the defendants were proceeding to rectify this inequality as well. 103 F. Supp. 920. The case is again here on direct appeal under 28 U. S. C. § 1253.

In the Virginia case, *Davis* v. *County School Board,* the plaintiffs are Negro children of high school age residing in Prince Edward County. They brought this action in the United States District Court for the Eastern District of Virginia to enjoin enforcement of provisions in the state constitution and statutory code which require the segregation of Negroes and whites in public schools. Va. Const., § 140; Va. Code § 22-221 (1950). The three-judge District Court, convened under 28 U. S. C. §§ 2281 and 2284, denied the requested relief. The court found the Negro school in-

In each of the cases, minors of the Negro race, through their legal representatives, seek the aid of the courts in obtaining admission to the public schools of their community on a non-segregated basis. In each instance, they had been denied admission to schools attended by white children under laws requiring or permitting segregation according to race. This segregation was alleged to deprive the plaintiffs of the equal protection of the laws under the Fourteenth Amendment. In each of the cases other than the Delaware case, a three-judge federal district court denied relief to the plaintiffs on the so-called "separate but equal" doctrine announced by this Court in *Plessy* v. *Ferguson,* 163 U.S. 537. Under that doctrine, equality of treatment is accorded when the races are provided substantially equal facilities, even though these facilities be separate. In the Delaware case, the Supreme Court of Delaware adhered to that doctrine, but ordered that the plaintiffs

---

ferior in physical plant, curricula, and transportation, and ordered the defendants forthwith to provide substantially equal curricula and transportation and to "proceed with all reasonable diligence and dispatch to remove" the inequality in physical plant. But, as in the South Carolina case, the court sustained the validity of the contested provisions and denied the plaintiffs admission to the white schools during the equalization program. 103 F. Supp. 337. The case is here on direct appeal under 28 U. S. C. § 1253.

In the Delaware case, *Gebhart* v. *Belton,* the plaintiffs are Negro children of both elementary and high school age residing in New Castle County. They brought this action in the Delaware Court of Chancery to enjoin enforcement of provisions in the state constitution and statutory code which require the segregation of Negroes and whites in public schools. Del. Const., Art. X, § 2; Del. Rev. Code § 2631 (1935). The Chancellor gave judgment for the plaintiffs and ordered their immediate admission to schools previously attended only by white children, on the ground that the Negro schools were inferior with respect to teacher training, pupil-teacher ratio, extra-curricular activities, physical plant, and time and distance involved in travel. 87 A. 2d 862. The Chancellor also found that segregation itself results in an inferior education for Negro children (see note 10, *infra*), but did not rest his decision on that ground. *Id.,* at 865. The Chancellor's decree was affirmed by the Supreme Court of Delaware, which intimated, however, that the defendants might be able to obtain a modification of the decree after equalization of the Negro and white schools had been accomplished. 91 A. 2d 137, 152. The defendants, contending only that the Delaware courts had erred in ordering the immediate admission of the Negro plaintiffs to the white schools, applied to this Court for certiorari. The writ was granted, 344 U.S. 891. The plaintiffs, who were successful below, did not submit a cross-petition.

be admitted to the white schools because of their superiority to the Negro schools.

The plaintiffs contend that segregated public schools are not "equal" and cannot be made "equal," and that hence they are deprived of the equal protection of the laws. Because of the obvious importance of the question presented, the Court took jurisdiction.[2] Argument was heard in the 1952 Term, and reargument was heard this Term on certain questions propounded by the Court.[3]

Reargument was largely devoted to the circumstances surrounding the adoption of the Fourteenth Amendment in 1868. It covered exhaustively consideration of the Amendment in Congress, ratification by the states, then existing practices in racial segregation, and the views of proponents and opponents of the Amendment. This discussion and our own investigation convince us that, although these sources cast some light, it is not enough to resolve the problem with which we are faced. At best, they are inconclusive. The most avid proponents of the post-War Amendments undoubtedly intended them to remove all legal distinctions among "all persons born or naturalized in the United States." Their opponents, just as certainly, were antagonistic to both the letter and the spirit of the Amendments and wished them to have the most limited effect. What others in Congress and the state legislatures had in mind cannot be determined with any degree of certainty.

An additional reason for the inconclusive nature of the Amendment's history, with respect to segregated schools, is the status of public education at that time.[4] In the South, the movement toward

[2] 344 U. S. 1, 141, 891.

[3] 345 U. S. 972. The Attorney General of the United States participated both Terms as *amicus curiae*.

[4] For a general study of the development of public education prior to the Amendment, see Butts and Cremin, A History of Education in American Culture (1953), Pts. I, II; Cubberley, Public Education in the United States (1934 ed.), cc. II–XII. School practices current at the time of the adoption of the Fourteenth Amendment are described in Butts and Cremin, *supra*, at 269–275; Cubberley, *supra*, at 288–339, 408–431; Knight, Public Education in the South (1922), cc. VIII, IX. See also H. Ex. Doc. No. 315, 41st Cong., 2d Sess. (1871). Although the demand for free public schools followed substantially the same pattern in both the North and the South, the development in the South did not begin to gain momentum until about 1850, some twenty years after that in the North. The reasons

free common schools, supported by general taxation, had not yet taken hold. Education of white children was largely in the hands of private groups. Education of Negroes was almost nonexistent, and practically all of the race was illiterate. In fact, any education of Negroes was forbidden by law in some states. Today, in contrast, many Negroes have achieved outstanding success in the arts and sciences as well as in the business and professional world. It is true that public education had already advanced further in the North, but the effect of the Amendment on Northern States was generally ignored in the congressional debates. Even in the North, the conditions of public education did not approximate those existing today. The curriculum was usually rudimentary; ungraded schools were common in rural areas; the school term was but three months a year in many states; and compulsory school attendance was virtually unknown. As a consequence, it is not surprising that there should be so little in the history of the Fourteenth Amendment relating to its intended effect on public education.

In the first cases in this Court construing the Fourteenth Amendment, decided shortly after its adoption, the Court interpreted it as proscribing all state-imposed discriminations against the Negro race.[5] The doctrine of "separate but equal" did not

---

for the somewhat slower development in the South (*e.g.*, the rural character of the South and the different regional attitudes toward state assistance) are well explained in Cubberley, *supra*, at 408–423. In the country as a whole, but particularly in the South, the War virtually stopped all progress in public education. *Id.*, at 427–428. The low status of Negro education in all sections of the country, both before and immediately after the War, is described in Beale, A History of Freedom of Teaching in American Schools (1941), 112–132, 175–195. Compulsory school attendance laws were not generally adopted until after the ratification of the Fourteenth Amendment, and it was not until 1918 that such laws were in force in all the states. Cubberley, *supra*, at 563–565.

[5] *Slaughter-House Cases,* 16 Wall. 36, 67–72 (1873); *Strauder* v. *West Virginia,* 100 U.S. 303, 307–308 (1879):

"It ordains that no State shall deprive any person of life, liberty, or property, without due process of law, or deny to any person within its jurisdiction the equal protection of the laws. What is this but declaring that the law in the States shall be the same for the black as for the white; that all persons, whether colored or white, shall stand equal before the laws of the States, and, in regard to the colored race, for whose protection the amendment was primarily designed, that no discrimination shall be made against them by law because of their color? The words of the amendment, it is true, are prohibitory, but they contain a necessary implication of a positive

make its appearance in this Court until 1896 in the case of *Plessy* v. *Ferguson, supra,* involving not education but transportation.[6] American courts have since labored with the doctrine for over half a century. In this Court, there have been six cases involving the "separate but equal" doctrine in the field of public education.[7] In *Cumming* v. *County Board of Education,* 175 U.S. 528, and *Gong Lum* v. *Rice,* 275 U.S. 78, the validity of the doctrine itself was not challenged.[8] In more recent cases, all on the graduate school level, inequality was found in that specific benefits enjoyed by white students were denied to Negro students of the same educational qualifications. *Missouri ex rel. Gaines* v. *Canada,* 305 U.S. 337; *Sipuel* v. *Oklahoma,* 332 U.S. 631; *Sweatt* v. *Painter,* 339 U.S. 629; *McLaurin* v. *Oklahoma State Regents,* 339 U.S. 637. In none of these cases was it necessary to reexamine the doctrine to grant relief to the Negro plaintiff. And in *Sweatt* v. *Painter, supra,* the Court expressly reserved decision on the question whether *Plessy* v. *Ferguson* should be held inapplicable to public education.

In the instant cases, that question is directly presented. Here, unlike *Sweatt* v. *Painter,* there are findings below that the Negro

---

immunity, or right, most valuable to the colored race,—the right to exemption from unfriendly legislation against them distinctively as colored,— exemption from legal discriminations, implying inferiority in civil society, lessening the security of their enjoyment of the rights which others enjoy, and discriminations which are steps towards reducing them to the condition of a subject race."

See also *Virginia* v. *Rives,* 100 U.S. 313, 318 (1879); *Ex parte Virginia,* 100 U.S. 339, 344–345 (1879).

[6] The doctrine apparently originated in *Roberts* v. *City of Boston,* 59 Mass. 198, 206 (1849), upholding school segregation against attack as being violative of a state constitutional guarantee of equality. Segregation in Boston public schools was eliminated in 1855. Mass. Acts 1855, c. 256. But elsewhere in the North segregation in public education has persisted until recent years. It is apparent that such segregation has long been a nationwide problem, not merely one of sectional concern.

[7] See also *Berea College* v. *Kentucky,* 211 U.S. 45 (1908).

[8] In the *Cumming* case, Negro taxpayers sought an injunction requiring the defendant school board to discontinue the operation of a high school for white children until the board resumed operation of a high school for Negro children. Similarly, in the *Gong Lum* case, the plaintiff, a child of Chinese descent, contended only that state authorities had misapplied the doctrine by classifying him with Negro children and requiring him to attend a Negro school.

and white schools involved have been equalized, or are being equalized, with respect to buildings, curricula, qualifications and salaries of teachers, and other "tangible" factors.[9] Our decision, therefore, cannot turn on merely a comparison of these tangible factors in the Negro and white schools involved in each of the cases. We must look instead to the effect of segregation itself on public education.

In approaching this problem, we cannot turn the clock back to 1868 when the Amendment was adopted, or even to 1896 when *Plessy* v. *Ferguson* was written. We must consider public education in the light of its full development and its present place in American life throughout the Nation. Only in this way can it be determined if segregation in public schools deprives these plaintiffs of the equal protection of the laws.

Today, education is perhaps the most important function of state and local governments. Compulsory school attendance laws and the great expenditures for education both demonstrate our recognition of the importance of education to our democratic society. It is required in the performance of our most basic public responsibilities, even service in the armed forces. It is the very foundation of good citizenship. Today it is a principal instrument in awakening the child to cultural values, in preparing him for later professional training, and in helping him to adjust normally to his environment. In these days, it is doubtful that any child may reasonably be expected to succeed in life if he is denied the opportunity of an education. Such an opportunity, where the state has undertaken to provide it, is a right which must be made available to all on equal terms.

We come then to the question presented: Does segregation of children in public schools solely on the basis of race, even though the physical facilities and other "tangible" factors may be equal,

[9] In the Kansas case, the court below found substantial equality as to all such factors. 98 F. Supp. 797, 798. In the South Carolina case, the court below found that the defendants were proceeding "promptly and in good faith to comply with the court's decree." 103 F. Supp. 920, 921. In the Virginia case, the court below noted that the equalization program was already "afoot and progressing" (103 F. Supp. 337, 341); since then, we have been advised, in the Virginia Attorney General's brief on reargument, that the program has now been completed. In the Delaware case, the court below similarly noted that the state's equalization program was well under way. 91 A. 2d 137, 149.

deprive the children of the minority group of equal educational opportunities? We believe that it does.

In *Sweatt v. Painter, supra,* in finding that a segregated law school for Negroes could not provide them equal educational opportunities, this Court relied in large part on "those qualities which are incapable of objective measurement but which make for greatness in a law school." In *McLaurin* v. *Oklahoma State Regents, supra,* the Court, in requiring that a Negro admitted to a white graduate school be treated like all other students, again resorted to intangible considerations: ". . . his ability to study, to engage in discussions and exchange views with other students, and, in general, to learn his profession." Such considerations apply with added force to children in grade and high schools. To separate them from others of similar age and qualifications solely because of their race generates a feeling of inferiority as to their status in the community that may affect their hearts and minds in a way unlikely ever to be undone. The effect of this separation on their educational opportunities was well stated by a finding in the Kansas case by a court which nevertheless felt compelled to rule against the Negro plaintiffs:

"Segregation of white and colored children in public schools has a detrimental effect upon the colored children. The impact is greater when it has the sanction of the law; for the policy of separating the races is usually interpreted as denoting the inferiority of the Negro group. A sense of inferiority affects the motivation of a child to learn. Segregation with the sanction of law, therefore, has a tendency to retard the educational and mental development of Negro children and to deprive them of some of the benefits they would receive in a racially integrated school system."[10]

Whatever may have been the extent of psychological knowledge at the time of *Plessy* v. *Ferguson,* this finding is amply supported by modern authority.[11] Any language in *Plessy* v. *Ferguson* contrary to this finding is rejected.

[10] A similar finding was made in the Delaware case: "I conclude from the testimony that in our Delaware society, State-imposed segregation in education itself results in the Negro children, as a class, receiving educational opportunities which are substantially inferior to those available to white children otherwise similarly situated." 87 A. 2d 862, 865.

[11] K. B. Clark, Effect of Prejudice and Discrimination on Personality Development (Midcentury White House Conference on Children and

We conclude that in the field of public education the doctrine of "separate but equal" has no place. Separate educational facilities are inherently unequal. Therefore, we hold that the plaintiffs and others similarly situated for whom the actions have been brought are, by reason of the segregation complained of, deprived of the equal protection of the laws guaranteed by the Fourteenth Amendment. This disposition makes unnecessary any discussion whether such segregation also violates the Due Process Clause of the Fourteenth Amendment.[12]

Because these are class actions, because of the wide applicability of this decision, and because of the great variety of local conditions, the formulation of decrees in these cases presents problems of considerable complexity. On reargument, the consideration of appropriate relief was necessarily subordinated to the primary question—the constitutionality of segregation in public education. We have now announced that such segregation is a denial of the equal protection of the laws. In order that we may have the full assistance of the parties in formulating decrees, the cases will be restored to the docket, and the parties are requested to present further argument on Questions 4 and 5 previously propounded by the Court for the reargument this Term.[13] The

---

Youth, 1950); Witmer and Kotinsky, Personality in the Making (1952), c. VI; Deutscher and Chein, The Psychological Effects of Enforced Segregation: A Survey of Social Science Opinion, 26 J. Psychol. 259 (1948); Chein, What are the Psychological Effects of Segregation Under Conditions of Equal Facilities?, 3 Int. J. Opinion and Attitude Res. 229 (1949); Brameld, Educational Costs, in Discrimination and National Welfare (McIver, ed., 1949), 44–48; Frazier, The Negro in the United States (1949), 674–681. And see generally Myrdal, An American Dilemma (1944).

[12] See *Bolling* v. *Sharpe, post,* p. 497, concerning the Due Process Clause of the Fifth Amendment.

[13] "4. Assuming it is decided that segregation in public schools violates the Fourteenth Amendment

"(*a*) would a decree necessarily follow providing that, within the limits set by normal geographic school districting, Negro children should forthwith be admitted to schools of their choice, or

"(*b*) may this Court, in the exercise of its equity powers, permit an effective gradual adjustment to be brought about from existing segregated systems to a system not based on color distinctions?

"5. On the assumption on which questions 4 (*a*) and (*b*) are based, and assuming further that this Court will exercise its equity powers to the end described in question 4 (*b*),

"(*a*) should this Court formulate detailed decrees in these cases;

Attorney General of the United States is again invited to participate. The Attorneys General of the states requiring or permitting
segregation in public education will also be permitted to appear as
amici curiae upon request to do so by September 15, 1954, and
submission of briefs by October 1, 1954.[14]

It is so ordered.

2. RESISTANCE AND REPRESSION

Black Monday *Tom P. Brady**

*Mississippi Congressman John Bell Williams called May 17, 1954,
the day of the Supreme Court's decision, "Black Monday"—and
so it has remained in the minds of racists ever since. Some two
months later the first White Citizens' Council was formed in
Indianola, Mississippi. Members of the "Uptown K.K.K.," the
"Klan in gray flannel suits," hoped to safeguard "racial integrity"
through economic, social, and political pressures. "Integration
represents darkness, regimentation, totalitarianism, communism
and destruction," Robert B. Patterson, one of its founders, wrote.
"Segregation represents the freedom to choose one's associates,
Americanism, State sovereignty and the survival of the white
race. . . . There is no middle ground!" The bible of the Citizens'
Council in its early days was Tom P. Brady's pamphlet* Black
Monday. *Brady, a Mississippi judge, had also taught sociology at
the University of Mississippi for two years. He gathered together
scraps of pseudo-history and pseudo-ethnology, mixed them with a
fear of spreading Communism, "mongrelization," and the welfare
state, and produced a book which reflected the malaise of the*

"(*b*) if so, what specific issues should the decrees reach;

"(*c*) should this Court appoint a special master to hear evidence with
a view to recommending specific terms for such decrees;

"(*d*) should this Court remand to the courts of first instance with directions to frame decrees in these cases, and if so what general directions
should the decrees of this Court include and what procedures should the
courts of first instance follow in arriving at the specific terms of more
detailed decrees?"

[14] See Rule 42, Revised Rules of this Court (effective July 1, 1954).

* From Tom P. Brady, *Black Monday* (Winona, Miss., 1955), pp. 9–14,
44–50.

Southern racist. On its cover were pictures of Thomas Jefferson and Joseph Stalin with the admonition: "Choose you this day whom ye will serve."

EVOLUTION AND CULTURE OF THE WHITE RACE

Before the birth of Christ and the beginning of Christianity, the yellow man, through the sublime teachings of Buddha, Confucius and Lao-tze, had developed a highly religious concept. The God of India, Brahma, had furnished to its followers the consolation and hope necessary for their spiritual peace. The other great religions of the world, including Sikhism, Zoroastrianism and Mohammedanism, all came into being because of the intellectual development which these races had obtained through the merciless evolutionary struggle which had been successfully made by them.

The works of the remarkable Leonardo da Vinci, born the year in which the brave Columbus discovered America, are ample proof of the great evolutionary development which was being made by the white race. It was during this period that civilization received the colors of Titian, the lines of Michelangelo and the grace of Raphael. Dante had already written his "Divine Comedy." The immortal Shakespeare and the sublime Milton were in the offing; "Hamlet" and "Paradise Lost" were to be conceived and created. Galileo was soon to explore the airy spheres of space and to advance the science of mathematics. The explorations of the Norsemen, Columbus, Balboa and Magellan, which followed, were great strides in development, but are of less importance because their discoveries were inevitable. The true miracles were those which were to follow and were to be discovered by Darwin, Huxley, Hall, Mendel and their contemporaries. It was from the white race that Millet came, who painted the "Angelus," indescribable in beauty; Reubens, who could give to the world the "Descent From the Cross," and Cervantes, who created the confounding "Don Quixote." From the white race came a Goethe, a Rousseau, a Molière, a Bacon and a Locke.

Granting that all animate life came from one common source, protoplasm, still there arose three different species of man. The majority of Americans believe in the existence of a Divine Being in

spite of sneers from so-called intellectual communistic and socialistic snobs. The Supreme Architect of the Universe saw fit that
there should be, and are today, on this planet, three distinct species
of man. If God had deemed it wise and just that there should be
only one specie of man on this earth, the laws of heredity and the
stimuli of environment would have produced this uniform man.
There are those today who would improve upon the handiwork of
the Divine Architect and would cause the amalgamation of all
races if they had the power to do so. If the Omnipotent Creator
had willed it, this single specie of man would have been located all
over the face of the earth. The three species of man would not
have been placed in different locales.

Let us pass over an interlude of time and again take stock. In
1620, a Dutch ship landed at Jamestown. The white man was
colonizing a New World. In this Dutch ship were negro captives
taken from the west coast of Africa, approximately 137 in number. Slavery was an accepted world custom, utilized by all peoples
and nations, including the negro race. The date that the Dutch ship
landed on the sandy beach of Jamestown was the greatest day in
the history of the American negro. He should have some fitting
ceremony to commemorate it. He should set it apart as his day of
Thanksgiving.

The white man had established the arts and sciences and had
conquered the oceans. Modern commerce and world trade had
been established. The white race had evolved into a somewhat
respectable piece of humanity, quite worthy of admiration. While
the sons of other races were being educated in schools and
colleges, while Parliaments and Versailles were being constructed,
what of our negroid brother?

There is no room for boasting or arrogance. Humility and
frankness are much more in order. We find the negro hidden in the
steaming jungle, afraid of his very shadow. Bound with the fetters
of daimonology, his back is pressed against the struggle for
existence. Before him burns a slow fire. Clothed only in a loin
cloth, with a churinga stone about his neck, his teeth sharpened by
rough rocks so that they can more easily tear human flesh, he
squats and utilizes the great discovery he has made, namely, that
the point of his green spear can be hardened by a flame of fire.
Here we find the negro only one-half step from the primordial

brute. The marvelous struggle for development had been naturally and completely side-stepped. He was impervious to the Divine urge and yearning for advancement because he was handcuffed by heredity, and the negro is still so handcuffed. These are the melancholy facts, and they cannot be refuted. That was his status in 1620, and is still his status in darkest Africa.

THE ADVENT OF THE NEGRO IN AMERICA

Yes, the Dutch, Spanish, English and Yankee slave traders conferred upon a small part of the negro race the greatest benefit one man ever conferred upon another. And yet slavery is morally wrong, and all nations have had to discover this truth the difficult way.

The American negro was divorced from Africa and saved from savagery. In spite of his basic inferiority, he was forced to do that which he would not do for himself. He was compelled to lay aside cannibalism, his barbaric savage customs. He was transported from aboriginal ignorance and superstition. He was given a language. A moral standard of values was presented to him, a standard he could never have created for himself and which he does not now appreciate. His soul was quickened. He was introduced to God! And the men of the South, whether we like it or not, were largely responsible for this miracle.

How is it, then, that the American negro has been so terribly wronged and mistreated? The benefits derived from the necessary evolutionary steps, mental and otherwise, which it took the white and yellow men thousands of years to achieve, were donated to the poor, mistreated negro in the twinkling of an eye. But nothing of true and lasting value is achieved in this world without great labor and sacrifice. Since the negro could and did not think of labor, since he would not sacrifice, his reception of the benefits offered by those who did, was and has been extremely limited. The veneer has been rubbed on, but the inside is fundamentally the same. His culture is yet superficial and acquired, not substantial and innate.

The purpose of this comparison is not to embarrass or humiliate anyone. You can dress a chimpanzee, housebreak him, and teach him to use a knife and fork, but it will take countless generations of evolutionary development, if ever, before you can convince him that a caterpillar or a cockroach is not a delicacy. Likewise the social, political, economic and religious preferences of the negro remain close to the caterpillar and the cockroach. This is not stated to ridicule or abuse the negro. There is nothing fundamentally wrong with the caterpillar or the cockroach. It is merely a matter of taste. A cockroach or caterpillar remains proper food for a chimpanzee.

Though we may at times have to turn our heads and look backward somewhat, still the ideas and events which transpired from 1620 to 1896 and from 1896 to 1936, are yet so vibrant, and are still exerting such a tremendous influence upon our national life in all of its many ramifications, that they can still be considered to circumscribe us. They are interwoven into our mores, and we are frequently not conscious of their influence whatsoever.

At the beginning of the seventeenth century, the Dutch, Spanish, French, English and Yankee slave traders proceeded to appropriate the energies of man. Slavery is one of the oldest of the professions. This gentle occupation was zealously followed by our Northern associates until about 1807. Hogsheads of rum were carried to the African chieftains, who in return therefor would assist the white man in capturing and enslaving their brothers. The negro slave was of no benefit to the Northern colonists, because of his rudimentary intelligence and susceptibility to cold and its attendant diseases, except as a piece of merchandise. As the slave trade prospered, the American colonists spread westward. Land was available merely for the taking. England, France, Holland and Spain fought for the mastery of this country, England being finally victorious.

The negro could not be expected to participate in the conquest of these United States. His language consisted mostly, at the time of the Revolutionary War, of grunts, a sign language and a few words. The jargon of the jungle was in his tongue and the Congo flowed deep in his brain. He was being taught and was learning words sufficient in his new language to make known his wants. The negro has always been adept at expressing his wants and lately his demands. In the tobacco fields and cotton fields, as a beast of burden, he earned his keep, just as slaves had been doing for thousands of years before him. Jews and Egyptians had been enslaved before the negro race had been discovered, and yet one would suppose the badly mistreated American negro held a monopoly on servitude.

The negro's contribution in our struggle for freedom with England was comparable to that of a well-broken horse. When Thomas Jefferson was composing the Declaration of Independence and wrote that it was evident that all men were created equal, he did not even remotely consider the negro slaves he had purchased, domesticated, and was watching from the veranda of his home, as being men. They were primitive savages and wholly beyond the consideration of our founding fathers. When did the negro fall within the purview of our Constitution? Approximately one hundred years later. When the sale of slaves had been prohibited in this country, when the Yankee traders had been paid in full, when no possible benefit could be derived from the slaves by the Northern States and there was nothing to trade for rum, then we hear from the Garrisons, the Stowes, the John Browns, the Thaddeus Stevenses, the Charles Sumners and the rest of the reformers. The demand is made that the slaves be freed. Whose slaves? The other man's slaves, of course.

"Ethically and morally where should the blame for slavery rest? On the man who captured, transported, subjugated and sold the slave, or on the man who purchased, fed, protected and worked him?" The Northern abolitionists had the glib answer to this question. (Digest from "Whither Solid South" by Collins.)

The white race, through evolutionary development and great labor, produced many geniuses. It seems almost impossible that during this period of approximately three hundred years, the white race could have produced a John Locke, a Bismarck, a Disraeli, a Gladstone; that a Victor Hugo, a Tolstoy and a Dumas could have given to the world their remarkable writings. That, likewise, a Tennyson, a Browning, a Shelley, a Keats, a Whittier, a Longfellow, a Poe and a Whitman could sing their songs for the enjoyment, consolation and inspiration of the world.

Puccini's "La Bohème," Verdi's "Rigoletto," Gounod's "Faust" and Wagner's "Siegfried," together with Beethoven's profound symphonies, and the works of Mozart, Handel and Mendelssohn, are nothing less than miracles.

The inventions of Whitney, Fulton, Edison, Bell, Morse,

Marconi and McCormick did more for the advancement of the human race during this interim of time than can be fully appreciated.

It was from the white race that we got our Websters, our Calhouns, our Clays, our Lincolns, our Grover Clevelands and our Woodrow Wilsons. Last but not least, we find our James G. Bennetts, our Horace Greeleys, our Charles A. Danas and our Joseph Pulitzers. Could all these geniuses have been accidental? Of course not; it is the same old story repeated over and over again—figs produce figs and from thistles come thistles.

A WORD TO THE WISE

Oh, High Priests of Washington, blow again and stronger upon the dying embers of racial hate, distrust and envy. Pour a little coal oil of political expediency and hope of racial amalgamation upon the flickering blaze which you have created, and you will start a conflagration in the South which all of Neptune's mighty ocean cannot quench. The decision which you handed down on Black Monday has arrested and retarded the economic and political and, yes, the social status of the negro in the South for at least one hundred years. Provided, of course, you do not by some similar legal legerdemain place the bayonet of the Welfare State through the throat of the average Southerner. The intelligence, the training, the experience and the character of a judicial tribunal is reflected in the timbre and quality of its decisions. One rudimentary truth, which is apparently unknown and unappreciated by the high priests, is simply this: A law is never paramount to mores. Habits and customs produce folkways which in turn evolve into mores. Laws limp behind and reflect as a mirror the essence of the mores. Perhaps in the spiritual world beyond our human life a law can establish mores, but not on this planet. The Supreme Court can play King Canute to its heart's content—but laws like bullets cannot kill a sacred custom. Laws cannot remake or revise the germ plasm of a race of men. Sacred mores are invulnerable to the dagger of any Brutus. When a law transgresses the moral and ethical sanctions and standards of the mores, invariably strife, bloodshed and revolution follow in the wake of its attempted enforcement.

The loveliest and the purest of God's creatures, the nearest thing to an angelic being that treads this terrestrial ball is a well-bred, cultured Southern white woman or her blue-eyed, golden-haired little girl.

The maintenance of peaceful and harmonious relationship, which have been conductive to the well-being of both the white and negro races in the South, has been possible because of the inviolability of Southern Womanhood. Cases of moral leprosy and degeneracy have produced sporadic instances of amalgamation of whites with negroes. It is such instances as these which produced the negro hybrids of America.

There is an octaroon, or some degree of roon, who has been capitalizing on his negro blood, and who, like Christophe, has anointed and proclaimed himself the champion of the American negro; and like Christophe he, too, will meet his destruction.* Unfortunately, he will carry down with him many misguided followers. There is many a negro in Sing Sing and other State prisons today who would be free had he remained in Mississippi, Georgia, Louisiana or Alabama. The contact and intermarriage of the negro with the Northern White has been injurious indeed to both races. Inquire of the wardens of the State penitentiaries of Illinois, Michigan, Pennsylvania, Ohio, New Jersey, New York and California, or wherever the negro has congregated, for what crimes he is incarcerated. You will find that theft, murder, rape, sex crimes and aggravated assault are the predominant ones. Remembering that there are only approximately three million negroes in the North, next ascertain what percentage of the inmates of your penal institutions is Negro. You will be astounded to discover that the ratio is fantastic. The Northerner has done poorly by the negro, and yet, in contrast, we find this high tribunal adjudicating that "Many negroes have achieved outstanding success in the arts and sciences as well as in the business and professional world." (U.S. Supreme Court decision.) All the briefs of counsel representing the appellants were not available, but we presume these celebrities were cited to the United States Supreme Court. It is also in order to assume that the Supreme Court fittingly had in mind Booker T. Washington and George Washington Carver, the only two great and wise American negroes this country has produced.

* Walter White.

Of course, we should include Jack Johnson and Joe Louis, capable ex-champion prize-fighters, some track stars, the few baseball and football players. Let us not overlook Father Divine with his white Northern wife, the octoroon Walter White, Secretary of the NAACP, Paul Robeson of Soviet connections, Dr. Bunche, who was recently cleared of Communist affiliation, and, of course, Thurgood Marshall, whose argument is reechoed in the erudite sociological opinion of the Supreme Court. There also are the Louis Armstrongs, Cab Calloways and Lena Hornes. These entertainers, athletes and leaders are the artistic, scientific, professional and business successes referred to by our fawning Supreme Court in citing the moral and cultural development of the negro race. This handful of negroes, not over one hundred and fifty in number, whose contribution to American life is appreciated, is given as proof of the entire race's evolutionary salvation. Such observations are proof indeed that the comprehension of the negro and his problems by the members of the United States Supreme Court, including Justices Black and Clark, is scarcely a squirrel's leap from total ignorance.

If the Southern-born Secretary of the National Association for the Advancement of Colored People does not know the Southern negro, and we assert this to be a fact, how could you expect a man from California, or Kentucky, or Vienna, Austria, or Minnesota, or Pennsylvania, or Massachusetts, or Indiana to comprehend the Southern negro and his relationship to the white men of the South? The gentlemen from Alabama and Texas should know and will one day answer for their stupidity. What the NAACP Secretary does know and states is what he would like to see in existence— and these other above the Mason-Dixon line Justices merely regurgitate this wishful thinking.

THE SOUTHERN NEGRO

To know a man you have to live with him—not read or "thob" about him. There is no substitute for daily association in learning the character, desires and habits of another human being.

Gunner Myrdal (who probably had never seen a dozen negroes in his life until the Carnegie Foundation brought him to this country) wrote a volume on the racial problem ("An American

Dilemma"). It is based on a few uncorrelated facts, impersonally obtained, together with much theory, "full of sound and fury signifying nothing." Such nonsense could have been the reservoir from which our Supreme Court obtained some of its conclusions.

If you had a negro mammy take care of you and keep you from eating dirt; if you played with negro boys when a boy; if you have worked with and among them, laughed at their ribald humor; if you have been stunned by their abysmal vulgarity and profanity; if you can find it in your heart to overlook their obscenity and depravity; if you can respect and love their deep religious fervor; if you can cherish their loyalty and devotion to you, then you are beginning to understand the negro.

If you have had a negro man and his wife and children live and work with you on your place; if he has worked your crops, tended your cattle and performed all other obligations; if his wife has cooked your meals, cleaned your home, and watched over your children; and you, in turn, have fed and clothed all of them and protected them from anyone *who would harm them;* if you bought the school books for their children; if you have paid the installments on the car which they own, permitted them to use your gas and oil; if you have bailed the husband out of jail on Monday morning after his "crab-apple switch" had been too active in a dice game or at some "tunk" on Saturday night; if you have taken him to the doctor and had his wounds treated, paid his bill and fine without expecting to be or having been reimbursed; if, when his wife or one of his little children became ill, you provided the best medical care possible without any cost to him because of the friendship which existed between you, and if death struck his little one, you grieved with him and you bought and gave the coffin to him, in honor of the dead, because of the affection which exists between you; if you have given him, in addition to his salary, extra money at Christmas and at other times in order that he might buy some presents for the three or four illegitimate children which he acknowledges as his own, THEN you are beginning to know the negro and understand his problems. And unless you have, to some degree, approximated this relationship, then you do not and cannot understand or know the negro and his problems. As a matter of fact, you are quite ignorant on this question.

What the Supreme Court needs to do is to spend about thirty

days in Georgia, Alabama, Louisiana, Mississippi or East Texas and associate intimately with the average negro family. It should do this in August, mind you, and then the Supreme Court would have a passing understanding of the negro and his problems, and its decision would not embody within it such foolishness as *"many negroes have achieved outstanding success in the arts and sciences, as well as in the business and professional world."*

Men of the "Bible Belt" realize fully that the negro has not received the treatment which he should have received at our hands. We know, too, that no human being can mistreat another and escape paying a terrific price—that God's law of retribution is as fixed and immutable as God's law of gravity.

We will give to the negro in good conscience all that he is justly entitled to, and what we in good conscience can afford. Let us leave our gift at the altar and go right the wrongs we have committed and then return and make our offering.

It is not too late. In so far as the South is concerned, the Southern negro knows we are his friend. We have provided his material necessities when he could not do so for himself. Gradually we have opened the door of opportunity to him and will continue to do so. The South has produced some negroes of considerable wealth and ability. Doctors, lawyers, educators, ministers, businessmen and farmers can be found among them, but "one swallow does not make a summer."

Harmony and peace has reigned and a renaissance was in the offing. In a steady, evolutionary manner, the only way in which it can be accomplished, the negroes of the South were coming into their own. Contrary to the propaganda of welfare state proponents, newspapers, radios and televisions of the North, the educational facilities of the negro in the South have advanced in the past twenty years by leaps and bounds. Neither the NAACP or the reign of Roosevelt had anything to do with it. The decision of "Black Monday" will fall far short of correcting our educational maladjustments for negroes or whites. Great gulfs and inequalities exist in the white schools. The city schools of both whites and negroes are excellent, while the country schools in the poorer sections are reminiscent of Reconstruction days.

If the sociological Supreme Court and the Administration yearn so for the welfare of the negro's education in the South, and are not primarily interested in his black vote everywhere, or if they actually desire to see education nationalized in this country, a great stride toward which has just been taken, let them collaborate further. The executive branch of this Government is responsible for the personnel of the Supreme Court.

Only the most credulous could believe that the judicial and the executive branches of government in this country are truly separate and distinct. Together they should have little trouble in getting the assistance needed from the powerful NAACP. Its executive secretary should approve. The left-wing liberals, the Communist-front organizations, the welfare staters are all standing by together with the Communist-infiltrated labor unions. Let them politically coerce if they cannot persuade Congress to set aside ten or twenty billion dollars of the sixty billion dollars we have already squandered and will continue to squander among the socialistic nations of this earth, who despise and laugh at us. Let it be spent instead in the hookwormy, shoeless South. Educational palaces can be built for the Southern negro. Fabulous salaries can be paid the colored teachers. A veritable educational heaven can be produced here on earth, but unfortunately not by October of 1954, the month in which the "when" and "how" mandate was handed down for the abolition of segregation in the four States involved.

Let's not require the white South to carry the cross upon which it is to be crucified.

That the Federal Government should go into the educational business, a "consummation greatly to be desired" by the Communisms of America, should not alarm the Supreme Court. Those persons in the teaching profession who could "pass muster," and who were found ideologically desirable by the Secretary of Education, which office will, incidentally, have to be created, could continue in their chosen vocations.

The others, less fortunate, could be given jobs of lesser importance, where they could still work for a benevolent and providential government.

Could this be the "psychological" ultimate intimated in the decision? A government under law is to be supplemented by a sociological, psychological, ideological organization. The minds of our youth, white and black, in but a few years could be completely captured and regimented.

In passing, the biographies of the members of the Supreme Court, including the new Chief Justice, do not indicate that they hold any degrees in sociology or psychology, or that they taught these new-born sciences. From whom, then, did they obtain their knowledge of these subjects? Their training has been in the political arena. The fact that Mr. Warren is now Chief Justice does not destroy any opportunity nor any aspiration which he may have to become President of these United States. This fact should be borne in mind as new, unanimous decisions are handed down.

Under the First Amendment, which yet remains inviolate, a loyal, constitutional American can still speak or write his mind without fear of reprisals. We have not yet arrived at the point where the people are intimidated and freedom of thought is tabooed, but the socialization of education will produce this state of affairs.

We have long since passed those conditions, similar in temper which caused Cicero to cry in anguish, "Oh, tempora, O, mores."

The Southern Manifesto*

Obsession with the Court's ruling dominated Southern legislative proceedings in the late 1950's. "Pupil-Placement" laws were enacted as a subterfuge by which Negroes might be excluded from schools without specific reference to race. Resolutions of "interposition" also proliferated. The one from Georgia is typical: "It is the duty of the State in flagrant cases such as this to interpose its powers between its people and the efforts of said Court to assert an unlawful dominion over them." In Congress, Senator Byrd attempted to organize the entire South to resist through the "Southern Manifesto," which pledged Southern senators and congressmen "to use all lawful means to bring about a reversal of this decision. . . ." The final draft of the "Manifesto" was written by Senator Richard B. Russell of Georgia. Three Southern senators and twenty-four congressmen refused to sign—all the others did, including the entire congressional delegations of Alabama, Arkansas, Georgia, Louisiana, Virginia, Mississippi and South

* From "Declaration of Constitutional Principles," March 12, 1956; 84th Cong., 2nd Sess., *Congressional Record* (1956), CII, 4460–4461.

Carolina. Obstructionism was the order of the day, and it proved quite successful in circumventing the Court's decision.

The unwarranted decision of the Supreme Court in the public school cases is now bearing the fruit always produced when men substitute naked power for established law.

The Founding Fathers gave us a Constitution of checks and balances because they realized the inescapable lesson of history that no man or group of men can be safely entrusted with unlimited power. They framed this Constitution with its provisions for change by amendment in order to secure the fundamentals of government against the dangers of temporary popular passion or the personal predilections of public officeholders.

We regard the decision of the Supreme Court in the school cases as a clear abuse of judicial power. It climaxes a trend in the Federal Judiciary undertaking to legislate, in derogation of the authority of Congress, and to encroach upon the reserved rights of the States and the people.

The original Constitution does not mention education. Neither does the 14th amendment nor any other amendment. The debates preceding the submission of the 14th amendment clearly show that there was no intent that it should affect the system of education maintained by the States.

The very Congress which proposed the amendment subsequently provided for segregated schools in the District of Columbia.

When the amendment was adopted in 1868, there were 37 States of the Union. Every one of the 26 States that had any substantial racial differences among its people, either approved the operation of segregated schools already in existence or subsequently established such schools by action of the same law-making body which considered the 14th amendment.

As admitted by the Supreme Court in the public school case (*Brown* v. *Board of Education*), the doctrine of separate but equal schools "apparently originated in *Roberts* v. *City of Boston* (1849), upholding school segregation against attack as being violative of a State constitutional guarantee of equality." This constitutional doctrine began in the North, not in the South, and it was followed not only in Massachusetts, but in Connecticut, New

York, Illinois, Indiana, Michigan, Minnesota, New Jersey, Ohio, Pennsylvania and other northern States until they, exercising their rights as States through the constitutional processes of local self-government, changed their school systems.

In the case of *Plessy* v. *Ferguson* in 1896 the Supreme Court expressly declared that under the 14th amendment no person was denied any of his rights if the States provided separate but equal public facilities. This decision has been followed in many other cases. It is notable that the Supreme Court, speaking through Chief Justice Taft, a former President of the United States, unanimously declared in 1927 in *Lum* v. *Rice* that the "separate but equal" principle is "within the discretion of the State in regulating its public schools and does not conflict with the 14th amendment."

This interpretation, restated time and again, became a part of the life of the people of many of the States and confirmed their habits, customs, traditions, and way of life. It is founded on elemental humanity and common-sense, for parents should not be deprived by Government of the right to direct the lives and education of their own children.

Though there has been no constitutional amendment or act of Congress changing this established legal principle almost a century old, the Supreme Court of the United States, with no legal basis for such action, undertook to exercise their naked judicial power and substituted their personal political and social ideas for the established law of the land.

This unwarranted exercise of power by the Court, contrary to the Constitution, is creating chaos and confusion in the States principally affected. It is destroying the amicable relations between the white and Negro races that have been created through 90 years of patient effort by the good people of both races. It has planted hatred and suspicion where there has been heretofore friendship and understanding.

Without regard to the consent of the governed, outside agitators are threatening immediate and revolutionary changes in our public-school systems. If done, this is certain to destroy the system of public education in some of the States.

With the gravest concern for the explosive and dangerous condition created by this decision and inflamed by outside meddlers:

We reaffirm our reliance on the Constitution as the fundamental law of the land.

We decry the Supreme Court's encroachments on rights reserved to the States and to the people, contrary to established law, and to the Constitution.

We commend the motives of those States which have declared the intention to resist forced integration by any lawful means.

We appeal to the States and people who are not directly affected by these decisions to consider the constitutional principles involved against the time when they too, on issues vital to them, may be the victims of judicial encroachment.

Even though we constitute a minority in the present Congress, we have full faith that a majority of the American people believe in the dual system of government which has enabled us to achieve our greatness and will in time demand that the reserved rights of the States and of the people be made secure against judicial usurpation.

We pledge ourselves to use all lawful means to bring about a reversal of this decision which is contrary to the Constitution and to prevent the use of force in its implementation.

In this trying period, as we all seek to right this wrong, we appeal to our people not to be provoked by the agitators and troublemakers invading our States and to scrupulously refrain from disorder and lawless acts.

The Use of Violence in the South*

When legal deterrents and economic pressures failed to work, violence was resorted to. The White Citizens' Councils and varieties of competing Klans—White Knights, United Klans, Dixie Klans, U.S. Klans, National Knights of the Ku Klux Klan, Inc.—spread throughout the South. Roy Harris, president of the Citizens' Councils of America, Inc., traveled from town to town and insisted that all political issues be reduced to the single question: "Who's the strongest man for segregation?" Defiance of federal court orders should be supported with "every means and at every cost,"

* From Southern Regional Council, *Intimidation, Reprisal and Violence in the South's Racial Crisis* (Atlanta, 1959), pp. 15–20.

Harris said. "Give me segregation or give me death," an Alabama legislator proclaimed. Beatings, anonymous phone calls in the middle of the night, social exclusion, cross burnings, and worse confronted those whites who were considered "moderates" on the racial issue. What follows is a brief history of some of the typical acts of violence in Alabama from January 1, 1955 to January 1, 1959. Needless to say, this is but a representative sampling of a considerably longer list of atrocities throughout the South.

There is no simple way to distinguish the events noted in this section from those earlier reported under the heading "Intimidation" except to say that these are bigger, and if anything more purposeless. This list of 225 acts against private liberties and public peace includes:

6 Negroes killed;

29 individuals, 11 of them white, shot and wounded in racial incidents;

44 persons beaten;

5 stabbed;

30 homes bombed; in one instance (at Clinton, Tenn.) an additional 30 houses were damaged by a single blast; attempted blasting of five other homes;

8 homes burned;

15 homes struck by gunfire, and 7 homes stoned;

4 schools bombed, in Jacksonville, Nashville, and Chattanooga, and Clinton, Tenn.

2 bombing attempts on schools, in Charlotte and Clinton;

7 churches bombed, one of which was for whites; an attempt made to bomb another Negro church;

1 church in Memphis burned; another church stoned;

4 Jewish temples or centers bombed, in Miami, Nashville, Jacksonville, and Atlanta;

3 bombing attempts on Jewish buildings, in Gastonia, N.C., Birmingham, and Charlotte;

1 YWCA building in Chattanooga and an auditorium in Knoxville dynamited;

2 schools burned;

In addition, 17 towns and cities were threatened by mob action.

The list also has an item which tells of the persecution of Koinonia Farm in Georgia.*

At the time of the bombings in Jacksonville, Ralph McGill wrote in *The Atlanta Constitution:*

> The mayors of a number of Southern cities have organized to try and prevent further such outrages. This is a good move.
>
> But let us not overlook the fact that these bombings are the fruit of the tree of defiance of law and of orderly process. In all the cities represented at the conference of disturbed mayors, there had been leaders in the press, and in public life who had attacked the Supreme Court, the President of the United States, and the U. S. Attorney-General in the most reckless and abusive terms. That this inspired the criminal fringe to action cannot be denied.
>
> It is one thing strongly to exercise the unquestioned American principle of dissenting from court and political decisions. But to abuse the institutions on which our country is based in violent, defiant terms cannot do otherwise than to encourage lawlessness and to excite the criminal fringe.
>
> Irrational abuse and preachments of defiance of due process by persons in public life constitute a tree which bears the bitter fruits of bombings of churches and schools.
>
> We should not blind ourselves to this fact. To do otherwise is to engage in self-deceit.

It has been frequently said that violence and direct action never have been far from Southern folkways. This may be correct. There are also, however, other characteristics woven closely into Southern culture: graciousness, good manners, relaxed living, and political sagacity. There would be little point in compiling the record set out in the following and preceding pages unless we believed that these latter qualities will in time prevail.

ALABAMA

Birmingham, Ala.: Two discharged Birmingham police officers and a city jail warden were acquitted in federal court of depriving a Negro prisoner of his civil rights. Indictments were brought against the three men after Charles Patrick claimed he was beaten

---

* An interracial farming community founded in the 1950's.

by the officers in the jail while the warden was present. He had been jailed after the wife of one of the policemen complained the Negro had threatened her during an argument over a parking space. He later was cleared of the charges. The warden was suspended from his post for 10 days. (April 18, 1955)

Wadley, Ala.: An interracial meeting at Southern Union College was broken up by 30 men who threatened that if the Negroes did not leave, "We'll blow up the place." College President Clyde C. Flannery said all those at the meeting were Southerners and members of the Congregational Christian Church, which operates the college. He said there was a widespread belief in town that the delegates were to discuss school segregation but that actually they met to talk about international relations and primarily the menace of Communism. Flannery said he could identify six of the 30 men but would consult his attorney to decide whether legal action should be taken. Apparently, the men were not identified publicly nor was any action brought. (July 22, 1955)

Carrollton, Ala.: Three white men were charged with a misdemeanor in the kidnapping of a 21-year-old Negro, who was hit with a shotgun in a mistaken identity reprisal. Pickens County Sheriff R. R. Shields said he arrested the men on a highway after they had released the beaten and frightened Negro, Mutt Jones. Shields described the three white men as "being well thought of around here." Asked why the men had kidnapped Jones, Shields explained, "It was just a case of mistaken identity. A Negro hit one of the men's father with a blackjack and they thought it was Jones." Shields described Jones as an ex-convict and added, "Jones didn't have a mark on him. They did hit him two or three times on the head and shoulder with an automatic shotgun, though." (September 13, 1955)

Selma, Ala.: A white couple poured gasoline on a Negro woman's home and set it ablaze. (September 23, 1955)

Selma, Ala.: Four white persons forced a Negro porter into a car and drove 10 miles into the country before releasing him. The abductors apparently believed him to be another individual accused of insulting a white woman. (October 23, 1955)

Montgomery, Ala.: A bomb which exploded at the home of the Rev. Martin Luther King, Jr., leader in the fight against bus segregation, blew out windows and damaged the front porch. Mrs.

King, their daughter and a visitor were in the house but were uninjured. (January 31, 1956)

Tuscaloosa, Ala.: After a three-year court fight, a young Negro woman, Autherine Lucy, was admitted to the University of Alabama in February 1956. Friday, February 3, she went to her first class as campus police manned the corridors. That night, a crowd of 1,200 students, attracted by a burning cross, assembled on University Avenue but after exploding firecrackers, singing "Dixie" and marching through a women's dormitory area, they dispersed. The next night students massed before the Student Union Building. Outsiders were noted, trying to whip the crowd into action. The University News Bureau director said three or four outside groups were in evidence—high school pupils, workers from a nearby plant and members of an extreme pro-segregation group from Birmingham. Monday, a crowd of about 3,000 roamed the campus, jeering and cursing university officials accompanying Miss Lucy and pelting them with eggs, rocks and mud. She was removed from the campus under heavy police escort. With demonstrations reaching uncontrollable proportions, University officials suspended Miss Lucy indefinitely, expressing fear for her life. In mid-February, two Negro brothers were arrested for kicking and beating a University student in what one said was an attempt to "get even" for "the way they treated Miss Lucy." At the end of the month, U.S. District Judge H. Hobart Grooms ordered she be readmitted. Hours later, the University Board of Trustees expelled her permanently because of her "outrageous, false and baseless accusations" in allegations that the university had "conspired" in the violent demonstrations which resulted in her temporary suspension. Later, the board announced a student leader in the campus riots had been expelled, four suspended and 25 students disciplined. Judge Grooms denied Miss Lucy's petition to re-enter the university and ruled the expulsion was justified. (March, April, September 1956)

Montgomery, Ala.: The home of a young white minister who was active in Montgomery's bus boycott by Negroes was bombed. The Rev. Robert Graetz and his family were away from home at the time. Graetz, 27, the white pastor of the all-Negro Trinity Lutheran Church, has actively supported the boycott and been a member of the Montgomery Improvement Association. (August 25, 1956)

Prichard, Ala.: The Rev. Joshua Barney, 68-year-old preacher and carpenter, who sought a city council post, narrowly escaped harm when four shots were fired into his home. Barney was warned anonymously to get out of the race, as was another Negro running for the council in Huntsville. Both Negroes were defeated. (September 7, 1956)

Mobile, Ala.: A Negro's home in a white section was damaged by fire, less than 24 hours after it was peppered by a shotgun. Fire Inspector J. B. Foster said it apparently was arson. Booker T. Gulley, the owner, said windows had been smashed frequently by bricks and he had received threatening telephone calls since moving into the house a few weeks earlier. He said that he had used all his money as a downpayment for the house after a Negro real estate agent told him, "The white people are going to move out and the colored people move in." Nevertheless, after the fire, Gulley said he would move out as soon as he could sell the house. (September 27, 1956)

Montgomery, Ala.: Acid was thrown on 10 cars within a week. All but one belonged to Negroes. The exception was a car-trailer owned by a white minister who participated in a Negro-sponsored institute. He reported that his parked vehicle, emblazoned with slogans of brotherhood, was struck by acid on two successive nights. (December 10, 1956)

Montgomery, Ala.: Acid was thrown on the car of a bus boycott leader. The complaint was made to police by the Rev. Ralph D. Abernathy, pastor of the Negro First Baptist Church. (December 19, 1956)

Carrollton, Ala.: Robed nightriders fired into the home of a Negro tenant and ordered him to move within 48 hours. Sheriff R. R. Shields waited at the house, which is near Palmetto in north Pickens County, as the deadline approached but the men did not reappear. The sheriff said he had been told of a false rumor that the Negro's children were going to ride a white school bus. (January 5, 1957)

Montgomery, Ala.: Four Negro churches and the home of a Negro minister, in addition to the home of a white minister (see

Graetz, above) were bombed, less than 12 hours after a racially integrated city bus was ambushed with gunfire. No injuries were reported. (January 10, 1957)

Montgomery, Ala.: A second attempt to blow up the home of the Rev. Martin Luther King misfired. Twelve sticks of dynamite tied around a metal tube were tossed on the porch but the bomb failed to explode. (January 27, 1957)

Montgomery, Ala.: A bomb tossed between a Negro house and a filling station exploded, damaging both buildings. Three Negroes suffered cuts and scratches. This, along with the attempted bombing of the King home (see above), was another in a series of outbreaks of violence which began shortly after bus segregation was ended by Federal Court order in December. (January 27, 1957)

Birmingham, Ala.: The home of the Rev. F. L. Shuttlesworth, Negro minister and leader of the Alabama Christian Movement for Human Rights, which staged a one-day defiance of city bus segregation laws, was heavily damaged by dynamite on Christmas night. (January 1957)

Birmingham, Ala.: A city bus with 30 passengers aboard was hit four times by gunfire. Six Negro boys were arrested in connection with the shooting. Earlier, shots were fired into the Negro section of a bus and two white youths were reported seen fleeing from the scene. (January 1957)

Birmingham, Ala.: A mob of rock-throwing whites, yelling threats, attacked a white integration leader who later was fined $30 for reckless driving in making his escape. Lamar Weaver, the victim, had just left the Terminal Railroad Station where a Negro couple had tested the integration policy in a waiting room, when he was slugged with a suitcase and stoned. He was convicted at a special hearing of running a red light and reckless driving as he drove his damaged car from a parking lot through a gauntlet of his tormentors. (March 6, 1957)

Birmingham, Ala.: Hooded Klansmen slugged a television newsman and knocked him to the ground when he attempted to take pictures at a public rally. Leo Willette, news director for WBRC-TV, arrived at the rally in East Lake Park as some 500 Klansmen listened to a speaker denounce the press as "Communist inspired." Four or five men grabbed Willette. By the time police dispersed the crowd around him his camera was missing. Willette's face was bruised and his clothing muddied. (An announcement was made at the end of the rally that the camera had been turned over to policemen and would be returned to the newsman.) (March 23, 1957)

Mobile, Ala.: The fifth of a series of recent bombing attempts in the city was reported by Walter Johnson, Negro cook. He said he supposed the small bomb, thrown by a white boy on a bicycle, was the result of his living "in a mixed neighborhood." Little damage was done. (March 1957)

Montgomery, Ala.: A white man and three Negro women were arrested after an argument over integrated seating on a Boylston bus. Detective Captain E. P. Brown said there were "several entirely different stories" but the only point of agreement seemed to be that several blows were struck. The Negroes said the white man cursed and hit two of the women with a wrench after one refused to move to the rear of the bus. The man said he asked one of the Negroes to move and she slapped him across the face. All were charged with assault and battery and released on their own bonds. (April 17, 1957)

Birmingham, Ala.: Nat King Cole, Negro singer and pianist, was attacked by a group of white men as he played for a white audience in Municipal Auditorium. Six white men rushed the band leader, knocking Cole and the microphone to the floor. Police rushed from the wings, grabbed the attackers and took them to jail. Cole apparently was not injured, only stunned. Later, police said they had learned that it had been planned that 100 or 150 white men would meet at the auditorium, infiltrate the audience, overpower the band, the police and anyone else who interfered. "But the expected mob failed to show," Detective C. B. Golden said. About a week later Recorders Court Judge Ralph E. Parker imposed maximum jail sentences on four of the attackers, members of the White Citizens Council; two others were fined. (April 10, 18, 1957)

Bessemer, Ala.: A dynamite explosion knocked out windows and the side of a Negro church during a service and another blast damaged the home of Negro civic leader and union officer. No one was injured, although there were 200 persons inside at the time the explosive was ignited in an alley behind the Allen Temple Methodist Church. Police knew of no motive. Neither the minister nor the man whose house was bombed had been active in any integration drive. (April 29, 1957)

Prattville, Ala.: Three Negroes were beaten by a robed KKK group during a Klan rally here. Police Chief O. C. Burton said the beatings occurred after the Negroes "shouted and cursed" during a talk by one of the speakers. He said one of the Negroes then claimed about "25 or 30" Klansmen attacked him and his companions. The men required medical treatment but were not seriously hurt, the police chief added. No arrests were made and Burton said the Klansmen he questioned denied any knowledge of the beatings. (May 23, 1957)

Birmingham, Ala.: Two young Negro men told of being kidnapped, taken into a woods and beaten with rubber hoses. Harold Cunningham, 19, and Henry Silent, 21, said they were beaten after being questioned about where they were "two Saturdays ago." The young men and their dates said they went to a white drive-in ice cream stand, but left because it was too crowded. Then, the girls told police, they were followed by two cars, which forced their automobile to stop in a section of north Birmingham. Four white men were in each car and they had "some pistols." The men forced the Negro youths to get down on the floor of a car and told them, "One of you is going to talk before you leave." After being beaten and threatened with hanging and shooting, the Negroes escaped when all but one of the men returned to the cars. (June 11, 1957)

Birmingham, Ala.: James Henry Brock, 27, a Birmingham Negro, told police he was abducted by a group of hooded white men and beaten near Prattville, about 20 miles north of Montgomery. Brock was hospitalized with multiple bruises and cuts over his face and body which he said were caused by whips trimmed from trees. Brock said he and his wife were visiting his parents in Autauga County when two carloads of white men drove behind a car in which he sat with three other Negroes in Prattville late Saturday night. The Negro said the men, who were wearing coveralls with hoods over their heads, told them, "Don't move— stand still or we'll shoot." The other Negroes ran and "the men started shooting at them with shotguns and pistols." Apparently none was injured. Brock said he was pulled from the car, beaten and kicked, then driven into the woods where he was beaten again. He quoted one of the assailants as saying finally, "Run if you want to live—and if you get back to Birmingham, tell those niggers this is what we do to them down here." Brock ran and walked about five miles to a farm home and the owner took him to a hospital. The Autauga County sheriff said he was making a full investigation and promised Negroes would be given "full protection" against any such future incidents. Later, he indicated some doubt the whipping had occurred. (July 8, 1957)

Birmingham, Ala.: A Negro, George Johnson, reported four white men attempted to burn his home by throwing two homemade incendiary bombs on his porch. Witnesses said they saw four young white men just before the bombs were thrown and that one left the car in which they were riding and threw milk bottles filled with gasoline on the porch. One set fire to the house. Johnson, an employee of a construction company, said he knew of no reason for anyone trying to burn his house. (July 27, 1957)

Bessemer, Ala.: Two Negroes taken into protective custody were released after police officials warned them against attempted violations of the city's segregation ordinances. Blevins Stout and William Thomas were held without charge during an investigation of their attempt to enter municipal Roosevelt Park. The two men, officers of the Alabama Association for Human Rights, had asked permission to use the tennis court at the park but were denied entry by an officer at the admission office. The two were met at the park by a group of irate white citizens who warned them against attempting to enter. The Negroes left without argument. They later were escorted to City Hall by a motorcycle scout when several of the white men pursued their cars. While officers questioned Stout and Thomas about their motives, members of the white protesting group milled about the corridors of City Hall. (Aug. 11, 1957)

Stanton, Ala.: The Saturday night flogging of a white sawmill worker spurred a country-wide investigation of possible connection with recent Klan activities in the area. The victim, a 37-year-old father of six, told county authorities he was beaten by 12 or 13 white men, strangers to him, in the front yard of his home after his assailants told him, "We're tired of the way you've been treating your wife and family and we're tired of you associating too freely with Negroes." The flogging came three weeks after the beatings in

Maplesville (see below), six miles to the north. (August 27, 1957)

Maplesville, Ala.: Six Negroes were beaten in what a newspaper account said appeared to be a senseless outrage. The six men, one a soldier on leave, were watching television in the home of one of them when Ku Klux Klansmen arrived. The masked men beat the Negroes from the rear, using rubber hoses or blackjacks; four of the victims then were taken out into the road and starting running, while four or five shots were fired. They hid in a wooded area. Earlier in the evening, 22 carloads of Klansmen pulled up in front of the town hall, donned robes and marched through town. After the beatings, two of the Negroes left town. Apparently the only thing which prevented a mass exodus of other Negroes from the small town was that several influential citizens, like Raymond Stremming, operator of a veneer company, promised there would be no repetition of the Klan incident. "It is going to be easier to run the Klan off than it is for the Klan to run the Negroes off," said Stremming. Later, Stremming was threatened and warned to leave town. The town police chief, a county deputy sheriff and several of his employees stood armed guard after the threat, Stremming said. (August 1957)

Marion, Ala.: A Bibb County white man was shot in the arm during a nightrider raid on the home of a part-time Negro preacher. Circuit Solicitor Blanchard McLeon said Nathaniel Benson, 40, the Negro whose home was raided, told this story: Robed white men in three cars tossed sulphur bombs in his house at midnight and then shot at him when he went outside with his shotgun. Benson said he went out the back door shooting his shotgun "in the air" and ran into woods nearby. The incident came to light when the white man was admitted to a hospital. (August 31, 1957)

Birmingham, Ala.: A 34-year-old Negro was kidnapped and emasculated by a group of white men wearing hoods and robes. The man, Judge Aaron, was taken to a Veterans Administration hospital, where doctors said he had been severely beaten and "100 per cent" emasculated. Two months later, two members of the Ku Klux Klan, Bart Floyd and Joe Pritchett, both 31, were convicted of mutilation and sentenced to 20 years, the maximum punishment provided in Alabama. A third Klansman, Jesse Mabry, later also was sentenced to 20 years. Witnesses said Pritchett commanded a night-riding detail which set out to prove the worthiness of Floyd, who was to be promoted to captain in the Klan lair. Floyd was described as the Klansman who mutilated Aaron. In sentencing Floyd, Circuit Court Judge Alta L. King said the deed was the "most cowardly, atrocious and diabolical crime ever to come to my attention." (September 4, November 7–8, 1957) *

Prattville, Ala.: A Negro minister reported to the Autauga County sheriff that two shots were fired into his car as he drove from a revival in Prattville. The Rev. J. W. Bonner, pastor of the First Christian Methodist Episcopal church in Montgomery, said neither he nor any of his three passengers were injured. A bullet was recovered from the upholstery of Bonner's automobile. The minister said the shots were fired from a car which "contained six or seven white people" as it passed him on the highway. During the boycott of city buses in Montgomery, the minister was one of 90 Negroes charged with violating Alabama's anti-boycott law. (September 6, 1957)

Birmingham, Ala.: The Rev. F. L. Shuttlesworth was beaten and threatened with death by an angry mob when he attempted to enroll four Negro children at all-white Phillips High School. Police arrested three white men and battled a dozen more until the Negro minister could escape. Two hours later four Negro men drove by the school and tossed rocks at a window. The next day Phillips was evacuated after a bomb threat which proved to be a hoax. The same day crowds gathered around Phillips, Woodlawn High and Graymont elementary school. Police kept order except for a demonstration at Woodlawn, where the crowd threw rocks at passing cars and buses occupied by Negroes. The three schools were the ones to which eight Negro children had asked admittance. The following day, 76 Negro high school pupils were taken from their bus and questioned by police after rock throwing incidents. Later, one was convicted of throwing a soft drink bottle at a car, sentenced to six months in jail and fined $100, the maximum sentence. Six others were turned over to juvenile authorities. Three white men were charged with assault with intent to murder in the

---

* For a detailed account of this case and its subsequent disposition, see William Bradford Huie, *Three Lives for Mississippi* (New York, 1965), pp. 18–35.

beating of the Negro minister. Shuttlesworth is president of the Alabama Christian Movement for Human Rights, a pro-integration group formed in Birmingham. (September 10, 11, 14, 1957)

Evergreen, Ala.: Four Negroes were beaten by a mob in Klan regalia. The victims said the robed men accused them of NAACP membership. Two of those beaten were ministers. They apparently were chance passersby at a spot where Klansmen were gathered. The other two were accused of neglecting their children. (September 1957)

Leeds, Ala.: About 50 carloads of parents showed up at Moody Junior High School in St. Clair County after a rumor spread that Negroes would attempt to enroll. When no Negroes appeared, the parents left. The school is at Moody Cross Roads, about five miles north of Leeds. (September 17, 1957)

Bessemer, Ala.: A dynamite blast damaged the home of a Negro attorney who was attempting to open two public parks in Bessemer to Negroes. Windows in the home of David Hood, Jr., were shattered and he said some of the glass fell on him as he slept on a living room couch with a loaded rifle nearby. Hood said he had received telephone threats against his life and only two nights earlier he had dismissed three guards who had protected his home for three weeks. The house is circled with floodlights. Hood recently was convicted of violating the state firearms law by carrying a pistol. He said he had a permit which expired and that he had been unable to get it renewed. (November 1, 1957)

Birmingham, Ala.: Four homes purchased by Negroes in the once all-white section of Fountain Heights were dynamited over a period of several months. One of the homes later was damaged by fire which police blamed on arsonists. White property owners in the area have formed an association designed to prevent sales of homes to Negroes. (November 2, 1957, December 7, 1957)

Centreville, Ala.: White men horse-whipped a Negro preacher north of here. Bibb County Sheriff Carl A. Griffin said the Rev. T. D. Wesley gave this account: After preaching at a Negro church, he was driving along a country road when men in two or three cars stopped him, handcuffed him and tied him with rope. They drove him up a side road and beat him with a horsewhip, then left him, still bound, in the unlocked trunk of his car. He managed to free himself and drive to Centreville, where he was taken to a Selma hospital. Wesley said one of his assailants wore a kind of hat or hood which came over his face. The sheriff said no explanation for the beating had been uncovered. He added that he was informed Wesley was threatened once before and that his assailants vowed to get him if he talked. (November 5, 1957)

Fort Deposit.: A young Negro, Rogers Hamilton, 19, was found shot to death near his farm home. Lowndes County Sheriff Frank Ryals said that according to the youth's mother, two unidentified men "called at the house for the boy and took him away in a truck." She told officers she followed the truck for a short distance and saw her son shot to death, but that she was some distance away and could not identify the men. The sheriff said the mother first claimed the men were white, then changed her story; he said she also thought her son might have been attacked as a result of an argument over a woman. "Reports reaching the Northern press tagged the death last October 22 a lynching," the sheriff said. "However, our investigation has revealed nothing that leads us to believe these reports." (November 13, 1957)

Clanton, Ala.: Armed with hand grenades, rifles and tear gas, sheriffs and highway patrolmen from eight counties, accompanied by 150 to 200 white townspeople, converged at a barricaded Negro home. One Negro was killed and two others captured. The crowd moved on the house the day after a deputy sheriff and another white man were wounded by gunfire from ambush. The affair began one Thursday night in November 1957, when a cross was burned near the Negro section in Lomax, a small community three miles from the Central Alabama town of Clanton. Then, according to police, some of the Negroes armed themselves Friday and Saturday night in fear of Klan violence. They were watching the hill in Lomax when Deputy Sheriff Floyd Porter stopped a white motorist to make a routine driver's license check. Suddenly, a shotgun blast ripped over the car and several pellets struck a passenger. (One officer later speculated the deputies might have been mistaken for Klansmen.) Porter gave chase through an open field and as he rounded a small Negro church he was struck by a shotgun blast which almost tore off a hand and punctured his left lung. Authorities brought bloodhounds from the state prison to the church and followed a trail to the home of Willie Dunigan, 43-year-old Negro farmhand. In the subsequent gun battle, Dunigan was killed, his wife wounded seriously and four deputies suffered minor wounds. Later, police reported they were holding at least eight Negroes for questioning. Sheriff Hugh Champion denied there was evidence of any basic racial trouble and said, "It was just an unfortunate incident arising out of a tense atmosphere." (November 18, 21, 1957)

Birmingham, Ala.: A Negro school janitor said he was abducted and beaten Tuesday night by a group of white men who identified themselves as Ku Klux Klansmen. Woodrow Johnson told school authorities three white men ordered him into a car in Bessemer, telling him he was under arrest. He became suspicious when they drove into a woods instead of to jail. The men asked him if he was working for racial integration and also if he was the Rev. (Martin Luther) King. Johnson said he was struck from behind and knocked unconscious and during this time was hit in the eye. The janitor said the men put him back in the car and drove him part way back to Bessemer. He said the first three men were joined by at least five others in the woods. (December 7, 1957)

Montgomery, Ala.: A group of Negroes beat a 20-year-old white man after a Negro woman was struck by a car he was driving, the highway patrol reported. Six or seven Negro men pulled Jimmy B. Rigsby of Montgomery from his car following the accident, beat him about the head and kicked him in the ribs, the patrol said. The report said the Negro woman apparently got out of a car and was searching for a loose part when she was struck by an outside rearview mirror on the Rigsby car. She suffered a broken arm and abrasions. The attackers had fled when patrolmen arrived. (December 13, 1957)

Birmingham, Ala.: The home of a Negro family who had moved into a white neighborhood and ignored a warning fiery cross was damaged by a bomb explosion. The house, in East Birmingham, was occupied by the Otis Flowers family. The blast blew out a wall of the house and Arthur Flowers, 12, suffered a cut hand. Detectives said it was the second bombing of a Negro home within a week. (December 31, 1957)

Birmingham, Ala.: A newspaper carrier boy underwent a nose operation after being hit by a brick he reported was thrown at him by Negroes. Tim Knight, 14, said he had dropped his papers and was picking them up when he was struck by the brick thrown from a bus carrying Negro children. The incident occurred in a white neighborhood. (March 12, 1958)

Dora, Ala.: Walker County deputies sought three to five white men for questioning in the shotgun wounding of a Negro man. Deputy Alvin Phillips said Joe Harris was taken to a doctor in Praco after being wounded in the arm and side. Three other Negroes sitting in a car with Harris in front of a store in downtown Dora gave this account: The four Negro men were talking when a car carrying three to five youths between 18 and 21 years old pulled alongside Harris' car. One of the white youths pulled out a shotgun and fired one blast. The pellets struck Harris. (April 14, 1958)

Birmingham, Ala.: Fifty-four sticks of dynamite left in a satchel at Temple Beth-El failed to go off when a fuse went out. The dynamite sticks had enough power to demolish the synagogue. Harry Horwitz, administrative director of the Temple, said he could offer no explanation. (April 28, 1958)

Bessemer, Ala.: A dynamite blast shattered windows in a house where seven Negro children were sleeping, but none was injured. Mrs. Dora Mauldin said several windows were broken, boards were knocked off the house and a large hole was found near the foundation. Mrs. Mauldin said she knew of no reason for anyone to throw the dynamite at the house, which is in an all-Negro district. (May 12, 1958)

Birmingham, Ala.: Police investigated the collapse of the broadcasting tower of Negro-operated radio station WEDR. Perry L. Thompson, an announcer at the station, said the guy wire had been cut. Thompson entered the May 6 Democratic primary race for lieutenant governor but later withdrew. When the station went on the air three years earlier, the tower was damaged by vandals. (May 17, 1958)

Birmingham, Ala.: The church of a Negro leader was saved from destruction when a volunteer guard moved dynamite away from the building moments before it exploded. The Rev. F. L. Shuttlesworth said the bomb would have demolished his Bethel Baptist Church if it had not been for the "heroic deed" of Will Hall. A retired coal miner, Hall is one of six volunteers who had guarded the church each Saturday night since it and the adjoining home of the minister were damaged heavily by bombing in December, 1956. The minister said Hall found a smoking can containing dynamite against a wall of the church. He moved it to the edge of the street 30 feet away about a minute before the blast, which shattered windows and cracked plaster in the church. Following the explosion, police said the only clues were a few pieces of the metal can which held the dynamite and a vague description of a carload of white men seen passing the church shortly before the bomb was found. (June 30, 1958)

Birmingham, Ala.: Three white men faced charges of bombing the home of a Negro. The blast shattered the porch and front wall of William Blackwell's house. One child suffered a neck cut but two others escaped injury. Police said Negroes caught and beat two of the white men until the latter were rescued by officers. A third man was picked up later. The police said the suspects apparently had planned to bomb four or five Negro homes but their plan went awry when the first bomb exploded prematurely. (July 18, 1958)

Birmingham, Ala.: A jeering, milling crowd of white men and teenagers chased Negroes from the vicinity of Phillips High School. The crowd, apparently standing guard against any attempts of Negroes to enroll in the white school, grew to more than 150 and remained at the scene for more than four hours until dispersed by police. A white boy suffered a head injury when, he said, he was struck by a rock thrown by a Negro youth. Police arrested three white men who, they said, refused to move on. Negroes had attempted to enroll at Phillips a year ago, but made no attempt this year. The Negroes chased away apparently were only pedestrians passing through the area. (September 3, 1958)

Maplesville, Ala.: A Negro pulpwood worker who reportedly was kidnaped by armed white men returned home safely several hours later, Police Chief Aubrey Morrison said. A search by deputies and the highway patrol began after a report that Robert Clint Warks, 24, was kidnaped. Officers said three Negroes reported seeing Warks forced into a car by four white men, three of whom had pistols. Morrison said Warks' family "wasn't talking much" and he didn't know any details of the incident. He said he was told that the Negro was unable to identify any of the white men. About an hour and a half after the alleged kidnaping, the Associated Press in Birmingham received an anonymous telephone call from someone who said, "There has been a Negro kidnaped at Maplesville. I thought you might want to know about it," and then hung up. (Sept. 20, 1958)

Montgomery, Ala.: A heavy chain was thrown across power lines serving television station WSFA, knocking it off the air minutes after the Steve Allen Show began. One of Allen's guests was Negro star Harry Belafonte. It was the second time in less than a year that the station had been knocked out. The station was blacked out the previous time just before it was to telecast an interview with the Rev. Martin Luther King, Jr., Negro leader in Montgomery. In the latest incident, power was restored after an hour. Last August a mob of about 100 white men forced the shutdown of a drive-in theater at nearby Wetumpka when it scheduled a movie in which Belafonte played opposite a white actress. (Nov. 10, 1958)

Birmingham, Ala.: An admitted Ku Klux Klansman was convicted of bombing a Negro home and sentenced to 10 years in prison by a jury which recommended probation. Judge Wallace Gibson said he would formally pass sentence for Hubert Eugene Wilcutt on Jan. 9. Defense Attorney George Rogers told the jury if it returned a guilty verdict, "you'll see Negroes spreading out like a cancer into every white community." (Dec. 5, 1958)

*A Revival of Scientific Racism Henry E. Garrett**

Times of racial tension and crisis in the past, as in the 1830's– 1850's, and the 1870's–1890's, have traditionally led to a revival of "scientific racism." The 1950's–1960's was again such a period in our history. The amateurish views of a man like Judge Brady were superseded by those of scholars with better credentials: Wesley C. George, Professor Emeritus of Anatomy at the University of North Carolina; Audrey M. Shuey, psychologist at Randolph-Macon Woman's College in Lynchburg, Virginia; Frank McGurk of Villanova University; Carleton Putman, Yankee businessman turned popular historian, scientist and author of Race and Reason *(1961)—the book which replaced Brady's as the handbook of the Citizens' Councils. George, who also headed the North Carolina*

---

* Henry E. Garrett, "The Equalitarian Dogma," *Mankind Quarterly,* I (1961), 253–257.

Patriots, Inc., put the case this way: "Racial differences are facts that cannot be wiped away by social or political theories or by 'freedom marches,' for they are hereditary and follow the laws of genetics." The chief spokesman of this school of "scientific racists" is Henry E. Garrett, former head of Columbia University's psychology department. Garrett is the author of many articles on the inherent inferiority of Negroes and he constantly berates what he calls the "equalitarian dogma" which limits the studies of scholars who reject his views.

Up to World War I, it is probable that American scientists who gave the matter any thought at all, believed the Negro to be natively less gifted as a race than the white. The Negro was generally considered to be less intelligent and more indolent than the white, and as often lacking in the fundamental traits of honesty and reliability. And these judgments were concurred in by most white Americans.

Modern social scientists do not often accept these common-sense judgments. Instead, they hold that racial differences are skin deep; that whereas the black African differs from the white European in the breadth and depth of his civilization, there are no genetic or native factors to account for these differences, that all races are potentially equal in mental ability and differ only in their opportunity to achieve. Usually they will include motivation as a cause of racial differences, together with discrimination and prejudice.

This view that, except for environmental differences, all races are fundamentally equal has been called the *equalitarian* dogma*. It has spread through many colleges and universities, is widely accepted by sincere humanitarians, by social reformers, by crusaders, by sentimentalists and (ostensibly) by politicians. Many ministers of religion, convinced that the concept of the "equality of man" is in keeping with the ideals of Christian brotherhood and of democracy, have joined the social scientists. Last, but by no means least, the Communists vigorously defend the equalitarian dogma. Only the man-in-the-street (uninstructed in modern anthropology) remains puzzled and unconvinced.

---

* Use of the word "equalitarian" in this paper is limited to the meaning indicated above.

Equalitarianism, or egalitarianism as it is often called, finds its strongest support from two sources: the allegedly scientific group who have "proved" equality, and the religious folk who accept this proof and, on the basis of it, assert that belief in racial differences implies "superiority" and "inferiority" and as such is unchristian, shameful and blameworthy. Each camp supplements the other. The social scientists turn to moral denunciation when their evidence grows feeble, and the religious fall back on "science" to bolster up their ethical preachments. From these two directions the American people have for more than 30 years been subjected to a barrage of propaganda unrivalled in its intensity and self-righteousness. Today, in many departments of psychology, anthropology and even genetics, the equalitarian dogma has been installed as a major premise not to be questioned. Budding young scientists of independent mind jeopardize their careers by challenging the dogma and may be silenced by strong disapproval. Many college students have been strongly indoctrinated and parrot the equalitarian arguments without competent familiarity with the evidence, shifting from the "scientific" to the moralistic as the occasion requires. The northern press and many influential magazines, together with the radio and TV, confidently proclaim equalitarianism.

How can we account for the shift from a general belief in native racial differences to the equalitarian dogma? There are, I believe, five main sources which have stimulated and directed the propaganda barrage mentioned above. Let us examine these in order.

The Rise of "Modern Anthropology"

By far the most potent assault upon native racial differences from the scientific side has come from the work of Franz Boas, who may be thought of as the "father" of equalitarianism. Boas came to the United States from Germany in 1886, and for 37 years (1899–1936) was Professor of Anthropology at Columbia University.

Boas accepted the idea of races, but held that such entities differ only in culture. In the 1938 edition of his The Mind of Primitive Man (perhaps his best known work), he wrote (p. 268) ". . . it seemed barely possible that perhaps (italics mine) the race

(Negro) would not produce *quite so many* (italics mine) men of highest genius as other races, while there was nothing at all that could be interpreted as suggesting any material difference in the mental capacity of the bulk of the Negro population as compared with the bulk of the white population." This is a curious statement. Could Boas say truthfully in 1938 that the African Negro had produced *any* men to compare with the best of the European whites: to compare, for example, with Aristotle, Cicero, Thomas Aquinas, Galileo, Voltaire, Goethe, Shakespeare or Newton? On the other hand, consider the Jews, Boas' own ethnic group. By almost any criterion, the Jews have produced a disproportionate number of intellectually gifted persons, and this despite the handicaps under which they have often lived and worked. Did "culture" alone produce these outstanding men or was there better native endowment to begin with? There is much indirect evidence that Boas' devotion to the equalitarian dogma in his later years was in part motivated by strong political and social convictions. But it is hard to document this.

Boas' followers have actively and aggressively championed equalitarianism, and have discounted (and often belittled) any evidence tending to show that Negro-white differences in mental tests may not be environmentally determined. But the cultural anthropologists rarely use objective measures recognized as valid for judging the comparative worth of racial groups. In consequence, their conclusions, though confidently announced, are often subjective and unconvincing.

The view held here is that psychological tests offer the best, i.e., most valid, quantitative data for the determination of race differences. The best recent survey of the comparative standing of American Negroes and American whites on a number of mental tests may be found in the book *The Testing of Negro Intelligence* by A. M. Shuey, published in 1958. (It is significant of the power and lack of tolerance of the equalitarians that none of the university presses to which this book was submitted was willing to publish it.)

The Testing of Negro Intelligence covers the 44 years from 1913 to 1957, and analyses some 200 studies. Negro-white comparisons are made of pre-school children, grade and high school children, college students, gifted and retarded children, soldiers, delinquents, racial hybrids and Negro migrants. A brief summary of relevant findings is as follows:

1. IQ's of American Negroes are from 15 to 20 points, on the average, below those of American whites.
2. Negro overlap of the white median IQ's ranges from 10% to 25% (equality would require 50%).
3. About six times as many Negroes as whites fall below IQ 70, that is, in the feeble-minded group.
4. About six times as many whites as Negroes fall in the "gifted child" category.
5. Negro-white differences in mean test score occur in all types of intelligence tests, but Negro lag is greatest in tests of an abstract nature, for example, problems involving reasoning, deduction, comprehension and the like.
6. Negro-white differences increase with age, the gap in performance being greatest in high school and college.
7. Large and significant differences in favour of whites appear even when socio-economic factors have been equated.

It seems clear that the evidence from psychometrics does not support the equalitarian dogma.

HITLER AND THE NAZIS

Undoubtedly Hitler's cruelties and the absurd racial superiority theories of the Nazis set up a favourable climate for the proponents of the equalitarian dogma. It is easy for the equalitarian to argue that acceptance of the *fact* of racial differences is a forerunner of notions of racial superiority, discrimination, prejudice and persecution. The argument is fallacious. Recognition of differences in ability between men and women and between adults and children does not lead forthwith to prejudice and persecution; in fact, the contrary is true. Recognition of the talents of many Negroes for sports and for various forms of entertainment has if anything improved the feelings of the white majority toward Negroes generally.

Hitler's persecution of the Jews has greatly oversensitized the American Jew toward anything which smacks of racial distinction. The preoccupation of the Jews with racial matters today is evident in the activities of various Jewish organizations. Most of these belligerently support the equalitarian dogma which they accept as having been "scientifically" proven.

THE RISE OF AFRICAN NATIONALISM

The struggle for freedom and self-determination by the various peoples of Africa has aroused the sympathy of many white people, and has undoubtedly fortified the emotional appeal in the idea that all men are born equally endowed. But emotionally-founded beliefs can be deceptive. It is well known that the African Negro has been self-governing throughout most of history, the colonial period being relatively short (only 80 years in the Belgian Congo). During his long period of self-government, we find not the fantasy of the happy savage free of modern tensions, but the reality of a miserable creature tormented by disease and enemies, living a life of indescribable squalor. In the nearly 6000 years of recorded history, the African has never constructed an alphabet, created a science or literature, or built up a civilization. Toynbee, the eminent British historian, has written that of the 21 great civilizations of the past, not one has been Negro. To be sure, we are often reminded of the Negro kingdoms of West Africa which, during the 12th century, briefly attained a level of civilization relatively high for that period. But these "magnificent civilizations" as the equalitarian anthropologists call them were hardly on a par with the then flourishing civilizations of France, Italy and the Near East. Moreover, Timbuktu with its allegedly "great university" was Moslem and Arabic, while the university itself was little more than a large mosque with a few teachers.

African history offers no comfort to the equalitarian unless carefully rewritten and "interpreted."

THE SUPREME COURT DECISION OF 1954

In May of 1954, the Supreme Court of the United States handed down its decision on desegregation of schools. This decree was hailed by proponents of the equalitarian dogma, who rightly regarded it is a great victory for their cause. A great many people, however, are disturbed by the confusion of legal and moral rights and their relation to biological and psychological differences.

Both the legal and psychological aspects of the Supreme Court's decision are questionable. When the Constitution means one thing for 60 years and then overnight means just the opposite, it is hard for the ordinary citizen to be convinced that we are ruled by laws and not by men. As to the psychological aspects of the decision, many critics have pointed to the dubious credentials of the "experts" cited by the Court, and the subjectivity of their evidence.

Perhaps the only justification for the Supreme Court's decision is the view that the end justifies the means, and that the end is sufficiently desirable to risk dispensing with the Constitution to attain it.

THE INFLUENCE OF THE COMMUNISTS

Undoubtedly Communists have aided in the spread and acceptance of the equalitarian dogma, though their motives have been anything but humanitarian. Direct action as well as subversion are in the Communist creed. Hence the forceful application of the equalitarian dogma, as in the school desegregation cases, inevitably foments dissension and bitterness on which the Communist thrives. Communists and their front-men have served the cause of equalitarianism well: in government, in entertainment, in radio and television.

The weight of the evidence favours the proposition that racial differences in mental ability (and perhaps in personality and character) are innate and genetic. The evidence is not all in, and further inquiry is sorely needed. Surely there are no good reasons why restrictions should be placed on further scientific research and discussion. At best, the equalitarian dogma represents a sincere if misguided effort to help the Negro by ignoring or even suppressing evidences of his mental and social immaturity. At worst, equalitarianism is the scientific hoax of the century.

Dissenters: The Liberal South*

It has taken great courage for white moderates and liberals in the South to oppose the dominant trends of the 1950's–1960's. Many who have voiced their dissent have suffered accordingly: Charles Morgan, James Silver, the Heffners of McComb, Mississippi. Those who stood their ground and refused to be driven from the South have done a great deal to promote the racial revolution: Paul Green, Hodding Carter, Ralph McGill, William Bradford Huie, the late Lillian Smith, among others. The leading institutional expression of white Southern moderation has been the Southern Regional Council. The Council, founded in 1944, was the successor to Will W. Alexander's Commission on Interracial Cooperation. It argued that forceful political leadership at the national and local levels in the 1950's would have significantly limited the rise of Southern resistance. There is no greater mistake than viewing the white South as a monolith, it insisted: "A large proportion [of Southerners] would welcome, or at least have no objection to, a broadening of civil rights because, more keenly than do persons in other regions, they want to be emancipated from the heavy, age-old weight." Disillusioned by the failures of the Eisenhower Administration, the Southern Regional Council presented the following proposals for executive action to President Kennedy as soon as he took office. "The South should be informed where the President stands," the Council insisted. "Statements ought to be more, and not less, frequent than in the past."

THE PROPOSALS

I. The Office of the President

    A. Internal Policies and Organization

      1. An adviser on race relations could perform valuable services for the President, and could also participate helpfully in the program planning of the Commission on Civil Rights and the Civil Rights Division of the Department of Justice. There is, further-

---

* From Southern Regional Council, *The Federal Executive and Civil Rights* (Atlanta, 1961), pp. ii–v.

more, a strong case for establishment of an office, with adequate staff, to review the execution of all governmental programs and expenditures of all government funds, for compliance with the policy of non-discrimination.

B. National Leadership

2. National unity will be served best if the President speaks forthrightly to and of the South, and if he and his administration confine their statements of policy regarding racial discrimination to that which they are prepared to enforce. The President and his administration could specially contribute to the abatement of sectionalism by frequent conferences and consultations, publicized or not as they see fit, with Southern economic and political leaders, to the end of broadening the base of Southern support for civil rights and equal opportunities.

II. The Powers of the President

A. Broad Policy

3. The President, by public statement, should set as a national goal the full and free development of all our human resources, and should pledge a painstaking effort by all federal departments and agencies to administer their programs in such ways as to hasten the end of discriminations.

4. The effort of America to establish racial harmony and justice enables our people to understand the aspirations of formerly colonial peoples, and for them to identify their hopes with ours. Those who represent America abroad should interpret our racial strife and change with truthfulness and candor.

B. Federal Employment

5. There should be overall review of federal employment practices, without waiting for complaints and with the aim of immediate compliance with the policy of non-discrimination. Agencies whose functions are critically related to civil rights have a pressing need for Negro staff. Mindful of the cumulative effects of past discrimination, the government could be a yardstick for private employers by careful experimentation with techniques for the measuring of job potential.

6. Real advantages would accrue to the country from frequent appointment of competent Negroes to high level administrative posts. Negroes can be valuable assets in the representation of the

United States abroad, but not if they are used primarily in non-white capitals.

C. Education

7. We urge upon the President that he

—publicly affirm his full support of the Supreme Court's 1954 decision and his intention to employ his executive powers as needed to assure orderly compliance with it;

—publicly affirm his administration's belief that segregation is an intolerable hindrance to the national goal of higher educational standards;

—direct the Attorney-General to look closely into the authorizations he has for initiating or intervening in school desegregation cases;

—direct the Secretary of Health, Education and Welfare to assemble and disseminate, for the use of educators and the instruction of the public, educational facts related to the integration process.

8. The vast federal outlays for public school education need to be administered with scrupulous regard for the basic federal policy against discrimination. At the present time, the two areas of vocational training and schooling for children of military personnel merit special attention to insure racial equality and fair-dealing.

9. An announcement ought to be made that, at a certain date, no research funds will be granted by the federal government to any institution of higher learning (or its faculty), public or private, which refuses admission to anyone because of race, creed, color, or national origin.

D. Security of Person and Property

10. While the present turmoil continues, the Department of Justice has an obligation to enforce vigilantly the existing statutes and precedents which protect personal security, and to discharge fully the federal government's duty to preserve the public peace; in particular, every available means should be used to assure orderly school desegregation and the right of peaceable assembly and protest.

E. Voting

11. The Civil Rights Division of the Department of Justice should be staffed with an adequate number of attorneys of first quality, and the Division's working relationships with the U.S.

District Attorneys should be so defined as to permit widespread enforcement of the voting provisions of the Civil Rights Acts of 1957 and 1960.

12. A national registration drive, under the personal sponsorship of the President, should be launched, and supported by publications describing registration and voting qualifications and procedures in each state.

F. Armed Services

13. The National Guard in Southern states is the remnant of segregation in the armed services; segregation in Southern colleges and universities, and the mode of selection of academy cadets and midshipmen, restrict the opportunities for Negroes to become military officers. All of these situations are within the power of the President to remedy or ameliorate.

G. Health, Recreation

14. Health and recreational programs, both of which bring the government into close personal touch with people, need to be constantly audited for discriminatory effects. Continued observance of the "separate, but equal" clause in the Hill-Burton Act* is Constitutionally dubious, and should be authoritatively examined.

H. Transportation

15. Interstate travel is a field in which a final federal effort could decisively end segregation. The clearly established unconstitutionality of segregation in common carriers operated intra-state invites serious study by the Department of Justice of means to require observance of the Constitutional principle.

I. Contractor Employment

16. There needs to be more effective enforcement of the bar against discriminatory employment by government contractors. Large contractors can be appropriately charged with a special responsibility for positive recruitment of Negroes; and appropriate means of requiring this would be prior certification as a condition for award of contract.

17. Federal cooperation with discrimination should be ended at once in the apprenticeship and employment services.

J. Housing

18. A declaration by the President that federal housing pro-

* Providing federal funds for the construction of hospitals.

grams will be guided by a belief in the values of integration would be the soundest basis for an Executive Order prohibiting discrimination. Because the federal government has been a principal architect of housing segregation, there is special reason for it continuously to evaluate its success in reversing the process. Adverse reactions, especially in the South, are to be expected to firm policies; Presidential leadership can be decisive in allaying and overcoming them.

3. REVOLUTION

*The Use of Nonviolence Martin Luther King, Jr.**

At the end of a long day in December, 1955, Mrs. Rosa Parks boarded a bus in Montgomery, Alabama. Her feet were tired, she said, and when the driver asked her to relinquish her seat so that a white person could sit down, she refused and was arrested. This was the rather inauspicious beginning of the Montgomery bus boycott. Three hundred and eighty-two days later, after continual prayer pilgrimages, arrests, economic boycotts, petitions, bombings, and court decisions, the buses were desegregated. Martin Luther King, Jr., president of the Montgomery Improvement Association, became a figure of national prominence, the most well-known leader of the civil rights revolution. In January, 1957, Dr. King established the Southern Christian Leadership Conference (SCLC) in Atlanta, and since then has brought his tactics of massive, nonviolent resistance to communities throughout the nation. Although allusion is often made to the Gandhian influence on King, the spirit of Jesus, Christianity, and the philosophic-religious training he received at Morehouse College, Crozer Theological Seminary, and Boston University were more directly the sources of his world view. Tactically, he has acted as a skillful broker between the right and left wings of the groups involved in civil rights protest. His attitudes toward nonviolence were succinctly outlined in the following essay written shortly after the victory at Montgomery. "Oh yes, I know the words by heart now," one of his

* From Martin Luther King, Jr., "Nonviolence and Racial Justice," *Christian Century*, LXXIV (February 6, 1957), 165–167.

parishioners said; "though I need not like Engelhardt [a local segregationist], I must love him."

It is commonly observed that the crisis in race relations dominates the arena of American life. This crisis has been precipitated by two factors: the determined resistance of reactionary elements in the south to the Supreme Court's momentous decision outlawing segregation in the public schools, and the radical change in the Negro's evaluation of himself. While southern legislative halls ring with open defiance through "interposition" and "nullification," while a modern version of the Ku Klux Klan has arisen in the form of "respectable" white citizens' councils, a revolutionary change has taken place in the Negro's conception of his own nature and destiny. Once he thought of himself as an inferior and patiently accepted injustice and exploitation. Those days are gone.

This new self-respect and sense of dignity on the part of the Negro undermined the south's negative peace, since the white man refused to accept the change. The tension we are witnessing in race relations today can be explained in part by this revolutionary change in the Negro's evaluation of himself and his determination to struggle and sacrifice until the walls of segregation have been finally crushed by the battering rams of justice.

The determination of Negro Americans to win freedom from every form of oppression springs from the same profound longing for freedom that motivates oppressed peoples all over the world. The rhythmic beat of deep discontent in Africa and Asia is at the bottom a quest for freedom and human dignity on the part of people who have long been victims of colonialism. The struggle for freedom on the part of oppressed people in general and of the American Negro in particular has developed slowly and is not going to end suddenly. Privileged groups rarely give up their privileges without strong resistance. But when oppressed people rise up against oppression there is no stopping point short of full freedom. Realism compels us to admit that the struggle will continue until freedom is a reality for all the oppressed peoples of the world.

Hence the basic question which confronts the world's oppressed is: How is the struggle against the forces of injustice to be waged? There are two possible answers. One is resort to the all too prevalent method of physical violence and corroding hatred. The danger of this method is its futility. Violence solves no social problems; it merely creates new and more complicated ones. Through the vistas of time a voice still cries to every potential Peter, "Put up your sword!" The shores of history are white with the bleached bones of nations and communities that failed to follow this command. If the American Negro and other victims of oppression succumb to the temptation of using violence in the struggle for justice, unborn generations will live in a desolate night of bitterness, and their chief legacy will be an endless reign of chaos.

The alternative to violence is nonviolent resistance. This method was made famous in our generation by Mohandas K. Gandhi, who used it to free India from the domination of the British empire. Five points can be made concerning nonviolence as a method in bringing about better racial conditions.

First, this is not a method for cowards; it *does* resist. The nonviolent resister is just as strongly opposed to the evil against which he protests as is the person who uses violence. His method is passive or nonaggressive in the sense that he is not physically aggressive toward his opponent. But his mind and emotions are always active, constantly seeking to persuade the opponent that he is mistaken. This method is passive physically but strongly active spiritually; it is nonaggressive physically but dynamically aggressive spiritually.

A second point is that nonviolent resistance does not seek to defeat or humiliate the opponent, but to win his friendship and understanding. The nonviolent resister must often express his protest through noncooperation or boycotts, but he realizes that noncooperation and boycotts are not ends themselves; they are merely means to awaken a sense of moral shame in the opponent. The end is redemption and reconciliation. The aftermath of nonviolence is the creation of the beloved community, while the aftermath of violence is tragic bitterness.

A third characteristic of this method is that the attack is directed against forces of evil rather than against persons who are caught in those forces. It is evil we are seeking to defeat, not the persons victimized by evil. Those of us who struggle against racial injustice must come to see that the basic tension is not between races. As I like to say to the people in Montgomery, Alabama: "The tension in this city is not between white people and Negro people. The tension is at bottom between justice and injustice, between the forces of light and the forces of darkness. And if there is a victory it will be a victory not merely for 50,000 Negroes, but a victory for justice and the forces of light. We are out to defeat injustice and not white persons who may happen to be unjust."

A fourth point that must be brought out concerning nonviolent resistance is that it avoids not only external physical violence but also internal violence of spirit. At the center of nonviolence stands the principle of love. In struggling for human dignity the oppressed people of the world must not allow themselves to become bitter or indulge in hate campaigns. To retaliate with hate and bitterness would do nothing but intensify the hate in the world. Along the way of life, someone must have sense enough and morality enough to cut off the chain of hate. This can be done only by projecting the ethics of love to the center of our lives.

In speaking of love at this point, we are not referring to some sentimental emotion. It would be nonsense to urge men to love their oppressors in an affectionate sense. "Love" in this connection means understanding good will. There are three words for love in the Greek New Testament. First, there is *eros*. In Platonic philosophy *eros* meant the yearning of the soul for the realm of the divine. It has come now to mean a sort of aesthetic or romantic love. Second, there is *philia*. It meant intimate affectionateness between friends. *Philia* denotes a sort of reciprocal love: the person loves because he is loved. When we speak of loving those who oppose us we refer to neither *eros* nor *philia;* we speak of a love which is expressed in the Greek word *agape*. *Agape* means nothing sentimental or basically affectionate; it means understanding, redeeming good will for all men, an overflowing love which seeks nothing in return. It is the love of God working in the lives of men. When we love on the *agape* level we love men not because we like them, not because their attitudes and ways appeal to us, but because God loves them. Here we rise to the position of loving the person who does the evil deed while hating the deed he does.

Finally, the method of nonviolence is based on the conviction that the universe is on the side of justice. It is this deep faith in the future that causes the nonviolent resister to accept suffering without retaliation. He knows that in his struggle for justice he has cosmic companionship. This belief that God is on the side of truth and justice comes down to us from the long tradition of our Christian faith. There is something at the very center of our faith which reminds us that Good Friday may reign for a day, but ultimately it must give way to the triumphant beat of the Easter drums. Evil may so shape events that Caesar will occupy a palace and Christ a cross, but one day that same Christ will rise up and split history into A.D. and B.C., so that even the life of Caesar must be dated by his name. So in Montgomery we can walk and never get weary, because we know that there will be a great camp meeting in the promised land of freedom and justice.

This, in brief, is the method of nonviolent resistance. It is a method that challenges all people struggling for justice and freedom. God grant that we wage the struggle with dignity and discipline. May all who suffer oppression in this world reject the self-defeating method of retaliatory violence and choose the method that seeks to redeem. Through using this method wisely and courageously we will emerge from the bleak and desolate midnight of man's inhumanity to man into the bright daybreak of freedom and justice.

The Sit-Ins: Student Letters*

The rebellion of the young began on February 1, 1960, when four freshmen from the all-Negro Greensboro, North Carolina, Agricultural and Technical College sat down at a Woolworth lunch counter and asked for service. Their action sparked student sit-ins throughout the South. The most significant point about the sit-ins was their spontaneity. Quickly, organizers from SCLC, CORE, and other groups began workshops in nonviolent resistance with them. Ella Baker of SCLC was a key figure in gathering together a number of the leaders of the student movement in 1961 and creating a permanent organization which represented their views. Distrustful of established rights' organizations and leaders, the students opted for independent action and created SNCC. Young Negroes in the South had forgotten their "proper place," and as the movement spread it destroyed the established etiquette and

* From CORE, *Sit-Ins: The Students' Report* (New York, 1960).

mythology of Southern race relations. The following letters were written by students who participated in the 1960 sit-ins.

TALLAHASSEE: THROUGH JAIL TO FREEDOM

by Patricia Stephens
Florida A & M

I am writing this in Leon County Jail. My sister Priscilla and I, five other A & M students and one high school student are serving 60-day sentences for our participation in the sit-ins. We could be out on appeal but we all strongly believe that Martin Luther King was right when he said: "We've got to fill the jails in order to win our equal rights." Priscilla and I both explained this to our parents when they visited us the other day. Priscilla is supposed to be on a special diet and mother was worried about her. We did our best to dispel her worries. We made it clear that we want to serve-out our full time.

Students who saw the inside of the county jail before I did and were released on bond, reported that conditions were miserable. They did not exaggerate. It is dank and cold. We are in what is called a "bull tank" with four cells. Each cell has four bunks, a commode and a small sink. Some of the cells have running water, but ours does not. Breakfast, if you can call it that, is served at 6:30. Another meal is served at 12:30 and in the evening, "sweet" bread and watery coffee. At first I found it difficult to eat this food. Two ministers visit us every day. Sundays and Wednesdays are regular visiting days, but our white visitors who came at first are no longer permitted by the authorities.

There is plenty of time to think in jail and I sometimes review in my mind the events which brought me here. It is almost six months since Priscilla and I were first introduced to CORE at a workshop in Miami. Upon our return we helped to establish a Tallahassee CORE group, whose initial meeting took place last October. Among our first projects was a test sit-in at Sear's and McCrory's. So, we were not totally unprepared when the south-wide protest movement started in early February.

Our first action in Tallahassee was on Feb. 13th. At 11 A.M. we sat down at the Woolworth lunch counter. When the waitress approached, Charles Steele, who was next to me, ordered a slice of cake for each of us. She said: "I'm sorry: I can't serve you" and moved on down the counter repeating this to the other participants. We all said we would wait, took out our books and started reading—or at least, we tried.

The regular customers continued to eat. When one man finished, the waitress said: "Thank you for staying and eating in all this indecency." The man replied: "What did you expect me to do? I paid for it."

One man stopped behind Bill Carpenter briefly and said: "I think you're doing a fine job: just sit right there." A young white hoodlum then came up behind Bill and tried to bait him into an argument. Unsuccessful, he boasted to his friends: "I bet if I disjoint him, he'll talk." When Bill didn't respond, he moved on. A number of tough looking characters wandered into the store. In most instances the waitress spotted them and had them leave. When a few of them started making derisive comments, the waitress said, about us: "You can see they aren't here to start anything." Although the counters were closed 20 minutes after our arrival, we stayed until 2 P.M.

The second sit-in at Woolworth's occurred a week later. The waitress saw us sitting down and said: "Oh Lord, here they come again!" This time a few white persons were participating, secretly. They simply sat and continued eating, without comment. The idea was to demonstrate the reality of eating together without coercion, contamination or cohabitation. Everything was peaceful. We read. I was reading the "Blue Book of Crime" and Barbara Broxton, "How to Tell the Different Kinds of Fingerprints"—which gave us a laugh in light of the arrests which followed.

At about 3:30 P.M. a squad of policemen led by a man in civilian clothes entered the store. Someone directed him to Priscilla, who had been chosen our spokesman for this sit-in. "As Mayor of Tallahassee, I am asking you to leave," said the man in civilian clothes.

"If we don't leave, would we be committing a crime?" Priscilla asked. The mayor simply repeated his original statement. Then he came over to me, pointed to the "closed" sign and asked: "Can you read?" I advised him to direct all his comments to our elected spokesman. He looked as though his official vanity was wounded but turned to Priscilla. We did too, reiterating our determination to stay. He ordered our arrest.

Two policemen "escorted" each of the eleven of us to the station. I use quotes because their handling of us was not exactly gentle nor were their remarks courteous. At 4:45 we entered the police station. Until recently the building had housed a savings and loan company, so I was not surprised to observe that our cell was a renovated bank vault. One by one, we were fingerprinted.

After about two hours, the charges against us were read and one of us was allowed to make a phone call. I started to call Rev. C. K. Steele, a leader of nonviolent action in Tallahassee whose two sons were involved in the sit-ins. A policeman stopped me on the grounds that Rev. Steele is not a bondsman. I heard a number of policemen refer to us as "niggers" and say we should stay on the campus.

Shortly, the police captain came into our cell and announced that someone was coming to get us out. An hour later we were released—through the back door, so that the waiting reporters and TV men would not see us and give us publicity. However, the reporters were quick to catch on and they circled the building to meet us.

We were arraigned February 22 and charged with disturbing the peace by riotous conduct and unlawful assembly. We all pleaded "not guilty!" The trial was set for March 3. A week prior to that date the entire A & M student body met and decided to suspend classes on March 3 and attend the trial. The prospect of having 3000 students converge on the small courtroom was a factor, we believe, in causing a 2-week postponement.

Our biggest single demonstration took place on March 12 at 9 A.M. The plan was for FSU students, who are white, to enter the two stores first and order food. A & M students would arrive later and, if refused service, would share the food which the white students had ordered. It was decided that I should be an observer this time rather than a participant because of my previous arrest.

The white and Negro students were sitting peacefully at the counter when the mayor and his corps arrived. As on the previous occasion, he asked the group to leave, but when a few rose to comply, he immediately arrested them. As a symbolic gesture of contempt, they were marched to the station in interracial pairs.

After the arrests many of us stood in a park opposite the station. We were refused permission to visit those arrested. I rushed back to report this on campus. When I returned to the station, some 200 students were with me. Barbara Cooper and I, again, asked to visit those arrested. Again, we were refused.

Thereupon, we formed two groups and headed for the variety stores. The 17 who went to McCrory's were promptly arrested. The group headed for Woolworth's was met by a band of white hoodlums armed with bats, sticks, knives and other weapons. They were followed by police. To avoid what seemed certain violence, the group called off the sit-in at Woolworth's and returned to the campus in an orderly manner.

We asked the president of the student body to mobilize the students for a peaceful march downtown. He agreed but first tried, without success, to arrange a conference with the mayor.

However, the mayor was not too busy to direct the city, county and state police who met us as we neared the downtown area. There were 1000 of us, in groups of 75—each with two leaders. Our hastily printed posters said: "Give Us Our Students Back," "We Will Not Fight Mobs," "No Violence," "We Want Our Rights: We are Americans, Too."

As we reached the police line-up, the mayor stepped forward and ordered us to disperse within three minutes. But the police did not wait: they started shooting tear gas bombs at once. One policeman, turning on me, explained: "I want you!" and thereupon aimed one of the bombs directly at me.

The students moved back toward campus. Several girls were taken to the university hospital to be treated for burns. Six students were arrested, bringing the total arrests for the day to 35. Bond was set at $500 each and within two days all were out.

The 11 of us arrested on February 20 were tried on March 17. There was no second postponement. The trial started promptly at 9:30. Five additional charges had been made against us, but were subsequently dropped. During the trial, Judge Rudd tried to keep race out of the case. He said it was not a factor in our arrest. But we realize it was the sole factor. The mayor in his testimony used the word "nigger" freely. We were convicted and sentenced to 60 days in jail or a $300 fine. All 11 had agreed to go to jail but three paid fines upon advice of our attorneys.

So, here I am serving a 60-day sentence along with seven other CORE members. When I get out, I plan to carry on this struggle. I feel I shall be ready to go to jail again if necessary.

PORTSMOUTH: A LESSON IN NONVIOLENCE

by Edward Rodman
Norcom High School

Life is and always has been unpredictable. Little did I or any one else know the startling effects the first sit-in at Greensboro would have on us in Portsmouth, Virginia. The only previous integration here had been on the buses, and, very recently, in the Public Library. The Negro youth of Portsmouth had good reason to be impatient.

Our story here begins on February 12th, Lincoln's birthday. Several girls decided to observe the occasion by staging a sit-in, in sympathy with the students of North Carolina. So, after school, the first sit-in of Portsmouth's history took place. There was no violence, but no one was served. We sat until the lunch counter at Rose's Variety Store closed.

Our group was a loosely-knit collection of high school students, each with the same ideal: "Equality for All." Frankly speaking, that is about all we had in common. We were lacking organization, leadership, and planning.

By February 15th, our numbers had increased considerably. We demonstrated at two stores at the Shopping Center. Again we met no obstruction—only a few hecklers, whose worst insults we passed off with a smile. Things were looking good. The newspaper and radio reporters were there getting our story.

Our spontaneous movement was gaining momentum quickly. We were without organization; we had no leader and no rules for conduct other than a vague understanding that we were not to fight back. We should have known the consequences, but we didn't.

I was late getting to the stores the following day, because of a meeting. It was almost 4:00 P.M. when I arrived. What I saw will stay in my memory for a long time. Instead of the peaceful, non-violent sit-ins of the past few days, I saw before me a swelling, pushing mob of white and Negro students, news-photographers,

T.V. cameras and only two policemen. Immediately, I tried to take the situation in hand. I did not know it at the time, but this day I became the sit-in leader.

I didn't waste time asking the obvious questions: "Who were these other Negro boys from the corner?" "Where did all the white hoods come from?" It was obvious. Something was going to break loose, and I wanted to stop it. First, I asked all the girls to leave, then the hoods. But before I could finish, trouble started. A white boy shoved a Negro boy. The manager then grabbed the white boy to push him out and was shoved by the white boy. The crowd followed. Outside the boy stood in the middle of the street daring any Negro to cross a certain line. He then pulled a car chain and claw hammer from his pocket and started swinging the chain in the air.

He stepped up his taunting with the encouragement of others. When we did not respond, he became so infuriated that he struck a Negro boy in the face with the chain. The boy kept walking. Then, in utter frustration, the white boy picked up a street sign and threw it at a Negro girl. It hit her and the fight began. The white boys, armed with chains, pipes and hammers, cut off an escape through the street. Negro boys grabbed the chains and beat the white boys. The hammers they threw away. The white boys went running back to their hot rods. I tried to order a retreat.

During the fight I had been talking to the store manager and to some newspaper men. I did not apologize for our sit-in—only for unwanted fighters of both races and for their counduct. Going home, I was very dejected. I felt that this outbreak had killed our movement. I was not surprised the following day when a mob of 3,000 people formed. The fire department, all of the police force and police dogs were mobilized. The police turned the dogs loose on the Negroes—but not on the whites. Peaceful victory for us seemed distant.

Next day was rainy and I was thankful that at least no mob would form. At 10:00 A.M. I received a telephone call that was to change our whole course. Mr. Hamilton, director of the YMCA, urged me to bring a few students from the original sit-in group to a meeting that afternoon. I did. That meeting was with Gordon Carey, a field secretary of CORE. We had seen his picture in the paper in connection with our recent campaign for integrated library facilities and we knew he was on our side. He had just left North Carolina where he had helped the student sit-ins. He told us about CORE and what CORE had done in similar situations elsewhere. I decided along with the others, that Carey should help us organize a nonviolent, direct action group to continue our peaceful protests in Portsmouth. He suggested that an all-day workshop on nonviolence be held February 20.

Rev. Chambers organized an adult committee to support our efforts. At the workshop we first oriented ourselves to CORE and its nonviolent methods. I spoke on "Why Nonviolent Action?" exploring Gandhi's principles of passive resistance and Martin Luther King's methods in Alabama. We then staged a socio-drama acting out the right and wrong ways to handle various demonstration situations. During the lunch recess, we had a real-life demonstration downtown—the first since the fighting. With our new methods and disciplined organization, we were successful in deterring violence. The store manager closed the counter early. We returned to the workshop, evaluated the day's sit-in and decided to continue in this manner. We established ourselves officially as the Student Movement for Racial Equality.

Since then, we have had no real trouble. Our struggle is not an easy one, but we know we are not alone and we plan to continue in accordance with our common ideal: equality for all through non-violent action.

NASHVILLE: A COMMUNITY STRUGGLE

by Paul Laprad
Fisk University

There were about 30 of us in the first group of sit-inners arrested in Nashville. It was approximately 1:30 P.M. on February 27. We were escorted from the store by police—not too gently. There were cheers from hundreds of people along the sidewalks. The cheers, I fear, were for the police, not for us.

During the few minutes it took the paddy wagon to get from the store to the city jail, I reflected on what a long way we had come since the idea of sit-ins first hit Nashville. The present action climaxes nearly two years of work by Jim Lawson of the Fellowship of Reconciliation, the Rev. Kelly Miller Smith of the Nashville Christian Leadership Conference, and Nashville CORE.

Back in 1958 following the opening of the new Cain-Sloan store with its segregated eating facilities, desegregation of restaurants became a prime objective. Starting last fall, Jim Lawson, as projects director of the NCLC, began holding training sessions on nonviolence, which were attended by Fisk and Tennessee A & I students. Although Nashville was almost completely unaware of it, test sit-ins were held at Harvey's department store on Nov. 28, 1959 and at Cain-Sloan's on December 5. Hence, the movement which spread from Greensboro did not strike a vacuum when it hit Nashville.

The morning of February 10, Jim Lawson called me to say that CORE's field secretary Gordon R. Carey and the Rev. Douglas Moore had called him from Durham asking Nashville to help the North Carolina sit-ins. I told him I would talk with some of the students on campus. They were already quite excited over the North Carolina developments.

The next evening we were able to get together about 50 students from Fisk, A & I and American Baptist Theological Seminary. We decided to go into action and the first sit-in took place February 13. About 100 students participated—at three stores: Woolworth's, McLellan's and Kress's. We were refused service and remained seated until the stores closed. There was no hostility. Five days later, we tried again. This time 200 students took part and we were able to cover a fourth store, Grant's.

First sign of possible violence came on February 20, a Saturday, with school out and the white teenagers downtown. Some of them jeered at the demonstrators. At Walgreens, the fifth store to be covered, a boy got into a violent argument with a white co-ed from Fisk.

Police were present during all of these sit-ins, but did not make arrests or attempt to interfere with the demonstrators. Between February 20 and 27, however, a merchants' committee called upon Mayor Ben West to halt the sit-ins. He said city attorneys had advised him that anyone has the right to sit at a lunch counter and request service. However, he expressed the viewpoint that it is a

violation of law to remain at a lunch counter after it has been
closed to the public.

This set the stage for February 27, again a Saturday. Every
available man on the police force had been ordered into the
downtown area at the time of our demonstration. I was with the
student group which went to Woolworth's. Curiously, no police
were inside the store when white teenagers and others stood in the
aisles insulting us, blowing smoke in our faces, grinding out ciga-
rette butts on our backs and, finally, pulling us off our stools and
beating us. Those of us pulled off our seats tried to regain them as
soon as possible. But none of us attempted to fight back in any
way.

Failing to disrupt the sit-in, the white teenagers filed out. Two or
three minutes later, the police entered and told us we were under
arrest. To date, none of the whites who attacked us have been
arrested, although Police Chief D. E. Hosse has ordered an
investigation to find out why.

As might be expected, even the jail cells in Nashville are
segregated. Two other white students and I were isolated from the
others in a fairly large room, but we managed to join in the singing
which came from the horribly crowded cells where the Negro
students were confined.

There were 81 of us, in all, arrested that day. We hadn't been in
jail more than a half hour before food was sent into us by the
Negro merchants. A call for bail was issued to the Negro community and within a couple of hours there was twice the amount
needed.

Our trials were February 29. The regular city judge refused on a
technicality to handle the cases and appointed a special judge
whose bias was so flagrant that Negro lawyers defending us were
shocked. At one point, Z. Alexander Looby, a well-known
NAACP attorney and City Council member, threw up his hands
and commented: "What's the use!" During the two days I sat in
court, every policeman who testified under oath, stated that we had
been sitting quietly at the lunch counters and doing nothing else.

The judge's verdict on disorderly conduct charges was "guilty."
Most of us were fined $50 and costs. A few of the cases are being
appealed as test cases. Next, we were all re-arrested on state
charges of conspiracy to obstruct trade and commerce, but the

district attorney general has expressed doubts as to the validity of this charge and to date no indictments have been returned by the grand jury.

On March 2 another 63 students were arrested at Nashville's two bus stations—Greyhound and Trailways. They too were charged with disorderly conduct and then conspiracy. It began to look as though we might well fill the jails. The next day, however, a new development occurred. At the urging of the Friends' Meeting, the Community Relations Conference, the Ministerial Association and other groups, Mayor West appointed a 7-man bi-racial committee to try to work out a solution.

Although some Negroes expressed doubts about whether the committee was truly representative, we decided to discontinue the sit-ins temporarily to give it a chance to deliberate. However a boycott of the stores by the Negro community was started at this time. By March 25 we felt the committee had had sufficient time to answer what is essentially a moral problem and we took action again. This time we covered an additional drugstore, Harvey's, and Cain & Sloan's. Only four students were arrested—all at the drugstore. Police appeared to have received orders not to molest us.

This sit-in provoked a violent reaction from Governor Buford Ellington, who charged that it was "instigated and planned by and staged for the convenience of Columbia Broadcasting System." The charge stemmed from the fact that two CBS documentary teams had been with us for a week, filming our meetings and getting material for "Anatomy of a Demonstration." Of course, the idea that we would stage a sit-in purely for the convenience of cameramen is too ridiculous.

Meanwhile, the first breaks in the pattern had occurred. On March 16, four Negro students were served at the Greyhound bus station. . . .

The Mayor's committee announced it had been ready to report but, because of the March 25 sit-in, was unable to do so. On April 5 the committee recommended that for a 90-day trial period the stores "make available to all customers a portion of restaurant facilities now operated exclusively for white customers" and that pending cases against the sit-in participants be dropped.

The plan of the Mayor's committee was rejected by the store management and by the student leaders. The students said "The suggestion of a restricted area involves the same stigma of which we are earnestly trying to rid the community. The plan presented by the Mayor's Committee ignores the moral issues involved in the struggle for human rights." We were not prepared to accept "integrated facilities" while "whites only" counters were maintained.

Demonstrations were resumed April 11.

One final note should be added about the effects of the sit-ins here. They have unified the Negro community in an unprecedented manner. The boycott proved effective in sharply curtailing seasonal Easter business in the variety stores. On April 19, within only a few hours after the bombing of Looby's home, over 2500 demonstrators marched on City Hall. Adult leaders have assured us that, even if the students suddenly vanished from the scene, the action campaign would continue unabated. In Nashville, this is *not* a students-only struggle.

I could not close without reference to the academic freedom fight involving Jim Lawson, one of three Negro students at Vanderbilt's divinity school. He was expelled March 3 because of his "strong commitment to a planned campaign of civil disobedience." He did not actually participate in the sit-ins, but he has been our advisor and counselor throughout. His expulsion has touched off a storm of protest not only in Nashville but in academic and ministerial circles from coast to coast.

ORANGEBURG: BEHIND THE CAROLINA STOCKADE

by Thomas Gaither
Claflin College

On March 16 many newspapers throughout the world carried a photo showing 350 arrested students herded into an open-air stockade in Orangeburg, South Carolina.

I was arrested later in the day while marching in protest in front of the courthouse. I didn't realize until scrutinizing the stockade photo much later, that the scene shown was unusual—to say the least—and would provoke questions from newspaper readers unfamiliar with the local scene.

What were all these well-dressed, peaceable-looking students doing in a stockade? Why weren't they inside the jail if they were under arrest? How come that such un-criminal-appearing youths were arrested in the first place?

The story begins about a month before when we students in the Orangeburg area became inspired by the example of the students in Rock Hill, first South Carolina city where lunch counter sit-ins occurred. We, too, feel that stores which graciously accept our money at one counter, should not rudely refuse it at another. We decided to request service at Kress's lunch counter.

But first, we felt that training in the principles and practice of nonviolence was needed. We formed classes of about 40 students each over a period of three to four days. Our chief texts were the pamphlet "CORE Rules for Action" and Martin Luther King's inspirational book, "Stride Toward Freedom." In these sessions we emphasized adherence to nonviolence and discussed various situations which might provoke violence. Could each one of us trust our God and our temper enough to not strike back even if kicked, slapped or spit upon? Many felt they could discipline themselves in violent situations. Others were honest enough to admit they could not and decided not to participate until they felt surer of themselves on this issue.

After the initial briefing session, two group spokesmen were chosen: one from Claflin College and one from South Carolina State College. Their duty was to chart action plans for February 25. They checked the entrances of the Kress store and counted the number of stools at the lunch counter. The number of minutes it takes to walk from a central point on campus to Kress's was timed exactly. From our training groups, we picked 40 students who felt confident in the techniques of nonviolence. After further training and some prayer we felt prepared for action.

At 10:45 A.M. on February 25, students from Claflin and South Carolina State left their respective campuses in groups of three or four, with one person designated as group leader. The groups followed three routes, walking at a moderate pace, which would ensure their arriving at the store simultaneously.

The first fifteen students went in and sat down at the lunch counter. After they had been there about a quarter of an hour, signs were posted saying that the counters were closed in the interest of public safety.

The first group then left and another group of about 20 students took their seats. The manager then started removing the seats from the stands. Each student remained seated until his seat was removed. A few students were jostled by police. A number of hoodlums were in the store, some of whom carried large knives and other weapons, unconcealed. However, no violence occurred. By closing time the seats were still off their stands and nobody was being served.

We returned to the store next day, following the same plan of action. At first the seats were still down but by 11:30 those at one end of the counter were screwed-on and some white people were served. We students stood along the rest of the counter until 3:30. By this time, additional students had joined us and we were several rows deep. At 4, the store closed.

The next day, Saturday, we decided against sitting-in. We had sought and obtained clearance from the chief of police to picket and we were prepared to start on Monday. However, no sooner had some 25 students started picketing than they were ordered to remove their signs or face arrest. They were informed that an anti-picketing ordinance had been enacted that same day.

Inside the store, the counters were stacked with trash cans. Not more than two Negroes at a time were being permitted to enter. Each day our spokesmen checked the counter. Meanwhile some 1,000 Claflin and South Carolina State students were receiving training for the mass demonstrations which were to follow.

The first such demonstration started at 12:30 on March 1. Over 1,000 students marched through the streets of Orangeburg with signs saying: "All Sit or All Stand," "Segregation is Obsolete," "No Color Line in Heaven" and "Down With Jim-crow."

Not long after reaching the main street, the marchers were met by a contingent of state police who requested identification of leaders and asked that the signs be taken down. The group leaders were informed that they would be held responsible for any outbreak of violence and that if this occurred, they would be charged with inciting to riot. There was no violence. Only two persons were arrested, and these were *not* participants.

After the March 1 demonstration, the lunch counters were closed for two weeks. With a view to strengthening our local movement and broadening it on a statewide basis, the South Carolina Student Movement Association was established. I was named chairman of the Orangeburg branch. We initiated a boycott of stores whose lunch counters discriminate.

March 15 was the day of the big march—the one in which 350 students landed in the stockade. The lunch counters had reopened the previous day and a sit-in was planned in addition to the march. Governor Hollings had asserted that no such demonstration would be tolerated. Regarding us, he said: "They think they can violate any law, especially if they have a Bible in their hands: our law enforcement officers have their Bibles too."

Of course, we were violating no law with our peaceful demonstration. As for the law enforcement officers having their Bibles, they may have them at home, but what they had in their hands the day of our demonstration were tear gas bombs and firehoses, which they used indiscriminately. The weather was sub-freezing and we were completely drenched with water from the hoses. Many of the girls were knocked off their feet by the pressure and floundered around in the water. Among the students thrown by the water were several physically handicapped students—one of them a blind girl.

Over 500 students were arrested. 150 filled the city and county jails. That's why some 350 were jammed into the stockade, surrounded by a heavy wire fence about seven feet high. The enclosure ordinarily serves as a chicken coop and storage space for chicken feed and lumber. There are two tall iron gates. It afforded no shelter whatsoever in the sub-freezing weather.

In contrast to the cold outside, students in the jail's basement were sweating in 90-degree temperatures emanating from the boiler room. One student drenched from head to toe was locked in solitary in a cell with water three inches deep. Requests for dry clothing were denied. The Claflin College nurse who came to give first aid was halted at the court house entrance and literally had to force her way inside.

I was arrested with a group of some 200 students marching around the court house in protest over the earlier mass arrests. At first police told us we would be permitted to march if we kept moving in an orderly manner but then they announced that unless we returned to the campus at once we would be arrested. I was seized first as one of the leaders and was held in jail for four hours.

The trials of the arrested students started next day, a few students at a time. All were eventually convicted of "breach of the peace" and sentenced to 30 days in jail or $100 fine. The cases are being appealed to the higher courts.

Meanwhile, our action program proceeds. We are set in our goal and, with the help of God, nothing will stop us short of that goal.

BATON ROUGE: HIGHER EDUCATION— SOUTHERN STYLE

by Major Johns
Southern University
(till March 30 when he was expelled for
his role in the student protest)

Some Negro University and College administrations have supported their students' lunch counter sit-ins or, at least, have remained neutral. Others have taken a stand in opposition to the students. Southern University in Baton Rouge and its president, Dr. Felton G. Clark fall in this latter category.

Dr. Clark had the opportunity of taking a courageous position and becoming one of the world's most respected educational leaders. Instead, he chose to buckle-under to the all-white State Board of Education, which administers the university.

Early in March the Board issued a warning that any student participating in a sit-in would be subject to "stern disciplinary action." The sit-in movement had not yet spread to Baton Rouge but, as one law student expressed it: "When the Board spoke, it became a challenge to us and we could not ignore it." A representative student committee then met with Dr. Clark and asked, specifically, what would happen to students who sat-in. He replied that the Board had left him no alternative but to expel them.

On March 28 seven students sat-in at the Kress lunch counter. In less than 20 minutes they were arrested. Bond was set at the astronomical figure of $1,500 each. However, the money was promptly raised by the Negro community and the students were released. A mass meeting was held on campus at which students pledged support of the jailed sit-iners. The following day, nine more students engaged in sit-ins at Sitman's drugstore and at the Greyhound bus station. They remained in jail six days pending a court hearing and were released on bond April 4.

The day after the second arrests, 3,500 students marched through the center of town to the State Capitol, where we held an hour-long prayer meeting. As chief speaker, I attacked segregation and discrimination not only here in Baton Rouge but in other parts of the country.

I was unaware that this speech would sever my connections with the university before the day was over. That afternoon Dr. Clark returned from a conference in Washington and immediately cast his lot against the students. He summoned faculty members who were known to oppose the sit-ins and were furthest removed from really knowing the students. Immediately following this meeting, he announced the expulsion of 17 students, the 16 who had participated in the two sit-ins and myself.

This suddenly shifted the focus of the Baton Rouge student protest from lunch counters to the university administration. As Marvin Robinson, participant in the first sit-in and president of the senior class expressed it, we had a choice: "Which is the more important, human dignity or the university? We felt it was human dignity."

The students voted to boycott all classes until the 17 of us were reinstated. Lines were tightly drawn: the students on one side, the administration, faculty, State Board of Education, and a group of hand-picked alumni on the other. We 17 were no longer permitted on campus. But twice daily, in the morning and afternoon, we would address the students from the balcony of a 2-story house across a railroad track from the campus. By using a loudspeaker we were able to make ourselves heard by the large groups of students assembled on the campus-side of the track. This went on for two days.

Unable to get the students back to class, administration officials started calling their parents and telling them that the student leaders were inciting to riot. This move boomeranged: it caused many parents to fear for their sons' and daughters' safety to the extent of summoning them home. The administration countered by announcing that any student who wanted to withdraw from the university and go home could do so. Such a sizeable number of students applied at the registrar's office for withdrawal slips that the administration amended its ruling to the effect that these slips would have to be co-signed by parents.

Meanwhile certain persons in the community and on campus moved to negotiate a settlement. They initiated several meetings with administration officials. Dr. Clark admitted to friends that he had acted in haste, but remained adamant in refusing to re-admit the 17 expelled students. Finally, he agreed to meet with eight of the student leaders. The meeting started at 5 P.M. on April 2 and lasted until 11:30. Throughout the 6½-hour meeting over 3,000 students sat in front of the building where the meeting was held. When the eight emerged, announced their decision to leave the university, but urged the other students to stay on and return to classes, there was an outcry. Some burst into tears, others shouted that they wanted to quit also. The student leaders reaffirmed their decision and gave assurance that they had reached it on their own after the administration had agreed not to dismiss anyone else.

The following morning, however, the administration broke its part of the agreement and expelled another student. The leaders thereupon called a meeting and urged that the students stay out of class. A local citizens' committee, which had raised bail bond money and had agreed to use some of it to help homegoing students pay their transportation, requested a meeting with Dr. Clark. The upshot was that the committee reversed itself and decided that money raised could be used only for bail bond and not for students' bus or rail fares home.

Jim McCain, CORE field secretary who had come to Baton Rouge to help us, tried to dissuade the committee from this decision, but without success.

"I tried my best to show them that helping the students to leave Southern, even if the university should close as a result, would strike a real blow at segregation," McCain said.

Withdrawal of the transportation funds was responsible for reducing considerably the total number of students who withdrew in protest. Nevertheless, the number who left on the weekend of April 2 was in the thousands. Of those, between 1,000 and 1,500 have not yet returned. As I write this, I do not know the exact number of students who permanently withdrew to protest an administration which serves segregation and discounts human dignity.

The protest movement by students at Southern will long be remembered in Baton Rouge. One instructor died, another had a heart attack and we are told that Dr. Clark is under medical care. It is reported by persons close to Dr. Clark that he has received several hundred letters and wires from all over the world—not one of them complimentary. Dr. Clark, I am sure, has lost many friends because of the position he has taken against his students. Until this protest, Southern University was an island unto itself. Dr. Clark was its president since 1938 and his father was its president from 1914 until 1938. Southern University will not be able to live by itself any longer. How far the community will proceed in continuing the movement which the students have started, only time will tell. But segregation in Baton Rouge has received a severe jolt.

The North: "We Walk So They May Sit"

by Martin Smolin
Columbia University

This slogan, used widely on picket signs, summarizes the aim of thousands outside the south. National picketing and boycott of variety-store chains which segregate at their counters in the south is aimed at showing them that segregation does not pay.

In an article headed "Campuses in North Back Southern Students," McCandlish Phillips wrote recently in the New York Times: "The present campus generation has been accused of self-concern and a pallid indifference to social or political questions. This issue appears to have aroused it as have few others."

This is definitely true, not only of students in the north but in the midwest and far west, from the smallest college to the "big three," Yale, Harvard and Princeton.

At New Haven, 35 Yale medical students picketed local variety stores in four shifts. At Saratoga Springs, 20 Skidmore College faculty members joined 200 college girls in a demonstration.

These are typical of student activities which are taking place from coast to coast. While initiated on individual campuses, these activities are supported by such national student organizations as the National Student Association and the National Student Christian Federation.

In college towns, picketing of the variety stores has been established by the students, themselves. In the cities, college, as well as high school students, have been the mainstay of picket lines organized by CORE, NAACP and other established organizations. Labor unions have helped by manning many picket lines.

This is the case in New York where I, a student at Columbia University, have been a CORE picket captain. We set up our orginal picket line at a Woolworth store in the heart of Harlem on the second Saturday after the Greensboro sit-in. Within a half hour the store was cleared of customers. Hardly anybody on this busy thoroughfare crossed our picket lines. I looked in through the glass doors and could see that the employees looked puzzled at the store's emptiness on such a busy Saturday afternoon.

Passersby voiced approval of the picketing. Many asked to join the line and some did.

One woman told me she would be glad to join, but she was waiting for her husband. For a while I observed her watching from a distance. Then, a man arrived and she came over to me saying: "My husband and I would like to help: what can we do?" They stayed three hours distributing leaflets and returned the following Saturday to hand them out the entire afternoon.

On a cold February afternoon, a young man appeared on the picket line looking half-frozen. "Am I glad you showed up: I've been waiting for you since 9 o'clock," he said. "But we weren't scheduled to start picketing until 2," I told him. "Well, I read in the newspaper that CORE was going to picket this store, but the article didn't give the starting time, so I just took the morning train in and decided to wait for you," he explained. "The train?," I asked in surprise. "Yes, I live in Lakewood, New Jersey," he said. Lakewood is 75 miles from New York.

Not everyone is this devoted, yet this is not an untypical example of the support our picket lines have received. At one Woolworth store the manager, himself, expressed support. As we were about to end our picketing for the day, he signaled to me and said: "I've heard about the work you people are doing and agree with you 100%. I think we must integrate our stores in the South."

At another Woolworth store, a Bible concessionaire came out and told me: "You're losing me business like crazy—but don't stop. I'd even join you if I didn't have my concession here." As he went back into the store, he added: "I guess people have been reading my product lately."

When nine southern students whom CORE brought north to tell their story, joined our picket line on 125th Street, I asked how it made them feel to observe our activities in this part of the country. "It makes us feel that we are not alone in our struggle," is the way Merritt Spaulding, a student who had been arrested in Tallahassee, expressed it. This, together with the sympathy demonstrated each week on the picket line, has given me great encouragement.

People have asked me why northerners—especially white people who have been in the majority in our picket demonstrations in New York—take an active part in an issue which doesn't concern them. My answer is that injustice anywhere is everybody's concern.

Sitting at a lunch counter may seem like a small thing to some, but the right to do so is inextricably bound up with the American idea of equality for all. The world's eyes are upon us. We and our democracy are on trial. All of us are being judged by what occurred in Little Rock in recent years and by what is happening in the south today.

That is why students in the north have identified themselves with the movement in the south. U.S. students have been challenged to shake off their traditional political apathy and take a stand.

As a student at Columbia University and as a member of New York CORE, I am aware that northern students have wanted to speak out for integration for some time. But, aside from listening to speeches with which we agreed—there was little to do.

We were waiting for the leadership to come from the south. Now, the lunch counter sit-ins have given us the awaited opportunity to act. We intend to keep up the picketing and the boycott of variety stores until lunch counter discrimination is eliminated in the south—as it has been in other parts of the country.

The Confrontation with the Southern Power Structure*

The sit-ins of 1960 were followed by the CORE-sponsored freedom rides of 1961 and SNCC's voter registration project. Those

* From CORE, *Justice?* (New York, 1962).

*involved received an instant course in sociology, as the hazy and
textbookish phrase "power structure" became the reality of the
mayors, merchants, sheriffs, and voter-registrars they confronted.
Plans to challenge established authority often had the air of battle
preparations: road maps were studied, engines fixed to permit high
speeds, rear lights rigged so that they might be turned off when
traveling at night, codes devised to confuse anyone tapping telephone lines, and so on. In May, 1962, a number of rights workers
described these experiences to an ad hoc committee of prominent
Americans interested in civil liberties. Their testimony follows.*

First witness Ronnie Moore, chairman of Baton Rouge, La.,
CORE, is twenty-one years old. A sophomore at Southern University majoring in sociology with the intention of becoming a minister, he was expelled last January for leading student civil rights
action. Charged with criminal anarchy, he goes to trial in Baton
Rouge in mid-September, 1962.

He said that in November, 1961, he helped organize a CORE
chapter at Southern University, the largest Negro university in the
world, and that month tried to negotiate with merchants of twelve
stores in nearby Baton Rouge toward desegregation of lunch
counters and jobs. When merchants refused to see him CORE
started a selective-buying program and, on December 7th and 8th,
he directed a CORE workshop for about 170 students.

Q. What is a workshop, Mr. Moore?

A. Something like a school. We teach the rights of American
citizenship, the right to picket, and we expose persons to the
philosophy of non-violence.

Q. What was the outcome of the workshop?

A. The students went into the community, sat-in at the lunch
counters.

Q. You were denied service, you were told to leave and you did
leave?

A. Right.

Q. Then what happened?

A. On December 14th we decided to exercise our right to
picket. We regarded that in America we had this right, and we still
believe we have this right. Twenty-three students who picketed the

stores for a minute and a half were arrested for obstructing the sidewalks.

Q. Were they obstructing the sidewalks?

A. They were picketing like the labor unions picket, in orderly manner, walking on the end of the sidewalk.

Q. Then what happened?

A. That evening I and a few others addressed a rally on campus. We discussed the unlawful arrest of the students, and decided we should go down to Baton Rouge the next day in non-violent fashion to redress our grievances with the parish officials.

Q. How did you intend to do that?

A. We intended to ride buses and catch cabs and go in automobiles down to Third Street and march two by two to the court house. We would sing and make a few statements in protest of the denial of the right to picket.

Q. Did you do that?

A. Well, as students moved off campus they were arrested, about fifty. Bus drivers were arrested.

Q. For what?

A. They claim the buses were overloaded and a lot of things, and ordered students back to the campus. As police pulled students off the buses, students continued to walk for seven miles to the courthouse.

Q. How many students participated?

A. Around 3,000 to 4,000.

Q. You were not in the walk but were operating a sound truck, directing students?

A. Right. I was arrested for illegal use of a sound truck. I created a nuisance by a protest of segregation in an all-Negro neighborhood.

Q. In your opinion you were welcome?

A. I think so.

Q. Is a license required?

A. A license is not required.

Q. Are sound trucks used generally in that area?

A. Politicians use them each and every year.

I was in jail about six hours, then my attorneys posted $1500 cash bond, and I came downstairs from the cell, and as I was going out of the door I was re-arrested, charged with conspiracy to commit criminal mischief, taken back to jail, and an additional $2000 bond.

Q. Do you know what criminal mischief is?

A. It was brought out that criminal mischief had something to do with the non-violent workshop.

Q. The additional bond was posted?

A. Twenty-one days later, when I was released.

Q. Have you comment about treatment in jail?

A. Well, there were three incidents of police brutality. I made three requests to see a doctor. They were ignored, so I knocked on the door to go out. One officer reached through the bars and choked me and slapped me.

I spoke of the incident to students there and Dave Dennis, of CORE, approached the door to inquire about the beating. They opened the door to the Negro cell and reached in and grabbed Dennis. One officer pulled him up and slammed him against the iron bars and put him in solitary. Jerome Smith, of CORE, was beaten.

When we came out of jail we reported these incidents to the local FBI and they went to investigate with local police officers, and came out with "no violation of civil rights."

(On January 4th, Ronnie Moore and seventy-two other students returned to Southern University with the pledge of Dr. Felton G. Clark, its Negro president, that he would not expel them although the all-white State Board of Education demanded their dismissal. On the night of the 17th when it became known that Dr. Clark would expel seven CORE leaders, 1500 students gathered before his home to ask why. Dr. Clark refused to appear. The next morning he announced the closing of the university by five o'clock that afternoon and ordered all students off-campus by that hour. After attending court, Ronnie Moore returned to campus shortly before five, and after half an hour met his friend, Weldon Rougeau, at the gymnasium.)

Q. Were you arrested?

A. Yes. It was raining so we went under the ramp of the gym

and two officers came up and asked our names and said, "You are
under arrest for criminal trespass and for disturbing the peace."

Q. Were there other students on campus?

A. Yes, over 500.

Q. Were any of them arrested?

A. No. The officers pointed out that all seven CORE leaders
will be arrested. "You find the seven, you arrest them."

Q. Were you doing anything other than standing out of the
rain?

A. I wasn't, no. We were talking.

Q. You were taken back to jail?

A. Yes, placed under $3000 cash bond.

Q. Bringing your collective bond to $6000?

A. Right.

Q. Do you know the maximum penalty for disturbing the
peace?

A. Six months in jail and a $50 or $100 fine, something like
that.

Well, we (Moore and Rougeau) had to stay in jail in the same
cell. It was a solitary confinement cell seven by seven feet. We
stayed there fifty-eight days until bond could be raised.

Q. An additional charge was placed against you on February
12th?

A. Yes, the charge was criminal anarchy. It means I advocated
in public and private opposition to the state of Louisiana by
unlawful means.

Q. Bond?

A. $12,500.

Q. What is the penalty for criminal anarchy?

A. The count is ten years in the state penitentiary at hard labor.

Roger Baldwin: You are the first person likely to be tried under
the criminal anarchy statute in Louisiana?

A. First likely to be tried.

Telford Taylor*: Did you say there is no specification in the
indictment as to what the basis of this criminal anarchy charge is?

Carl Rachlin†: None whatsoever. I hope to stay proceedings

---

* Prosecutor at Nuremburg trials.
† CORE's counsel.

until a bill of particulars is supplied and test whether this is a denial of due process, if necessary all the way to the Supreme Court. Because, if Ronnie Moore should be convicted the sentence could be more than five years, and it's my understanding of Louisiana law that if the sentence is more than five years we may not have a right to bail and he will rot in jail while we appeal the case, which may take years, as you know.

The Rev. Elton B. Cox, Congregational minister of High Point, N.C., and CORE field secretary, helped direct the non-violent workshop, addressed the student rally at which it was decided to march to Baton Rouge, and after Ronnie Moore's arrest took charge of the protest at the court house.

The Rev. Cox: When we arrived there was the whole fire department waiting for us, and 300 sheriff's deputies and the city police force. With officials we discussed the program. We intended to sing one stanza of "God Bless America," recite the Lord's Prayer, make allegiance to the flag and hear an address by me, to protest the arrest of the twenty-three. An officer said, "Get on with it, get it over."

At the close of the program the students upstairs in the jail sang back to us. When the songs came out of the jail students in the street shouted in praise. It was at this moment that the tear gas shells were thrown, about forty-seven just in front of the court house. Students ran, trying to get to higher ground.

When we regathered and marched on Third Street and Main Street we were tear-gassed again and they sicked the dogs on us. The city of Baton Rouge has two German shepherd police dogs. Dogs attacked the college students, tore the student's coats. More than 300 students were treated later at the college infirmary for dog bites, or being trampled, or inhaling tear gas.

I was arrested, charged with failing to obey an officer, and criminal mischief, and remained in solitary confinement for ten days.

Q. What was the original bond?

A. $2000. When this was brought to jail by my attorney, they raised my bond to $4000.

Q. Any reason given for doubling your bond?

A. Not to me.

Q. Was this additional $2000 posted?

A. Yes, and when the attorney came to get me out of jail for $4000, they raised it to $6000, and when he returned with $6000, they raised it to $8000. This in a sequence of days. He protested and they reduced it to $6000, and I was bonded out on that.

Q. Have you been tried?

A. Yes, in a very hostile situation. The Fire Department was called out to maintain what they call order in the hallways. In the court room deputies were lined up along the wall, very often holding their hands on their thirty-eights, looking very hostile. I was cursed many times.

They said I was trying to overthrow the social system of the South by talking about integration—

Dr. Kenneth Clark*: Weren't you?

A. Indeed, so I am trying with most of my remarks.

(The Rev. Cox was found guilty, sentenced to twenty-one months, fined $5700. He was out on appeal bond of $8125.)

Robert Zellner of SNCC told of his arrest with Charles McDew in Baton Rouge. The two had tried to bail out Dion Diamond, also of SNCC, arrested on campus, charged with criminal anarchy. Bail having been raised from $6000 to $13,000, they were unsuccessful and left town, returning later to visit Diamond in jail.

Mr. Zellner: They told us we could not see him. We asked if we could leave him some fruit, cigarettes and reading material. They said we could. We left the jail and bought some books, fruit, cigarettes, and returned to give him this, and they put us in jail.

Q. What were you charged with?

A. Vagrancy, though we had about $150. Also, criminal anarchy.

Q. How long did you stay in jail?

A. Twelve days.

Q. Has the indictment been dropped against you.

A. No. I assume they won't try it but they haven't dropped it. They haven't released the $6000 bond.

* Social psychologist.

Robert Moses of SNCC, Harvard graduate, told of working on voter registration in southern Mississippi in the summer of 1961, and of the killing, on September 25th, of Herbert Lee.

Mr. Moses said that police rode around the area where voting schools were held, intimidating people; that some who attended meetings lost their jobs; that in Liberty a cousin of the sheriff attacked him in sight of officers, his head wound requiring eight stitches.

Q. Mr. Moses, did you know a person named Herbert Lee?

A. Yes, he was a Negro farmer who lived near Liberty.

Q. Would you tell the Committee what Mr. Lee was doing and what happened?

A. He was killed on September 25th. That morning I was in McComb. The Negro doctor came by the voter registration office to tell us he had just taken a bullet out of a Negro's head.

We went over to see who it was because I thought it was somebody in the voting program, and were able to identify the man as Mr. Herbert Lee, who had attended our classes and driven us around the voting area, visiting other farmers.

That night we went into the county to track down people who had seen the killing. Three Negroes told more or less the same story.

That they were at the cotton gin in Liberty and Mr. Lee drove up to gin the cotton in his truck, followed by Mr. Herst in his car. He is representative to the Mississippi state legislature.

Q. Mr. Herst is white?

A. Mr. Herst is white. That he got out of his car and went over to the cab of Mr. Lee's truck. That they began talking. That Mr. Herst was waving a gun. That Mr. Lee got out of his cab on the right side. That Mr. Herst ran around the front and shot Mr. Lee one shot in his temple.

A Negro witness said a deputy sheriff asked him, "Did you see the tire tool?" The witness said he didn't see any tire tool in Mr. Lee's hand. The deputy replied, "Well, there was one."

The witness testified at the coroner's jury that there was a tire tool. When they had a grand jury, about a month later, the witness came to us to know whether he should testify that there was a tool, which he said there wasn't, though he had testified this at the coroner's jury.

We called Washington and Justice Department officials explained that they could not guarantee protection for individual witnesses. The man testified at the grand jury that there was a tire tool.

Q. The grand jury found no basis for an indictment against Rep. Herst, is that correct?

A. Yes.

Albert Bigelow, Quaker of Cos Cob, Conn., told of apparent police cooperation with the mob that attacked and burned the bus carrying the first Freedom Riders at Anniston, Ala., in May, 1961. He credited Eli Cowling of the state highway police, who was on the bus in plainclothes and kept the mob off, with saving riders' lives. Mr. Bigelow's story refers to police action outside the bus.

Mr. Bigelow: As we came into the station there was a mob of about 150. There were no police in sight. The crowd started to attack the bus. They cut a tire. None of us got off the bus. We were there fifteen minutes before any police appeared. Then one policeman in a brown uniform came and talked in a very friendly way to the men.

Eventually police formed a path through this crowd and we were able to leave.

Q. How many police at the time you left?

A. I saw, I think, three.

About six miles out of Anniston the tire blew. A mob, following in automobiles, surrounded the bus, in a more angry mood than in Anniston. They had pipes and chains as well as clubs. Mr. Cowling stood at the door of the bus.

They really went to work on the bus for about fifteen, perhaps twenty minutes. The safety glass was all sagging. Now, a state policeman in uniform drove up. He did absolutely nothing about the vandalism. He seemed to almost collaborate with the mob. He called on the radio in his car in a very leisurely manner.

In five minutes the bus burst into flames. People in the back got out of the window. We got out of the front door. Some were clubbed as they got out. Many had smoke poison. Mr. Cowling directed two state police who had arrived tardily; they fired pistols in the air. The mob drew away.

James Peck, editor of the CORElator, followed.

Mr. Peck: Regarding the men that were arrested for burning the bus. First there was a mistrial because one of the jurors belonged to the Klan and had perjured himself. Finally the men pleaded guilty to bombing and burning the bus and received suspended sentences.

J. B. Culbertson*: It appears they perpetrated that crime on the bus up in the United States District Court where the judge was appointed by the president of the United States. It is one of the problems that President Kennedy will have.

If you have that type of federal judge, they will pat the fellows on the back and say, don't do it any more, we are going to let you go this time. If we expect that type of judge in the federal court, what can we expect in the state court?

I hope and pray our administration will not appoint members of the White Citizens Council to the judiciary.

Mrs. Eleanor Roosevelt: I think you have to realize that under our political system judges have to be endorsed by the senators and congressmen of their district. Unless you can awaken public opinion to have some effect in the South, on these representatives who are elected, you are asking the President to risk a vote on his policy bills.

Now this is in our system and points up, I think, the need for the individual citizen to be awakened and held responsible, because it is the people in these areas who are responsible.

They elect their representatives. They are the ones who feel this way. I think they will respond to the real feeling of the rest of the country if it is brought out what they are doing to their country.

We are not a divided people in this country. We are of one country and we have to awaken this feeling in the country.

(Mr. Peck was among riders on the second bus arriving at Anniston two hours after the first.)

Mr. Peck: There were no police on hand. Word soon got around of what had happened. Other passengers got off our bus. As the bus was about to leave, eight white men climbed aboard. The driver announced that if Negroes did not move back he would not drive on.

* South Carolina lawyer.

There were no police. The gang started forcibly moving our men back. Walter Bergman and I went forward to try to intercede. The next moment I was flat on my face on the floor. The leader slugged me and then he slugged Bergman. They slugged us and kicked us until we were all in the back of the bus.

Bergman looked very bad. His face was all swollen and he was bleeding. We didn't know he had received this very serious injury for which he is still in the hospital. I was bleeding.

These men sat in the very front seats. The bus proceeded to Birmingham.

As we got off the bus we saw a mob carrying ill-concealed metal pipes. This was no surprise. I had called Rev. Shuttlesworth. He said, "You are going to get this greeting. It has been in the organization for the past week. There is going to be a mob."

They carried me into this alleyway and went to work with pipes and fists. Before long I was unconscious. Later Walter Bergman found me and helped me into a cab.

Q. This was Mothers Day, 1961?

A. Yes, Mothers Day. Police Chief Connor later explained the absence of police by saying his men were all visiting their mothers. I mean all, because there were none there.

Dr. Clark: How long were you in the hospital?

A. Oh, from six in the evening until two in the morning, after they had completed the fifty-three stitches in my head.

Dr. Clark: Were you in communication with the FBI?

A. Yes, in New Orleans, a couple of days later.

Dr. Clark: Did the FBI ask you, using pictures that had appeared in the public press, to identify your assailants?

A. I don't believe they asked that.

Rowland Watts*: Would it be fair to say that the FBI took your story and made no effort to explore it, to get identification?

A. That is exactly it.

Jerome Smith, twenty-three years old, CORE field secretary in New Orleans, La., followed.

Q. How many times have you been arrested in civil rights activities?

* American Civil Liberties Union representative.

A. It's complicated. In 1960, in New Orleans, about seven times for sitting-in. In April, 1961, I served thirty days there for picketing. In May, 1961, I served eighty days in Jackson, Miss., for my part in the Freedom Rides. In December, 1961, I was arrested in Baton Rouge. I took part in the mass march. I served twenty-one days and was beaten in jail. I was arrested in August, 1961, in New Orleans, for protesting police brutality. I have no official count of the rest.

Dr. Clark: Have you a count of beatings?

Mr. Watts: We have counted twelve so far. Perhaps we have overlooked a few.

Q. On November 29th, five days after the ICC ruling outlawing discrimination in interstate travel, a group from New Orleans CORE went to McComb to test the Greyhound station?

A. Yes, five of us. We arrived in the morning but the station was closed. Later when we returned we were met by a mob. George Raymond and several girls were kicked, coffee was thrown on George, I was beaten by brass knuckles and what have you. Tom Gaither was pitched into the street several times.

There were no police in the station, none on the outside of the station. I was informed later that the police station is a block or two from the bus station.

Mr. Rachlin: Subsequently the mayor of McComb obtained an injunction against CORE forbidding it from participating in any civil rights activities in McComb. The owner of a lunch counter inside the station was a plaintiff. He had never served Negroes at his counter. He admitted to a violation of federal law, yet the federal judge did not find difficulty in issuing the injunction.

Frank Nelson, civil engineer of New York City, was in New Orleans in August, 1961, expecting to go to Jackson, Miss., for hearing as a Freedom Rider.

Mr. Nelson: On August 13, myself and two other Freedom Riders, also white, were awaiting dinner in New Orleans at the home of a Negro CORE member and her family. Half a dozen police came into the house and began to question us.

Q. Did you ask if they had a warrant?

A. They said no, they didn't need one. We were taken to the

police station, questioned and booked on no visible means of support, though we had money.

We were put in a wagon for transfer to another station. In the wagon we found another white male prisoner. As we stopped outside the parish station he started swinging at us. Police opened the door, came in swinging blackjacks and kicking at us. They threw us out.

As I landed on the ground an officer grabbed me and while hitting me over the head with his blackjack yelled, "He's trying to escape."

John Dolan got thrown out face first and an officer leaped onto him. We were told to stand, face the wall, put our hands on the wall. Police beat us with blackjacks, with cursing between. About a dozen officers watched.

They took us inside for questioning. George Blevins had a bad cut on his head, his shirt was covered with blood. An officer grabbed him by the hair and dug his hand into the wound. Later George had four stitches.

John Dolan was taken into a little alcove. I edged forward so I could see. They were slapping him and hitting him with a blackjack and kicking him in the stomach and groin, trying to get him to tell where other Freedom Riders were.

After hospital treatment we were put in jail. We asked to phone our lawyer and they gave us a flat *no*.

Our lawyers came. Later we were tried and acquitted of no visible means of support. But charges of simple assault, aggravated assault and attempt to escape stand against us. We had to put up $1,000 bond apiece. There has been no further trial.

Later the FBI called us in for investigation. I was not given pictures to identify but volunteered information. Far as I know, nothing came of the investigation.

Eric Weinberger of Norwich, Conn., was sent by CORE to Brownsville, Tenn., in December, 1961, to teach unemployed Negro sharecroppers to make leather bags for sale. Some sharecroppers, evicted after registering to vote, continue to live in tents.

Mr. Weinberger showed the Committee a sample of the soft leather tote bag.

Mr. Weinberger: It was designed by a teacher in a Quaker school.

Within three hours of my first arrival in Brownsville I was urged, "Mr. Weinberger, get out of town." Police were following me.

After taking a few bags to New York and arranging for orders I went back to Brownsville in February and conducted classes. We began making bags. This went on for three days.

There was a young man with me, Jeffrey Gordon, taking a trip. I offered him a lift to Memphis, fifty miles away. About ten in the morning we got into the station wagon and headed up to Memphis.

We got about three blocks. There was a police car waiting for us. A deputy said to follow him to the court house.

There, the deputy said we would have to spend the night in jail.

Q. Did he give you a reason?

A. No.

Q. Was he charging you with any crime?

A. He wouldn't tell us whether we were under arrest. We refused to go with him. He started to grab us and we didn't cooperate. We were dragged out of the court house by the feet with our heads bouncing on the cement steps, and put in the county jail.

Three hours later they came for fingerprints. Jeffrey was first. He didn't cooperate. He was dragged out of the cell by a device, a clamp over the wrist.

Q. Metal clamp or leather?

A. Metal, like a single handcuff, adjustable to various sizes of wrists. But they keep tightening it.

Then I was dragged out by this instrument. I felt this was a horror of police injustice and when they put my hand on the ink pad, I would move my finger a half inch to smear it.

This infuriated them. I was beaten and punched in my eye. The wrist clamp was used to an extreme. This finger was bent back to the ultimate. I passed out several times. They slapped me back to consciousness.

My pants were torn off. An electric stock probe, used in stockyards to make cattle move along, was used around the private parts, it was very painful stuff. I was picked up and held in the air by the private parts.

They gave up. They did not get the fingerprints. The beating lasted fifteen minutes. I was dragged back to the cell. The deputy came by to curse me.

Next day I was taken to the adjacent cell, tied with a rope to the base of the cell. The clamp was used on the hand they wanted to fingerprint. A plier was used to pull the fingers and they got the prints. We were released at the end of seventy-two hours.

Q. Were you charged with any crime?

A. No. The deputy wanted to hold us because we were at the house of a Negro but the sheriff said there was no statute on that. They released a story to the paper that we were held in connection with a burglary but nobody asked us about burglary.

After going to Memphis I returned, was arrested within 24 hours for speeding, convicted and fined $50. I knew I wasn't speeding and went to jail for two weeks, fasting.

Mr. Baldwin*: Did you make a complaint against this scandalous treatment?

A. No. The FBI was sent around. I didn't wish to make a statement.

Mr. Baldwin: Because?

A. Because these police have community support. If one man with the worst reputation were removed from the force, they can find another to replace him.

Q. How is the bag project now?

A. Orders are coming in at a nice rate.

Henry Thomas, 20 years old, CORE field secretary. In Huntsville, Ala., in January, 1962, he organized student sit-ins. Police, he said, followed him "all the while. Sometimes kept a 24-hour tag on me."

On the 15th, he noticed a strange odor in his car. Police standing nearby denied having seen anyone tamper with it.

Mr. Thomas: Someone had torn the battery leads, but we got the car started. After about a block I got a stinging sensation in the

* James Baldwin.

seat of my pants. It was very bad. A little later I was in so much pain, I couldn't concentrate on anything.

We found a doctor and he smelled my coat and said, "That's just like mustard gas."

I was put in hospital, under sedation.

Later doctors at the Redstone Arsenal said there is not supposed to be any of this stuff loose, it must be homemade and could be very powerful.

Police were more interested in what I was doing in town than in what happened. They concluded some of my friends did this to me.

Q. Can you say who Marshall Keith is?

A. He was a white man who worked at the Arsenal. He came to our meetings and sat-in once with the students.

Next morning, about two o'clock, he was taken from his home at gunpoint, blindfolded and taken to a remote part of the city, stripped of his clothes and this chemical sprayed on him. He was left out there and made his way to a Negro home and got medical attention.

Q. He was a Huntsville boy?

A. He was a Huntsville boy. We could not contact him after he was released from the hospital. I was told his grandma had been threatened, that he had resigned his job. He left town for New York City. That was the last we heard of him.

Gerald Johnson, student at Talledega College, Talledega, Ala., took part in sit-ins, kneel-ins and picketings there in April, 1962. Fifty-three faculty and students were arrested.

Mr. Baldwin: How much integration is there in Talledega?

A. We have got nothing.

April 6th was our first march downtown. That day six of us tried to go in the public library. We tried many days. We could never get in.

When we picketed the theatre, tear gas was thrown. Mustard oil was thrown on me and on my buddy.

When we picketed a store, white men jumped on a Negro, beat him and pushed him through a plate glass window. He was arrested for breaking and entering. A white man was arrested. When the policeman searched the white man he handed to the policeman a knife. The policeman put the knife in his pocket, searched the man and gave him the knife back.

On the 27th we organized a march of 250 students to go downtown. On the first corner we could see the fire truck and police there to stop us. We said we couldn't turn back. Policemen came down the line saying we would be arrested, tear gas would be used, and water hoses, and if necessary, bullets. Nobody moved.

So they started pushing us. They beat us and poked us in the back with these clubs. One policemen had a sharp instrument at the end of his club. He put it in my back with all his might. The president of the college, Dr. Arthur D. Gray, was beaten.

A state policeman came up behind us, putting the club between our legs, swinging upwards. But we walked with our knees together and all of the clubs were caught on the knee.

That same week-end we were served with an injunction by a state court. This injunction has killed entirely our movement.

Charles McLaurin, twenty-one year old Army veteran of Jackson, Miss., told of police use of dogs at the State Fair at Jackson in October, 1961. Commonly the first five Fair days are for whites, the last three for Negroes.

Q. How different is the Fair for the second three days?
A. The best exhibits are taken down and a lot of the rides.

The NAACP called a boycott. Three of us went down to see if it would come off. We asked people at the ticket booth if they wanted to pay for second best, for segregation. Soon four police surrounded us. We told them what we were doing. They told us to leave. We tried to. They crowded around us, waving their sticks. We couldn't know which way to go.

Police began to run back students in front of the Fair. I was arrested, and at the gate I saw two policemen with dogs. Another dog was being taken out of a police car.

From the van I could see people running, fleeing over the hill, police after them with the dogs. Later I learned a dog got off the leash and bit a policeman.

Mr. Thomas: The dog had a better sense of justice than some men.

Mr. McLaurin: When the NAACP pickets arrived, police took the signs from them. Seven of us were arrested.

Q. What were you charged with?

A. Obstructing pedestrian traffic. We were found guilty, given six months and $500 fine. We're out on $500 appeal bond. The appeal hasn't been heard.

Q. Were police dogs used in Jackson on other occasions?

A. Yes, to break up the people peaceably assembled on the sidewalk at the court building, at the city jail and the library. Where they were holding a Negro dance the police brought out all six dogs to run the Negroes away from the dance.

In most Negro neighborhoods and in jail police use dogs to frighten people into giving information. The dogs really are used to frighten the Negroes.

Joseph Rauh*: How long have they been using dogs in this way?

A. I think now over a year.

Mr. Rauh: How long after the sit-ins started did the dogs come into Jackson?

A. Immediately after the sit-ins. I think the dogs were mostly brought in because of the sit-ins.

Mr. Rauh: It is obviously related to keeping Negroes in their place.

Robert Zellner told the story of Brenda Travis, seventeen-year-old high school student of McComb, Miss., under parole forbidding her to engage in civil rights action and hence unable to appear at the hearing.

Mr. Zellner: Brenda is a very dynamic person with great courage and determination. With two friends, she was arrested in the white section of the McComb bus station, on August 30, 1961. They had bought interstate tickets.

Sixteen then, she was convicted in adult court of disturbing the peace, sentenced to six months, fined $200, put on bond of $1000. She spent September in adult jail, awaiting bond.

October 4th she went back to her school. The principal said he'd sent her records off somewhere and she couldn't get back in.

About 115 students walked out of school in protest. Also the killing of Herbert Lee had fired them up. They determined to walk

* Of Americans for Democratic Action.

in orderly fashion to the county court house about eight miles away. I joined their march.

But it was late in the afternoon and it was decided to go into McComb. By the city hall there was a large mob. About twenty white men shoulder to shoulder across the sidewalk, with two police in front, stopped the march.

I was the only white person marching. About fifteen police standing around allowed seven or eight men to attack me. Some students stood on the bottom step to pray and were arrested. Then we were all arrested.

Brenda was in jail three or four days. Then the prosecutor and the judge decided she should be treated as a juvenile. Two plainclothesmen took her out of her cell and told her they were taking her to a lawyer. They drove her eighty miles to the Oakley Training School. Brenda didn't know where she was. The men left and a lady told her she was in the reform school.

She was there six months and three weeks. There was no class for her, she only went to one in home economics. She couldn't continue her education and this upset her. The food was very terrible with bugs. It was very degrading there.

Q. Tell about Brenda's release.

A. Professor Einsman, he had been an anti-Nazi in Germany and teaches German at Talledega College, was tremendously concerned when he heard Brenda's story. He said, "I'm going to Mississippi and talk to the judge."

(After several visits Dr. Einsman persuaded the judge to release Brenda in his custody.)

Mr. Zellner: So they drew up papers for her release and Dr. Einsman took Brenda to Talledega College, where she is living with his family.

4. THE KENNEDY AND JOHNSON ADMINISTRATIONS

*President Kennedy's Address on Civil Rights**

One of the paradoxes of the largely nonviolent protest movement is that some of its great victories have come as a consequence of

* From the *New York Times*, June 12, 1963.

violence: the brutal treatment of freedom riders led to the ICC order desegregating interstate transportation facilities; the bomb that killed four young Negro girls in Birmingham was a prelude to the Civil Rights Act of 1964; Selma preceded the Voting Rights Act of 1965. Public outrage was transformed into political pressure, and congressmen, senators, and Presidents responded accordingly. Increasing presidential commitment to the demands of racial equality characterized the Kennedy and Johnson Administrations. President Kennedy's well-known address declaring civil rights "a moral issue"—which follows—was occasioned by Governor George C. Wallace's attempt to prevent the registration of two Negro students at the University of Alabama.

This afternoon, following a series of threats and defiant statements, the presence of Alabama National Guardsmen was required on the University of Alabama to carry out the final and unequivocal order of the United States District Court of the Northern District of Alabama.

That order called for the admission of two clearly qualified young Alabama residents who happened to have been born Negro.

That they were admitted peacefully on the campus is due in good measure to the conduct of the students of the University of Alabama who met their responsibilities in a constructive way.

I hope that every American, regardless of where he lives, will stop and examine his conscience about this and other related incidents.

This nation was founded by men of many nations and backgrounds. It was founded on the principle that all men are created equal, and that the rights of every man are diminished when the rights of one man are threatened.

Today we are committed to a worldwide struggle to promote and protect the rights of all who wish to be free. And when Americans are sent to Vietnam or West Berlin we do not ask for whites only.

It ought to be possible, therefore, for American students of any color to attend any public institution they select without having to be backed by troops. It ought to be possible for American consumers of any color to receive equal service in places of public accommodation, such as hotels and restaurants, and theaters and retail stores without being forced to resort to demonstrations in the street.

And it ought to be possible for American citizens of any color to register and to vote in a free election without interference or fear of reprisal.

It ought to be possible, in short, for every American to enjoy the privileges of being American without regard to his race or his color.

In short, every American ought to have the right to be treated as he would wish to be treated, as one would wish his children to be treated. But this is not the case.

The Negro baby born in America today, regardless of the section or the state in which he is born, has about one-half as much chance of completing a high school as a white baby, born in the same place, on the same day; one-third as much chance of completing college; one-third as much chance of becoming a professional man; twice as much chance of becoming unemployed; about one-seventh as much chance of earning $10,000 a year; a life expectancy which is seven years shorter and the prospects of earning only half as much.

This is not a sectional issue. Difficulties over segregation and discrimination exist in every city, in every state of the Union, producing in many cities a rising tide of discontent that threatens the public safety.

Nor is this a partisan issue. In a time of domestic crisis, men of goodwill and generosity should be able to unite regardless of party or politics.

This is not even a legal or legislative issue alone. It is better to settle these matters in the courts than on the streets, and new laws are needed at every level. But law alone cannot make men see right.

We are confronted primarily with a moral issue. It is as old as the Scriptures and is as clear as the American Constitution. The heart of the question is whether all Americans are to be afforded equal rights and equal opportunities; whether we are going to treat our fellow Americans as we want to be treated.

If an American, because his skin is dark, cannot eat lunch in a restaurant open to the public; if he cannot send his children to the best public school available; if he cannot vote for the public officials who represent him; if, in short, he cannot enjoy the full and free life which all of us want, then who among us would be content to have the color of his skin changed and stand in his place?

Who among us would then be content with the counsels of patience and delay? One hundred years of delay have passed since President Lincoln freed the slaves, yet their heirs, their grandsons, are not fully free. They are not yet freed from the bonds of injustice; they are not yet freed from social and economic oppression.

And this nation, for all its hopes and all its boasts, will not be fully free until all its citizens are free.

We preach freedom around the world, and we mean it. And we cherish our freedom here at home. But are we to say to the world—and much more importantly to each other—that this is the land of the free, except for Negroes; that we have no second-class citizens, except for Negroes; that we have no class or caste system, no ghettos, no master race, except with respect to Negroes.

Now the time has come for this nation to fulfill its promise. The events of Birmingham and elsewhere have so increased the cries for equality that no city or state or legislative body can prudently choose to ignore them.

The fires of frustration and discord are burning in every city, North and South. Where legal remedies are not at hand, redress is sought in the streets in demonstrations, parades and protests, which create tensions and threaten violence—and threaten lives.

We face, therefore, a moral crisis as a country and a people. It cannot be met by repressive police action. It cannot be left to increased demonstrations in the streets. It cannot be quieted by token moves or talk. It is a time to act in the Congress, in your state and local legislative body, and, above all, in all our daily lives.

It is not enough to pin the blame on others, to say this is a problem of one section of the country or another, or deplore the facts that we face. A great change is at hand, and our task, our obligation is to make that revolution, that change peaceful and constructive for all.

Those who do nothing are inviting shame as well as violence. Those who act boldly are recognizing right as well as reality.

Next week I shall ask the Congress of the United States to act, to make a commitment it has not fully made in this century to the proposition that race has no place in American life or law.

The Federal judiciary has upheld the proposition in a series of forthright cases. The Executive Branch has adopted that proposition in the conduct of its affairs, including the employment of Federal personnel, and the use of Federal facilities, and the sale of Federally financed housing.

But there are other necessary measures which only the Congress can provide, and they must be provided at this session.

The old code of equity law under which we live commands for every wrong a remedy. But in too many communities, in too many parts of the country wrongs are inflicted on Negro citizens and there are no remedies in law.

I am, therefore, asking the Congress to enact legislation giving all Americans the right to be served in facilities which are open to the public—hotels, restaurants and theaters, retail stores and similar establishments. This seems to me to be an elementary right. Its denial is an arbitrary indignity that no American in 1963 should have to endure, but many do.

I have recently met with scores of business leaders, urging them to take voluntary action to end this discrimination. And I've been encouraged by their response. And in the last two weeks over 75 cities have seen progress made in desegregating these kinds of facilities.

But many are unwilling to act alone. And for this reason nationwide legislation is needed, if we are to move this problem from the streets to the courts.

I'm also asking Congress to authorize the Federal government to participate more fully in lawsuits designed to end segregation in public education. We have succeeded in persuading many districts to desegregate voluntarily. Dozens have admitted Negroes without violence.

Today a Negro is attending a state-supported institution in every one of our 50 states. But the pace is very slow.

Too many Negro children entering segregated grade schools at the time of the Supreme Court's decision nine years ago will enter segregated high schools this fall, having suffered a loss which can never be restored.

The lack of an adequate education denies the Negro a chance to get a decent job. The orderly implementation of the Supreme Court decision therefore, cannot be left solely to those who may not have the economic resources to carry their legal action or who may be subject to harassment.

Other features will be also requested, including greater protection for the right to vote.

But legislation, I repeat, cannot solve this problem alone. It must be solved in the homes of every American in every community across the country.

In this respect, I want to pay tribute to those citizens, North and South, who've been working in their communities to make life better for all.

They are acting not out of a sense of legal duty but out of a sense of human decency. Like our soldiers and sailors in all parts of the world, they are meeting freedom's challenge on the firing line and I salute them for their honor—their courage.

My fellow Americans, this is a problem which faces us all, in every city of the North as well as the South.

Today there are Negroes unemployed—two or three times as many compared to whites—inadequate education; moving into the large cities, unable to find work; young people particularly out of work, without hope, denied equal rights, denied the opportunity to eat at a restaurant or a lunch counter, or go to a movie theater; denied the right to decent education; denied, almost today, the right to attend a state university even though qualified.

It seems to me that these are matters which concern us all—not merely Presidents, or Congressmen, or Governors, but every citizen of the United States.

This is one country. It has become one country because all of us and all the people who came here had an equal chance to develop their talents.

We cannot say to 10 per cent of the population that "you can't have that right. Your children can't have the chance to develop whatever talents they have, that the only way they're going to get their rights is to go in the street and demonstrate."

I think we owe them and we owe ourselves a better country than that.

Therefore, I'm asking for your help in making it easier for us to move ahead and provide the kind of equality of treatment which we would want ourselves—to give a chance for every child to be educated to the limit of his talent.

As I've said before, not every child has an equal talent or an equal ability or equal motivation. But they should have the equal right to develop their talent and their ability and their motivation to make something of themselves.

We have a right to expect that the Negro community will be responsible, will uphold the law. But they have a right to expect the law will be fair, that the Constitution will be color blind, as Justice Harlan said at the turn of the century.

This is what we're talking about. This is a matter which concerns this country and what it stands for, and in meeting it I ask the support of all our citizens.

The Civil Rights Act of 1964*

On June 19, 1963, President Kennedy sent a draft of his proposed legislation to Congress. Despite the mood of the country and the March on Washington that summer the act continued to run into congressional road blocks. After Kennedy's assassination forceful executive leadership was given the measure by President Johnson. After many maneuvers, bipartisan agreement was finally reached to end debate in the Senate—it had gone on for 534 hours—and on July 2, 1964, the most far-reaching civil rights bill in American history became law.

Title I—Voting

Prohibits registrars from applying different standards to white and Negro voting applicants and from disqualifying applicants because of inconsequential errors on their forms. Requires that literacy tests be in writing, except under special arrangements for blind persons, and that any applicant desiring one be given a copy of the questions and his answers. Makes a sixth-grade education a rebuttable presumption of literacy. Allows the Attorney General or defendant state officials in any voting suit to request trial by a three-judge Federal Court.

---

* The following digest of the act's provisions is from *The New York Times,* June 20, 1964.

TITLE II—PUBLIC ACCOMMODATIONS

Prohibits discrimination or refusal of service on account of race in hotels, motels, restaurants, gasoline stations and places of amusement if their operations affect interstate commerce or if their discrimination "is supported by state action." Permits the Attorney General to enforce the title by suit in the Federal courts if he believes that any person or group is engaging in a "pattern or practice of resistance" to the rights declared by the title. The latter language was added in the Senate, which also authorized three-judge courts for suits under this title.

TITLE III—PUBLIC FACILITIES

Requires that Negroes have equal access to, and treatment in, publicly owned or operated facilities such as parks, stadiums and swimming pools. Authorizes the Attorney General to sue for enforcement of these rights if private citizens are unable to sue effectively.

TITLE IV—PUBLIC SCHOOLS

Empowers the Attorney General to bring school desegregation suits under the same conditions as in Title III. Authorizes technical and financial aid to school districts to assist in desegregation. The Senate strengthened a provision in the House bill saying that the title does not cover busing of pupils or other steps to end "racial imbalance."

TITLE V—CIVIL RIGHTS COMMISSION

Extends the life of the Civil Rights Commission until Jan. 31, 1968.

TITLE VI—FEDERAL AID

Provides that no person shall be subjected to racial discrimination in any program receiving Federal aid. Directs Federal agencies to take steps against discrimination, including—as a last resort, and after hearings—withholding of Federal funds from state or local agencies that discriminate.

Title VII—Employment

Bans discrimination by employers or unions with 100 or more employes or members the first year the act is effective, reducing over four years to 25 or more. Establishes a commission to investigate alleged discrimination and use persuasion to end it. Authorizes the Attorney General to sue if he believes any person or group is engaged in a "pattern or practice" of resistance to the title, and to ask for trial by a three-judge court. The Senate added the "pattern-or-practice" condition and shifted the power to sue from the commission to the Attorney General.

Title VIII—Statistics

Directs the Census Bureau to compile statistics of registration and voting by race in areas of the country designated by the Civil Rights Commission. This might be used to enforce the long-forgotten provision of the 14th Amendment that states that discriminate in voting shall lose seats in the House of Representatives.

Title IX—Courts

Permits appellate review of decisions by Federal District judges to send back to the state courts criminal defendants who have attempted to remove their cases on the ground that their civil rights would be denied in state trials. Permits the Attorney General to intervene in suits filed by private persons complaining that they have been denied the equal protection of the laws.

Title X—Conciliation

Establishes a Community Relations Service in the Commerce Department to help conciliate racial disputes. The Senate removed a House ceiling of seven employes.

TITLE XI—MISCELLANEOUS

Guarantees jury trials for criminal contempt under any part of the act but Title I—a provision added in the Senate. Provides that the statute shall not invalidate state laws with consistent purposes, and that it shall not impair any existing powers of Federal officials.

The Voting Rights Act of 1965

A Digest of the Act*

Few people expected a major new rights bill in the next session of Congress, but recalcitrant Southern voting registrars and the atrocities at Selma demonstrated that the franchise provisions of the Civil Rights Acts of 1957, 1960, and 1964 were inadequate. The new bill eliminated literacy tests for voter applicants and permitted the use of federal examiners in areas where Negroes seemed to be systematically disfranchised. The Voting Rights Act of 1965 may in time have greater impact on the South than any other legislation of the recent period.

On January 4, 1965, President Johnson proposed in his State of the Union Message that ". . . we eliminate every remaining obstacle to the right and the opportunity to vote."

In March, a week after Negro civil rights marchers had been attacked by Alabama law enforcement officers as they attempted to walk from Selma to Montgomery to dramatize their appeal for full voting rights, the President appeared before a special session of Congress to urge speedy enactment of voting legislation and told Congress that ". . . the harsh fact is that in many places in this country men and women are kept from voting simply because they are Negroes." He added, "No law we now have on the books . . . can ensure the right to vote when local officials are determined to deny it."

The Administration's proposal to eliminate barriers to the right to vote was introduced in the House of Representatives on March 17 and in the Senate the following day. The Administration bill

* From the United States Commission on Civil Rights, *The Voting Rights Act: The First Months* (Washington, D.C., 1965), pp. 10–13.

contained two central features, similar to proposals previously made by the Commission on Civil Rights, which were designed to attack the problem of systematic discrimination by local voting officials.

It provided that all literacy tests and other devices used to deny Negroes their voting rights would be suspended in States where less than 50 percent of the population had been registered or had voted in the 1964 Presidential election.

The proposal also provided for the appointment of Federal examiners who would list voters in designated areas covered by the legislation. It gave the Attorney General of the United States broad discretionary power to designate the counties in which the U.S. Civil Service Commission would appoint examiners.

In determining the political subdivisions to which examiners would be assigned, the Attorney General could assign examiners to any political subdivision from which he had received 20 meritorious complaints alleging voter discrimination or upon a determination that in his judgment examiners were needed to prevent denial of the right to vote in a subdivision.

Although the Administration bill was modified during the more than four months it was considered by Congress, its two central features—elimination of literacy tests and assignment of Federal examiners—remained in the final version.

The bill contained a provision dealing with poll taxes—a device which has been used to effect both racial and economic discrimination. The original measure modified State poll tax procedures by allowing new voters to vote if they tendered poll tax payment for the current year within 45 days before an election. The House bill abolished all poll taxes. The Senate-approved measure, however, provided for accelerated court challenge by the Attorney General of State poll tax requirements rather than outright abolition. As finally approved, the bill contained the Senate's proposal for challenging the poll tax and retained the Administration's provision for its payment.

The Attorney General's discretionary power to assign examiners was clarified by a provision that in exercising his discretion he could consider such factors as differences in registration level for whites and nonwhites and affirmative indications of compliance with the law.

The Administration bill required a would-be voter to allege to a Federal examiner that he had been refused registration or found not qualified to register by State officials sometime during a 90-day period before he appeared before the examiner. Some Congressmen argued that in counties where disfranchisement was most acute, registration would continue to be limited by reluctance of Negroes to confront hostile State officials. The Act, as passed, did not contain this requirement.

To assure the proper conduct of an election, Congress added a provision giving the Civil Service Commission authority to appoint, at the request of the Attorney General, poll watchers to be stationed at polling places in examiner counties to observe whether any persons were denied the opportunity to vote and to observe the tabulation of ballots.

The Senate added to the Administration bill a provision dealing with language literacy. It allows a prospective voter to qualify, without taking a literacy test, by demonstrating that he has completed at least six grades in a school under the American flag conducted in a language other than English. This provision will result in enfranchising persons educated in Puerto Rico who now reside on the mainland of the United States.

The Senate began debating the Administration measure on April 13 and approved its version on May 26. The bill was called up in the House on July 6 and passed after three days of debate. The Senate-House Conference Committee reported out its version on August 2. The House approved the Voting Rights Act of 1965 with a 328–74 vote on August 3 and the Senate added its approval by a vote of 79–18 on August 4.

THE FINAL BILL

The Voting Rights Act of 1965, signed by the President on August 6, suspends all literacy tests and other devices as qualifications for voting in any Federal, State, local, general, or primary election. It applies to the States of Alabama, Alaska, Georgia, Louisiana, Mississippi, South Carolina, Virginia, at least 26 counties in North Carolina, and one county in Arizona. The Act also covers election to political party office.

In effect, the Act requires the registration of any otherwise qualified person even though he may be unable to read or write.

It provides for the assignment of Federal examiners to list voters and poll watchers to observe voting and the counting of ballots in the counties covered by the Act.

Congress found that the payment of poll tax had been used in some areas to abridge the right to vote and directed the Attorney General to initiate immediate suits to test the constitutionality of poll taxes.

The foreign language literacy provision adopted by the Senate was retained in the final bill.

The Act provides civil and criminal sanctions against anyone who interferes with persons seeking to vote and those who urge or help others to vote. It also provides administrative and civil remedies for persons prevented from voting.

President Johnson's Speech on the Voting Rights Act*

Today is a triumph for freedom as huge as any victory that's ever been won on any battlefield.

Yet to seize the meaning of this day we must recall darker times.

Three and a half centuries ago the first Negroes arrived at Jamestown. They did not arrive in brave ships in search of a home for freedom. They did not mingle fear and joy in expectation that in this new world anything would be possible to a man strong enough to reach for it.

They came in darkness and they came in chains. And today we strike away the last major shackle of those fierce and ancient bonds.

Today the Negro story and the American story fuse and blend. And let us remember that it was not always so. The stories of our nation and of the American Negro are like two great rivers. Welling up from that tiny Jamestown spring, they flow through the centuries along divided channels.

When pioneers subdued a continent to the need of man they did not tame it for the Negro. When the Liberty Bell rang out in Philadelphia it did not toll for the Negro. When Andrew Jackson

* From the *New York Times,* August 7, 1965.

threw open the doors of democracy they did not open for the Negro. It was only at Appomattox a century ago that an American victory was also a Negro victory. And the two rivers, one shining with promise, the other dark-stained with oppression, began to move toward one another.

Yet for almost a century the promise of that day was not fulfilled.

Today is a towering and certain mark that in this generation that promise will be kept. In our time the two currents will finally mingle and rush as one great stream across the uncertain and the marvelous years of the America that is yet to come.

This act flows from a clear and simple wrong. Its only purpose is to right that wrong. Millions of Americans are denied the right to vote because of their color. This law will ensure them the right to vote. The wrong is one which no American in his heart can justify. The right is one which no American, true to our principles, can deny.

In 1957, as the leader of the majority in the United States Senate, speaking in supporting legislation to guarantee to the rights of all men a right to vote, I said:

"This right to vote is the basic right without which all others are meaningless. It gives people—people as individuals—control over their own destinies."

Last year I said: "Until every qualified person, regardless of the color of his skin, has the right unquestioned and unrestrained, to go in and cast his ballot in every precinct in this great land of ours I am not going to be satisfied."

Immediately after the election I directed the Attorney General to explore as rapidly as possible the ways to ensure the right to vote.

And then last March, with the outrage of Selma still fresh, I came down to this Capitol one evening and asked the Congress and the people for swift and for sweeping action to guarantee to every man and woman the right to vote.

In less than 48 hours I sent the Voting Rights Act of 1965 to the Congress.

In a little more than four months the Congress, with over-whelming majorities, enacted one of the most monumental laws in the entire history of American freedom.

The members of the Congress, the many private citizens who worked to shape and pass this bill, will share a place of honor in our history for this one act alone.

There were those who said this is an old injustice and there is no need to hurry. But 95 years have passed since the 15th Amendment gave all Negroes the right to vote and the time for waiting is gone. There were those who said smaller and more gradual measures should be tried, but they had been tried.

For years and years they had been tried and tried and tried and they had failed and failed and failed. And the time for failure is gone.

There were those who said that this is a many-sided and very complex problem. But however viewed, the denial of the right to vote is still a deadly wrong and the time for injustice has gone.

This law covers many pages but the heart of the act is plain. Wherever, by clear and objective standards, states and counties are using regulations or laws or tariffs to deny the right to vote then they will be struck down.

If it is clear that state officials still intend to discriminate, then Federal examiners will be sent in to register all eligible voters. When the prospect of discrimination is gone the examiners will be immediately withdrawn.

And under this act if any county anywhere in this nation does not want Federal intervention it need only open its polling places to all of its people.

This good Congress—the 89th Congress—acted swiftly in passing this act. And I intend to act with equal dispatch in enforcing this act.

And tomorrow at 1 P.M. the Attorney General has been directed to file a lawsuit challenging the constitutionality of the poll tax in the State of Mississippi.

And this will begin the legal process, which I confidently believe will very soon prohibit any state from requiring the payment of money in order to exercise the right to vote. And also by tomorrow the Justice Department through publication in the Federal Register will have officially certified the states where discrimination exists.

I have in addition requested the Department of Justice to work all through this weekend so that on Monday morning next they can designate many counties where past experience clearly shows that

Federal action is necessary and required. And by Tuesday morning trained Federal examiners will be at work registering eligible men and women in 10 to 15 counties.

And on that same day next Tuesday, additional poll tax suits will be filed in the states of Texas, Alabama and Virginia. And I pledge you that we will not delay or we will not hesitate, or we will not turn aside until Americans of every race and color and origin in this country have the same rights as all others to share in the process of democracy.

So through this act and its enforcement an important instrument of freedom passes into the hands of millions of our citizens. But that instrument must be used.

Presidents and Congresses, laws and lawsuits, can open the doors to the polling places and open the doors to the wondrous rewards which await the wise use of the ballot. But only the individual Negro and all the others who have been denied the right to vote can really walk through those doors and can use that right and can transform the vote into an instrument of justice and fulfillment.

So let me now say to every Negro in this country: you must register; you must vote; you must learn so your choices advance your interests and the interests of our beloved nation.

Your future and your children's future depend upon it and I don't believe you're going to let them down.

This act is not only a victory for Negro leadership; this act is a great challenge to that leadership. It is a challenge which cannot be met simply by protests and demonstrations. It means that dedicated leaders must work around the clock to teach people their rights and their responsibilities and to lead them to exercise those rights and to fulfill those responsibilities and those duties to their country.

And if you do this then you will find, as others have found before you, that the vote is the most powerful instrument ever devised by man for breaking down injustice and destroying the terrible walls which imprison men because they are different from other men.

Today what is perhaps the last of the legal barriers is tumbling and there will be many actions and many difficulties before the rights woven into law are also woven into the fabric of our nation.

But the struggle for equality must now move to a different battlefield. It is nothing less than granting every American Negro his freedom to enter the mainstream of American life—not the conformity that blurs enriching differences of culture and tradition, but rather the opportunity that gives each a chance to choose, for centuries of oppression and hatred have already taken their painful toll.

It can be seen throughout our land, in men without skills, in children without fathers, in families that are imprisoned in slums and in poverty. For it is not enough just to give men rights; they must be able to use those rights in the personal pursuit of happiness.

The wounds and the weaknesses, the outward world and the inward scars, which diminish achievement are the work of American society and we must all now help to end them—help to end them through expanding programs already devised and through new ones to search out and forever end the special handicap of those who are black in a nation that happens to be mostly white.

So it is for this purpose—to fulfill the rights that we now secure—that I have already called a White House conference to meet here in the nation's capital this fall. And so we will move step by step, often painfully, but I think with clear vision, along the path toward American freedom.

It is difficult to fight for freedom, but I think I also know how difficult it can be to bend long years of habit and custom to grant it. There is no room for injustice anywhere in the American mansion.

But there is always room for understanding toward those who see the old ways crumbling and to them today I say simply this: It must come.

It is right that it should come and when it has you will find a burden that has been lifted from your shoulders, too. It is not just a question of guilt, although there is that. It is that men cannot live with a lie and not be stained by it.

The central fact of American civilization, one so hard for others to understand, is that freedom and justice and the dignity of man are not just words to us. We believe in them. Under all the growth, and the tumult, and abundance, we believe. And so, as long as some among us are oppressed and we are part of that oppression it must blunt our faith and sap the strength of our high purpose.

Thus, this is a victory for the freedom of the American Negro, but it is also a victory for the freedom of the American nation. And every family across this great entire searching land will live stronger in liberty, will live more splendid in expectation and will be prouder to be American because of the act that you have passed that I will sign today.

5. THE NEGRO COMMUNITY IN THE SIXTIES

A Muslim's Account of the Story of Creation Elijah Muhammad*

The Nation of Islam—commonly known as Black Muslims —was founded in 1930 but came to the attention of the general public during the late 1950's and early 1960's. Characteristically, the selective vision of white America saw the Muslims only as a hate group and worried about their potential for violence. The broader aspects of Muslim ideology—its emphasis on a puritanical standard of behavior, respect for law and authority, self-help and pride in blackness—were generally ignored. Among the most interesting strains of Muslim theology is the way it selects the traditional stereotype of Negroes, reverses it, and applies it to whites. Proslavery advocates, for example, wrote that the serpent in the Garden of Eden was a black man; Elijah Muhammad proves to his followers that it was really the white man. Some scientists claim Negroes are innately inferior; Elijah Muhammad insists that all whites are born with smaller brains and less intelligence than Negroes. In the following selection Elijah Muhammad rewrites the story of creation and explains how all whites are devils created by an ancient Dr. Frankenstein, "Mr. Yakub."

Our 66 trillion years from the moon has proven a great and wise show of the original power, to build wonders in the heavens and

* From Elijah Muhammad, *Message to the Blackman in America* (Chicago, 1965), pp. 110–122.

earth. Six thousand years ago, or to be more exact 6,600 years ago, as Allah taught me, our nation gave birth to another God whose name was Yakub. He started studying the life germ of man to try making a new creation (new man) whom our twenty-four scientists had foretold 8,400 years before the birth of Mr. Yakub, and the Scientists were aware of his birth and work before he was born, as they are today of the intentions or ideas of the present world.

According to the word of Allah to me, "Mr. Yakub was seen by the twenty-three Scientists of the black nation, over 15,000 years ago. They predicted that in the year 8,400 (that was in our calendar year before this world of the white race), this man (Yakub) would be born twenty miles from the present Holy City, Mecca, Arabia. And, that at the time of his birth, the satisfaction and dissatisfaction of the people would be:—70 per cent satisfied, 30 per cent dissatisfied."

And, that when this man is born, he will change civilization (the world), and produce a new race of people, who would rule the original black nation for 6,000 years (from the nine thousandth year to the fifteen thousandth year).

After that time, the original black nation would give birth to one, whose wisdom, Knowledge and power would be infinite. One, whom the world would recognize as being the greatest and mightiest God, since the creation of the universe. And, that He would destroy Yakub's world and restore the original nation, or ancient nation, into power to rule forever.

This mighty One is known under many names. He has no equal. There never was one like Him. He is referred to in the Bible as God Almighty, and in some places as Jehovah, the God of Gods, and the Lord of Lords.

The Holy Qur-an refers to Him as Allah, the One God; beside Him, there is no God and there is none like Him; the Supreme Being; the mighty, the wise; the best knower; the light; the life giver; the Mahdi (this is He, Whom I have met and am missioned by).

He, also, is referred to as the Christ, the second Jesus. The Son of Man, who is wise and is all-powerful. He knows how to reproduce the universe, and the people of His choice. He will remove and destroy the present, old warring wicked world of

Yakub (the Caucasian world) and set up a world of peace and righteousness, out of the present so-called Negroes, who are rejected and despised by this world.

Mr. Yakub was, naturally, born out of the 30 per cent dissatisfied. As we know, wherever there is a longing or demand for a change, nature will produce that man, who will bring it about.

Allah taught me that the present percentage is 98 per cent near, 100 per cent, with the present ruling powers. This 100 per cent dissatisfied will bring about a 100 per cent change. Yakub did not bring about a 100 per cent change, but near (90 per cent). Allah said: "When Yakub was six years old, one day, he was sitting down playing with two pieces of steel. He noticed the magnetic power in the steel attracting the other. He looked up at his uncle and said: "Uncle, when I get to be an old man, I am going to make a people who shall rule you." The uncle said: "What will you make; something to make mischief and cause bloodshed in the land?" Yakub said: "Nevertheless, Uncle, I know that which you do not know."

And, it was at that moment, the boy Yakub, first came into the knowledge of just who he was—born to make trouble, break peace, kill and destroy his own people with a made enemy to the black nation.

He learned his future from playing with steel. It is steel and more steel that his made race (the white race), are still playing with. Steel has become the most useful of all metal for the people. What he really saw in playing with the two pieces of steel was the magnetic power of attraction.

The one attracting and drawing the other under its power. In this, he saw an unlike human being, made to attract others, who could, with the knowledge of tricks and lies, rule the original black man—until that nation could produce one greater and capable of overcoming and making manifest his race of tricks and lies, with a nation of truth.

Yakub was the founder of unlike attracts and like repels, though Mr. Yakub was a member of the black nation. He began school at the age of four. He had an unusual size head. When he had grown up, the others referred to him as the "big head scientist."

At the age of 18 he had finished all of the colleges and universities of his nation, and was seen preaching on the streets of

Mecca, making converts. He made such impressions on the people, that many began following him.

He learned, from studying the germ of the black man, under the microscope, that there were two people in him, and that one was black the other brown.

He said if he could successfully separate the one from the other he could graft the brown germ into its last stage, which would be white. With his wisdom, he could make the white, which he discovered was the weaker of the black germ (which would be un-alike) rule the black nation for a time (until a greater one than Yakub was born).

This new idea put him to work finding the necessary converts to begin grafting his new race of people. He began by teaching Islam, with promises of luxury to those who would believe and follow him.

As Mr. Yakub continued to preach for converts, he told his people that he would make the others work for them. (This promise came to pass.) Naturally, there are always some people around who would like to have others do their work. Those are the ones who fell for Mr. Yakub's teaching, 100 per cent.

As he made converts in and around the Holy City of Mecca, persecutions set in. The authorities became afraid of such powerful teachings, with promises of luxury and making slaves of others. As they began making arrests of those who believed the teaching, the officers would go back and find, to their surprise, others still teaching and believing it.

Finally they arrested Mr. Yakub. But, it only increased the teachings. They kept persecuting and arresting Yakub's followers until they filled all the jails.

The officers finally reported to the King that there was no room to put a prisoner in—if arrested. "All the jails are filled; and, when we go out into the streets, we find them still teaching. What shall we do with them?" The King questioned the officers on just what the teachings were; and of the name of the leader.

The officers gave the King the answers to everything. The King said: "This is not the name of that man." On entering the prison, the King was shown Yakub's cell. "Wa-Alaikum." The King said: "So you are Mr. Yakub?" He said: "Yes, I am." The King said: "Yakub, I have come to see if we could work out some agreement that would bring about an end to this trouble. What would you suggest?"

Mr. Yakub told the King: "If you give me and my followers everything to start civilization as you have, and furnish us with money and other necessities of life for twenty years, I will take my followers and we will go from you."

The King was pleased with the suggestion or condition made by Yakub, and agreed to take care of them for twenty years, until Yakub's followers were able to go for themselves.

After learning who Mr. Yakub was, they all were afraid of him, and were glad to make almost any agreement with him and his followers.

The history or future of Mr. Yakub and his people was in the Nation's Book, by the writers (23 Scientists) of our history, 8,400 years before his birth. So, the Government began to make preparation for the exiling of Mr. Yakub and His followers. The King ordered everyone rounded up who was a believer in Mr. Yakub. They took them to the seaport and loaded them on ships.

After rounding them all up into ships, they numbered 59,999. Yakub made 60,000. Their ships sailed out to an Isle in the Aegean Sea called "Pelan" (Bible "Patmos"). After they were loaded into the ships, Mr. Yakub examined each of them to see if they were 100 per cent with him; and to see if they were all healthy and productive people. If not, he would throw them off. Some were found to be unfit and overboard they went.

When they arrived at the Isle, Mr. Yakub said to them: "See how they (the Holy People) have cast us out. Now—if you will choose me to be your King, I will teach you how to go back and rule them all."

Of course, they had already chosen Yakub to be their King at the very start. So, Yakub chose doctors, ministers, nurses and a cremator for his top laborers. He called these laborers together and told them his plan for making a new people, who would rule for 6,000 years.

He called the doctor first and said: "Doctor, let all the people come to you who want to marry; and if there come to you two real black ones, take a needle and get a little of their blood and go into your room and pretend to be examining it, to see whether their blood would mix. Then, come and tell them that they will each have to find another mate, because their blood does not mix." (It was the aim of Yakub to get rid of the black and he did.) "Give them a certificate to take to the minister, warning the minister against marrying the couple because their blood does not mix. When there comes to you two browner ones, take a pretended blood test of them; but, give them a certificate saying that they are eligible to marry."

Mr. Yakub's charge to his laborers was very strict—death if one disobeyed. They didn't know what Yakub had in mind until they were given their labor to do. He made his laborers, from the chief to the least, liars. The doctor lied about the blood of the two black people who wanted to marry, that it did not mix.

The brown and black could not be married (brown only). The doctors of today hold the same position over the people. You go to them to get a blood test to see if you are fit to be married.

Today, they say it is done to see if there are any contagious germs in the blood. I wish that they would enforce such a law today (keep the white from mixing with black—just the opposite). Perhaps we could remain black and not be disgraced by a mixture of all colors.

In the days of Yakub's grafting of the present white race, a new and unalike race among the black nation for 600 years, his law was—that they should not allow the birth of a black baby in their family, but the white (devil) should mix their blood with the black nation, in order to help destroy black; but, they should not allow the black to mix with their blood.

His aim was to kill and destroy the black nation. He ordered the nurses to kill all black babies that were born among his people, by pricking the brains with a sharp needle as soon as the black child's head is out of the mother.

If the mother is alert (watching the nurse), then the nurse would lie and fool the mother to get possession of child to murder it, by saying that she (mother) gave birth to an "angel child." And that she (the nurse) would like to take the baby to heaven, so when the mother dies, she would have a room with her child in heaven, for her baby was an angel.

This is the beginning of the first lie or liar; and, it was so that the nurse would take the black baby away on this falsehood and claim that they were taking the poor black baby to heaven. As Yakub had taught them, they would feed it to wild beasts and if they did not [have] a wild beast to feed the black babies to, Yakub told the nurses to give it to the cremator to burn.

Mr. Yakub warned the laborers, from the doctor down to this cremator, that if anyone of them failed to carry out his orders, off go their heads.

When there was a birth of a brown baby, the nurse would come and make much ado over it, and, would tell the mother that she had given birth to a holy child and that she would nurse it for the next six weeks, for her child was going to be a great man (that is when it was a boy baby).

After the first 200 years, Mr. Yakub had done away with the black babies, and all were brown. After another 200 years, he had all yellow or red, which was 400 years after being on "Pelan." Another 200 years, which brings us to the six hundredth year, Mr. Yakub had an all-pale white race of people on this Isle.

Of course, Mr. Yakub lived but 150 years; but, his ideas continued in practice. He gave his people guidance in the form of literature. What they should do and how to do it (how to rule the black nation). He said to them: "When you become unalike (white), you may return to the Holy Land and people, from whom you were exiled."

The Yakub-made devils were really pale white, with really blue eyes; which we think are the ugliest of colors for a human eye. They were call[ed] Caucasian—which means, according to some of the Arab scholars, "One whose evil effect is not confined to one's self alone, but affects others."

There was no good taught to them while on the Island. By teaching the nurses to kill the black baby and save the brown baby, so as to graft the white out of it; by lying to the black mother of the baby, this lie was born into the very nature of the white baby; and, murder for the black people also born in them—or made by nature a liar and murderer.

The black nation is only fooling themselves to take the Caucasian race otherwise. This is what Jesus learned to their history, before He gave up His work of trying to convert the Jews or white race to the religion of Islam.

And, the same knowledge of them was given to Muhammad by the Imams (or scientists) of Mecca. That is why the war of the Muslims against them came to a stop.

Muhammad was told that he could not reform the devils and

that the race had 1,400 more years to live; the only way to make righteous people (Muslims) out of them was to graft them back into the black nation.

This grieved Muhammad so much that it caused him heart trouble until his death (age sixty-two and one half years). The old scientists used to laugh at Muhammad for thinking that he could convert them (the devils) to Islam. This hurt his heart.

Mr. Yakub taught his made devils on Pelan: "That—when you go back to the holy black nation, rent a room in their homes. Teach your wives to go out the next morning around the neighbors of the people, and tell that you heard her talking about them last night.

"When you have gotten them fighting and killing each other, then ask them to let you help settle their disputes, and restore peace among them. If they agree, then you will be able to rule them both." This method the white race practices on the black nation, the world over. They upset their peace by putting one against the other, and then rule them after dividing them.

This is the reason why the American so-called Negroes can never agree on unity among themselves, which would put them on top overnight. The devils keep them divided by paid informers from among themselves. They keep such fools among us. But, the real truth of the devils sometimes converts the informers, and brings them over to us as true believers. We don't bother about killing them, as I am not teaching that which I want to be kept as a secret, but that which the world has not known and should know.

After Yakub's devils were among the Holy people of Islam (the black nation) for six months, they had our people at war with each other. The holy people were unable to understand, just why they could not get along in peace with each other, until they took the matter to the King.

The King told the holy people of the black nation that the trouble they were having was caused by the white devils in their midst, and that there would be no peace among them until they drove these white-made devils from among them.

The holy people prepared to drive the devils out from among them. The King said: "Gather every one of the devils up and strip them of our costume. Put an apron on them to hide their naked-ness. Take all literature from them and take them by way of the desert. Send a caravan, armed with rifles, to keep the devils going westward. Don't allow one of them to turn back; and, if they are lucky enough to get across the Arabian Desert, let them go into the hills of West Asia, the place they now call Europe."

Yakub's-made devils were driven out of Paradise, into the hills of West Asia (Europe), and stripped of everything but the language. They walked across that hot, sandy desert, into the land where long years of both trouble and joy awaited them; but—they finally made it. (Not all: many died in the desert.)

Once there, they were roped in, to keep them out of Paradise. To make sure, the Muslims, who lived along the borders of East and West Asia, were ordered to patrol the border to keep Yakub's devils in West Asia (now called Europe), so that the original nation of black men could live in peace; and that the devils could be alone to themselves, to do as they pleased, as long as they didn't try crossing the East border.

The soldiers patrolled the border armed with swords, to prevent the devils from crossing. This went on for 2,000 years. After that time, Musa (Moses) was born: the man whom Allah would send to these exiled devils to bring them again into the light of civilization. Before we take up this first 2,000 years of the devils exiled on our planet, let us not lose sight of what and how they were made, and of the god who made them, Mr. Yakub.

Since we have learned that Mr. Yakub was an original man (black) the ignorant of our people may say: "If Yakub was a black man and the father of the devils, then he was a devil." That is like one saying "The horse is as much a mule as the mule."

Or, that an orange or lemon is as much grapefruit as the grapefruit: because the grapefruit is grafted from the orange and lemon. They are not alike because the grafted is no longer original.

Just what have we learned, or rather are learning from this divine revelation of our enemies, the devils? Answer: We are learning the truth, which has been kept a secret for 6,000 years concerning the white race, who have deceived us. We learn what is meant by the Bible's symbolic teachings: that they were made from dust.

This only tends to convey the idea that they were created from nothing; which means the low and humble origin of such creation.

Again, we learn who the Bible (Genesis 1:16) is referring to in the saying: "Let us make man." This "US" was fifty-nine thousand, nine hundred and ninety-nine (59,999) black men and women; making or grafting them into the likeness or image of the original man.

Now that they are the same, but have the ways of a human being they are referred to as "mankind"—not the real original man, but a being made like the original in the sense of human beings.

The Holy Qur-an throws a great light on the truth of the creation of this pale, white race of devils. "O mankind, surely we have created you from a male and a female" (Chap. 49:15). This makes it very easy to understand to whom it is referring. "What mankind?" Surely we created man from sperm mixed (with ovum) to try him, so we have made him hearing and seeing" (Chap. 76:2).

Inasmuch as these chapters have a further reference to the spiritual creation of the Last Messenger, it is equally true that they refer to the physical creation of the white race. In another place, the Holy Qur-an says: "We have created man, and now he is an open disputer."

Yakub's race of devils were exiled in the hills and caves of West Asia (now called Europe). They were without anything to start civilization and became savages. They remained in such condition for 2,000 years—no guide or literature.

They lost all knowledge of civilization. The Lord, God of Islam, taught me that some of them tried to graft themselves back into the black nation, but they had nothing to go by. A few were lucky enough to make a start, and got as far as what you call the gorilla. In fact, all of the monkey family are from this 2,000 year history of the white race in Europe.

Being deprived of divine guidance for their disobedience, the making of mischief and causing bloodshed in the holy nation of the original black people by lies, they became so savage that they lost all their sense of shame.

They started going nude as they are doing today (and leading the so-called Negroes into the very acts).

They became shameless. In the winter they wore animal skins for clothes and grew hair all over their bodies and faces like all the other wild animals.

In those days, they made their homes in the caves on hillsides. There is a whole chapter devoted to them in the Holy Qur-an. They had it very hard, trying to save themselves from being destroyed by wild beasts which were plentiful at that time in Europe.

Being without a guide, they started walking on their hands and feet like all animals; and, learned to climb trees as well as any of the animals. At night, they would climb up into trees, carrying large stones and clubs, to fight the wild beasts that would come prowling around at night, to keep them from eating their families.

Their next and best weapons were the dogs. They tamed some of these dogs to live in the caves with their families, to help protect them from the wild beasts. After a time, the dog held a high place among the family because of his fearlessness to attack the enemies of his master. Today, the dog is still loved by the white race and is given more justice than the so-called Negroes, and, is called the white man's best friend. This comes from the cave days.

After 2,000 years of living as a savage, Allah raised up Musa (Moses) to bring the white race again into civilization: to take their place as rulers, as Yakub had intended for them. Musa (Moses) became their God and leader. He brought them out of the caves; taught them to believe in Allah; taught them to wear clothes; how to cook their food; how to season it with salt; what beef they should kill and eat; and, how to use fire for their service. Moses taught them against putting the female cow under burden.

He established for them Friday as the day to eat fish, and not to eat meat (beef) on that day. And, fish is the main menu on Fridays in many of the whites' homes today.

They were so evil (savage) that Moses had to build a ring of fire around him at night; and, he would sleep in the center of the ring to keep the devils from harming him. They were afraid of fire, and are still afraid of fire.

Allah said that: "One day, Moses told them he was going to have fish come up from the sea so that tomorrow we will have some fish."

On the next day, the fish were there. Moses had a boat load sent up from Egypt. Moses said: "See! The sea came up last night and brought us some fish." One of the savages was a little smart and he said to Moses: "Where is the water?"

From then on, Moses recognized the fact that he could not say just anything to them. He had a hard time trying to civilize them. Once they gave Moses so much trouble that he took a few sticks of dynamite, went up on the mountainside, placed them into the ground, and went back to get those who were giving him the most trouble.

He said to them: "Stand there on the edge of this mountain and you will hear the voice of God." They stood there about 300 in number. Moses set the fuse off and it killed all of them.

The Imams got after Moses for performing this trick on the devils. Moses said to the Imams: "If you only knew how much trouble these devils give me, you would do as I do." Moses taught the devils that if they would follow him and obey him, Allah would give them a place among the holy people. Most of them believed Moses, just to get out of the caves.

The Imams recognized the tremendous job Musa (Moses) had, trying to civilize the savages. These enemies of the righteous black nation of earth now had to take the place as the rulers and conquerors of the earth. The devils were given the knowledge and power to bring every living thing, regardless of its kind of life, into subjection.

And God said: "Let us make man in our image, after our likeness; Let them have dominion over the fish of the sea; and over the fowl of the air; and over the cattle, and over all the earth; and over every creeping thing that creepeth upon the earth": and God said unto them: "Be fruitful and multiply; and replenish the earth, and subdue it" (Gen. 1:26, 28).

The above was all necessary if the devils were to rule as a God of the world. They must conquer, and bring into subjection, all life upon the earth—not land life alone, but they must subdue the sea and the like therein—master everything, until a greater master of God comes, which would mean the end of their power over the life of our earth.

We all bear witness that the scripture quoted above refers to the Caucasian race. They are the only people who answer that description and work for the past 4,000 years.

They have subdued the people and most every kind of living thing upon the earth. God has blessed them to exercise all their knowledge, and blessed them with guides (prophets) from among our own people; and, with the rain and seasons of the earth.

Today, their wealth is great upon the earth. Their sciences of worldly good have sent them, not only after the wealth of other than their own people, but even after the lives and property of their own kind. They have tried to re-people (replenish) the earth with their own kind, by skillfully killing off the black man and mixing their blood into the black woman.

But, the job is too big for them to ever conquer. The black nation, including its other three colors, brown, red and yellow, outnumber the Caucasian race, eleven to one.

"God created them in His image" (Gen. 1:27). They are in the image and likeness of a human being (black man), but are altogether a different kind of human being than that of the human beings.

Their pale white skin; their blue eyes (even disliked by themselves) tells any black man or woman, that in those blue and green eyes, there just can't be any sincere love and friendship for them. They are unlike and we are like. Like repels—unlike attracts. The very characteristics of black and white are so very different.

Black people have a heart of gold, love and mercy. Such a heart, nature did not give to the white race. This is where the so-called Negroes are deceived in this devil race. They think they have the same kind of heart; but the white race knows better. They have kept it as a secret among themselves, that they may be able to deceive the black people.

They have been, and still are, successful in deceiving the black man, under the disguise of being the ones who want peace, love and friendship with the world, and with God—at the same time making war with the world, to destroy peace, love and friendship of the black nation.

A brother loves and desires for his brother what he desires for himself. So-called Negroes, do you have this kind of love and desire from the white race for you? Why? Because as I have shown to you, they are not your brothers, by nature. They are fully showing you, this day, openly, that they are different from you; and, you are different from them.

Why not try making brotherly love and friendship with your own kind first? To see you trying to integrate with the very enemy of yours, and God, shows beyond a shadow of a doubt, that you don't know yourself nor your enemies; or rather are lost in love for our enemies, I know you, who love your enemy, don't like that I tell you this truth. But, I can't help it—come what may. God has put upon me this mission, and I must do His will or burn.

Are you with me to do the will of God, or the will of the devil and the disbelieving people? I know you are, for you have learned and are learning more truth than you have ever read or ever will read. Fear not! Allah is on our side, to give you and me the Kingdom.

An Affirmation of Blackness Malcolm X*

Malcolm X spoke a language that no one could misunderstand. He paraded America's brutal racial history before the eyes of every audience he met. A respected figure among many Negroes as a Muslim, he has since his assassination become a venerated personality for some. His presence, his charisma, his so-obvious manliness, were part of the appeal. As Ossie Davis said, ". . . whatever else he was or was not—Malcolm was a man! White folks do not need anybody to remind them they are men. We do!" As important were Malcolm's faith in the ability of black people to direct their own destinies, his willingness to express longings and hates that are rarely made public, his sense of kinship with the aspirations of black people in America and throughout the world, his race pride. Malcolm's affirmation of Blackness expressed a fundamental mood of Negro America which has been restated in the call for "Black Power," and in different form in the poetry and plays of LeRoi Jones, and in Daniel H. Watt's journal, Liberator. The following speech was delivered in Cleveland on April 3, 1964. Malcolm had already left the Nation of Islam. Sponsored by Cleveland's CORE, Louis Lomax and Malcolm X spoke on the subject, "The Negro Revolt—What Comes Next?"

Mr. Moderator, Brother Lomax, brothers and sisters, friends and enemies: I just can't believe everyone in here is a friend and I don't want to leave anybody out. The question tonight, as I understand it, is "The Negro Revolt, and Where Do We Go From Here?" or "What Next?" In my little humble way of understanding it, it points toward either the ballot or the bullet.

* From "The Ballot or the Bullet," in *Malcolm X Speaks: Selected Speeches and Statements* (New York, 1965), pp. 23–38.

Before we try and explain what is meant by the ballot or the bullet, I would like to clarify something concerning myself. I'm still a Muslim, my religion is still Islam. That's my personal belief. Just as Adam Clayton Powell is a Christian minister who heads the Abyssinian Baptist Church in New York, but at the same time takes part in the political struggles to try and bring about rights to the black people in this country; and Dr. Martin Luther King is a Christian minister down in Atlanta, Georgia, who heads another organization fighting for the civil rights of black people in this country; and Rev. Galamison, I guess you've heard of him, is another Christian minister in New York who has been deeply involved in the school boycotts to eliminate segregated education; well, I myself am a minister, not a Christian minister, but a Muslim minister; and I believe in action on all fronts by whatever means necessary.

Although I'm still a Muslim, I'm not here tonight to discuss my religion. I'm not here to try and change your religion. I'm not here to argue or discuss anything that we differ about, because it's time for us to submerge our differences and realize that it is best for us to first see that we have the same problem, a common problem—a problem that will make you catch hell whether you're a Baptist, or a Methodist, or a Muslim, or a nationalist. Whether you're educated or illiterate, whether you live on the boulevard or in the alley, you're going to catch hell just like I am. We're all in the same boat and we all are going to catch the same hell from the same man. He just happens to be a white man. All of us have suffered here, in this country, political oppression at the hands of the white man, economic exploitation at the hands of the white man, and social degradation at the hands of the white man.

Now in speaking like this, it doesn't mean that we're anti-white, but it does mean we're anti-exploitation, we're anti-degradation, we're anti-oppression. And if the white man doesn't want us to be anti-him, let him stop oppressing and exploiting and degrading us. Whether we are Christians or Muslims or nationalists or agnostics or atheists, we must first learn to forget our differences. If we have differences, let us differ in the closet; when we come out in front, let us not have anything to argue about until we get finished arguing with the man. If the late President Kennedy could get together with Khrushchev and exchange some wheat, we certainly

have more in common with each other than Kennedy and
Khrushchev had with each other.

If we don't do something real soon, I think you'll have to agree
that we're going to be forced either to use the ballot or the bullet.
It's one or the other in 1964. It isn't that time is running out—
time has run out! 1964 threatens to be the most explosive year
America has ever witnessed. The most explosive year. Why? It's
also a political year. It's the year when all of the white politicians
will be back in the so-called Negro community jiving you and me
for some votes. The year when all of the white political crooks will
be right back in your and my community with their false promises,
building up our hopes for a letdown, with their trickery and their
treachery, with their false promises which they don't intend to
keep. As they nourish these dissatisfactions, it can only lead to one
thing, an explosion; and now we have the type of black man on the
scene in America today—I'm sorry, Brother Lomax—who just
doesn't intend to turn the other cheek any longer.

Don't let anybody tell you anything about the odds are against
you. If they draft you, they send you to Korea and make you face
800 million Chinese. If you can be brave over there, you can be
brave right here. These odds aren't as great as those odds. And if
you fight here, you will at least know what you're fighting for.

I'm not a politician, not even a student of politics; in fact, I'm
not a student of much of anything. I'm not a Democrat, I'm not a
Republican, and I don't even consider myself an American. If you
and I were Americans, there'd be no problem. Those Hunkies that
just got off the boat, they're already Americans; Polacks are
already Americans; the Italian refugees are already Americans.
Everything that came out of Europe, every blue-eyed thing, is
already an American. And as long as you and I have been over
here, we aren't Americans yet.

Well, I am one who doesn't believe in deluding myself. I'm not
going to sit at your table and watch you eat, with nothing on my
plate, and call myself a diner. Sitting at the table doesn't make you
a diner, unless you eat some of what's on that plate. Being here in
America doesn't make you an American. Being born here in
America doesn't make you an American. Why, if birth made you
American, you wouldn't need any legislation, you wouldn't need
any amendments to the Constitution, you wouldn't be faced with

civil-rights filibustering in Washington, D.C., right now. They don't have to pass civil-rights legislation to make a Polack an American.

No, I'm not an American. I'm one of the 22 million black people who are the victims of Americanism. One of the 22 million black people who are the victims of democracy, nothing but disguised hypocrisy. So, I'm not standing here speaking to you as an American, or a patriot, or a flag-saluter, or a flag-waver—no, not I. I'm speaking as a victim of this American system. And I see America through the eyes of the victim. I don't see any American dream; I see an American nightmare.

These 22 million victims are waking up. Their eyes are coming open. They're beginning to see what they used to only look at. They're becoming politically mature. They are realizing that there are new political trends from coast to coast. As they see these new political trends, it's possible for them to see that every time there's an election the races are so close that they have to have a recount. They had to recount in Massachusetts to see who was going to be governor, it was so close. It was the same way in Rhode Island, in Minnesota, and in many other parts of the country. And the same with Kennedy and Nixon when they ran for president. It was so close they had to count all over again. Well, what does this mean? It means that when white people are evenly divided, and black people have a bloc of votes of their own, it is left up to them to determine who's going to sit in the White House and who's going to be in the dog house.

It was the black man's vote that put the present administration in Washington, D.C. Your vote, your dumb vote, your ignorant vote, your wasted vote put in an administration in Washington, D.C., that has seen fit to pass every kind of legislation imaginable, saving you until last, then filibustering on top of that. And your and my leaders have the audacity to run around clapping their hands and talk about how much progress we're making. And what a good president we have. If he wasn't good in Texas, he sure can't be good in Washington, D.C. Because Texas is a lynch state. It is in the same breath as Mississippi, no different; only they lynch you in Texas with a Texas accent and lynch you in Mississippi with a Mississippi accent. And these Negro leaders have the audacity to go and have some coffee in the White House with a Texan, a Southern cracker—that's all he is—and then come out and tell you and me that he's going to be better for us because, since he's from the South, he knows how to deal with the Southerners. What kind of logic is that? Let Eastland be president, he's from the South too. He should be better able to deal with them than Johnson.

In this present administration they have in the House of Representatives 257 Democrats to only 177 Republicans. They control two-thirds of the House vote. Why can't they pass something that will help you and me? In the Senate, there are 67 senators who are of the Democratic Party. Only 33 of them are Republicans. Why, the Democrats have got the government sewed up, and you're the one who sewed it up for them. And what have they given you for it? Four years in office, and just now getting around to some civil-rights legislation. Just now, after everything else is gone, out of the way, they're going to sit down now and play with you all summer long—the same old giant con game that they call filibuster. All those are in cahoots together. Don't you ever think they're not in cahoots together, for the man that is heading the civil-rights filibuster is a man from Georgia named Richard Russell. When Johnson became president, the first man he asked for when he got back to Washington, D.C., was "Dicky"—that's how tight they are. That's his boy, that's his pal, that's his buddy. But they're playing that old con game. One of them makes believe he's for you, and he's got it fixed where the other one is so tight against you, he never has to keep his promise.

So it's time in 1964 to wake up. And when you see them coming up with that kind of conspiracy, let them know your eyes are open. And let them know you got something else that's wide open too. It's got to be the ballot or the bullet. The ballot or the bullet. If you're afraid to use an expression like that, you should get on out of the country, you should get back in the cotton patch, you should get back in the alley. They get all the Negro vote, and after they get it, the Negro gets nothing in return. All they did when they got to Washington was give a few big Negroes big jobs. Those big Negroes didn't need big jobs, they already had jobs. That's camouflage, that's trickery, that's treachery, window-dressing. I'm not trying to knock out the Democrats for the Republicans, we'll get to them in a minute. But it is true—you put the Democrats first and the Democrats put you last.

Look at it the way it is. What alibis do they use, since they control Congress and the Senate? What alibi do they use when you and I ask, "Well, when are you going to keep your promise?" They blame the Dixiecrats. What is a Dixiecrat? A Democrat. A Dixiecrat is nothing but a Democrat in disguise. The titular head of the Democrats is also the head of the Dixiecrats, because the Dixiecrats are a part of the Democratic Party. The Democrats have never kicked the Dixiecrats out of the party. The Dixiecrats bolted themselves once, but the Democrats didn't put them out. Imagine, these lowdown Southern segregationists put the Northern Democrats down. But the Northern Democrats have never put the Dixiecrats down. No, look at that thing the way it is. They have got a con game going on, a political con game, and you and I are in the middle. It's time for you and me to wake up and start looking at it like it is, and trying to understand it like it is; and then we can deal with it like it is.

The Dixiecrats in Washington, D.C., control the key committees that run the government. The only reason the Dixiecrats control these committees is because they have seniority. The only reason they have seniority is because they come from states where Negroes can't vote. This is not even a government that's based on democracy. It is not a government that is made up of representatives of the people. Half of the people in the South can't even vote. Eastland is not even supposed to be in Washington. Half of the senators and congressmen who occupy these key positions in Washington, D.C., are there illegally, are there unconstitutionally.

I was in Washington, D.C., a week ago Thursday, when they were debating whether or not they should let the bill come onto the floor. And in the back of the room where the Senate meets, there's a huge map of the United States, and on that map it shows the location of Negroes throughout the country. And it shows that the Southern section of the country, the states that are most heavily concentrated with Negroes, are the ones that have senators and congressmen standing up filibustering and doing all other kinds of trickery to keep the Negro from being able to vote. This is pitiful. But it's not pitiful for us any longer; it's actually pitiful for the white man, because soon now, as the Negro awakens a little more and sees the vise that he's in, sees the bag that he's in, sees the real game that he's in, then the Negro's going to develop a new tactic.

These senators and congressmen actually violate the constitutional amendments that guarantee the people of that particular state or county the right to vote. And the Constitution itself has within it the machinery to expel any representative from a state where the voting rights of the people are violated. You don't even need new legislation. Any person in Congress right now, who is there from a state or a district where the voting rights of the people are violated, that particular person should be expelled from Congress. And when you expel him, you've removed one of the obstacles in the path of any real meaningful legislation in this country. In fact, when you expel them, you don't need new legislation, because they will be replaced by black representatives from counties and districts where the black man is in the majority, not in the minority.

If the black man in these Southern states had his full voting rights, the key Dixiecrats in Washington, D.C., which means the key Democrats in Washington, D.C., would lose their seats. The Democratic Party itself would lose its power. It would cease to be powerful as a party. When you see the amount of power that would be lost by the Democratic Party if it were to lose the Dixiecrat wing, or branch, or element, you can see where it's against the interests of the Democrats to give voting rights to Negroes in states where the Democrats have been in complete power and authority ever since the Civil War. You just can't belong to that party without analyzing it.

I say again, I'm not anti-Democrat, I'm not anti-Republican, I'm not anti-anything. I'm just questioning their sincerity, and some of the strategy that they've been using on our people by promising them promises that they don't intend to keep. When you keep the Democrats in power, you're keeping the Dixiecrats in power. I doubt that my good Brother Lomax will deny that. A vote for a Democrat is a vote for a Dixiecrat. That's why, in 1964, it's time now for you and me to become more politically mature and realize what the ballot is for; what we're supposed to get when we cast a ballot; and that if we don't cast a ballot, it's going to end up in a situation where we're going to have to cast a bullet. It's either a ballot or a bullet.

In the North, they do it a different way. They have a system that's known as gerrymandering, whatever that means. It means when Negroes become too heavily concentrated in a certain area, and begin to gain too much political power, the white man comes along and changes the district lines. You may say, "Why do you keep saying white man?" Because it's the white man who does it. I haven't ever seen any Negro changing any lines. They don't let him get near the line. It's the white man who does this. And usually, it's the white man who grins at you the most, and pats you on the back, and is supposed to be your friend. He may be friendly, but he's not your friend.

So, what I'm trying to impress upon you, in essence, is this: You and I in America are faced not with a segregationist conspiracy, we're faced with a government conspiracy. Everyone who's filibustering is a senator—that's the government. Everyone who's finagling in Washington, D.C., is a congressman—that's the government. You don't have anybody putting blocks in your path but people who are a part of the government. The same government that you go abroad to fight for and die for is the government that is in a conspiracy to deprive you of your voting rights, deprive you of your economic opportunities, deprive you of decent housing, deprive you of decent education. You don't need to go to the employer alone, it is the government itself, the government of America, that is responsible for the oppression and exploitation and degradation of black people in this country. And you should drop it in their lap. This government has failed the Negro. This so-called democracy has failed the Negro. And all these white liberals have definitely failed the Negro.

So, where do we go from here? First, we need some friends. We need some new allies. The entire civil-rights struggle needs a new interpretation, a broader interpretation. We need to look at this civil-rights thing from another angle—from the inside as well as from the outside. To those of us whose philosophy is black nationalism, the only way you can get involved in the civil-rights struggle is give it a new interpretation. That old interpretation excluded us. It kept us out. So, we're giving a new interpretation to the civil-rights struggle, an interpretation that will enable us to come into it, take part in it. And these handkerchief-heads who have been dillydallying and pussyfooting and compromising—we don't intend to let them pussyfoot and dillydally and compromise any longer.

How can you thank a man for giving you what's already yours?

How then can you thank him for giving you only part of what's already yours? You haven't even made progress, if what's being given to you, you should have had already. That's not progress. And I love my Brother Lomax, the way he pointed out we're right back where we were in 1954. We're not even as far up as we were in 1954. We're behind where we were in 1954. There's more segregation now than there was in 1954. There's more racial animosity, more racial hatred, more racial violence today in 1964, then there was in 1954. Where is the progress?

And now you're facing a situation where the young Negro's coming up. They don't want to hear that "turn-the-other-cheek" stuff, no. In Jacksonville, those were teenagers, they were throwing Molotov cocktails. Negroes have never done that before. But it shows you there's a new deal coming in. There's new thinking coming in. There's new strategy coming in. It'll be Molotov cocktails this month, hand grenades next month, and something else next month. It'll be ballots, or it'll be bullets. It'll be liberty, or it will be death. The only difference about this kind of death—it'll be reciprocal. You know what is meant by "reciprocal"? That's one of Brother Lomax's words, I stole it from him. I don't usually deal with those big words because I don't usually deal with big people. I deal with small people. I find you can get a whole lot of small people and whip hell out of a whole lot of big people. They haven't got anything to lose, and they've got everything to gain. And they'll let you know in a minute: "It takes two to tango; when I go, you go."

The black nationalists, those whose philosophy is black nationalism, in bringing about this new interpretation of the entire meaning of civil rights, look upon it as meaning, as Brother Lomax has pointed out, equality of opportunity. Well, we're justified in seeking civil rights, if it means equality of opportunity, because all we're doing there is trying to collect for our investment. Our mothers and fathers invested sweat and blood. Three hundred and ten years we worked in this country without a dime in return—I mean without a *dime* in return. You let the white man walk around here talking about how rich this country is, but you never stop to think how it got rich so quick. It got rich because you made it rich.

You take the people who are in this audience right now. They're poor, we're all poor as individuals. Our weekly salary individually amounts to hardly anything. But if you take the salary of everyone in here collectively it'll fill up a whole lot of baskets. It's a lot of wealth. If you can collect the wages of just these people right here for a year, you'll be rich—richer than rich. When you look at it like that, think how rich Uncle Sam had to become, not with this handful, but millions of black people. Your and my mother and father, who didn't work an eight-hour shift, but worked from "can't see" in the morning until "can't see" at night, and worked for nothing, making the white man rich, making Uncle Sam rich.

This is our investment. This is our contribution—our blood. Not only did we give of our free labor, we gave of our blood. Every time he had a call to arms, we were the first ones in uniform. We died on every battlefield the white man had. We have made a greater sacrifice than anybody who's standing up in America today. We have made a greater contribution and have collected less. Civil rights, for those of us whose philosophy is black nationalism, means: "Give it to us now. Don't wait for next year. Give it to us yesterday, and that's not fast enough."

I might stop right here to point out one thing. Whenever you're going after something that belongs to you, anyone who's depriving you of the right to have it is a criminal. Understand that. Whenever you are going after something that is yours, you are within your legal rights to lay claim to it. And anyone who puts forth any effort to deprive you of that which is yours, is breaking the law, is a criminal. And this was pointed out by the Supreme Court decision. It outlawed segregation. Which means segregation is against the law. Which means a segregationist is breaking the law. A segregationist is a criminal. You can't label him as anything other than that. And when you demonstrate against segregation, the law is on your side. The Supreme Court is on your side.

Now, who is it that opposes you in carrying out the law? The police department itself. With police dogs and clubs. Whenever you demonstrate against segregation, whether it is segregated education, segregated housing, or anything else, the law is on your side, and anyone who stands in the way is not the law any longer. They are breaking the law, they are not representatives of the law. Any time you demonstrate against segregation and a man has the audacity to put a police dog on you, kill that dog, kill him, I'm telling you, kill that dog. I say it, if they put me in jail tomorrow, kill—that—dog. Then you'll put a stop to it. Now, if these white people in here don't want to see that kind of action, get down and tell the mayor to tell the police department to pull the dogs in. That's all you have to do. If you don't do it, someone else will.

If you don't take this kind of stand, your little children will grow up and look at you and think "shame." If you don't take an uncompromising stand—I don't mean go out and get violent; but at the same time you should never be nonviolent unless you run into some nonviolence. I'm nonviolent with those who are non-violent with me. But when you drop that violence on me, then you've made me go insane, and I'm not responsible for what I do. And that's the way every Negro should get. Any time you know you're within the law, within your legal rights, within your moral rights, in accord with justice, then die for what you believe in. But don't die alone. Let your dying be reciprocal. This is what is meant by equality. What's good for the goose is good for the gander.

When we begin to get in this area, we need new friends, we need new allies. We need to expand the civil-rights struggle to a higher level—to the level of human rights. Whenever you are in a civil-rights struggle, whether you know it or not, you are confining yourself to the jurisdiction of Uncle Sam. No one from the outside world can speak out in your behalf as long as your struggle is a civil-rights struggle. Civil rights comes within the domestic affairs of this country. All of our African brothers and our Asian brothers and our Latin-American brothers cannot open their mouths and interfere in the domestic affairs of the United States. And as long as it's civil rights, this comes under the jurisdiction of Uncle Sam.

But the United Nations has what's known as the charter of human rights, it has a committee that deals in human rights. You may wonder why all of the atrocities that have been committed in Africa and in Hungary and in Asia and in Latin America are brought before the UN, and the Negro problem is never brought before the UN. This is part of the conspiracy. This old, tricky, blue-eyed liberal who is supposed to be your and my friend, supposed to be in our corner, supposed to be subsidizing our struggle, and supposed to be acting in the capacity of an adviser, never tells you anything about human rights. They keep you wrapped up in civil rights. And you spend so much time barking up the civil-rights tree, you don't even know there's a human-rights tree on the same floor.

When you expand the civil-rights struggle to the level of human rights, you can then take the case of the black man in this country before the nations in the UN. You can take it before the General Assembly. You can take Uncle Sam before a world court. But the only level you can do it on is the level of human rights. Civil rights keeps you under his restrictions, under his jurisdiction. Civil rights keeps you in his pocket. Civil rights means you're asking Uncle Sam to treat you right. Human rights are something you were born with. Human rights are your God-given rights. Human rights are the rights that are recognized by all nations of this earth. And any time any one violates your human rights, you can take them to the world court. Uncle Sam's hands are dripping with blood, dripping with the blood of the black man in this country. He's the earth's number-one hypocrite. He has the audacity—yes, he has—imagine him posing as the leader of the free world. The free world!—and you over here singing "We Shall Overcome." Expand the civil-rights struggle to the level of human rights, take it into the United Nations, where our African brothers can throw their weight on our side, where our Asian brothers can throw their weight on our side, where our Latin-American brothers can throw their weight on our side, and where 800 million Chinamen are sitting there waiting to throw their weight on our side.

Let the world know how bloody his hands are. Let the world know the hypocrisy that's practiced over here. Let it be the ballot or the bullet. Let him know that it must be the ballot or the bullet.

When you take your case to Washington, D.C., you're taking it to the criminal who's responsible; it's like running from the wolf to the fox. They're all in cahoots together. They all work political chicanery and make you look like a chump before the eyes of the world. Here you are walking around in America, getting ready to be drafted and sent abroad, like a tin soldier, and when you get over there, people ask you what are you fighting for, and you have to stick your tongue in your cheek. No, take Uncle Sam to court, take him before the world.

By ballot I only mean freedom. Don't you know—I disagree with Lomax on this issue—that the ballot is more important than the dollar? Can I prove it? Yes. Look in the UN. There are poor nations in the UN; yet those poor nations can get together with their voting power and keep the rich nations from making a move. They have one nation—one vote, everyone has an equal vote. And when those brothers from Asia, and Africa and the darker parts of this earth get together, their voting power is sufficient to hold Sam in check. Or Russia in check. Or some other section of the earth in check. So, the ballot is most important.

Right now, in this country, if you and I, 22 million African-Americans—that's what we are—Africans who are in America. You're nothing but Africans. Nothing but Africans. In fact, you'd get farther calling yourself African instead of Negro. Africans don't catch hell. You're the only one catching hell. They don't have to pass civil-rights bills for Africans. An African can go anywhere he wants right now. All you've got to do is tie your head up. That's right, go anywhere you want. Just stop being a Negro. Change your name to Hoogagagooba. That'll show you how silly the white man is. You're dealing with a silly man. A friend of mine who's very dark put a turban on his head and went into a restaurant in Atlanta before they called themselves desegregated. He went into a white restaurant, he sat down, they served him, and he said, "What would happen if a Negro came in here?" And there he's sitting, black as night, but because he had his head wrapped up the waitress looked back at him and says, "Why, there wouldn't no nigger dare come in here."

So, you're dealing with a man whose bias and prejudice are making him lose his mind, his intelligence, every day. He's frightened. He looks around and sees what's taking place on this earth, and he sees that the pendulum of time is swinging in your direction. The dark people are waking up. They're losing their fear of the white man. No place where he's fighting right now is he winning. Everywhere he's fighting, he's fighting someone your and my complexion. And they're beating him. He can't win any more. He's won his last battle. He failed to win in the Korean War. He couldn't win it. He had to sign a truce. That's a loss. Any time Uncle Sam, with all his machinery for warfare, is held to a draw by some rice-eaters, he's lost the battle. He had to sign a truce. America's not supposed to sign a truce. She's supposed to be bad. But she's not bad any more. She's bad as long as she can use her hydrogen bomb, but she can't use hers for fear Russia might use hers. Russia can't use hers, for fear that Sam might use his. So, both of them are weaponless. They can't use the weapon because each's weapon nullifies the other's. So the only place where action can take place is on the ground. And the white man can't win another war fighting on the ground. Those days are over. The black man knows it, the brown man knows it, the red man knows it, and the yellow man knows it. So they engage him in guerrilla warfare. That's not his style. You've got to have heart to be a guerrilla warrior, and he hasn't got any heart. I'm telling you now.

I just want to give you a little briefing on guerrilla warfare because, before you know it, before you know it—It takes heart to be a guerrilla warrior because you're on your own. In conventional warfare you have tanks and a whole lot of other people with you to back you up, planes over your head and all that kind of stuff. But a guerrilla is on his own. All you have is a rifle, some sneakers and a bowl of rice, and that's all you need—and a lot of heart. The Japanese on some of those islands in the Pacific, when the American soldiers landed, one Japanese sometimes could hold the whole army off. He'd just wait until the sun went down, and when the sun went down they were all equal. He would take his little blade and slip from bush to bush, and from American to American. The white soldiers couldn't cope with that. Whenever you see a white soldier that fought in the Pacific, he has the shakes, he has a nervous condition, because they scared him to death.

The same thing happened to the French up in French Indochina. People who just a few years previously were rice farmers got together and ran the heavily-mechanized French army out of Indochina. You don't need it—modern warfare today won't work. This is the day of the guerrilla. They did the same thing in Algeria. Algerians, who were nothing but Bedouins, took a rifle and sneaked off to the hills, and de Gaulle and all of his highfalutin' war machinery couldn't defeat those guerrillas. Nowhere on this earth does the white man win in a guerrilla warfare. It's not his speed. Just as guerrilla warfare is prevailing in Asia and in parts of Africa and in parts of Latin America, you've got to be mighty naive, or you've got to play the black man cheap, if you don't think some day he's going to wake up and find that it's got to be the ballot or the bullet.

The Watts Riot *John A. McCone**

Despite the seeming differences in appearance of black ghettos throughout the nation, their enduring difficulties are similar: economic and family dislocation, high rents, inadequate services, second-rate schools. This fact became strikingly clear in August, 1965, in Watts. A short time before an Urban League study rated life for the Negro community of Los Angeles superior to sixty-eight other cities in which Negroes lived throughout the country. But beneath the outward pleasantries of small houses and front lawns conditions were much the same in Watts as they were in Harlem, Chicago's South Side, or Cleveland's Hough. For 144 hours, from August 11 to August 16, 1965, Watts was turned into a battlefield, the worst racial outbreak in America since Detroit's riot of 1943. This description of the fury that was Watts is from the much-criticized McCone Commission report. John A. McCone, former director of the CIA, headed the Governor's Commission on the Los Angeles Riots.

THE FRYE ARRESTS

On August 11, 1965, California Highway Patrolman Lee W. Minikus, a Caucasian, was riding his motorcycle along 122nd Street, just south of the Los Angeles City boundary, when a passing Negro motorist told him he had just seen a car that was being driven recklessly. Minikus gave chase and pulled the car over at 116th and Avalon, in a predominantly Negro neighborhood, near but not in Watts. It was 7:00 P.M.

The driver was Marquette Frye, a 21-year-old Negro, and his older brother, Ronald, 22, was a passenger. Minikus asked Marquette to get out and take the standard Highway Patrol sobriety test. Frye failed the test, and at 7:05 P.M., Minikus told him he was under arrest. He radioed for his motorcycle partner, for a car to take Marquette to jail, and a tow truck to take the car away.

* John A. McCone, "144 Hours in August 1965," from *Violence in the City—An End or a Beginning?* (Los Angeles, 1965), pp. 10–25.

They were two blocks from the Frye home, in an area of two-story apartment buildings and numerous small family residences. Because it was a very warm evening, many of the residents were outside.

Ronald Frye, having been told he could not take the car when Marquette was taken to jail, went to get their mother so that she could claim the car. They returned to the scene about 7:15 P.M. as the second motorcycle patrolman, the patrol car, and tow truck arrived. The original group of 25 to 50 curious spectators had grown to 250 to 300 persons.

Mrs. Frye approached Marquette and scolded him for drinking. Marquette, who until then had been peaceful and cooperative, pushed her away and moved toward the crowd, cursing and shouting at the officers that they would have to kill him to take him to jail. The patrolmen pursued Marquette and he resisted.

The watching crowd became hostile, and one of the patrolmen radioed for more help. Within minutes, three more highway patrolmen arrived. Minikus and his partner were now struggling with both Frye brothers. Mrs. Frye, now belligerent, jumped on the back of one of the officers and ripped his shirt. In an attempt to subdue Marquette, one officer swung at his shoulder with a night stick, missed, and struck him on the forehead, inflicting a minor cut. By 7:23 P.M., all three of the Fryes were under arrest, and other California Highway Patrolmen and, for the first time, Los Angeles police officers had arrived in response to the call for help.

Officers on the scene said there were now more than 1,000 persons in the crowd. About 7:25 P.M., the patrol car with the prisoners, and the tow truck pulling the Frye car, left the scene. At 7:31 P.M., the Fryes arrived at a nearby sheriff's substation.

Undoubtedly the situation at the scene of the arrest was tense. Belligerence and resistance to arrest called for forceful action by the officers. This brought on hostility from Mrs. Frye and some of the bystanders, which, in turn, caused increased actions by the police. Anger at the scene escalated and, as in all such situations, bitter recriminations from both sides followed.

Considering the undisputed facts, the Commission finds that the arrest of the Fryes was handled efficiently and expeditiously. The sobriety test administered by the California Highway Patrol and its use of a transportation vehicle for the prisoner and a tow truck to remove his car are in accordance with the practices of other law enforcement agencies, including the Los Angeles Police Department.

THE SPITTING INCIDENT

As the officers were leaving the scene, someone in the crowd spat on one of them. They stopped withdrawing and two highway patrolmen went into the crowd and arrested a young Negro woman and a man who was said to have been inciting the crowd to violence when the officers were arresting her. Although the wisdom of stopping the withdrawal to make these arrests has been questioned, the Commission finds no basis for criticizing the judgment of the officers on the scene.

Following these arrests, all officers withdrew at 7:40 P.M. As the last police car left the scene, it was stoned by the now irate mob.

As had happened so frequently in riots in other cities, inflated and distorted rumors concerning the arrests spread quickly to adjacent areas. The young woman arrested for spitting was wearing a barber's smock, and the false rumor spread throughout the area that she was pregnant and had been abused by police. Erroneous reports were also circulated concerning the treatment of the Fryes at the arrest scene.

The crowd did not disperse, but ranged in small groups up and down the street, although never more than a few blocks from the arrest scene. Between 8:15 P.M. and midnight, the mob stoned automobiles, pulled Caucasian motorists out of their cars and beat them, and menaced a police field command post which had been set up in the area. By 1:00 A.M., the outbreak seemed to be under control but, until early morning hours, there were sporadic reports of unruly mobs, vandalism, and rock throwing. Twenty-nine persons were arrested.

A MEETING MISFIRES

On Thursday morning, there was an uneasy calm, but it was obvious that tensions were still high. A strong expectancy of further trouble kept the atmosphere tense in the judgment of both police and Negro leaders. The actions by many individuals, both

Negro and white, during Thursday, as well as at other times, to attempt to control the riots are commendable. We have heard many vivid and impressive accounts of the work of Negro leaders, social workers, probation officers, churchmen, teachers, and businessmen in their attempts to persuade the people to desist from their illegal activities, to stay in their houses and off the street, and to restore order.

However, the meeting called by the Los Angeles County Human Relations Commission, at the request of county officials, for the purpose of lowering the temperature misfired. That meeting was held beginning about 2:00 P.M. in an auditorium at Athens Park, eleven blocks from the scene of the arrest. It brought together every available representative of neighborhood groups and Negro leaders to discuss the problem. Members of the press, television, and radio covered the meeting. Various elected officials participated and members of the Los Angeles Police Department, Sheriff's Office and District Attorney's Office were in attendance as observers.

Several community leaders asked members of the audience to use their influence to persuade area residents to stay home Thursday evening. Even Mrs. Frye spoke and asked the crowd to "help me and others calm this situation down so that we will not have a riot tonight." But one Negro high school youth ran to the microphones and said the rioters would attack adjacent white areas that evening. This inflammatory remark was widely reported on television and radio, and it was seldom balanced by reporting of the many responsible statements made at the meeting. Moreover, it appears that the tone and conduct of the meeting shifted, as the meeting was in progress, from attempted persuasion with regard to the maintenance of law and order to a discussion of the grievances felt by the Negro.

Following the main meeting, certain leaders adjourned to a small meeting where they had discussions with individuals representing youth gangs and decided upon a course of action. They decided to propose that Caucasian officers be withdrawn from the troubled area, and that Negro officers in civilian clothes and unmarked cars be substituted. Members of this small group then went to see Deputy Chief of Police Roger Murdock at the 77th Street Station, where the proposals were rejected by him at about

7:00 P.M. They envisaged an untested method of handling a serious situation that was rapidly developing. Furthermore, the proposal to use only Negro officers ran counter to the policy of the Police Department, adopted over a period of time at the urging of Negro leaders, to deploy Negro officers throughout the city and not concentrate them in the Negro area. Indeed, when the proposal came the police had no immediate means of determining where the Negro officers on the forces were stationed. At this moment, rioting was breaking out again, and the police felt that their established procedures were the only way to handle what was developing as another night of rioting. Following those procedures, the police decided to set up a perimeter around the center of trouble and keep all crowd activity within that area.

AN ALERT IS SOUNDED

About 5:00 P.M. Thursday, after receiving a report on the Athens Park meeting, Police Chief William H. Parker called Lt. Gen. Roderic Hill, the Adjutant General of the California National Guard in Sacramento, and told him that the Guard might be needed. This step was taken pursuant to a procedure instituted by Governor Brown and agreed upon in 1963 and 1964 between the Los Angeles Police Department, the Governor and the Guard. It was an alert that the Guard might be needed.

Pursuant to the agreed-upon procedure, General Hill sent Colonel Robert Quick to Los Angeles to work as liaison officer. He also alerted the commanders of the 40th Armored Division located in Southern California to the possibility of being called. In addition, in the absence of Governor Brown who was in Greece, he called the acting Governor, Lieutenant Governor Glenn Anderson, in Santa Barbara, and informed him of the Los Angeles situation.

The Emergency Control Center at Police Headquarters—a specially outfitted command post—was opened at 7:30 P.M. on Thursday. That day, one hundred and ninety deputy sheriffs were asked for and assigned. Between 6:45 and 7:15 P.M., crowds at the scene of the trouble of the night before had grown to more than 1,000. Firemen who came into the area to fight fires in three overturned automobiles were shot at and bombarded with rocks. The first fire in a commercial establishment was set only one block from the location of the Frye arrests, and police had to hold back rioters as firemen fought the blaze.

Shortly before midnight, rock-throwing and looting crowds for the first time ranged outside the perimeter. Five hundred police officers, deputy sheriffs and highway patrolmen used various techniques, including fender-to-fender sweeps by police cars, in seeking to disperse the mob. By 4:00 A.M. Friday, the police department felt that the situation was at least for the moment under control. At 5:09 A.M., officers were withdrawn from emergency perimeter control.

During the evening on Thursday, Lt. Gov. Anderson had come to his home in suburban Los Angeles from Santa Barbara. While at his residence, he was informed that there were as many as 8,000 rioters in the streets. About 1:00 A.M. Friday, he talked by phone to John Billett of his staff and with General Hill, and both advised him that police officials felt the situation was nearing control. About 6:45 A.M., at Lt. Gov. Anderson's request, Billet called the Emergency Control Center and was told by Sergeant Jack Eberhardt, the intelligence officer on duty, that "the situation was rather well in hand," and this information was promptly passed on to Anderson. Anderson instructed Billett to keep in touch with him and left Los Angeles at 7:25 A.M. for a morning meeting of the Finance Committee of the Board of Regents of the University of California in Berkeley, and an afternoon meeting of the full Board.

FRIDAY, THE 13TH

Around 8:00 A.M., crowds formed again in the vicinity of the Frye arrests and in the adjacent Watts business area, and looting resumed. Before 9:00 A.M., Colonel Quick called General Hill in Sacramento from the Emergency Control Center and told him riot activity was intensifying.

At approximately 9:15 A.M., Mayor Sam Yorty and Chief Parker talked on the telephone, and they decided, at that time, to call the Guard. Following this conversation, Mayor Yorty went to the airport and boarded a 10:05 flight to keep a speaking engagement at the Commonwealth Club in San Francisco. Mayor Yorty told our Commission that "by about 10:00 or so, I have to decide whether I am going to disappoint that audience in San Francisco and maybe make my city look rather ridiculous if the rioting doesn't start again, and the mayor has disappointed that crowd." The Mayor returned to the City at 3:35 P.M.

The riot situation was canvassed in a Los Angeles Police Department staff meeting held at 9:45 A.M. where Colonel Quick, of the California National Guard, was in attendance, along with police officials. At 10:00 A.M., according to Colonel Quick, Chief Parker said, "It looks like we are going to have to call the troops. We will need a thousand men." Colonel Quick has said that Chief Parker did not specifically ask him to get the National Guard. On the other hand, Chief Parker has stated that he told Colonel Quick that he wanted the National Guard and that Quick indicated that he would handle the request.

In any event, at 10:15, Colonel Quick informed General Hill by telephone that Chief Parker would probably request 1,000 national guardsmen. General Hill advised Colonel Quick to have Chief Parker call the Governor's office in Sacramento. At 10:50 A.M., Parker made the formal request for the National Guard to Winslow Christian, Governor Brown's executive secretary, who was then in Sacramento, and Christian accepted the request.

By mid-morning, a crowd of 3,000 had gathered in the commercial section of Watts and there was general looting in that district as well as in adjacent business areas. By the time the formal request for the Guard had been made, ambulance drivers and firemen were refusing to go into the riot area without an armed escort.

CALLING THE GUARD

At approximately 11:00 A.M., Christian reached Lt. Gov. Anderson by telephone in Berkeley and relayed Chief Parker's request. Lt. Gov. Anderson did not act on the request at that time. We believe that this request from the chief law enforcement officer of the stricken city for the National Guard should have been honored without delay. If the Lieutenant Governor was in doubt about conditions in Los Angeles, he should, in our view, have confirmed Chief Parker's estimate by telephoning National Guard officers in Los Angeles. Although we are mindful that it was natural and prudent for the Lieutenant Governor to be cautious in acting in the absence of Governor Brown, we feel that, in this instance, he hesitated when he should have acted.

Feeling that he wished to consider the matter further, Lt. Gov. Anderson returned to Los Angeles by way of Sacramento. A propeller-driven National Guard plane picked him up at Oakland at 12:20 P.M., and reached McClellan Air Force Base, near Sacramento, at 1:00 P.M. Anderson met with National Guard officers and civilian staff members and received various suggestions, ranging from advice from Guard officers that he commit the Guard immediately to counsel from some civilian staff members that he examine the situation in Los Angeles and meet with Chief Parker before acting. Although Anderson still did not reach a decision to commit the Guard, he agreed with Guard officers that the troops should be assembled in the Armories at 5 P.M., which he had been told by General Hill was the earliest hour that it was feasible to do so. Hill then ordered 2,000 men to be at the armories by that hour. Anderson's plane left Sacramento for Los Angeles at 1:35 P.M. and arrived at 3:35 P.M.

At the time Lt. Gov. Anderson and General Hill were talking in Sacramento, approximately 856 Guardsmen in the 3rd Brigade were in the Long Beach area 12 miles to the south, while enroute from San Diego, outfitted with weapons, to summer camp at Camp Roberts. We feel it reasonable to conclude, especially since this unit was subsequently used in the curfew area, that further escalation of the riots might have been averted if these Guardsmen had been diverted promptly and deployed on station throughout the riot area by early or mid-afternoon Friday.

Friday afternoon, Hale Champion, State Director of Finance, who was in the Governor's office in Los Angeles, reached Governor Brown in Athens. He briefed the Governor on the current riot situation, and Brown said he felt the Guard should be called immediately, that the possibility of a curfew should be explored, and that he was heading home as fast as possible.

Early Friday afternoon, rioters jammed the streets, began systematically to burn two blocks of 103rd Street in Watts, and drove off firemen by sniper fire and by throwing missiles. By late afternoon, gang activity began to spread the disturbance as far as fifty and sixty blocks to the north.

Lieutenant Governor Anderson arrived at the Van Nuys Air

National Guard Base at 3:35 P.M. After talking with Hale Champion who urged him to call the Guard, Anderson ordered General Hill to commit the troops. At 4:00 P.M., he announced this decision to the press. At 5:00 P.M., in the Governor's office downtown, he signed the proclamation officially calling the Guard.

By 6:00 P.M., 1,336 National Guard troops were assembled in the armories. These troops were en route to two staging areas in the rioting area by 7:00 P.M. However, neither the officials of the Los Angeles Police Department nor officers of the Guard deployed any of the troops until shortly after 10:00 P.M. Having in mind these delays, we believe that law enforcement agencies and the National Guard should develop contingency plans so that in future situations of emergency, there will be a better method at hand to assure the early commitment of the National Guard and the rapid deployment of the troops.

The first death occurred between 6:00 and 7:00 P.M. Friday, when a Negro bystander, trapped on the street between police and rioters, was shot and killed during an exchange of gunfire.

THE WORST NIGHT

Friday was the worst night. The riot moved out of the Watts area and burning and looting spread over wide areas of Southeast Los Angeles several miles apart. At 1:00 A.M. Saturday, there were 100 engine companies fighting fires in the area. Snipers shot at firemen as they fought new fires. That night, a fireman was crushed and killed on the fire line by a falling wall, and a deputy sheriff was killed when another sheriff's shotgun was discharged in a struggle with rioters.

Friday night, the law enforcement officials tried a different tactic. Police officers made sweeps on foot, moving en masse along streets to control activity and enable firemen to fight fires. By midnight, Friday, another 1,000 National Guard troops were marching shoulder to shoulder clearing the streets. By 3:00 A.M. Saturday, 3,356 guardsmen were on the streets, and the number continued to increase until the full commitment of 13,900 guardsmen was reached by midnight on Saturday. The maximum commitment of the Los Angeles Police Department during the riot period was 934 officers; the maximum for the Sheriff's Office was 719 officers.

Despite the new tactics and added personnel, the area was not under control at any time on Friday night, as major calls of looting, burning, and shooting were reported every two to three minutes. On throughout the morning hours of Saturday and during the long day, the crowds of looters and patterns of burning spread out and increased still further until it became necessary to impose a curfew on the 46.5 square-mile area on Saturday. Lieutenant Governor Anderson appeared on television early Saturday evening to explain the curfew, which made it a crime for any unauthorized persons to be on the streets in the curfew area after 8:00 P.M.

THE BEGINNING OF CONTROL

Much of the Saturday burning had been along Central Avenue. Again using sweep tactics, the guardsmen and police were able to clear this area by 3:30 P.M. Guardsmen rode "shotgun" on the fire engines and effectively stopped the sniping and rock throwing at firemen. Saturday evening, road blocks were set up in anticipation of the curfew. The massive show of force was having some effect although there was still riot activity and rumors spread regarding proposed activity in the south central area.

When the curfew started at 8:00 P.M., police and guardsmen were able to deal with the riot area as a whole. Compared with the holocaust of Friday evening, the streets were relatively quiet. The only major exception was the burning of a block of stores on Broadway between 46th and 48th Streets. Snipers again prevented firemen from entering the area, and while the buildings burned, a gun battle ensued between law enforcement officers, the Guard, and the snipers.

During the day Sunday, the curfew area was relatively quiet. Because many markets had been destroyed, food distribution was started by churches, community groups, and government agencies. Governor Brown, who had returned Saturday night, personally toured the area, talking to residents. Major fires were under control but there were new fires and some rekindling of old ones. By Tuesday, Governor Brown was able to lift the curfew and by the following Sunday, only 252 guardsmen remained.

Coordination between the several law enforcement agencies during the period of the riot was commendable. When the California Highway Patrol called for help on Wednesday evening, the Los Angeles Police Department responded immediately. When the situation grew critical Thursday evening, the Los Angeles Sheriff's Office committed substantial forces without hesitation. Indeed, the members of all law enforcement agencies—policemen, sheriff's officers, Highway Patrolmen, city Marshalls—and the Fire Departments as well—worked long hours, in harmony and with conspicuous bravery, to quell the disorder. However, the depth and the seriousness of the situation were not accurately appraised in the early stages, and the law enforcement forces committed and engaged in the several efforts to bring the riots under control on Thursday night and all day Friday proved to be inadequate. It required massive force to subdue the riot, as demonstrated by the effectiveness of the Guard when it moved into the position late Friday night and worked in coordination with the local law enforcement units.

OTHER AREAS AFFECTED

As the word of the South Los Angeles violence was flashed almost continuously by all news media, the unrest spread. Although outbreaks in other areas were minor by comparison with those in South Central Los Angeles, each one held dangerous potential. San Diego, 102 miles away, had three days of rioting and 81 people were arrested. On Friday night, there was rioting in Pasadena, 12 miles from the curfew zone. There, liquor and gun stores were looted and Molotov cocktails and fire bombs were thrown at police cars. Only prompt and skillful handling by the police prevented this situation from getting out of control.

Pacoima, 20 miles north, had scattered rioting, looting, and burning. There was burning in Monrovia, 25 miles east. On Sunday night, after the curfew area was quiet, there was an incident in Long Beach, 12 miles south. About 200 guardsmen and Los Angeles police assisted Long Beach police in containing a dangerous situation which exploded when a policeman was shot when another officer's gun discharged as he was being attacked by rioters. Several fires were set Sunday night in the San Pedro-Wilmington area, 12 miles south.

Was There a Pre-established Plan?

After a thorough examination, the Commission has concluded that there is no reliable evidence of outside leadership or pre-established plans for the rioting. The testimony of law enforcement agencies and their respective intelligence officers supports this conclusion. The Attorney General, the District Attorney, and the Los Angeles police have all reached the conclusion that there is no evidence of a pre-plan or a pre-established central direction of the rioting activities. This finding was submitted to the Grand Jury by the District Attorney.

This is not to say that there was *no* agitation or promotion of the rioting by local groups or gangs which exist in pockets throughout the south central area. The sudden appearance of Molotov cocktails in quantity and the unexplained movement of men in cars through the areas of great destruction support the conclusion that there was organization and planning after the riots commenced. In addition, on that tense Thursday, inflammatory handbills suddenly appeared in Watts. But this cannot be identified as a master plan by one group; rather it appears to have been the work of several gangs, with membership of young men ranging in age from 14 to 35 years. All of these activities intensified the rioting and caused it to spread with increased violence from one district to another in the curfew area.

The Grim Statistics

The final statistics are staggering. There were 34 persons killed and 1,032 reported injuries, including 90 Los Angeles police officers, 136 firemen, 10 national guardsmen, 23 persons from other governmental agencies, and 773 civilians. 118 of the injuries resulted from gunshot wounds. Of the 34 killed, one was a fireman, one was a deputy sheriff, and one a Long Beach policeman.

In the weeks following the riots, Coroner's Inquests were held regarding thirty-two of the deaths.* The Coroner's jury ruled that

* The Coroner's Inquest into one of the deaths was cancelled at the request of the deceased's family. There was no inquest into the death of the deputy sheriff because of pending criminal proceedings.

twenty-six of the deaths were justifiable homicide, five were homicidal, and one was accidental. Of those ruled justifiable homicide, the jury found that death was caused in sixteen instances by officers of the Los Angeles Police Department and in seven instances by the National Guard.*

It has been estimated that the loss of property attributable to the riots was over $40 million. More than 600 buildings were damaged by burning and looting. Of this number, more than 200 were totally destroyed by fire. The rioters concentrated primarily on food markets, liquor stores, furniture stores, clothing stores, department stores, and pawn shops. Arson arrests numbered 27 and 10 arson complaints were filed, a relatively small number considering that fire department officials say that all of the fires were incendiary in origin. Between 2,000 and 3,000 fire alarms were recorded during the riot, 1,000 of these between 7:00 A.M. on Friday and 7:00 A.M. on Saturday. We note with interest that no residences were deliberately burned, that damage to schools, libraries, churches and public buildings was minimal, and that certain types of business establishments, notably service stations and automobile dealers, were for the most part unharmed.

There were 3,438 adults arrested, 71% for burglary and theft. The number of juveniles arrested was 514, 81% for burglary and theft. Of the adults arrested, 1,232 had never been arrested before; 1,164 had a "minor" criminal record (arrest only or convictions with sentence of 90 days or less); 1,042 with "major" criminal record (convictions with sentence of more than 90 days). Of the juveniles arrested, 257 had never been arrested before; 212 had a "minor" criminal record; 43 had a "major" criminal record. Of the adults arrested, 2,057 were born in 16 southern states whereas the comparable figure for juveniles was 131. Some of the juveniles arrested extensively damaged the top two floors of an auxiliary jail which had been opened on the Saturday of the riots.

Those involved in the administration of justice—judges, prosecutors, defense counsel, and others—merit commendation for the steps they took to cope with the extraordinary responsibility thrust on the judicial system by the riots. By reorganizing calendars and

---

* A legal memorandum analyzing the procedures followed in the inquests, which was prepared at the request of the Commission, has been forwarded to the appropriate public officials for their consideration.

making special assignments, the Los Angeles Superior and Municipal Courts have been able to meet the statutory deadlines for processing the cases of those arrested. Court statistics indicate that by November 26, the following dispositions had been made of the 2,278 felony cases filed against adults: 856 were found guilty; 155 were acquitted; 641 were disposed of prior to trial, primarily by dismissal; 626 are awaiting trial. Of the 1,133 misdemeanor cases filed, 733 were found guilty, 81 were acquitted, 184 dismissed and 135 are awaiting trial.

The police and Sheriff's Department have long known that many members of gangs, as well as others, in the south central area possessed weapons and knew how to use them. However, the extent to which pawn shops, each one of which possessed an inventory of weapons, were the immediate target of looters, leads to the conclusion that a substantial number of the weapons used were stolen from these shops. During the riots, law enforcement officers recovered 851 weapons. There is no evidence that the rioters made any attempt to steal narcotics from pharmacies in the riot area even though some pharmacies were looted and burned.

Overwhelming as are the grim statistics, the impact of the August rioting on the Los Angeles community has been even greater. The first weeks after the disorders brought a flood tide of charges and recriminations. Although this has now ebbed, the feeling of fear and tension persists, largely unabated, throughout the community. A certain slowness in the rebuilding of the fired structures has symbolized the difficulty in mending relationships in our community which were so severely fractured by the August nightmare.

A Study of the Negro Family Daniel Patrick Moynihan*

Daniel P. Moynihan's study of the Negro family has been much debated and much misunderstood. No one can question the existence of serious family dislocation among the Negro lower classes. The argument centered around the origins of the trouble, and hasty readers charged Moynihan with racism or undue emphasis on the

* From the Moynihan Report: United States Department of Labor, *The Negro Family: The Case for National Action* (Washington, D.C., 1965), pp. 5–14.

heritage of slavery. The fact is that Moynihan demonstrated a close correlation between present economic conditions and family instability. "During times when jobs were reasonably plentiful . . . the Negro family became stronger and more stable," Moynihan wrote. "As jobs became more and more difficult to find, the stability of the family became more and more difficult to maintain."

At the heart of the deterioration of the fabric of Negro society is the deterioration of the Negro family.

It is the fundamental source of the weakness of the Negro community at the present time.

There is probably no single fact of Negro American life so little understood by whites. The Negro situation is commonly perceived by whites in terms of the visible manifestations of discrimination and poverty, in part because Negro protest is directed against such obstacles, and in part, no doubt, because these are facts which involve the actions and attitudes of the white community as well. It is more difficult, however, for whites to perceive the effect that three centuries of exploitation have had on the fabric of Negro society itself. Here the consequences of the historic injustices done to Negro Americans are silent and hidden from view. But here is where the true injury has occurred: unless this damage is repaired, all the effort to end discrimination and poverty and injustice will come to little.

The role of the family in shaping character and ability is so pervasive as to be easily overlooked. The family is the basic social unit of American life; it is the basic socializing unit. By and large, adult conduct in society is learned as a child.

A fundamental insight of psychoanalytic theory, for example, is that the child learns a way of looking at life in his early years through which all later experience is viewed and which profoundly shapes his adult conduct.

It may be hazarded that the reason family structure does not loom larger in public discussion of social issues is that people tend to assume that the nature of family life is about the same throughout American society. The mass media and the development of suburbia have created an image of the American family as a highly standardized phenomenon. It is therefore easy to assume that whatever it is that makes for differences among individuals or groups of individuals, it is not a different family structure.

There is much truth to this; as with any other nation, Americans are producing a recognizable family system. But that process is not completed by any means. There are still, for example, important differences in family patterns surviving from the age of the great European migration to the United States, and these variations account for notable differences in the progress and assimilation of various ethnic and religious groups. A number of immigrant groups were characterized by unusually strong family bonds; these groups have characteristically progressed more rapidly than others.

But there is one truly great discontinuity in family structure in the United States at the present time: that between the white world in general and that of the Negro American.

The white family has achieved a high degree of stability and is maintaining that stability.

By contrast, the family structure of lower class Negroes is highly unstable, and in many urban centers is approaching complete breakdown.

N.b. There is considerable evidence that the Negro community is in fact dividing between a stable middle-class group that is steadily growing stronger and more successful, and an increasingly disorganized and disadvantaged lower-class group. There are indications, for example, that the middle-class Negro family puts a higher premium on family stability and the conserving of family resources than does the white middle-class family. The discussion of this paper is not, obviously, directed to the first group excepting as it is affected by the experiences of the second—an important exception. . . .

There are two points to be noted in this context.

First, the emergence and increasing visibility of a Negro middle-class may beguile the nation into supposing that the circumstances of the remainder of the Negro community are equally prosperous, whereas just the opposite is true at present, and is likely to continue so.

Second, the lumping of all Negroes together in one statistical measurement very probably conceals the extent of the disorganization among the lower-class group. If conditions are improving for one and deteriorating for the other, the resultant statistical averages might show no change. Further, the statistics on the Negro family and most other subjects treated in this paper refer only to a specific point in time. They are a vertical measure of the situation at a given moment. They do not measure the experience of individuals over time. Thus the average monthly unemployment rate for Negro males for 1964 is recorded as 9 percent. But *during* 1964, some 29 percent of Negro males were unemployed at one time or another. Similarly, for example, if 36 percent of Negro children are living in broken homes *at any specific moment,* it is likely that a far higher proportion of Negro children find themselves in that situation *at one time or another* in their lives.

NEARLY A QUARTER OF URBAN NEGRO MARRIAGES ARE DISSOLVED

Nearly a quarter of Negro women living in cities who have ever married are divorced, separated, or are living apart from their husbands.

The rates are highest in the urban Northeast where 26 percent of Negro women ever married are either divorced, separated, or have their husbands absent.

On the urban frontier, the proportion of husbands absent is even higher. In New York City in 1960, it was 30.2 percent, *not* including divorces.

Among ever-married nonwhite women in the nation, the proportion with husbands present *declined* in *every* age group over the decade 1950–60, as follows:

Age	Percent with Husbands Present	
	1950	1960
15–19 years	77.8	72.5
20–24 years	76.7	74.2
25–29 years	76.1	73.4
30–34 years	74.9	72.0
35–39 years	73.1	70.7
40–44 years	68.9	68.2

Although similar declines occurred among white females, the proportion of white husbands present never dropped below 90 percent except for the first and last age group.

NEARLY ONE-QUARTER OF NEGRO BIRTHS ARE NOW ILLEGITIMATE

Both white and Negro illegitimacy rates have been increasing, although from dramatically different bases. The white rate was 2 percent in 1940; it was 3.07 percent in 1963. In that period, the Negro rate went from 16.8 percent to 23.6 percent.

The number of illegitimate children per 1,000 live births increased by 11 among whites in the period 1940–63, but by 68 among nonwhites. There are, of course, limits to the dependability of these statistics. There are almost certainly a considerable number of Negro children who, although technically illegitimate, are in fact the offspring of stable unions. On the other hand, it may be assumed that many births that are in fact illegitimate are recorded otherwise. Probably the two opposite effects cancel each other out.

On the urban frontier, the nonwhite illegitimacy rates are usually higher than the national average, and the increase of late has been drastic.

In the District of Columbia, the illegitimacy rate for nonwhites grew from 21.8 percent in 1950, to 29.5 percent in 1964.

A similar picture of disintegrating Negro marriages emerges from the divorce statistics. Divorces have increased of late for both whites and nonwhites, but at a much greater rate for the latter. In 1940 both groups had a divorce rate of 2.2 percent. By 1964 the white rate had risen to 3.6 percent, but the nonwhite rate had reached 5.1 percent—40 percent greater than the formerly equal white rate.

ALMOST ONE-FOURTH OF NEGRO FAMILIES ARE HEADED BY FEMALES

As a direct result of this high rate of divorce, separation, and desertion, a very large percent of Negro families are headed by females. While the percentage of such families among whites has been dropping since 1940, it has been rising among Negroes.

The percent of nonwhite families headed by a female is more than double the percent for whites. Fatherless nonwhite families increased by a sixth between 1950 and 1960, but held constant for white families.

It has been estimated that only a minority of Negro children reach the age of 18 having lived all their lives with both their parents.

Once again, this measure of family disorganization is found to be diminishing among white families and increasing among Negro families.

THE BREAKDOWN OF THE NEGRO FAMILY HAS LED TO A STARTLING INCREASE IN WELFARE DEPENDENCY

The majority of Negro children receive public assistance under the AFDC program at one point or another in their childhood.

At present, 14 percent of Negro children are receiving AFDC assistance, as against 2 percent of white children. Eight percent of white children receive such assistance at some time, as against 56 percent of nonwhites, according to an extrapolation based on HEW data. (Let it be noted, however, that out of a total of 1.8 million nonwhite illegitimate children in the nation in 1961, 1.3 million were *not* receiving aid under the AFDC program, although a substantial number have, or will, receive aid at some time in their lives.)

Again, the situation may be said to be worsening. The AFDC program, deriving from the long established Mothers' Aid programs, was established in 1935 principally to care for widows and orphans, although the legislation covered all children in homes deprived of parental support because one or both of their parents are absent or incapacitated.

In the beginning, the number of AFDC families in which the father was absent because of desertion was less than a third of the total. Today it is two-thirds. HEW estimates "that between two-thirds and three-fourths of the 50 percent increase from 1948 to 1955 in the number of absent-father families receiving ADC may be explained by an increase in broken homes in the population."

A 1960 study of Aid to Dependent Children in Cook County, Ill. stated:

The "typical" ADC mother in Cook County was married and had children by her husband, who deserted; his whereabouts are unknown, and he does not contribute to the support of his children. She is not free to remarry and has had an illegitimate child since her husband left. (Almost 90 percent of the ADC families are Negro.)

The steady expansion of this welfare program, as of public assistance programs in general, can be taken as a measure of the steady disintegration of the Negro family structure over the past generation in the United States.

Race Hatred in the North*

The Reverend Dr. Martin Luther King, Jr., came to Chicago in the winter of 1965. SCLC's decision to come north reflected the current recognition that most of the legislative victories of the past had left the ghettos untouched; and that the problems in the city threatened to erode previous gains. CORE and SNCC, in different ways, came to the same conclusion. In this period of transition, Negro leadership was groping for solutions to problems not readily solved by acts of Congress or court decisions. That the new racial frontier was a tough one was demonstrated on the streets of Chicago in the summer of 1966. Just as few suspected the depth of Southern resistance in 1954–1955, many contemporaries were shocked to see the virulence of race hatred among whites that came to the surface of Northern cities in 1966.

The Rev. Dr. Martin Luther King, Jr., was struck by a rock today as civil rights demonstrators marched through a crowd of 2,000 cursing and bottle-throwing whites on Chicago's Southwest Side.

Dr. King fell briefly to his knees, but was helped up and walked on, preceded by a cordon of 50 policemen. Volleys of rocks, eggs and bottles whizzed past him as the rioting continued. The rock that struck him, just above the right ear, left a visible mark.

One Negro marcher assigned to protect Dr. King was left dazed and bleeding by rocks that struck him above the nose.

The march was the latest in a series led by Dr. King, who is

* This special to *The New York Times* by Gene Roberts, datelined "Chicago, Aug. 5," was headed: "Rock Hits Dr. King as Whites Attack March in Chicago/Felled Rights Leader Rises and Continues Protest as Crowd of 2,000 Riots." It appeared in the *Times* of August 6, 1966.

chairman of the Southern Christian Leadership Conference, to protest racial discrimination in housing in Chicago. The rioting today erupted in the Marquette Park neighborhood.

The Police Department used 1,960 officers to hold back the shouting crowd of whites. The patrolmen did not hesitate to use their nightsticks.

After Dr. King had been helped to his feet he told newsmen:

"I have seen many demonstrations in the South but I have never seen any so hostile and so hateful as I have seen here today. I have to do this—to expose myself—to bring this hate into the open."

When Dr. King arrived in Marquette Park, a public recreational area, about 2,000 whites were gathered to meet him. The whites carried signs reading "KKK, We Need a Ku Klux Klan" and "King Would Look Good With a Knife in His Back."

Fifty policemen helped Dr. King out of his car and escorted him to the head of a column of about 500 Negro marchers. It was while he was being led to the head of the column that the rock struck him.

While Dr. King was assembling his marchers, scores of whites swarmed over the marchers' cars, trying to turn them over. Some whites jumped atop cars owned by the marchers and danced on them. Others smashed car lights. The whites retreated only when policemen used clubs on them.

Most of the whites appeared to be teen-agers. About 500 adults were in the crowd, many inciting the youngsters to "get those niggers."

Police Superintendent O. W. Wilson said much of the trouble was caused by "curiosity seekers and bystanders." He called on Chicagoans to stay out of "trouble" areas.

During the first hour of the march, 75 policemen walked in the forefront, clearing the way. Two hundred policemen encircled the marching column, and the rest were dispersed around the marching area.

About 150 white teen-agers roamed ahead of the marching column, stoning Negroes on buses and in cars that happened to be in the area. The marching and the violence created a number of traffic jams.

The march route included the Gage Park, Chicago Lawn, and Marquette Park areas, in which, according to the 1960 Census, about one-third of the 100,000 residents are of "foreign stock." Many residents are of Polish and Lithuanian backgrounds.

Only six Negroes are known to live in the area, and they are housemaids who live in.

In the same area last Sunday, about 40 civil rights marchers protesting housing discrimination there were injured when violence erupted and 20 cars were damaged.

Black Power *Stokely Carmichael**

The heated debate over the meaning of "Black Power" stems in part from the indefinability of the phrase. It is a hazy concept and, like the literature of another nebulous concept, "race," it provides a sounding board for every type of predisposed view. Those who wish to see violence in it, find it; others who don't, don't. Although Richard Wright and W. E. B. Du Bois used the phrase in the past, it was popularized in the summer of 1966 by SNCC's chairman, Stokely Carmichael. As Carmichael uses it, "Black Power" seems a utopian concept—a romantic longing for Black people to unite and sacrifice their personal interests for the advance of the race. It is quite similar to the nationalistic arguments that have usually arisen during other periods of intensified inter-racial alienation, such as Martin R. Delany's program in the 1850's, Bishop Turner's theme in the 1890's, Marcus Garvey's views in the 1920's and Du Bois' attitude in the Great Depression. Carmichael tries to define what he means by the idea in the following speech.

This is 1966 and it seems to me that it's "time out" for nice words. It's time black people got together. We have to say things nobody else in this country is willing to say and find the strength internally and from each other to say the things that need to be said. We have to understand the lies this country has spoken about black people and we have to set the record straight. No one else can do that but black people.

I remember when I was in school they used to say, "If you work real hard, if you sweat, if you are ambitious, then you will be

---

* Speech delivered in Chicago on July 28, 1966, and printed by the Chicago SNCC. A copy of this address is in the Urban Historical Collection, University of Illinois, Chicago Circle.

successful." I'm here to tell you that if that was true, black people would own this country, because we sweat more than anybody else in this country. We have to say to this country that you have lied to us. We picked your cotton for $2.00 a day, we washed your dishes, we're the porters in your bank and in your building, we are the janitors and the elevator men. We worked hard and all we get is a little pay and a hard way to go from you. We have to talk not only about what's going on here but what this country is doing across the world. When we start getting the internal strength to tell them what should be told and to speak the truth as it should be spoken, let them pick the sides and let the chips fall where they may.

Now, about what black people have to do and what has been done to us by white people. If you are born in Lowndes County, Alabama, Swillingchit, Mississippi or Harlem, New York and the color of your skin happens to be black you are going to catch it. The only reason we have to get together is the color of our skins. They oppress us because we are black and we are going to use that blackness to get out of the trick bag they put us in. Don't be ashamed of your color.

A few years ago, white people used to say, "Well, the reason they live in the ghetto is they are stupid, dumb, lazy, unambitious, apathetic, don't care, happy, contented," and the trouble was a whole lot of us believed that junk about ourselves. We were so busy trying to prove to white folks that we were everything they said we weren't that we got so busy being white we forgot what it was to be black. We are going to call our black brothers' hand.

Now, after 1960, when we got moving, they couldn't say we were lazy and dumb and apathetic and all that anymore so they got sophisticated and started to play the dozens with us.* They called conferences about our mamas and told us that's why we were where we were at. Some people were sitting up there talking with

---

* Here is how Richard Wright describes "The Dirty Dozens": "Out of the folk songs of the migrant Negro there has come one form of Negro folklore that makes even Negroes blush a little among themselves. . . . These songs, sung by more adult Negroes than would willingly admit it, sum up the mood of despairing rebellion. They are called The Dirty Dozens. Their origin is obscure but their intent is plain. . . . They jeer at life; they leer at what is decent, holy, just, wise, straight, right, and uplifting." *White Man, Listen!* (New York, 1964), p. 89.

Johnson while he was talking about their mamas. I don't play the dozens with white folks. To set the record straight, the reason we are in the bag we are in isn't because of my mama, it's because of what they did to my mama. That's why I'm where I'm at. We have to put the blame where it belongs. The blame does not belong on the oppressed but on the oppressor, and that's where it is going to stay.

Don't let them scare you when you start opening your mouth—speak the truth. Tell them, "Don't blame us because we haven't ever had the chance to do wrong." They made sure that we have been so blocked-in we couldn't move until they said, "Move." Now there are a number of things we have to do. The only thing we own in this country is the color of our skins and we are ashamed of that because they made us ashamed. We have to stop being ashamed of being black. A broad nose, a thick lip and nappy hair is us and we are going to call that beautiful whether they like it or not. We are not going to fry our hair anymore but they can start wearing their hair natural to look like us.

We have to define how we are going to move, not how they say we can move. We have never been able to do that before. Everybody in this country jumps up and says, "I'm a friend of the civil rights movement. I'm a friend of the Negro." We haven't had the chance to say whether or not that man is stabbing us in the back or not. All those people who are calling us friends are nothing but traitorous enemies and we can take care of our enemies but God deliver us from our "friends." The only protection we are going to have is from each other. We have to build a strong base to let them know if they touch one black man driving his wife to the hospital in Los Angeles, or one black man walking down a highway in Mississippi or if they take one black man who has a rebellion and put him in jail and start talking treason, we are going to disrupt this whole country.

We have to say, "Don't play jive and start writing poems after Malcolm is shot." We have to move from the point where the man left off and stop writing poems. We have to start supporting our own movement. If we can spend all that money to send a preacher to a Baptist convention in a Cadillac then we can spend money to support our own movement.

Now, let's get to what the white press has been calling riots. In the first place don't get confused with the words they use like "anti-white," "hate," "militant" and all that nonsense like "radical" and "riots." What's happening is rebellions not riots. . . . The extremists in this country are the white people who force us to live the way we live. We have to define our own ethic. We don't have to (and don't make any apologies about it) obey any law that we didn't have a part to make, especially if that law was made to keep us where we are. We have the right to break it.

We have to stop apologizing for each other. We must tell our black brothers and sisters who go to college, "Don't take any job for IBM or Wall Street because you aren't doing anything for us. You are helping this country perpetuate its lies about how democracy rises in this country." They have to come back to the community, where they belong and use their skills to help develop us. We have to tell the Doctors, "You can't go to college and come back and charge us $5.00 and $10.00 a visit. You have to charge us 50¢ and be thankful you get that." We have to tell our lawyers not to charge us what they charge but to be happy to take a case and plead it free of charge. We have to define success and tell them the food Ralph Bunche eats doesn't feed our hungry stomachs. We have to tell Ralph Bunche the only reason he is up there is so when we yell they can pull him out. We have to do that, nobody else can do that for us.

We have to talk about wars and soldiers and just what that means. A mercenary is a hired killer and any black man serving in this man's army is a black mercenary, nothing else. A mercenary fights for a country for a price but does not enjoy the rights of the country for which he is fighting. A mercenary will go to Viet Nam to fight for free elections for the Vietnamese but doesn't have free elections in Alabama, Mississippi, Georgia, Texas, Louisiana, South Carolina and Washington, D.C. A mercenary goes to Viet Nam and gets shot fighting for his country and they won't even bury him in his own home town. He's a mercenary, that's all. We must find the strength so that when they start grabbing us to fight their war we say, "Hell no."

We have to talk about nonviolence among us, so that we don't cut each other on Friday nights and don't destroy each other but move to a point where we appreciate and love each other. That's the nonviolence that has to be talked about. The psychology the man has used on us has turned us against each other. He says nothing about the cutting that goes on Friday night but talk about raising one finger-tip towards him and that's when he jumps up. We have to talk about nonviolence among us first.

We have to study black history but don't get fooled. . . . You have to know what Mr. X said from his own lips not the Chicago Sun-Times. That responsibility is ours. The Muslims call themselves Muslims but the press calls them black Muslims. We have to call them Muslims and go to their mosque to find out what they are talking about firsthand and then we can talk about getting together. Don't let that man get up there and tell you, "Oh, you know those Muslims preach nothing but hate. You shouldn't be messing with them." "Yah, I don't mess with them, yah, I know they bad." The man's name is the Honorable Elijah Muhammad and he represents a great section of the black community. Honor him.

We have to go out and find our young blacks who are cutting and shooting each other and tell them they are doing the cutting and shooting to the wrong people. We have to bring them together and spend the time if we are not just shucking and jiving. This is 1966 and my grandmother used to tell me, "The time is far spent." We have to move this year.

There is a psychological war going on in this country and it's whether or not black people are going to be able to use the terms they want about their movement without white people's blessing. We have to tell them we are going to use the term "Black Power" and we are going to define it because Black Power speaks to us. We can't let them project Black Power because they can only project it from white power and we know what white power has done to us. We have to organize ourselves to speak from a position of strength and stop begging people to look kindly upon us. We are going to build a movement in this country based on the color of our skins that is going to free us from our oppressors and we have to do that ourselves.

We have got to understand what is going on in Lowndes County, Alabama, what it means, who is in it and what they are doing so if white people steal that election like they do all over this country then the eyes of black people all over this country will be focused there to let them know we are going to take care of business if they mess with us in Lowndes County. That responsibility lies on all of us, not just the civil rights workers and do-gooders.

If we talk about education we have to educate ourselves, not with Hegel or Plato or the missionaries who came to Africa with the bible and we had the land and when they left we had the bible and they had the land. We have to tell them the only way anybody eliminates poverty in this country is to give poor people money. You don't have to headstart, uplift and upward-bound them into your culture. Just give us the money you stole from us, that's all. We have to say to people in this country, "We don't really care about you. For us to get better, we don't have to go to white things. We can do it in our own community, ourselves if you didn't steal the resources that belong there." We have to understand the Horatio Alger lie and that the individualist, profit-concept nonsense will never work for us. We have to form cooperatives and use the profits to benefit our community. We can't tolerate their system.

When we form coalitions we must say on what grounds we are going to form them, not white people telling us how to form them. We must build strength and pride amongst ourselves. We must think politically and get power because we are the only people in this country that are powerless. We are the only people who have to protect ourselves from our protectors. We are the only people who want a man called Willis* removed who is a racist, that have to lie down in the street and beg a racist named [Mayor] Daley to remove the racist named Willis. We have to build a movement so we can see Daley and say, "Tell Willis to get hat," and by the time we turn around he is gone. That's Black Power.

Everybody in this country is for "Freedom Now" but not everybody is for Black Power because we have got to get rid of some of the people who have white power. We have got to get us some Black Power. We don't control anything but what white people say we can control. We have to be able to smash any political machine in the country that's oppressing us and bring it to its knees. We have to be aware that if we keep growing and multiplying the way we do in ten years all the major cities are

* Benjamin C. Willis, former superintendent of Chicago's public school system.

going to be ours. We have to know that in Newark, New Jersey, where we are 60% of the population, we went along with their stories about integrating and we got absorbed. All we have to show for it is three councilmen who are speaking for them and not for us. We have to organize ourselves to speak for each other. That's Black Power. We have to move to control the economics and politics of our community so the southside cannot be controlled by a Daley. We have to tell Daley, "Don't you dare arrest anybody for treason. If you should arrest anybody it should be yourself and your whole corrupt political machinery that's been exploiting and oppressing us, Daley." We have to let them know when they arrest some of our black brothers we are going to make them heroes in our community.

I want to show you what the man does to our minds. Do you remember watching Tarzan and how we used to yell for him to beat up the black, uncivilized, cannibal natives? Well, they are putting Tarzan back on TV this September and we ought to yell for the black people to beat the hell out of Tarzan and send him back to Europe.

Now I want to explain about this "Western Civilization" we are being upgraded into. The man got on [the] radio and said, "Well, when they start rioting they are nothing else but savages," and we got mad but you know the man was right, because a savage throws a Molotov Cocktail, civilized man just drops a bomb, that's all. Civilized Lyndon is just dropping bombs and daring the people to touch the men who dropped the bombs on them. That's civilization.

Well anyway, a Lt. Colonel was shot down in Africa and landed among some of the brothers. They saw this big bird coming down and they got afraid but when my man landed they took care of him. After a couple of months they got so they could talk, so the tribe got everybody together because they wanted to hear what my man had to say. And they said, "Well, look here. Who are you? I mean what's all this?" And well, my man stood off and said, "I'm a Lt. Colonel in the United States Airforce." And the cat said, "Wow. What does that mean?" He said, "Well, it means that I'm a high-ranking officer. I have under my command several thousand men and I'm a well educated man. I graduated from Harvard University with a Ph.D. in Military Science." And so the chief said, "Well, what's happening with this bird?" He said, "Well that's a war plane and we're engaged in a war." And the tribesmen understood war and they started jumping up and down, "Wow. You in a war. Are you winning?" He said, "Yes, my good man, all these medals here represent at least thirty men I have killed single-handedly. Three-zero men, by myself and these are the medals." And the tribe went wild, "Wow, is he a hero." And the tribesman said, "Wow, baby, you must have had some feast!" And the white Lt. Colonel from the civilized United States jumped back, snorted and said, "My good man, where I come from we don't eat people when we kill them. We're civilized." And the chief said, "Well, baby, why you kill them?"

Bibliographic Note

❁

A considerable number of books deal with the meaning of race in American life. This bibliographic note points to some of the most significant works but is hardly comprehensive. Those who wish to undertake studies in depth should consult the following bibliographies: Monroe N. Work, *A Bibliography of the Negro in Africa and America* (New York, 1928); Elizabeth W. Miller, *The Negro in America: A Bibliography* (Cambridge, Mass., 1966); Erwin A. Salk, *A Layman's Guide to Negro History* (Chicago, 1966); Edgar T. and Alma M. Thompson, *Race and Region: A Descriptive Bibliography* (Chapel Hill, N.C., 1949); Dwight L. Dumond, *A Bibliography of Anti-Slavery in America* (Ann Arbor, Mich., 1961).

Issues of the following journals over the years are a rich source for information and bibliography: *Journal of Negro History; Journal of Negro Education; Journal of Southern History; Phylon; Journal of Intergroup Relations; Crisis; Opportunity; Integrated Education; The New South; CORE-later; Student Voice; Freedomways; The Citizen.*

A number of books of outstanding quality cover the entire history of American race relations. Among the most perceptive are: E. Franklin Frazier, *The Negro in the United States* (New York, 1957); John Hope Franklin, *From Slavery to Freedom* (New York, 1956); Gunnar Myrdal, *An American Dilemma* (New York, 1944), 2 vols.; C. Vann Woodward, *The Strange Career of Jim Crow* (New York, 1966); W. J. Cash, *The Mind of the South* (New York, 1941); Talcott Parsons and Kenneth B. Clark, eds., *The Negro American* (Boston, 1966); Jack Greenberg, *Race Relations and American Law* (New York, 1959); August Meier and Elliott M. Rudwick, *From Plantation to Ghetto* (New York, 1966).

Social scientists and historians have studied the origins of prejudice and the meaning of race in the modern world. Some representative volumes are: Gordon V. Allport, *The Nature of Prejudice* (Cambridge, Mass., 1954); Ruth Benedict, *Race: Science and Politics* (New York, 1940); Thomas F. Pettigrew, *A Profile of the Negro American*

637

(Princeton, N.J., 1964); UNESCO, *Race and Science: The Race Question in Modern Science* (New York, 1961); Kenneth B. Clark, *Prejudice and Your Child* (Boston, 1963); L. C. Dunn and T. Dobzhansky, *Heredity, Race and Society* (New York, 1964); Mary E. Goodman, *Race Awareness in Young Children* (Cambridge, Mass., 1952); Thomas F. Gossett, *Race: The History of an Idea in America* (Dallas, 1963); William Stanton, *The Leopard's Spots: Scientific Attitudes toward Race in America, 1815–59* (Chicago, 1960); I. A. Newby, *Jim Crow's Defense: Anti-Negro Thought in America, 1900–1930* (Baton Rouge, La., 1965).

There are individual histories of slavery for most states. The more important surveys deal with the institution in its sectional, national and international setting: Elizabeth Donnan, ed., *Documents Illustrative of the History of the Slave Trade to America* (Washington, D.C., 1930–1935), 4 vols.; Daniel P. Mannix and Malcolm Cowley, *Black Cargoes: A History of the Atlantic Slave Trade* (New York, 1962); Basil Davidson, *Black Mother: The Years of the African Slave Trade* (Boston, 1961); Helen H. Catterall, ed., *Judicial Cases Concerning American Slavery and the Negro* (Washington, D.C., 1926–1937), 5 vols.; Kenneth M. Stampp, *The Peculiar Institution* (New York, 1956); Frank Tannenbaum, *Slave and Citizen: The Negro in the Americas* (New York, 1947); Stanley M. Elkins, *Slavery: A Problem in American Institutional History and Intellectual Life* (Chicago, 1959); Eugene D. Genovese, *The Political Economy of Slavery: Studies in the Economy and Society of the Slave South* (New York, 1965); Herbert Aptheker, *American Negro Slave Revolts* (New York, 1943); Ulrich B. Phillips, *American Negro Slavery* (New York, 1918); Herbert S. Klein, *Slavery in the Americas: A Comparative Study of Cuba and Virginia* (Chicago, 1967); Eric Williams, *Capitalism and Slavery* (Chapel Hill, N.C., 1944); Lorenzo J. Greene, *The Negro in Colonial New England* (New York, 1942); David B. Davis, *The Problem of Slavery in Western Culture* (Ithaca, N.Y., 1966); Arthur Zilversmit, *The First Emancipation: The Abolition of Negro Slavery in the North* (Chicago, 1967).

The nature of race relations in the ante-bellum South and North is explored in the following works: Leon F. Litwack, *North of Slavery: The Negro in the Free States, 1790–1860* (Chicago, 1961); John Hope Franklin, *The Militant South* (Cambridge, Mass., 1956); William W. Freehling, *Prelude to Civil War: The Nullification Controversy in South Carolina, 1816–1836* (New York, 1966); Frederic Bancroft, *Slave Trading in the Old South* (Baltimore, 1931); John M. Lofton, *Insurrection in South Carolina: The Turbulent World of*

Denmark Vesey (Yellow Springs, Ohio, 1964); Charles Sydnor, *The Development of Southern Sectionalism, 1819–1848* (Baton Rouge, La., 1948); Clement Eaton, *The Freedom-of-Thought Struggle in the Old South* (New York, 1964); Harvey Wish, *George Fitzhugh: Propagandist of the Old South* (Baton Rouge, La., 1943); William S. Jenkins, *Pro-Slavery Thought in the Old South* (Gloucester, Mass., 1960); Dwight L. Dumond, *Antislavery Origins of the Civil War in the United States* (Ann Arbor, Mich., 1961), and *Anti-Slavery: The Crusade for Freedom in America* (Ann Arbor, 1961); E. Franklin Frazier, *The Free Negro Family* (Nashville, 1932); Philip Foner, ed., *The Life and Writings of Frederick Douglass* (New York, 1950), 4 vols.; Charlotte L. Forten, *A Free Negro in the Slave Era* (New York, 1961); Carter G. Woodson, *Free Negro Heads of Families in the United States in 1830* (Washington, D.C., 1925), and *The Education of the Negro Prior to 1861* (New York, 1915); Bernard Mandel, *Labor: Free and Slave* (New York, 1955); Richard C. Wade, *Slavery in the Cities: The South, 1820–1860* (New York, 1964); Martin Duberman, ed., *The Antislavery Vanguard: New Essays on the Abolitionists* (Princeton, N.J., 1965); Irving H. Bartlett, *Wendell Phillips: Brahmin Radical* (Boston, 1961); John L. Thomas, *The Liberator, William Lloyd Garrison: A Biography* (Boston, 1963); Walter M. Merrill, *Against Wind and Tide: A Biography of William L. Garrison* (Cambridge, Mass., 1963); Benjamin P. Thomas, *Theodore Weld: Crusader for Freedom* (New Brunswick, N.J., 1950); Whitney R. Cross, *The Burned Over District* (Ithaca, N.Y., 1950); Gilbert H. Barnes, *The Anti-Slavery Impulse, 1830–1844* (New York, 1964).

The significance of race in American life from the Civil War to the early twentieth century is discussed in John Hope Franklin, *The Emancipation Proclamation* (New York, 1963); Benjamin Quarles, *Lincoln and the Negro* (New York, 1962); Dudley Taylor Cornish, *The Sable Arm: Negro Troops in the Union Army* (New York, 1956); Benjamin Quarles, *The Negro in the Civil War* (Boston, 1953); C. Vann Woodward, *Reunion and Reaction* (New York, 1956), and *Origins of the New South, 1877–1913* (Baton Rouge, La., 1951); W. E. B. Du Bois, *Black Reconstruction in America, 1860–1880* (Cleveland, 1964), and *The Souls of Black Folk* (Chicago, 1903); Vernon L. Wharton, *The Negro in Mississippi, 1865–1890* (Chapel Hill, N.C., 1947); George B. Tindall, *South Carolina Negroes, 1877–1900* (Columbia, S.C., 1952); C. L. Wagandt, *The Mighty Revolution: Negro Emancipation in Maryland* (Baltimore, 1965); Joel Williamson, *After Slavery: The Negro in South Carolina During Reconstruction, 1861–1877* (Chapel Hill, N.C., 1965); Willie Lee

Rose, *Rehearsal for Reconstruction: The Port Royal Experiment* (Indianapolis, 1964); James M. McPherson, *Abolitionists and the Negro in the Civil War and Reconstruction* (Princeton, N.J., 1964); Stanley P. Hirshson, *Farewell to the Bloody Shirt: Northern Republicans and the Southern Negro, 1877–1893* (Bloomington, Ind., 1962); Vincent P. DeSantis, *Republicans Face the Southern Question: The New Departure Years, 1877–1897* (Baltimore, 1959); LaWanda and John Cox, *Politics, Principle and Prejudice, 1865–1866* (New York, 1963); Frenise A. Logan, *The Negro in North Carolina, 1876–1894* (Chapel Hill, N.C., 1964); Rayford W. Logan, *The Betrayal of the Negro* (New York, 1965); August Meier, *Negro Thought in America, 1880–1915* (Ann Arbor, Mich., 1963); Samuel R. Spencer, *Booker T. Washington and the Negro's Place in American Life* (Boston, 1955); Louis Harlan, *Separate and Unequal: Public School Campaigns and Racism in the Southern Seaboard States, 1901–1915* (Chapel Hill, N.C., 1958); Paul Lewinson, *Race, Class, and Party* (New York, 1965).

Some important studies of twentieth-century conditions are: Francis L. Broderick, *W. E. B. Du Bois: Negro Leader in Time of Crisis* (Stanford, 1959); Elliott M. Rudwick, *W. E. B. Du Bois: A Study in Minority Group Leadership* (Philadelphia, 1961); Mary White Ovington, *The Walls Came Tumbling Down* (New York, 1947); E. Franklin Frazier, *Black Bourgeoisie* (New York, 1962); David M. Chalmers, *Hooded Americanism: The First Century of the Ku Klux Klan* (New York, 1965); Edmund David Cronon, *Black Moses: The Story of Marcus Garvey* (Madison, Wis., 1955); St. Clair Drake and Horace R. Cayton, *Black Metropolis: A Study of Negro Life in a Northern City* (New York, 1945); Gilbert Osofsky, *Harlem: The Making of a Ghetto* (New York, 1966); Wilson Record, *The Negro and the Communist Party* (Chapel Hill, N.C., 1951); Allen K. Chalmers, *They Shall Be Free* (New York, 1951); Sara Harris, *Father Divine* (New York, 1953); Horace R. Cayton and George C. Mitchell, *Black Workers and the New Unions* (Chapel Hill, N.C., 1939); Herbert Garfinkel, *When Negroes March* (Glencoe, Ill., 1949); Louis Ruchames, *Race, Jobs and Politics: The Story of FEPC* (New York, 1953); Loren Miller, *The Petitioners: The Story of the Supreme Court of the United States and the Negro* (New York, 1966); L. D. Reddick, *Crusader Without Violence* (New York, 1959); Lerone Bennett, Jr., *What Manner of Man: A Biography of Martin Luther King* (Chicago, 1964); Benjamin Muse, *Virginia's Massive Resistance* (Bloomington, Ind., 1961), and *Ten Years of Prelude: The Story of Integration Since the Supreme Court's 1954 Decision* (New York,

1964); Lillian Smith, *Killers of the Dream* (New York, 1949); Charles Morgan, Jr., *A Time to Speak* (New York, 1964); Hodding Carter, *So the Heffners Left McComb* (New York, 1965); James Silver, *Mississippi: The Closed Society* (New York, 1964); James Q. Wilson, *Negro Politics: The Search for Leadership* (New York, 1960); Harold F. Gosnell, *Negro Politicians* (Chicago, 1935); C. Eric Lincoln, *The Black Muslims in America* (Boston, 1961); E. U. Essien-Udom, *Black Nationalism: A Search for Identity in America* (Chicago, 1962); James Peck, *Freedom Ride* (New York, 1962); Howard Zinn, *SNCC: The New Abolitionists* (Boston, 1964); Nat Hentoff, *The New Equality* (New York, 1965); Elizabeth Sutherland, ed., *Letters from Mississippi* (New York, 1965); Louis E. Lomax, *The Negro Revolt* (New York, 1962); Harold R. Isaacs, *The New World of Negro Americans* (New York, 1963); *The Autobiography of Malcolm X* (New York, 1965); Len Holt, *The Summer That Didn't End: The Story of the Mississippi Civil Rights Project of 1964* (New York, 1965); Kenneth B. Clark, *Dark Ghetto* (New York, 1965); Wilma Dykeman and James Stokley, *Seeds of Southern Change: The Life of Will Alexander* (Chicago, 1962); Sally Belfrage, *Freedom Summer* (New York, 1965); John Ehle, *The Free Men* (New York, 1965); Nicholas Von Hoffman, *Mississippi Notebook* (New York, 1964); Erskine Caldwell, *In Search of Bisco* (New York, 1965); Lee Rainwater and William L. Yancey, *The Moynihan Report and the Politics of Controversy* (Cambridge, Mass., 1967).

Index